# THE COMPLETE
# HARLEY 2253 MANUSCRIPT

## Volume 2

# MIDDLE ENGLISH TEXTS SERIES

The Middle English Texts Series is designed for classroom use. Its goal is to make available to teachers, scholars, and students texts that occupy an important place in the literary and cultural canon but have not been readily available in student editions. The series does not include those authors, such as Chaucer, Langland, or Malory, whose English works are normally in print in good student editions. The focus is, instead, upon Middle English literature adjacent to those authors that teachers need in compiling the syllabuses they wish to teach. The editions maintain the linguistic integrity of the original work but within the parameters of modern reading conventions. The texts are printed in the modern alphabet and follow the practices of modern capitalization, word formation, and punctuation. Manuscript abbreviations are silently expanded, and *u/v* and *j/i* spellings are regularized according to modern orthography. Yogh (3) is transcribed as *g, gh, y,* or *s,* according to the sound in Modern English spelling to which it corresponds; thorn (þ) and eth (ð) are transcribed as *th.* Distinction between the second person pronoun and the definite article is made by spelling the one *thee* and the other *the,* and final *-e* that receives full syllabic value is accented (e.g., *charitê*). Hard words, difficult phrases, and unusual idioms are glossed either in the right margin or at the foot of the page. Explanatory and textual notes appear at the end of the text, often along with a glossary. The editions include short introductions on the history of the work, its merits and points of topical interest, and brief working bibliographies.

This series is published in association with the University of Rochester.

Medieval Institute Publications is a program of
The Medieval Institute, College of Arts and Sciences

 WESTERN MICHIGAN UNIVERSITY

# THE COMPLETE
# HARLEY 2253 MANUSCRIPT
## Volume 2

Edited and Translated by

Susanna Fein

with

David Raybin and Jan Ziolkowski

TEAMS • Middle English Texts Series

MEDIEVAL INSTITUTE PUBLICATIONS
Western Michigan University
*Kalamazoo*

**Library of Congress Cataloging-in-Publication Data**

The Complete Harley 2253 Manuscript / edited and translated by Susanna Fein with David Raybin and Jan Ziolkowski.
     volumes cm. -- (Middle English texts series)
  Harley's contents are presented according to booklet structure; the grouping of seven booklets to make the Harley manuscript's full 140 leaves seems to have happened when the scribe was alive.
  For the Latin texts, Jan Ziolkowski provided translations of those obscure works; for translations of French, David Raybin has been a collaborator; initially, there was another collaborator for the French portions of Harley, Barbara Nolan, who before her death, had drafted English versions of some fabliaux, the translation of Gilote and Johane.
  Includes bibliographical references and indexes.
  ISBN 978-1-58044-205-3 (pbk. : alk. paper) -- ISBN 978-1-58044-198-8 (pbk. : alk. paper) -- ISBN 978-1-58044-199-5 (pbk. : alk. paper)
  1.  English literature--Middle English, 1100-1500. 2.  Anglo-Norman literature. 3.  Latin literature, Medieval and modern--England. 4.  Middle Ages--Literary collections. 5.  Manuscripts, Medieval--England--London. 6.  British Library. Manuscript. Harley 2253.  I. Fein, Susanna Greer, editor, translator. II. Raybin, David B., 1951- translator. III. Ziolkowski, Jan M., 1956- translator. IV. Consortium for the Teaching of the Middle Ages. V. British Library. Manuscript. Harley 2253. VI. British Library. Manuscript. Harley 2253. English. VII. Title: Harley 2253.
  PR1120.M77 2014
  820.8'001--dc23

                                        2014011645

ISBN 978-1-58044-198-8

P   5   4   3   2   1

# ✿ CONTENTS

ACKNOWLEDGMENTS                                                    ix

INTRODUCTION                                                        1

MS HARLEY 2253: TEXTS AND TRANSLATIONS

BOOKLET 3

| | | |
|---|---|---|
| 8. ABC a femmes | 8. ABC of Women | 18 |
| 9. De l'Yver et de l'Esté | 9. Debate between Winter and Summer | 34 |
| 10. Vorte make cynople | 10. How to Make Red Vermilion | 46 |
| 11. Vorte temprene asure | 11. How to Temper Azure | 46 |
| 12. Vorte make gras-grene | 12. How to Make Grass-Green | 48 |
| 13. Vorte maken another maner grene | 13. How to Make Another Kind of Green | 48 |
| 14. Yet for gaude-grene | 14. Another for Yellow-Green | 48 |
| 15. Vorte couche selverfoyl | 15. How to Apply Silverfoil | 48 |
| 16. Vorte maken iren as hart as stel | 16. How to Make Iron as Hard as Steel | 50 |
| 17. Vorte maken blankplum | 17. How to Make White Lead | 50 |

BOOKLET 4

| | | |
|---|---|---|
| 18. Incipit vita sancti Ethelberti | 18. The Life of Saint Ethelbert | 50 |
| 19. Anima Christi, sanctifica me | 19. Soul of Christ, Sanctify Me | 58 |
| 20. Quant voy la revenue d'yver | 20. A Goliard's Feast | 58 |
| 21. Alle herkneth to me nou | 21. Harrowing of Hell | 66 |
| 22. In a thestri stude Y stod | 22. Debate between Body and Soul | 78 |
| 23. Sitteth alle stille ant herkneth to me | 23. A Song of Lewes | 86 |
| 24. Chaunter m'estoit | 24. Lament for Simon de Montfort | 88 |
| 24a. Charnel amour est folie | 24a. Carnal Love Is Folly | 96 |
| 24a*. Momentaneum est quod delectat | 24a*. What Allures Is Momentary | 96 |
| 24b. Erthe toc of erthe | 24b. Earth upon Earth | 96 |
| 25. Lystneth, lordynges! A newe song Ichulle bigynne | 25. The Execution of Sir Simon Fraser | 98 |
| 25a. Lord that lenest us lyf | 25a. On the Follies of Fashion | 108 |
| 26. Enseignement sur les amis | 26. Lesson for True Lovers | 112 |
| 27. Middelerd for mon wes mad | 27. The Three Foes of Man | 116 |

| | | |
|---|---|---|
| 28. Ichot a burde in a bour ase beryl so bryht | 28. Annot and John | 120 |
| 29. Bytuene Mersh ant Averil | 29. Alysoun | 122 |
| 30. With longyng Y am lad | 30 The Lover's Complaint | 126 |
| 31. Ich herde men upo mold | 31. Song of the Husbandman | 128 |
| 32. Herketh hideward ant beoth stille | 32. The Life of Saint Marina | 130 |
| 33. Weping haveth myn wonges wet | 33. The Poet's Repentance | 140 |
| 34. Most I ryden by Rybbesdale | 34. The Fair Maid of Ribblesdale | 144 |
| 35. In a fryht as Y con fare fremede | 35. The Meeting in the Wood | 148 |
| 36. A wayle whyt ase whalles bon | 36. A Beauty White as Whale's Bone | 150 |
| 37. Gilote e Johane | 37. Gilote and Johane | 156 |
| 38. Les pelrinages communes que crestiens fount en la Seinte Terre | 38. Pilgrimages in the Holy Land | 172 |
| 39. Les pardouns de Acres | 39. The Pardons of Acre | 184 |
| 40. Ne mai no lewed lued libben in londe | 40. Satire on the Consistory Courts | 188 |
| 41. Of a mon Matheu thohte | 41. The Laborers in the Vineyard | 192 |
| 43. Lenten ys come with love to toune | 43. Spring | 194 |
| 44. In May hit murgeth when hit dawes | 44. Advice to Women | 196 |
| 45. Heye Louerd, thou here my bone | 45. An Old Man's Prayer | 198 |
| 46. Ichot a burde in boure bryht | 46. Blow, Northern Wind | 204 |
| 47. Alle that beoth of huerte trewe | 47. The Death of Edward I | 210 |
| 48. Lustneth, lordinges, bothe yonge ant olde | 48. The Flemish Insurrection | 214 |
| 49. Marie, pur toun enfaunt | 49. The Joys of Our Lady | 222 |
| 50. Suete Jesu, king of blysse | 50. Sweet Jesus, King of Bliss | 224 |
| 51. Jesu Crist, heovene kyng | 51. Jesus Christ, Heaven's King | 228 |
| 52. Wynter wakeneth al my care | 52. A Winter Song | 228 |
| 53. When Y se blosmes springe | 53. A Spring Song on the Passion | 230 |
| 54. Ferroy chaunsoun | 54. I Pray to God and Saint Thomas | 232 |
| 55. Dum ludis floribus | 55. While You Play in Flowers | 234 |
| 56. Quant fu en ma juvente | 56. Song on Jesus' Precious Blood | 236 |
| 57. Marie, mere al Salveour | 57. Mary, Mother of the Savior | 244 |
| 58. Dulcis Jesu memoria | 58. Jesus, Sweet Is the Love of You | 246 |
| 59. Une petite parole | 59. Sermon on God's Sacrifice and Judgment | 258 |
| 60. Stond wel, moder, under rode | 60. Stand Well, Mother, under Rood | 264 |
| 61. Jesu, for thi muchele miht | 61. Jesus, by Your Great Might | 266 |
| 62. I syke when Y singe | 62. I Sigh When I Sing | 270 |
| 63. Nou skrinketh rose ant lylie-flour | 63. An Autumn Song | 272 |
| 64. My deth Y love, my lyf Ich hate | 64. The Clerk and the Girl | 276 |
| 65. When the nyhtegale singes | 65. When the Nightingale Sings | 278 |

66. Blessed be thou, Levedy        66. Blessed Are You, Lady              278
67. Ase Y me rod this ender day    67. The Five Joys of the Virgin       280
68. Herkne to my ron               68. Maximian                          284
69. Mayden, moder milde            69. Maiden, Mother Mild               296
70. The Geste of Kyng Horn         70. King Horn                         300

EXPLANATORY NOTES                                                        371

TEXTUAL NOTES                                                            455

APPENDIX: FULL CONTENTS OF MS HARLEY 2253                                481

VOLUME 2: INDEX OF FIRST LINES                                           485

VOLUME 2: INDEX OF MANUSCRIPTS CITED                                     489

VOLUME 2: INDEX OF PROPER NAMES                                          491

BIBLIOGRAPHY                                                             503

 # ACKNOWLEDGMENTS

This edition of MS Harley 2253 is indebted beyond words to many individuals. Most of all, Russell Peck's patient, unwavering support for the project and his own example as a great medieval scholar have motivated me in profound ways. Carter Revard has been ever-generous in sharing research and insights about the manuscript, and of course it is Carter's ground-breaking work that has allowed the main scribe to be precisely localized. When my Anglo-Norman transcriptions were still new and somewhat crude, Tony Hunt selflessly reviewed them all. As I have sought to emulate the stellar standards of the Anglo-Norman Text Society, his learned scholarship has been my model. For the Latin texts, Jan Ziolkowski was very good to provide, early on, faithful translations of those obscure works. For translations of French, David Raybin has been, as always, an incomparable collaborator; his work has enabled me to hear each Anglo-Norman author's distinctive style and voice. Initially, there was another collaborator for the French portions of MS Harley 2253: Barbara Nolan. Before her death, Barbara had drafted English versions of some fabliaux. The translation of *Gilote and Johane* published here bears witness to her splendid ear for lively comedy. For errors that remain in these volumes, in texts or translations, I bear responsibility.

Other debts accrued over the years have been either individual or institutional. I owe much to the wisdom of those who contributed essays to *Studies in the Harley Manuscript* in 2000 to advance research on a then-still-opaque textual artifact: besides Carter and Barbara, they include Marilyn Corrie, the late Mary Dove, David Jeffrey, Michael Kuczynski, Frances McSparran, Richard Newhauser, Helen Phillips, Karl Reichl, John Scattergood, Elizabeth Solopova, Theo Stemmler, and John Thompson. Ongoing conversations with each of them have been mainstays of my work, and Mary Dove is much missed. With others I have discussed the pioneering challenges of manuscript editing and scribal mapping. Here, particularly, I thank Julia Boffey, Martin Camargo, Martha Driver, Tony Edwards, Simon Horobin, Kathryn Kerby-Fulton, Linne Mooney, Derek Pearsall, Wendy Scase, Carl Schmidt, George Shuffelton, Eric Stanley, Thorlac Turville-Petre, and Míceál Vaughan. A new wave of Harley scholars has also emerged, and for sharing their insights, I am grateful to Daniel Birkholz, Nancy Durling, John Hines, Seth Lerer, Ingrid Nelson, Justin O'Hearn, Jason O'Rourke, and Catherine Rock. I also reserve special thanks for my Kent State Latinist colleague Radd Ehrman and for the friendly counsels I depend on from Richard Firth Green, Kristen Figg, and John Block Friedman.

My first transcription of MS Harley 2253 was supported by an NEH Summer Stipend in 1997, a grant spurred by an invitation to create the *Harley Lyrics* chapter for *A Manual of Writings in Middle English*. For this impetus, I gratefully acknowledge the late Al Hartung and his editorial successor Peter Beidler. Unflagging institutional support has been granted by Kent State University through the Research Council, the Institute for Bibliography and Editing, the Department of English, and the library staff. David Raybin's translations were supported by a grant from the Council on Faculty Research at Eastern Illinois University. The British Library has lent aid whenever I have had need to see Harley and related manuscripts; I thank especially Julian Harrison, curator of Early Modern Manuscripts. The Medieval Song Network at University College London, organized by Ardis Butterfield and Helen Deeming, has created an innovative, supportive context for new work on lyrics. Finally, but not at all least, I thank the Harvard English Department, which is responsible not just for setting me on this path long ago when I was Larry Benson and Morton Bloomfield's student but also for inviting me to return in fall 2010 as a Bloomfield Fellow, lending momentum to this project. For this privilege, I must thank Daniel Donoghue, James Simpson, and Nicholas Watson, ever-gracious hosts.

At the University of Rochester, I sincerely thank METS Assistant Editor Martha M. Johnson-Olin and staff editors Katie VanWert, Kara L. McShane, Pamela M. Yee, and Alison Harper, whose sharp-eyed diligence improved the final product. At Western Michigan University's Medieval Institute Publications, I thank Patricia Hollahan and her dedicated staff. At each location, Rochester and Kalamazoo, it is gratifying to experience great editorial care. The NEH has generously funded the Middle English Texts Series in which this volume appears. Thanks are also due to David White, who provided early technical assistance, and to Rebecca Sargent, who worked meticulously on large swathes of the unedited Anglo-Norman poetry that appears in volume 1.

Above all, this edition of MS Harley 2253 owes its being to my family, and I therefore dedicate it with love to Elizabeth, Carolyn, and Jonathan.

 **INTRODUCTION**

Manuscripts from medieval England are rarely presented to readers of today in the manner given here: each item edited beside a modern English translation.[1] No medieval book, however, warrants this exceptional treatment so much as does the famous Harley Lyrics manuscript.

London, British Library, MS Harley 2253 is one of the most important literary books to survive from the English medieval era. In rarity, quality, and abundance, its secular love lyrics comprise an unrivaled collection. Intermingled with them are additional treasures for the student of Middle English: contemporary political songs as well as delicate lyrics designed to inspire religious devotion. And digging beyond these English gems, one readily discovers more prizes — less well known ones — in French and Latin: four fabliaux (the largest set from medieval England), three lives of Anglo-Saxon saints, and a wealth of satires, comedies, debates, interludes, collected sayings, conduct literature, Bible stories, dream interpretations, and pilgrim guides. Rich in texts in three languages, the book's overall range is quite astounding. The Ludlow scribe, compiler and copyist of folios 49–140, shows himself to have been a man of unusual curiosity, acquisitiveness, and discerning connoisseurship.

THE HARLEY MANUSCRIPT: FOLIOS 1–48

Volume 1 of this three-volume edition prints what were originally two booklets, matched to each other in size and format and holding a rich assortment of religious narratives in Anglo-French verse and prose. These booklets are uniformly copied by an older scribe (not the Ludlow scribe) in a formal textura script. The texts themselves are complete, but Scribe A left open spaces at the heads of sections for the insertion of rubricated initials. The Ludlow scribe (Scribe B) clearly had these books in his possession, for he supplied in red ink titles for each work and four initials on folio 1r. Although not made by the main scribe of

---

[1] There are few precedents for this manner of presentation, but the approach seems to be gathering momentum. See, for example, recent editions of the Anglo-Saxon *Beowulf* manuscript (Fulk); the Latin *Cambridge Songs* manuscript, termed "the grandfather of the *Harley Lyrics*" (Ziolkowski 1998, p. xxx); and the Middle English *Pearl* manuscript, translated on CD-ROM (Andrew and Waldron). The English texts of the Kildare manuscript have been edited with translations (Lucas), and similar treatment has been given to the English saints' lives of Cambridge, St. John's College, MSS N. 16 and N. 17 (Waters). Meanwhile, editions of entire codices, glossed but not translated, have started to appear in the Middle English Texts Series: MS Ashmole 61 (Shuffelton) and the Audelay manuscript (Fein 2009). Digital whole-manuscript transcriptions with facsimile images are also gradually emerging: the Auchinleck manuscript online (Burnley and Wiggins) and the Vernon manuscript on DVD-ROM (Scase and Kennedy).

interest, this portion of Harley 2253 represents what the Ludlow man had access to in his library. It contains lively works with imaginative appeal: moral sayings and exempla from the ancient desert fathers, absorbing accounts of Christ's trial and passion, and a well-crafted set of apostolic saints' legends.

THE HARLEY MANUSCRIPT: FOLIOS 49–140

The Ludlow scribe's robust achievement (printed in volumes 2 and 3) appears on the codex's folios 49–140, leaves that are accessible in their original form by means of a high-quality facsimile (Ker). Excluded from that facsimile are the first forty-eight leaves because a different scribe — Scribe A — was responsible for their content. Working several decades earlier, this older scribe copied texts of religion exclusively in Anglo-Norman. At some point his products came into the possession of the Ludlow scribe (chronologically, Scribe B), whom we know owned and read these works because in around 1331 he wrote the titles in red found at the head of Scribe A's texts.[2] Thus what folios 49–140 represent is a long addendum produced by the Ludlow scribe from about 1331 to 1341 and then affixed by him to a preexisting older book, extending it to nearly three times its original length.

It is difficult to know how to classify a book so singular as the Harley manuscript. Is it a miscellany or an anthology? In reference to the Ludlow scribe's portion, one must categorize the book as something of a hybrid, that is, a miscellany that idiosyncratically and frequently veers toward the nature and purposes of an anthology.[3] That is to say, there is much evidence of meaningful layouts, linkages, and juxtapositions that work not only to join texts alike in language and genre but also to create junctures that bridge the divides. This feature of the Harley manuscript has fascinated many modern readers, yet it also tends to make the book maddeningly hard to comprehend as a whole entity.

In this METS edition, the making available of the whole contents of MS Harley 2253 — edited texts set next to faithful translations of them — is designed to overcome what has been the major obstacle to study of the whole book, that is, simply put, the difficulty students and scholars encounter in *reading all of it*. The Ludlow scribe worked fluently in three languages. Sometimes, the mixing occurs within individual poems: different poets blended two or three languages in macaronic fashion, as in *Mary, Maiden Mild* and *Against the King's Taxes*. But at a most basic level it is the scribe's own work that is macaronic when he sets texts of different languages side by side in significant ways. Multilingual fluency is thus a constant, and with it one may detect a well-developed, ever-alert deployment of diverse linguistic registers, displayed by juxtaposition and textual selection. This fundamental

---

[2] Revard 2007, p. 98 n. 5. See also O'Rourke 2005, p. 55.

[3] The terms *miscellany* and *anthology* are often in flux as scholars work to categorize medieval manuscripts of mixed content (see, for example, the attempts at definition in Nichols and Wenzel). Codicological intentions frequently cannot be known, so organizing principles come to be detected internally and, hence, may seem overly ruled by subjective interpretation. The Harley manuscript is, as Scattergood observes, "organized to a degree" (2000a, p. 167). Wanley first described it as a trilingual miscellany: a book "upon several Subjects; partly in old French, partly in Latin, and partly in old English; partly in Verse, & partly in Prose" (2:585). More recently, Connolly has characterized it as "a complex compilation of secular and devotional material in verse and prose which has no discernible perinciple of organization" (p. 132). On categorizing the arrangement of contents in Harley, see especially Revard 1982, 2007; Stemmler 2000; Fein 2000b, 2007; and O'Rourke 2005.

feature suggests how the Ludlow scribe must have enjoyed interlingual wit unleashed for social play, piety, and pedagogy. Given how modern conventions of editing tend to downplay medieval contexts, this critically important aspect of the Harley reading experience has been largely unavailable to a modern audience.

My goal in making this edition is to give students the capacity to read and experience the whole book alongside viewing it in the facsimile, and also to enable scholars to better study and appraise the Ludlow scribe and the compilation he so creatively made. With texts printed continuously and translations at hand, the trilingualism of the Harley manuscript is here rendered transparent.[4] Readers may explore the scribe's accomplishment in its entirety rather than merely in its parts, as has typically characterized Harley studies. By printing everything in order, this edition exhibits the linguistic crossover points while simultaneously lessening temporal and verbal impediments: the flavor of the medieval texts can be experienced in original words *and* with modern English equivalencies. Students may thereby bridge linguistic boundaries with the fluency practiced by the scribe.[5]

Compartmented within linguistic spheres of study reinforced by traditional disciplines, many scholars of medieval texts work mainly inside single-language frameworks. In the case of MS Harley 2253, such a method is far less than ideal and will yield myopic results. Broadly speaking, it is Middle English scholars who have dealt with the English texts, especially the famous lyrics and political songs, while they have relegated to Anglo-Normanists the task of handling the French ones — the matter that comprises, in fact, the bulk of the collection. Consequently, the book's French has long lain in a state of neglect — often barely edited or not edited at all — because relatively few literary scholars in English *or* French departments work in the vast textual terrain of post–Norman Conquest, French-speaking England. Lately, hopeful signs have emerged that, by means of valuable new tools and collaborative projects, this barren state is to be steadily remedied.[6] This METS edition contributes to the broader, sweeping impetus to bring the French of England — as well as much more early Middle English — to greater clarity and understanding.

Likewise has the book's "Latin of England" been largely ignored.[7] The versatile Ludlow scribe worked professionally in this *third* language, too, as legal scrivener and most probably

---

[4] One can, of course, see this diversity in the facsimile, but reading handwritten texts in three languages and medieval script is not easy for most, and the existence of the facsimile has not spurred scholarship of Harley 2253 much beyond examination of isolated textual clusters or themes. For notable exceptions, see Turville-Petre 1996 and Revard 2000b. That a comprehensive approach is ripe for adoption is indicated by two recent dissertations that embrace Harley's English and Anglo-Norman contents as a unified field (Maulsby, Nelson 2010), and another that does the same for the Ludlow scribe's three manuscripts (Rock).

[5] For translations, I am indebted to my collaborators David Raybin for Anglo-Norman and Jan Ziolkowski for Latin. For the final form each translation takes, I am responsible for errors.

[6] Some of these new tools and projects include the valuable comprehensive catalogue *Anglo-Norman Literature* (R. Dean and Boulton); the online *Anglo-Norman Dictionary*; the online *Production and Use of English Manuscripts 1060 to 1220* Project (Da Rold et al.); a ground-breaking collection of essays (Wogan-Browne et al.); and the French of England Translation Series (FRETS) of ACRMS Publications. All of these occurrences augment the already steady output of editorial scholarship from the Anglo-Norman Text Society (ANTS).

[7] MS Harley 2253 is never mentioned, for example, in the authoritative study of Anglo-Latin literature in Rigg 1992.

as chaplain. In the book's Latin one finds selections as intriguingly provocative as the vernacular ones. All of this Latin material appears, of course, in this edition in proper sequence with the French and English matter. Many bits of it — such as the prose lives of Ethelbert, Etfrid, and Wistan, each a foundational story of the region's Anglo-Saxon heritage — are here edited and printed for the first time.

The innovation of this full-manuscript edition-with-translation is, therefore, critical to its goal. The format is designed to treat Middle English, Anglo-Norman, and Latin evenly and to translate each in a manner that invites inspection of the originals.[8] In the past, individual Harley texts have been accessible only in scattered places and scattered ways. Many are in modern anthologies that typically reinforce divides of language or genre. Only a handful of editors have striven to include groups of Harley texts in one place, and anthologies of medieval verse typically print a number of English lyrics without the French ones.[9] Thomas Wright anthologized and translated the Harley political verse — English, French, and Latin — arranging them not together but rather in a broad selection of political songs from England (Wright 1839). Likewise, the Harley Anglo-Norman fabliaux appear in the definitive *Nouveau recueil complet des fabliaux*, but they must be sought there in separate volumes because they are treated within categories of Old French fabliaux.[10] Here, at last, is the Harley manuscript *in toto*.

## BOOKLETS

The presentation of Harley's contents according to booklet structure introduces another significant breakthrough. Internal booklets were first delineated by N. R. Ker,[11] and they were given some attention in the 2000 collection *Studies in the Harley Manuscript*.[12] Reading the Harley manuscript according to its physical makeup — that is, by the individual quires or groups of quires that constitute independent blocks of texts — sheds light on what the

---

[8] As I initially planned the format (in discussions with METS general editor Russell A. Peck), it was thought that Middle English texts would be glossed rather than translated, in accord with METS style. However, texts written in dialects of early Middle English bear a greater than normal need for the close analysis that modern translation brings, and they demand full utilization of the online *Middle English Dictionary*. Moreover, as my translation work proceeded, I was surprised to see how rarely the *Harley Lyrics* have been translated; how existing translations tend to be versified rather than close; how the very challenging vernacular satires (arts. 25a, 31, 40, 81, 88) have never been translated; and how some English items (i.e., arts. 32, 68, 85, 89) have seldom been printed, much less subjected to critical editing and translation.

[9] The major anthologies of select English contents are Böddeker, Brown 1932, Brown 1952, and Brook. The only anthology to mix English and French lyrics is Wright 1842. Editions of select Anglo-Norman are also found in Jeffrey and Levy, and in the unpublished dissertations of Dove and Kennedy.

[10] Noomen and van den Boogard; see also Montaiglon and Raynaud; and Short and Pearcy. Revard has printed the fabliaux and some comic French items with verse translations (2004, 2005a, 2005b, 2005c).

[11] Ker, p. xvi. In listing the "independent blocks" of MS Harley 2253, Ker omitted the division that marks booklet 1 as separate from booklet 2.

[12] Fein 2000c (with a chart on pp. 371–76), Nolan, and Thompson 2000. See also O'Rourke 2005, Revard 2007, and Fein 2007. O'Rourke 2000 examines the booklets of London, British Library, Royal 12.C.12, another codex belonging to the Ludlow scribe.

first two scribes strove to accomplish within their portions of the book. We cannot assert that the Ludlow scribe's textual productions ever circulated in multiple booklets. Individual articles *did* get copied, however, into booklets in the manuscript's early making, even if only at the scribe's desk. Although now in a modern binding, the codex as we have it seems to date from the scribe's own time — an assumption based on the fact that the first two booklets (inscribed by Scribe A) were also the property of the Ludlow scribe. So the grouping of seven booklets to make the Harley manuscript — its full 140 leaves — seems to have happened when the scribe was alive.[13]

The booklet makeup yields tangible clues as to the two main scribes' local purposes. In particular, it begins to reveal rationales that underlie the Ludlow scribe's anthologizing impulses, showing how he arranged texts with an eye to clustering topics, themes, and/or antithetical arguments inside units smaller than the whole book. The following paragraphs provide an overview of the contents of each booklet in the manuscript.[14]

**Booklet 1 (quires 1–2, fols. 1–22).** This booklet holds the lengthy text of the *Vitas patrum* in Anglo-Norman verse with the story of Thais (drawn from the same work) appended at the end. The hand is that of the earlier Scribe A. The Ludlow scribe has written in red the title *Vitas patrum* on fol. 1. This booklet and the next one constitute the volume that the Ludlow scribe had in hand when he commenced his own copying endeavor.

**Booklet 2 (quires 3–4, fols. 23–48).** Scribe A's work continues in this booklet with more Anglo-Norman religious texts in both verse and prose. First there is a long verse paraphrase of the Gospels: Herman de Valenciennes's *La Passioun Nostre Seignour*. Coming next is the anonymous prose *Gospel of Nicodemus*, a work of biblical apocrypha enjoying broad dissemination in many languages throughout medieval Europe. Appended to *The Gospel of Nicodemus* are two of its traditional accretions, *The Letter of Pilate to Tiberius* and *The Letter of Pilate to Emperor Claudius*. Then Scribe A adds four prose saints' lives — those of John the Evangelist, John the Baptist, Bartholomew, and Peter — a textual cluster that has analogues in Old French manuscripts.[15] A history of the Passion and its aftermath (including saints from that historical era) is the spiritual knowledge conveyed by this booklet to a reader. Here again, the Ludlow scribe inserts titles in red. It is intriguing to think that he may have been acquainted with the elder Scribe A, for as the first scribe left lines blank for titles, it was the Ludlow scribe who filled them in when he acquired the book. The Ludlow scribe's titles indicate, at the very least, that he knew the contents of the book in his possession.

---

[13] Alternatively, it may have happened soon after his death, when his library was still intact and an executor, relative, or associate sought to preserve it. Revard assumes that it was the Ludlow scribe who acted to join the fifteen quires (2007, pp. 98–99). Ker notes only that, because of the booklet makeup, "the quires need not be in their original order" (p. xvi). See also Fein 2013.

[14] In the presentation of texts in this edition, the divisions of booklet, quire, and folio are designated, and each item is keyed to its article number in the facsimile (Ker, pp. ix–xvi). Here I have occasionally refined Ker's numbering, that is, I have given separate numbers to arts. 1a, 3a, and 3b in volume 1, and to art. 24a* in volume 2 (see Appendix).

[15] This collection of lives has been edited by D. Russell 1989. Revard relates them to Ludlow-area churches having the same patron saints: "St John Evangelist is patron of the Palmers' Gild in Ludlow parish Church of St Lawrence; St John Baptist is patron saint of the Ludlow Hospital of St John Baptist; the parish Church of St Bartholomew is three miles south of Ludlow in Richard's Castle; and the Church of St Peter is at Leominster Priory, ten miles south of Ludlow" (2007, p. 100). Saint Peter also figures centrally in the Leominster-based life of Saint Etfrid found in booklet 6 (see art. 98).

***Booklet 3 (quire 5, fols. 49–52).*** This booklet marks the start of the Ludlow scribe's portion of MS Harley 2253. Choosing a purposeful beginning and a radical shift in topic from booklets 1 and 2, the scribe starts off with an alphabet poem, the *ABC of Women*, followed by the *Debate between Winter and Summer*. Both of these entertainments are in Anglo–Norman verse. The booklet consists of just one quire of four leaves, and it originally ended with a column and a half of blank space (fol. 52v), on which a later person (hence, chronologically, Scribe C) added paint recipes. Such recipes pertain to the technical interests of a manuscript illuminator, and they may offer a clue as to the further ownership or use of MS Harley 2253 after its completion by the Ludlow scribe — perhaps, that is, after his death. The first evident user of the book (after the scribe or his patron) was someone who wished to retain instructions on how to make paint colors and apply silverfoil to parchment. This same person may have added the decorative initial *W* appearing on the last folio of MS Harley 2253 (fol. 140v). The break in topic from Scribe A's religious texts to the Ludlow scribe's courtly entertainments likely indicates that this booklet was initially separate from booklets 1–2 and was at first conceived to be so.

***Booklet 4 (quire 6, fols. 53–62).*** Like booklet 3, this one consists of a single quire, yet, having ten leaves, it is more than twice the length. Distinctly moral in nature, it is filled with exempla of tragic men — wicked traitors and fallen heroes alike — who pass on to death and implicitly to the afterlives they deserve. The booklet starts off with the local, sanctified example of Saint Ethelbert, Anglo-Saxon patron martyr of Hereford Cathedral, delivered in Latin prose.[16] But the tone is most fully established by the presence of the English *Harrowing of Hell* and *Debate between Body and Soul* — humanity's cosmic fate beside that of the individual. Next there appear political poems on Richard of Cornwall ("Richard the trichard"), Simon de Montfort, William Wallace, and Simon Fraser, and tucked in between is a triad of moral proverbs in English, French, and Latin — the stark message universalized in every language. *The Three Foes of Man* closes this booklet with stern warning to watch one's own behavior and consider the eventual fate. Interlopers in this moralistic booklet introduce an edge of comedy or courtliness: *A Goliard's Feast*, *On the Follies of Fashion*, and *Lesson for True Lovers*. Read a certain way, these texts expose human foibles, but they veer more toward the lightheartedness of booklet 3.

***Booklet 5 (quires 7–11, fols. 63–105).*** Numbering forty-three leaves, booklet 5 is the longest and most complex of the sections of MS Harley 2253. Its first half constitutes an extraordinary anthology of lyrics mostly in English, the finest such collection to survive from medieval Britain. In this sequence, secular love lyrics come first with religious poems following later, although such categories are not strictly maintained. In the secular section appears a comic monk's tale (a pseudo-saint's life), *The Life of Saint Marina*. Roughly dividing the secular from the religious sections are the rollicking French interlude *Gilote and Johane* and a pair of pilgrimage texts in French prose. This cluster seems to enact a meandering transition from sexual desires to Holy Land travels. It also marks an exit from quire 7 into quires 8–9, which hold delicate lyrics (still largely in English) that, for the most

---

[16] Revard suggests that *The Life of Saint Ethelbert* is the earliest of the texts appearing on fols. 49–140 (2007, p. 101), which might suggest that the Ludlow scribe initially designed booklet 4 to follow immediately on booklets 1 and 2. Like them (and unlike booklet 3), it is ruled in columns. The scribe evidently regarded the three Latin lives as texts of special reverence. He copied the others (Etfrid and Wistan) as the *concluding* items of their respective booklets.

part, honor Christ and Mary, with two historical poems paired and mixed in: *The Death of Edward I* and *The Flemish Insurrection*.

Anchoring the second half of booklet 5 are two long works: the English verse romance *King Horn* and the Ludlow scribe's never-before-edited Anglo-Norman prose translation of stories from Genesis, Exodus, and Numbers. These somewhat freely adapted stories stress the exploits of Joseph, Moses, and the priestly Levite tribe. *King Horn*, coming with a preface (a prayer-poem in French and English), occupies almost ten full folios on its own. The succeeding Bible stories occupy thirteen. In sheer length, then, these two texts constitute the core of the Ludlow scribe's continuous labor as represented on folios 49–140. Quires 10–11 were appended to the lyric anthology in order to provide room for *Horn* and the stories. On the last verso of booklet 5 — that is, its back cover if it once stood alone — the scribe has written in Latin a list of the books of the Bible. This list signals, perhaps, a pedagogical function residing behind this compilation of superb specimens in verse and dynamic models of virtuous male behavior.

**Booklet 6 (quires 12–14, fols. 106–133).** This booklet contains the largest collection of Anglo-Norman fabliaux to be found in England. In all, there are four here, each one told very cleverly, with two of them not recorded elsewhere. They seem grouped with many poems that argue the inherent flaws and merits of women (obviously a perennially favorite topic). Designed for social repartee, this theme is also evident in several booklet 5 items, although in booklet 6 it is more pronounced and more typically expressed in French. Displays of wit continue in the comic *Jongleur of Ely and the King of England*, which also participates in the booklet's deep interest in conveying wise advice and inculcating proper male conduct, especially as passed from father to son (Urbain to his son, Saint Louis to Philip) or from a named sage (Saint Bernard, Thomas of Erceldoune, Hending, and so on). Anglo-Norman prevails in this booklet, but there are still some interesting English items, such as the *Book of Dreaming*, the remarkable *Man in the Moon*, and the *contrefacta* on Jesus' love versus woman's love. The booklet also contains the second Latin saint's life, *The Legend of Saint Etfrid*, which commemorates another Anglo-Saxon saint with local resonance. Geographic lore with a crusading edge surfaces in texts on Saracen lands, international heraldic arms, and the relics housed in the cathedral of the Spanish city of Oviedo. In overall makeup, booklet 6 is an intriguing miscellany that suggests an audience of young men, perhaps pupils, as well as scripts for mixed-gender social settings at which comic entertainments could be read aloud, and perhaps enacted, for enjoyment and discussion.

**Booklet 7 (quire 15, fols. 134–140).** Consisting of one quire of seven leaves, booklet 7 is written entirely in French and Latin and mainly in prose. It is a handbook of practical religion that provides the reader with lists of occasions for prayers, masses, and psalms to be said in times of adversity, along with more lists of the reasons to fast on Friday, the propitious attributes of herbs, and Anselm's questions to be asked of the dying. A few longer texts stand out as somewhat detached from this purpose, and they give the booklet a more miscellaneous though still devout feel: the Latin moralization *All the World's a Chess Board*, which the scribe may have drawn from a copy of John of Wales's *Communeloquium*; the macaronic French/Latin political diatribe *Against the King's Taxes*; an intense, affective meditation focused on the hours of the Passion; and a commemoration of the life of Saint Wistan, Anglo-Saxon patron saint of the Ludlow scribe's neighboring Wistanstow. To judge by the script, this last text was added several years after the other texts were copied, in around 1347. As an end to the Harley manuscript, booklet 7 displays the piety of daily worship tied to the worldly concerns of a clergy opposed to oppressive taxation by the state. It is another booklet that might once have stood alone, although it should be noted that the last text of booklet 6, *Prayer for Protection*, offers a bridge to the practices and beliefs detailed here.

PROFILE OF THE LUDLOW SCRIBE

Much has been written about the Ludlow scribe, especially since Carter Revard's landmark research that dates his hand as it appears in three manuscripts and forty-one legal writs. Revard's report of these discoveries appeared just when the study of scribes exploded on the investigative scene of Middle English as an important technique by which to bring historical precision to the cultural mapping of manuscripts, their contents, and their readers. Such work has recently revolutionized the study of Chaucer, Langland, Gower, Trevisa, and Hoccleve, revealing previously unknown networks of metropolitan scribes — in particular, a pivotal group of men centered in the London Guildhall — who assiduously copied and promoted these authors.[17] Work on the Ludlow scribe runs parallel to this movement while illustrating a strand of the scribal networks operating outside of London. In this realm of Middle English literary-historical studies, the Ludlow scribe is someone of special interest, akin to the intriguing Rate (main scribe of MS Ashmole 61) and Robert Thornton of Yorkshire (compiler of two manuscripts in the fifteenth century). Many such scribes are like the Ludlow scribe in being entirely anonymous yet recognizable in their handiwork and proclivities. As the maker of a key manuscript, the Ludlow scribe is a leading figure among a growing company of copyists now recognized for the value of what they preserved. Increasingly, scholars are focusing on these figures so as to understand the historical purposes for which texts were made and to learn how texts circulated, were used, and were selected to be copied. For a scribe as provocative and idiosyncratic in his choices as was the Ludlow scribe of MS Harley 2253, we also just want to know more about who he was, who he might have worked for, how he was educated, how he was trained as a scribe, and in what circles he moved in society.

Documents reveal that the scribe who copied folios 49–140 of the Harley manuscript flourished as a professional legal scribe in the vicinity of Ludlow from 1314 to 1349. The forty-one writs and charters in his hand recovered by Revard are dated from December 18, 1314, to April 13, 1349. If he was in his twenties when he inscribed the first of these documents, then he was born in the last decade of the thirteenth century. He may have died during the Black Death, which swept through England from 1348 to 1350, so his dates can roughly be set from about 1290 to about 1350.

The earliest writs hail from Ludlow, the scribe's apparent home base. There are sixteen documents from Ludlow itself, including one probably written for Sir Lawrence Ludlow of Stokesay Castle, which is located west of Ludlow in the direction of Wistanstow. In that village is the church built on the site of Saint Wistan's martyrdom as chronicled in the last text of MS Harley 2253. The most outlying document is from Edgton, a village west of Wistanstow. Another is from Stanton Lacy, which is to the north of Ludlow. All others are set south of Ludlow: in the town's neighboring outskirts, four from Ludford and one each from Sheet and Steventon; and from further south: fifteen from Overton, two from Ashford Carbonel, and one from Richard's Castle. With the exception of Edgton, all the writs and

---

[17] See Horobin; Mooney and Stubbs; and the important new online resource *Late Medieval English Scribes* (Mooney et al.).

charters are located within a three-mile radius of Ludlow. And Edgton is but two miles from Wistanstow, which is merely three miles from Stokesay Castle.

The other two Latin saints' lives affiliate the Harley manuscript with major centers directly on the road south from Ludlow. *The Life of Saint Ethelbert* commemorates the patron saint of Hereford and its cathedral.[18] *The Legend of Saint Etfrid* recounts the colorful story of a lion tamed by the saint's offer of bread, a dreamlike encounter that predicts an Anglo-Saxon king's conversion and the founding of a monastery in Leominster. The three saints' lives share a common thread of interest in regional saints from Anglo-Saxon times, that is, foundational stories for religious centers in the vicinity of the scribe's activity. In the case of *The Martyrdom of Saint Wistan*, it is conceivable that the scribe himself redacted the story and preached it to a congregation in Wistanstow to mark a feast day, or that it came from such a local source written for such a parochial purpose.

A considerable amount of further evidence about the Ludlow scribe's reading, collection habits, and tastes exists in two additional manuscripts, where his hand frequently appears in such a way as to suggest that he once owned them as well. These books are MS Harley 273 and MS Royal 12.C.12. Both are housed with the Harley manuscript in London at the British Library, and, to judge from the scribe's script, both predate it. Revard supplies good overviews of these books and dates the scribe's handwriting in each one.[19] Yet, except for attention paid to the Ludlow scribe's copies of some major works — such as the *Short Metrical Chronicle* (an abridgement of the Middle English *Brut*) and *Fouke le Fitz Waryn* (an outlaw tale in Anglo-Norman prose) — the intricate range of contents found in these two books and the various, sometimes stray insertions made by the scribe have not yet been systematically described.[20]

In characterizing who the Ludlow scribe was and exploring his probable occupations and training, one may borrow from an informed speculation as to the compiler-scribe of a comparable, older West Midland book, Oxford, Bodleian Library MS Digby 86. Here, it has been said, the scribe was likely "a cleric, perhaps the local parish-priest, more probably a private chaplain in a manorial household. . . . He had a dual function, to provide both spiritual guidance and also what one might call book-based entertainment."[21] This profile for the Digby scribe seems a good fit for the Ludlow scribe, too.[22] We may readily surmise

---

[18] The Ludlow scribe's seeming connections to Hereford and to Hereford Cathedral, a sophisticated center of learning with international ties, have long piqued scholarly curiosity. See especially Ker, pp. xxi–xxiii; Salter, pp. 32–33; Revard 2000b, pp. 23–30; Corrie 2003, pp. 78–79; Birkholz; and Fein 2013. McSparran notes that the scribe's orthography and dialect localize him to the vicinity of Leominster, which lies twelve miles north of Hereford and nine miles south of Ludlow, all lying on the same route (pp. 393–94, citing Samuels).

[19] Revard 2000b, pp. 65–73.

[20] The content of the writs and charters is presented in Revard 2000b, pp. 30–64, 91–107. On MS Royal 12.C.12, see especially Ker, pp. xx–xxi; Hathaway et al., pp. xxxvii–liii; O'Farrell-Tate, pp. 46–50; and O'Rourke 2000. On all three books, see Walpole, pp. 29–40; and O'Rourke 2005, pp. 52–53.

[21] Frankis, p. 183. On the affiliations between the Harley and Digby manuscripts, see Corrie 2000; and Boffey, pp. 8–10.

[22] Scholars have, furthermore, detected a degree of cosmopolitan sophistication in the Ludlow scribe, whose selections "drew on material written abroad as well as works written more locally" (Corrie 2003, p. 79) and probably derived from "contact with high ecclesiastics, noble benefactors,

that his training was in Latin, religion, and law, subjects that all point to a clerical education. A distinct taste for secular performance pieces suggests his additional role as a master of entertainments, no doubt as a speaking reader, possibly even as a performer or director of others in performance. Marginal speech markers in *Harrowing of Hell* and *Gilote and Johane* preserve these articles' original theatricality, and many more of the Ludlow scribe's preserved debates, dialogues, and expressive monologues seem designed for dramatic show. Oral delivery is often announced from the start, and such openings surely indicate real occasions and are not just literate convention.[23] The scribe seems to have held some particular political leanings, which were probably common to his region: patriotic toward nation and king; sympathetic, however, to the barons' cause as formerly led by Simon de Montfort; and strongly opposed to petty, corrupt officialdom and unreasonable taxation. These attitudes show an empathy for the common populace, but they were also shared by many clergy, and a good degree of identification with the clerical authors expressing these views probably accounts for the scribe's inclusion of these outlooks.[24]

Of course, it may be that the scribe's social attitudes were also shaped to please a patron; various scholars have sought to identify who the scribe's patron might have been.[25] Because we cannot know the name of the patron any more than we can know the name of the scribe, it seems wisest to glean what we can of attitudes and social outlooks as they are suggested by the articles of MS Harley 2253 taken in aggregate and in combination. The meanings built by juxtaposition and selection would seem best explained as deriving from the intelligence of the scribe — someone with literary leanings and a freedom to pursue his own whims, choices, chance finds, and networks of texts. If an externally directed pattern is perceptible here, it runs toward edification and instruction. It would seem likely that the Ludlow scribe had some responsibility in the inculcation of manners and learning for a male heir or heirs in a well-bred, perhaps aristocratic setting. In this environment, he, his charges, and his patrons were accustomed to interact with one another in Anglo-Norman. Toward household members, his duties must also have included spiritual guidance, as from a professional chaplain.

The inclusion of the adventure stories of *King Horn* in the Harley manuscript and of *Fouke le Fitz Waryn* in MS Royal 12.C.12 seems well explained as directed toward an audience of boys whose morals were to be shaped by a clerical tutor or schoolmaster.[26] The Old Testament stories devote space to the God-ordained exploits of Joseph and Moses. The political and geographical works offer more instruction on history and knowledge of the world and local environs. And the debates on women's nature, the lyrics on secular love, and even the outrageously profane fabliaux provide provocative matter to be absorbed by inquisitive young men about the mysterious nature of the opposite gender. Most overtly, the literature

---

as well as with travelling scholars and minstrels" (Salter, p. 32). For other profiling insights, see especially O'Rourke 2000 (p. 222), 2005; and Revard 2007, pp. 99–102.

[23] Fein 2007, pp. 81, 88–91.

[24] See, for example, the explanatory notes to arts. 31, 109, and 114. On the collective political outlook of the Harley contents, see Scattergood 2000a; and also O'Rourke 2005, pp. 50–52.

[25] For recent proposals as to the unknown patron, patrons, or milieus, see Revard 2000b, esp. pp. 74–90; O'Rourke 2000; Hines, pp. 71–104; and Birkholz.

[26] For *Fouke le Fitz Waryn*, the chronicled history of a local family and namesake heir was surely a factor that compelled interest in the narrative, too. See Revard 2000b, pp. 87–90, 108–09; and Hanna.

of conduct and good manners clustered in booklet 6 seems designed for the schoolroom, whether directed at a single scion of a household or a group of pupils from aspirant Anglo-Norman homes.

Most interesting, perhaps, in considering the roles of the Ludlow scribe, is to observe how he sometimes assumed the task of author as well as a redactor and compiler. The Bible stories and *Fouke le Fitz Waryn* are now accepted as his own literate productions created by translating and adapting inherited material. For the former, extracts from the Vulgate Bible (and sometimes Peter Comestor) were converted from Latin to Anglo-Norman prose, with the scribe adding occasional lessons: a mnemonic couplet on the ten plagues, a multilingual explanation of the word *manna*, and a typological reading of the Synagogue as the "Church for Christians" ("eglise a chretiens"). For *Fouke*, an Anglo-Norman verse romance was remade as prose in the same language. Certain turns of phrase show the scribe to have been anglophone by birth, francophone by social standing and daily habit — as were, no doubt, his associates, his patrons, and their children.[27] To these French works now ascribed to him, works in other languages contend as more possibilities. One is *The Martyrdom of Saint Wistan*, a Latin redaction from a longer Latin prose life.[28] In English, too, he may have devised *A Bok of Swevenyng* by cobbling it from the Latin dreambook *Somniale Danielis* in his possession in MS Royal 12.C.12.

The lines that distinguish scribe from compiler and even from the higher offices of an author are sometimes blurred, therefore, as we reach for an accurate profile of this interesting man from medieval Ludlow. Regarding poetry of this period, Derek Pearsall has commented that "the scribe as much as the poet is the 'author' of what we have in extant copies."[29] Nowhere is this more true than in the command performance of the Ludlow scribe. He collected ephemeral songs, entertainments, and diatribes that survive nowhere else because they floated on broadsheets never intended for appearance among the records of a book. For some of the most vernacular items of local politics and social satire, the Ludlow scribe became, perhaps unconsciously, an innovator in preservation by new media when he inscribed *into booklets* comic complaints delivered in colorful alliterative idiom to ventriloquize the outlooks of monoglot, unlettered English people. Such scripts designed for performance and class-based mockery acquire a new, more politicized valence when — marked exclusively as *utterance* — they come eventually to dwell inside the boards of a bound document, thereby officially "recording" a marginal point of view.[30]

---

[27] Wilshere, and see explanatory notes to art. 71. The author of *Urbain the Courteous* (art. 79) advocates that French be taught to English children. In it, a father instructs his son: "I want, first of all, / For you to be wise and full of kindness, / Gracious and courteous, / And that you know how to speak French, / For highly is this language praised / By noblemen" (lines 15–20).

[28] This vita seems the most likely of the three to be the Ludlow scribe's own redaction, although the other two Latin lives — both adapted from longer vitae — may also have sprung from his efforts. See the explanatory notes to arts. 18, 98, and 114.

[29] Pearsall, p. 120.

[30] I have argued elsewhere that the scribe preserved these particular vernacular satires because he saw significant ways to pair and juxtapose them with other works (Fein 2007, pp. 91–94). When the English vernacular enters this textual/oral world as biting satire, there are subtle enactments of social class and register in play. So, too, when Latin enters, there are uplifted tones of clerical learning and moral teaching.

The Ludlow scribe's remarkable manuscript captures for us myriad snapshots of lived moments in the literate culture of the French-speaking English from the western Marches, giving us multiple perspectives on how that society sought entertainment and pursued mental enrichment a half-century before Chaucer. When we closely examine vernacular performance texts extant in other copies, like the *Harrowing of Hell* and *King Horn*, we readily discover how the scribe's distinct touch has perceptibly inflected his versions. At the same time, in the Ludlow scribe's selections and insertions, one may potentially trace his preferences and influences: Peter Comester, John of Wales, Albertus Magnus, Anselm of Canterbury, Hilary of Poitiers, Chrétien de Troyes, for example. The Hereford Franciscan poet and preacher William Herebert might have been one of his acquaintances.[31] In addition, the imaginatively rich, stylistically versatile narratives copied by Scribe A enhance our sense of the Anglo-French literary influences swirling within the scribe's easy reach. The Ludlow scribe's milieus, sources, range of training, professional activities, and goals as a copyist pose a challenging, fascinating domain for scholarly investigation. With this edition and translation, that domain is now fully open for reading and exploration.

FURTHER READING

*Facsimile*
Ker, N. R. Intro. to *Facsimile of British Museum MS. Harley 2253*. EETS o.s. 255. London, 1965.

*Standard Edition of the English "Harley Lyrics"*
Brook, G. L., ed. *The Harley Lyrics: The Middle English Lyrics of Ms. Harley 2253*. Fourth ed. Manchester: Manchester University Press, 1968.

*Descriptive Bibliography of the English "Harley Lyrics"*
Fein, Susanna. "XXVII. The Lyrics of MS Harley 2253." In *A Manual of the Writings in Middle English, 1050–1500*. Vol. 11, ed. Peter G. Beidler. New Haven: Connecticut Academy of Arts and Sciences, 2005. Pp. 4168–4206, 4311–61.

*Other Editions of Multiple Harley Items*
Böddeker, Karl, ed. *Altenglische Dichtungen des MS. Harl. 2253*. Berlin: Weidmannsche, 1878.
Brown, Carleton, ed. *English Lyrics of the XIIIth Century*. Oxford: Clarendon, 1932.
———, ed. *Religious Lyrics of the XIVth Century*. Oxford: Clarendon, 1924. Second edition. Rev. G. V. Smithers. Oxford: Clarendon, 1952.
Dove, Mary. "A Study of Some of the Lesser-Known Poems of British Museum Ms. Harley 2253." D.Phil. dissertation, Girton College, Cambridge, 1969.
Jeffrey, David L., and Brian J. Levy, eds. *The Anglo-Norman Lyric: An Anthology*. Toronto: Pontifical Institute of Mediaeval Studies, 1990.

---

[31] The Ludlow scribe includes one or two poems by the Franciscan Nicholas Bozon, whose writings appear in the Herebert manuscript (London, British Library, MS Add. 46919). See explanatory notes to arts. 9 (often attributed to Bozon), 24a (also in the Herebert manuscript), and 78 (a Bozon text in the Herebert manuscript). The links are discussed by Jeffrey 2000, pp. 263, 269–70; and Revard 2007, pp. 104–05 n. 17.

Kennedy, Thomas Corbin. "Anglo-Norman Poems about Love, Women, and Sex from British Museum MS. Harley 2253." Ph.D. dissertation, Columbia University, 1973.

Montaiglon, Anatole de, and Gaston Raynaud, eds. *Recueil général et complet des fabliaux des XIIIᵉ et XIVᵉ siècles*. 6 vols. Paris, 1872–90; repr. New York, 1964.

Noomen, Willem, and Nico van den Boogard, eds. *Nouveau recueil complet des fabliaux*. 10 vols. Assen: Van Gorcum, 1983–98.

Robbins, Rossell Hope, ed. *Historical Poems of the XIVth and XVth Centuries*. New York: Columbia University Press, 1959.

Turville-Petre, Thorlac, ed. *Alliterative Poetry of the Later Middle Ages: An Anthology*. Washington, DC: Catholic University of America Press, 1989.

Wright, Thomas, ed. *Political Songs of England, from the Reign of John to That of Edward II*. 1839; repr. with an intro. by Peter Coss. Cambridge: Cambridge University Press, 1996.

———, ed. *The Latin Poems Commonly Attributed to Walter Mapes*. London: John Bowyer Nichols and Son (for the Camden Society), 1841; repr. New York: AMS Press, 1968.

———, ed. *Specimens of Lyric Poetry, Composed in England in the Reign of Edward the First*. Percy Society, 1842; repr. New York: Johnson Reprint Corporation, 1965.

———, ed. "Early English Receipts for Painting, Gilding, &c." *Archaeological Journal* 1 (1844), 64–66.

*Recent Editions of Select Harley Items*

Hunt, Tony, ed., and Jane Bliss, trans. *"Cher alme": Texts of Anglo-Norman Piety*. French of England Translation Series. Tempe: Arizona Center for Medieval and Renaissance Studies, 2010.

Lerer, Seth. "'Dum ludis floribus': Language and Text in the Medieval English Lyric." *Philological Quarterly* 87 (2008), 237–55.

Millett, Bella. *Wessex Parallel WebTexts*. 2003. Online at http://www.soton.ac.uk/~wpwt/.

Pringle, Denys. *Pilgrimage to Jerusalem and the Holy Land, 1187–1291*. Burlington, VT: Ashgate, 2012. Pp. 229–36.

Revard, Carter. "*The Wife of Bath's Grandmother*: or How Gilote Showed Her Friend Johane That the Wages of Sin Is Worldly Pleasure, and How Both Then Preached This Gospel throughout England and Ireland." *Chaucer Review* 39 (2004), 117–36.

———. "Four Fabliaux from London, British Library MS Harley 2253, Translated into English Verse." *Chaucer Review* 40 (2005), 111–40.

———. "*A Goliard's Feast* and the Metanarrative of Harley 2253." *Revue Belge de Philologie et d'Histoire* 83 (2005), 841–67.

———. "The Outlaw's Song of Trailbaston." In *Medieval Outlaws: Twelve Tales in Modern English Translation*. Ed. Thomas H. Ohlgren. Second edition. West Lafayette, IN: Parlor Press, 2005. Pp. 151–64.

Short, Ian, and Roy Pearcy, eds. *Eighteen Anglo-Norman Fabliaux*. ANTS Plain Texts Series 14. London: Anglo-Norman Text Society, 2000.

Treharne, Elaine, ed. *Old and Middle English c.890–c.1450*. Third edition. Chichester: Wiley-Blackwell, 2010.

Woolgar, C. M., ed. *Household Accounts from Medieval England*. Part 1: *Introduction, Glossary, Diet Accounts (I)*. Records of Social and Economic History n.s. 17. Oxford: Oxford University Press for The British Academy, 1992. Pp. 174–77.

*Essay Collection on MS Harley 2253*

Fein, Susanna, ed. *Studies in the Harley Manuscript: The Scribes, Contents, and Social Contexts of British Library MS Harley 2253*. Kalamazoo, MI: Medieval Institute Publications, 2000. *Contents:*

- Susanna Fein. "British Library MS Harley 2253: The Lyrics, the Facsimile, and the Book." Pp. 1–20.
- Carter Revard. "Scribe and Provenance." Pp. 21–109.
- Theo Stemmler. "Miscellany or Anthology? The Structure of Medieval Manuscripts: MS Harley 2253, for Example." Pp. 111–21.
- Michael P. Kuczynski. "An 'Electric Stream': The Religious Contents." Pp. 123–61.
- John Scattergood. "Authority and Resistance: The Political Verse." Pp. 163–201.
- Richard Newhauser. "Historicity and Complaint in *Song of the Husbandman*." Pp. 203–17.
- Karl Reichl. "Debate Verse." Pp. 219–39.
- Helen Phillips. "Dreams and Dream Lore." Pp. 241–59.
- David L. Jeffrey. "Authors, Anthologists, and Franciscan Spirituality." Pp. 261–70.
- John J. Thompson. "'Frankis rimes here I redd, / Communlik in ilk[a] sted . . .': The French Bible Stories in Harley 2253." Pp. 271–88.
- Barbara Nolan. "Anthologizing Ribaldry: Five Anglo-Norman Fabliaux." Pp. 289–327.
- Mary Dove. "Evading Textual Intimacy: The French Secular Verse." Pp. 329–49.
- Susanna Fein. "A Saint 'Geynest under Gore': Marina and the Love Lyrics of the Seventh Quire." Pp. 351–76.
- Elizabeth Solopova. "Layout, Punctuation, and Stanza Patterns in the English Verse." Pp. 377–89.
- Frances McSparran. "The Language of the English Poems: The Harley Scribe and His Exemplars." Pp. 391–426.
- Marilyn Corrie. "Harley 2253, Digby 86, and the Circulation of Literature in Pre-Chaucerian England." Pp. 427–43.

*Other Recent Criticism*

Birkholz, Daniel. "Harley Lyrics and Hereford Clerics: The Implications of Mobility, c. 1300–1351." *Studies in the Age of Chaucer* 31 (2009), 175–230.

Boffey, Julia. "Middle English Lyrics and Manuscripts." In *A Companion to the Middle English Lyric*. Ed. Thomas G. Duncan. Cambridge: D. S. Brewer, 2005. Pp. 1–18.

Butterfield, Ardis. "English, French and Anglo-French: Language and Nation in the Fabliau." In *Mittelalterliche Novellistik im europaischen Kontext: Kulturwissenschaftliche Perspektiven*. Ed. Mark Chinca, Timo Peuvekamp-Felber, and Christopher Yound. Berlin: Erich Schmidt, 2006. Pp. 238–59.

Cable, Thomas. "Foreign Influence, Native Continuation, and Metrical Typology in Alliterative Lyrics." In *Approaches to the Metres of Alliterative Verse*. Ed. Judith Jefferson and Ad Putter. Leeds Texts and Monographs, new series 17. Leeds: University of Leeds, 2009. Pp. 219–34.

Choong, Kevin Teo Kia. "Bodies of Knowledge: Embodying Riotous Performance in the Harley Lyrics." In *"And Never Know the Joy": Sex and the Erotic in English Poetry*. Ed. C. C. Barfoot. Amsterdam: Rodopi, 2006. Pp. 13–32.

Corrie, Marilyn. "Kings and Kingship in British Library MS Harley 2253." *Yearbook of English Studies* 33 (2003), 64–79.

D'Arcy, Anne Marie. "The Middle English Lyrics." In *Readings in Medieval Texts: Interpreting Old and Middle English Literature*. Ed. David F. Johnson and Elaine Treharne. Oxford: Oxford University Press, 2005. Pp. 306–22.

Durling, Nancy Vine. "British Library MS Harley 2253: A New Reading of the Passion Lyrics in Their Manuscript Context." *Viator* 40 (2009), 271–307.

Fein, Susanna. "Harley Lyrics." In *The Oxford Encyclopedia of British Literature*. Ed. David Scott Kastan and Gail McMurray Gibson. 5 vols. Oxford: Oxford University Press, 2006. 2:519–22.

———. "Compilation and Purpose in MS Harley 2253." In *Essays in Manuscript Geography: Vernacular Manuscripts of the English West Midlands from the Conquest to the Sixteenth Century*. Ed. Wendy Scase. Turnhout: Brepols, 2007. Pp. 67–94.

———. "The Four Scribes of MS Harley 2253." *Journal of the Early Book Society* 16 (2013), 27–49.

———. "Literary Scribes: The Harley Scribe and Robert Thornton as Case Studies." In *Insular Books: Vernacular Miscellanies in Late Medieval Britain*. Ed. Margaret Connolly and Raluca Radulescu. Proceedings of the British Academy. London: British Academy, forthcoming.

Fisher, Matthew. *Scribal Authorship and the Writing of History in Medieval England*. Columbus: Ohio State University Press, 2012. Pp. 100–45.

Hanna, Ralph. "The Matter of Fulk: Romance and the History of the Marches." *Journal of English and Germanic Philology* 110 (2011), 337–58.

Hines, John. *Voices in the Past: English Literature and Archaeology*. Cambridge: D. S. Brewer, 2004.

Kerby-Fulton, Kathryn, Maidie Hilmo, and Linda Olson. *Opening Up Middle English Manuscripts: Literary and Visual Approaches*. Ithaca, NY: Cornell University Press, 2012.

Kinch, Ashby. "Dying for Love: Dialogic Response in the Lyrics of BL MS Harley 2253." In *Courtly Literature and Clerical Culture*. Ed. Christopher Huber and Henrike Lähnemann. Tübingen: Attempto, 2002. Pp. 137–47.

Lerer, Seth. "Medieval English Literature and the Idea of the Anthology." *PMLA* 118 (2003), 1251–67.

Maulsby, Stephen C. "The Harley Lyrics Revisited: A Multilingual Textual Community." Ph.D. dissertation, Catholic University of America, 2008.

Nelson, Ingrid Lynn. "The Lyric in England, 1200–1400." Ph.D. dissertation, Harvard University, 2010.

———. "The Performance of Power in Medieval English Households: The Case of the *Harrowing of Hell*." *Journal of English and Germanic Philology* 112 (2013), 48–69.

O'Rourke, Jason. "British Library MS Royal 12 C. xii and the Problems of Patronage." *Journal of the Early Book Society* 3 (2000), 216–25.

———. "Imagining Book Production in Fourteenth-Century Herefordshire: The Scribe of British Library, Harley 2253 and His 'Organizing Principles.'" In *Imagining the Book*. Ed. Stephen Kelly and John J. Thompson. Turnhout: Brepols, 2005. Pp. 45–60.

Revard, Carter. "From French 'Fabliau Manuscripts' and MS Harley 2253 to the *Decameron* and the *Canterbury Tales*." *Medium Ævum* 69 (2000), 261–78.

———. "Oppositional Thematics and Metanarrative in MS Harley 2253, Quires 1–6." In *Essays in Manuscript Geography: Vernacular Manuscripts of the English West Midlands from the Conquest to the Sixteenth Century*. Ed. Wendy Scase. Turnhout: Brepols, 2007. Pp. 95–112.

Rock, Catherine A. "Romances Copied by the Ludlow Scribe: Purgatoire Saint Patrice, Short Metrical Chronicle, Fouke le Fitz Waryn, and King Horn." Ph.D. dissertation, Kent State University, 2008.

Scahill, John. "Trilingualism in Early Middle English Miscellanies: Languages and Literature." *Yearbook of English Studies* 33 (2003), 18–52.

Scase, Wendy. *Literature and Complaint in England 1272–1553*. Oxford: Oxford University Press, 2007.

Scattergood, John. *The Lost Tradition: Essays on Middle English Alliterative Poetry*. Dublin: Four Courts Press, 2000.

———. "The Love Lyric before Chaucer." In *A Companion to the Middle English Lyric*. Ed. Thomas G. Duncan. Cambridge: D. S. Brewer, 2005. Pp. 39–67.

NOTE ON THE PRESENTATION OF TEXTS

The texts of MS Harley 2253 are printed in the modern alphabet and follow the conventions of the Middle English Texts Series. I list here several details of presentation that require special notice.

*Transcriptions.* Final *h* or final *k* with a medial horizontal line (often a looped flourish) is rendered as *he* or *ke*.

Final yogh is rendered as *s* in English texts, *z* in French texts.

The Ludlow scribe's form of *homme* ("man") consistently lacks a minim; previous editors have transcribed the word as either *houme* or *honme*. The form used in this edition is *honme*.

The distinction between the Ludlow scribe's *t* and *c* is frequently slight or nonexistent. Consequently, transcription of those letters may be governed by the language in question. For example, in French texts, *-cio(u)n* is the standard spelling of the suffix; in Latin texts, it is *-tion*.

In Latin texts, the letter *i* remains and does not become *j*.

Other editors' variations of the practices cited here are not recorded in the textual notes.

*Abbreviations.* The Ludlow scribe's ampersand is rendered *ant* in English texts, *e* in French texts, *et* in Latin texts, in accordance with his evident usage when the forms are spelled out. Scribe C's ampersand found in the English paint recipes (arts. 10–17) is also rendered *ant* (although he spells out both *ant* and *et*). The frequent transcription of ampersand in English texts as *and* by previous editors is not noted in the textual notes.

Scribe A's abbreviation *Jh'u* is rendered *Jhesu*. The Ludlow's scribe's abbreviation *ihc* is rendered *Jesu*, as supported by Ker (p. xix) and by the scribe's normal usage. There is only one occurrence of the spelling *ihesu* in the Ludlow scribe's work: *ABC of Women* (art. 8), line 63 (the first appearance of the word). Transcription as *Ihesu* or *Jhesu* by previous editors is not noted in the textual notes.

In French texts copied by the Ludlow scribe, *ns* with an expansion mark is rendered *nous*, as found at *ABC of Women* (art. 8), line 228; *vs* with an expansion mark is rendered *vous*, as found at *Debate between Winter and Summer* (art. 9), line 126. Expansions as *vus* and *nus* by previous editors are not recorded in the textual notes. In Scribe A's texts, these abbreviations are expanded to *nus* and *vus*, in accordance with the scribe's practice.

The abbreviation for *par* in French, English, and Latin texts (*p* with a medial line through the descender) is normally rendered *par*, but in some lexical contexts the form indicates *per* (i.e., *pernez*, *perdu*, *apertenant*, *spere*, etc.).

Likewise, the abbreviation *mlt* is rendered *molt* in French texts (the Ludlow scribe's attested spelling), *mult* in Latin texts. However, in some lexical contexts, the French abbreviation indicates *mult* (for example, *mlteplia* on fol. 95v near *multiplierent* spelled out).

In French texts, *q* with a macron is expanded to *que*, not *qe*. Expansion to *qe* by other editors (i.e., Kennedy) is not listed in the textual notes.

In French texts, the abbreviation *seign* with a flourish on the *n* is rendered *seignur*. The Ludlow scribe's spelling of this word fluctuates. For example, in *Debate between Winter and Summer* (art. 9), one finds the word abbreviated and spelled out as *seignur*, *seignor*, *seigneur*, and *seignour*.

*Paragraphs and initials.* Paraphs and large initials, typically in red ink, adorn the opening word of most texts and may also appear internally. All paraphs are recorded. Red initials are not indicated; wherever their placement may be meaningful, they are discussed in the explanatory notes. Boldface initials corresponding to scribal initials appear in two texts: first, in *ABC of Women* (art. 8) to highlight the ABC formula, and, second, in *The Life of Saint Ethelbert* (art. 18) to record how the scribe presents its divisions by initial letter and not by paraph.

*Refrains and burdens.* The Ludlow scribe's abbreviated indicators for lyric refrains and carol burdens are expanded and printed in full, in the manner in which they were intended to be recited or sung after each stanza. Refrains and burdens appear in italic font. The lines of the opening burden of carols (arts. 36 and 46) are not numbered.

*Article numbers.* The numbering of items in MS Harley 2253 is keyed to the Ker facsimile (pp. ix–xvi). It follows the enumeration first created by Wanley and then refined by Ker. Article 42 is vacant and therefore omitted (see Ker, p. ix). A Latin couplet (art. 24a*) is presented here as a separate article for the first time.

*Foliation.* Material from the manuscript is cited in the left margin by folio number, recto or verso ("r" or "v"), and column ("a," "b," or "c"). A vertical line appears in prose texts wherever a folio or column break occurs. Folio breaks rarely occur within lines of verse; where they do, the break is indicated by a vertical line.

*Titles.* The Middle English, Anglo-Norman, and Latin titles of original works found in MS Harley 2253 derive from first lines, incipits, or scholarly consensus. The titles of the translated texts reflect their standard modern English titles. Where no modern nomenclature exists, titles have been created by the editor.

*Variant readings.* Variant readings recorded by previous editors are compiled in the textual notes. Editions that modernize texts or regularize spellings are omitted. These notes are keyed to the editions listed for each work in the explanatory notes. Differences in word breaks and in the use of apostrophes in French words are not recorded. Words or letters clearly marked for deletion by the scribe are also not recorded. For a broader listing of the numerous editions of the famous *Harley Lyrics* (that is, the thirty-two poems selected by Brook), see Fein 2005.

**BOOKLET 3**                                                    **QUIRE 5**

### ABC a femmes                                                  [art. 8]

49r]     Quy a la Dame de parays
         Deyvent foy e leauté
         Ore entendent a mes dis,
         E je lur dirroy verité.
5        Si nul y soit qe eit mespris
         Vers femme par mavesté,
         De corteysie soit forbanys
         Ou hastivement soit redressé
             A dreyt,
10          Quar il pert sa noreture
               Certes que femme deceit.

         Dieu m'avaunce, par charité,
         Auxi come j'ay mestier;
         Je froi a femmes un a b c,
15       A l'escole si eles vueillent aler.
         Celes que sunt lettree
         As autres purront recorder
         Coment eles sunt honoree
         En dreyture, sauntz fauser
20           De nulle.
            Ou va femme, la vet joie:
               Ele ne va pas soule.

         **A**mour de femme moun cuer entame
         De fere un poy enveysure
25       Pur sauver femme de tote blame.
         Chescun devereit mettre cure
         Pur l'amour de une dame
         Que tot le mound en terre honure.
         Que femme esclaundre e met en fame
30       Ne vint unqe de bone nature,
             A veyr dyre.

**BOOKLET 3**    QUIRE 5

### ABC of Women    [art. 8]

49r]   Those who to heaven's Lady
        Owe faith and loyalty
        May listen now to my words,
        And I'll tell them the truth.
5       If there's anyone who's done wrong
        To women through wickedness,
        May he be banished from courtesy
        Or immediately be corrected
            Justly,
10      For surely he betrays his breeding
            Whoever deceives a woman.

        May God assist me, in charity,
        As far as I have need;
        I will make for women an ABC,
15      Should they wish to go to school.
        Those who are literate
        Can inform others
        How they are honored
        Properly, without falsifying
20          Anything.
            Where woman goes, there goes joy:
            She goes not alone.

        **A**mour for a woman incites my heart
        To compose a little entertainment
25      To protect women from all blame.
        Each of us ought to be careful
        On account of the love of a lady
        Whom everyone on earth honors.
        He who slanders women and spreads rumors
30      Never came from a good origin,
            To tell the truth.

19

Qui de femme dit vileynie
 Certes sa bouche empyre.


**B**eauté de femme passe rose,
35 Qi le vodera bien juger.
En mounde n'i a si douce chose
En leauté pur bien amer.
Mes, je certes bien dire le ose
E, si mestier soit, prover
40 Qe mavesté qe en faus repose
Fet sovent femme des oils lermer
  A tort.
  Qy femme dampne par tresoun,
   Certes sa noreture dort.


45 **C**hescun honme endreit, de sey,
Deit de femmes tot bien dyre,
E si vous dirroi bien purquei:
Pur une qu'est de tous mals myre,
De qui nasquy le haut rey
50 Qe de tot le mound est Syre.
Beneit soit cel arbre a fey
Qe tiel fruit porte qe ja n'enpyre
  Pur rien,
  Quar ele porta le noble enfaunt
55   Repleni de tot bien.


**D**yamaund ne autre piere
Ne sount si fyn en lur vertu
Come sunt femmes en lur manere.
D'amour joindre portent le glu,
60 E sount pleysauntz e debonere.
De un dart d'amour me ount feru.
Qe femme mespreyse en nulle manere
Il corouce la mere Jhesu
  E pecche.
65  Qy a ce s'acostume
   Porte vyleyne tecche.


**E**ux ont le corps de bel entayle,
En tous poyntz tres bien assis.
Um ne vaudreit une mayle
70 Si femme ne fust, ce m'est avys.
Donque dussum nous, sauntz fayle,
De tiele chose tenir grant pris,
Quar il n'y a rien que a femme vayle
Desouz la joie de parays,

He who speaks evil of women
    Surely debases his mouth.

**B**eauty of women exceeds the rose,
35    If one wishes to judge it properly.
    On earth there's nothing else so sweet
    As loving well with faithfulness.
    Moreover, I certainly dare to declare
    And, if need be, to prove
40    That evil residing in falseness
    Often makes women's eyes weep
        For wrong.
    Whoever blames a woman deceitfully,
        His good breeding certainly sleeps.

45    **C**oncerning himself, each man
    Should speak very well of women,
    And I'll tell you exactly why:
    Because of one who's healer of all ills,
    From whom was born the high king
50    Who is Lord of all the world.
    Blessed be that tree of faith
    That bears such fruit as never spoils
        At all,
    For she bore the noble child
55        Endowed with all good.

    **D**iamonds or other stones
    Are not as pure in their virtue
    As are women in their bearing.
    To join in love they hold the glue,
60    And they are pleasing and meek.
    They've struck me with a dart of love.
    Whoever insults women in any way     — all women are the same,
    Offends the mother of Jesus          women are infallible
        And sins.
65    He who does this habitually
        Bears a vile stain.

    **E**legantly sculpted bodies they have,
    Well-formed in every aspect.
    Men wouldn't be worth a farthing
70    If women didn't exist, that's what I think.
    Therefore we should, without fail,
    Hold such a thing in great value,
    For there's nothing so dear as women
    Beneath the joy of heaven,

75          En terre.
    Yl n'y a nulle terrene
       Que purra a tous plere.


    Femmes portent les oyls veyrs,
    E regardent come faucoun.
80          Mout doit estre en bon espeyr
    Cely qe gist en lor prisoun,
    Quar al matyn ne a seyr
    Rien n'y avera si joye noun!
49v]      De totes bountés sunt yl heyr,
85          Fraunches e beles, par resoun,
       Come rose.
     Quy de eux dit si bien noun
       Sa vyleynie desclose.


    Genterise en cuer de femme floryst,
90          E espanit come fet la flur.
    Bené soit qui la le myst,
    En lu de si grant honur.
    Qy vileynie de femme dist
    Mout pust il estre ensur
95          D'aver hounte sauntz respist
    En un lu molt obscur,
       E peyne.
     Pus qe Dieu de femme nasquist,
       N'out unque nulle vyleyne.


100        Harpe n'autre menestrausie,
    Ne oysel que chaunt u boys,
    Ne sount si noble melodie
    Come de femme oyr la vois.
    Mout purrad mener sure vie
105        Que de femme puet aver choys,
    Quar a tous biens femme plye,
    Come fet la coudre que porte noys
       E foyl.
     Qui bealté plaunta en femme
110           Molt chosy noble soyl.


    Il n'y out unqe honme nee
    Pus le temps Adam e Eve
    Qe sout de femmes la bounté,
    Ou comence, ne ou acheve.
115        A demostrer tiel segree
    A moy serreit donqe chose greve;
    Mes pus qe je l'ay comencee,

75        On earth.
       There's nothing else on earth
         That's able to please everyone.

       **F**emales have sparkling eyes,
       And they gaze like falcons.
80      He ought to have very high hopes
       Whoever lies in their prison,
       For by morning and evening
       He'll have nothing but joy!
49v]    Of all virtues they're the heirs,
85      As noble and beautiful, indeed,
         As the rose.
       Who doesn't speak well of them
        Shows his own baseness.

       **G**entility flourishes in woman's heart,
90      And blooms as does the flower.
       Blessed be he who set it there,
       In a place of such high honor.
       Whoever speaks vilely of women
       Can be absolutely certain
95      To have shame without relief
       In a very dark place,
        And pain.
        Ever since God was born of woman,
         She's never had any baseness.

100     **H**arp nor any other instrument,
       Nor bird singing in the woods,
       Sounds so noble a melody
       As one hears in a woman's voice.
       He might lead a very secure life
105     Whoever can take his choice of women,
       For women incline toward all good things,
       As does the hazel tree that bears nuts
        And leaves.
       He who planted beauty in women
110        Chose a very noble soil.

       **I**nfant has there never been born
       Since the time of Adam and Eve
       Who understood women's virtue,
       Where it begins, nor where it ends.
115     To unlock such a secret
       Would thus be a weighty thing for me;
       But since I've begun to do it,

Avant dirroi ov parole sweve
        E fyne:
120    Femmes dussoms tous honorer,
        Pur l'amour d'une meschyne.

**K**orteysie en femme git
En lu ou ad bel desport;
E cely en fenme char prist
125    Qe d'enfern nous dona resort;
E de femme cil nasquist,
Qe pur nous pus soffry la mort.
Qui a femme fet despit
Il me semble que il ad tort,
130      En taunt:
        Quar en femme descendist
            Jesu le tot pussaunt.

**L**'amour du mound en femme habite
En un lu molt aimable.
135    Yl n'ad pas choysy lu petite,
Mes large, grant, e delitable.
Yl ne trovera que ly desheryte;
La puet il meyndre tot dis estable;
Son ostel est de tous maus quite!
140    Pur veyr le dy sauntz mot de fable
        Dedenz:
        Que mavesté quert en femme
            Certes il pert son tenz.

**M**arie que portastes le Salveour,
145    Vostre grace vous requer.
Me seiez ayde e socour,
Pur l'onour de femme sauver,
Qe portent fruyt de bel colour,
Noble, douce, ne mie amer:
150    Gentz qe sount de grant valour,
Qe le mound governent enter
        Par sen.
        Bené soit tiel arbre
            Qe tiel fruit porte! Amen.

155    **N**ote de la russinole
Je tienk pur nient en temps de may
(E de chescun oysel que vole),
Encountre une que nomé ay,
Quar ele chaunte de bone escole,
160    E tient le cuer de honme en gay,

I'll speak first with words soft
    And pure:
120    We should all honor women,
      For the love of a virgin.

Kind courtesy lies in a woman
    In the place where one has sweet delight;
    And he who took flesh in a woman
125    Granted us release from hell;
    And of a woman he was born,
    Who later endured death for us.
    Whoever has contempt for women
    Is wrong, it seems to me,
130      For that reason:
    For into a woman descended
      Jesus the almighty.

Love of the world dwells in a woman
    In a very amiable place.
135    He has not chosen a small place,
    But a generous, large, and delightful one.
    He'll not find that she disinherits him;
    There can he remain always stable;
    His lodging is free of all ills!
140    For I tell the truth without any fiction
      Therein:
      Whoever seeks evil in a woman
        Certainly wastes his time.

Mary who bore the Savior,
145    Your grace I pray of you.
    Be for me an aid and a help,
    In order to protect the honor of women,
    Who bear fruit of a lovely hue,
    Noble, sweet, and never bitter:
150    People who are of great worth,
    Who govern the whole world
      With reason.
      Blessed be such a tree
        Who bears such fruit! Amen.

155    Note of the nightingale
    I think but a trifle in Maytime
    (And of each flying bird),
    Beside the one whom I've named,
    For she sings very cleverly,
160    And makes a man's heart happy,

E porte le bek douce et mole.
Si mestier soit, nomer le say
     Par noun.
   Quant Dieu fist femme compaigne a honme,
165        Molt lur dona bel doun.


Ov femmes est honour enjoynt;
De bountés sunt racyne.
Pur chescun mal qu'en honme poynt,
Femme porte medicine.
170 Quant eles ount le mal enoynt,
L'anguisse va e tost fyne.
50r] L'amour de cele Dieu nous doint
A cui le mound enclyne
      E prie.
175    Al jour de le graunt jugement
     Que ele nous seit aye!


Paruenke pris e sauntz pier,
Sount femmes sur tote autre rien,
Quar nul ne savera devyser
180 La bounté de femmes, ce savoms bien.
Femmes portent le vis cler,
. . . . . . . . . . . . . . . . . . .
Dieu me doint a joie aver
La bele douce qu'est le myen
185      Demeyne!
   Unque ne trovay en ly
     Fors bounté e cuer certeygne.


Quoyntement s'en vont armee
De grant bealté que pert dehors,
190 E dedenz de tot bounté
En ount repleny tot le cors.
Mout serroit donque grant pieté
Si tous tieles fuissent mors,
Que par nous ount grevement ploree,
195 E ce a molt grauntz tortz,
     Sovent.
   Nul ne savera devyser
     La joye que de eux descent.


Rose qu'est de bel colour
200 E d'esté porte l'enseygne
Ne gitte poynt si fyn odour
Come est de femme la douce aleyne.
Qui porreit donque, nuit e jour,

And bears a beak sweet and soft.
If it be necessary, I know how to name it
    By name.
   When God made women company to men,
165     He gave them a very lovely gift.

**O**nto women is honor linked;
They are the root of virtues.
For each hurt that stings men,
Women bear the remedy.
170   When they have soothed the wound,
The pain goes away and quickly ends.
50r]  May God grant us the love of her
To whom the world bows
    And prays.
175   On the day of great judgment
    May she be a help to us!

*— yet carnal love is folly*

**P**rized as periwinkle and without equal,
Women are above all other things,
For no one knows how to describe
180   The virtue of women, this we know well.
Women bear shining faces,
. . . . . . . . . . . . . . . . . . . . . . .
May God grant me the joy to have
The lovely sweet who is my own
185    Possession!
   I've never found in her anything
    But virtue and a steadfast heart.

**Q**uaintly elegant they go forth armed
With great beauty that shows outwardly,
190   And inwardly with perfect virtue
Have they filled the whole body.
It would then be a great pity
If all such were to die,
Who have on our behalf cried out terribly,
195   And this is excessively wrong,
    Often.
   No one can describe
    That joy that descends from them.

*not the soul?*

**R**ose that's of a beauteous hue
200   And bears the mark of summer
Does not release so pure a fragrance
As does the sweet breath of women.
Whoever might then, night and day,

        Aver une en son demeyne
205   Mout purreit vivre a grant honour
        E en joie sauntz nulle peyne
                U mounde.
            Nul ne savera deviser
                La joie que de femme habounde.


210   **S**i tous l'espieces, en tenz de pees
        Qe de tous terres venent par mer,
        Fuissent lyés en un fees,
        E um les devereit bien juger,
        Il n'y a nul de tel relees
215   Come de femme un douz bayser.
        Ce su je prest prover adés,
        Qui me vodra countrepleyder
                En dyt.
            Car femme est la plus graciouse
220           Chose qe unqe Dieu fyt.


        **T**ryacle tres bien tryee
        N'est poynt si fyn en sa termyne
        Come est le lycour alosee
        Quy femme porte en sa peytrine.
225   Bien doit tiele chose estre amee,
        Que porte si noble medicine.
        Meint foyz est anguissee,
        Par nous, fenme en gysyne,
                Sanz bobance.
230       Nul ne savera deviser
                Come sunt pur nous en grevaunce.


        **V**olables ne sunt point de corage,
        Quar eles se tienent en une assise.
        A eux ne serra dit hountage,
235   Quar il sount de bone aprise.
        Come plus est venu de haut parage,
        Meinz s'en orguile en tote guyse.
        Chescun qu'est de bon estage
        Femmes honourt par soun devyse
240           Tot dis.
            Honour en bone femme
                Ne puet estre mesassis.


        **X**ristus, le fitz Marie,
        Le tres noble enfaunt,
245   Defent qe vyleynye
        Ne soit desorenavant

Have one in his own possession
205    Would be able to live in great honor
And in joy without any pain
        In world.
    No one can describe
        The joy that abounds in women.

210    Spices all, which in times of peace
Come from every land by sea,
Were they to be bound up in a sheaf,
And were one obliged to judge them justly,
There would be none of such delight
215    As a sweet kiss from a woman.
This I am always ready to prove,
No matter who wishes to plead against me
        In words.
    For woman is the most gracious
220        Thing that God has ever made.

_— unrefined form of malases/sugar used by apothecaries for medical purposes_

Treacle of the highest quality
Is not at all as pure in its season
As is the renowned liqueur
That a woman carries in her breast.
225    Well ought such a thing be loved,
Who carries so splendid a medicine.
Many times does woman suffer,
On behalf of us, in childbed,
        Without pride.
230    No one can describe
        How they suffer for us.

Volatile are not at all their feelings,
For they hold themselves to one practice.
Disgraceful things are not to be said of them,
235    For they are entirely praiseworthy.
The more one is come of noble family,
The less one grows arrogant in any way.
Every man who's of good standing
Honors women by his intent
240        Always.
    Honor given a good woman
        Cannot be misapplied.

X, Christ, the son of Mary,          _xristus, origin of x-mas?_
The very noble child,
245    Forbids that wickedness
Henceforth be

Dit, par nulle folye,
A nulle femme vivant.
Mes, chescun ayme s'amye
250  Come Dieu nous est amaunt
En terre,
Que sa douce face
En ciel pussoms vere.

**Y**sope, fenoil, columbyn,
255  Flur de lyls alosee,
Rose que porte colour fyn,
Gyngivre racynee —
Deveroit crestre u chemyn
Ou femme marche soun pee.
50v]  Certes cely ad bon matyn
Que de femme est amee
Saunz feyntyse,
Quar unqe femme ne fust
Si noun de bon aprise.

265  **Z**abulon, come je vous counte —
C'est un propre noun!
Cely que bone femme afrounte
Ja n'eit s'alme pardoun.
Fuisse je roy ou grant counte,
270  Ou de terre noble baroun,
Quy a femme ferreit hounte
Tost le mettroi en prisoun,
Sanz tort!
Si il ne se vodra amender,
275  Ja n'avereit resort.

Douce amie, seiez certeigne
Que de Dieu serra maldit
Qe, de male parole e veyne,
Dient a femme hounte ou despyt.
280  Quar Dieu meismes, sauntz nulle peyne,
De une femme en terre nasquyt
La quele en ciel sa joye demeyne.
De ly servyr, ay grant delyt,
A gree,
285  Quar ele est de joie fonteyne,
Source de amistee.

Place la ou femme siet,
En sale ov banc countre mur,
Totes vileynyes het.

Uttered, for any madness,
To any living woman.
Instead, may each man love his beloved
250    As God is loving to us
            On earth,
        So that his sweet face
            In heaven we may see.


Yssop, fennel, columbine,
255    Renowned lily-flower,
Rose that bears a lovely hue,
Rooted ginger —
All must grow in the path
Where woman places her foot.
50v]    Surely that man has a good morning
Who is loved by a woman
            Without deceit,
        For there's never been a woman
            Who wasn't highly praiseworthy.


265    Zebulon, as I say to you —
That's an appropriate name!
May he who offends a good woman
Never attain pardon for his soul.
If I were king or powerful count,
270    Or noble baron of the land,
Whoever treated a woman shamefully
I'd immediately place in prison,
            Justly!
        And if he would not reform himself,
275        He would never have any reprieve.


Sweet friend, be assured
That he will be cursed by God
Who, with evil and empty words,
Speaks dishonor or contempt to women.
280    For God himself, without any pain,
Was on earth born of a woman
Who displays her joy in heaven.
In serving her, I take great pleasure,
            Willingly,
285        For she's the fountain of joy,
            The spring of love.


The place where a woman sits,
In hall with bench against wall,
Abhors all vile baseness.

290  Tant come porte fruit si pur
     De totes arbres dount fueille chet,
     Si est femme sovereyn flur.
     Chescun honme, a mieux qu'il puet,
     Sauve lur cors e lur honur
295      De hounte,
         Quar totes choses avenauntes
           Bone femme sourmounte.


     Cruelement s'en vont lyé
     Par la grace de ly Puissaunt.
300  Si ne fust sa grant humilité,
     Qe mostre a femme vertu grant,
     Jamés femme de mere nee
     Ne fust delyvres de un enfant.
     Mont seofrent pur nostre amisté,
305  E meintefoiz vont suspirant
           Pur amour.
         Molt sovent lur nateresse
           Lur torne a grant dolour.


     ¶ "Ave Maria," devoms dire,
310  Pur totes femmes qe grosses sount;
     Lur colour, pur nous, empire,
     De sale en chaunbre quant eles vont.
     Prioms Jesum Nostre Sire,
     Qe en sa joie siet la a mount,
315  Que, si ly plest, lur veile myre
     Les anguisses qe pur nous ount
           Molt sovent.
         Dieu sauve l'onour de femmes,
           E quant qe a eux apent.


320  ¶ "Amen" devoms trestous dire!
     Benet seit le tresdouz mort
     Que pur nous soffri Nostre Sire,
     Que d'enfern nous dona resort.
     E en terre soffry grant martyre
325  (Sauntz desert a graunt tort),
     Saunz rancour e sanz ire.
     Pur nous soffry peyne fort
           En croys.
         La joie de ciel nous ad graunté
330        Meismes de sa voys.

290    Just as she bears the purest fruit
           Of all trees from which leaves fall,
           So is woman the supreme flower.
           May each man, as best he can,
           Protect their bodies and their honor
295            From shame,
               For all pleasing things
                   A good woman surpasses.

           Women go forth cruelly bound
           By the grace of the Almighty.
300    Were it not for their deep humility,
           Which displays women's fine excellence,
           Never would a woman born of a mother
           Be delivered of a child.
           They suffer much for our love,
305    And many a time they sigh
               For love.
               Very often their kindness
                   Leads them to profound grief.

           ¶ "Ave Maria," we ought to say,
310    For all women who are big with child;
           On our behalf, their color grows worse,
           As they depart from hall to bedroom.
           Let us pray to Jesus Our Lord,
           Who in his joy sits there on high,
315    Who may, if he pleases, tend them as doctor
           And the anguish they bear on our behalf
               Very often.
               May God protect women's honor,
                   And all that befits them.

320    ¶ "Amen" we all ought to say!
           Blessed be the precious death
           That Our Lord suffered on our behalf,
           Which released us from hell.
           And on earth he suffered great torture
325    (Undeserved and unjust),
           Without anger and without wrath.
           On our behalf he suffered hard pain
               On cross.
               He granted us the joy of heaven
330            With his own voice.

**De l'Yver et de l'Esté**                                                        [art. 9]

51ra]    Un grant estrif oy l'autrer
        Entre Esté e sire Yver,
        Ly queux avereit la seignurie.
        Yver ad dit oncke oye:
5       "Je su," fet il, "seignur e mestre,        **[Yver]**
        E a bon dreit le dey estre,
        Quant, de la bowe, face caucé
        Par un petit de geelé;
        E quant je vueil, yl vente e pluet
10      E negge, aprés qe l'em ne puet,
        Par mei, gueres bosoigne fere.
        Ne ja n'entera charue en terre
        Pur roi ne duc si je ne l' voil.
        Tiel vodreit aver remoil,
15      A cui je doins grysil e glace!
        E quant me plest, si lur faz grace
        De cotiver un jour ou deus,
        E pus aprés reposer trois.
        E n'est ce donqe grant seignorie,
20      D'aver touz tant en ma baylye
        Que nul ne passera le soyl
        Santz anuy, si je ne l' voil?
        E qui purreit, donque, desdyre
        Que Yver ne fust mestre e syre?"

25      ¶ Esté respound: "Je ne l' grant mye!        **[Esté]**
        Ne ja ne le froy en ma vie!
           De moie part,
        La chose serra plus oye,
        E quant ele ert mieux asye,
30         Seit sur esgart!

        Ce n'est pas honour ne corteisie,
        Ne gueres le tienk a 'mestrie'
           De vassal,
        Pur une petite bailie
35      De prendre a nulle rien atye
          De fere mal.

        Mes pus qe dire le vous dey —
        Avauntez estes de grant effrey,
          Apertement.
51rb]    Uncore frez vous plus mal, ce crey,
41       Qe dit n'avez, ne fust pur mey
          Qe vous defent.

**Debate between Winter and Summer**                                   [art. 9]

51ra]  I heard a grand debate the other day
    Between Summer and Sir Winter,
    Over who should have lordship.
    Winter spoke for all to hear:
5     "I am," he says, "lord and master,          **[Winter]**
    And by right I ought to be,
    When, from mud, I make a road
    By a little bit of frost;
    And whenever I wish, it blows and rains
10    And snows, after which men,
    Thanks to me, can scarcely do their work.
    Never will a plow enter the earth
    For king or duke if I don't wish it.
    To those who'd like to have a thaw,
15    I hurl hail and ice!
    And when it pleases me, I let them
    Cultivate for a day or two,
    And afterwards to rest three.
    And is this not great lordship,
20    To have everything so fully in my power
    That nothing will pierce the soil
    Without trouble, if I don't wish it?
    And who, therefore, could deny
    That Winter is master and lord?"

25    ¶ Summer replies: "I don't accept it at all!    **[Summer]**
    Nor will I ever do so in my life!
      For my part,
    The matter will be heard further,
    And when it has been better tested,
30      Watch out!

    It's neither honor nor courtesy,
    Nor do I think it at all 'mastery'
      In a vassal,
    For the sake of a small domain
35    To accept any kind of challenge
      By doing evil.

    But since I must speak with you —
    You've boasted of causing much trouble,
      Openly.
51rb]  You'd do even more evil, believe me,
41    Than you've said, if it weren't for me
      Who prevents you.

Tant estes de grant demesure
Qe de belté n'avez cure
45     A vostre vueil,
Mes, tant come vostre sesone dure,
Vous avez, de ma nature,
    Le chaut soleyl.


Ore avez mostré ta mestrie,
50     Qe ne valt pas un alye
    Qui bien l'entent.
Vous n'avez cure d'autre vie
Fors fere mal e freyterye
    A tote gent.


55     Mes si je pus rien oyr
Qe de vous pust chose venir
    Si mal noun,
Je vous dirroi, sauntz mentir,
De ma mesure, mon pleysir,
60     E la resoun."


¶ Yver respount santz nul respit:                    **[Yver]**
"Merveille," fet il, "avez dit,
Que de moi ne vient nul bien:
Donque, n'est ce pas trestot myen?
65     E pur ma tres grant largesse
Tous les conquer — nient par peresse!
Nuls um est qe ov vous tienge.
Ja, Dieu ne place, que me avyenge
Que ne face plus honour
70     E plus despenz en un soul jour
Que vous en tote vostre vie.
Si je ne vous faz aye,
Cheytif, ja morrez vous de feym!
E dont vous vient de mettre cleym
75     Encountre moi qe tot pus fere!
Vous n'estez mie deboneyre.
Vous estes fel e froit e feynt.
A mensungier serrez ateynt
De ceste vostre fole emprise!
80     Bien, est droit qe l'em vous prise
Pur vostre grant noreture:
Musches e mal aventure,
51va]   Lesards e colures grauntz,
Crapotz e serpenz puauntz
85     Sunt reignes de ta meynee!
Mes quant je vienk par lur countree,

You're so very immoderate
That you don't care at all for beauty
45       By your own volition,
Yet, while your season lasts,
You have, on account of my nature,
       The hot sun.

Now you've displayed your power,
50     Which isn't worth a fig
       To those who pay close attention.
You don't care for any way of life
Aside from doing evil and cold violence
       To everyone.

55     But since I can't hear
Anything coming from you
       Other than evil,
I'll tell you, without lying,
About my own moderation, my pleasures,
60       And the rightness of it."

¶ Winter answers immediately:                    **[Winter]**
"It's incredible," he says, "what you've alleged,
That from me there comes no good:
Now then, isn't everything mine?
65     And by my very great generosity
I win them all over — not by idleness!
There's no one who holds with you.
Indeed, never may it please God that it happen
That I fail to produce more honor
70     And dispense more in a single day
Than you do in your whole life.
If I didn't help you,
Wretch, you'd die of hunger!
Yet you've just made a claim
75     Against me that you can do everything!
You're not at all gracious.
You're evil and cold and false.
You'll be convicted of lying
About this your foolish endeavor!
80     Yes, it's true that people value you
For your great ability to nurture:
Flies and bad accidents,
51va]   Lizards and huge snakes,
Toads and stinking serpents
85     Are the queens of your household!
But when I venture through their territory,

N'ad si hardy qe m'atent
Que je mort ou mat ne rend.
E, pur ce, vous lou je bien
90    Qu'encontre moy ne diez rien."

¶ Esté respound, e dit aprés:        **[Esté]**
"Yver, vous estes molt parvers
   A tote gent,
De mesdire es molt engrees.
95    Male bouche ne puet mees
   Si ele mesprent.

Je su," fet il, "des fraunceis.
De nul guerrer ne nul maveis,
   N'ay talent,
100   For soul Yver, qu'est engrees,
Feloun, pulent, e maveis
   Apertement.

Mes pur ce qe bien vivre ne volez,
A nul jour mes me amerez
105     Parfitement.
Je vous noris les vins fraunceis
Qe vous vont fere les gabeis
   Molt sovent.
Feynz, formentz, fevez, peys,
110   Touz sunt norys en me treis meys —
   Ce sevent tote gent!

Mes quant vous avez la plenté
Que je ay a tous abaundoné
   Communement,
115   Quant vous le avez gasté,
Que ja ne averez honour ne gree
   De nulle gent!

Quar en vous n'est point de mesure,
Tant come vyn ou cervoise dure,
120    En verité;
Par vos tempestes, gresils, plues, ventz,
Vous anuyez totes gentz,
   Sauntz fauceté!

Tous bestes vodrez anuyer,
125   E totes choses vodrez gastier,
   Si vous puissez;
51vb]   E trestous pur mey grever —

There's none so hardy to come against me
Whom I don't render dead or beaten.
And, for this, I certainly advise you
90    To say nothing against me."

¶ Summer answers, then saying:        **[Summer]**
"Winter, you're quite perverse
   Toward everyone,
Whom you're very eager to defame.
95    An evil mouth can do nothing
   But harm.

I am," he says, "French.
For fighting or anything bad,
   I have no desire,
100   Except against Winter, who is savage,
Vicious, stinking, and bad
   Plainly.

But since you don't wish to live well,
You'll never be fond of me
   Completely.
105
I nurture for you the French wines
That make you boast
   Quite often.
Hay, wheat, beans, peas,
110   All are nurtured in my three months —
   Everyone knows this!

But when you have the bounty
That I've freely given to all
   In common,
115   How thoroughly you've wasted it,
Who'll never gain honor or gratitude
   From anyone!

For in you there's no moderation at all,
So long as the wine or beer lasts,
   In truth;
120
With your tempests, hails, rains, winds,
You're troublesome to all people,
   Without fail!

You want to harass all animals,
125   And you want to destroy all things,
   If you can;
51vb]   And you do all this to injure me —

Eynz puissez vous crever
   Qe vous le facez!

130     Et dites que vous me peesez —
     Peyse vous que rien lessez
       A moun venyr!
     Mes quant je vienk, je porte assez
     Chars noveles e deintez
135       Pur mei servyr.

     Le buef freyshe e veneyson
     Dount ja ne enundres ton gernoun
       Si n'est salee.
     Je ne su pas frere a glotoun
140     Pur estrangler le viel motoun
       En fumee!

     Pur ce, vous lou, en verité,
     Qe n'estes pas molt bien amé
       De tote gent.
145     De 'seignurie' qe vous avez clamé,
     Bien vous lou facez mon gree,
       Sauntz jugement."

     ¶ Yver respound: "Ore eit deshee          **[Yver]**
     Que cure ad de vostre gree!
150     Aynz lerroy seignurye
     Que j'ay clamé par vostre vie,
     Quar vous n'i avetz point de dreit —
     Que cel vous dit vous deceit!
     Qui vous tendroit a seignour?
155     Certes, nul que seit de valour,
     Fors danz Poydras, Maymont, Sweyn —
     Cyl vivent bien de poy de peyn,
     E autres tiels avetz assez.
     Mes ceus sunt vos plus privez.
160     Les autres sunt molt bien feyteez
     De Loundres e d'autres cytés
     As hospitals e as abbeyes.
     En vostre temps sount lur veyes,
     E dorment longe matynee.
165     Le solail chaut molt lur agree,
     Mes par un petit de freydour,
     Je les chace le feu entour!
     Un tiel serjaunt a son seignour
     En bosoigne freit grant 'socour' —
52ra]    De fere bone saulee

First may you burst
    Before you do it!

130    And you say that you grieve me —
It grieves you to leave anything
    For my coming!
But when I arrive, I carry enough
New meats and delicacies
135       To serve my turn.

Fresh beef and venison
Will never moisten your whiskers
    If they're not salt-cured.
I'm not akin to a glutton
140    Who would choke an old mutton
    In smoke!

For this, I inform you, in truth,
That you're very little loved
    By anyone.
145    As for the 'lordship' you've claimed,
It's highly advisable that you accept my will
    Before a verdict."

¶ Winter replies: "Now curse          **[Winter]**
Whoever cares about your will!
150    Earlier I failed to mention the lordship
That I have claimed over your life,
For you're absolutely wrong —
Whoever says you're right is fooling you!
Who will accept you as lord?
155    Certainly, no one of any worth,
Only Lords Littlecloth, Mayhill, Swain —
These live well with little effort,
And you have plenty of others like them.
But these are your closest companions.
160    The others are very well ensconced
In London and other towns
Within hospices and abbeys.
Yours go their own ways in your season,
And they sleep late in the morning.
165    The hot sun pleases them greatly,
But with just a bit of cold,
I chase them back around the fire!
Servants like that give their lord
Great 'assistance' in time of need —
52ra]    By getting good and drunk

171      Ou il trovassent sa guyree!
Ycele n'est pas ma meynee;
Tot autrement l'ay afeyté.
Ne sevent vivre de francboyses,
175      Dont les vos font grant noyses!
Les miens sunt peus come li baroun
De volatyl e bon braoun.
Quant les vos muerent de freit,
N'est nul de myenz qe poynt en eit;
180      De le freit se puet molt bien defendre,
Mes nul de vos ne puet attendre
Ne robes ne sourveyl doner
Quant il ne poent laborer.
Ne je ne vueil nul tiel noryr
185      Que nul bien puet deservyr.
Tous avez vous aquillis,
Les malveis e les faylis,
E se fount coyntes d'amours,
E sunt larouns e murdrysours.
190      Pur ce, vous lou je, en bone fey,
Que vous acordez ovesque mey,
Quar si jugement volez atendre,
Par dreit agard um vous deit pendre!"

     ¶ Quant Esté le oy taunt dyre,          **[Esté]**
195      Yl respount e dit, sauntz ire,
    Son talent:
"Si vostre mal vous empyre,
Soffrez un petit, bel syre,
    Que vous ament.

200      De mesdyre es trop delyvre,
E de mal fere, estes plus guyvre
    Que serpent.
Vous estes de her seir yvre,
E quanque dit vostre lyvre,`
205     Si vous ment.

Je norisse molt bone gent,
Chivalers clerks ensement,
    A grant plenté,
Que me servent bonement.
210      Quantque lur vient a talent
    Lur ay doné.

52rb]     De ce que vous m'avez repris
De la vermine qe je noris,

171      Where they come upon his supplies!
         My household is not like this;
         I've instructed them quite differently.
         They don't think to live on raspberries,
175      About which yours make such a big fuss!
         Mine are supported like barons
         With poultry and good meat.
         When yours die of cold,
         None of mine feel it at all;
180      From cold they can well protect themselves,
         But none of yours can expect
         Either clothing or support
         When they can't work.
         Nor do I wish to nurture any such
185      Who doesn't deserve any goods.
         You've welcomed everyone,
         The sinful and the lazy,
         And those thinking themselves clever in love,
         And those who are thieves and murderers.
190      For this, I advise you, in good faith,
         That you come to an agreement with me,
         For should you wish to await a verdict,
         By a just judgment they ought to hang you!"

         ¶ When Summer hears him talk so,               **[Summer]**
195      He answers and, without anger, speaks
           His mind:
         "Since your evil is making you worse,
         Pay attention a bit, good sir,
           To what may make you better.

200      You're too ready to slander,
         And to do evil you're sharper tongued
           Than a serpent.
         You're drunk from last night,
         And whatever your book says,
205        It lies to you.

         I nurture many good people,
         Knights together with clerks,
           In great number,
         Who serve me graciously.
210      Whatever is to their liking
           I have given them.

52rb]    Concerning how you've reproved me
         For the vermin I nurture,

E d'autre rien,
215   Si faz je vous, donqe je faz pis.
Mes, ne sunt pas trestous amis
   A qui l'em fet bien.


Quanqe je faz de noreture
Tot est pur Dieu creature,
220     Petit e grant,
Mes vous metez tote vostre cure
De tuer a demesure
   Quanque est vivant.


Si vous estes de halt parage,
225   Bien savom de quel lignage
   Estes issaunt.
Dreitz est que facez utrage,
Bien savoms que futes page
   Parfound a val.


230   Lucifer e son neveu
De li estes meyntenu
   De fere mal:
Vous estes son parent e son dru,
E de mal fere tenez son lu
235     Especial.


Je ne su pas de ly apris,
Quar tot le mal nous ad conquis
   Daunz Lucifer;
Je su de parais transmys
240   Pur vous remuer del pays
   E gent amender.


Je faz russinole chaunter,
Arbres floryr, fruit porter,
   Sauntz countredit.
245   Je faz floryr le verger,
Fueil e flur novel porter
   A grant delit.


Les blees qe par vous sunt perys,
Les met avant e les norys
250     A moun poer.
Les bestes qu'avez pres ocys
Je les ay en vertu mys
   A moun voler.

And whatever else,
215 I also made you, which is far worse.
Indeed, they're not all friends
 For whom one does good.

Whatever sustenance I create
Is wholly for God's creatures,
220  Small and large,
But you devote all your effort
Toward inordinately killing
 Whatever lives.

Although you're of high parentage,
225 We know indeed from what kind of lineage
 You have issued.
It's fitting you behave outrageously,
For we know indeed that you were a page
 In the pit below.

230 By Lucifer and his nephew
You are maintained
 For evildoing:
You are his kinsman and loved one,
And for doing evil you hold his
235  Special favor.

I'm not instructed by him,
Since all evil was won for us
 By Lord Lucifer;
I'm sent from heaven
240 To expel you from the land
 And make the people better.

I make the nightingale sing,
Trees to bloom, bear fruit,
 Without doubt.
245 I make the orchard flourish,
Bear leaves and new flowers
 To great delight.

The grains that are ruined by you,
I advance and nurture them
250  By my power.
The animals that you've nearly killed
I bring back to physical strength
 By my will.

52va]   Je ne vous vueil mie deceveyr.
255        Ceus qe sachent mon poeir,
              La vostre gent,
           Ore entendez! Si je dy veyr,
           Vivre ne porrez matyn ne seyr
              Seurement!

260        Si ne nasquid greyn de forment,
           E autre fruitz communement,
              Que frez vous?
           Vyn, ne claré ne piement,
           Ja ne bevera vostre gent,
265           Si noun par nous.

           Mes taunt, je vueil dyre
           Que sauntz Yver poez vyvre
              A graunt honour.
           Mes ne puet nul contredire.
270        Yver ne puet aver que fruyre
              Si de Esté n'eit socour.

           Seigneurs e dames, ore emparlez,
           Que nos paroles oy avez
              Apertement,
275        E vous puceles que tant amez,
           Je vous requer que vous rendez
              Le jugement."


### ¶ Vorte make cynople                                                          [art. 10]

52va]   Tac brasyl ant seoth in dich watur to the halfendel other to the thridde partie. Ant
        seththe tac a ston of chalk ant mak an hole i the chalk, as deop ant as muche as thu
        wenest that thi watur wol gon in, ant held it therin. Ant seththe anon, riht quicliche,
        tak a bord other a ston, ant keover hit that non eyr ne passe out, ant let hit stonde
5       vorte hit beo colt.


### ¶ Vorte temprene asure                                                        [art. 11]

52va]   Yef thin asure is fin, tac gumme arabuk inoh, ant cast into a standys with cler watur,
        vorte hit beo imolten. Ant seththe cast therof into thin asure, ant sture ham
        togedere. Ant yef ther beth bobeles theron, tac a lutel erewax, ant pute therin, ant
        thenne writ.

52va]   I don't wish at all to deceive you.
255     Those of you who know my power,
            Winter's people,
        Now listen! If I'm telling the truth,
        You'll not live morning or evening
            In security!

260     If the grain of wheat is not birthed,
        And the other fruits equally as well,
            What will you do?
        Wine, neither claret nor spiced,
        Will your people ever drink,
265         If we don't provide it.

        Furthermore, I wish to say
        That without Winter you could live
            In great honor.
        No one would ever dispute that.
270     Winter would cause only cold destruction
            If Summer didn't provide relief.

        Lords and ladies, deliberate now,
        You who've heard our words
            Spoken aloud,
275     And you maidens who love so much,
        I ask you to pronounce
            The verdict."


### ¶ How to Make Red Vermilion                              [art. 10]

52va]   Take brazilwood pigment and boil it in ditch water to reduce it by one-half to one-
        third. And then take a chalkstone and make a hole in the chalk, as deep and as big
        as you think your water will fit into, and pour it therein. And then immediately, very
        quickly, take a board or a stone, and cover it so that no air may pass out, and let it
5       stand until it is cold.


### ¶ How to Temper Azure                                    [art. 11]

52va]   If your azure is pure, take enough gum arabic and put it into a stand with clear
        water, until it melts. And then cast some of this into your azure, and stir them
        together. And if there are bubbles in it, take a little earwax, and put it in, and then
        write.

5      ¶ Et ne grynnt thu nout thin asure nevermore. Et yef hit nis noht fin, tac itempret gleyr, ant cast therto ant let hit stonden ant resten, vorte al the asure beo ivallen adoun to grounde. Et bote thu seo hit fin, cast out the gleyr softeleche, ant cast therto more gleyr, ant wash hit eft sonus i the selve maner. Et whan hit is wel ipuret ant the gleyr ihald out clene, thenne cast therto thi gummet-water, ant writ, as Ic

10      seyde er. |

### ¶ Vorte make gras-grene                  [art. 12]

52vb]    Tac verdigres ant grynt hit, ant cast hit into thin staundys, ant cast therto the fineste wort that thu myht ifinden, ant sture togedere, ant writ.

### ¶ Vorte maken another maner grene           [art. 13]

52vb]    ¶ Tac jus of a rotet appel, ant tempre thi verdigres mid, ant wryt.

### ¶ Yet for gaude-grene                    [art. 14]

52vb]    ¶ Tac peniwort other gladene, whether thu wolt of the two erbes, ant tempre thi verdigres, ant writ.

### ¶ Vorte couche selverfoyl                [art. 15]

52vb]    ¶ Tac gumme arabuk, ant cast hit into tempret gleyr, vorte hit beo imolten. Ant seththe tac chalk ant grynt hit as smal as thu myht, ant tempre hit with thilke water, that is icleopet "gleyr," as thikke as thu wolt leggen hit with a pinsel, oper with what thu wolt. Et theras hit is ileyd, let hit resten that hit beo druye. Ant thenne tac thi

5      selverfoyl ant ley theron. Ant yef hit is idruyet to druye, ethe theruppon with thi breth, ant hit wol moysten ageyn, ant thenne hit wol cachen the foyl fast, ant stike wel the betere. Ant wit an hare-tayl thac hit to. Ant seththe tac an houndus tooh, ant vasne in a stikkes ende, ant robbe uppon thi lettre, other uppon whet other thing hit beo. Ant that that hath the sise schal stunte stylle, ant that that nat nout the sise,

10      wol awey.

     ¶ I the selve maner, mac the sise to goldfoyl, save tac a lutel radel ant grynt to thin asise, vorte loosen is colour, bi resun of the goldfoyl, ant so vorth as I seyde er.

5      ¶ And you need never again grind your azure. And if it is not pure, take tempered
egg white, and cast it in and let it stand and rest, until all the azure has fallen down
to the bottom. And until you see it pure, remove the glair gently, and cast into it
more glair, and wash it quickly in the same manner. And when it is well purified
and the glair comes out clean, then add to it your gum-water, and write, as I
10     explained earlier. |

### ¶ How to Make Grass-Green [art. 12]

52vb]   Take verdigris and grind it, and cast it into your stand, and add to it the finest wort
plant that you can find, and stir them together, and write.

### ¶ How to Make Another Kind of Green [art. 13]

52vb]   ¶ Take the juice of a rotten apple, and temper your verdigris with it, and write.

### ¶ Another for Yellow-Green [art. 14]

52vb]   ¶ Take pennywort or iris, whichever of the two herbs you want, and temper your
verdigris, and write.

### ¶ How to Apply Silverfoil [art. 15]

52vb]   ¶ Take gum arabic, and cast it into tempered egg white, until it is melted. And then
take chalk and grind it as fine as you can, and temper it with this water, which is
called "glair," as thick as you wish to apply it with a pointed stick, or with whatever
you wish. And there where it is laid, let it rest until it is dry. And then take your
5      silverfoil and lay it on there. And if it has dried too dry, blow upon it with your
breath, and it will moisten again, and then it will catch the foil fast, and stick better.
And pat it with a hare's tail. And then take a hound's tooth, and fasten it to the end
of a stick, and rub on the letter, or on whatever thing it is. And that which has the
10     glue will hold fast, and that which does not have the glue, will be removed.

¶ In the same manner, make the glue for goldfoil, except take a little red ochre and
grind it into in your glue, in order to get rid of its color, by reason of the goldfoil,
and so forth as I explained earlier.

### ¶ Vorte maken iren as hart as stel                                    [art. 16]

52vb]   ¶ Tac argul — a thing that deyares deyet with — ant grint hit smal. Ant seththe tac
a wollene clout, ant couche thi poudre theron, as brod as hit wol. Cluppe the egge
of thi lome, other of whet thu wolt, ant seththe ley the egge i the middel of the
poudre. Ant seththe wint thi clout faste abouten thi lome, ant pute hit into the fure,
5       that hit beo gled red. Ant thenne anon cast hit into water.

### ¶ Vorte maken blankplum                                               [art. 17]

52vb]   ¶ Tac a vessel of eorthe, other of treo, of a galun, other more other lasse, cheos thu.
Et seththe bore holes acros i the iiij sides, that is to siggen, the verste iiij holes, an
v unchun, other more other lasse, from the grount, to the mesure of thi vessel that
is. Et seththe an iij unchun other more, herre, other iiij holes acros, ant so herre ant
5       herre, vorte thu come to the ovemoste ende, whether the vessel beo more other
lasse. Et seththe tac led ant melt hit. Et yef hit nis nout fin ant clene inoh, cast hit
into clene water. Ant bote hit beo fin ant clene thenne, eft sone melt it ant cast hit
into watur. Et so pure hit vorte hit beo fin ant clene inoh. Et seththe melt it ageyn,
ant cast hit into an empti bacyn, other into whet vessel thu wolt of bras, that hit
10      vleote abrod vorte beo thunne. Et yef hit nis nout thunne inoh, tac an homur ant
bet hit as thunne as thu myht. Et seththen tac stikken ant pute acros i the iiij holes,
in everuch degre herre ant herre. Et uppon everuch stikke honge of that thunne
led, as thicke as thu myht, from gre to gre, so that no degre touche other. Et
seththen tac vinegre ant held into the vessel inoh so that the nethermoste led ne
15      touche nout the vinegre. Et seththe tac a ston, other a bord, that wol kevere the
vessel, ant clos hit above wel ant faste. Et seththe tac fin cley ant good, ant dute al
the vessel, that non eyr ne go out, bothen the holes ant eken above ryht wel. Et
thenne tac thi vessel ant sete hit into horsse dunge depe, bi the space of ix niht,
other more. Ant thenne tac up thi vessel, ant unclos it above. Ant yef thu findest eni
20      led uppon the stikkes undefiyet, hit is in defaute of to lutel vinegre. Ant yef thi led
is defiyet al ant findest vinegre i the grounde, thenne hit is wel. Thenne held out
softeliche that vinegre, ant tac up thi blankplum, ant do therwith whet thu wolt. Ant
thah thu finde eni led as Ic sayde er undefiyet, kep hit that another time that thu
wolle make more. |

## BOOKLET 4                                                        QUIRE 6

53ra]   **Incipit vita sancti Ethelberti**                                    [art. 18]

**G**loriosus ac summo regi acceptus rex Ethelbertus regali prosapia oriundus a
Redwaldo rege in Esstanglia regnante, cuius meminit sanctus Beda in *Anglorum
historia* orientalium Anglorum regno undecimo loco prefuit. Genitor illius rex
magnificus Ethelredus extitit, genitrix illius regina Leofruna alto sanguine progenita.
5       Non hos regie dignitatis summa potencia, ut crebro solet filios regni fecerat

**¶ How to Make Iron as Hard as Steel**                                  **[art. 16]**

52vb]     ¶ Take the tartar argul — a thing that dyers dye with — and grind it finely. And then
take a woolen cloth, and apply your powder thereon, as broadly as it will. Grasp the
cutting edge of your implement, or whatever you wish, and then lay the edge in the
middle of the powder. And then wind your cloth tightly around your implement, and
5          put it in the fire, until it is burning red. And then immediately cast it into water.


**¶ How to Make White Lead**                                            **[art. 17]**

52vb]     ¶ Take a vessel of clay, or of wood, a gallon in size, more or less, as you choose. And
then bore holes across in the four sides, that is to say, the first four holes, about five
inches, more or less, from the ground, according to the size of your vessel. And then
about three inches or more, higher, another four holes across, and so higher and
5          higher, until you come to the furthermost end, whether the vessel is large or small.
And then take lead and melt it. And if it is not pure and clean enough, cast it into
clean water. And unless it is then pure and clean, melt it soon again and cast it into
water. And so purify it until it is fine and clean enough. And then melt it again, and
cast it into an empty basin, or into whatever vessel of brass you want, so that it will
10         flow over a broad surface and become thin. And if it is not thin enough, take a
hammer and beat it as thin as you can. And then take sticks and put them across in
the four holes, in each part higher and higher. And on every stick hang some of
that thin lead, as thickly as you can, from rung to rung, so that no part touches
another. And then take vinegar and pour enough into the vessel so that the bottom-
15         most lead does not touch the vinegar. And then take a stone, or a board, that will
cover the vessel, and close it well and tightly on top. And then take pure and good
clay, and seal tight the vessel, so that no air may escape at all, neither from the
holes nor from above. And then take your vessel and set it deeply in horse dung, for
a period of nine nights, or more. And then pick up your vessel, and uncover it from
20         above. And if you find any lead upon the sticks undissolved, it is because of too little
vinegar. And if your lead is entirely dissolved and you find vinegar on the ground,
then it is good. Then gently pour out that vinegar, and take up your white lead, and
do with it as you wish. And if you find any lead as I explained before undissolved,
keep it until another time when you wish to make more. |


**BOOKLET 4**                                                          **QUIRE 6**

53ra]     **The Life of Saint Ethelbert**                                 **[art. 18]**

Glorious King Ethelbert, pleasing to the highest king, arisen of royal stock from
King Redwald who ruled in East Anglia, whom saintly Bede recalls in *The History of
the English*, was the eleventh to hold dominion over the East Anglians. His father
was the magnificent King Ethelred, his mother Queen Leofruna born of noble
5          blood. The highest power of royal office did not cause, as often happens,

oblivisci quam ineffabilia sint gaudia celestibus. Hec adquirere, hec possidere tota mente affectabant.

Anno incarnationes Dominice septingentesimo, septuagesimo nono, ab adventu Anglorum in Britanniam, trescentesimo vicesimo nono, regiis parentibus nascitur
10    Ethelbertus, et baptismi sacramento renascitur Cristo; ablutus aqua salutari, confirmatus dextera pontificali, Sancti Spiritus gratiam suscipit qua benigne preventus ad omnium virtutum incrementa in dies proficiebat. In puerili etate, nil puerile actitare dulce habebat, set adolescenciam suam litteris et moribus sacris studuit informare; gravitas enim quedam morum que ei divinitus innata fuerat,
15    nullatenus illum vanis substerni sinebat.

Processu temporis, post funus paternum, inclitus Ethelbertus heres patris factus est,
53rb]  etatis | quartum decimum tunc gerens annum. Electus, et a Domino preelectus, regni Estanglie sublimatur solio. Erat itaque hic rex iuvenis forme elegantis, deo acceptabilis, virtute laudabilis, alloquio affabilis, pius ac benignus. Consulunt ei
20    optimates sui, ut dignitate regia puellam dignam accipiat in congugem. Obstat ille tempore non modico, cor gerens signatum castitatis pudore. Tandem consilii communis instantia rex victus, ne in aliquo regni periculo scandalum fiat suis suorum cedit consilio. Cui unus de optimatibus suis ait, "Australe regnum Anglie cui quondam iure regali quidam Eglan nomine preerat novi rege carere. Sola
25    regnat filia eius ibi virgo vocabulo, Sindritha, virgo satis honesta facie et moribus. Hanc regali thoro dignam censeo fore." Ad quem rex ait, "Huiusmodi consilium acceptarem, virginis laudate speciositati me copularem, si patris eius precordia dudum noscem sine fraudis macula subsistere. Nam cum patre meo rege Ethelredo initum pacis fedus fraude virulenta creberrime maculavit. Abscit inquam abscit, ut
30    dolosi generis consortio ullatenus jungar."

Deinde quidam comes Oswaldus nomine ita regem affatus, inquit, "Cunctis Anglie regnis, ut michi videtur, regnum Mercie prestat. In hac rex Offa, filius Ehinferti quondam ducis Merciorum, regnat. Etatis provecte, capud canicie circumfusus, agitur nunc annus duodetricesimus, ex quo, Mercensibus preesse ceperat. Regine | nomen
53va]  Kynedryda; filie vero virginis decore nomen, Elphryda. Hec ut res expostulat solium
36    reginale conscendere digna est." Laudatur huius consilium. Rex cum omnibus suis illud acceptat. Sola tamen regina Leofruna mater regis id revocat et reclamat, dicens Offam regem Merciorum tyrannum et plurimo experimento plenum dolo pronunciat. Mercenses omnino sine fide probat unde nec illi huiusmodi placet
40    consilium; rex autem contra, quod tota curia consulit, quod acceptat, licet mater eius contraveniat, fieri oportere proclamat.

these children of royal power to forget how indescribable are the joys of those in heaven. They aspired with their whole heart to acquire and possess these.

In the 779th year of the Lord's incarnation, in the 329th year after the arrival of the Angles in Britain, Ethelbert is born to kingly parents, and is reborn to Christ
10 through the sacrament of baptism; cleansed by the salvational water and confirmed by the bishop's right hand, he receives the grace of the Holy Ghost, under the kindly protection of which he progressed from day to day to the increase of all virtues. In his childhood he considered it sweet to do nothing childish, but rather he was eager to shape his youth through book learning and sacred morals; for a certain solemnity
15 of morals which had been divinely innate in him permitted him in no way to be subverted by vanities.

With the passage of time, after his father's death, renowned Ethelbert became his
53rb] father's heir | when he was fourteen years of age. King elect (and already elected by the Lord), he is elevated to the throne of East Anglia. This king was a young man of elegant appearance, pleasing to God, praiseworthy in virtue, attractive in conver-
20 sation, dutiful, and kindly. His noblemen advise him to take as wife a girl worthy of royal office. He resists for a long time, since he had a heart distinguished by the modesty of chastity. At length the king, overcome by the pressure of common opinion, lest in some crisis of his reign there should be a stumbling block for his people, gives in to the opinion of his nobles. One of them says to him: "The southern realm of England, over which a certain man named Eglan formerly held
25 rule, is without a new king. His daughter rules there by herself, a maiden named Sindritha, a maiden quite chaste in appearance and morals. I judge that she is worthy of a king's bed." The king says to him, "I would accept advice of this sort, I would join myself to the beauty of the maiden you have praised, if I could know that her father's heart was without the taint of deceit. For he most frequently tainted with virulent deceit the peace treaty he had entered with my father, King Ethelred. Far
30 be it, I say, far be it that ever I should be joined in alliance with a treacherous king."

Then a certain count named Oswald, having thus addressed the king, said, "As it seems to me, the realm of Mercia is preeminent over all the realms of England. In it reigned King Offa, son of Einfert who was formerly duke of the Mercians. His head is encircled with the white hair of advanced age, and it is now the twenty-eighth
53va] year from when he started to rule over the Mercians. The queen's | name [is]
36 Cynethryth; the name of the daughter who has the grace of being a virgin, Alfrida. As this circumstance demands, she is worthy to ascend a queen's throne." The advice of this man is praised. The king, together with all his men, accepts it. Only Queen Leofruna, mother of the king, rejects it and cries out against it, saying that King Offa of the Mercians is a tyrant, and she pronounces him deceitful on the basis of many experiences. She finds the Mercians altogether faithless and for that reason
40 advice of this sort does not please her; but in contrast the king, although his mother is opposed, decrees that it is appropriate to do what the whole court advises and what he accepts.

**P**uer Dei gloriosus rex Ethelbertus iter parat in Merciam, hanc martirii sui gloria, totam illustraturus, scutoque meritorum perpetuo tuitorus. Set ecce! Dum in conspectu omnium, regium equum ascendit, terra dat motum maximum, exercitum

45 territat universum. Attonita signo vidua mater regina fit anxia et dubia, utrum vita comitante rex filius suus unquam constat rediturus. "Dei," tamen ait, "fiat voluntas fiat." Terre signo celi mox respondet signum, sol enim per orbem radios spargens fulcerat lucide, et ecce! Obscuratur toti curie, in medio itinere, densitas nebularum subito orbata, itinerantes sese, alterutrum videre negat. Dumtaxat vocis per sonum,

50 quislibet alterum novit. Obstupescit rex Ethelbertus, dum sic radiosus phebus obtenebrascit. Ad stupidam celi curiam clamare cepit, "Genua," inquit, "flectamus, prece polum pulsemus ut nostri misereatur omnipotens Deus." Vix oratione completa, fit aurora tota, serena. Tunc rex hillaris effectus, ait, "Sit nomen Domini

53vb] | benedictum, ex hoc nunc et usque in seculum."

55 **S**ummi Patris tandem preordinante gratia, sanctus Ethelbertus iam egressus de Estanglia, velut Abraham patriarcha de terra et cognatione sua [*Genesis 12:1*], Merciam venit ubi viva hostia sancta, Deo placens offertur, sicque repromissionis terram lacte et melle manantem cum corona martirii ingredietur. Hospitatur in villa regia Sottone nominata, non longe a loco ubi Offa rex Merciorum tunc

60 temporis degebat. Eadem vero nocte rex Ethelbertus fatigatus ex itinere cum se sopori dedisset, cuncta que illi futura erant per sompnium videbat, vidit nanque per sompnium aule regie sue tectum decidisse; cornua eciam thalami sui in quo quiescere solebat tectum cum parietibus subito in terram comminui; vestem quam induebatur sanguine madefactam; trabem longam et latam in medio urbis in altum

65 erectam, se ipsum in avem transfiguratum et levi volatu eam supervolitasse. Quam visionem Oswaldo comiti suo plane revelabat; et comes omnia consolandi et obsequendi gratia interpretari satagebat. Rex tamen de dissolutione sui corporis et regni sui desolatione hec cuncta considerans intrepide fiduciam habens in Domino, et quicquid accideret gratias reddens, viam vitamque suam Deo comendabat.

70 **P**remiserat autem rex viros discretos cum regiis donariis ad Offam regem adventum suum ei nunciantes. Reversis itaque amicus, tam prosperus quaque ab Offa rege missis veniendi securitatem cum benivolencia regis reportabant. Veniens insuper

54ra] rex Ethelbertus | in apparatu regio coram Offa rege, existente regina Kynedryda cum filia sua Elphryda regis Ethelberti pulcritudine plurimum admirantes, interloquia

75 diversa optinentes. Ac regina iuvenis formam conspiciens, hora captata, pudenda cordis, vocis expressione detexit. Ille ut erat Dei plenus gratia, sponsam regis Offe et coniugium maritale necnon animam propriam violare penitus necglexit.

The renowned boy of God, King Ethelbert, journeys to Mercia, all of which he will make illustrious with the renown of his martyrdom and which he will protect unceasingly with the shield of his merits. But look! As in everyone's view he mounts the royal horse, the earth gives a very great quake and frightens the whole army. As-

45 tonished by this sign, his widowed mother, the queen, becomes anxious and doubtful whether it is certain that her son the king is ever going to return alive. Nevertheless she says, "Let the will of God be done." Soon a sign in the sky replies to the sign in the earth, for the sun, spreading its rays over the world, had shone brightly, but now look! A thick bank of clouds is made dark before the whole court in the middle of their route, and the sudden absence of the sun prevents them as they are journeying

50 from seeing each other. At best, by sound of voice does one recognize another. King Ethelbert is stunned as the radiant sun thus grows dark. He begins to shout out to the court, which is stunned by the sky. He says, "Let us get down on our knees and entreat heaven with prayers that all-powerful God have mercy on us." No sooner had their prayer been finished than the whole sky becomes bright. Then the king,

53vb] made jubilant, says, "Blessed be the name of the Lord | for this now and forever."

55 At last, foreordained by the grace of the highest Father, Saint Ethelbert, having set forth from East Anglia, like father Abraham from his country and from his kin [*Genesis 12:1*], comes to Mercia where a living holy offering — one pleasing to God — is made, and so he will enter the promised land, dripping with milk and honey, with the crown of martyrdom. He takes lodging in the royal palace named Sutton, not far from the place where Offa, king of the Mercians, was then living. When on

60 the same night King Ethelbert, tired from the journey, had fallen alseep, he saw in a dream everything that was going to happen to him, for he saw in the dream that the roof of his royal hall and even the corners of his bedchamber in which he was accustomed to rest fell down; that the roof together with the walls at once broke into pieces; that the garment he was wearing was drenched in blood; and that he was

65 metamorphosed into a bird and flew over the long and broad roofbeam that had been raised aloft in the middle of the city. He revealed this vision thoroughly to his companion, Oswald; and the companion took pains to interpret everything for the sake of providing solace and complaisance. The king, considering fearlessly all these things about the dissolution of his body and the desolation of his realm, having faith in the Lord, and rendering thanks no matter what should happen, commended his way and his life to God.

70 The king had sent in advance men of discernment with royal gifts to King Offa, to announce to him his arrival. When the emissaries[?] returned from King Offa, they brought back certainty of safe passage together with the good will of the king. More-

54ra] over, when King Ethelbert came | in royal splendor before King Offa, Queen Cynethryth and her daughter Alfrida much admired the handsomeness of King

75 Ethelbert and had many conversations. And the queen, seeing the attractive appearance of the young man, seized a moment and uncovered the shameful impulses of her heart with an utterance of her voice. Inasmuch as he was filled with the grace of God, he refrained entirely from violating the spouse of King Offa, their marriage bond, and his own soul. Instead he requested her daughter in accord with the law of

Set ad Dei legem et copulam maritalem filiam suam postulavit. Videns igitur trux belua se contemptam in beati viri necem maturat consilia. Accessit autem ad 80 tyrannum virum suum mulier scelera, ait, "Rumor quem hausisti olim auribus, nunc extat verus. Ecce rex Ethelbertus manu militum stipatus venit, menia subintrat; filiam tuam, velis nolis, in coniugem accepturus. Si non precaveris tibi regnum tuum invadet, regnoque te omnio expellet. Surge, tibi et tuis consule, percipe vt morte crudelissima moriatur, et obprobrium gentis nostre auferatur."

85 Hiis male suasoriis verbis rex accensus dolos parat, morte scitit innocentis. Cui quidam Gwynbertus ait, "Patratum a me homicidium, ad te o rex confugium me eligere compulit. Ad hunc autem occidendum, dum tibi placet, peratus existo; nam 54rb] et ego in domo patris sui Ethelredi per quindecim annos nutritus | fui, et post mortem eius filio suo Ethelberto obsequio strenue probitatis adhesi. Solus ego pre 90 omnibus in actubus meis, illis placui. Ergo istud melius alio, scelere effectu possum adimplere." Qui mercede constituta peccuniaque suscepta hospitium Ethelberti fraudulenter adivit, inquiens ad eum, "Prospera tibi sint cuncta, princeps desiderabilis. Quicquid petiturus accessisti, indificiliter optinebis; hoc pollicetur rex Offa dominus meus. In accubitu enim suo illum invenies. Minuit quippe sanguinem 95 nec audet eius infirmitas diei admittere claritatem. Introeamus igitur pariter ad eum, absque frequencia militari, sine strepitu et armis, adventus tui causam illi quamtocius exposituri." Fecit fortis atleta Dei secundum consilium viri dolosi, proditorem suis brachiis amplectens. Cumque thalamum ad hoc provisum fuissent ingressi exilientibus Gwynberti complicibus, capitur Ethelbertus atque ligatur. Suoque ipsius 100 gladio evaginato, capud Gwynbertus amputavit. Iussu autem regis Offe corpus cum capite in paludem prope ripam fluminis Lugge proiectum est. Sic innocens peremptus in terris rex et martir gaudia regni celestis conscendit.

Adveniens virgo regia Elphryda regem extinctum priusquam a thalamo fuerat eiectus, spectat. Materno consilio patratum scelus exhorescit et ait, "Nullus nunciorum 105 ad me ulterius ingredietur, nuncians de sponsi alicuius amplexibus." Vovens itaque 54va] Deo virginitatem suam in | insula Cruland nomine, anachoretica conversatione vitam finiebat.

Exurexit itaque eadem nocte super sepulcrum beati martiris Ethelberti tam inmensi luminis splendor ut totus locus igne putaretur accensus. Quo signo viso multe regionis 110 illius gentes Offam tyrannum superbum graviter exterruerunt, eumque ut peniteret ad viam humilitatis reduxerunt. Qui decimam ecclesie Dei omnium que possidebat tribuens, facinus quod in Ethelberto exercuit penitendo deflevit. Passus est autem beatus Ethelbertus die Dominica xiii° kalendas Iunii. Cuius gloriosa intercessio nobis veniam porrigat delictorum.

God and marriage bonds. Seeing herself spurned, therefore, the savage beast ripens plots to slaughter the blessed man. Moreover, the outrageous woman approached
80     her husband, the tyrant, and said, "The report that you once heard now shows itself true. Look, King Ethelbert comes, surrounded by a band of soldiers, and enters the city walls; he is going to take your daughter as wife, whether you want it or not. If you do not watch out for yourself, he will invade your realm and will expel you altogether from the realm. Rise up, take thought for yourself and your followers, order that he die a death most cruel, and let the disgrace of our people be removed."

85     The king, incensed by these wicked exhortations, prepares treacheries and thirsts after the death of an innocent man. To him a certain Gwinbert says, "A murder I committed obliged me to seek refuge with you, O king. Since it pleases you, I am prepared to kill him; for I was raised in the home of his father Ethelred for fifteen
54rb]    years, | and after his death I clung fast eagerly to his son Ethelbert in compliance
90     with uprightness. I alone, before all others, pleased them in my actions. Therefore better than another, I can put this misdeed into effect." When the reward had been determined and the money received, he entered Ethelbert's quarters deceitfully, saying to him, "May everything prosper for you, desirable prince. What you have come to seek, you will obtain without difficulty; my lord King Offa promises this.
95     Indeed, you will find him lying down. Truly, he had his blood let, and in his weakness he does not dare admit the brightness of daylight. Therefore let us go in together to him, without a retinue of soldiers, without the clatter of arms, to explain to him as quickly as possible the motive of your visit." The brave athlete of God, embracing his betrayer in his arms, acted in accordance with the advice of the treacherous man. And when they entered the bedroom provided for this purpose,
100     Ethelbert is taken and bound by the accomplices of Gwinbert who leap out. Gwinbert cut off his head with his own unsheathed sword. At the bidding of King Offa, the body together with the head is cast into a swamp near the bank of the river Lugg. Thus the innocent king and martyr, having been slain on earth, ascends to the joys of the heavenly realm.

The royal maiden Alfrida arrives and sees the murdered king before he has been removed from the bedroom. She shudders in horror at the crime committed upon
105    her mother's advice, and she says, "No messenger will approach me henceforth to carry messages about the embraces of some betrothed." And so devoting her
54va]    virginity to God, she ended her life on | the island named Croyland, leading an anchorite's existence.

And so on the same night there arose over the tomb of the blessed martyr Ethelbert the radiance of a light so measureless that the whole place was thought to be
110    akindle with fire. Having seen this sign, the many peoples of that region took fright severely at Offa, the proud tyrant, and they led him back to the way of humility to repent. Contributing to God's church a tithe of everything he possessed, he wept repentantly for the misdeed he had committed against Ethelbert. Morover, blessed Ethelbert suffered his passion on the twentieth of May. May his glorious intercession grant us forgiveness for our failings.

115    **T**ercia vero nocte apparuit sanctus Ethelbertus cuidam viro Brythfrido nomine cum
       inmenso lumine et ut velociter surgeret imperavit, dicens, "Vade dilectissime ad
       sepulcrum meum et accipe corpus meum. Et ad Stratum Waye fluminis ferre satage
       et ibidem cum honore reconde." Expergefactus a sompno vir probus oculos aperuit,
       et claritate celesti totam domum illustratam prospexit. Qui brachia sua ut sanctum
120    Dei comprehenderet extendit, set beatus martir cum splendore abscedens non
       comparuit. Exurexit vir ille velociter, visione letus gracias agentes Deo, et advocans
       Egmundum virum illustre. Perrexerunt ambo ad sepulcrum eius. Elevantes corpus
       sanctum, vestibus preciosis induerunt, ac in quodam curru corpus sacrum
       imponentes, versus locum assignatum abierunt. Cum autem iter inceptum agressi
125    fuissent, per Dei dispositionem capud sancti glorisum amiserunt. Ad quod cum
54vb]  quidam cecus pedem offenderet, | sic nescius, scienter clamavit, "Adiuva me, serve
       Dei Ethelberte," statimque eadem hora in momento visum recepit. Et accipiens
       gloriosum capud in manibus, Deo omipotenti et beato Ethelberto gratias referebat.
       Insequitur itaque iter initum, capud deportans et ad currum sequentes clamavit,
130    "Expectate, et munus quod baiulo accipite!" Et narrabat eis quid acciderat. Qui
       gratias agentes Deo ad locum preordinatum portaverunt ibique cum maximo honore
       sepelierunt pro cuius amore maxima mirabilia altissimus operatur per infinita
       seculorum secula.

### Anima Christi, sanctifica me                                                     [art. 19]

54vb]  Anima Christi, sanctifica me.
       Corpus Christi, salva me.
       Sanguis Christi, inebria me.
       Aqua lateris Christi, lava me.
5      Passio Christi, conforta me.
       O bone Iesu, exaudi me
       Et non me permittas separari a te.
       Ab hoste maligno defende me.
       In hora mortis voca me,
10     Et pone me iuxta te
       Ut cum angelis tuis laudem te
       In secula seculorum. Amen.

       Qui hanc orationem devote dixerit iii^m dies veniale possidebit.

### Quant voy la revenue d'yver                                                      [art. 20]

55ra]  Quant voy la revenue
       D'yver qe si me argue
       Qe ly temps se remue,
       Lors aym buche fendue,

115     **O**n the third night Saint Ethelbert appeared with immeasurable light to a certain man
        named Brithfrid and commanded him to rise swiftly, saying, "Go, most beloved, to
        my tomb and receive my body. Endeavor to take it to the Street of the river Wye
        [i.e., Hereford] and bury it there with honor." Wakened from sleep, the righteous
        man opened his eyes and looked out upon the whole house illuminated by heavenly
120     brightness. He stretched out his arms to embrace God's saint, but the blessed
        martyr, leaving with his radiance, was not to be found. That man arose swiftly,
        joyously rendering thanks to God for the vision and calling a distinguished man,
        Egmund. Both of them proceeded to his tomb. Raising up the saintly body, they
        dressed it in precious garments, and, placing the sacred body on a cart, they went
125     off toward the designated place. But when they had set out and begun the journey,
        by God's disposition they lost the glorious head of the saint. When a certain blind
54vb]   man stumbled | unknowingly upon it, he cried out knowingly, "Aid me, Ethelbert,
        God's servant," and immediately at that instant in the very same hour he regained his
        sight. Taking the glorious head in his hands, he offered thanks to all-powerful God
        and to blessed Ethelbert. And so, carrying the head, he pursued the route they had
130     undertaken, and he cried to those following the cart, "Wait, and take the gift that
        I am bearing!" And he related to them what had happened. Offering thanks to God,
        they carried to the designated place and buried with greatest honor the one for love
        of whom highest God works the greatest miracles for endless centuries of centuries.


        **Soul of Christ, Sanctify Me**                                                    **[art. 19]**

54vb]   Soul of Christ, sanctify me.
        Body of Christ, save me.
        Blood of Christ, intoxicate me.
        Water from the side of Christ, wash me.
5       Passion of Christ, comfort me.
        O good Jesus, hearken to me
        And do not allow me to be separated from you.
        Defend me from the evil enemy.
        Call me at the hour of death,
10      And set me beside you
        So that I may praise you with your angels
        Forever and ever. Amen.


        The person who pronounces this prayer devoutly for three days will gain forgiveness.


        **A Goliard's Feast**                                                             **[art. 20]**

55ra]   When I see the return
        Of winter that so afflicts me
        As the weather changes,
        Then I love a split log,

5      Charboun clykant,
Tysoun flambaunt;
Feu de souche meisné
De joie chaunt;
Quar je l'eym tant,
10    Tot le cors me tressue.

Quaunt vient acochier,
Certes molt me agree
Fagot en fournil,
Secche sauntz fumee,
15    Qe tost esprent
E brese rent.
E je me degrat molt sovent
(Le pys e l'eschyne!),
Quar la char bien pue,
20    E de draps mal vestue.

Ayme molt la jorné,
Quar quaunt, pur chalour se sue
Taunt, qe fors soit issue
La freydour e alee.
25    Ceo est moun delit:
De aver beau lit
De dras blaunchys
Fleyre la buee.

La tenue coverture
30    C'est ma desconfiture,
Lange sauntz foreure —
De celi n'ai je cure
Quar il n'est preuz.
Mieux aym les feus:
35    Quant je voy la refroidure,
A ly m'en vou;
Mieux aym son jou
Qe dous dees detorsure!

Quaunt l'yver s'esteynt
40    Par la matynee,
Certes, molt me grevee
La noyf e la gelee,
Mes en verglaz
Atourner faz,
45    Menues hastes en bruaz.

5      The crackling coal,
       The blazing brands;
       The big-logged hearth fire
       Sings with joy;
       Indeed I love it so much,
10     My whole body sweats.

       When bedtime comes,
       What surely pleases me
       Is a faggot in the hearth,
       Dry without smoke,
15     Which burns entirely
       And turns to embers.
       I quite often scratch myself
       (The worst is the spine!),
       For the flesh stinks a lot,
20     And is ill-dressed in clothes.

       I love greatly the daytime,
       For then, by means of heat
       Chasing it so, the cold
       Is sent outside and is gone.
25     This is my delight:
       To have a good bed
       Of white cloth
       With a fresh smell.

       A thin blanket
30     Makes me miserable,
       Wool not fur-lined —
       I don't care for that
       For it's of no use.
       I like the fires better:
35     When I see the cold,
       I go to the fire;
       I like its play better
       Than two weighted dice!

       When the winter extends
40     Through the morning,
       Indeed, I'm sorely grieved
       By the snow and frost,
       As into slick ice
       It is transformed,
45     Little slivers in the fog.

De pourcel madle ostee
Pris en bone pasture,
La loygne sauntz arsure,
En la broche botee —
50      Quar c'est ma noreture!
Tout ay ma tenure
En bon morsel donee
En bon claré,
En fort raspee —
55      Q'eym mieux d'assez
Que cervoyse enfumee!


¶ Taverne ay molt amee
(N'est pas droit qe la hee!);
Tout ay m'amour donee
60      En savour destempré
En gavigaut,
En cetewaut,
Mys en chaudee peveré —
Ne fet pas mal
65      Entour Noal,
Mostarde ove char salee.


¶ Oues e madlarz,
Plongons e blaryes,
Chapouns chanevaus,
70      Gelynes rosties,
Cygnes, pouns,
Grues, heyrouns,
Cerceles, jauntes,
E morillons.


75      E purcel enfarcie,
La loygne entrelardé —
De cele ay molt amee!
Venesoun ne haz mie,
Ne char de cerf venee,
80      Ne deym, ne porcke, velee
Une pome flestrye;
¶ Jamboun
De fresche salesoun
55rb]   Mi ad ren|du la vie!


85      Quaunt je su leez la tonne,
E yl ploit e yl tonne,
Tout adees ma fosoyne:
Vyn de haute persone,

Some roasted boar
From good pasturage,
The loin unburnt,
Thrust on a skewer —
50    That's to my taste!
I've given all my holdings
For one good morsel
With a good claret,
With a strong table wine —
55    I much prefer that
To smoky beer!

¶ I've much loved the tavern
(There's no reason to hate it!);
I've given all my love
60    To a flavored brew
With galingale,
With zedoary,
Mixed with hot pepper —
It's not bad
65    Around Christmas,
Mustard with salted meat.

¶ Geese and mallards,
Coots and moorhens,
Capons on canvas,
70    Roasted hens,
Swans, peacocks,
Cranes, herons,
Teals, wild geese,
And tufted ducks.

75    And stuffed pig,
The interlarded loin —
I've much loved that!
I don't hate venison at all,
Nor flesh from hunted deer,
80    Nor buck, nor boar, veal
With dried apple;
¶ Ham
Freshly salted
55rb]    Has re|stored me to life!

85    When I'm beside the tun,
And it rains and thunders,
There's always plenty for me:
Wine of the best quality,

Levre encine, conin lardee;
90 Molt est fous qe saonne
Formage rees
Quaunt rostie ay
E je le faz corouné
E pui grosoiller.

95 Nuilles e oblees,
Royssolees e guaffres,
E tostiz doreez.
Perdryz, plovers,
Coloms croysers.
100 Le wydecoks est bon mangiers!

E andoilles lardés —
Je tienk pur fol qe doune
Son aver enprisonee
Pur tripes enfumés.
105 Quar quant revient a noune,
My hoste m'a resoune:
Si dit qu'il ad trovee,
Countre la nuyt,
Un chaudon quit
110 A chasteyne paree.

¶ En quaresme a Lentre,
Lors eym perche paree,
La tenche enversee
E en souz botee,
115 Harang, plays,
E peschoun freshe,
E alosee en pastee,
Gastieu rostiz,
Menu brayz,
120 E flamiche salee.

¶ Dars ne heez je mie,
Fenduz de quonie,
Anguille de gors,
De sa pieu veudie,
125 Conger, estorgoun,
Luz, salmoun,
Vendoise, breme, ne gerdon,
Ne morue ov l'aille,
Ne crevice pelle,
130 Ne roches, ne lampré,
Ne ray refreidé,

Stewed hare, larded rabbit;
90      He's crazy who'd refuse
A bit of soft cheese
When I've toasted it
And crowned it
With gooseberries.

95      Cookies and cakes,
Rissoles and waffles,
Toasted golden brown.
Partridges, plovers,
Doves from dovecote.
100     Woodcock is good to eat!

And larded chitterlings —
I take for a fool any who puts
His goods in hock
For smoked tripe.
105     For when I revive around noon,
My innkeeper has a word with me:
He says he recommends,
At bedtime,
A hot pot
110     Of peeled chestnuts.

¶ During the forty days of Lent,
Then I love scaled perch,
Tench turned over
And immersed in broth,
115     Herring, plaice,
And fresh fish,
And shad in pastry,
Baked breads,
Lightly grilled,
120     And salted custard tart.

¶ Dace I don't at all hate,
Split elegantly,
Freshwater eel,
Its skin removed,
125     Conger eel, sturgeon,
Pike, salmon,
Gudgeons, bream, nor gurnard,
Nor cod with garlic,
Nor shelled crayfish,
130     Nor roach, nor lamprey,
Nor cold skate,

Ly makerel
Freshe e novel,
E tot cist autre bon morsel
135      Mout al bourse veydee.

¶ Quant la Pasche repoire,
Je m'y last tayre;
Tart e flaon faz fere
Pur la sesoun retrere.
140      Molt aym motoun
A gras reynoun,
E l'aignel faz fors trere
De pelicoun,
M'entencioun
145      Met au poyvre defere.

¶ Droyz est qe l'en eyt motoun
En porree, pucynz,
En verynz,
Oue en franke gardé
150      (Atant novel
Jus de tuel!),
La teste en rost, aprés l'owel,
E gras cheveryl lardé
Ne me doit pas desployré,
155      Pur le manger retrere,
Pee de porcke en socié
(A froit celer
E haut soler),
Herbe mugier
160      Menuement poudré —
E je m'envoys donks dormyr!

**Alle herkneth to me nou**                                    [art. 21]

55va]      Alle herkneth to me nou!                        [Narrator]
A strif wolle Y tellen ou
Of Jesu ant of Sathan.
Tho Jesu wes to helle ygan
5          Forte vacche thenne hys
Ant bringen hem to parays,
The Devel hevede so muche pousté
That alle mosten to helle te.
Nas non so holy prophete
10         Seththe Adam ant Eve then appel ete
Ant he were, at this worldes fyne,

art. 21 – Tale of Jesus after death and before resurrection when he frees souls from Hell.
Debate follows between Christ and Satan

ART. 21. HARROWING OF HELL                                                     67

Mackerel
Fresh and newly caught,
And all other good morsels
135    That have emptied many a purse.

¶ When Easter returns,
I quit being quiet;
I have tarts and flan made
To close up the season.
140    I dearly like mutton
With fat kidneys,
So I have a lamb skinned
Out of its fleece,
Intending to
145    Spice it with crushed pepper.

¶ It's good to have mutton
With leek potage, chicken,
On weekdays,
Goose fattened in a pen
150    (Then new
Stains on tablecloth!),
A roast head, after cooked goose,
And a fat kid in lard
Wouldn't displease me,
155    To close up the meal,
Pigs' feet in sauce
(From the cold storeroom
And the upper sunroom),
With spicy nutmeg
160    Sprinkled on lightly —
And then I send myself to sleep!

## Harrowing of Hell                                    [art. 21]

55va]    All listen to me now!                          [Narrator]
I'll tell you of a contest
Between Jesus and Satan.
When Jesus had gone to hell
5    To fetch from there his own
And bring them to paradise,
The Devil had so much power
That all were made to go to hell.
There was never a prophet so holy
10    Since Adam and Eve had eaten the apple
That he, at this world's end,

That he ne moste to helle-pyne;
Ne shulde he never thenne come
Nere Jesu Crist, Godes Sone,
15    Vor that wes seid to Adam ant Eve,
That were Jesu Crist so leeve,
Ant so wes seyd to Habraham,
That wes sothfast holy man,
Ant so wes seid to Davyd the kyng,
20    That wes of Cristes oune ofspryng,
Ant to Johan the Baptist,
That folewede Jesu Crist,
Ant to Moyses the holy whyt,
The hevede the lawe to yeme ryht,
25    Ant to mony other holy mon —
Mo then Ich telle con —
That weren alle in more wo
Then Y con ou telle fro.
Jesu Crist arew hem sore
30    Ant seide he wolde vacche hem thore.
He lyhte of ys heye tour
Into Seinte Marie bour;
He wes bore for oure nede
In this world in pore wede;
35    In this world he wes ded
Forte losen us from the qued.     *deliver us from evil*
Tho Jesu hevede shed ys blod
For our neode upon the rod,
In godhed toke he then way
40    That to helle-gates lay;
Then he com there, tho seide he
Alse Y shal nouthe telle the.

55vb]   "Harde gates hav Y gon,               **[Dominus]**
Sorewen soffred mony on!
45    Thritty wynter ant thridde half yer
Hav Y woned in londe her.
Almost ys so muche agon
Seththe Y bycom furst mon —
Ich have seththe tholed ant wyst
50    Hot, cold, honger, ant thurst.
Mon hath do me shome ynoh
Wyth word ant dede, in heore woh —
Bounden ant bueten, yron of blode —
Demeden me to deye on rode.
55    For Adames sunne fol, ywis,
Ich have tholed al this!
Adam, thou havest aboht sore!

Narrator explains Jesus's connection to king David, the passions, and what Biblical characters are trapped in Hell.

Jesus explains that he became man and suffered for Adam's sin.

Could avoid going to hell-pain;
Nor could he ever escape from thence
Were it not for Jesus Christ, God's Son,
15     For it was prophesied to Adam and Eve,
Who were so dear to Jesus Christ,
And thus was said to Abraham,
Who was a steadfast holy man,
And thus was said to David the king,
20     Who was of Christ's own lineage,
And to John the Baptist,
Who followed Jesus Christ,
And to Moses the holy man,
Who had the law to govern rightly,
25     And to many other holy men —
More than I can name —
Who were all in more agony
Than I can describe to you.
Jesus Christ pitied them deeply
30     And said he would fetch them from there.
He descended from his high tower
Into Saint Mary's womb;
He was born for our need
In this world in a poor garment;
35     In this world he died
To deliver us from an evil contract.
When Jesus had shed his blood
For our sake upon the cross,
In godhead he went the next way
40     That led to hell-gates;
When he came there, then he spoke
As I will now tell you.

55vb]    "Hard experiences I've endured,                  **[Lord]**
Suffered many a sorrow!
45     Thirty-three and a half years
Have I dwelled here on earth.
So very much has happened
Since I first became man —
I've since then suffered and known
50     Hot, cold, hunger, and thirst.
Men have done me extreme dishonor
By word and deed, in their wickedness —
Bound and beaten, dripping in blood —
They judged me to die on cross.
55     For Adam's foul sin, indeed,
I've suffered all of this!
Adam, you've paid grievously!

— interesting to state exactly how old Jesus is/was

I nul soffre that no more!
Adam, thou hast duere aboht
60       That thou levedest me noht.
Y shal the bringe of helle-pyne
Ant with the alle myne!"

"Who ys that Ych here thore?                    **Sathan ait**
Ich him rede speke na more!
65       For he may so muche do
That he shal us come to
Forte buen oure fere
Ant fonden hou we pleyen here!"

"Thou miht wyten, in thy lay,                    **Dominus ait**
70       That mine woll Y have away.
Wost thou never whet Ych am?
Almost ys thritti wynter gan
That thou hast fonded me
Forte knowe wet Y be.
75       Sunne fond thou never non
In me as in other mon,
Ant thou shalt wyte wel today
That mine wolle Y have away.
Wen thou bilevest al thyn one,
80       Thenne myht thou grede ant grone!"

"Par ma fey, Ich holde myne                    **Sathan**
Alle tho that bueth heryne!
Resoun wol Y telle the,
Ther ageyn myht thou nouht be:
56ra]    Whose buyth any thyng,
86       Hit is hys ant hys ofspryng.
Adam hungry com me to —
Monrade dude Y him me do —
For on appel Ich yef hym,
90       He is myn, ant al hys kun!"

"Sathanas, hit wes myn —                        **Dominus**
The appel that thou yeve hym,
The appel ant the appel tre —
Bothe were maked thourh me!
95       Hou myhstest thou on eny wyse
Of other monnes thyng make marchandise?
Seththe he wes boht wyth myn,
Wyth resoun wolle Ich haven hym!"

Jesus says he's came to claim the souls, Satan says he had a legal right to them b/c he sold Adam an apple for his soul, Jesus argues that the apple never belonged to him.

ART. 21. HARROWING OF HELL                                              71

I'll not tolerate it anymore!
Adam, you've paid a high price
60      Because you didn't believe in me.
I shall deliver you from hell-pain
And all of mine with you!"

"Who is that I hear there?                  **Satan speaks**
I command him to speak no more!
65      For he may create so much havoc
Were he to approach us
As our peer in combat
And discover how we operate here!"

"Be informed that, in your domain,           **Lord speaks**
70      My property I will take away.
Don't you know who I am?
Almost thirty years have elapsed
Since you tested me
To find out who I am.
75      You never found any sin
In me as in other men,
And you'll surely see today
How I will take mine away.
When you give up all of yours,
80      Then may you wail and groan!"

"By my faith, I claim as mine             **Satan**
All those who are in here!
I'll explain to you a legal fact,
Against which you can't dispute:
56ra]    Whoever buys anything,
86      It and its offspring belong to him.
Adam came to me hungry —
I made him pledge himself to me —
For an apple that I gave to him,
90      He is mine, and all his kin!"

"Satan, it was mine —                     **Lord**
The apple that you gave to him,
The apple and the apple tree —
Both were created by me!
95      How might you in any way
Make a purchase with another man's thing?
Since he was bought with my property,
By legal right I will claim him!"

|          | "Jesu, wel Y knowe the                    | **Sathan** |
|----------|-------------------------------------------|
| 100      | (That ful sore reweth me!),               |
|          | Thou art Louerd over al;                  |
|          | Wo ys him that the knowe ne shal!         |
|          | Heovene ant erthe tac to the;             |
|          | Soules in helle lef thou me —             |
| 105      | Let me haven hem ant helde.               |
|          | That thou havest wel mote thou welde!"    |

|          | "Stille be thou, Sathanas!                | **Dominus** |
|----------|-------------------------------------------|
|          | The ys fallen ambes aas!                  |
|          | Wendest thou Ich were ded for noht?       |
| 110      | Thourh my deth ys monkune boht!           |
|          | They that haved served me                 |
|          | Wyth me he shulen in hevene be.           |
|          | Thou shalt buen in more pyne              |
|          | Then eny that ther is heryne."            |

| 115      | "Ne may non me worse do                   | **Sathan** |
|----------|-------------------------------------------|
|          | Then Ich have had hiderto!                |
|          | Ich have had so muche wo                  |
|          | That Y ne recche whyder Y go!             |
|          | Yef thou revest me of myne,               |
| 120      | Y shal reve the of thyne —                |
|          | Y shal gon from mon to mon                |
|          | Ant reve the of mony on!"                 |

|          | "God wot, Y shal speke the wyht,          | **Dominus** |
|----------|-------------------------------------------|
|          | Ant do the to holde gryht!                |
| 125      | So faste shal Y bynde the                 |
|          | Lutel shalt thou reve me;                 |
|          | Thou shalt buen in bondes ay              |
|          | O that come Domesday.                     |
| 56rb]    | Thou shalt never outwende                 |
| 130      | Monkunne forte shende,                    |
|          | For were thou among men,                  |
|          | Thou woldest me reven moni of hem.        |
|          | The smale fendes that bueth nout stronge, |
|          | He shulen among men yonge;                |
| 135      | Thilke that nulleth ageyn hem stonde,     |
|          | Ichulle he habben hem in honde!           |
|          | Helle-gates Y come nou to,                |
|          | Ant Y wole that heo undo!                 |
|          | Wer ys nou this gateward?                 |
| 140      | Me thuncheth he is a coward!"             |

*Jesus will bind Satan in Hell until Doomsday. Satan may send demons to earth and claim whatever souls they acquire.*

|  | | |
|---|---|---|
| 100 | "Jesus, I know you well | **Satan** |

"Jesus, I know you well
100  (I'm very sorry about that!),    *interesting*
You are Lord over all,
Woe is he who'll never know you!
Heaven and earth belong to you;
Leave the souls in hell to me —
105  Let me have and keep them.
May you rule well what you already have!"

**Satan**

"Be quiet, Satan!
To you fall double aces!
Do you think I died for nothing?
110  By my death mankind's redeemed!
They who have served me
Will be with me in heaven.
You will be in more pain
Than any who are here."

**Lord**

115  "No one can do any worse to me
Than I've already experienced!
I've had so much agony
That I don't care which way I go!
If you rob me of mine,
120  I'll rob you of yours —
I'll go from man to man
And rob you of many a one!"

**Satan**

"God knows, I'll speak to you boldly,
And bid you to hold your peace!
125  I'll bind you so tightly
That you'll rob me of little;
You'll remain bound forever
Till the coming of Doomsday.
56rb]  You'll never escape
130  To destroy mankind,
For were you among men,
You would rob me of many of them.
The minor fiends who aren't strong,
They shall go among men;
135  Those who will not resist them,
I decree that they take them in hand!
I now arrive at hell-gates,
And I bid that they be opened!
Where's now this gatekeeper?
140  I think he's a coward!"

**Lord**

"Ich have herd wordes stronge —                          **Ianitor**
Ne dar Y her no lengore stonde!
Kepe the gates whose may —
Y lete hem stonde ant renne away!"

145     "Helle-gates wolle Y falle                          **Dominus**
Ant out taken myne alle!
Sathanas, Y bynde the! Her shalt thou lay
O that come Domesday!"

"Welcome, Louerd, God of londe,                          **Adam**
150     Godes Sone, ant Godes sonde!
Welcome, Louerd, mote thou be,
That thou wolt us come ant se!
Louerd, nou thou art come to ous,
Bring ous of this lothe hous,
155     Bryng us of this lothe lond,
Louerd, henne, into thyn hond!
Louerd, wost thou whet Ych am?
Thou me shuptest of eorthe: Adam!
For Y thyn heste hueld noht,
160     Duere Ich habbe hit her aboht!
Have merci of us, Godes sone;
Let ous no more her wone!
Alle that herynne be
Yore haveth yyrned after the!
165     We hopeth wel thourh thy comyng
Of oure sunnes haven froryng."

"Knou me, Louerd — Ich am Eve!                          **Eva**
Ich ant Adam the were so leove,
56va]  Thou laddest ous to parays.
170     We hit forgulten ase unwys;
We thin heste dude forleten
Tho we then appel eten.
So longe we haveth buen herynne —
Deore have we aboht ur synne!
175     Louerd God, yef us leve,
Adam ant me, ys wyf Eve,
To faren of this lothe wyke
To the blisse of hevene ryke!"

"Adam, Ich have yeve mi lyf                          **Dominus**
180     For the ant for Eve, thi wyf;
Wendest thou Ich were ded for noht?
For my deth wes monkune yboht."

*Jesus binds Satan.*
*Adam and Eve appear and beg to be taken out of Hell.*

|  | "I've heard forceful words — | **Gatekeeper** |
|  | I don't dare stand here any longer! |  |
|  | Keep the gates whoever wants to — |  |
|  | I leave them standing and run away!" |  |

| 145 | "I'll make hell-gates fall, | **Lord** |
|  | And take out all of mine! |  |
|  | Satan, I bind you! Here will you lie |  |
|  | Till the coming of Doomsday!" |  |

|  | "Welcome, Lord, God of earth, | **Adam** |
| 150 | God's Son, and God's gift! |  |
|  | Welcome, Lord, may you be, |  |
|  | Who wished to come and see us! |  |
|  | Lord, now that you've come to us, |  |
|  | Deliver us from this hateful house, |  |
| 155 | Deliver us from this hateful land, |  |
|  | Lord, from hence, into your hand! |  |
|  | Lord, do you know who I am? |  |
|  | You created me of earth: Adam! |  |
|  | Because I disobeyed your command, |  |
| 160 | Dearly have I paid for it here! |  |
|  | Have mercy on us, God's Son; |  |
|  | Let us dwell here no more! |  |
|  | All who are in here |  |
|  | Long have yearned for you! |  |
| 165 | We hope dearly by your coming |  |
|  | To have solace for our sins." |  |

|  | "Know me, Lord — I am Eve! | **Eve** |
|  | I and Adam were so precious to you, |  |
| 56va] | You led us to paradise. |  |
| 170 | We forfeited it unwisely; |  |
|  | We utterly neglected your command |  |
|  | When we ate the apple. |  |
|  | So long we've been in here — |  |
|  | Dearly have we paid for our sin! |  |
| 175 | Lord God, give us permission, |  |
|  | Adam and me, his wife Eve, |  |
|  | To travel from this hateful home |  |
|  | To the bliss of heaven's realm!" |  |

|  | "Adam, I have given my life | **Lord** |
| 180 | For you and for Eve, your wife; |  |
|  | Do you think that I died for nothing? |  |
|  | For by my death was mankind bought." |  |

"Louerd Crist, Ich am                                    **Habraham**
That thou calledest Habraham!
185    Thou me seidest that of me
Shulde such a child ybore be
That us shulde brynge of pyne —
Me ant (wyth me) alle myne.
Thou art the child! Thou art the man
190    That wes ybore of Habraham!
Do nou that thou byhihstes me:
Bring me to hevene up with the."

"Habraham, Ych wot ful wel                               **Dominus**
Wet thou seidest, everuch del —
195    That mi leve moder wes
Boren ant shaped of thi fleyhs."

"Louerd, Ich am David the kyng                           **[David]**
That bore was of thyn ofspring.
Do me ase thou bihete
200    Thourh the lawe of the prophete.
Nou thou art come to ous,
Bring us from this dredful hous."

"David, thou were bore of my kyn.                        **Dominus**
For thi godnesse art thou myn,
205    More for thi godnesse
Then for eny sibnesse."

"Louerd Crist, Ich am Johan,                             **Iohannes**
That the folewede in Flum Jordan.
56vb]    Tuelf moneth is agon
210    That Y tholede martirdom.
Thou sendest me the ryhte wey
Into helle, forte sey
That thou, Crist, Godes Sone,
Sone shuldest to helle come
215    Forto lesen of helle-pyne
Alle that thou holdest thyne.
Nou thou art come! Nou thou do
That thou seidest fer ant tho."

"Johan, Johan, Ich wot ful wel                           **Dominus**
220    Whet thou seidest everuch del —
Thou shalt seo whet Y shal do
That Y seyde er the to."

      "Lord Christ, I am                                     **Abraham**
      He whom you called Abraham!
185   You said that from me
      Such a child would be born
      Who would deliver us from pain —
      Me and (with me) all mine.
      You are the child! You are the man
190   Who was born of Abraham!
      Do now what you promised me:
      Bring me up to heaven with you."

      "Abraham, I acknowledge fully                      **Lord**
      What you've said, every word —
195   That my dear mother was
      Born and created of your flesh."

      "Lord, I am David the king,                         **[David]**
      Who was born of your lineage.
      Do to me as you promised
200   Through the law of the prophet.
      Now that you have come to us,
      Deliver us from this dreadful house."

      "David, you were born of my kin.                **Lord**
      For your goodness you are mine,
205   More for your goodness
      Than for any kinship."

      "Lord Christ, I am John,                     **John [the Baptist]**
      Who followed you in the River Jordan.
56vb]  Twelve months have passed
210   Since I suffered martyrdom.
      You sent me on the right way
      Into hell, in order to prophesy
      That you, Christ, God's Son,
      Soon would come to hell
215   To release from hell-pain
      All whom you consider yours.
      Now you have come! Now do
      What you proclaimed far and long ago."

      "John, John, I acknowledge fully              **Lord**
220   What you've said, every word —
      You shall see that I will do
      What I said before to you."

      "Louerd, thou knowest al wyth skyl                          **Moyses**
      The lawe of Synay upon the hyl.
225   Ich am Moyses the prophete,
      That hueld the lawes that thou byhete,
      That thou, Jesu, Godes Sone,
      Woldest to the helle come,
      Ant that thou woldest come to bete
230   The sunnes that Adam thohte suete."

      "Moyses, that Ich hihte the                                **Dominus**
      In the Olde Lawe, thou dudest me,
      Ant alle the other that mine buen
      Shule to blisse with me tuen.
235   They that nolden on me leven
      Shule with Sathanas bileven.
      Ther hue shulen wonen ay
      O that come Domesday."

      God, for is moder love,                                    **[Narrator]**
240   Let us never thider come!
      Louerd, for thi muchele grace,
      Graunte us in heovene one place.
      Let us never be forloren
      For no sunne, Crist ycoren.
245   Ah, bring us out of helle-pyne,
      Louerd, ous ant alle thyne,
      Ant yef us grace to libbe ant ende
      In thi service ant to hevene wende.
        Amen.


      **In a thestri stude Y stod**                              **[art. 22]**

57r]  In a thestri stude Y stod a lutel strif to here              **[Narrator]**
      Of a Body that was ungod, ther hit lay on a bere.
      Tho speke the Gost wyth drery mod ant myd sorful chere:    **[Gost]**
      "Wo wrht thy fleyshe, thi foule blod! Whi lyst thou nou here?

5     "Ful kene thou were in halle, whil thou were alyve,
      False domes deme, chaunge two for fyve;
      Falsnesse ant swykedom thou wrohstes ful ryve —
      Tharefore pyne stronge maketh me thunne thryve."

      Tho spac the Body so dymme to that drery Gaste:           **[Body]**
10   "Was me noht of synne, that byndeth me so faste!
      I wende my worldes wynne me wolde ever laste;
      The bondes that Y am ynne, to helle he wolleth me caste."

"Lord, you wisely know all        **Moses**
The law of Sinai upon the hill.
225 I am Moses the prophet,
Who held the laws wherein you vowed
That you, Jesus, God's Son,
Would come to hell,
And that you would come to atone for
230 The sins that Adam considered sweet."

"Moses, what I ordered you to do     **Lord**
By the Old Law, you did for me,
And all the others who are mine
Shall proceed to bliss with me.
235 They who wouldn't believe in me
Shall remain with Satan.
There they shall dwell forever
Till the coming of Doomsday."

May God, for his mother's love,     **[Narrator]**
240 Let us never come thither!
Lord, by your abundant grace,
Grant us a place in heaven.
Let us never be damned
For any sin, as Christ's chosen.
245 Ah, bring us out of hell-pain,
Lord, us and all that's yours,
And give us grace to live and die
In your service and go to heaven.
  Amen.

**Debate between Body and Soul**     **[art. 22]**

*— seperate enteties w/ conciousness*

57r] I stood in a dark place to overhear a little quarrel  **[Narrator]**
Of an unrighteous Body, where it lay on a bier.
Then the Soul spoke miserably and with sad countenance:  **[Soul]**
"Woe to your flesh, your foul blood! Why lie you now here?

5 "You were quite eager in hall, when you were alive,
To dispense false judgments, change two for five;
Deception and treachery you created everywhere —
Thus does fierce pain make me barely to thrive."

Then the Body spoke quite faintly to that sad Soul:  **[Body]**
10 "Would that I weren't filled with sin, which binds me so hard!
I thought that my worldly gain would last forever;
The bonds that I'm in, they'll cast me to hell."

Tho spake the Gost with ryht red soth al to wys:                    **[Gost]**
    "Wher ys thi muchele prude, thy veyr ant thi gris?
15    Thine palefreis ant steden, ant al thi purpris?
    Thou ne shalt with the beren, wrecche, ther thou lis."

Tho saide the Body with drery mod on bere ther hit lay:            **[Body]**
    "Nou ys come her my deth, ant myn ende day.
    Bounden am Y hond ant fot that Y ne may away.
20    Nou aren mi dawes done. Y wende ha lyved ay!"

"Thou havest ylyved to longe! Wo wruth the so suykel!            **[Gost]**
    Ever whil thou lyvedest, fals thou were ant fykel.
    Turne ryht to wronge thou lovedest al to mukel.
    Pynen harde ant stronge to the bueth nou ful tykel."

25    "Wrecche Gost, thou wen away! Hou longe shal thi strift laste?   **[Body]**
    Wormes holdeth here mot, domes byndeth faste.
    Maked he habbeth here lot on my fleyshe to caste.
    Mony fre bodi shal roten — ne be Y nout the laste!"

"Body, miht thou nout lepen to pleyen ant rage,                   **[Gost]**
30    Wilde bueres bete, bynde lyouns savage,
    Pore men to threte ant reven here heritage.
    Wormes shulen ete thy fleyshe for al thyn heye parage."

"Wrecche Gost, thou wend away! Ful wel thou const chyde!         **[Body]**
    Y wot that Y shal rotien for al my muchele pride;
35    Wormes shule ete myn herte, ant my whyte syde
    Stynken worse then any hound, so hit may bytyde."

"Body, wher aren thy solers, thi castles, ant thy toures?        **[Gost]**
    Thine ryche clothes ant thine covertoures?
    Ful lowe shalt thou lyggen for alle thine heye boures.
40    Jesu, Vader, ant Holy Gost, shild me from helle shoures!"

57v]    "Wrecche Gost, thou wend away! Fare ther thou shalt fare.   **[Body]**
    Me is nou wo ynoh. Myn bones aren al bare.
    Min hous ys maked of erthe. Yturnd ys al to kare.
    Thah thou chyde nyht ant day, of me tyd the no mare."

45    "Body, why nere thou bythoht, whiles thou myhtes the welde,   **[Gost]**
    On him that made us alle of noht, whet thou hedest to yelde?
    For oure synnes, for hyse noht, ys oune fleyshe he selde.
    His body wes on rode don, so the prophete us telde.

"Body, wyld thou nou lythe, ant Y wol telle the
50    Of wondres fele ant ryve er Domesday shal be.

Then spoke the Soul with good counsel to reveal the truth: **[Soul]**
"Where is your haughty pride, your fancy and gray fur?

15  Your palfreys and steeds, and all your worldly goods?
You'll not bear them with you, wretch, where you lie."

*— material goods do not exist in Heaven*

Then said the Body miserably where it lay on the bier: **[Body]**
"Now is come here my death, and my last day.
Hand and foot I am bound so I can't get away.

20  Now are my days over. I expected to live forever!"

"You have lived too long! You wrought so much woe! **[Soul]**
Always while you lived, you were false and fickle.
All too much you enjoyed turning right to wrong.
Hard and sharp pains now afflict you severely."

25  "Wretched Soul, go away! How long will your quarrel last? **[Body]**
Worms hold council here, with fast-binding judgments.
They have cast their lot on my flesh.
Many noble bodies will rot — I'll not be the last!"

"Body, you're not able to leap up to play and strut, **[Soul]**
30  To beat wild bears, bind savage lions,
Threaten poor men and steal their inheritance.
Worms will eat your flesh despite all your high breeding."

"Wretched Soul, go away! So well you can chide! **[Body]**
I know that I'll rot on account of my excessive pride;
35  Worms will eat my heart, and my white sides
Will stink worse than a hound, as it will happen."

"Body, where are your chambers, your castles, and your towers? **[Soul]**
Your rich clothes and your outward trappings?
Very low will you lie despite all your grand rooms.
40  Jesus, Father, and Holy Ghost, shield me from hell's torments!"

57v]  "Wretched Soul, go away! Go where you should. **[Body]**
Already I'm woeful enough. My bones are all bare.
My house is made of earth. All is turned to despair.
Though you chide night and day, I'm no longer your business."

45  "Body, why didn't you think, while you could govern yourself, **[Soul]**
About him who made us from nothing, and what you ought to offer?
For our sins, not for his own, he sold his own flesh.
His body was tortured on the cross, as the prophet tells us.

"Body, confused now you lie, and I'll explain to you
50  Wonders many and plenteous before Doomsday befalls.

The mon that ys on lyve he may hit here ant see
That world shal al todryve, stones breke on thre.

"The furste day shal springe ase blod a red deu,
That al this world shal sprede, bynymen gomen ant gleu;
55      The grene tren shule blede that Crist himself seu.
Wel his him thenne that hath be god ant treu.

"The other day shal fur brenne al that hire forestond;
Ne may hit no water quenche, ne nout that hire forewond.
The world shal al o-fure ben, ant these brode londes.
60      Thenne shal oure Louerd sayen, 'Suche aren myne sondes.'

"The thridde day shal flowe a flod, that al this world shal hyle,
Bothe heye ant lowe the flume shal hit swyle,
Herre then eny hul opo the herthe a myle.
Wel ys him that ys trewe al that ilke while.

65      "The furthe day shal blowe a wynd; so longe so hit dures
Castles adoun falleth, bothe halles ant bures.
The hulles maketh evene smethe wyth the dales.
Him Y telle a louerd that thus con bete bales.

        "The fyfte day him cometh ywys!
70      Everuch best that lyves ys
        Toward hevene ys hed halt
        Ant thuncheth wonder wed this byhalt,
        Ant wolde clepe to oure Dryhte —
        Ah hy to speke ne habbeth myhte.

75      "The seste day ayen the dom shule four aungles stonde,
Blowe that this world shal quaque, with beme in here honde.
Yef hit ys any soule that flet bi water other by londe,
Up hit shal aryse anon ant to the dom gonge.

58r]    "The sevethe day shule upryse, ase the Bok us tolde,
80      In stat of thrytty wynter bothe yunge and olde —
Thilke that God han ydon. He mowe be ful bolde
When Jesu Crist wol come his harde domes holde.

"We mowe ther noud chyde ne have wordes stronge;
The aungles shule quakye, that Crist shup wyth hys honde,
85      Ant the apostles xii that eoden with Crist in londe,
Ant alle Cristes ycoren that never loveden wronge.

"Thenne shal segge oure Louerd to Seinte Marie,
Bringinde the rode opon ys bake that stod on Calvarie,

The one who's alive will hear it and see
That the world will be destroyed, stones break into three.

*— revelation*

"On the first day there will spring up like blood a red dew,
Which will spread through this world, removing gladness and glee;
55    The green wood will bleed, that accompanied Christ himself.
Then well is he who has been good and true.

"On the next day fire will burn all that stands before it;
No water may quench it, nor may anything stop it.
The world will be entirely on fire, and these broad lands too.
60    Then our Lord will say, 'Such are my signs.'

"On the third day a flood will flow, covering all this world,
The river will swell both high and low,
Higher by a mile than any hill on earth.
Well is he who is true during all that time.

65    "On the fourth day a wind will blow; as long as it lasts
Castles will fall down, both halls and chambers.
The hills will be made level with the dales.
I call him a lord who then can escape misery.

    "On the fifth day he comes indeed!
70    Every creature who is alive
Holds his head toward heaven
And thinks it a wonder what this betokens,
And wants to cry out to our Lord —
But they don't have the power to speak.

75    "On the sixth day four angels will stand before the judgment,
Blow until the world quakes, with trumpets in their hands.
If there's any soul who wanders by sea or by land,
It will arise immediately and proceed to judgment.

*— superficial of this part of revelation*

58r]    "On the seventh day there will arise, as the Book told us,
80    Both young and old in their conditions of thirty winters —
The same length that God lived. One must be very steadfast
When Jesus Christ comes to exact his stern judgments.

"There we may neither chide nor have bold words;
The angels will tremble, whom Christ shaped with his hand,
85    As will the twelve apostles that went with Christ on earth,
And all Christ's chosen who never loved sin.

"Then will our Lord speak to Saint Mary,
Carrying on his back the cross that stood on Calvary,

*(where he was crucified)*

Ant schowen us hise fet ant honden al blody.
90    For oure soule fode deth tholede hy.

"Thenne sayth Jesu Crist to Sathanas the unhende,    **[Jesus]**
'Fare awey the, foule swyke, ant thi cursede genge!'"

Thenne saith the Gost, "Weylawey!" Ant at the ende: "Alas,    **[Gost]**
Body, wo wurth the time that thou ybore was!
95    Hy shal into helle for thi trespas,
Ant tholien harde pinen wyth that sory Judas."

Such pleyntes makyeth the Soule to the Fleyshe,    **[Narrator]**
Ant thus heo departeth wyth muche reunes:
The Soule into helle, ant that nis nout les;
100    The Body to the erthe, ant rotieth endeles.

Whiles he wes in worlde, he hevede frend ant kyn.
When he is graved under mold, al cold ys hys yn.
The wormes sitteth on ys brest ant eteth of ys chyn.
Ne haveth he frend on erthe that thenketh opon hym.

105    Al this worldes pride ant al this worldes ahte
Ne mihte holde a monnes lyf a day to the nahte.

Were ther eny in londe that myhte charre ded,
Shulde no mon deye that hevede eny red;
He wolde with ys catel, bote he were aqued
110    Wyten from the dethe the body ant the hed.

Jesu Crist himselven is so corteis
For ous he soffrede deth, ase the Boc hit seys.

Alle we shule deye, be we never so proude.
For alle oure toures heye, ligge we shule throute,
115    In forstes ant in snowes, in shures ant in cloude.
Of all oure riche clothes, tid us never a shroude.
Whose hath don for Godes love, he may be ful stoude.

Her we haveth houses of lym ant of ston,
58v]    Ant alle we shulen hem leven, everuchon;
120    Fare we shule to a bour that is oure long hom —
Nouther more ne lasse bote from the hed to ton;
Ther shal rotie ure fleyshe al to the bon.

When the flor is at thy rug, the rof ys at thy neose,
Al this worldes blisse nis nout worth a peose.

And showing us his feet and hands all bloody.
90     For our soul's nourishment he suffered death.

"Then Jesus Christ will say to Satan the vile:          **[Jesus]**
'Be gone, foul traitor, and your cursed hell-hole!'"

Then says the Soul, "Wailaway!" And finally: "Alas,    **[Soul]**
Body, woe is the time when you were born!
95     You will hasten to hell for your sins,
And suffer harsh pains with that wretched Judas."

The Soul makes such complaints to the Flesh,    **[Narrator]**
And thus they depart with much regret:
The Soul into hell, and that's not a lie;
100    The Body to the earth where it rots endlessly.

While he was in the world, he had friends and kin.
When he is buried underground, all cold is his inn.
The worms sit on his breast and eat from his chin.
He hasn't a friend on earth who thinks upon him.

*— the dead are not remembered?*

105    All this world's pride and all this world's wealth
Might not extend a man's life by even a day.

Were there any on earth who might escape death,
No man would die who had any counsel;
Unless he were miserly, he would with his property
110    Protect the body and head from death.

Jesus Christ himself is so courteous
That for us he suffered death, as the Book says.

We all will die, be we never so proud.
For all our high towers, we will lie in plain view,
115    In frosts and in snows, under showers and clouds.
Despite all our rich clothes, not a shroud falls to us.
Whoever has acted for God's love, he may be full noble.

*— who is being spoken about here? we good christians? is the narrator's audience?*

Here we have houses of lime and of stone,
58v]    And we will relinquish them all, every one;
120    We will travel to a bower that is our lasting home —
Neither more nor less than from the head to the toe;
There will our flesh rot entirely to the bone.

When the floor is at your back, the roof is at your nose,
All this world's bliss is not worth a pea.

125     Bote yef Jesu Cristes merci among us more were,
        To wrothere hele that ever we in londe comen here.
        To thin holy halewen, Crist, bring us alle yfere.
            Amen.


**Sitteth alle stille ant herkneth to me**                [art. 23]

58v]    Sitteth alle stille ant herkneth to me!
        The Kyng of Alemaigne, bi mi leaute,
        Thritti thousent pound askede he
        Forte make the pees in the countre,
5           Ant so he dude more.
                *Richard,*
                *Thah thou be ever trichard,*
                *Tricchen shalt thou nevermore!*


        Richard of Alemaigne, whil that he wes kyng,
10      He spende al is tresour opon swyvyng,
        Haveth he nout of Walingford o ferlyng;
        Let him habbe ase he brew, bale to dryng,
                Maugre Wyndesore.
                *Richard,*
15              *Thah thou be ever trichard,*
                *Tricchen shalt thou nevermore!*


        The Kyng of Alemaigne wende do ful wel,
        He saisede the mulne for a castel,
        With hare sharpe swerdes he grounde the stel.
20      He wende that the sayles were mangonel
                To helpe Wyndesore.
                *Richard,*
                *Thah thou be ever trichard,*
                *Tricchen shalt thou nevermore!*


25      The Kyng of Alemaigne gederede ys host,
        Makede him a castel of a mulnepost,
        Wende with is prude ant is muchele bost,
        Brohte from Alemayne mony sori gost
                To store Wyndesore.
30              *Richard,*
                *Thah thou be ever trichard,*
                *Tricchen shalt thou nevermore!*


        By God that is aboven ous, he dude muche synne
        That lette passen over see the Erl of Warynne;
35      He hath robbed Engelond, the mores ant the fenne,

125    Unless Jesus Christ's mercy be greater among us,
    We on earth will always come here to an evil outcome.
    To your holy saints, Christ, bring us all together.
      Amen.


**A Song of Lewes** [art. 23]

58v]    Sit very still and listen to me!
    The King of Germany, on my honor,
    Thirty thousand pounds he asked
    To make the peace in the country,
5        And thus he did more.
        *Richard,*
      *Though you're forever a traitor,*
      *You'll never more betray!*


    Richard of Germany, while he was king,
10    He spent all his treasure upon whoring,
    He has no more than a farthing from Wallingford;
    Let him have as he brews, evil to drink,
        In spite of Windsor.
        *Richard,*
15    *Though you're forever a traitor,*
      *You'll never more betray!*


    The King of Germany thought to do very well,
    He seized the windmill for a castle,
    With their sharp swords they secured their position.
20    They thought that the windsails were catapults
        To help Windsor.
        *Richard,*
      *Though you're forever a traitor,*
      *You'll never more betray!*


25    The King of Germany gathered his host,
    Made him a castle of a windmill post,
    Marched with his pride and his great boast,
    Brought from Germany many wretched souls
        To supply Windsor.
30        *Richard,*
      *Though you're forever a traitor,*
      *You'll never more betray!*


    By God that's above us, he did much sin
    To allow the Earl of Warenne to pass over the sea;
35    He has robbed England, the moors and the fen,

The gold ant the selver, ant yboren henne
    For love of Wyndesore.
       *Richard,*
      *Thah thou be ever trichard,*
40      *Tricchen shalt thou nevermore!*

Sire Simond de Mountfort hath suore bi ys chyn,
Hevede he nou here the Erl of Waryn,
Shulde he never more come to is yn,
Ne with sheld, ne with spere ne with other gyn,
45    To help of Wyndesore.
       *Richard,*
      *Thah thou be ever trichard,*
      *Tricchen shalt thous nevermore!*

Sire Simond de Montfort hath suore bi ys top,
50   Hevede he nou here Sire Hue de Bigot,
Al he shulde quite here tuelfmoneth scot;
Shulde he nevermore with his fot pot
    To helpe Wyndesore.
       *Richard,*
55     *Thah thou be ever trichard*
      *Tricchen shalt thou nevermore!*

59r]    Be the luef, be the loht, Sire Edward,
Thou shalt ride sporeles o thy lyard
Al the ryhte way to Dovere-ward;
60   Shalt thou nevermore breke foreward!
    Ant that reweth sore!
Edward, thou dudest ase a shreward,
    Forsoke thyn emes lore!
       *Richard,*
65     *Thah thou be ever trichard,*
      *Tricchen shalt thou nevermore!*

## Chaunter m'estoit                                                     [art. 24]

59r]    Chaunter m'estoit,
    Mon cuer le voit,
    En un dure langage.
    Tut en ploraunt
5    Fust fet le chaunt
    De nostre duz baronage,
    Qe pur la pees
    (Si loynz aprés)
    Se lesserent detrere,

The gold and the silver, and borne it away
    For love of Windsor.
        *Richard,*
        *Though you're forever a traitor,*
40      *You'll never more betray!*

Sir Simon de Montfort has sworn by his chin,
That were he now to have here Sir Earl of Warenne,
He should never again come to his lodging,
With shield nor with spear nor with more craft,
45      Come to help Windsor.
        *Richard,*
        *Though you're forever a traitor,*
        *You'll never more betray!*

Sir Simon de Montfort has sworn by his head,
50      That were he now to have here Sir Hugh of Bigot,
He would entirely repay their twelvemonth's royal tax;
He would never again kick with his foot
        To help Windsor.
        *Richard,*
55      *Though you're forever a traitor,*
        *You'll never more betray!*

59r]    Be you loved, be you hated, Sir Edward,
        You'll ride spurless on your poor horse
        All the straight way toward Dover;
60      You'll never again break a vowed contract!
            May you bitterly regret that!
        Edward, you acted like a scoundrel,
            Abandoned your uncle's teaching!
                *Richard,*
65          *Though you're forever a traitor,*
            *You'll never more betray!*

## Lament for Simon de Montfort                                        [art. 24]

59r]    Sing I must,
        My heart wishes it,
        In a sorrowful strain.
        Entirely in tears
5       Was made the song
        Of our gentle baronage,
        Who for the sake of peace
        (So long deferred)
        Let themselves be destroyed,

10  Lur cors trencher
   E demenbrer,
   Pur salver Engletere.
    *Ore est ocys,*
    *La flur de pris,*
15   *Qe taunt savoit de guere;*
    *Ly quens Mountfort,*
    *Sa dure mort*
    *Molt en plorra la terre.*


   Si com je qui,
20  Par un mardi
   Firent la bataile;
   Tot a cheval
   Fust le mal,
   Sauntz nulle pedaile.
25  Tres malement
   Y ferirent
   De le espie forbie,
   Qe la part
   Sire Edward
30  Conquist la mestrie.
    *Ore est ocis,*
    *La flur de pris,*
    *Qe taunt savoit de guere;*
    *Ly quens Mountfort,*
35   *Sa dure mort*
    *Molt en plorra la terre.*


   Mes par sa mort
   Le cuens Mountfort
   Conquist la victorie.
40  Come ly martyr
   De Caunterbyr,
   Finist sa vie.
   Ne voleit pas,
   Li bon Thomas,
45  Qe perist seinte Eglise.
   Ly cuens auxi
   Se combati
   E morust sauntz feyntise.
    *Ore est ocys,*
50   *La flur de pris,*
    *Qe taunt savoit de guere;*
    *Ly quens Mountfort,*
    *Sa dure mort*
    *Molt en plorra la terre.*

10     Their bodies hacked
       And dismembered,
       To save England.
           *Now he is slain,*
           *The flower of fame,*
15         *Who knew so much of war;*          } *refrain*
           *The Earl Montfort,*
           *His cruel death*
           *The land will deeply mourn.*


       As I believe,
20     On a Tuesday
       They fought the battle;
       All on horseback
       Was the disaster,
       Without any foot soldiers.
25     Very poorly
       They struck blows there
       With burnished sword,
       So that the side
       Of Lord Edward
30     Won the mastery.
           *Now he is slain,*
           *The flower of fame,*
           *Who knew so much of war;*
           *The Earl Montfort,*
35         *His cruel death*
           *The land will deeply mourn.*


       But by his death
       The Earl Montfort
       Won the victory.
40     Like the martyr
       Of Canterbury,
       He concluded his life.
       He did not wish,
       The good Thomas,
45     That Holy Church should perish.
       The count also
       Entered combat
       And died without deceit.
           *Now he is slain,*
50         *The flower of fame,*
           *Who knew so much of war;*
           *The Earl Montfort,*
           *His cruel death*
           *The land will deeply mourn.*

55　　Sire Hue le fer
　　　Ly Despencer,
　　　Tres noble justice,
　　　Ore est a tort
　　　Lyvré a mort,
60　　A trop male guise,
　　　Sire Henri
　　　(Pur veir le dy),
　　　Fitz le cuens de Leycestre,
　　　Autres assez,
65　　Come vous orrez,
　　　Par le cuens de Gloucestre.
　　　　　*Ore est ocis,*
　　　　　*La flur de pris,*
　　　　　*Qe taunt savoit de guere;*
70　　　　*Ly quens Mountfort,*
　　　　　*Sa dure mort*
　　　　　*Molt en plorra la terre.*

　　　Qe voleint moryr
　　　E mentenir
75　　La pees e la dreyture,
　　　Le seint martir
　　　Lur fra joyr,
　　　Sa conscience pure.
　　　Qe velt moryr
80　　E sustenir
　　　Les honmes de la terre,
　　　Son bon desir
　　　Acomplir,
　　　Quar bien le quidom fere.
85　　　　*Ore est ocys,*
　　　　　*La flur de pris,*
　　　　　*Qe taunt savoit de guere;*
　　　　　*Ly quens Mountfort,*
　　　　　*Sa dure mort*
90　　　　*Molt en plorra la terre.*

　　　Pres de son cors
　　　(Le bon tresors)
　　　Une heyre troverent.
　　　Les faus ribaus
95　　Tant furent maus,
　　　E ceux qe le tuerent.
　　　Molt fust pyr
　　　Qe demenbryr
　　　Firent le prodhonme

55      The fierce Sir Hugh
        The Despenser,
        Most noble justiciar,
        Now is wrongly
        Delivered to death,
60      In a most shameful way,
        And Sir Henry
        (To tell the truth),
        Son of the Earl of Leicester,
        And many others,
65      As you will hear,
        By the Earl of Gloucester.
          *Now he is slain,*
          *The flower of fame,*
          *Who knew so much of war;*
70        *Count Montfort,*
          *His cruel death*
          *The land will deeply mourn.*

        Those willing to die
        And maintain
75      Peace and righteousness,
        The holy martyr
        Will bring them joy,
        His conscience clean.
        Whoever's willing to die
80      And sustain
        The men of the land,
        His good desire
        To accomplish,
        We think he does quite well.
85        *Now he is slain,*
          *The flower of fame,*
          *Who knew so much of war;*
          *The Earl Montfort,*
          *His cruel death*
90        *The land will deeply mourn.*

        Near his body
        (The good treasure),
        They found a hair shirt.
        The false knaves
95      Were so wicked,
        And those who slew him.
        It was even worse
        That they dismembered
        The worthy man

100     Qe de guerrer
        E fei tener,
        Si bien savoit la sonme.
            *Ore est ocys,*
            *La flur de pris,*
105         *Qe taunt savoit de guere;*
            *Ly quens Mountfort,*
            *Sa dure mort*
            *Molt en plorra la terre.*


        Priez touz,
110     Mes amis douz,
        Le fitz seinte Marie,
        Qe l'enfant,
        Her puissant,
        Meigne en bone vie.
115     Ne vueil nomer
        Li escoler
        (Ne vueil qe l'em die),
        Mes pur l'amour
        Le Salveour,
120     Priez pur la clergie.
            *Ore est ocys,*
            *La flur de pris,*
            *Qe tant savoit de guere;*
            *Ly quens Montfort,*
125         *Sa dure mort*
            *Molt en plurra la terre.*


59v]    Ne say trover rien
        Qu'il firent bien,
        Ne baroun ne counte,
130     Les chivalers
        E esquiers.
        Touz sunt mys a hounte
        Pur lur lealté
        E verité,
135     Que tut est anentie.
        Le losenger
        Purra reigner,
        Le fol pur sa folie.
            *Ore est ocis,*
140         *La flur de pris,*
            *Qe taunt savoit de guere;*
            *Ly quens Mountfort,*
            *Sa dure mort*
            *Molt en plorra la terre.*

| 100 | Who understood fighting |
|     | And keeping faith, |
|     | Everything so well. |

*Now he is slain,*
*The flower of fame,*
105     *Who knew so much of war;*
    *The Earl Montfort,*
    *His cruel death*
    *The land will deeply mourn.*


     Pray all of you,
110   My gentle friends,
     To blessed Mary's son,
     That the child,
     The powerful heir,
     Be led to a good life.
115   I will not name
     The youth
     (I don't wish it said),
     But for the love
     Of the Savior,
120   Pray for the clergy.
     *Now he is slain,*
     *The flower of fame,*
     *Who knew so much of war;*
     *The Earl Montfort,*
125   *His cruel death*
     *The land will deeply mourn.*


59v]   I can find nothing
     That they did right,
     Neither baron nor earl,
130   The knights
     And squires.
     All are brought low
     On account of their loyalty
     And truthfulness,
135   Entirely come to nought.
     The flatterer
     Will be able to reign,
     The fool through his folly.
     *Now he is slain,*
140   *The flower of fame,*
     *Who knew so much of war;*
     *The Earl Montfort,*
     *His cruel death*
     *The land will deeply mourn.*

145     Sire Simoun,
        Ly prodhom,
        E sa compagnie
        En joie vont
        En ciel amount
150     En pardurable vie.
        Mes Jesu Crist
        Qe en croyz se mist,
        Dieu, enprenge cure
        Qe sunt remis
155     E detenuz
        En prisone dure.
            *Ore est ocys,*
            *La flur de pris,*
            *Qe taunt savoit de guere;*
160         *Ly quens Mountfort,*
            *Sa dure mort*
            *Molt en plorra la terre.*


**Charnel amour est folie**                                    [art. 24a]

59v]    ¶ Charnel amour est folie!
        Qe velt amer sagement
        Eschywe ce quar breve vie
        Ne lesse durer longement.
5       Ja n'ert la char si florie
        Que a purreture ne descent.
        Brief delit est lecherie,
        Mes santz fyn dure le torment.


**Momentaneum est quod delectat**                              [art. 24a*]

59v]    Momentaneum est quod delectat,
        Set eternum quod cruciat.


**Erthe toc of erthe**                                         [art. 24b]

59v]    ¶ Erthe toc of erthe erthe wyth woh;
        Erthe other erthe to the erthe droh;
        Erthe leyde erthe in erthene throh;
        Tho hevede erthe of erthe erthe ynoh.

145 Sir Simon,
The worthy man,
And his company
Proceed in joy
In heaven above
150 In everlasting life.
But may Jesus Christ
Who put himself on cross,
God, take care
Of those confined
155 And detained
In harsh prison.
*Now he is slain,*
*The flower of fame,*
*Who knew so much of war;*
160 *The Earl Montfort,*
*His cruel death*
*The land will deeply mourn.*

## Carnal Love Is Folly

[art. 24a]

*distinction between sexual and romantic love*

59v] ¶ Carnal love is folly!
He who wishes to love wisely
Avoids it because life's brevity
Doesn't allow it to endure long.
5 Never did flesh exist or flourish
That didn't descend to rottenness.
Lechery is a brief pleasure,
But torment lasts without end.

## What Allures Is Momentary

[art. 24a*]

59v] What allures is momentary,
But what torments is eternal.

## Earth upon Earth

[art. 24b]

59v] ¶ Earth took of earth earth with woe;
Earth another earth to the earth drew;
Earth laid earth in earthen trough;
Then had earth of earth earth enough.

**Lystneth, lordynges! A newe song Ichulle bigynne**                    [art. 25]

59v]      Lystneth, lordynges! A newe song Ichulle bigynne
          Of the traytours of Scotlond that take beth wyth gynne.
          Mon that loveth falsnesse ant nule never blynne
          Sore may him drede the lyf that he is ynne,
5                    Ich understonde.
                 Selde wes he glad
                 That never nes asad
                 Of nythe ant of onde.


          That Y sugge by this Scottes that bueth nou todrawe,
10        The heuedes o Londone Brugge, whose con yknawe.
          He wenden han buen kynges, ant seiden so in sawe;
          Betere hem were han ybe barouns ant libbe in Godes lawe
                   Wyth love.
                 Whose hateth soth ant ryht
15               Lutel he douteth Godes myht,
                 The heye kyng above.


          To warny alle the gentilmen that bueth in Scotlonde,
          The Waleis wes todrawe, seththe he was anhonge,
          Al quic biheueded, ys boweles ybrend.
20        The heued to Londone Brugge wes send
                     To abyde.
                 After Simond Frysel,
                 That wes traytour ant fykel
                 Ant ycud ful wyde.


25        Sire Edward, oure kyng, that ful ys of piete,
          The Waleis quarters sende to is oune contre
          On four half to honge, huere myrour to be
          Theropon to thenche, that monie myhten se
                   Ant drede.
30               Why nolden he be war,
                 Of the bataile of Donbar,
                 Hou evele hem con spede?


60r]      Bysshopes ant barouns come to the kynges pes,
          Ase men that weren fals, fykel, ant les;
35        Othes hue him sworen in stude ther he wes,
          To buen him hold ant trewe for alles cunnes res,
                   Thrye,
                 That hue ne shulden ageyn him go.
                 So hue were "temed" tho.
40               Weht halt hit to lye?

**The Execution of Sir Simon Fraser**                    [art. 25]

59v]    Listen, lords! I'll begin a new song
        About the traitors of Scotland captured by craft.
        One who loves treachery and won't ever quit
        May bitterly fear the life that he's in,
5               I'm certain.
            Seldom was he merry
            Who was never content
            For malice and for envy.

        I speak of these Scotsmen who've now been dismembered,
10      Their heads on London Bridge, for anyone to recognize.
        They planned to be kings, and said so in speech;
        Better for them to have been barons and live in God's law
                With love.
            Whoever hates truth and right
15          Little fears God's power,
            The high king above.

        To warn all the nobles who dwell in Scotland,
        The Wallace was dismembered, then he was hanged,
        Beheaded while alive, his bowels burned.
20      The head was sent to London Bridge
                To abide.
            Afterwards Simon Fraser,
            Who was traitor and dangerous
            And known very widely.

25      Sir Edward, our king, who's full of piety,
        Sent the quarters of Wallace to his own country
        To hang in four regions, to be their mirror
        To reflect thereon, so that many might see
                And feel dread.
30          Why wouldn't they take warning,
            By the battle of Dunbar,
            How poorly they might fare?

60r]    Bishops and barons came to the king's peace,
        As men who were false, crafty, and untruthful;
35      Oaths to him they swore in the place where he was,
        To be loyal and true to him in every kind of crisis,
                At all times,
            That they'd not go against him.
            So then were they "tamed."
40          What does it profit to lie?

*[handwritten marginal note beside lines 9–13:]* they tried to be gods / they lived in unchristian ways

To the Kyng Edward hii fasten huere fay —
Fals wes here foreward so forst is in May,
That sonne from the southward wypeth away!
Moni proud Scot therof mene may,

45              To yere.
         Nes never Scotlond
         With dunt of monnes hond
         Allinge aboht so duere!


     The Bisshop of Glascou, Ychot he was ylaht;
50   The Bisshop of Seint Andre, bothe, he beth ycaht;
     The Abbot of Scon with the kyng nis nout saht.
     Al here purpos ycome hit ys to naht,
              Thurh ryhte.
         Hii were unwis
55       When hii thohte pris
         Ageyn huere kyng to fyhte.


     Thourh consail of thes bisshopes ynemned byfore,
     Sire Robert the Bruyts furst kyng wes ycore.
     He mai everuche day ys fon him se byfore —
60   Yef hee mowen him hente, Ichot he bith forlore
              Sauntz fayle!
         Soht forte sugge,
         Duere he shal abugge
         That he bigon batayle.


65   Hii that him crounede proude were ant bolde.
     Hii maden Kyng of Somere, so hii ner ne sholde;
     Hii setten on ys heued a croune of rede golde,
     Ant token him a kyneyerde, so me kyng sholde,
              To deme.
70       Tho he wes set in see,
         Lutel god couthe he
         Kyneriche to yeme.


     Nou Kyng Hobbe in the mures yongeth;
     Forte come to toune nout him ne longeth.
75   The barouns of Engelond, myhte hue him gripe,
     He him wolde techen on Englysshe to pype
              Thourh streynthe.
         Ne be he ner so stout,
         Yet he bith ysoht out
80       O brede ant o leynthe.


     Sire Edward of Carnarvan (Jesu him save ant see!)
     Sire Emer de Valence, gentil knyht ant free,

To King Edward they plight their faith —
Their contract was as false as frost is in May,
Which the sun from the south wipes away!
Many a proud Scotsman may complain about that,
45          This year.
          Never was Scotland
          By dint of human hand
          Bought altogether so dear!

The Bishop of Glasgow, I know he was captured;
50    The Bishop of St. Andrew, too, he is caught;
The Abbot of Scone is not at peace with the king.
Their entire plot has come to nothing,
          By right.
          They were unwise
55          When they thought it praiseworthy
          To fight against their king.

Through the counsel of these bishops named before,
Sir Robert the Bruce first was chosen king.
He may every day see his enemies before him —
60    If they should capture him, I know he'll be destroyed
          Without fail!
          To say the truth,
          Dearly shall he pay
          For having begun battle.

65    They who crowned him were arrogant and bold.
They made him King of Summer, as they never should;
They set on his head a crown of red gold,
And gave him a scepter as one should to a king,
          By which to judge.
70          When he was set on throne,
          Little good knew he
          How to rule a kingdom.

Now King Hob walks on the moors;
It doesn't suit him to come to town.
75    The barons of England, if they might seize him,
They would teach him to pipe in English
          By force.
          Though he be never so brave,
          Yet he is hunted out
80          Far and wide.

Sir Edward of Carnarvon (may Jesus save and protect him!)
And Sir Aymer de Valence, fine knight and noble,

Habbeth ysuore huere oht that, par la grace Dee,
Hee wolleth ous delyvren of that false contree,
85            Yef hii conne.
       Muche hath Scotlond forlore —
       Whet alast, whet bifore —
       Ant lutel pris wonne.


       Nou Ichulle fonge ther Ich er let,
90     Ant tellen ou of Frisel, ase Ich ou byhet.
       In the batayle of Kyrkenclyf, Frysel wes ytake
       (Ys continaunce abatede eny bost to make)
              Biside Strivelyn —
       Knyhtes ant sweynes,
95     Fremen ant theynes,
       Monye with hym.


60v]   So hii weren byset on everuche halve.
       Somme slaye were, ant somme dreynte hemselve.
       Sire Johan of Lyndeseye nolde nout abyde:
100    He wod into the water, his feren him bysyde,
              To adrenche.
       Whi nolden hii be war?
       Ther nis non ageyn star.
       Why nolden hy hem bythenche?


105    This wes byfore Seint Bartholomeus Masse,
       That Frysel wes ytake, were hit more other lasse.
       To Sire Thomas of Multoun, gentil baroun ant fre,
       Ant to Sire Johan Jose bytake tho wes he
              To honde.
110    He wes yfetered weel,
       Bothe with yrn ant wyth steel,
       To bringen of Scotlonde.


       Sone therafter the tydynge to the kyng com.
       He him sende to Londone with mony armed grom;
115    He com yn at Newegate, Y telle yt ou aplyht;
       A gerland of leves on ys hed ydyht,
              Of grene.
       For he shulde ben yknowe
       Bothe of heye ant of lowe
120    For treytour, Y wene.


       Yfetered were ys legges under his horse wombe;
       Bothe with yrn ant with stel mankled were ys honde;
       A gerland of peruenke set on ys heued;
       Muche wes the poer that him wes byreved

Have sworn their oath that, by the grace of God,
They will deliver us from that false country,
85              If they can.
            Much has Scotland lost —
            What in the end, what before —
            And won little praise.

Now I shall resume where I left off,
90        And tell you about Fraser, as I promised you.
          In the battle of Kirkencliff, Fraser was captured
          (His countenance ceased to make any boast)
                    Near Stirling —
            Knight and swains,
95          Freemen and thanes,
            Many with him.

60v]      Thus were they beset on every side.
          Some were slain and some drowned themselves.
          Sir John of Lindsay would not wait:
100       He waded into the water, his companions beside him,
                    To drown.
            Why wouldn't they beware?
            There is no opposing star.
            Why wouldn't they reflect?

105       This was before St. Bartholomew's Mass,
          That Fraser was captured, or thereabouts.
          To Sir Thomas of Multon, a fine and noble baron,
          And to Sir John Jose he was then delivered
                    Into custody.
110         He was well fettered,
            Both with iron and steel,
            To be brought out of Scotland.

Sone thereafter the news came to the king.
He sent him to London with many armed men;
115       He entered Newgate prison, I tell you faithfully;
          A garland of leaves put on his head,
                    Of green,
            Because he should be displayed
            Before both high and low
120         As a traitor, I think.

Fettered were his legs under his horse's belly;
Both with iron and steel his hands were manacled;
A garland of periwinkle was set on his head;
Great was the power that was taken from him

125          In londe.
             So God me amende,
             Lutel he wende
             So be broht in honde.


        Sire Herbert of Morham, feyr knyht ant bold,
130     For the love of Frysel ys lyf wes ysold.
        A wajour he made, so hit wes ytold,
        Ys heued of to smhyte yef me him brohte in hold,
                Wat so bytyde.
             Sory wes he thenne,
135          Tho he myhte him kenne
             Thourh the toun ryde.


        Thenne seide ys scwyer a word anon-ryht:
        "Sire, we beth dede; ne helpeth hit no wyht!"
        (Thomas de Boys the scwyer wes to nome.)
140     "Nou Ychot oure wajour turneth ous to grome,
                So Y bate!"
             Y do ou to wyte,
             Here heued was ofsmyte
             Byfore the Tour gate.


145     This wes on Oure Levedy Even, for sothe, Ych understonde;
        The justices seten for the knyhtes of Scotlonde:
        Sire Thomas of Multoun, an hendy knyht ant wys,
        Ant Sire Rauf of Sondwyche, that muchel is told in pris,
                Ant Sire Johan Abel.
150          Mo Y mihte telle by tale,
             Bothe of grete ant of smale —
             Ye knowen suythe wel.


        Thenne saide the justice, that gentil is ant fre:
        "Sire Simond Frysel, the kynges traytour hast thou be,
155     In water ant in londe, that monie myhten se.
        What sayst thou thareto?  Hou wolt thou quite the?
                Do say."
             So foul he him wiste,
             Nede waron truste
160          Forto segge nay.


61r]    Ther he wes ydemed so hit wes londes lawe:
        For that he wes lordswyke, furst he wes todrawe,
        Upon a retheres hude forth he wes ytuht —
        Sumwhile in ys time he wes a modi knyht
165             In huerte.
             Wickednesse ant sunne

| 125 | On earth. |
| | As God may amend me, |
| | Little did he expect |
| | To be brought so into custody. |

| | Sir Herbert of Morham, a fair and bold knight, |
| 130 | For the love of Fraser his life was sold. |
| | A wager he made, as it was told, |
| | To have his head cut off if they captured Fraser, |
| | Whatever betide. |
| | Sorry was he then, |
| 135 | When he might see him |
| | Ride through the town. |

| | Then his squire spoke a word immediately: |
| | "Sir, we're dead; there's no creature to help us!" |
| | (Thomas de Bois was the squire's name.) |
| 140 | "Now I know that our wager brings us to harm, |
| | So my courage ends!" |
| | I give you to know, |
| | Their heads were cut off |
| | Before the Tower gate. |

| 145 | This occurred on Our Lady's Eve, indeed, I believe; |
| | The justices sat for the knights of Scotland: |
| | Sir Thomas of Multon, a courteous and wise knight, |
| | And Sir Ralph of Sandwich, who's much praised in worth, |
| | And Sir John Abel. |
| 150 | More I could disclose, |
| | Both great and small — |
| | You know very well. |

| | Then said the justice, who's excellent and noble: |
| | "Sir Simon Fraser, you've been the king's traitor, |
| 155 | By water and by land, as many might see. |
| | How do you answer thereto? How acquit yourself? |
| | Do respond." |
| | He knew himself to be so foul, |
| | He had no reliable means |
| 160 | By which to say no. |

| 61r] | There he was judged according to the land's law: |
| | Because he was traitor to his lord, first he was drawn, |
| | Upon an ox's hide he was dragged forth — |
| | Once in his life he'd been a brave knight |
| 165 | In heart. |
| | Wickedness and sin |

Hit is lutel wunne;
That maketh the body smerte.


For al is grete poer, yet he was ylaht —
170    Falsnesse ant swykedom, al hit geth to naht!
Tho he wes in Scotlond, lutel wes ys thoht
Of the harde jugement that him wes bysoht
        In stounde.
        He wes four sithe forswore
175        To the kyng ther bifore,
        Ant that him brohte to grounde.


With feteres ant with gyves Ichot he wes todrawe,
From the Tour of Londone, that monie myhte knowe,
In a curtel of burel, a selkethe wyse,
180    Ant a gerland on ys heued, of the newe guyse,
        Thurh Cheepe.
        Moni mon of Engelond,
        Forto se Symond,
        Thideward con lepe.


185    Tho he com to galewes, furst he was anhonge,
Al quic, byheueded (thah him thohte longe);
Seththe he was yopened, is boweles ybrend,
The heued to Londone Brugge wes send,
        To shonde.
190        So Ich ever mote the,
        Sumwhile wende he
        Ther lutel to stonde.


He rideth thourh the site, as Y telle may,
With gomen ant wyth solas, that wes here play,
195    To Londone Brugge hee nome the way.
Moni wes the wyves chil that theron loketh a day,
        Ant seide: "Alas,
        That he wes ibore,
        Ant so villiche forlore,
200        So feir mon ase he was!"


Nou stont the heued above the tu-brugge,
Faste bi Waleis, soth forte sugge,
After socour of Scotlond longe he mowe prye,
Ant after help of Fraunce. Wet halt hit to lye?
205        Ich wene
        Betere him were in Scotlond
        With is ax in ys hond
        To pleyen o the grene.

Bring little gain;
They make the body smart.

Despite all his great power, still he was taken —
170    Falseness and treachery, it all turns to nothing!
When he was in Scotland, little did he consider
The hard judgment that was prepared for him
    In a short time.
    He was four times perjured
175    There before the king,
And that caused him to fall.

With fetters and manacles I know he was dragged,
From the Tower of London, so that many might be aware,
In a tunic of sackcloth, in a strange manner,
180    And a garland on his head, of the latest fashion,
    Through Cheapside.
    Many men of England,
    In order to see Simon,
    Began thither to rush.

185    When he came to the gallows, first he was hanged,
While alive, beheaded quickly (though it seemed to him long);
Afterwards he was opened, his bowels burned,
The head was sent to London Bridge,
    To his disgrace.
190    As ever I may thrive,
    Little had he once thought
    To stand there.

They ride through the city, as I may tell,
With game and with fun, that was their play,
195    To London Bridge they took their way.
Many a woman's child looks thereon by day,
    And said: "Alas,
    That he was born,
    And so vilely undone,
200    So fair a man as he was!"

Now the head stands above the drawbridge,
Close by Wallace, to tell the truth,
Long may they pray for relief from Scotland,
And for help from France. What good's it to lie?
205    I suppose
    It was better for him in Scotland
    With his ax in his hand
    To play on the green.

Ant the body hongeth at the galewes faste
210    With yrnene claspes, longe to laste.
       Forte wyte wel the body, ant Scottyshe to gaste,
       Foure ant tuenti ther beoth, to sothe ate laste,
               By nyhte —
               Yef eny were so hardi
215            The body to remuy —
               Al so to dyhte.


       Were Sire Robert the Bruyts ycome to this londe,
       Ant the Erl of Asseles, that hardé is an honde,
       Alle the other pouraille, for sothe, Ich understonde,
220    Mihten be ful blythe ant thonke Godes sonde,
               With ryhte:
               Thenne myhte uch mon
               Bothe riden ant gon
               In pes, withoute vyhte.


61v]   The traytours of Scotlond token hem to rede
226    The barouns of Engelond to brynge to dede;
       Charles of Fraunce, so moni mon tolde,
       With myht ant with streynthe hem helpe wolde —
               His thonkes!
230            Tprot! Scot! For thi strif!
               Hang up thyn hachet ant thi knyf!
               Whil him lasteth the lyf
               With the longe shonkes!


**Lord that lenest us lyf**                                    [art. 25a]


61v]   ¶ Lord, that lenest us lyf
       Ant lokest uch an lede,
       Forte cocke with knyf
       Nast thou none nede;
5      Bothe wepmon ant wyf
       Sore mowe drede
       Lest thou be sturne with strif
       For bone that thou bede
               In wunne:
10             That monkune
               Shulde shilde hem from sunne.


       Nou hath prude the pris
       In everuche plawe;
       By mony wymmon unwis
15     Y sugge mi sawe,

And the body hangs fast on the gallows
210   With iron clasps, long to last.
To guard well the body and scare the Scottish,
There are four and twenty, truly, at least,
        By night —
        Were any so hardy
215       As to remove the body —
        Ready to attack.

Were Sir Robert the Bruce to come to this land,
And the Earl of Asceila, who's strong of might,
All the other poor people, truly, I understand,
220   Might be very happy and thank God's gift,
        With good reason:
        Then might every man
        Both ride and go
        In peace without fighting.

61v]   The traitors of Scotland took counsel among themselves
226   To bring the barons of England to death;
Charles of France, as many a man said,
Would help them with might and with strength —
        Thanks to him!
230       Fah! Scot! For your strife!
        Hang up your hatchet and your knife!
        While life lasts to him
        With the long shanks!

**On the Follies of Fashion**                                    **[art. 25a]**

61v]   ¶ Lord, who lends us life
And watches over everyone,
To point a knife
You have no need;
5     Both man and woman
Must fearfully dread
Lest you be stern with strife
Over the request you made
        In bliss:
10      That mankind
        Should refrain from sin.

Nowadays pride takes the praise
At every social occasion;
By example of many foolish women
15    I express my verdict,

For yef a ledy lyne is
Leid after lawe,
Uch a strumpet that ther is
Such drahtes wol drawe
20          In prude:
          Uch a screwe wol hire shrude
          Thah he nabbe nout a smoke hire foule ers to hude!


Furmest in boure
Were boses ybroht;
25   Levedis to honoure
Ichot he were wroht;
Uch gigelot wol loure
Bote he hem habbe soht;
Such shrewe fol soure
30   Ant duere hit hath aboht
          In helle:
          With develes he shule duelle
          For the clogges that cleveth by here chelle!


Nou ne lacketh hem no lyn
35   Boses in to beren:
He sitteth ase a slat swyn
That hongeth is eren.
Such a joustynde gyn
Uch wrecche wol weren;
40   Al hit cometh in declyn,
This gigelotes geren
          Upo lofte:
          The Devel may sitte softe
          Ant holden his halymotes ofte!


45   Yef ther lyth a loket
By er outher eye,
That mot with worse be wet
For lac of other leye.
The bout ant the barbet
50   Wyth frountel shule feye.
Habbe he a fauce filet,
He halt hire hed heye
          To shewe
          That heo be kud ant knewe,
55          For strompet in rybaudes rewe!

For if a lady's clothing is
Fitted according to fashion,
Every strumpet that's around
Will follow such tricks

20         Haughtily:
    Every shrewish girl will dress herself up
    Though she hasn't a smock to hide her foul arse!

*oh my!*

    First into lady's chamber
    Were brought hair buns over cheeks;
25   For the honor of ladies
    I know they were devised;
    Every vain girl will scowl
    Unless she's obtained them;
    This shrew full bitterly
30   And dearly has bought it
        In hell:
    With devils she shall dwell
    For the clumps that cling in her hairnet!

    Nowadays they don't lack linen
35   To support their hair buns:
    They sit like a baited pig
    That hangs its ears.
    Such a jousting device
    Each wench will wear;
40   All comes to decline,
    This vain girl's fashion
        Up on top:
    The Devil may sit comfortably
    And hold his court sessions often!

45   If there lies a curl
    By either ear or eye,
    It may be wet down with a worse fluid
    For lack of any other lye.
    The loop and the cloth band
50   Has to match the forehead piece.
    She has a faux-silk headband,
    Yet she holds her head high
        To show
    That she's recognized and known,
55   As a strumpet in rogues' company!

**Enseignement sur les amis**                              [art. 26]

61v]    ¶ Cyl qe vodra oyr mes chauns,
            En soun cuer se remyre:
        Si il, en fet ou en semblauns,
            Rien touche a la matire
5       De un chauncon en romauns
            Ou la en orrez descrire
        La lessoun a leals amantz,
            Vous y comencez a lyre!

        Meint honme quide aver ami
10          Conquis en sa richesse,
        Q'assez tost le avera gerpi,
            Si il veit pus sa destresse;
        E primes le avera escharni
            Pur sa tresgrant largesse.
15      Si nul vous ad de ce servi,
            Ne creez mes sa promesse.

62r]    Si toun ami as esprové
            Ne ly deves pas offendre,
        Mez seiez de une volenté:
20          Grant bien en purrez prendre.
        Ne seiez pas de ly grevé
            Quei qe um vous face entendre,
        Quar meint um quide aver trové
            Qe puis ly estuit rendre.

25      Si te avient qe eiez mester
            De counsail ou de aye,
        Ne le devez pas a tous mostrer —
            Tant ad le siecle envie!
        A toun ami n'estuit celer
30          Ton consail ne ta vie,
        Quar si il te puet de ren valer,
            Il ne vous faudra mie.

        E vostre bon ami tenez,
            Ne devez pas retrere;
35      E lealment li consilez,
            Com leals amis doit fere.
        Vostre counsail a ly mostrez,
            A ly ne devez tere;
        Si lealment vous entreamez,
40          Le un puet l'autre crere.

**Lesson for True Lovers**                    *A lesson for men from a man's perspective.*          [art. 26]

61v]    ¶ He who would hear my songs,
            Let him examine his heart:
        If it should, in deed or likeness,
            Touch at all upon the subject
5       Of a song in plain French
            In which you'll hear described
        The lesson for true lovers,
            Begin to read there!

        Many a man thinks to have won
10          A lover when he's wealthy,
        Whom she'll abandon quickly,
            When she later sees his penury;
        And she'll have mocked him first
            For his very great generosity.
15      If anyone has treated you this way,
            No longer believe her promise.

62r]    If you've tested your lover
            You shouldn't offend her,
        But be of one will:
20          You can reap great benefit by it.
        Don't get upset with her
            Whatever people may cause you to hear,
        For many a man thinks he's learned
            Something he may later have to disavow.

25      If it happens that you're in need
            Of advice or assistance,
        You oughtn't reveal it to all —
            So envious is the world!
        From your lover you shouldn't conceal
30          Your secrets or your way of life,
        For if she can help you in anything,
            She'll not fail you at all.

        And hold fast to your lover,
            You shouldn't withdraw;
35      And advise her loyally,
            As true lovers should.
        Show her your thoughts,
            You must not be silent with her;
        If you love each other faithfully,
40          Each can believe the other.

Si vostre ami velt mesaler,
  La main le devez tendre.
Ne ly soffrez pas soun voler
  Si vous le poez defendre.
45  Mes bel ly devez chastier,
  E entre vous reprendre,
E come vous meismes en le ester,
  Sauntz nulle rien offendre.


Si vous oiez de vostre ami
50    Parler par aventure,
Ne devez mettre en obly
  De preisir sa porture.
Les bienz diez derere ly;
  Devant ly, a mesure,
55  Quar losenger e leal ami
  Diversent par nature.


Entre amis seit oweleté,
  Senz e corteysie,
Amour e deboneraté,
60    E tele compagnie
Qe tant me volez de bounté,
  De solas, e de aye
Come vodrez qe feisse je
  Si je usse grant mestrie.


65  Uncore, y a en fyn amour
  Chose qe molt me agree,
Par ount si pasent ly plusour
  Dount ja n'ert regardee:
Si vostre ami est en dolour,
70    En play ou en mellee,
Ne le guerpez a deshonour
  Pur coup ne pur colee.


Vostre ami cherissez,
  Si me volez crere.
75  De nulle rien ly priez
  Si il ne le pust bien fere.
Quar si il ne le fet, vous ly grevez
  Quant il ne le puet parfere;
E si il mesfet, vous meserrez,
80    Car ce fet pur vous plere.


Uncore, y a en la lessoun
  Un petit plus a fere:

If your lover wishes to go astray,
   You should extend your hand to her.
Don't let her have her desire
   If you can prevent it.
45   But you must admonish her gently,
   And handle it privately,
And as if you yourself were in her place,
   Without offending her at all.

If you hear your lover
50   Spoken of by chance,
You shouldn't forget
   To compliment her character.
Say good things out of her presence;
   In her presence, be moderate,
55   For a flatterer and a true lover
   Differ by nature.

Equality should exist between lovers,
   Good sense and courtesy,
Love and graciousness,
60   And such companionship
That you'd wish for me as much good,
   Pleasure, and help
As you'd like me to perform
   If I had enough power.

65   In addition, there exists in pure love
   Something that greatly pleases me,
Which most people overlook ‒ ?
   And which hasn't yet been considered:
If your lover is in distress,
70   In a plight or in a conflict,
Don't leave her to be dishonored
   For fear of a strike or a blow.

Cherish your lover,
   If you care to believe me.
75   Ask nothing at all of her
   Unless she can do it well.
For if she doesn't do it, you upset her
   Because she's unable to do it;
And if she acts badly, you act badly,
80   For it was done to please you.

In addition, the lesson includes
   A little more to be done:

La privité ton compaignoun
   Ne devez pas retrere.
85   Soun consail te est confessioun,
   Assez en devez tere.
Si en tant ly feissez tresoun,
   A envis vous dust um crere.

Si vostre ami est en pecchié,
90   Qei qe nul autre en die,
Tot sachez vous la verité,
   Ne le descoverez mie.
Car meint um fust plus avilee
   Si l'em sust sa folie,
95   E meint um pecche en privitee
   E pus prent bone vie.

Ore ai mostré un poi de pas
   Ou amour est foundé.
En ce vers trover purras
100   Si tu les as bien gardé.
62v]   A toun ami ne diez pas
   Quanque son cuer agree,
Mes ce qe a soun honour verras,
   Si en ert amour payé.

105   Ore pri a tous lais e clers,
   Si ne me chaut qe l'oye,
Qe nul ne prenge le travers
   De fyn amour verroie,
Car leal cuer n'est pas divers;
110   Eynz ayme droite voie.
Ly "Tu autem" est en ce vers;
   Ly respounz soit de joye!
   Amen.

## Middelerd for mon wes mad          [art. 27]

62v]   ¶ Middelerd for mon wes mad.
Unmihti aren is meste mede.
This Hedy hath on honde yhad
That hevene hem is hest to hede.
5   Icherde a blisse budel us bad
The dreri Domesdai to drede,
Of sunful sauhting sone be sad.
That derne doth this derne dede,
   Thah he ben derne done,

Your companion's secrets
   You must never divulge.
85   Her secret is a confession to you,
      You must be very quiet about it.
   And insofar as you betray her,
      Scarcely should anyone believe you.

If your lover's engaged in sin,
90   In a way that no one else speaks of,
While you know the whole truth,
   Don't let it ever be discovered.
   For many a one would be more reviled
      Were her foolishness known,
95   And many a one sins in private
      And later adopts a good life.

Now I've shown a few of the steps
   Upon which love is founded.
   In this poem you can discover
100      Whether you've guarded them well.
62v]   Do not say to your lover
      Whatever pleases her heart,
But what will be true to her honor,
      And by this will love be requited.

105   Now I pray of all laity and clergy,
      And I don't care who hears it,
   That no one go against
      Pure true love,
   For a loyal heart is not fickle;
110      Instead it loves correctly.
   The "Tu autem" is in this poem;
      Let the response be joyful!
         Amen.

**The Three Foes of Man**                    [art. 27]

62v]   ¶ Middle-earth was made for men.
      Puny are its best rewards.
      Blessed God has brought this about
      That heaven is essential for them to heed.
5   I heard a herald of joy hearken us
      To dread the terrifying Doomsday,
      To grow weary soon of sinful pursuit.
      Those who secretly do these hidden deeds,
         Though they be privately performed,

10      This wrakeful werkes under wede
            In soule soteleth sone.

        Sone is sotel, as Ich ou sai,
        This sake, althah hit seme suete
        That I telle a poure play
15      That furst is feir ant seththe unsete.
        This wilde wille went awai
        With mone ant mournyng muchel unmete.
        That liveth on likyng out of lay
        His hap he deth ful harde on hete
20          Ageyns he howeth henne —
            Alle is thrivene thewes threte
                That thenketh nout on thenne.

        Ageynes thenne, us threteth thre:
        Yef he beth thryven ant thowen in theode,
25      Ur soule bone so brotherli be
        As berne best that bale forbeode.
        That wole wihtstonden streynthe of theo,
        Is rest is reved with the reode.
        Fyth of other ne darth he fleo
30      That Fleishshes faunyng furst foreode —
                That falsist is of fyve!
            Yef we leveth eny leode,
                Werryng is worst of wyve.

        Wyves wille were ded wo,
35      Yef he is wicked forte welde;
        That burst shal bete for hem bo:
        He shal him burewen thah he hire belde.
        By body ant soule, Y sugge also
        That some beeth founden under felde
40      That hath to fere is meste fo!
        Of gomenes he mai gon al gelde
                Ant sore ben fered on folde,
            Lest he to harmes helde
                Ant happes hente unholde.

45      Hom unholdest her is on —
        Withouten helle — ase Ich hit holde:
        So fele bueth founden monnes fon!
        The furst of hem biforen Y tolde.
        Ther afterward: this Worldes won
50      With muchel unwynne us woren wolde;
        Sone beth this gomenes gon
        That maketh us so brag ant bolde

10          These wicked deeds under cover
                 Are exposed soon in the soul.

            Soon is exposed, I say to you,
            This sin, although it seems sweet
            I judge it a poor pleasure
15          Which first is fair and then later repulsive.
            This unruly willfulness passes away
            With highly extreme lament and grief.
            He who lives in unlawful desire
            Will violently cry out against his fate
20              When he goes from here —
                 All his good virtues will rebuke
                    Whoever fails to think on what comes later.

            Regarding later, three threaten us:
            So that they may thrive and flourish among men,
25          Our souls' slayers act as brotherly
            As the best men who forestall harm.
            Any who'd withstand the strength of them,
            His rest is disturbed like the swaying reed.
            He need not flee the assault of any other
30          Who's first withstood the Flesh's caressing —
                 That one is falsest of five!
                 If we believe any man,
                    The worst is war-crafty woman.

            A woman's will is a deadly peril,
35          Especially if she's hard to control;
            He must fix the damage for them both:
            He must save himself though he shelter her.
            By analogy to body and soul, I say also
            That some are found under earth
40          Who have as his worst enemy a wife!
            Of idle games he ought to stay gelded
                 And be very fearful on earth,
                 Lest he fall to harm
                    And seize a disastrous outcome.

45          The most disastrous home is here —
            Not counting hell — as I assert:
            So many are found to be man's foes!
            The first of them I already told you about.
            The next: this World's riches
50          Would disturb us with deep sorrow;
            Soon are gone these idle games
            That make us so boisterous and bold

Ant biddeth us ben blythe;<br>
An ende he casteth ous fol colde<br>

55         In sunne ant serewe sythe.

In sunne ant sorewe Y am seint,<br>
That siweth me so sully sore.<br>
My murthe is al with mournyng meint,<br>
Ne may Ich mythen hit namore.<br>
60      When we beth with this world forwleynt<br>
That we ne lustneth lyves lore,<br>
The Fend in fyht us fynt so feynt,<br>
We falleth so flour when hit is frore,<br>
     For folkes Fader al fleme.<br>
65      Wo him wes ywarpe yore<br>
       That Crist nul nowyht queme.

To queme Crist we weren ycore,<br>
Ant kend ys craftes forte knowe.<br>
Leve we nout we buen forlore<br>
70      In lustes thah we lyggen lowe;<br>
We shule aryse ur Fader byfore<br>
Thah fon us fallen umbe throwe:<br>
To borewen us all, he wes ybore!<br>
This bonnyng when him bemes blowe,<br>
75      He byt us buen of hyse,<br>
     Ant on ys ryht hond hente rowe<br>
      Wyth ryhtwyse men to aryse.

**BOOKLET 5**                                   **QUIRES 7–11**

**Ichot a burde in a bour ase beryl so bryht**         **[quire 7]**<br>
                                                 **[art. 28]**

63r]    ¶ Ichot a burde in a bour ase beryl so bryht,<br>
       Ase saphyr in selver, semly on syht,<br>
       Ase jaspe the gentil that lemeth with lyht,<br>
       Ase gernet in golde, ant ruby wel ryht,<br>
5      Ase onycle he ys, on yholden on hyht,<br>
       Ase diamaund the dere in day, when he is dyht.<br>
       He is coral ycud with cayser ant knyht;<br>
       Ase emeraude amorewen, this may haveth myht.<br>
         The myht of the margarite haveth this mai mere;<br>
10       For charbocle Ich hire ches bi chyn ant by chere.

       Hire rode is ase rose, that red is on rys;<br>
       With lilye-white leres, lossum he is;<br>
       The primerole he passeth, the peruenke of pris,

        And cause us to be merry;
      In the end they cast us very cruelly
55         To sin and time of sorrow.

     In sin and sorrow I am sunk,
     They pursue me so exceedingly hard.
     My mirth's all mingled with mourning,
     Nor may I conceal it any more.
60    When we become so proud with this world
     That we don't listen to life's advice,
     The fighting Fiend finds us so feeble,
     We fall as a flower when it is withered,
       Fully exiled from mankind's Father.
65      Woe was assigned to him long ago
       Who wishes not to please Christ at all.

     To please Christ we were chosen,
     And taught to know his power.
     We ought not believe that we are lost
70    Even though we lie sunk in desires;
     We shall arise before our Father
     Even though foes defeat us at times:
     To save us all, he was born!
     When trumpets blow this summons for him,
75      He will bid us be among his,
      And at his right hand take position
       With righteous men to arise!

**BOOKLET 5**                                           **QUIRES 7–11**

     **Annot and John**                                 **[quire 7]**
*— shady place or under trees or plants*            **[art. 28]**

63r]  ¶ I know a lady in a bower as bright as beryl,
     As sapphire in silver, lovely to see,
     As fine jasper that gleams with light,
     As garnet in gold, and ruby well set,
5    As onyx she is, one highly regarded,               *— comparisons to precious stones*
     As precious diamond by day, when she's adorned.
     She is coral valued by emperor and knight;
     As emerald by morning, this girl has power to heal.
      The power of pearl this fair girl possesses;
10     I choose her as my precious gem in every way.

     Her complexion's as rose, red on the stem;
     With lily-white cheeks, she is lovable;               *— colors / flowers*
     She excels the primerole, the prized periwinkle,

With alisaundre, thareto, ache, ant anys.
15   Coynte ase columbine, such hire cunde ys,
Glad under gore, in gro ant in grys.
He is blosme opon bleo, brihtest under bis,
With celydoyne ant sauge, ase thou thiself sys:
      That syht upon that semly to blis he is broht!
20         He is solsecle, to sauve ys forsoht!

He is papejai in pyn, that beteth me my bale;
To trewe tortle in a tour, Y telle the mi tale;
He is thrustle thryven in thro, that singeth in sale,
The wilde laveroc, ant wolc, ant the wodewale;
25   He is faucoun in friht, dernest in dale,
Ant with everuch a gome, gladest in gale.
From Weye he is wisist into Wyrhale;
Hire nome is in a note of the nyhtegale,
      In an note is hire nome. Nempneth hit non?
30         Whose ryht redeth, roune to Johon.

Muge he is, ant mondrake, thourh miht of the mone,
Trewe triacle ytold with tonges in trone;
Such licoris mai leche from Lyne to Lone;
Such sucre mon secheth that saveth men sone;
35   Blithe yblessed of Crist, that bayeth me mi bone
When derne dede is in dayne derne are done.
Ase gromyl in greve, grene is the grone,
Ase quibibe ant comyn, cud is in crone,
      Cud comyn in court, canel in cofre,
40         With gyngyure ant sedewale, ant the gylofre.

He is medicyne of miht, mercie of mede,
Rekene ase Regnas resoun to rede,
Trewe ase Tegeu in tour, as Wyrwein in wede,
Baldore then Byrne, that oft the bor bede;
63v]   Ase Wylcadoun he is wys, dohty of dede,
46   Feyrore then Floyres, folkes to fede,
Cud ase Cradoc in court, carf the brede,
Hendore then Hilde, that haveth me to hede.
      He haveth me to hede, this hendy, anon;
50         Gentil ase Jonas, heo joyeth with Jon!

**Bytuene Mersh ant Averil**                                   [art. 29]

63v]   ¶ Bytuene Mersh ant Averil
When spray biginneth to springe,
The lutel foul hath hire wyl

Horse parsley, too, wild celery, and anise.
15   Pretty as columbine, such is her nature,
Merry under skirt, with gray and rich furs.
She's a flower in color, radiant under dress,
With celandine and sage, as you yourself see:
   Who sees that beauty is transferred to bliss!
20      She is marigold, sought out for health!

She's a parrot in a pine, who conquers my sorrow;
To true turtledove in a tower, I tell you my tale;
She's a thrush doughty in dispute, who sings in the hall,
The wild lark, and hawk, and the golden oriole;
25   She's a falcon in forest, most hidden in valley,
And among everyone, most glad in merriment.
She is wisest from the Wye into the Wirral;
Her name's in a note of the nightingale,
   In a note is her name. Can anyone name it?
30      Whoever guesses correctly, whisper to John.

*– comparisons to birds*

Nutmeg she is, and mandrake, by power of the moon,
True remedy attested to by courtly report;
Such licorice may bring cure from Lynn to Lune;
Such sought-after sugar that heals men quickly;
35   I'm happily blessed by Christ, who grants me my prayer
When private daytime deeds are performed secretly.
As gromwell in grove, whose seed is green,
As peppercorn and cumin, prized for its crown,
   Court-prized cumin, cinnamon in chest,
40      With ginger and setwall, and the clove.

She is medicine with potency, mercy with reward,
Ready as Regnas to counsel reasonably,
True as Tegeu in tower, as Wyrwein in fine dress,
Bolder than Byrne, who often challenged the boar;
63v]   As Wylcadoun she's wise, doughty of deed,
46   Fairer than Floyres, a pleasure to folks,
Famous as Cradoc in court, who carved the roast,
More courteous than Hilde, who takes care of one.
   She takes care of one, this fair one, indeed;
50      Gracious as Jonas, she finds pleasure with John!


**Alysoun**                                                                    [art. 29]

63v]   ¶ Between March and April
When sprig begins to sprout,
The little bird fulfills her desire

On hyre lud to synge.
5       Ich libbe in love-longinge
For semlokest of alle thynge:
He may me blisse bringe;
   Ich am in hire baundoun!
     *An hendy hap Ichabbe yhent!*
10      *Ichot from hevene it is me sent;*
     *From alle wymmen mi love is lent*
     *Ant lyht on Alysoun.*

On heu hire her is fayr ynoh,
Hire browe broune, hire eye blake;
15      With lossum chere he on me loh,
With middel smal ant wel ymake.
Bote he me wolle to hire take
Forte buen hire owen make,
Longe to lyven Ichulle forsake
20         Ant feye fallen adoun.
     *An hendy hap Ichabbe yhent!*
     *Ichot from hevene it is me sent;*
     *From alle wymmen mi love is lent*
     *Ant lyht on Alysoun.*

25      Nihtes when Y wende ant wake
(Forthi myn wonges waxeth won),
Levedi, al for thine sake,
Longinge is ylent me on!
In world nis non so wyter mon
30      That al hire bounte telle con:
Hire swyre is whittore then the swon,
   Ant feyrest may in toune.
     *An hendi hap Ichabbe yhent!*
     *Ichot from hevene it is me sent;*
35           *From alle wymmen mi love is lent*
     *Ant lyht on Alysoun.*

Ich am for wowyng al forwake,
Wery so water in wore,
Lest eny reve me my make
40      Ychabbe yyyrned yore.
Betere is tholien whyle sore
Then mournen evermore.
Geynest under gore,
   Herkne to my roun!
45           *An hendi hap Ichabbe yhent!*
     *Ichot from hevene it is me sent;*

To sing in her own words.
5        I live in love-longing
For the prettiest of all things:
She may bring me to bliss;
    I am in her control!
      *A happy fate have I found!*
10        *I know from heaven to me it's sent;*
      *From all women my love has leapt*
        *And lit on Alysoun.*

In hue her hair is fair enough,
Her brows brown, her eyes black;
15      With a lovely face she smiled at me,
With waist small and well made.
Unless she draws me to herself
To be her own companion,      *– unless she loves me I'll die*
I'll have to give up living long
20      And am destined to decline.
      *A happy fate have I found!*
      *I know from heaven to me it's sent;*
      *From all women my love has leapt*
        *And lit on Alysoun.*

25      Nightly when I toss and wake
(For which my cheeks grow pale),
Lady, entirely for your sake,
I'm overtaken by longing!
In all the world there's none so wise
30      That he may describe all her bounty:
Her neck is whiter than the swan,
    And she the fairest girl in town.
      *A happy fate have I found!*
      *I know from heaven to me it's sent;*
35      *From all women my love has leapt*
        *And lit on Alysoun.*

I am with wooing all worn out,
As weary as water by the shore,
Lest any rob me of my mate
40      For whom I long have yearned.
It's better to feel pain awhile
Than grieve forevermore.
Most kind under skirt,
    Listen to my song!
45      *A happy fate have I found!*
      *I know from heaven to me it's sent;*

*From alle wymmen mi love is lent*
*Ant lyht on Alysoun.*

## With longyng Y am lad [art. 30]

63v]     ¶ With longyng Y am lad;
On molde Y waxe mad;
    A maide marreth me.
Y grede, Y grone, unglad,
5     For selden Y am sad
    That semly forte se.
    Levedi, thou rewe me!
To routhe thou havest me rad!
Be bote of that Y bad:
10     My lyf is long on the!

Levedy, of alle londe
Les me out of bonde —
    Broht Ich am in wo!
Have resting on honde —
15     Ant sent thou me thi sonde,
    Sone, er thou me slo!
    My reste is with the ro.
Thah men to me han onde,
To love nul Y noht wonde,
20     Ne lete for non of tho.

Levedi, with al my miht,
My love is on the liht,
    To menske, when Y may.
Thou rew ant red me ryht!
25     To dethe thou havest me diht:
    Y deye longe er my day!
    Thou leve upon mi lay!
Treuthe, Ichave the plyht
To don that Ich have hyht
30     Whil mi lif leste may.

Lylie-whyt hue is,
Hire rode so rose on rys,
    That reveth me mi rest;
Wymmon war ant wys,
35     Of prude hue bereth the pris:
    Burde, on of the best.
    This wommon woneth by west,
Brihtest under bys.

> *From all women my love has leapt*
> *And lit on Alysoun.*

## The Lover's Complaint

63v]    ¶ With longing I am led;
        On earth I go mad;
            A maiden injures me.
        I wail, I groan, unhappy,
5       For seldom am I satisfied
            By sight of that fair one.
            Lady, pity me!
        You've brought me to grief!
        Be the cure for which I've prayed:
10          My life depends on you!

        Lady, from everywhere
        Release me from bondage —
            I am brought to woe!
        You have relief in hand —
15      And send me your response,
            Soon, before you slay me!
            I am restless as a roe.
        Though men are envious of me,
        I'll not hesitate to love,
20          Nor cease for any of them.

        Lady, with all my might,
        My love is settled on you,
            To honor, when I may.
        Pity and guide me justly!
25      To death you've condemned me:
            I die long before my time!
            Believe my song!
        In truth, I've pledged to you
        To do what I have promised
30          While my life may last.

        She is lily-white,
        Her cheeks like rose on stem,
            Who robs me of my rest;
        Among women cautious and wise,
35      She takes the prize for pride:
            This lady, one of the best.
            This woman lives to the west,
        Radiant under linen.

Hevene Y tolde al his
40      That o nyht were hire gest!


**Ich herde men upo mold**                                          [art. 31]

64r]    ¶ Ich herde men upo mold make muche mon,
        Hou he beth itened of here tilyynge:
        "Gode yeres ant corn, bothe beth agon!"
        Ne kepeth here no sawe ne no song synge:
5       "Nou we mote worche — nis ther non other won —
        Mai Ich no lengore lyve with mi lesinge!
        Yet ther is a bitterore bid to the bon,
        For ever the furthe peni mot to the kynge!
            Thus we carpeth for the kyng ant carieth ful colde,
10          Ant weneth forte kevere, ant ever buth acast;
            Whose hath eny god, hopeth he nout to holde,
            Bote ever the levest we leoseth alast.


        "Luther is to leosen ther ase lutel ys,
        Ant haveth monie hynen that hopieth therto.
15      The hayward heteth us harm to habben of his;
        The bailif bockneth us bale ant weneth wel do;
        The wodeward waiteth us wo, that loketh under rys.
        Ne mai us ryse no rest, rycheis, ne ro!
        Thus me pileth the pore that is of lute pris,
20      Nede in swot ant in swynk, swynde mot swo:
            Nede he mot swynde, thah he hade swore,
            That nath nout en hod his hed forte hude!
            Thus Wil walketh in lond, ant Lawe is forlore,
            Ant al is piked of the pore the prikyares prude!


25          "Thus me pileth the pore ant pyketh ful clene;
        The ryche me raymeth withouten eny ryht;
        Ar londes ant ar leodes liggeth fol lene;
        Thorh biddyng of baylyfs, such harm hem hath hiht!
        Meni of religioun me halt hem ful hene —
30      Baroun ant bonde, the clerc ant the knyht.
        Thus Wil walketh in lond, ant Wondred ys wene;
        Falsshipe fatteth ant marreth wyth myht:
            Stont stille y the stude ant halt him ful sturne,
            That maketh beggares go with bordon ant bagges.
35          Thus we beth honted from hale to hurne;
            That er werede robes, nou wereth ragges!


        "Yet cometh budeles with ful muche bost:
        'Greythe me selver to the grene wax!

I'd consider heaven entirely his
40      Who one night were her guest!


**Song of the Husbandman**                                    [art. 31]

64r]     ¶ I heard men of the land harshly complain,
         About how they're harassed in their farming:
         "Good years and corn crops, both are gone!"
         They don't care to hear platitudes nor sing any song:
5        "Now we must labor — there's no other option —
         No longer can I live with my losses!
         And still there's a cut more bitter to the bone,
         For every fourth penny must go to the king!
             Thus we complain about the king and are cruelly vexed,
10           And hope to recover, and are repeatedly cast down;
             Whoever has any goods, he expects not to keep them,
             But always the dearest possessions we lose in the end.

         "It is dreadful to lose where there is little,
         And we have many laborers who look for their share.
15       The hayward threatens us harm to get his bit;
         The bailiff promises us grief and expects to do well;
         The woodward brings us sorrow, who peers under trees.
         There may arise for us no rest, wealth, or peace!
         Thus they rob the poor man who's of little account,
20       Who thereby needs must perish, in sweat and in toil:
             He needs must perish, though he'd sworn not to,
             He who hasn't a hood to cover his head!
         Thus Will walks the land, and Law is abandoned,
             And all horsemen's finery is plundered from the poor!

25       "Thus they rob the poor and strip them quite clean;
         The powerful plunder them without any right;
         Their lands and their property lie fully barren;
         With demands of bailiffs, such harm is promised them!
         They hold many of religion in utter contempt —
30       Baron and bondsman, the clerk and the knight.
         Thus Will walks on earth, and Poverty is expected;
         Falsehood grows fat and mightily brings ruin:
             He stands still in the place and behaves most sternly,
             Which causes beggars to go with staff and bags.
35           Thus are we hunted from corner to corner;
             He who formerly wore robes, now wears rags!

         "Still tax collectors come with excessive arrogance:
         'Pay me silver for the green wax!

Thou art writen y my writ, that thou wel wost!'
40      Mo then ten sithen told Y my tax!
'Thenne mot Ych habbe hennen arost,
Feyr on fyhshe-day, launprey ant lax:
Forth to the chepyn!' Geyneth ne chost.
Thah Y sulle mi bil ant my borstax,
45          Ich mot legge my wed wel, yef Y wolle,
Other sulle mi corn on gras that is grene;
Yet I shal be 'foul cherl,' thah he han the fulle!
That Ich alle yer spare, thenne Y mot spene!

"Nede Y mot spene that Y spared yore.
50      Ageyn this cachereles cometh thus Y mot care!
Cometh the maister-budel, brust ase a bore,
Seith he wole 'mi bugging bringe ful bare';
Mede Y mot munten — a marke other more —
Thah Ich at the set dey sulle mi mare!
55      Thus the grene wax us greveth under gore
That me us honteth ase hound doth the hare:
He us honteth ase hound hare doth on hulle.
Seththe Y tek to the lond, such tene me wes taht.
Nabbeth ner budeles boded ar fulle,
60          For he may scape, ant we aren ever caht.

"Thus Y kippe ant cacche cares ful colde
Seththe Y counte ant cot hade to kepe;
To seche selver to the kyng, Y mi seed solde,
Forthi mi lond leye lith ant leorneth to slepe!
65      Seththe he mi feire feh fatte y my folde —
When Y thenke o mi weole, wel neh Y wepe!
Thus bredeth monie beggares bolde,
Ant ure ruye ys roted ant ruls er we repe:
Ruls ys oure ruye, ant roted in the stre,
70          For wickede wederes, by broke ant by brynke.
Thus wakeneth in the world Wondred ant Wee:
Ase god is swynden anon, as so forte swynke!"

**Herketh hideward ant beoth stille**                           [art. 32]

64va]       ¶ Herketh hideward ant beoth stille,
Y preie ou, yef hit be or wille,
Ant ye shule here of one virgine
That wes ycleped Seinte Maryne.
5          Hit wes a mon by oldre dawe
That muche lovede Godes lawe,
Ant streinthede him bi al ys miht

You are entered in my writ, as you well know!'
40      More than ten times I have paid my tax!
'Then must I have roast hens,
Generously on fish-day, lamprey and salmon:
Off to the market!' No argument helps.
Even though I sell my hoe and my logging-axe,
45          My deposit I must put down in full, if I'm able,
Or else sell my corn while it's still green;
Even so I'll be 'foul peasant,' though he be paid in full!
What all year I save, then I must spend!

"I must needs spend what I previously saved.
50      Thus I must worry about these tax collectors coming!
The chief collector comes, bristling as a boar,
Says he will 'strip my home completely bare';
I must offer a bribe — a mark or more —
Even were I on the due date to sell my mare!
55      Thus the green wax grieves us to the quick
While they hunt us like a hound does the hare:
They hunt us like a hound hunts hare on hill.
Since I took to the land, such trouble's been taught me.
Never have tax collectors declared their full gains,
60          For *he* can escape, and *we* are always caught.

"Thus I receive and catch very cruel grievances
Ever since I've had to keep accounts and cottage;
To find silver for the king, I sold my seed,
For which reason my land lies fallow and falls asleep!
65      Later they took my fine livestock from my fold —
When I think about my goods, well nigh I weep!
Thus are many beggars bred by arrogance,
And our rye is rotted and useless before we reap it:
Useless is our rye, and rotted on the stalk,
70          On account of bad storms, by brooks and by banks.
Thus Poverty and Woe awaken in the world:
It's as good to perish at once, as toil so hard!"

**The Life of Saint Marina**                                                        [art. 32]

64va]      ¶ Hearken this way and be still,
I pray you, if it be your will,
And you shall hear about one virgin
Who was named Saint Marina.
5          There was a man of former days
Who greatly loved God's command,
And exerted himself by all his strength

To serve God bo day ant nyht.
He wes a mon of werkes gode,
10      Ant wel he lovede is soule fode.
He bysohte Louerd Jesu
To sende in him sum vertu
The Fend to shende ant is myht,
Ant God to serven, that is best ryht.
15      Hit bifel is wyf wes ded,
Ant he bithohte him such a reed:
He wolde be monke in alle wyse,
Ant yelden him to Godes servise.
Ant so he dude, withoute les.
20      Marie milde to wyf he ches
Ant the ordre dude underfonge.
He wes therinne swithe longe,
Seve yer ant sumdel mo;
Tho warth this monke swithe wo
25      For is dohter from him wes.
Nyht ne day, ne hevede he pes;
He mournede ant wep among,
Ant thohte o day seve yer long
That he ne may is dohter sen —
30      In more serewe ne may mon ben!
For duel ant serewe he morneth so
That al is murthe is turnd to wo —
Gret duel to him, forsothe, he nom.
The abbot that seh ant to him com,
35      Ant bed him telle for whet thing
He wes in so muche mournyng.
"Thah Y the telle, hit helpeth noht —
Y ne may hit leten of my thoht!"
"Why hit be thou telle hit me,
40      Ant Y wol fonde to helpe the."
"The to telle null Y spare
For why hit is that Y care:
64vb]   Tho my wyf wes to God ygon,
Ant alle myn children boten on;
45      Yore is that ich that on seh —
Alas, that hit nere me neh!"
"Tharefore, doute the noht.
That child shal hider ben ybroht
Ant susteined in this abbe,
50      Sone, for the love of the.
Wether his hit, grom other mayde?"
"Sire, a grome, forsothe," he sayde.
He nolde be knowe for no thyng
That hit wes a mayde yyng.

To serve God both day and night.
He was a man of good works,
10    And deeply he loved his soul's comfort.
He prayed to Lord Jesus
To send him some spiritual force
To destroy the Fiend and his might,
And God to serve, as is most proper.
15         It happened that his wife was dead,
And he conceived such a plan:
He would be a monk in every way,
And yield himself to God's service.
And so he did, without lie.
20    He chose to marry Mary mild
And of the order did take vows.
         He was in there a long time,
Seven years and somewhat more;
Eventually this monk became very sad
25    For his daughter was away from him.
He had no peace, night nor day;
He mourned and wept continually,
And reflected then how for seven years
He hadn't seen his daughter —
30    In more sorrow a man could not be!
For grief and sorrow he mourned so
That all his mirth is turned to woe —
He felt great inward sorrow, indeed.
The abbot saw that and came to him,
35    And bade him reveal the cause why
He was in so much mourning.
         "Were I to tell you, it wouldn't help —
I can't take my mind off of it!"
         "Tell me why it is,
40    And I'll endeavor to help you."
         "I won't hold back from telling you
The reason why I'm so upset:
64vb]    A while ago my wife went to God,
And all my children except for one;
45    It's been long since I saw that one —
Alas, that it's not near me!"
         "Of that cause, have no fear.
That child shall be brought here
And nurtured in this abbey,
50    Son, for the love of you.
Which is it, boy or girl?"
         "Sir, a boy, truly," he said.
He wouldn't reveal for anything
That it was a young girl.

55      "Nou wend ant seh wher hit be,
        Ant bring hit bifore me."
            "God the yelde that best may,
        Sire, have wel godneday!"
            Nou is this monke forth ywend,
60      Ant glad is of the avauncement
        That this child shal underfonge.
        He hyyede blyve ant nes nout longe;
        A robe he dude hire apon
        Ant evesede hire ase a mon.
65      The maidnes nome, withoute lees,
        Maryne ycleped wes;
        Hire fader hire made be cleped Maryn,
        Ant nou heo ys don in shryn.
            Hire fader hire brohte to that abbe:
70      Feir chil it ys forte se!
        Swythe wel it wes ytaht:
        Hit wolde aryse to the mydnaht,
        Ant go to matines the monkes yfere,
        Ant wel leornede huere manere.
75      Sone therafter the habit he nom,
        Ant holi monke this may bicom!
            Such cas this child wes byfalle:
        His fader wes ded — so we shulen alle!
        The abbot ant the covent bo
80      Loveth Maryn, the yonge monke, so
        That hue him putten to baylye,
        Ant maden him maister of panetrie.
65ra]   He heveden a stude ther biside,
        Ant Maryn moste thider ryde.
85      Thider he eode to houses neode
        Ant for no shome — God forbeode!
            Ther wes a deye in that won
        A dohter hevede, a feyr womon.
        Thider com a knyht of valour
90      Ant lovede this may "par amour"
        (So he speken), ant weren at on,
        That with childe wes that womon.
            Tho seide hire moder with wordes milde:
        "Leve dohter, thou art mid childe.
95      Who is the fader? Tel me anon."
            "The yonge monke, bi Seint Jon!"
            "Wher mette ye on yfere?"
            "Y the berne, ther we were
        Ant toke me forth, ageyn the pes —
100     Al to sothe, so hit wes!"
            Hit byfel the child wes bore

| | |
|---|---|
| 55 | "Now go and see where it is, |
| | And bring it before me." |
| | "May God bring you the best, |
| | Sir, and have good day!" |
| | Now this monk is departed forth, |
| 60 | And is glad of the advancement |
| | That this child shall experience. |
| | He hurried quickly and wasn't long; |
| | He set a robe upon her |
| | And clothed her like a man. |
| 65 | The maiden's name, without lie, |
| | Was called Marina; |
| | Her father made her be named Marin, |
| | And now she is set in shrine. |
| | Her father brought her to that abbey: |
| 70 | It is a fair child to behold! |
| | Thoroughly it was educated: |
| | It would arise at midnight, |
| | And go to matins together with the monks, |
| | And learn well their way of life. |
| 75 | Soon thereafter he took the habit, |
| | And a holy monk this maiden became! |
| | Then an event befell this child: |
| | His father died — so shall we all! |
| | The abbot and the convent both |
| 80 | So greatly loved Marin, the young monk, |
| | That they assigned him the role of bailiff, |
| | And made him master of the pantry. |
| 65ra] | They owned a neighboring place, |
| | And Marin had to ride there. |
| 85 | Thither he went for household needs |
| | And for no shame — God forbid! |
| | There was a dairyman in that place |
| | Who had a daughter, a fair woman. |
| | Thither came a valorous knight |
| 90 | Who loved this maiden "with noble love" |
| | (So he said), and they were as one, |
| | And then pregnant was that woman. |
| | Then said her mother with gentle words: |
| | "Dear daughter, you are with child. |
| 95 | Who is the father? Tell me now." |
| | "The young monk, by Saint John!" |
| | "Where did you meet together?" |
| | "In the barn, there we were |
| | And he took me forth, unlawfully — |
| 100 | All in truth, so it was!" |
| | It happened that the child was born |

Ant ybroht the monke byfore.
The word sprong to al the covent.
The tolde the monke him yshent;
105    Lutel he speke ant sihte sore,
Ant seide, "On God me leh wel more."
   The abbot lette after the monke sende,
Ant seide: "Thou ne dudest nout ase hende
To bynymen that may hire wareisoun
110    For eny-kunnes gersoun.
Al to sothe, Y the sugge,
Thou hit shalt ful dere abugge —
Penaunce the tid, allegate —
Buen yput out at the gate;
115    Thre yer ther thou shalt ligge,
Ant thi gult ful deore abugge.
Bringeth him out that Y se,
Y preye ou, for the love of me!"
   "Ich habbe ysunged, 'Merci, Y crie!'
120    Thou me help, sone Marie!
Help me, yef thi wille beo,
Louerd, that restest on rode-treo!"
   The monke is to the gate ybroht,
For al is bone him geyneth noht.
125    Tho he wes at the gate outthrast;
Anon that child wes on him cast.
65rb]    Ther he dreyede muche wo,
The chil ant the monk also,
Ant heden deyed for poverete
130    Nede help of the othere monkes be:
Uch day heo him yeven anhyse bred,
Elles for hunger he hevede be ded,
Ant him arewede ful sore
That he hevede leye ther so yore.
135      Thenne speke the porter:
"Habbeth reuthe of this monk her,
Ant bitime doh him to dethe —
For hunger her, he liveth unnethe!"
   Thenne speke the priour
140    (God him yeve muchel honour):
"Tymliche he shal tolyvred be
Thourh myn help ant my pouste."
The priour com to the covent
Ant seide: "Sires, verreyment,
145    Delivre we this prisoun among us alle;
We nuten wet cas us may byfalle."
   Thenne saide the abbot:
"That is soht, God hit wot."

And brought before the monks.
Word spread throughout the convent.
The monks told him he was disgraced;
105    He spoke little and sighed deeply,
And said, "In God I trust all the more."
   The abbot had the monk sent for,
And said: "You acted ungraciously
To rob that maid of her treasure
110    For any kind of possession.
All in truth, I say to you,
You shall pay for it quite dearly —
Penance shall be with you, indeed —
You shall be put out at the gate;
115    Three years there you shall lie,
And pay quite dearly for your guilt.
Take him out of my sight,
I pray you, for the love of me!"
   "I have sung, 'Mercy, I cry!'
120    Help me, son of Mary!
Help me, if it be your will,
Lord, who rests on rood-tree!"
   The monk is brought to the gate,
For all his pleas gain him nothing.
125    Then he was thrust out at the gate;
Quickly that child was cast on him.
65rb]   There they suffered great hardship,
The child and the monk also,
And would have died of poverty
130    Were it not for the other monks' help:
Each day they gave him anise bread,
Or else for hunger he would have died,
And he lamented very mournfully
That he had lain there for so long.
135     Then spoke the porter:
"Have pity on this monk here,
Or else eventually he will die —
Here on account of hunger, he barely lives!"
   Then spoke the prior
140    (God give him much honor):
"Soon he shall be delivered
Through my help and my power."
The prior came to the convent
And said: "Sirs, truly,
145    Let's free this wretch among us all;
We don't know what may befall us."
   Then said the abbot:
"That is true, God knows."

He letten after him sende,
150     For he wes bothe god ant hende.
Tho he wes after ysent,
Tho he tolde him, al yshent,
He wende forte ha ben anhon
Other o worse deth ydon.
155       He com byfore the abbot:
"Maryn, thuncheth the god
Such penaunce forte dreye
For eny-cunnes foleye?"
          "Jesu, yef thi wille be,
160     Y preye that thou foryeve me
That Ich habbe misdon ageynes the —
Merci, Y crie, par charité!"
Ant thah his herte wes ful lyht,
That hevede be so ydyht
165     Thourh penaunce, ther forte ligge,
The joie of hyre ne may mon sugge!
Heo livede therinne with muche wo,
Tuo yer, forsothe, ant namo.
Nou heo is ded, wyterly;
170     Hyre soule is with Oure Levedy.
65va]       Thenne spec a monk to another:
"Go we whosshen ur dede brother,
For thah he habbe don a synne,
Yet he is brother of herynne."
175     A nome the body ant brohte to bathe —
Alas, that he wes ded so rathe!
          "Hit is a wommon!" seide that on.
          "That is soth, bi Seint Jon!
Jesu, shilde us from pyne,
180     For we han lowen on Maryne,
Ant penance duden hire on stronge,
Ant letten hire pyne to longe!"
          Letten after the abbot sende,
Ant tolden him the ord ant ende,
185     Ant the covent everuchon,
Ant shouueden hit wes a womon.
          The abbot for duel falleth to grounde,
Ant ther he lith a longe stounde,
Ant tho he mihte upstonde,
190     Yerne thonketh Godes sonde —
He ant the monkes alle ifere,
Ant other men, mo, ther were.
          "Nou hit is thus bifalle,
We moten thenchen, among us alle,
195     Hire onoure in alle wyse,

He had him sent for,

150    For he was both good and gentle.

When he had arrived,

Then he told him, all ashamed,

That he would rather have been hanged

Or been given some other worse death.

155    He came before the abbot:

"Marin, do you think it good

To suffer such penance

For any kind of folly?"

"Jesus, if it be your will,

160    I pray that you forgive me

Whatever I've sinned against you —

Mercy, I cry, for charity!"

And though his heart was very relieved,

It had been so transformed

165    Through penance, there to endure,

The joy of her may no man see!

She lived in there with much distress,

Two years, truly, and no more.

Now she has died, certainly;

170    Her soul is with Our Lady.

65va]    Then spoke a monk to another:

"Let's go wash our dead brother,

For though he has committed a sin,

Yet he's a brother in this place."

175    They took the body and brought it to bath —

Alas, that he had died so quickly!

"It is a woman!" said that one.

"That is true, by Saint John!

Jesus, shield us from pain,

180    For we have injured Marina,

And imposed tough penance on her,

And let her suffer too long!"

They had the abbot sent for,

And told him from beginning to end,

185    And everyone in the convent,

And showed that it was a woman.

The abbot for grief falls to ground,

And there he lies a long while,

And when he might stand up,

190    Earnestly thanks God for this gift —

He and the monks all together,

And other men, more, who were there.

"Now that it is thus befallen,

We must remember, among us all,

195    To honor her in every way,

        For heo is ded in Godes servise,
        Ant heo mey to him biseche
        For ous that is oure soule leche."
            The wommon that on Marine the child ber
200     Nuste that heo wes mayden er.
        So sone so Marine wes ded,
        Such shute com in the womones hed,
        Ase thah heo couthe lutel god;
        Ant therafter wax riht wod,
205     Ant com thider ase ley Marine,
        With muche shome ant muche pine.
        Ther heo lay mid unsounde,
        Fourteniht faste ybounde,
        Ant soffrede ther muche wo
210     O that fourteniht were ago.
            This monkes heden muche care
        That heo hire seyen so fare,
        Ant bysohten Jesu, for love of Marine,
        Delyveren hire of thilke pyne.
65vb]   Whil heo theraboute speke,
216     Anon riht hire bondes breke,
        Ant toc to hire womones cunde,
        Ant warth into hire ryhte munde;
        Ant kneulachede ho hade misdon
220     To bere that child hire apon,
        Ant tolde opeliche, alle byfore,
        Hou that child wes geten ant bore,
        Ant bisohte him foryevenesse
        That is kyng of hevene blisse.
225     To thilke blisse God us sende
        That lesteth ever withouten ende.

        He that made ant wrot this vie
        Ant hyre hath in memorie,
            From shome Crist him shilde!
230     Levedi, yef thi wille be,
        Thou have merci of me,
            For love of thine childe.
                Amen.


**Weping haveth myn wonges wet**                                    [art. 33]

66r]    ¶ Weping haveth myn wonges wet                  **Dunprest**
        For wikked werk ant wone of wyt!
        Unblithe Y be til Y ha bet
        Bruches broken, ase Bok byt,

        For she is dead in service to God,
        And she may beseech for us
        He who is our souls' physician."
           The woman who on Marina bore the child

200      Knew not earlier that she was a girl.
        As soon as Marina was dead,
        Such harm came into the woman's head,
        As if she could do little good;
        And thereafter went entirely mad,

205      And came there where Marina lay,
        With much shame and much pain.
        There she lay in her madness,
        Tightly restrained for a fortnight,
        And suffered there much distress

210      Until that fortnight had passed.
           These monks had much concern
        When they saw her condition,
        And prayed to Jesus, for love of Marina,
        To deliver her from this suffering.

65vb]   While they spoke about this,
216      Immediately her bonds broke,
        And she regained her woman's nature,
        And returned to her right mind;
        And she acknowledged that she had sinned

220      To bear that child upon her,
        And confessed openly, before everyone,
        How that child was begotten and born,
        And besought forgiveness of him
        Who is king of heaven's bliss.

225      God send us to this bliss
        That lasts forever without end.

        He that made and wrote this life
        And has her in memory,
           May Christ shield him from shame!

230      Lady, if it be your will,
        Have mercy on me,
           For love of your child.
           Amen.

## The Poet's Repentance                                     [art. 33]

66r]    ¶ Weeping has made my cheeks all wet           **Dunprest**
        For wicked deed and lack of wit!
        Unhappy I am till I've atoned
        For broken breaches, as the Book commands,

5      Of levedis love, that Y ha let,
         That lemeth al with luefly lyt.
         Ofte in song Y have hem set,
         That is unsemly — ther hit syt!
           Hit syt ant semeth noht,
10        Ther hit ys seid in song:
           That Y have of hem wroht,
           Ywis, hit is al wrong!

         Al wrong Y wrohte for a wyf
         That made us wo in world ful wyde:
15        Heo rafte us alle richesse ryf,
         That durthe us nout in reynes ryde!
         A stythye stunte hire sturne stryf,
         That ys in heovene hert in hyde.
         In hire, lyht on — ledeth lyf —
20        Ant shon thourh hire semly syde:
           Thourh hyre side he shon
           Ase sonne doth thourh the glas.
           Wommon nes wicked non
           Seththe he ybore was!

25        Wycked nis non, that Y wot,
         That durste for werk hire wonges wete;
         Alle heo lyven from last of lot,
         Ant are al hende ase hake in chete.
         Forthi on molde Y waxe mot
30        That Y sawes have seid unsete —
         My fykel fleishe, mi falsly blod! —
         On feld hem feole Y falle to fete:
           To fet Y falle hem feole
           For falsleke fifti-folde,
35        Of alle untrewe on tele
           With tonge ase Y her tolde!

         Thah told beon tales untoun in toune
         (Such tiding mei tide, Y nul nout teme),
         Of brudes bryht with browes broune,
40        Our blisse heo beyen, this briddes breme!
         In rude were roo with hem roune,
         That hem mihte henten ase him were heme;
         Nys kyng, cayser, ne clerk with croune,
         This semly serven that mene may seme:
45        Semen him may on sonde,
           This semly serven so,
           Bothe with fet ant honde,
           For on that us warp from wo.

5    Regarding ladies' love, which I have hindered,
     Who shine entirely with a lovely hue.
     Often in song I have described them,
     In an unseemly way — there it stands!
        It stands and is not seemly,
10      Where it is said in song:
        What I've written about them,
        Indeed, it is all wrong!

     All wrongly I acted because of a woman
     Who caused us grief in the very wide world:
15   She robbed us all of abundant wealth,
     Who needed not to ride us on reins!
     An excellent one stopped her fierce strife,
     Who dwells in heaven's heart in flesh.
     In her, one alighted — he who leads life —
20   And shone through her seemly side:
        Through her side he shone
        As does the sun through the glass.
        No woman has ever been wicked
        Since the time that he was born!

25   There's none who's wicked, of whom I know,
     Who must for sin dampen her cheeks;
     They all live free of blameful conduct,
     And are all as gracious as hawk in hall.
     Therefore on earth I grow sorry
30   That I have unbecomingly spoken words —
     My deceitful flesh, my false blood! —
     On ground before them I fall oft at their feet:
        At their feet I often fall
        For falsehood fiftyfold,
35      For all falsehoods in slander
        With tongue as I've here told!

     Though wanton tales be told in public
     (Such a thing may happen, I won't vouch for it),
     About fair ladies with brown brows,
40   They restore our bliss, these lovely ladies!
     To share secrets with them is peace mid discord,
     For he might obtain from them what befits him;
     There's no king, emperor, or clerk with tonsure,
     Who'd seem small for serving these seemly ones:
45      It may become him to do an errand,
        These fair ones so to serve,
        Both with feet and hands,
        For one who casts us from woe.

         Nou wo in world ys went away,
50       Ant weole is come, ase we wolde,
         Thourh a mihti, methful mai,
         That ous hath cast from cares colde.
         Ever wymmen Ich herie ay,
         Ant ever in hyrd with hem Ich holde,
55       Ant ever, at neode, Y nyckenay
         That Y ner nemnede that heo nolde:
             Y nolde ant null yt noht,
             For nothyng nou, a nede,
             Soth is that Y of hem ha wroht,
60           As Richard erst con red.


         Richard, rote of resoun ryht,
         Rykening of rym ant ron,
         Of maidnes meke thou hast myht!
         On molde Y holde the murgest mon,
65       Cunde comely ase a knyht,
         Clerk ycud, that craftes con,
         In uch an hyrd thyn athel ys hyht,
         Ant uch an athel thin hap is on:
             Hap that hathel hath hent,
70           With hendelec in halle!
             Selthe be him sent
             In londe of levedis alle!


         **Most I ryden by Rybbesdale**                           [art. 34]


66v]     ¶ Most I ryden by Rybbesdale
         Wilde wymmen forte wale,
             Ant welde wuch Ich wolde,
         Founde were the feyrest on,
5        That ever wes mad of blod ant bon,
             In boure best with bolde.
         Ase sonnebem, hire bleo ys briht —
         In uche londe heo leometh liht,
             Thourh tale, as mon me tolde.
10       The lylie lossum is ant long,
         With riche rose ant rode among,
             A fyldor fax to folde.


         Hire hed when Ich biholde apon,
         The sonnebeem aboute noon
15           Me thohte that Y seye;
         Hyre eyyen aren grete ant gray ynoh;
         That lussom, when heo on me loh,

Now woe in the world has gone away,
50    And joy has arrived, as we wish,
Through a mighty, gentle maiden,
Who's released us from cruel concerns.
Always I praise women continually,
And always in public I defend them,
55    And always, when necessary, I deny
That I ever said anything they didn't like:
    I didn't and wouldn't say anything,
    For nothing now, necessarily,
    Is true that I've written of them,
60      As Richard was first to point out.

Richard, source of good sense,
Paragon of verse and poetry,
Over gracious maidens you hold sway!
On earth I consider you the most pleasing man,
65    Of parentage as fine as a knight,
Scholar of fame, versed in skills,
In every household your excellence is mentioned,
And every man follows your fortune:
    Fortune has that man obtained,
70      With courtesy in hall!
    Happiness be sent to him
    In the land of ladies all!

### The Fair Maid of Ribblesdale                    [art. 34]

66v]    ¶ If I were to ride through Ribblesdale
To choose among sensuous women,
    And possess whichever one I wanted,
I would discover the fairest one,
5    Who was ever made of blood and bone,
    In the finest bower for the bold.
Like a sunbeam, her face is radiant —
In every land she shines brightly,
    By all accounts, as someone told me.
10    The lily is lovely and slender,
With pink and rose richly intermingled,
    A gold thread to bind her hair.

When I gaze upon her head,
The sunbeam at around noon
15      I thought I saw;
Her eyes are large and deeply blue;
That lovely one, when she smiled at me,

Ybend wax eyther breye.
The mone with hire muchele maht
20  Ne leneth non such lyht anaht
    (That is in heovene heye)
Ase hire forhed doth in day!
For wham, thus, muchel Y mourne may
    For duel to deth Y dreyye!

25  Heo hath browes bend an heh,
Whyt bytuene ant nout to neh;
    Lussum lyf heo ledes.
Hire neose ys set as hit wel semeth;
Y deye for deth that me demeth,
30      Hire speche as spices spredes.
Hire lockes lefly aren ant longe,
For sone he mihte hire murthes monge
    With blisse, when hit bredes.
Hire chyn ys chosen, ant eyther cheke
35  Whit ynoh ant rode on eke
    Ase roser when hit redes.

Heo hath a mury mouht to mele,
With lefly rede lippes lele,
    Romauns forte rede;
40  Hire teht aren white ase bon of whal,
Evene set ant atled al,
    Ase hende mowe taken hede;
Swannes swyre swythe wel ysette,
A sponne lengore then Y mette,
45      That freoly ys to fede.
Me were levere kepe hire come
Then beon pope ant ryde in Rome,
    Stythes upon stede.

When Y byholde upon hire hond,
50  The lylie-white lef in lond,
    Best heo mihte beo;
Eyther arm an elne long
(Baloygne mengeth al bymong),
    Ase baum ys hire bleo.
55  Fyngres heo hath feir to folde:
Myhte Ich hire have ant holde,
    In world wel were me!
Hyre tyttes aren anunder bis
As apples tuo of parays —
60      Ouself ye mowen seo.

Curved became both her brows.
The moon with her great power
20 Does not grant such light at night
  (Which is high in heaven)
As does her forehead in the day!
For this one, thus, I must sorely yearn
  As mortal anguish I endure!

_is there significance in a brighter forehead?_

25 She has brows arched and nobly high,
White between and not too close;
  A delightful life she leads.
Her nose is shaped as well beseems it;
I die a death, as she condemns me,
30   Her speech wafts like spices.
Her locks are beautiful and long,
And readily she might be festive
  With joy, when it falls loose.
Her chin is adorable, and each cheek
35 Beautifully white and also rosy
  Like the rosebush when it reddens.

She has a merry mouth for speaking,
With lips a lovely red and true,
  By which to read romances;
40 Her teeth are white as bone of whale,
Evenly set and all arranged,
  As the courteous may observe;
A swan's neck very well proportioned,
A span longer than any other I've met,
45   Is there to feed that beauty.
I would rather await her arrival
Than be the pope and ride in Rome,
  Most powerful on a steed.

When I gaze upon her hand,
50 The lily-white treasure on earth,
  Best she must be;
With either arm an ell long
(Whale-bone white mingles overall),
  Like balsam is her skin.
55 She has fingers fair to clasp:
Were I her to have and hold,
  In world I would be well!
Her breasts are under fine linen
Like two apples of paradise —
60   As you yourself may see.

Hire gurdel of bete gold is al:
Umben hire middel smal,
    That triketh to the to,
Al whith rubies on a rowe
65   Withinne corven, craft to knowe,
    Ant emeraudes mo.
The bocle is al of whalles bon:
Ther withinne stont a ston
    That warneth men from wo;
70   The water that hit wetes yn,
Ywis, hit wortheth al to wyn!
    That seyen seyden so.

Heo hath a mete myddel smal,
Body ant brest wel mad al,
75      Ase feynes withoute fere:
Eyther side soft ase sylk,
Whittore then the moren mylk,
    With leofly lit on lere.
Al that Ich ou nempne noht,
80   Hit is wonder wel ywroht —
    Ant elles wonder were!
He myhte sayen that Crist hym seye
That myhte nyhtes neh hyre leye —
    Hevene he hevede here!


**In a fryht as Y con fare fremede**                                   [art. 35]


66v]   ¶ In a fryht as Y con fare, fremede,
Y fonde a wel feyr fenge to fere;
Heo glystnede ase gold when hit glemede;
Nes ner gome so gladly on gere.
5    Y wolde wyte in world who hire kenede,
This burde bryht, yef hire wil were.
Heo me bed go my gates lest hire gremede;
Ne kepte heo non henyng here.

"Yhere thou me nou, hendest in helde,                [Man]
10   Nav Y the none harmes to hethe.
Casten Y wol the from cares ant kelde;
Comeliche Y wol the nou clethe."

"Clothes Y have on forte caste,                       [Maid]
Such as Y may weore with wynne;
15   Betere is were thunne boute laste
Then syde robes, ant synke into synne.

Her belt is all of delicate gold leaf:
Around her slender waist,
    It hangs down to the toe,
Adorned with rubies in a row
65      Exquisitely carved, with knowing craft,
    And emeralds besides.
The buckle is of pure whale's bone:
There within stands a stone
    Guarding men from woe;
70      The water in which it's dipped,
Indeed, completely turns to wine!
    They who've seen have said so.

She has a well-shaped narrow waist,
Body and breast all well designed,
75          Like phoenix without peer:
Either side as soft as silk,
Whiter than the morning milk,
    With lovely hue in cheek.
Everything I don't name for you
80      Is itself wondrously well made —
    Or else that would be strange!
He might claim Christ favors him
Who can at night lie near her —
    Heaven he would have here!

## The Meeting in the Wood                              [art. 35]

66v]    ¶ In a wood as I, a stranger, did walk,
I found as companion a very fair prize;
She glistened as gold when it gleams;
Never was a creature so splendid in clothes.
5       I wished to know who in the world created her,
This bright maiden, if she were willing.
She told me to go away lest she grow angry;
She didn't wish to hear any lewd proposal.

"Hear me now, most gracious in grace,          [Man]
10      I bear no insults by which to mock you.
I will rescue you from hardships and cold;
Beautifully will I clothe you now."

"I have clothes to put on,                      [Maid]
Such as I may wear with propriety;
15      It's better to wear thin items blamelessly
Than ample robes, and sink into sin.

Have ye or wyl, ye waxeth unwraste;
Afterward, or thonke be thynne;
Betre is make forewardes faste
20      Then afterward to mene ant mynne."

67r]    "Of munnyng ne munte thou namore;                    **[Man]**
Of menske thou were wurthe, by my myht;
Y take an hond to holde that Y hore,
Of al that Y the have byhyht.
25      Why ys the loth to leven on my lore
Lengore then my love were on the lyht?
Another myhte yerne the so yore
That nolde the noht rede so ryht."

"Such reed me myhte spaclyche reowe                    **[Maid]**
30      When al my ro were me atraht;
Sone tho woldest vachen an newe,
Ant take another withinne nyye naht.
Thenne miht I hongren on heowe,
In uch an hyrd ben hated ant forhaht,
35      Ant ben ycayred from alle that Y kneowe,
Ant bede clevyen ther Y hade claht.

"Betere is taken a comeliche yclothe,
In armes to cusse ant to cluppe,
Then a wrecche ywedded so wrothe
40      Thah he me slowe, ne myht I him asluppe!"
"The beste red that Y con to us bothe                  **[Man]**
That thou me take, ant Y the toward huppe;
Thah Y swore by treuthe ant othe,
That God hath shaped mey non atluppe."

45      "Mid shupping ne mey hit me ashunche —               **[Maid]**
Nes Y never wycche ne wyle.
Ych am a maide — that me ofthunche!
Luef me were gome boute gyle!"


**A wayle whyt ase whalles bon**                          [art. 36]

67r]    Wose wole of love be trewe, do lystne me!

*Ich wolde ich were a threstelcok,*
*A bountyng other a lavercoke,*
*Swete bryd!*
*Bituene hire curtel ant hire smoke*
*Y wolde ben hyd!*

Should you have your will, you'll prove inconstant;
Afterwards, your gratitude will be thin;
It's better to make binding pledges
20    Than afterwards to be sorry and mindful."

67r]    "Don't think any more about remembering;      **[Man]**
You're worthy of honor, by my power;
I pledge to be faithful until I grow gray,
By everything that I've promised to you.
25    Why are you reluctant to trust my advice
Any longer than my love has settled on you?
Another might entreat you for a long time
Who wouldn't ever advise you so well."

"Such advice I may soon regret      **[Maid]**
30    When all my peace is taken from me;
Soon you will fetch a new love,
And take another within nine nights.
Then I might starve within my own family,
In every household be hated and despised,
35    And be separated from all I've known,
And told to cling there where I'd embraced.

"Yet it's better to accept one beautifully clothed,
To kiss and to embrace him in arms,
Than be wed to a wretch so ill-tempered
40    That were he to beat me, I might not escape!"
"The best advice that I know for us both      **[Man]**
Is that you take me, and I skip toward you;
Even were I to swear by truth and oath,
None may evade what God has shaped."

45    "It can't be altered for me by shape-shifting —      **[Maid]**
I was never a witch or a sorceress.
I'm a virgin — that vexes me!
Dear to me would be a man without guile!"

### A Beauty White as Whale's Bone            **[art. 36]**

67r]    Who would of love be true, do listen to me!

*I wish I were a throstle-cock,*
*A bunting or a laverock,*
    *Sweet bird!*
*Between her kirtle and her smock*
    *I would be hid!*

Herkneth me! Y ou telle,
In such wondryng for wo Y welle!
Nys no fur so hot in helle
    Al to mon
5      That loveth derne ant dar nout telle
        Whet him ys on.
          *Ich wolde ich were a threstelcok,*
          *A bountyng other a lavercoke,*
            *Swete bryd!*
10         *Bituene hire curtel ant hire smoke*
           *Y wolde ben hyd!*

    Ich unne hire wel ant heo me wo;
    Ych am hire frend and heo my fo;
    Me thuncheth min herte wol breke atwo
15      For sorewe ant syke.
    In Godes greting mote heo go,
      That wayle whyte!
          *Ich wolde ich were a threstelcok,*
          *A bountyng other a lavercoke,*
20         *Swete bryd!*
          *Bituene hire curtel ant hire smoke*
          *Y wolde ben hyd!*

    ¶ A wayle whyt ase whalles bon;
    A grein in golde that godly shon;
25     A tortle that min herte is on,
        In tounes trewe!
    Hire gladshipe nes never gon
      While Y may glewe!
          *Ich wolde ich were a threstelcok,*
30         *A bountyng other a lavercoke,*
           *Swete bryd!*
          *Bituene hire curtel ant hire smoke*
          *Y wolde ben hyd!*.

    When heo is glad,
35    Of al this world namore Y bad
    Then beo with hire, myn one, bistad
      Withoute strif.
    The care that Ich am yn ybrad
      Y wyte a wyf.
40         *Ich wolde ich were a threstelcok,*
          *A bountyng other a lavercoke,*
           *Swete bryd!*
          *Bituene hire curtel ant hire smoke*
          *Y wolde ben hyd!*

Hearken to me! I tell you,
In such anxious distress I suffer!
There's no fire so hot in hell
 As burns for him
5 Who loves in private and dares not say
 What afflicts him.
  *I wish I were a throstle-cock,*
  *A bunting or a laverock,*
   *Sweet bird!*
10  *Between her kirtle and her smock*
   *I would be hid!*

I wish her well and she wishes me woe;
I am her friend and she's my foe;
I think my heart will break in two
15  For sorrow and longing.
In God's favor may she go,
 That beauty white!
  *I wish I were a throstle-cock,*
  *A bunting or a laverock,*
20   *Sweet bird!*
  *Between her kirtle and her smock*
   *I would be hid!*

¶ A beauty white as whale's bone;    ——— Harley MS begins the piece
A gem in gold that radiantly shone;           here.
25 A turtledove my heart's set on,
 Truest one in town!
Her blissfulness will never be gone
 While I can sing!
  *I wish I were a throstle-cock,*
30  *A bunting or a laverock,*
   *Sweet bird!*
  *Between her kirtle and her smock*
   *I would be hid!*

When she is blissful,
35 Of all this world I ask no more
Than to be with her, my own, lodged
 Without argument.
The distress I'm entangled in
 I blame upon a woman.
40  *I wish I were a throstle-cock,*
  *A bunting or a laverock,*
   *Sweet bird!*
  *Between her kirtle and her smock*
   *I would be hid!*

45      A wyf nis non so worly wroht!
        When heo ys blythe to bedde ybroht,
        Wel were him that wiste hire thoht,
            That thryven ant thro!
        Wel Y wot heo nul me noht;
50          Myn herte is wo.
                *Ich wolde ich were a threstelcok,*
                *A bountyng other a lavercoke,*
                    *Swete bryd!*
                *Bituene hire curtel ant hire smoke*
55                  *Y wolde ben hyd!*


        Hou shal that lefly syng,
        That thus is marred in mournyng?
        Heo me wol to dethe bryng
            Longe er my day!
60      Gret hire wel, that swete thing
            With eyenen gray.
                *Ich wolde ich were a threstelcok,*
                *A bountyng other a lavercoke,*
                    *Swete bryd!*
65              *Bituene hire curtel ant hire smoke*
                    *Y wolde ben hyd!*


        Hyre heye haveth wounded me ywisse,
        Hire bende browen that bringeth blisse!
        Hire comely mouth that mihte cusse —
70          In muche murthe he were!
        Y wolde chaunge myn for his
            That is here fere.
                *Ich wolde ich were a threstelcok,*
                *A bountyng other a lavercoke,*
75                  *Swete bryd!*
                *Bituene hire curtel ant hire smoke*
                    *Y wolde ben hyd!*


        Wolde hyre fere beo so freo,
        Ant wurthes were, that so myhte beo,
80      Al for on Y wolde geve threo,
            Withoute chep!
        From helle to hevene, ant sonne to see,
            Nys non so yeep,
            Ne half so freo.
85              *Ich wolde ich were a threstelcok,*
                *A bountyng other a lavercoke,*
                    *Swete bryd!*

45    No other woman's so splendidly formed!
      When she's merrily brought to bed,
      He's well who knows her thought,
            That excellent one!
      I know well she doesn't want me;
50          My heart is woeful.
                  *I wish I were a throstle-cock,*
                  *A bunting or a laverock,*
                        *Sweet bird!*
                  *Between her kirtle and her smock*
55                      *I would be hid!*


      How shall a desirous lover sing,
      Who's so marred by grief?
      She'll bring me to death
            Long before my day!
60    Greet her well, that sweet thing
            With eyes of gray.
                  *I wish I were a throstle-cock,*
                  *A bunting or a laverock,*
                        *Sweet bird!*
65                *Between her kirtle and her smock*
                        *I would be hid!*


      Those eyes have certainly wounded me,
      Her curved eyebrows bringing bliss!
      Her comely mouth that might kiss —
70          He'd be in ecstasy!
      I would change my lot for his
            Who is her companion.
                  *I wish I were a throstle-cock,*
                  *A bunting or a laverock,*
75                      *Sweet bird!*
                  *Between her kirtle and her smock*
                        *I would be hid!*


      Would that her companion be so generous,
      And worthy were, that it might happen,
80    All for one woman I'd give three,
            Without haggling!
      From hell to heaven, from sun to sea,
            There's no one so beguiling,
            Nor half so gracious.
85                *I wish I were a throstle-cock,*
                  *A bunting or a laverock,*
                        *Sweet bird!*

*Bituene hire curtel ant hire smoke*
*Y wolde ben hyd!*


**Gilote e Johane**                                                    [art. 37]

67va]    ¶ En may par une matyné s'en ala juer,              **[Narrator]**
         En un vert bois ramé, un jeuene chivaler,
         Si oyd deus femmes entremedler.
         Ly chevaler se arestut privément pur oyer:
5        Les damoyseles ne le aparsurent mie.
         E si lur nouns voletz qe je les vous die,
         Gilote e Johane nomer se feseyent,
         E de lur vies entreparleyent.


         Primes dit Gilote, de jolyf cuer:                   **[Gilote]**
10       "Je ay un amy que fet apreyser,
         Coynte e sage e beal bachiler,
         E tot me treove quanqe j'ay mester."


         "Veyre," dit Johane, "je su pucele,                 **[Johane]**
         Entre la gent tenu pur bele,
15       E, de mon cors, tenue pur lele:
         De ce meint prodhome parle novele,
         E uncore outre plus qe je vous die.
         Ne su mie apayé de tote vostre vie.
         Vous vivez malement en vileynie,
20       En manere de pecchié e de lecherie.
         Pur ce je vous lou qe vous lessez
         Ceste male vie e vous amendez,
         E fetez vous tost bien marier
         Pur doute de pecché e d'enconbrer."


25       "Veyre," dit Gilote, "vous estez desçue,            **[Gilote]**
         E de un ben nyent estes vous mué.
         Je estoie pucele, mes ore ne su mie,
         Ne jamés serroi, pur perdre la vie.
         Par la ou vous deites je su en pecché,
30       Certes, c'est voirs, si su je nee.
         Pus qe je primes fu engendré,
         Je ne me poey garder de pecché.
         Unqe ne fust femme, ne ja serra,
         Pus qe Deus Adam primes crea,
35       Damoisele ne dame, de sa ne de la,
         Qe a la foyz ne pecche, coment qe il va.
         Vous qe vous tenez digne en virginité,
         Plus qe je ne ay si avez vous pecché,

*Between her kirtle and her smock*
*I would be hid!*


**Gilote and Johane**                                                    [art. 37]

67va]  ¶ In May on a morning there went out to play,              [Narrator]
        In a green wood thick with branches, a young knight,
        And he heard two women debating.
        In secret the knight stopped to listen:
5       The young ladies weren't at all aware of him.
        And if you want me to tell you their names,
        They were called Gilote and Johane,
        And they were talking about their lives.

        First says Gilote, with a happy heart:                   [Gilote]
10      "I have a lover worth prizing,
        A clever and prudent and handsome young man,
        And he finds me whatever I need."

        "In truth," says Johane, "I'm a virgin,                  [Johane]
        Held as beautiful among people,
15      And, regarding my body, considered virtuous:
        Many a good man speaks about this fact,
        And even more than I tell you.
        I am not a bit pleased by your life.
        You live wickedly in baseness,
20      In a manner of sin and lechery.
        Therefore I admonish you to give up
        This wicked life and amend yourself,
        And get yourself quickly married
        For fear of sin and embarrassment."

25      "In truth," says Gilote, "you're deceived,               [Gilote]
        And you're bothered by a mere nothing.
        I was a virgin, but now I'm not at all,
        Nor will I ever be, so may I lose my life.
        As for your saying that I'm in sin,
30      Certainly, it's true, as I'm born.
        Since I was first begotten,
        I couldn't keep from sin.
        Never has there been a woman, nor ever will be,
        Since God first created Adam,
35      Single or married, here or there,
        Who doesn't sin sometimes, however it goes.
        You who hold yourself worthy in virginity,
        You've sinned more than I have,

Tes parens e tes amys sovent corocé,
40      E de jours e de nuytz malement tempté.
67vb]   E si vous purrez, privément a leysyr
        Sauntz aparteynaunce, a pleysyr,
        Tot parfere vostre voler,
        A peyne si vous vodrez le jeu lesser.
45      Vous estes al hostiel tot demoraunt,
        Mesdit e repris cum un enfaunt.
        E ne avez qe vous troeve kerchief ne gant,
        Creaunt serez pucele e tenez vous a taunt.
        Je su en joie e en jolyveté,
50      Pres de mon cher ami, qe me fet lee,
        De fere ce qe me plest a ma volenté.
        Qui qe l'en corouce, vyt il maugree.
        La ou vous parlez endreit de mariage,
        Noun frai je, Johane. Ce serreit outrage
55      De vivre en peyne e en damage.
        Qe malement se marie ne fet pas qe sage.
        Je serroi pris de su en ma mesoun,
        Desolé e batu pur poi d'enchesoun;
        E aver les enfauntz a trop de foysoun,
60      E ja ne departyrai de tel laroun.
        Unqe ne savoy femme que prist mary,
        Qe tost ou tart ne se repenty.
        A noun Dieu, Johane, ne est pas issi
        Entre moi meismes e mon amy.
65      Je pus quaunt je vueil partyr de ly
        Sauntz congié de prestre ou de autruy,
        E choyser un autre tauntost aprés,
        E vivre en joie e tous jours en pes,
        A dreyn de mes pecchiés estre confés
70      E de touz mesfetz aver relés."


        "Vous avetz molt parlé a desresoun,                        **[Johane]**
        Par maveise creaunce e abusioun,
        Quar lele pucelage e virginité
        Sunt en ciel e terre sovereyn digneté.
75      Par plusours ensamples puet estre prové
        Qe ce est la fyn de tote bounté.
        La premere ensample, qe tot conclud,
        Est de la Dame qe primes consut
67*ra]  Nostre douz Salveour, si come ly plust,
80      Pure virgine de jour e de nuyt;
        Virgine estoit devant e aprés,
        Virgine e dame demorant en pes.
        De totes virgines porta le fes.
        Douce Virgine, nous grauntez relés!

Often vexed your parents and friends,
40 Wickedly tempted [them] day and night.
67vb] And if you could, secretly in leisure
Without being seen, at your pleasure,
Achieve all you wanted,
Scarcely would you want to give up the game.
45 You're always staying at home,
Criticized and corrected like a child.
And you don't have anyone who finds you kerchiefs or gloves,
For they believe you'll be a virgin and keep yourself as such.
I'm in joy and in delight,
50 Near my dear lover, who makes me happy,
By doing what pleases me at my will.
Whoever's mad about it, let him be.
While you speak about marriage,
I won't have it, Johane. It would be outrageous
55 To live in suffering and in harm.
Whoever marries badly doesn't act prudently.
I would be trapped in my house,
Oppressed and beaten for little cause,
[I'd have] to have way too many children,
60 And I'd never be separated from such a rogue.
I've never known a woman who took a husband,
Who sooner or later didn't regret it.
In God's name, Johane, it's not thus
Between myself and my lover.
65 I can leave him when I want
Without permission from a priest or anyone else,
And choose another immediately afterwards,
And live in joy and always in peace,
And at the end be confessed of my sins
70 And be absolved of all my misdeeds."

"You've spoken very unreasonably,     **[Johane]**
In bad faith and error,
For steadfast maidenhood and virginity
Enjoy the highest status in heaven and earth.
75 It can be proved by many examples
That this is the goal of all goodness.
The first example, which includes all others,
Is that of the Lady who first conceived
67*ra] Our sweet Savior, as it was pleasing to him,
80 Pure virgin both day and night;
She was virgin before and after,
Virgin and lady living in peace.
Of all virgins she bore the burden.
Sweet Virgin, grant us absolution!

85      E autres ensamples de meintes virgines
        Que ore sunt en ciel pures meschines.
        E pur ce vous di je, par ceste resoun,
        Pucele su e de ce ay le noun,
        Come les virgines de salvacioun.
90      E je de virginale su condicioun,
        E vous estes de un degré descendi plus bas.
        E si estes del tot passé le pas.
        Ja en ta vie ne le recoveras
        Le pucelage qe tu perdu as.”

95      “Vos paroles,” dit Gilote, “sunt a entendre,          **[Gilote]**
        Mes en moltz des pointz vous vueil je reprendre.
        De Nostre douce Dame vous estes molt meyndre.
        Entre vous e ly ne poez ensaunple feyndre.
        Vous estes molt fole, e bien le savom,
100     De fere nulle ensample ou comparisoun
        Entre vous e la Dame de salvacioun,
        De qui nostre joie nous tous avom,
        Ou de fere ensample de seinte virgines,
        Qe sunt en ciel divine meschynes.
105     Vous estes terrene e si ne savez
        Coment a drein vous meismes cheverez.
        Vostre virginité ne vous valt rien
        Si de mal penser le cuer ne gardez bien.
        E Dieu dist meismes par comandement,
110     ‘Multiplier e crestre la gent,
        E rendre les almes a ly, Omnipotent.
        Celi qe me dedit sei meismes dement.’
        E tant come en terre soule viverez,
        Une alme a Dieu rendre ne poez.”

115     ¶ “Vous me ditez tro bien, en veritez,              **J[ohane]**
        Si en esposailles fuissent engendrez.
        Dreite engendrure est naturele chose;
        Ce est la soume de ce e la parclose.”

        “Dieu ne exepte par nulle escripture                **Gilote**
120     Nulle cristene gent par engendrure.
67*rb]  Quant mon ami de rien ne mesfet,
        Je prendroi un autre sauntz fere plet,
        E tendroi a ly a ma volenté.
        Si bien ne se porte, tost serra chaungé.
125     De la Magdaleyne vous avez oy retrere,
        Qe peccheresse fust quant fust en terre.
        Ore est en ciel gloriouse mere
        Par sa repentance e sa priere.

85      And there are other examples of many virgins
       Who are now pure maidens in heaven.
       And therefore I tell you, based on this argument,
       I am a maiden and I am known for this,
       Like the virgins of salvation.
90      And I am in a virginal state,
       And you have descended to a lower state,
       And you have absolutely passed the limit.
       Never in your life will you recover
       The maidenhood that you've lost."

95      "Your words," says Gilote, "are understandable,      **[Gilote]**
       But I want to correct you on many of the points.
       You are much less than Our sweet Lady.
       Between you and her you can't feign comparison.
       You're very foolish, and we know it well,
100     To make any example or comparison
       Between yourself and the Lady of salvation,
       From whom we have all our joy,
       Or to make an example of holy virgins,
       Who are divine maidens in heaven.
105     You are of this world and so you don't know
       How you yourself will fare at the end.
       Your virginity is worth nothing to you
       If you don't shield your heart from bad thoughts.
       And God himself said as a commandment,
110     'Multiply and increase the human race,
       And render souls to him, the Omnipotent.
       He who contradicts me opposes himself.'
       As long as you live alone on earth,
       You cannot give God a soul."

115     ¶ "You speak to me very well, in truth,      **J[ohane]**
       If they were begotten in marriage.
       Legal procreation is a natural thing:
       It's the culmination of it and its completion."

       "God doesn't cast out in any Scripture      **Gilote**
120     Any Christian person on account of begetting.
67*rb]  When my lover behaves badly in anything,
       I'll take another without making a plea,
       And I'll keep him according to my desire.
       If he doesn't conduct himself well, he'll soon be exchanged.
125     You've heard tell of the Magdalen,
       Who was a sinner when she was on earth.
       Now she's a glorious mother in heaven
       On account of her repentance and her prayer.

Si avez oi dire qe ele fust lors,
130 La plus orde femme qe unque fust, de cors,
Pleyne de pecchié dedenz e dehors.
E pus de ces pecchez Dieu fist devors.
Autres ensamples dient plusour
Qe Dieus plus ayme un peccheour
135 Qe se converte a chief de tour
Qe nulle virgine, par escriptour."

Johane respount santz nulle destaunce:         **[Johane]**
"Que pecchié de gree en operaunce,
Yl vet en doute e en balaunce
140 Si Dieu ne ly face de ce aleggaunce."

¶ "Chescun cristen qe se conust de gré       **G[ilote]**
Vers soun Creatour aver pecchié,
E cri merci de bone volenté,
Yl serra bien oy e serra salvé.
145 Turnez le Byble desus e dejus:
Vous ne troverez frere qe vous dirra plus.
Afeytez vous, file! Afeitez vous, fole!
Vous estes meynz sage. Venez a l'escole!
Fetez come je face. Dieu vous avaunce!
150 Aydez al siecle pur fere creaunce."

¶ "Vous me avetz conclud, mes ore vueil aprendre   **J[ohane]**
Coment je me purroi donque defendre
Si de mes parentz soie reprové."

"De ce je vous dirroi la fyne verité.       **[Gilote]**
155 Vous averez un bachiler jeouene e vaillant,
E a matin e a seir vous serra joyant,
E quant le gu d'amour avez asayee
Sys foiht ou seet, a vostre volentee,
Vous a vostre mere vendrez arere,
160 E la mere pur vous priera le pere.
Quar naturele chose est a la mere
Eyder la fille en tote manere.
67*va] E si vostre pere aprés vous reprent
E vous ledenge a soun talent,
165 Que vous avez fet noun pas sagement,
Lessez le passer. Ce n'est rien qe vent.
E si devez dire: 'Sire, si vous plet,
Meinte pucele ad issi fet.
Ne su pas la dreine ne la premere,
170 E purquoi serroi je lesse derere?
Si vous me ussez bel part avant mariee,

And you've heard it said that she was then,
130    Of body, the filthiest woman who ever was,
Full of sin within and without.
And then God separated her from these sins.
Many tell other examples of
How God loves more a sinner
135    Who's converted at the very end
Than any virgin, according to Scripture."

Johane answers without any delay:                          **[Johane]**
"He who sins willingly in deed,
He lives in fear and peril
140    Unless God gives him relief from this."

¶ "Each Christian who knows himself willingly          **G[ilote]**
To have sinned against his Creator,
And begs mercy with a good will,
He'll be well heard and will be saved.
145    Turn the Bible up and down:
You won't find a friar who will tell you more.
Educate yourself, girl! Educate yourself, fool!
You're not very prudent. Come to school!
Do as I do. May God prosper you!
150    Help the world to foster belief."

¶ "You've convinced me, but now I want to learn      **J[ohane]**
How I'd be able to defend myself
If I were reproved by my parents."

"I'll tell you the pure truth about that.                    **[Gilote]**
155    You'll have a young and brave man,
And morning and evening he'll be delighted with you,
And when you have tried the game of love
Six times or seven, according to your desire,
You'll come back to your mother,
160    And your mother will approach your father for you.
For it's a natural thing for a mother
To help her daughter in every way.
67*va]  And if your father then reproves you
And rails at you as he wants,
165    That you haven't acted prudently,
Let it go. It's nothing but wind.
And you must say: 'Lord, if it please you,
Many a maiden has done this.
I'm neither the last nor the first,
170    And why should I be left behind?
If you'd arranged for me to be married well before,

Ne fuisse je ore de cest arettee.
Fete vos files tost marier,
Quar nulle pucele se puet garder.
175 La pensee lur dampne e le voler —
Tant ad de joie en le mestier!'"

Donqe ceste Johane un amy prist,           **[Narrator]**
Plus bel bachiler unqe ne vist.
E come Gilote la out eynz dit,
180 En totes choses issi le fit.
Johane se cocha ov cel bachiler
Come pucele prest a soun voler,
E il se entremist de son mester.
La gist un 'hoho' e un teyser.

185 ¶ Donqe dit Gilote, a chief de tour,        **[Gilote]**
"Coment vous resemble de le gu d'amour?"

¶ "Certes, Gilote, c'est dreit gu!           **[Johane]**
Unqe en terre meilour ne fu
A reigne ne dame ne autre vivant!
190 Par mon ami ai je trové taunt,
Tant juay ov ly ou seme plat,
Qe par un simple 'escheke' si ly di 'mat.'"

¶ Donqe dit Gilote, e parla a Jone,       **[Gilote]**
"Coment vous resemble? Est la vie bone?"

195 "La beneson Dieu e sa douce mere        **[Johane]**
Puissez vous aver, come bone counsilere,
Car je su en joye e en jolyf chere
E su molt amendé en meinte manere,
Si fu bien fole e mal avysee
200 Qe j'ay pucele tant demoree
E perdu mon temps en vidueté,
Mes si ne fray je mes, en ma leauté."

¶ Tant ad Johane alé par Wyncestre       **[Narrator]**
E Gilote sa compaigne, qe fust chef mestre,
205 De dire ceste aventure e de precher,
Qe a peyne une puet um trover
67*vb] Que ne s'entremettra de tiel mestier;
Si ele soit requise de jeouene bachiler,
A peyne si ele savera son amour deveyer.

210 Si, com il alerent un matyn deduaunt,
Une jeuene espose lur vient acontrant,

I wouldn't now be accused of this.
Have your daughters marry early,
For no virgin can protect herself.
175  Thought and desire condemn them —
There's so much joy in the craft!'"

Then this Johane took a lover,                        **[Narrator]**
A more handsome young man she never saw.
And just as Gilote had told her earlier,
180  Thus she did in everything.
Johane went to bed with that young man
As a virgin prepared to do her will,
And he busied himself with his task.
There lay an 'oo-oo' and a hush.

185  ¶ Then Gilote says, when it's all over,               **[Gilote]**
"How does the game of love seem to you?"

¶ "Certainly, Gilote, it's a proper game!              **[Johane]**
Never was there a better one on earth
For a queen or a lady or any other living creature!
190  I've discovered so much through my lover,
I've played so much with him where we lie down,
That by a simple 'check' I called him 'mated.'"

¶ Then Gilote speaks, and said to Johane,             **[Gilote]**
"How does it seem to you? Is life good?"

195  "God's blessing and his sweet mother's              **[Johane]**
May you have, as a good adviser,
For I'm in delight and in a happy mood
And I'm much improved in many ways,
And I was really foolish and badly advised
200  That I've remained a virgin so long
And lost my time in chastity,
But I'll no longer do it, by my faith."

¶ Johane went so much about Winchester               **[Narrator]**
With her companion Gilote, who was headmaster,
205  Telling and preaching about this adventure,
That one can scarcely find a woman
67*vb]  Who won't engage in such a task;
If she should be asked by a young man,
She scarcely knows how to turn down his love.

210  So, as they went out one morning enjoying themselves,
A young wife came upon them,

E quant vist Gilote, si la salua
E counsail e aye ly demaunda,
E dit qe un chivaler ly aveit counté
215    Qe Gilote fust femme bien enloquyné,
"E dit qe il out oy la desputeysoun                    **[Uxor]**
Qe vous venquistes l'autrer a grant resoun,
E que vous avez Johane ensi consilee
Qe c'est grant joie e grant dentee."

220    Gilote assez bien la entendist,                        **[Gilote]**
E, tauntost aprés, la demaundist
Quei fust la chose qe ele coveytoit
Sur totes choses; qe rien ne celeroit.

"Mout y ad a dyre c'est verité,                        **[Uxor]**
225    Mes a vous, Gilote, ne serra rien cele.
E molt est a dire e a mostrer,
Mes 'bosoigne fet la voie deforcer.'
Je su jeouene espouse, si ay un baroun,
Mes trop est il fieble en sa mesoun.
230    Ce est la verité, il ad un vit
Trop est il plyant e trop petit,
E je su molt pres si me tienk clos,
E son vit est touzjours derere mon dors,
E pur fin anguisse me toud mon repos,
235    E me fet palyr e fremyr le cors.
Me covient moryr pur anguisse fyn
Si je n'eie l'amour de jolif hokekyn."

"Veyre," dit Gilote, "vous estes trahy,                **[Gilote]**
E de ce ne serrez rien abay.
240    Je mettroi consail; vous averez aye.
Vous averez medicine, si serrez garye.
Trop est femme desçu malement
E forement trahy, qe tiel honme prent.
Yl ne puet foutre ne fere talent.
245    Alas, alas, for Godes deth, such womon ys yshent!
Demayn quant vostre mary vet de mesoun,
Je vous froy venyr un jeouene clerjoun,
Qe de geu vous trovera grant foissoun,
De meyne e de tresble e de bordoun."

68ra]  "Si usse je fet graunt temps passé,                   **[Uxor]**
251    Mes je me dotay molt de pecché,
E pur ce le ai je uncore lessé
Tant qe je seie mieux avysé.
Car prestres nous dient en lur sermoun,

And when she saw Gilote, she greeted her
And asked her for advice and help,
And said that a knight had told her
215  That Gilote was a very eloquent woman,
"And he says that he'd heard the disputation   **[Wife]**
That you won the other day by impressive logic,
And that you've advised Johane in such a way
That it's a great joy and a great delight."

220  Gilote listened to her very well,        **[Gilote]**
And, immediately afterwards, she asked
What thing it was that she coveted
Above all things; she should hide nothing.

"It's true that there's a lot to say,        **[Wife]**
225  But from you, Gilote, nothing will be hidden.
And there's a lot to say and to show,
But 'need determines the path.'
I am a young wife, and I have a husband,
But he's too feeble at home.
230  The truth is, he has a prick
That's too pliant and too little,
And I'm very near and he holds me close,
And his prick is always behind my back,
And for pure anguish he steals my rest,
235  And makes me turn pale and my body tremble.
I'm ready to die on account of pure anguish
If I don't have the love of a jolly rascal."

"Truly," says Gilote, "you've been betrayed,   **[Gilote]**
And you will not be at all troubled by this.
240  I'll give advice; you'll have help.
You'll have medicine, and you'll be healed.
Too much is a woman badly deceived
And severely betrayed, who takes such a man.
He can't fuck or fulfill her desire.
245  Alas, alas, for God's death, such a woman is ruined!
Tomorrow when your husband leaves the house,
I'll have a young clerk come to you,
Who will compose for you an abundance of loveplay,
In the middle and the treble and the bass."

68ra]  "So I'd have done a long time ago,    **[Wife]**
251  But I was very afraid of sinning,
And therefore I've still put it aside
Until I might be better advised
For priests tell us in their sermons,

255    E si fount les freres en predicacioun,
       Qe ce est la mort e confusioun
       Femme de prendre autre qe son baron.
       E ce ne serroit pur moy de aver amour
       E perdre ma alme santz nul retour."

260    "N'est il pas baroun tenuz en terre          **G[ilote]**
       Qe ne puet ov sa femme engendrure fere,
       Ne il ne puet foutre, ne il ne puet trere.
       A force covent medicine quere.
       Prestres ne freres, pur lur sermoun,
265    Ne devez mie doter, par ceste resoun:
       Pus qe le frere qe list de son art
       Preche al pueple e foute de sa part.
       Nous jeouene femmes n'averom regart,
       Qe unqe ne veymes lettre ne art."

270    "Mes uncore vous vueil prier de plus,        **Uxor**
       Qe n'est avant dit ne mostré desus.
       Le roi ad fet fere fortz estatus
       Qe font grantz mals en plusours lyws:
       Si femme espousé ad guerpi
275    Par soun eyn de gré son propre mari
       E un autre honme ad choysy
       En manere de avoutre ov de amy,
       E se fet demorer ov son avoter
       Un demi an ou un an enter,
280    E son baron seit mis en cymeter,
       Mort e enterré santz revenyr . . . ?"

       "Certes," dit Gilote, "je vous dy veir,       **[Gilote]**
       La femme, en cel cas, pert son doweyr.
       Mes la ou le baroun ov bone volentee
285    Ad sa compaigne a ly recounsilee,
       Rien n'i est perdu, mes tot est gaygné,
       E accion par bref si serra graunté."

       "E quei si le baron reprendre ne la voleit?"   **[Uxor]**

       "Play de seinte Eglise quei ly valdreit?      **[Gilote]**
290    Par play de seinte Eglise la femme esposé
       Serra reprise son baroun malgré.
       Mes vous frez autre coyntise
       Par quei qe vous serrez arere reprise:
68rb]  Devant vostre baroun vendrez humblement;
295    Vous li crierez merci molt dulcement,
       E prierez qe il eit, pur l'amour de Dee,

255 And so do friars in their preaching,
That it is death and confusion
For a woman to take someone other than her husband.
And it wouldn't serve for me to have love
And lose my soul without any recourse."

260 "He's not considered a husband anywhere     **G[ilote]**
If he can't procreate with his wife,
Or if he can't fuck, or if he can't shoot.
He must perforce seek medical help.
Neither priests nor friars, for their sermons,
265 Should you fear a bit, for this reason:
Since the friar who has read about his art
Preaches to the people and fucks as well.
We young women will pay no attention,
Who never saw writing or a liberal art."

270 "But still I want to ask you more,     **Wife**
Which hasn't been said or demonstrated above.
The king has had firm statutes made
That cause great trouble in many places:
If a married woman has renounced
275 By her own choice her own husband
And has chosen another man
As her adulterer or lover,
And goes to stay with her adulterer
A half-year or an entire year,
280 And her husband is put in the cemetery,
Dead and buried with no coming back . . . ?"

"Indeed," says Gilote, "I tell you truly,     **[Gilote]**
The woman, in this case, loses her dowry.
But there where the husband with good will
285 Has reconciled his mate to himself,
Nothing is lost, but everything is gained,
And action by brief will be granted."

"And what if the husband doesn't want to take her back?"     **[Wife]**

"What would a tenet of Holy Church be worth to him?     **[Gilote]**
290 By tenet of Holy Church the married woman
Will be taken back despite her husband.
But you'll perform another clever act
By which you'll be taken back:
68rb] You'll come humbly before your husband;
295 You'll beg his mercy very tenderly,
And you'll pray that he have, for God's love,

Merci de vous e pietee:
'Je vous ay mesfet en ma vyleynye,
Si ne frai je jamés tant come je ay la vie.
300    Beau sire baroun, pernez bone cure
Quey me promistes par premesse dure.
Regardez a Dieu e a dreyture.
Vous ne me poez refuser pur nulle aventure.
Quant nous venimes le prestre devant,
305    Coment vous me deytes avisez vous a tant.
Veiez si la femme; veiez si l'enfant.
Douz sire baroun, tenez covenant.'
Prestres e freres e autre bone gent
Vendront e dirront communement:
310    'Recevez ta femme par digne talent,
Pur salver vostre alme hors de torment.'
Quant ceste chose serra mostré,
Vous vendrez devant ly bien atyré.
Le cuer li changera, si avera pieté,
315    E vous serrez dame bien recounsilé,
E serrez mestresse si come devant,
E serrez riche dame e plus puissant."

E si come Gilote cestes choses dist,                      **[Narrator]**
¶ Ceste jeouene espouse issi le fist.
320    E de totes choses qe Gilote la aprist,
Unqe en nul point rien ne faylist.
Cestes bones femmes s'en alerent juer,
Gilote e Johane ensemble a moster.
Ceste matere la comencerent.
325    Le tixt e la glose desputerent;
Apertement distrent lur argument.

Les femmes respondyrent comunement:                       **[Uxores]**
"Vous avez bien dit e clergialment;
Unqe ne oymes tiel prechement."

330    E totes bone femmes al hostel alerent,                **[Narrator]**
Quar hastive bosoignes lur chacerent,
E solum cet aprise tous feseient,
Si fount il uncore, ou qu'il seient.
68va]  Tant sunt celes damoiseles alé avant
335    Que il n'y a femme ore vivant,
En quel lu que ele soit demorant,
Qe bien ne siet juer a talevas devant.
En Engletere e Yrlaund yl precherent.
Meynt bone terre si envyronerent.

Mercy on you and pity:
'I have done you ill in my baseness,
And I will never again do it as long as I have life.
300       Handsome lord husband, bear well in mind
What you promised me by a firm promise.
Look to God and to justice.
You cannot refuse me on account of any chance event.
When we came before the priest,
305       Remember how you spoke to me.
Behold the woman; behold the child.
Sweet lord husband, keep your covenant.'
Priests and friars and other good people
Will come and speak as one:
310       'Receive your wife with a worthy desire,
In order to save your soul from torment.'
When this argument is brought forward,
You'll come before him well attired.
His heart will change, and he'll have pity,
315       And you'll be a lady well reconciled,
And you'll be mistress just as before,
And you'll be a wealthy lady and more powerful."

And just as Gilote had described these things,          **[Narrator]**
¶ So this young wife did.
320       And of all the things that Gilote had taught her,
Never in any way at all was she deficient.
These good women went forth to play,
Gilote and Johane together at church.
There they introduced this matter.
325       They debated the text and the gloss;
They spoke their argument openly.

The wives responded as one:                              **[Wives]**
"You've spoken well and in a clerkly way;
We've never heard such preaching."

330       And all the good women went to the hostelry,      **[Narrator]**
For urgent needs drove them,
And they did everything according to this teaching,
And they still do, wherever they may be.
68va]     So many of these young ladies have gone forth
335       That there isn't a woman now alive,
In whatever place she may be dwelling,
Who doesn't know how to play the game of love.
In England and Ireland they preached.
They traversed many a good land.

340        A la vile de Pount-Freint demorerent,
           E a lur aprise plusours tornerent.

           C'est une bourde de reheyter la gent,
           A Wyncestre fet, verroiement,
           Le mois de septembre le jour quinsyme,
345        Le an roy Edward vyntenuefyme,
           Le fitz roy Henry qe ama seinte Eglise.
           E quant vous avez lu tote ceste aprise,
           Priez a Dieu de ciel, roy glorious,
           Qe il eit merci e pieté de nous.


           **Les pelrinages communes que crestiens fount en la Seinte Terre**        [art. 38]

68va]      ¶ Ces sunt les pelrinages communes que crestiens fount en la Seinte Terre:

           De la vyle de ACRES a SEYNT ELYE, iiij liws de cele terre.

           E de la CAVE SEYNT ELYE a la CARME, j liwe.

           E de la Carme a SEINT JOHAN DE TYR, j liwe.

5          La yl y a une vile de seint Johan le Baptistre.

           E a j liwe de ileque est le peroun sur qui Dieu se resposa, devant le CHASTIEL
           PELRYN. E dedenz le chastel gist le cors seint Eufemie. E deprés est MERLE. La seint
           André nasquy [John 1:44]. E deprés si est la CAVE la ou Nostre Dame se mussa ov
           son fitz pur doute des Gyws.

10         E de ileqe a NOSTRE DAME DE MARREIS , iij liwes. La Nostre Dame se resposa.

           E d'yleoque a CESARIE, j liwe.

           E de yleqe a JAPHET, xij liwes. La est um peron qe um apele le PEROUN SEINT JAKE,
           e une CHAPELE ou seint Abakuc soleint meindre.

           E de yleqe a RAMES, la ou seint George fust martirizé, iiij liwes.

15         E d'ileqe a BETYNOBLE, maveis chymyn, iij liwes.

           E ii liwes a EMAUS, la ou Jesu parla ov Cleophas, e le conust par fraccion de pain
           [Luke 24:13–35].

           E de yleqe a MONT JOIE, ij liwes, e la fust ensevely Samuel le prophete [1 Samuel
           25:1].

340 They stayed in the town of Pontefract,
  And they converted many to their teaching.

  This is a jest to please the people,
  Performed at Winchester, truly,
  On the fifteenth day of September,
345 In the twenty-ninth year of King Edward,
  The son of King Henry who loved Holy Church.
  And when you've read all this teaching,
  Pray to God in heaven, the glorious king,
  That he may have mercy and compassion on us.


**Pilgrimages in the Holy Land**        **[art. 38]**

68va] ¶ These are the usual pilgrimages that Christians make in the Holy Land:

  From the city of ACRE to [the Monastery of] ST. ELIJAH, four leagues of that land.

  And from ST. ELIJAH'S CAVE to CARMEL, one league.

  And from Carmel to [the Church of] ST. JOHN OF TYRE, one league.

5 There is a dwelling there of Saint John the Baptist.

  And at one league from there is the rock on which God rested, in front of the PILGRIMS' CASTLE. And inside the castle lies the body of Saint Euphemia. And close by is TANTURA. There was Saint Andrew born [John 1:44]. And close by is the CAVE where Our Lady hid herself with her son for fear of the Jews.

10 And from there to OUR LADY OF THE MARSHES, three leagues. There Our Lady rested.

  And from there to CAESAREA, one league.

  And from there to JAFFA, twelve leagues. There is a rock there that is called ST. JAMES'S ROCK, and a CHAPEL where Saint Habakkuk was wont to dwell.

  And from there to RAMATH, where Saint George was martyred, four leagues.

15 And from there to BAIT NUBA, by a bad road, three leagues.

  And two leagues to EMMAUS, where Jesus spoke with Cleophas, and he knew him by the breaking of bread [Luke 24:13–35].

  And from there to MOUNT JOY, two leagues, and there the prophet Samuel was buried [1 Samuel 25:1].

68vb]   | E d'yleque a la cité de Jerusalem sunt ij liwes de bel chymyn. E le entre en la cité
21      est parmy la Porte ou seint Estevene fust lapidé [*Acts 7:58–59*]. E pus vous vendrez
        a Seint Sepulcre, e la frez vous vos oreysouns.

        Le compas dedentz le cuer ne est mie loyns de le Sepulcre. E la est un peroun,
        lequel Dieu dit qe fust la meene du mounde.

25      ¶ Mount Calvarie, ou Jesu fust crucefié, est al destre part de le cuer, e uncore est
        le sang apparysant sur la roche q'est apelé Golgatha.

        E deprés yl y a une tounbe de piere ou gisent les vij roys qe furent jadis de la cité,
        e Godefroy de Boylloun. Delees le haut auter la est le piler a qui Jesu fust lyé quant
        fust flaelé.

30      Deprés est la prisone e la cheyne dont Dieu fust encheyné en meisme la prisone. E
        la furent vewes le jour de Pashe treis Maries [Mark 16:1]. E delees descendrez xl
        degrees, e la trova seinte Eleyne la seinte Croyz.

        E deprés, descendaunt xl degreez, la est la Chapele Gryffoune. E la est une
        ymage de Nostre Dame, qe parla a la Egipciene e la emprist la loy.

35      E de coste la Sepulcre, ne mie molt loyns, est le Hospital Seint Johan, e la deprés
        si est la Eglise Seint Caryout, e delees si est la Latyne. La les treis Maries
        decyrerent lur chevels quant Dieu dust estre crucifié.

        E de yleque, le tret de un arc, si est Templum Domini, e la dedenz sunt plusours
        merveilles. E dedenz sunt xx hus e fortz portes. La est est la piere sur qui Dieu fust
40      mys le jour de la Chandelour devant le vyel Symeon [Luke 2:25–32].

        La vist Jacob l'eschele par ount descendirent angles de ciel a terre [Genesis 28:12].
        E par cele eschele vint un angle a Zacarie, qe ly anuncia qu'il avereit un fitz, qe
69ra]   a|nunciereit la advenement Dieu [Luke 1:13]. E la, dedenz un arch, si est la verge
        Aaron, e les vij chaundelabres de or, e les tables Moyses. E la pres Dieu pardona la
45      femme que fust pris en avoterie, come le Ewangelie tesmoigne [John 8:3–11].

        E la pres est la porte ou seint Pere e seint Johan troverent le countret qe lur
        demanda bien. E seint Pere ly dist: "Je n'ay or ne argent, mes ce qe j'ay, je vous
        dorray; levez, fi alez seyn" [Acts 3:1–7]. E cele porte est apelé Jerusalem, e la porte
        del north est apelé Parays. La est la founteyne qe est apelé Parays, dont seint
50      Eglise list qe eawe vyne en issist.

        La porte de west est apelé Speciouse.

68vb]     | And from there to the city of JERUSALEM are two leagues of good road. And the
21        way into the city is through the GATE where Saint Stephen was stoned [*Acts
          7:58–59*]. And then you will come to the HOLY SEPULCHER, and there you will say
          your prayers.

          The compass inside the choir is not far at all from the Sepulcher. And there is a
          rock, which God said was the center of the world.

25        ¶ MOUNT CALVARY, where Jesus was crucified, is to the right side of the choir, and
          the blood is still visible on the rock that is called GOLGOTHA.

          And close by there is a stone tomb where lie the seven kings who were formerly of
          that city, and Godfrey of Bouillon. Alongside the high altar there is the pillar to
          which Jesus was tied when he was flagellated.

30        Close by is the prison and the chain with which God was enchained in the same
          prison. And there were seen on Easter the three Marys [Mark 16:1]. And from there
          you will descend forty degrees, and there Saint Helena found the Holy Cross.

          And close by, descending forty degrees, there is the GRIFFIN CHAPEL. And there is
          an image of Our Lady, who spoke to the Egyptian woman and taught her the faith.

35        And alongside the Sepulcher, not at all far, is the HOSPITAL OF ST. JOHN [THE
          BAPTIST], and close by it is also the CHURCH OF ST. CHARITON, and also nearby is
          the [ABBEY CHURCH OF ST. MARY] LATIN. There the three Marys tore their hair
          when God had to be crucified.

          And from there, the flight of an arrow, is the TEMPLUM DOMINI, and inside it are
          many wonders. And inside are twenty doors and strong gates. East of there is the
40        stone on which God was placed on Candlemas Day before aged Simeon [Luke
          2:25–32].

          There saw Jacob the ladder by which angels descended from heaven to earth
          [Genesis 28:12]. And by this ladder an angel came to Zachary, who announced to
69ra]     him that he would have a son, who would an|nounce the coming of God [Luke
          1:13]. And there, inside an arch, are also Aaron's staff, and the seven candlesticks
          of gold, and the tablets of Moses. And near there God forgave the woman who was
45        taken in adultery, as the Evangelist attests [John 8:3–11].

          And near there is the door where Saint Peter and Saint John found the adversary
          who asked them for money. And Saint Peter said to him: "I do not have gold or
          silver, but what I have, I will give you; rise, and go in health" [Acts 3:1–7]. And this
          gate is called JERUSALEM, and the north gate is called PARADISE. There is the spring
50        that is called PARADISE, from which Holy Church teaches that water issued as wine.

          The west gate is called BEAUTIFUL.

La porte de le est si est apellé PORTE ORRYENE, e par cele porte entra Dieu, chevalchant le asne [John 12:14], e uncore sur la dure roche les pies de la asne sunt apparissauntz.

55      E de la part del north est PROBATICA PISCINA [John 5:2], e la soleit un angle mover le ewe, e celi qe primes y entroit soleit recoveryr saunté de chescune enfermeté.

E bien de yleque est le TEMPLE SALOMON. E plus amount est le bayn ou Nostre Dame soleit bayner soun fitz. E la molt pres est le lyt ou Jesu soleit cocher. E delees si est la TOUR DAVID. E devant la Tour si est une CHAPELE, e leynze est seint Johan bouche orriene [Luke 1:64–66] e autres reliques plusours. De la est est une EGLYSE
60      ou seint Jame fust decolé [Acts 12:2]. E par la poez passer vers le MOUNT SYON. La
69rb]   devya Nostre Dame, e les apostles la ensevelyrent | graunt piece de yleque en le val de Josaphat.

En le Mount Syon fist Dieu sa cene e lava les pyés de ces apostles [John 13:2–20].

65      E la vint Jesu a eux e lur dit, "Pax vobis." E la mostra ces playes a seint Thomas [John 20:21–29].

E noun pas loins de yleque est le liw ou Jesu fust desolee e coroné d'espynes, e la fust le paleis e la PRETORIE CAYPHAS [Matthew 26:3, 57; 27:29]. E la pres est la eglise ou le seint Espirit descendi le jour de Pentecoste desuz les apostles [Acts 2:1–4].

70      E la pres est la CAVE GALYGANT ou seint Pere refusa conustre Jesu [Luke 22:54–62].

E delees est la NATORYE SYLOE, e la Jesu eslumina le um qe fust nee veogle [John 9:1–41], e la fust ensevely Ysaye le prophete.

E de coste est ACHELDEMAC [Matthew 27:8].

Entre le MOUNT OLYVETE e la cyté est le VAL DE JOSAPHAT, dont avant est dit. E
75      deprés le val yl y a un lyw qe um apele SEINT ANNE. La fust Nostre Dame primes norye.

E la pres est JESSEMANY, la fust Jesu pris, e ces deis sunt uncore aparisauntz sur la dure roche ou yl mist sa meyn. E un petit de yleque est une EGLISE DE SEINT SALVEOUR — la ala Dieu tot soul pur orer a son piere devant sa Passioun [Matthew
80      26:36–46], e la sua Dieu sang. E desuz le Mount de Olyvete, dont eynz est dit, est un lyw ou Dieu veauntz ces disciples mounta en ciel.

The east gate there is called the GOLDEN GATE, and through this gate God entered, riding on the ass [John 12:14], and the tracks of the ass are still visible on the hard rock.

55     On the north side is the SHEEP POOL [John 5:2], and there an angel was accustomed to move the water, and the one who entered there first was bound to recover health from every illness.

       And a ways from there is SOLOMON'S TEMPLE. And higher up is the bath where Our Lady used to bathe her son. And very near there is the bed where Jesus used to sleep. And in that vicinity there is also DAVID'S TOWER. And in front of the tower is

60     a CHAPEL, and therein is Saint John [the Baptist]'s golden mouth [Luke 1:64–66] and many other relics. East of there is a CHURCH where Saint James was beheaded [Acts 12:2]. And through there you can pass toward MOUNT ZION. Our Lady died

69rb]  there, and the apostles buried her | a good ways from there in the Valley of Jehoshaphat.

       On Mount Zion God made his supper and washed the feet of his apostles [John 13:2–20].

65     And there Jesus came to them and said to them, "Peace be with you." And there he showed his wounds to Saint Thomas [John 20:21–29].

       And not far from there is the place where Jesus was defiled and crowned with thorns, and there were the palace and PRAETORIUM OF CAIAPHAS [Matthew 26:3, 57; 27:29]. And near there is the church where the Holy Spirit descended on the day of Pentecost upon the apostles [Acts 2:1–4].

70     And near there is the GALLICANT CAVE where Saint Peter denied knowing Jesus [Luke 22:54–62].

       And near from there is the POOL OF SILOAM, and there Jesus gave sight to the man who was born blind [John 9:1–41], and there was buried the prophet Isaiah.

       And alongside is the FIELD OF BLOOD [Matthew 27:8].

       Between the MOUNT OF OLIVES and the city is the VALLEY OF JEHOSHAPHAT, which

75     is spoken of above. And near the valley is a place that people call ST. ANNE. There was Our Lady first nurtured.

       And near there is GETHSEMANE, where Jesus was taken, and [the imprint of] his fingers is still visible on the hard rock where he put his hand. And a little way from there is the CHURCH OF THE HOLY SAVIOR — God went there all alone to pray to his

80     father before his Passion [Matthew 26:36–46], and there God sweat blood. And below the Mount of Olives, which is spoken of already, is a place where God in the sight of his disciples rose into the sky.

E la est un peroun sur qui Dieu mist soun un pié, qe uncore est apparisaunt e tous jours serra.

69va]    E la pres est ensevely une seynte femme, par quy nul peccheour puet passer ne aproscher | a sa tounbe.

86       La pres est le lu ou Dieu fist la Pater Nostre [Luke 11:2–4; Matthew 6:9–15].

E la pres est un lu ou Dieu se mostra le jour de Pasche a ces disciples [Luke 24:36–53].

90       E de ileque, a le amountance de une lywe Englesshe, est BETHPHAGE. De yleqe maunda Dieu Phelip e Johan a Jerusalem pur le asne le jour de Palmes. A quel jour le greindre honour qe Dieu avoit en terre les enfauntz Hebreus li fyrent [John 12:12–13].

E de yleqe avez, a BETHANYE ou Dieu resuscita Lazer [John 11:1–44], ij liwes, e pres fust evesque de Marcille. E yleque en la mesoun Symond Dieu pardona la 95       Magdaleyne ces pecchiés [Luke 7:36–50].

E de ileque a la QUARANTEYNE, ou Dieu iuna xl jours e nuytz [Matthew 4:1–2], sunt vij liwes.

E la pres si est JERICO.

E de yleque a le FLUM JORDAN sunt ij liwes a le lu ou seint Johan baptiza Dieu 100      [Matthew 3:13–15], e une colombe descendi sur Dieu en forme de seinte Espyryt [Matthew 3:16; Luke 3:22; John 1:32]. E par cest chemyn ne poez vous passer avant. Mes si vous alez de Jerusalem vers la cité de Bedlehem, vous irrez par SEINTE ELYE, j liwe de la cyté de Jerusalem. E la delees si est le CHAMP FLORY, un tres bel lu. E la recevera, a ce qe um dit, chescuny solum ce qu'il avera si deservi. E la déprés gist 105      SEINT RACHEL.

E de yleque a une liwe est BEDLEHEM. E la vindrent les Trois Rois fere lur present — Jaspar, Melchyor, e Baltazar — e chescun de eux porta or, mirre, e encenz [Matthew 2:1–12]. Delees le cuer est un PUT ou la esteyle chey qe amena les Treis Rois. De l'autre part sunt les Innocens que furent ocis [Matthew 2:16–18].

69vb]    E a j liwe de yleoqe apparust le aungel as berchers, | anunciant la nativeté Dieu 111      [Luke 2:8–14].

E de Jerusalem a SEINT HABRAHAM sunt vij liwes, e la fust Adam fourmé.

And there is a rock on which God placed his own foot, which still is visible and always will be.

And near there is buried a holy woman, by whom no sinner can pass nor approach
69va]    | her tomb.

86      Near there is the place where God performed the Paternoster [Luke 2–4; Matthew 6:9–15].

And near there is a place where God showed himself on Easter to his disciples [Luke 24:36–53].

And from there, at the distance of an English league, is BETHPHAGE. From there
90      God sent Philip and John to Jerusalem for the ass on Palm Sunday. On that day the greatest honor that God had on earth was accorded him by the Hebrew children [John 12:12–13].

And from there you have, to BETHANY where God revived Lazarus [John 11:1–44], two leagues, and nearby was the bishop of Marseilles [i.e., Lazarus's tomb]. And there
95      in Simon's house God pardoned the Magdalen for her sins [Luke 7:36–50].

And from there to the [PRIORY OF] QUARANTENA, where God fasted for forty days and nights [Matthew 4:1–2], are seven leagues.

And near there also is JERICHO.

And from there to the RIVER JORDAN are two leagues to the place where Saint John
100     baptized God [Matthew 3:13–15], and a dove descended on God in the form of the Holy Spirit [Matthew 3:16; Luke 3:22; John 1:32]. And on this road you cannot go any further. But if you go from Jerusalem toward the city of Bethlehem, you will go by [the MONASTERY OF] ST. ELIJAH, one league from the city of Jerusalem. And in that vicinity also is the FIELD OF FLOWERS, a very beautiful place. And there one will receive, so it is said, each according to what he deserves. And near there lies [the
105     TOMB OF] ST. RACHEL.

And from there at one league is BETHLEHEM. And there came the Three Kings to make their gifts — Jaspar, Melchior, and Balthazar — and each among them carried gold, myrrh, and frankincense [Matthew 2:1–12]. In the vicinity of the choir is a WELL where the starlight fell that led the Three Kings. On the other side are the Innocents who were killed [Matthew 2:16–18].

69vb]   And at one league from there the angel appeared to the shepherds, | announcing
111     the nativity of God [Luke 2:8–14].

And from Jerusalem to [the CATHEDRAL CHURCH OF] ST. ABRAHAM are seven leagues, and Adam was fashioned there.

E la deprés est SPELUNCA DUPPLICI [Genesis 23:9–20]. E la fount enclos de mur en char e en os le treis patriarkes Habraham, Ysaac, e Jacob. E la est la SEPULTURE EVE
115    e les treis femmes des patriarkes, en un lyw.

E de coste la vile est une CAVE ou Adam longement habita. E autres merveilles sunt yleque.

E de Jerusalem est j liwe a le lyw ou crust le arbre dount la seinte Croiz fut fet.

E de ileque a ij liwes est SEINT JOHAN DE BOYS, e la nasqui seint Johan le Baptist
120    [Luke 1:57]. E la sunt autres pelrynages plusours.

E de Jerusalem a NAPLES sunt xij liwes. La est PUYTZ JACOB, ou Dieu parla ov la Samaritane [John 4:5–26].

E de ileque a BASQUE, la ou seint Johan le Baptist fust decolee [Matthew 14:8–11], sunt ij liwes.

125    E de yleque a MOUNT HERMON sunt ix liwes.

E de south est la cyté NAMES, e a la porte de la vile Jesu resuscita le fitz de une vedue [Luke 7:11–15].

E de yleque a MOUNT TABOUR sunt ij liwes. E la est une EGLISE ou Dieu se mostra a Piere e a Johan qe il fust Dieu e homme, e tot fust vestu de blanc, e ceux qe la
130    furent cheyerent palmes a terre [Matthew 17:1–8; Mark 9:2–8; Luke 9:28–36].

E de yleque a BEBIE sunt v lyws. E de la si est la MER DE GALYLEE e la entour, en diverse lyws, Dieu fist meinte myracle. E la pres Dieu pust ov ij pesshouns e v payns v^m de homes [Matthew 14:13–21; Mark 6:32–44; Luke 9:10–17; John 6:1–15]. E Piere e André la pres lesserent lur batyl e siwerent Dieu e autres myracles feseient
135    la plusours [Matthew 4:18–20; Mark 1:16–18].

E la de coste est la CHASTIEL MAGDALON la fust la Magdaleyne nee.

E de ileque poez aler a NAZAREZ, la ou Nostre Dame nasqui, e al lu ou le Annunciacioun fust fet a Nostre Dame qe ele concevereit le Salveour de ciel e de terre [Luke 1:26–31].

140    La est une FONTEYNE DE SEINT GABRIEL. La soleit Nostre Dame e soun fitz Jesu quere eawe.

And there nearby is the DOUBLE CAVE [Genesis 23:9–20]. And there are enclosed in a wall the flesh and bones of the three patriarchs Abraham, Isaac, and Jacob. And there is EVE'S SEPULCHER along with the three wives of the patriarchs, in one place.

115

And next to the city is a CAVE where Adam lived for a long time. And other wonders are there.

And from Jerusalem it is one league to the place where grew the tree from which the Holy Cross was made.

And from there at two leagues is [the CHURCH OF] ST. JOHN OF THE WOODS, and there was born Saint John the Baptist [Luke 1:57]. And there are many other pilgrimages there.

120

And from Jerusalem to NABLUS are twelve leagues. There is JACOB'S WELL, where God spoke to the Samaritan [John 4:5–26].

And from there to SEBASTE, where Saint John the Baptist was beheaded [Matthew 14:8–11], are two leagues.

125

And from there to MOUNT HERMON are nine leagues.

And below is the city of NAMES, and at the gate of the city Jesus revived the son of a widow [Luke 7:11–15].

And from there to MOUNT TABOR are two leagues. And a CHURCH is there where God showed himself to Peter and John that he was God and man, and was all clothed in white, and those who were there fell swooning to the ground [Matthew 17:1–8; Mark 9:2–8; Luke 9:28–36].

130

And from there to TIBERIAS are five leagues. And also there is the SEA OF GALILEE about which, in various places, God performed many miracles. And near there God with two fish and five loaves fed five thousand people [Matthew 14:13–21; Mark 6:32–44; Luke 9:10–17; John 6:1–15]. And Peter and Andrew near there left their boat and followed God and performed there many other miracles [Matthew 4:18–20; Mark 1:16–18].

135

And alongside there is the MAGDALEN CASTLE where the Magdalen was born.

And from there you can go to NAZARETH, where Our Lady was born, and to the place where the Annunciation was made to Our Lady that she would conceive the Savior of heaven and earth [Luke 1:26–31].

140

There is a WELL OF ST. GABRIEL. There Our Lady and her son Jesus were accustomed to seek water.

70ra]   E la pres est le saut la ou le Gyws comaunderent Jesu sayler [Luke 4:29] | **[quire 8]**
        pur ce que il lur aprist la parole Dieu, e ileque dist Dieu qe nully serra tenu pur
        prophete in soun pays demeyne [Luke 4:24; compare Matthew 13:57; Mark 6:4; John
145     4:44].

        E de Nazarez a ZAPHORY est j liwe. E ileque nasqui seint Anne, la mere Marie, la
        mere Dieu.

        E de yleqe est j liwe a la CANE GALYLEE, la ou Nostre Seignour fist vyn de eawe en
        la mesoun Architelin [John 2:1–11], e ce fust un des primere myracles que Dieu
150     apartement fist.

        E de yleque a la EGLISE DE SEINT SOFFROUN sunt ij liwes, e la furent seint Johan te
        seint Jame nee.

        E de yleque sunt iij liwes a la EGLISE SEINT NYCHOLAS. E la gist meynt seint cors, e
        pardoun a demesure graunt est graunté a tous que la vendront.

155     De Acres a KOKET est j liwes.

        La devynt Dieu aignel e prist fourme de aignel [John 1:29, 36; compare 1 Corinthians
        5:7].

        E de yleque a SUR sunt ix liwes.

        La precha Jesus la parole Dieu. E une femme ly dit, "Benet seit le ventre qe vous
160     porta e les mameles qe vous aletterent." E Jesu la respondy, "Benet soient que oyent
        la parole Dieu e que la garde bien" [Luke 11:27–28].

        E de ileque a PUTEUS AQUARUM est j liwe [compare Canticles 4:15].

        E de Sur a SERPHENT sunt iiij liwes. La fust seint Elye maundé a une povre femme
        pur delyverer ly e sa meisné de poverté [1 Kings 17:8–24; 2 Kings 4:1–7].

165     E de yleque a SEETE sunt iij liwes. La est une EGLISE DE SEINT SALVEOUR, e la sunt
        relykes plusours. La delivera la femme Cananee Dieu par sa pieté [Matthew
        15:21–28; compare Mark 7:24–30], e autres merveilles sunt la plusours.

        E de yleque a BARUTH par terre ou par eawe sunt ix liwes. La fust en temps auncien
        un ymage de Nostre Seignour, e un Giwz le fery de une launce e le coste, e
70rb]   meyntenaunt en issi sang e eawe. | E pur ceste myracle plusours Gyws se
171     convertyrent a Dieu, e de cet sang est en plusours terres — a Rome, Fraunc,
        Engletere, e en autres liws devers — de qy Dieu fet meynte myracle.

And near there is the leap where the Jews ordered Jesus to leap forth [Luke 4:29]
70ra] | **[quire 8]** since he taught them the word of God, and there God said that none
would be held as a prophet in his own land [Luke 4:24; compare Matthew 13:57;
145 Mark 6:4; John 4:44].

And from Nazareth to SAFFURIYA is one league. And there was born Saint Anne, the
mother of Mary, the mother of God.

And from there is one league to CANA GALILEE, where Our Lord made wine from
water in Architelin's house [John 2:1–11], and this was one of the first miracles that
150 God performed openly.

And from there to the CHURCH OF ST. SAFFRAN are two leagues. And there were
born Saint John and Saint James.

And from there are three leagues to the CHURCH OF ST. NICHOLAS. And many holy
bodies lie there, and pardon of extraordinary magnitude is granted to all those who
come there.

155 From Acre to COQUET is one league.

There God became a lamb and took the form of a lamb [John 1:29, 36; compare 1
Corinthians 5:7].

And from there to TYRE are nine leagues.

Jesus preached the word of God there. And a woman said to him, "Blessed be the
160 womb that carried you and the breasts that nursed you." And Jesus answered her,
"Blessed are those who hear the word of God and keep it well" [Luke 11:27–28].

And from there to the WELL OF WATERS is one league [compare Canticles 4:15].

And from Tyre to SAREPTA are four leagues. There was Saint Elijah sent to a poor
woman to deliver her and her household from poverty [1 Kings 17:8–24; 2 Kings
4:1–7].

165 And from there to SIDON are three leagues. There is the CHURCH OF THE HOLY
SAVIOR, and there are many relics. There God delivered the Canaanite woman for
her piety [Matthew 15:21–28; compare Mark 7:24–30], and many other wonders are
there.

And from there to BEIRUT by land or by sea are nine leagues. There was in ancient
times an image of Our Lord, and a Jew struck it with a lance in the side, and now
70rb] blood and water issue from it. | And on account of this miracle many Jews converted
171 to God, and some of this blood is in many lands — in Rome, France, England, and
in various other places — by which God performs many miracles.

Plusours autre pelrynages sunt en cele terre, que je ne pus, ne ne say, trestouz nomer. De Sardayné, de la Mont Synay, e autres pelrynages qe sunt en celes

175    countrés, ne ay je parlé rien quar les passages sunt estroytes e les veyes longes.


**Les pardouns de Acres**                                          [art. 39]

70rb]   ¶ Ces sunt les pardouns de Acres:

A la bourde la vile: iiij aunz, karantaine.

A Seint Nicholas: iiij aunz, iiij karantaines.

As Alemayns: iiij auns; chescun jour, c jours.

5       A Seint Leonard: j an, c jours.

A Seint Romaunt: xl jours.

A Seint Estevene: iiij aunz, xl jours.

A Seint Samuel: j an, xl jours.

A Seint Lazer de Bethayne: viij aunz, iiij karantaines.

10      A Sepulcre: vij aunz, iiij karataines.

A Nostre Dame de Chevalers: v aunz.

A Nostre Dame de Sur: iij aunz.

A Seinte Croyz: iij aunz, xl jours.

A Seint Marc de Venyse: v aunz.

15      A Seint Lorenz: xl jours.

A Josaphat: iiij aunz, xl jours.

Many other pilgrimages exist in this land, of which I'm either unable, or know not how, to name them all. Of Sardenay, Mount Sinai, and other pilgrimages in these regions, I have said nothing because the paths are narrow and the ways long.

175

**The Pardons of Acre**                                                   [art. 39]

70rb]     ¶ These are the pardons of Acre:

To the edge of the city: four years, one quarantain [forty days].

To [the Cemetery Chapel of] St. Nicholas: four years, four quarantains.

To [the Church and Hospital of St. Mary of the] Germans: four years; each additional day, one hundred days.

5          To [the Abbey Church of] St. Leonard: one year, one hundred days.

To [the Church of] St. Romanus [in the Gardens]: forty days.

To [the Church and Hospital of] St. Stephen: four years, forty days.

To [the Abbey Church of] St. Samuel: one year, forty days.

To [the Church and Monastery of] St. Lazarus of Bethany: eight years, four quarantains.

10         To [the Church of the Holy] Sepulcher: seven years, four quarantains.

To [the Church of] St. Mary of the Knights: five years.

To [the Abbey Church of the Sisters of] St. Mary of Tyre: three years.

To [the Cathedral Church of the] Holy Cross: three years, forty days.

To [the Parish Church of] St. Mark of the Venetians: five years.

15         To [the Parish Church of] St. Laurence [of the Genoese]: forty days.

To [the Abbey Church of St. Mary of the Valley of] Jehoshaphat: four years, forty days.

A la Latyne: j an.

A Seint Pere de Pyse: v aunz.

A Seint Anne: v aunz.

20    A Seint Espyrit: vij aunz.

A Bedlehem: vij aunz.

A Seint André: v aunz.

Al Temple: iiij aunz, vj vintaines jours.

As Frere Prechours: iij aunz, xl jours.

25    A Seint Michel: iiij aunz, iiij karantaines.

As Freres de Sake: c xl jours.

A le Hospital Seint Johan: vij aunz; e tant de foyz come vous alez entour le Paleis de malades: xl jours, e le digmange a processioun: vj karantaines.

A Seint Gyle: v karantaines.

30    A la Magdaleyne: xj aunz.

A la Katerine: iiij aunz, iiij karantaines.

A la Trinité: j an.

A Seinte Bryde: viij aunz.

A Seint Martin de Bretons: iiij aunz, xl jours.

35    A Lazer de Chevalers: xv karantaines.

A Seint Thomas: xv aunz; e chescun mardi, vij aunz.

A Seint Bartholomeu: iiij aunz, iiij karantaines.

To the [Abbey Church of St. Mary] Latin: one year.

To [the Church of] St. Peter of the Pisans: five years.

To [the Abbey Church of] St. Anne: five years.

20      To [the Hospital of] the Holy Spirit: seven years.

To [the Hospital of the Brothers and/or Sisters of] Bethlehem: seven years.

To [the Church of] St. Andrew: five years.

To [the Church and Castle of] the Templars: four years, sixscore days.

To [the Church of] the Preaching Friars [i.e., Dominicans]: three years, forty days.

25      To [the Parish Church of] St. Michael: four years, four quarantains.

To [the House of] the Friars of the Sack: one hundred and forty days.

To the [Church and] Hospital of St. John [the Baptist]: eight years; and as many times as you go around the Palace of the Sick: forty days; and the Sunday procession: six quarantains.

To [the Church and Hospital of] St. Giles: five quarantains.

30      To the [Abbey Church of St. Mary] Magdalen: eleven years.

To the [Hospital of St.] Katherine [of the Battlefield]: four years, four quarantains.

To the [House of the Holy] Trinity [and Captives]: one year.

To [the Church and Hospital of] St. Brigid: eight years.

To [the Hospital of] St. Martin of the Bretons: four years, forty days.

35      To [the Church and Hospital of St.] Lazarus of the Knights: fifteen quarantains.

To [the Church and Hospital of] St. Thomas [the Martyr]: fifteen years; and each Tuesday, seven years.

To [the Leper Hospital of] St. Bartholomew [of Beirut]: four years, four quarantains.

A Seint Antoyne: iiij aunz, xl jours. |

70va]   As Frere Menours: ccc jours.

40   A Repentires: j an, xl jours.

A Seint Denys: iiij anz, iiij karantaines.

A Seint George: vij aunz.

A taunt finent le pelrynages de celes parties e les pardouns de Acres. Qe Dieus eit merci de los vyfs e les mortz. Amen.

**Ne mai no lewed lued libben in londe**          [art. 40]

70va]   ¶ Ne mai no lewed lued libben in londe
        Be he never in hyrt so haver of honde
            So lerede us biledes.
        Yef Ich on molde mote with a mai,
5       Y shal falle hem byfore ant lurnen huere lay,
            Ant rewen alle huere redes!
        Ah bote Y be the furme day on folde hem byfore,
        Ne shal Y nout so skere scapen of huere score —
            So grimly he on me gredes!
10     That Y ne mot me lede ther with mi lawe
        On alle maner othes that heo me wulleth awe
           (Heore boc ase unbredes),
              Heo wendeth bokes unbrad,
              Ant maketh men a moneth amad!
15             Of scathe Y wol me skere,
              Ant fleo from my fere.
              Ne rohte hem whet yt were,
                Boten heo hit had.

        Furst ther sit an old cherl in a blake hure;
20     Of alle that ther sitteth, semeth best syre,
           Ant leyth ys leg o lonke —
        An heme in an herygoud with honginde sleven! —
        Ant mo then fourti him byfore my bales to breven
            In sunnes yef Y songe.
25     Heo pynkes with heore penne on heore parchemyn,
        Ant sayen Y am breved ant ybroht yn
           Of al my weole wlonke;
        Alle heo bueth redy myn routhes to rede!
        Ther Y mot "for menske munte sum mede"

To [the Church and Hospital of] St. Anthony: four years, forty days. |

70va]    To [the House of] the Friars Minor [i.e., Franciscans]: three hundred days.

40       To [the House of] the Penitents [i.e., Magdalenes]: one year, forty days.

To [the Church and Hospital of] St. Denis: four years, four quarantains.

To [the Church of] St. George [of Lydda]: seven years.

Thus end the pilgrimages of these regions and the pardons of Acre. May God have mercy on the living and the dead. Amen.


## Satire on the Consistory Courts                                      [art. 40]

70va]    ¶ No unlettered man may survive in the land
         Unless he be always in court so craftily skilled
              As the learned who lead us about.
         If I should happen to lie on earth with a girl,
5        I must bow before them and learn their law,
              And suffer all their decrees!
         Unless I be before them on the first day in session,
         I shall not entirely escape from their register —
              So angrily do they cry out on me!
10       So that I may not testify for myself in my own defense
         Against many sworn charges by which they'd subdue me
              (As they censure with their book),
                   They turn over unclasped books,
                   And cause men to go mad for a month!
15                      I will clear myself of the charge,
                        And flee from my mistress.
                        They don't care what it was,
                             Except that she made it.


         First there sits an old churl in a black cap;
20       Of all who sit there, he seems most magisterial,
              And lays his leg stretched out —
         A yokel in a cloak with hanging sleeves! —
         And more than forty sit before him to record my penalty
              Should I sink in sins.
25       They stab with their pens on their parchment,
         And say I'm arraigned and brought in
              Despite all my rich respectability;
         All of them are ready to declare my punishments!
         I could "pay there some money for a favor"

30      Ant thonkfulliche hem "thonke."
            Shal Y thonke hem ther er Y go?
            Ye, the maister ant ys men, bo!
                Yef Y am wreint in heore write,
                Thenne am Y bacbite,
35              For moni mon heo maketh wyte
                    Of wymmene wo.


        Yet ther sitteth somenours, syexe other sevene,
        Mysmotinde men alle, by here evene,
            Ant recheth forth heore rolle.
71ra]   Hyrdmen hem hatieth, ant uch mones hyne,
41      For everuch a parosshe heo polketh in pyne,
            Ant clastreth wyth heore colle.
        Nou wol uch fol-clerc that is fayly
        Wende to the bysshop ant bugge bayly
45          (Nys no wyt in is nolle!),
        Come to countene court, couren in a cope,
        Ant suggen he hath privilegie proud of the pope,
            Swart ant al toswolle.
                Aren heo toswolle forswore?
50              Ye, the hatred of helle beo heore:
                    For ther heo beodeth a Boke
                    To sugge ase Y folht toke;
                    Heo shulen in helle on an hoke,
                        Honge therefore!


55      Ther stont up a yeolumon (yeyeth with a yerde)
        Ant hat out an heh (that al the hyrt herde),
            Ant cleopeth "Magge!" ant "Malle!"
        Ant heo cometh bymodered ase a morhen,
        Ant scrynketh for shome ant shometh for men,
60          Uncomely under calle.
        Heo biginneth to shryke ant scremeth anon,
        Ant saith: "By my gabbyng, ne shal hit so gon!"
            Ant "That beo on ou alle!
        That thou shalt me wedde ant welde to wyf!"
65      Ah me were levere with lawe leose my lyf
            Then so to fote hem falle!
                Shal Y to fote falle for mi fo?
                Ye, monie byswyketh heo swo
                    Of thralles Y am ther thrat
70                  That sitteth swart ant forswat;
                    Ther Y mot hente me en hat
                        Er Ich hom go.

30        And gratefully "thank" them.
                  Shall I "thank" them there before I go?
                  Yes, it's the master and his men, both!
                     If I'm written into their record,
                     Then am I in disrepute,
35                   For they lay blame on many a man
                        For women's woe.


          In addition, there sit summoners, six or seven,
          False accusers all, by their appearance,
                  And they stretch out their rolls.
71ra]     Retainers hate them, as does each man's servant,
41        For in every parish they make painful exactions,
                  And ensnare with their nets.
          Now will every fool-clerk who's a loser
          Go to the bishop and buy off a court bailiff
45                (There's no wit in his head!),
          Come to the shire court, squat in a church robe,
          And say he's got exalted privileges of the pope,
                  Threatening and all puffed up.
                     Are they puffed up in perjury?
50                   Yes, hell's hatred is theirs:
                        For there they ask for a Bible
                        To swear that I took a filthy girl;
                        They shall go to hell on a hook,
                           And hang there for that!


55        There stands up a court-crier (goes with a stick)
          And shouts out on high (so all the court heard),
                  And calls "Maggie!" and "Moll!"
          And she comes covered with mud like a moorhen,
          And shrinks for shame and is ashamed before men,
60                Unbecoming under hairnet.
          She begins at once to shriek and scream,
          And says: "By my gabbing, it shall not go so!"
                  And "It's all your fault!
          You must wed me and make me a wife!"
65        But I'd rather by law lose my life
                  Than bow so at their feet!
                     Shall I bow at the foot of my foe?
                     Yes, she deceives so many
                        That I'm threatened there with thralldom,
70                      By those who sit dark and sweaty;
                        There I'm sentenced by force
                           Before I go home.

Such chaffare Y chepe at the chapitre
That maketh moni thryve mon unthenfol to be,
75          With thonkes ful thunne!
Ant seththe Y go coure at constory,
Ant falle to fote uch a fayly:
          Heore is this worldes wynne!
Seththen Y pleide at bisshopes plee,
80     Ah me were levere be sonken y the see,
          In sor, withouten synne.
71va]  At chirche ant thourh cheping ase dogge Y am dryve,
That me were levere of lyve then so forte lyve,
          To care of al my kynne!
85               Atte constorie heo kenneth us care,
          Ant whissheth us evele, ant worse to fare.
                    A pruest proud ase a po
                    Seththe weddeth us bo —
                    Wyde heo worcheth us wo
90                         For wymmene ware!


**Of a mon Matheu thohte**                                    [art. 41]


70vb]  ¶ Of a mon Matheu thohte
Tho he the wynyord whrohte,
          Ant wrot hit on ys boc.
In marewe men he sohte;
5      At under, mo he brohte,
          Ant nom, ant non forsoc.
At mydday ant at non,
He sende hem thider fol son
          To helpen hem with hoc;
10     Huere foreward wes to fon
So the furmest heuede ydon,
          Ase the erst undertoc.


At evesong even neh,
Ydel men yet he seh,
.15       Lomen habbe an honde;
To hem he sayde an heh
That suythe he wes undreh
          So ydel forte stonde.
So hit wes bistad
20     That no mon hem ne bad
          Huere lomes to fonde.
Anon he was byrad
To werk that he hem lad;
          For nyht, nolde he nout wonde.

Such merchandise do I buy at the chapter
As causes many a thriving man to come to grief,
75      With very thin gratitude!
And ever after I go cower at the consistory,
And bow at the foot of every loser:
      Here is the reward of this world!
At that time I played in the bishop's game,
80    But I'd rather have been sunk in the sea,
      In grief, without sin.
71va]  At church and through market I'm driven like a dog,
And I'd rather be dead than live such a way,
      To the sorrow of all my kin!
85       At consistory they teach us grief,
      And wish us evil, and worse to have.
        A priest proud as a peacock
        Afterwards married us both —
        Far and wide they give us woe
90         For the ware of women!

### The Laborers in the Vineyard            [art. 41]

70vb]  ¶ Matthew reflected upon a man
When he worked in the vineyard,
   And wrote it in his book.
In the morning he sought workers;
5    At undern, he brought more,
   And hired, and none dismissed.
At midday and at nones,
He sent them thither quickly
   To help them with cutting hook;
10   Their contract was to receive
The same as the first had done,
   And as the first received.

At close to evensong,
He saw men remaining idle,
15   Having tools in hand;
To them he said emphatically
That he was quite unwilling
   To see them stand so idly.
Then it was determined
20   That none had ordered them
   To use their tools.
Immediately he resolved
That they should work as he assigned them;
   Despite nightfall, he didn't hesitate.

25      Huere hure anyht hue nome,
        He that furst ant last come:
            A peny brod ant bryht.
        This other swore, alle ant some —
        That er were come with lome —
30          That so nes hit nout ryht!
        Ant swore somme unsaht
        That hem wes werk bytaht
            Longe er hit were lyht,
        For ryht were that me raht
35      The mon that al day wraht
            The more mede anyht.


        Thenne seith he, ywis:
        "Why, nath nout uch mon his?
            Holdeth nou or pees!
71rb]   Away, thou art unwis!
41      Tak al that thin ys,
            Ant fare ase foreward wees.
        Yef Y may betere beode
        To mi latere leode,
45          To leve nam Y nout lees;
        To alle that ever hider eode
        To do today my neode,
            Ichulle be wraththelees."


        This world me wurcheth wo!
50      Rooles ase the roo,
            Y sike for unsete,
        Ant mourne, ase man doh mo,
        For doute of foule Fo,
            Hou Y my sunne may bete.
55      This mon that Matheu yef
        A peny that wes so bref —
            This "frely" folk unfete —
        Yet he yyrnden more,
        Ant saide he come wel yore,
60          Ant gonne is love forlete.


**Lenten ys come with love to toune**                          [art. 43]


71va]   ¶ Lenten ys come with love to toune,
        With blosmen ant with briddes roune,
            That al this blisse bryngeth.
        Dayeseyes in this dales,
5       Notes suete of nyhtegales —

25    Their pay at night they accepted,
      They who first and last came:
        A penny broad and bright.
      These others swore, one and all —
      They who had come early —
30       That it wasn't at all right!
      And some unhappy ones swore
      That work had been assigned to them
        Long before it dawned,
      And that it's proper to give
35      The one who worked all day
        The greater reward at night.

      Then he says, indeed:
      "Why, doesn't each have his?
        Hold now your peace!
71rb]   Away, you are foolish!
41      Take all that is yours,
        And behave as was agreed.
      If I may offer better terms
      To my more recent workers,
45       Don't consider me unjust;
      To all who ever came here
      To serve today my need,
        I shall be without anger."

      This world provokes misery in me!
50      Restless as the roe,
        I sigh at the presence of evil,
      And grieve, like the man who labored more,
      In fear of the foul Devil,
        Over how I may atone for my sin.
55      This man to whom Matthew gave
      A penny that was so little —
        This unsatisfied "generous" man —
      Still he desired more,
      And said he had come long before,
60       And did forfeit his master's love.

## Spring                                                                 [art. 43]

71va]   ¶ Springtime comes with love to town,
      With blossoms and birds' secret tunes,
        Bringing all this bliss.
      Daisies spring in these dales,
5      Sweet notes of the nightingales —

Uch foul song singeth!
The threstelcoc him threteth oo;
Away is huere wynter wo,
  When woderove springeth.
10  This foules singeth, ferly fele,
Ant wlyteth on huere wynter wele,
  That al the wode ryngeth!

The rose rayleth hire rode;
The leves on the lyhte wode
15    Waxen al with wille.
The mone mandeth hire bleo;
The lilie is lossom to seo,
  The fenyl ant the fille.
Wowes this wilde drakes;
20  Miles murgeth huere makes,
  Ase strem that striketh stille.
Mody meneth, so doh mo —
Ichot, Ych am on of tho —
  For love that likes ille.

25  The mone mandeth hire lyht;
So doth the semly sonne bryht,
  When briddes singeth breme.
Deawes donketh the dounes;
Deores with huere derne rounes
30    Domes forte deme;
Wormes woweth under cloude;
Wymmen waxeth wounder proude,
  So wel hit wol hem seme,
Yef me shal wonte wille of on,
35  This wunne weole Y wole forgon
  Ant wyht in wode be fleme.

**In May hit murgeth when hit dawes**                    **[art. 44]**

71vb]  ¶ In May hit murgeth when hit dawes
In dounes, with this dueres plawes —
  Ant lef is lyht on lynde,
Blosmes bredeth on the bowes!
5  Al this wylde wyhtes wowes,
  So well Ych underfynde.
Y not non so freoli flour
Ase ledies that beth bryht in bour,
  With love, who mihte hem bynde.
10  So worly wymmen are by west;

                    Each bird sings a song!
                    The song thrush chides o'er and o'er;
                    Departed is their winter woe,
                        When woodruff grows.
10                  These birds sing, amazingly many,
                    And warble about their wealth of joys,
                        Making all the woods to ring!


                    The rose puts on her rosy hue;
                    The leaves on the shimmery wood
15                      Grow large with desire.
                    The moon sends forth her radiance;
                    The lily is gorgeous to behold,
                        The fennel and the chervil.
                    In wooing go these wild drakes;
20                  Animals make merry with their mates,
                        Like stream that flows contentedly.
                    Moody ones complain, and yet do more —
                    I know, for I am one of those —
                        Of love that hardly pleases.


25                  The moon sends forth her light;
                    So does the lovely brilliant sun,
                        While birds sing gloriously.
                    Morning dews soak the downs;
                    Animals with their secret sounds
30                      Wishes may express;
                    Worms make love under ground;
                    Women grow wondrously proud,
                        As well it beseems them.
                    If I shall lack the favor of one,
35                  Such joyful abundance I must forgo
                        And flee to woods in exile.


**Advice to Women**                                    **[art. 44]**


71vb]    ¶ In May it makes us merry when it dawns
                    In hillsides, with these frolicking animals —
                        And leaf is light on linden tree,
                    Blossoms flourish on the boughs!
5                   All these wild creatures woo,
                        As well I perceive.
                    I know no flower so excellent
                    As ladies who shine bright in bower,
                        With love, whoever might bind them.
10                  Such splendid women live to the west;

One of hem Ich herie best
   From Irlond into Ynde!

Wymmen were the beste thing
That shup our heye hevene kyng,
15     Yef feole false nere;
Heo beoth to rad upon huere red
To love ther me hem lastes bed
   When heo shule fenge fere.
Lut in londe are to leve,
20   Thah me hem trewe trouthe yeve,
    For tricherie to yere;
When trichour hath is trouthe yplyht,
Byswyken he hath that suete wyht,
   Thah he hire othes swere.

25   Wymmon, war the with the swyke,
That feir ant freoly ys to fyke;
    Ys fare is o to founde;
So wyde in world ys huere won,
In uch a toune untrewe is on
30     From Leycestre to Lounde.
Of treuthe nis the trichour noht
Bote he habbe is wille ywroht
   At stevenyng, umbe-stounde.
Ah, feyre levedis, be onwar —
35   To late cometh the yeynchar
   When love ou hath ybounde!

72ra]   Wymmen bueth so feyr on hewe,
Ne trow Y none that nere trewe,
    Yef trichour hem ne tahte.
40   Ah, feyre thinges, freoly bore,
When me ou woweth, beth war bifore
   Whuch is worldes ahte!
Al to late is send ageyn
When the ledy liht byleyn
45    Ant lyveth by that he lahte!
Ah, wolde lylie-leor in lyn
Yhere lively lores myn,
   With selthe we weren sahte!

**Heye Louerd, thou here my bone**                          [art. 45]

72ra]   ¶ Heye Louerd, thou here my bone,
That madest middelert ant mone

One of them I praise the most
   From Ireland to India!

Women would be the best thing
Created by our high heaven's king,
15     If many were not false;
They are too hasty in their counsel
To love where men offer them vices
   When they should take a mate.
Few in land may be believed,
20   Though men give them a true pledge,
   Too ready for treachery;
When traitor has plighted his troth,
Deceived he has that sweet creature,
   Though he swears oaths to her.

25   Women, guard yourself from the dissembler,
Who fair and freely comes to flatter;
   His conduct's ever to be tested;
So prevalent in the world is their manner,
In every town there's one untrue
30     From Leicester to Lounde.
Truth means nothing to the traitor
Provided he has performed his will
   In tryst, for a brief time.
Ah, fair ladies, be on guard —
35   Too late comes the turning back
   When love has bound you!

72ra]   Women are so fair in appearance,
I know of none who are not true,
   Unless a traitor taught them.
40   Ah, fair creatures, nobly born,
When men woo you, be well warned
   About the world's peril!
It's all too late to turn back
When the lady lies deflowered
45     And lives by what she got!
Ah, were the lily-cheeked in linen
To listen lovingly to my advice,
   With bliss we would be joined!

**An Old Man's Prayer**                                                    [art. 45]

72ra]   ¶ High Lord, hear my prayer,
Who created earth and moon

   Ant mon of murthes munne.
   Trusti kyng, ant trewe in trone,
5  That thou be with me sahte sone,
    Asoyle me of sunne.
   Fol Ich wes, in folies fayn;
   In luthere lastes Y am layn,
    That maketh myn thryftes thunne.
10  That semly sawes wes woned to seyn;
   Nou is marred al my meyn,
    Away is al my wunne!
     Unwunne haveth myn wonges wet,
     That maketh me routhes rede.
15    Ne semy nout ther Y am set:
    Ther me calleth me "fulle-flet"
     Ant "waynoun-wayteglede"!

   Whil Ich wes in wille wolde,
   In uch a bour among the bolde,
20   Yholde with the heste;
   Nou Y may no fynger folde,
   Lutel loved ant lasse ytolde,
    Yleved with the leste.
   A goute me hath ygreythed so,
25  Ant other eveles monye mo —
    Y not whet bote is beste!
   Thar er wes wilde ase the ro,
   Nou Y swyke — Y mei nout so —
    Hit siweth me so faste!
30    Faste Y wes on horse heh
     Ant werede worly wede;
    Nou is faren al my feh —
    With serewe that Ich hit ever seh —
     A staf ys nou my stede.

72rb]  When Y se steden stythe in stalle,
36  Ant Y go haltinde in the halle,
    Myn huerte gynneth to helde;
   That er wes wildest inwith walle
   Nou is under fote yfalle,
40   Ant mey no fynger felde.
   Ther Ich wes luef, Ich am ful loht,
   Ant alle myn godes me atgoht,
    Myn gomenes waxeth gelde.
   That feyre founden me mete ant cloht,
45  Hue wrieth awey as hue were wroht —
    Such is evel ant elde!
     Evel ant elde ant other wo

    And salvation-minded man.
    Trustworthy king, and true in throne,
5   So you soon accord with me,
     Absolve me of sin.
    I was a fool, pleased with follies;
    In wicked vices I'm embroiled,
     Which makes my assets thin.
10  I once was prone to say wise saws;
    Now damaged is all my strength,
     Away is all my joy!
      Joylessness has wet my cheeks,
       Making me speak of regret.
15    I'm not suited for where I sit:
     There they call me "floor-filler"
      And "good-for-nothing fire-gazer"!

    Once I was in pleasure's power,
    In every room among the noble,
20    Counted among the highest;
    Now I may no finger clasp,
    Little loved and less esteemed,
     Abandoned with the lowest.
    A gout has so afflicted me,
25  And many more ills besides —
     I don't know what remedy's best!
    Where once I was wild as the roe,
    Now I refrain — I'm not able —
     It pursues me so fast!
30    Set I was on lofty horse
     And wore expensive clothes;
     Now gone is all my property —
     I'm sorry I ever saw it —
      A staff is now my steed.

72rb] When I see spirited steeds in stall,
36   While I go haltingly in the hall,
     My heart begins to sink;
    Who once was wildest inside walls
    Am now fallen underfoot,
40    And may no finger clasp.
    Where once beloved, I'm fully despised,
    And all my goods gone from me,
     My pleasures have grown barren.
    They who kindly gave me food and cloth,
45  Now turn away as if they're angry —
     Such is distress and age!
      Distress and age and other woe

   Foleweth me so faste,
   Me thunketh myn herte breketh atuo!
50  Suete God, whi shal hit swo?
    Hou mai hit lengore laste?


  Whil mi lif wes luther ant lees,
  Glotonie mi glemon wes;
   With me he wonede a while.
55  Prude wes my plowe-fere;
  Lecherie my lavendere;
   With hem is Gabbe ant Gyle.
  Coveytise myn keyes bere;
  Nithe ant Onde were mi fere —
60   That bueth folkes fyle!
  Lyare wes mi latymer;
  Sleuthe ant Slep mi bedyver,
   That weneth me unbe-while.
    Umbe-while Y am to whene
65    When Y shal murthes meten;
   Monne mest Y am to mene!
   Lord that hast me lyf to lene,
    Such lotes lef me leten!


  Such lyf Ich have lad fol yore.
70  Merci, Louerd! Y nul namore!
   Bowen Ichulle to bete.
  Syker, hit siweth me ful sore —
  Gabbes les ant luthere lore;
   Sunnes bueth unsete!
75  Godes heste ne huld Y noht,
  Bote ever ageyn is wille Y wroht;
   Mon lereth me to lete!
  Such serewe hath myn sides thurhsoht
  That al Y weolewe away to noht,
80   When Y shal murthes mete.
72va]   To mete murthes Ich wes wel fous,
    Ant comely mon ta calle
    (Y sugge by other ase bi ous),
    Alse ys hirmon halt in hous,
85    Ase heued hount in halle.


  Dredful Deth, why wolt thou dare
  Bryng this body that is so bare
   Ant yn bale ybounde?
  Careful mon ycast in care,
90  Y falewe as flour ylet forthfare;
   Ychabbe myn dethes wounde!

        Pursue me so fast,
       It seems my heart breaks in two!
50         Sweet God, why should it be so?
        How much longer may it last?

When my life was wicked and false,
Gluttony was my minstrel;
  With me he dwelled for a time.
55   Pride was my playmate;
Lechery my laundress;
   With them are Gossip and Guile.
Covetousness carried my keys;
Envy and Anger were my companions —
60     They are vile folks!
Liar was my interpreter;
Sloth and Sleep my bedfellows,
   Who still entertain me from time to time.
    From time to time I'm entertained
65      When I encounter pleasure;
    Of men I'm most to be pitied!
    Lord who has granted me life,
      Such evils let me abandon!

Such a life I've led very long.
70   Mercy, Lord! I won't anymore!
   I'll bow down to atone.
Certainly, they pursue me fiercely —
Gossip's lies and wicked words;
   Sins are unattractive!
75   God's command I didn't uphold,
But ever I acted against his will;
   One teaches me too late!
Such sorrow has pierced through my sides
So that wholly I wither away to nought,
80     When I encounter pleasure.
72va]     To encounter pleasure I was too eager,
      And to be called a fine fellow
    (I speak of others as well as me),
    Regarded as retainer in house,
85     And chief huntsman in hall.

Dreadful Death, why do you delay
To take this body that is so barren
   And bound in misery?
As an anxious man cast in care,
90   I wither as a flower left to die;
   I have my death wound!

Murthes helpeth me no more!
Help me, Lord, er then Ich hore,
     Ant stunt my lyf a stounde!
95   That yokkyn hath yyyrned yore;
Nou hit sereweth him ful sore,
     Ant bringeth him to grounde!
          To grounde hit haveth him ybroht.
               Whet ys the beste bote?
100          Bote heryen him that haht us boht,
               Ure Lord, that al this world hath wroht,
                    Ant fallen him to fote!


Nou Ich am to dethe ydyht.
     Ydon is al my dede.
105  God us lene, of ys lyht,
That we of sontes habben syht
     Ant hevene to mede!
          Amen.


**Ichot a burde in boure bryht** *strategic reading*                              [art. 46]

72va]   ¶ *Blow, northerne wynd,*
*Sent thou me my suetyng!*
*Blow, northerne wynd,*
*Blou! Blou! Blou!*

Ichot a burde in boure bryht
That sully semly is on syht:
Menskful maiden of myht,
     Feir ant fre to fonde.
5    In al this wurhliche won,
A burde of blod ant of bon
Never yete Y nuste non
     Lussomore in londe!
          *Blow, northerne wynd,*
10        *Sent thou me my suetyng!*
          *Blow northerne wynd,*
          *Blou! Blou! Blou!*


With lokkes lefliche ant longe,
With frcount ant face feir to fonde,
15   With murthes monie mote heo monge —
     That brid so breme in boure!
72vb]   With lossom eye grete ant gode,
With browen blysfol under hode —
He that reste him on the rode

        Merriment helps me no more!
        Help me, Lord, before I turn gray,
           And end my life in an instant!
95      He who's yoked to life has yearned long;
        Now it brings him deep sorrow,
           And throws him to the ground!
             To the ground it has thrown him.
              What is the best remedy?
100            Only to praise him who's redeemed us,
            Our Lord, who's created all this world,
             And bow at his foot!

        Now I am prepared for death.
           Done is all my deed.
105     God grant us, of his light,
        That we may envision saints
           And heaven as reward!
           Amen.


**Blow, Northern Wind** *strategic reading*        **[art. 46]**

72va]  ¶ *Blow, northern wind,*
*Send me my sweetheart!*
*Blow, northern wind,*
*Blow! Blow! Blow!*

        I know a lady in a bright bower
        Who's wondrously perfect to behold:
        Graceful maiden of power,
           Fair and excellent to discover.
5       In all this splendid place,
        No woman of blood and bone
        Have I ever yet known
           More lovely in the land!
           *Blow, northern wind,*
10          *Send me my sweetheart!*
           *Blow, northern wind,*
           *Blow! Blow! Blow!*

        With locks beautiful and long,
        With forehead and face fair to see,
15      With many people she may be festive —
           That lady so sparkling in bower!
72vb]  With lovely eyes large and good,
        With eyebrows blissful under hood —
        May he who rests himself on the cross

20          That leflich lyf honoure!
               *Blou, northerne wynd,*
               *Sent thou me my suetyng!*
               *Blow northerne wynd,*
               *Blou! Blou! Blou!*

25          Hire lure lumes liht
            Ase a launterne anyht;
            Hire bleo blykyeth so bryht —
               So feyr heo is, ant fyn!
            A suetly suyre heo hath, to holde,
30          With armes, shuldre, ase mon wolde,
            Ant fyngres feyre forte folde.
               God wolde hue were myn!
                  *Blow, northerne wynd,*
                  *Sent thou me my suetyng!*
35                *Blow northerne wynd,*
                  *Blou! Blou! Blou!*

            Middel heo hath menskful smal;
            Hire loveliche chere as cristal;
            Theghes, legges, fet, ant al,
40             Ywraht wes of the beste.
            A lussum ledy, lasteles
            That sweting is, ant ever wes —
            A betere burde never nes,
               Yheryed with the heste.
45                *Blow, northerne wynd,*
                  *Sent thou me my suetyng!*
                  *Blow northerne wynd,*
                  *Blou! Blou! Blou!*

            Heo is dereworthe in day:
50          Graciouse, stout, ant gay,
            Gentil, jolyf so the jay,
               Wohrliche when heo waketh.
            Maiden murgest of mouth —
            Bi est, bi west, by north, ant south,
55          Ther nis fiele ne crouth
               That such murthes maketh!
                  *Blow, northerne wynd,*
                  *Sent thou me my suetyng!*
                  *Blow northerne wynd,*
60                *Blou! Blou! Blou!*

            Heo is coral of godnesse;
            Heo is rubie of ryhtfulnesse;

20          Honor that lovable life!
                *Blow, northern wind,*
                *Send me my sweetheart!*
                *Blow, northern wind,*
                *Blow! Blow! Blow!*

25          Her cheek gleams with light
            Like a lantern by night;
            Her face shines so bright —
                So fair she is, and refined!
            A pretty neck she has, for embracing,
30          With arms, shoulder, as one would like,
            And fingers fair to clasp.
                Would to God she were mine!
                    *Blow, northern wind,*
                    *Send me my sweetheart!*
35              *Blow, northern wind,*
                *Blow! Blow! Blow!*

            She has a waist delicately small;
            Her lovely face like crystal;
            Thighs, legs, feet, and all,
40              Shaped in the best way.
            A lovely lady, faultless
            That sweetheart is and always was —
            A better woman there's never been,
                Praised among the highest.
45              *Blow, northern wind,*
                *Send me my sweetheart!*
                *Blow, northern wind,*
                *Blow! Blow! Blow!*

            She is precious by day:
50          Gracious, dignified, and amiable,
            Noble, lively as the bluejay,
                Beautiful when she awakens.
            Maiden merriest of mouth —
            By east, by west, by north, and south,
55          There's neither fiddle nor viol
                That creates such joys!
                    *Blow, northern wind,*
                    *Send me my sweetheart!*
                    *Blow, northern wind,*
60              *Blow! Blow! Blow!*

            She is coral of goodness;
            She is ruby of uprightness;

Heo is cristal of clannesse;
    Ant baner of bealte.
65    Heo is lilie of largesse;
Heo is paruenke of prouesse;
Heo is solsecle of suetnesse,
    Ant ledy of lealte.
      *Blow, northerne wynd,*
70       *Sent thou me my suetyng!*
      *Blow northerne wynd,*
      *Blou! Blou! Blou!*

To Love, that leflich is in londe,
Y tolde him, as Ych understonde,
75    Hou this hende hath hent in honde
    On huerte that myn wes,
Ant hire knyhtes me han so soht —
Sykyng, Sorewyng, ant Thoht —
Tho thre me han in bale broht
80    Ageyn the poer of Pees.
      *Blow, northerne wynd,*
      *Sent thou me my suetyng!*
      *Blow northerne wynd,*
      *Blou! Blou! Blou!*

73ra]    To Love Y putte pleyntes mo:
86    Hou Sykyng me hath siwed so;
Ant eke Thoht me thrat to slo
    With maistry, yef he myhte;
Ant Serewe, sore in balful bende,
90    That he wolde, for this hende,
Me lede to my lyves ende,
    Unlahfulliche in lyhte.
      *Blow, northerne wynd,*
      *Sent thou me my suetyng!*
95      *Blow northerne wynd,*
      *Blou! Blou! Blou!*

Hire Love me lustnede, uch word,
Ant beh him to me over bord,
Ant bed me hente that hord
100    Of myne huerte hele:
73rb]    "Ant bisecheth that swete ant swote,
Er then thou falle ase fen of fote,
That heo with the wolle, of bote,
    Dereworthliche dele."
105      *Blow, northerne wynd,*
      *Sent thou me my suetyng!*

She is crystal of chastity;
    And banner of beauty.
65    She is lily of generosity;
She is periwinkle of excellence;
She is marigold of sweetness,
    And lady of loyalty.
      *Blow, northern wind,*
70      *Send me my sweetheart!*
      *Blow, northern wind,*
      *Blow! Blow! Blow!*

To Love, who's beloved everywhere,
I told him, as I understand,
75    How this courteous one has captured in hand
    A heart that was mine,
And her knights have so sought after me —
 Sighing, Sorrowing, and Thought —
Those three have brought me to misery
80    Against the authority of Peace.
      *Blow, northern wind,*
      *Send me my sweetheart!*
      *Blow, northern wind,*
      *Blow! Blow! Blow!*

73ra]    To Love I made further complaints:
86    How Sighing has so pursued me;
And also Thought threatened to slay me
    With force, if he could;
And Sorrow, injured by grievous bondage,
90    Would, on account of this courteous one,
Lead me to my life's end,
    Unlawfully and plainly.
      *Blow, northern wind,*
      *Send me my sweetheart!*
95      *Blow, northern wind,*
      *Blow! Blow! Blow!*

Her Love listened to me, every word,
And bent himself toward me over the table,
And ordered me to embrace that treasure
100    For my heart's cure:
73rb]    "And beseech that sweet and gentle one,
Before you fall like mud off a foot,
That she will with you, for remedy, —
    Affectionately negotiate."
105      *Blow, northern wind,*
      *Send me my sweetheart!*

> *Blow northerne wynd,*
> *Blou! Blou! Blou!*

For hire love Y carke ant care;
110    For hire love Y droupne ant dare;
For hire love my blisse is bare,
        Ant al Ich waxe won!
For hire love in slep Y slake;
For hire love al nyht Ich wake;
115    For hire love mournyng Y make
        More then eny mon!
            *Blow, northerne wynd,*
            *Sent thou me my suetyng!*
            *Blow northerne wynd,*
120        *Blou! Blou! Blou!*

## Alle that beoth of huerte trewe                                    [art. 47]

73r]    ¶ Alle that beoth of huerte trewe,
A stounde herkneth to my song
Of duel that Deth hath diht us newe,
That maketh me syke ant sorewe among:
5      Of a knyht that wes so strong,
Of wham God hath don ys wille.
Me thuncheth that Deth hath don us wrong
That he so sone shal ligge stille.

Al Englond ahte forte knowe
10     Of wham that song is that Y synge:
Of Edward Kyng that lith so lowe;
Yent al this world is nome con springe:
Trewest mon of alle thinge,
Ant in werre war ant wys.
15     For him we ahte oure honden wrynge;
Of Cristendome he ber the pris!

Byfore that oure kyng wes ded,
He speke ase mon that wes in care:
"Clerkes, knyhtes, barouns," he sayde,
20     "Y charge ou, by oure sware,
That ye to Engelonde be trewe.
Y deye! Y ne may lyven na more!
Helpeth mi sone, ant crouneth him newe,
For he is nest to buen ycore.

*Blow, northern wind,*
*Blow! Blow! Blow!*

        For her love I fret and sorrow;
110    For her love I droop and falter;
        For her love my bliss is barren,
            And I grow pale!
        For her love in sleep I slacken;
        For her love all night I awaken;
115    For her love I make mourning
            More than any man!
                *Blow, northern wind,*
                *Send me my sweetheart!*
                *Blow, northern wind,*
120            *Blow! Blow! Blow!*


**The Death of Edward I**                                                 [art. 47]

73r]    ¶ All who are true of heart,
        Listen awhile to my song
        Of a grief Death dealt us recently,
        Making me sigh and constantly mourn:
5        Of a knight who was most strong,
        Through whom God enacted his will.
        I think Death has done us wrong
        That he should lie still so soon.

        All of England ought to know
10      Of whom I sing that song:
        It's of King Edward who lies most low;
        Throughout this world his name grows:
        Truest man in every way,
        And in war prudent and wise.
15      For him we ought to wring our hands;
        Of Christendom he bears the prize!

        Before it happened our king was dead,
        He spoke as a man who felt concern:
        "Clerks, knights, barons," he said,
20      "I charge you, by your oath,
        That you be true to England.
        I die! I may no longer live!
        Help my son, and crown him soon,
        For he is next in line to be chosen.

25    "Ich biquethe myn herte, aryht,
      That hit be write at mi devys:
      Over the see, that hue be diht,
      With fourscore knyhtes, al of pris,
      In werre that buen war ant wys,
30    Agein the hethene forte fyhte
      To wynne the crois that lowe lys;
      Myself Ycholde yef that Y myhte."

      Kyng of Fraunce, thou hevedest sunne
      That thou the counsail woldest fonde
35    To latte the wille of Kyng Edward
      To wende to the Holy Londe,
      That oure kyng hede take on honde
      Al Engelond to yeme ant wysse,
      To wenden into the Holy Londe
40    To wynnen us heveriche blisse!

      The messager to the pope com
      Ant seyde that oure kyng wes ded.
      Ys oune hond the lettre he nom;
      Ywis, is herte wes ful gret.
45    The pope himself the lettre redde,
      Ant spec a word of gret honour:
      "Alas!" he seide, "Is Edward ded?
      Of Cristendome he ber the flour!"

      The pope to is chaumbre wende;
50    For del ne mihte he speke namore.
      Ant after cardinals he sende,
      That muche couthen of Cristes lore
      Bothe the lasse ant eke the more,
      Bed hem bothe rede and synge.
55    Gret deol me myhte se thore!
      Mony mon is honde wrynge!

73v]  The Pope of Peyters stod at is masse,
      With ful gret solempnete.
      Ther me con the soule blesse:
60    "Kyng Edward, honoured thou be!
      God lene thi sone come after the,
      Bringe to ende that thou hast bygonne:
      The Holy Crois ymad of tre —
      So fain thou woldest hit han ywonne!"

65    Jerusalem, thou hast ilore
      The flour of al chivalerie!

25      "I dedicate my heart, truly,
        As shall be written by my command:
        That it be arranged, over the sea,
        With fourscore knights, all of repute,
        Who are in war prudent and wise,
30      To fight against the heathens
        To win the cross that lies low;
        I would go myself were I able."

        King of France, you are to blame
        That you would accept the counsel
35      To stop King Edward's mission
        To travel to the Holy Land,
        Which our king had undertaken
        To rule and guide all of England,
        To travel to the Holy Land
40      To win us heavenly bliss!

        The messenger came to the pope
        And said our king was dead.
        With his own hand he took the letter;
        Indeed, his heart was very heavy.
45      The pope himself read the letter,
        And spoke a word of great honor:
        "Alas!" he said, "Is Edward dead?
        Of Christendom he bore the flower!"

        The pope went to his chamber;
50      For sorrow he couldn't say more.
        And then he sent for the cardinals,
        Who knew much about Christ's lore
        Both lesser and also greater ones,
        Asked them to both read and sing.
55      Men might see great sorrow there!
        Many a man wrung his hands!

73v]    The Pope of Poitiers stood at his mass,
        With very dignified solemnity.
        There men began to bless the soul:
60      "King Edward, may you be honored!
        God grant that your son succeed you,
        And bring to an end what you've begun:
        The Holy Cross made of wood —
        You did so eagerly wish to win it!"

65      Jerusalem, you have lost
        The flower of all chivalry!

Nou Kyng Edward liveth namore.
Alas, that he yet shulde deye!
He wolde ha rered up fol heyye
70   Oure baners that bueth broht to grounde.
Wel longe we mowe clepe and crie
Er we a such kyng han yfounde!

Nou is Edward of Carnarvan
King of Engelond al aplyht.
75   God lete him ner be worse man
Then is fader, ne lasse of myht!
To holden is pore men to ryht,
Ant understonde good consail
Al Engelond forte wisse ant diht,
80   Of gode knyhtes darh him nout fail!

Thah mi tonge were mad of stel,
Ant min herte yyote of bras,
The godnesse myht Y never telle
That with Kyng Edward was.
85   Kyng, as thou art cleped conquerour,
In uch bataille thou hadest pris!
God bringe thi soule to the honour
That ever wes ant ever ys,
That lesteth ay withouten ende.
90   Bidde we, God ant Oure Ledy
        To thilke blisse
            Jesus us sende!
                Amen.

## Lustneth, lordinges, bothe yonge ant olde                    [art. 48]

73v]   ¶ Lustneth, lordinges, bothe yonge ant olde,
Of the Freynsshe men that were so proude ant bolde —
Hou the Flemmysshe men bohten hem ant solde
        Upon a Wednesday.
5    Betere hem were at home in huere londe
Then forte seche Flemmysshe by the see stronde,
Wharethourh moni Frenshe wyf wryngeth hire honde
        Ant singeth "weylaway"!

The Kyng of Fraunce made status newe
10   In the lond of Flaundres, among false ant trewe,
That the commun of Bruges ful sore con arewe,
        And seiden amonges hem:
"Gedere we us togedere hardilyche at ene;

Now King Edward lives no more.
Alas, that he should ever have died!
He would have raised up very high
70      Our banners that are dashed to ground.
We may very long call out and cry
Before we'll have found such a king!

Now is Edward of Carnarvon
All enthroned as king of England.
75      May God never let him be a worse man
Than his father, nor less of strength!
To hold his commons to the law,
And understand good counsel
To guide and instruct all of England,
80      May he not fail to have good knights!

Though my tongue were made of steel,
And my heart constructed of brass,
I might never tell the goodness
That rested with King Edward.
85      King, as you are named conqueror,
In every battle you had the prize!
God bring your soul to the honor
That ever was and ever is,
That lasts forever without end.
90      God and Our Lady, we pray,
    To this bliss
        Jesus us send!
            Amen.

### The Flemish Insurrection                                                [art. 48]

73v]    ¶ Listen, lords, both young and old,
Of the French men who were so proud and arrogant —
How the Flemish men bought and sold them
        On a Wednesday.
5       Better for them to have been home in their country
Than to have sought the Flemish by the seashore,
For which event many a French wife wrings her hands
        And sings "wailaway"!

The King of France made new statutes
10      In the land of Flanders, among false and true,
Which the commons of Bruges began much to resent,
        And said amongst themselves:
"Let's gather ourselves together courageously at once;

Take we the bailifs bi tuenty ant by tene;
15      Clappe we of the heuedes anonen o the grene,
                Ant caste we y the fen."

The webbes ant the fullaris assembleden hem alle
Ant makeden huere consail in huere commune halle,
Token Peter Conyng huere "kyng" to calle
20              Ant beo huere cheveuteyn.
Hue nomen huere rouncyns out of the stalle,
Ant closeden the toun withinne the walle;
Sixti baylies ant ten hue maden adoun falle
                Ant moni another sweyn.

25      Tho wolde the baylies that were come from Fraunce
Dryve the Flemisshe that made the destaunce;
Hue turnden hem ageynes with suerd and with launce,
                Stronge men ant lyht.
Y telle ou, forsothe, for al huere bobaunce,
30      Ne fore the avowerie of the Kyng of Fraunce,
Tuenti score ant fyve haden ther meschaunce
                By day ant eke by nyht.

74r]    Sire Jakes de Seint Poul yherde hou hit was,
Sixtene hundred of horsmen asemblede o the gras!
35      He wende toward Bruges, pas pur pas,
                With swithe gret mounde.
The Flemmysshe yherden telle the cas,
Agynneth to clynken huere basyns of bras,
Ant al hem todryven, ase ston doth the glas,
40              Ant fellen hem to grounde.

Sixtene hundred of horsmen hede ther here fyn;
Hue leyyen y the stretes ystyked ase swyn!
Ther hue loren huere stedes any mony rouncyn
                Thourh huere oune prude.
45      Sire Jakes ascapede by a coynte gyn:
Out at one posterne ther me solde wyn,
Out of the fyhte, hom to ys yn,
                In wel muchele drede.

Tho the Kyng of Fraunce yherde this anon,
50      Assemblede he is dousse pers everuchon
(The proude Eorl of Artoys ant other mony on)
                To come to Paris.
The barouns of Fraunce thider conne gon
Into the paleis that paved is with ston,

Seize the bailiffs by twenty and by ten;
15    We'll chop off the heads at once on the green,
            And cast them in the fen."

The weavers and the fullers all assembled
And held their council in their common hall,
Chose Peter Coning their "king" to be called
20            And be their leader.
They took their horses out of the stall,
And closed the town within the wall;
Sixty bailiffs and ten they made down fall
            And many another man.

25    The bailiffs who'd come from France then attempted
To drive out the Flemish who caused the rebellion;
They turned against them with sword and lance,
            Strong men and nimble.
I tell you, truly, despite all their insolence,
30    And despite the sanction of the King of France,
Twenty score and five met their misfortune
            By day and also by night.

74r]    Sir Jacques de St. Pol heard how it was,
Sixteen hundred horsemen assembled on grass!
35    He traveled toward Bruges, step by step,
            With great military force.
The Flemish heard of the situation,
Begin to clang their gongs of brass,
And smashed them all, as stone breaks glass,
40            And crushed them to ground.

Sixteen hundred horsemen had there their end;
They lay in the street stabbed like swine!
There they lost their steeds and many horses
            Through their own pride.
45    Sir Jacques escaped by a clever trick:
Out at one postern where men sold wine,
Away from the fight, home to his lodging,
            In extreme terror.

As soon as the King of France heard this,
50    He assembled every one of his gentle peers
(The proud Count of Artois and many more)
            To come to Paris.
The barons of France began thither to go
Into the palace that's paved with stone,

55      To jugge the Flemmisshe, to bernen ant to slon
                Thourh the flour-de-lis!

        Thenne seide the Kyng Phelip: "Lustneth nou to me,
        Myn eorles ant my barouns gentil ant fre,
        Goth, faccheth me the traytours ybounde, to my kne,
60              Hastifliche ant blyve."
        Tho suor the Eorl of Seint Poul: "Par la goul De,
        We shule facche the rybaus, wher thi wille be,
        Ant drawen hem with wilde hors out of the countre,
                By thousendes fyve!"

65      Sire Rauf de Nel sayth, the Eorl of Boloyne:
        "Nous ne lerrum en vie chanoun ne moyne
        (Wende we forth anon ritht, withoute eny assoygne),
                Ne no lyves man.
        We shule flo the Conyng and make roste is loyne!
70      The word shal springen of him into Coloyne,
        So hit shal to Acres and into Sesoyne,
                Ant maken him ful wan."

        Sevene eorles ant fourti barouns, ytolde,
        Fiftene hundred knyhtes, proude ant swythe bolde,
75      Sixti thousent swyers, among yunge ant olde,
                Flemmisshe to take.
        The Flemmisshe hardeliche hem com togeynes:
        This proude Freinsshe eorles, huere knyhtes ant huere sweynes,
        Aquelleden ant slowen by hulles ant by pleynes,
80              Al for huere kynges sake!

        This Frenshe come to Flaundres so liht so the hare;
        Er hit were mydnyht, hit fel hem to care!
        Hue were laht by the net so bryd is in snare,
                With rouncin and with stede.
85      The Flemmisshe hem dabbeth o the het bare;
        Hue nolden take for huem raunsoun ne ware;
        Hue doddeth of huere heuedes, fare so hit fare,
                Ant thareto haveth hue nede.

74v]    Thenne seyth the Eorl of Artois: "Y yelde me to the,
90      Peter Conyng by thi nome; yef thou art hende ant fre,
        That Y ne have no shame ne no vylte,
                That Y ne be noud ded."
        Thenne swor a bocher: "By my leaute,
        Shalt thou ner more the Kyng of Fraunce se,
95      Ne in the toun of Bruges in prisone be,
                Thou woldest spene bred!"

55       To judge the Flemish, to burn and to slay
            For the fleur-de-lis!

       Then King Philip said: "Listen to me now,
       My noble and gracious earls and barons,
       Go, fetch me the bound traitors, at my knee,
60            Hastily and quickly."
       Then swore the Count of St. Pol: "By God's throat,
       We'll fetch the rascals, as is your will,
       And drag them with wild horses out of the land,
            By five thousand!"

65       The Count of Bologne, Sir Rauf de Nel, says:
       "We'll not leave alive either canon or monk
       (We'll go forth instantly, without any delay),
            Nor any man living.
       We'll flay the Coning and make his loin roast!
70       The news of him shall carry as far as Cologne,
       And shall also to Acre and as far as Saxony,
            And make him quite pale."

       Seven counts and forty barons, in number,
       Fifteen hundred knights, proud and very bold,
75       Sixty thousand squires, young along with old,
            Set off to take the Flemish.
       The Flemish courageously fought against them:
       These proud French counts, their knights and their men,
       Were slaughtered and slain by hills and by plains,
80            All for their king's sake!

       These French came to Flanders as nimbly as the hare;
       Before it was midnight, the time came to mourn!
       They were caught by the net like a bird in a snare,
            With horse and with steed.
85       The Flemish struck them on the bare head;
       They wouldn't exchange them for ransom or goods;
       They lopped off their heads, happen as it may,
            And that they needed to do.

74v]     Then the Count of Artois says: "I surrender to you,
90       Peter Coning by name; as you're kind and honorable,
       See that I receive neither shame nor disgrace,
            For I'd rather not be dead."
       Then swore a butcher: "By my loyal honor,
       You'll never more see the King of France,
95       Nor be imprisoned in the town of Bruges,
            Where you'd eat bread!"

Ther hy were knulled y the put-falle,
This eorles ant barouns and huere knyhtes alle.
Huere ledies huem mowe abide in boure ant in halle
100        Wel longe!
For hem, mot huere kyng other knyhtes calle,
Other stedes taken out of huere stalle!
Ther hi habbeth dronke bittrere then the galle
        Upon the drue londe!

105    When the Kyng of Fraunce yherde this tydynge,
He smot doun is heued; is honden gon he wrynge!
Thourhout al Fraunce the word bygon to springe.
        Wo wes huem tho!
Muche wes the sorewe ant the wepinge
110    That wes in al Fraunce, among olde ant yynge;
The meste part of the lond bygon forte synge,
        "Alas ant weylawo!"

Awey, thou yunge pope! Whet shal the to rede?
Thou hast lore thin cardinals at thi meste nede,
115    Ne keverest thou hem, nevere for nones kunnes mede —
        Forsothe, Y the telle!
Do the forth to Rome to amende thi misdede;
Bide gode halewen hue lete the betere spede;
Bote thou worche wysloker, thou losest lond ant lede;
120        The coroune wel the felle.

Alas, thou seli Fraunce, for the may thunche shome
That ane fewe fullaris maketh ou so tome;
Sixti thousent on a day hue maden fot-lome,
        With eorl and knyht!
125    Herof habbeth the Flemysshe suithe god game,
Ant suereth bi Seint Omer and eke bi Seint Jame,
Yef hy ther more cometh, hit falleth huem to shame,
        With huem forte fyht!

I telle ou, forsothe, the bataille thus bigon
130    Bituene Fraunce ant Flaundres, hou hue weren fon,
Vor Vrenshe the Eorl of Flaundres in prison heden ydon
        With tresoun untrewe.
Yef the Prince of Walis his lyf habbe mote,
Hit falleth the Kyng of Fraunce bittrore then the sote;
135    Bote he the rather therof welle do bote,
        Wel sore hit shal hym rewe.

There they were knocked into the pit,
These earls and barons and all their knights.
Their ladies must await them in bower and hall
100            Very long!
In their place, their king must call on other knights,
And have other horses taken from their stalls!
There they've drunk more bitterly than the gall
                Upon the dry land!

105     When the King of France heard this tiding,
He cast down his head; his hands he wrung!
Throughout all France the word began to spread.
                Woeful were they then!
Deep was the sorrow and the weeping
110     That happened in all France, among old and young;
Most of the country began to sing,
                "Alas and wailaway!"

Away, you young pope! What advice should you take?
You've lost your cardinals in your greatest need,
115     And never regained them, not for any type of reward —
                Truly, I tell you!
Go forth to Rome to atone for your misdeed;
Pray to the good saints that they let you fare better;
Unless you act more wisely, you'll lose land and people;
120            The crown will defeat you.

Alas, foolish France, for it's to your shame
That just a few fullers can make you so tame;
They crippled sixty thousand in a day,
                Along with count and knight!
125     In this the Flemish have an extremely good sport,
And swear by Saint Omer and also Saint James,
If anymore come there, it'll be to their shame,
                With them to fight!

I tell you, truly, how the battle thus began
130     Between France and Flanders, how they became foes,
Because the French had put the Count of Flanders in prison
                With faithless treason.
If the Prince of Wales might stay alive,
The King of France will suffer more bitterly than soot;
135     Unless he quickly provide full remedy thereof,
                He'll be utterly sorry!

**Marie, pur toun enfaunt**                                      [art. 49]

75ra]  ¶ Marie, pur toun enfaunt,
          Qe est roi tot puissaunt
            E tot le mounde guye,
          Nous seiez de la mort garaunt,
5        Qe li maufé mescreaunt
            Nous ne eit en baylie.

          Ma douce Dame, en vous me fy,
          Car ta doçour me hardy
            De aver en vous fiaunce.
10       Pur ce, Dame, vous cri merci:
          Ne soffrez qe soi maubaily,
            Pur ta seinte puissaunce.

          Par la joie e le douçour
          Que vous aviez icel jour
15          Quant le angle dit, "Marie,
          Virgine seiez, sauntz nul retour,
          Sicome te envoit ton Creatour,
            Mar serrez esbaye."

          Pur la joie, uncore, vous pri,
20       Qe aviez quant il nasqui
            E virgine remeytes:
          Vous noristes, je le vous dy,
          Le fitz Dieu, Jesu, par qui
            En joie vous en estes.

25       Uncore, vous pri pur cel confort
          Qe aviez quant il de mort
            Releva en vie,
          E enfern brusa com ly fort,
          E remena a soun deport
30          Sa douce compagnie.

          Marie, mere Jesu Crist,
          Pur la joie que il vous fist
            Quant il en ciel mounta,
          E la char qe de vous prist,
35       A la destre son pere assist,
            Hautement la corona.

          Pur la joie, mere Marie,
          Qu'il vous fist en ceste vie,
            File Joachyn:

**The Joys of Our Lady**                                             [art. 49]

75ra]     ¶ Mary, on behalf of your child,
          Who is king all-powerful
              And rules the entire world,
          Protect us from death,
5         So that the evil miscreant
              May not have us in his power.

          My gentle Lady, I entrust myself to you,
          For your sweet kindness emboldens me
              To have confidence in you.
10        Therefore, Lady, I beg mercy of you:
          Do not permit that I be seized,
              Through your holy might.

          By the joy and the sweetness
          That you had that day
15            When the angel said, "Mary,
          Be a virgin, without any turning back,
          Whatever your Creator sends to you,
              You will not be dismayed."

          For the joy, also, I pray you,
20        That you had when he was born
              And you remained a virgin:
          You suckled, as I affirm to you,
          The son of God, Jesus, by whom
              You reside in joy.

25        Also, I pray to you for that comfort
          You had when he from death
              Was raised to life,
          And vanquished hell by his power,
          And brought back for his own delight
30            His sweet company.

          Mary, mother of Jesus Christ,
          For the joy that he made for you
              When he ascended to heaven,
          And the flesh that he took from you,
35        Seated at the right hand of his father,
              Crowned by him on high.

          For the joy, mother Mary,
          That he gave you in this life,
              Daughter of Joachim:

75rb]    Ore estes en sa compagnie,
         Des aungles haltement servye,
             E serrez sauntz fyn.

         Pur celes joies qe je vous chaunt,
         De moi qe su repentant,
45           Gloriouse mere,
         Eyez merci quar en mon vivant;
         Serroi vostre lige serjaunt
             En ma povre manere.

         Marie, mere Dee,
50       Pur le tue seinte pieté
             E pur ta grant fraunchise,
         Escu me seiez vers le malfé,
         Que par tey seye salvé
             E ma alme en ciel myse.


**Suete Jesu, king of blysse**                                    **[art. 50]**

75rb]    ¶ Suete Jesu, king of blysse,
         Myn huerte love, min huerte lisse,
         Thou art suete, myd ywisse;
         Wo is him that the shal misse.

5        Suete Jesu, min huerte lyht,
         Thou art day withoute nyht;
         Thou yeve me streinthe ant eke myht
         Forte lovien the aryht.

         Suete Jesu, min huerte bote,
10       In myn huerte thou sete a rote
         Of thi love, that is so swote,
         Ant leve that hit springe mote.

         Suete Jesu, myn huerte gleem,
         Bryhtore then the sonnebeem,
15       Ybore thou were in Bedleheem;
         Thou make me here thi suete dreem.

         Suete Jesu, thi love is suete;
         Wo is him that the shal lete.
         Tharefore me shulden ofte the grete
20       With salte teres ant eye wete.

75rb]    Now you are in his company,
        Waited on by angels on high,
          And shall be without end.

        For these joys that I sing to you,
        Upon me who am repentant,
45        Glorious mother,
        Be merciful for as long as I live;
        I will be your liege servant
          In my poor fashion.

        Mary, mother of God,
50       For your holy compassion
          And for your great generosity,
        Be my shield against the evil one,
        So that through you I may be saved
          And my soul brought to heaven.

## Sweet Jesus, King of Bliss                 [art. 50]

75rb]    ¶ Sweet Jesus, king of bliss,
        My heart's love, my heart's joy,
        You are sweet, most certainly;
        Woe to him who may lack you.

5        Sweet Jesus, my heart's light,
        You are day without night;
        You give me strength and also might
        So to love you truly.

        Sweet Jesus, my heart's remedy,
10      In my heart may you plant a root
        Of your love, which is so sweet,
        And grant that it must grow.

        Sweet Jesus, my heart's gleam,
        Brighter than the sunbeam,
15      You were born in Bethlehem;
        You make me hear your sweet song.

        Sweet Jesus, your love is sweet;
        Woe to him who forsakes you.
        Therefore I should often greet you
20      With salty tears and wet eyes.

Suete Jesu, kyng of londe,
Thou make me fer understonde
That min herte mote fonde
Hou suete bueth thi love-bonde.

75va]     Swete Jesu, Louerd myn,
26        My lyf, myn huerte al is thin;
          Undo myn herte ant liht theryn,
          Ant wite me from Fendes engyn.

          Suete Jesu, my soule fode,
30        Thin werkes bueth bo suete ant gode;
          Thou bohtest me upon the rode;
          For me, thou sheddest thi blode.

          Suete Jesu, me reoweth sore
          Gultes that Y ha wrotht yore;
35        Tharefore Y bidde thin mylse ant ore:
          "Merci, Lord, Y nul na more!"

          Suete Jesu, Louerd God,
          Thou me bohtest with thi blod;
          Out of thin huerte orn the flod;
40        Thi moder hit seh, that the by stod.

          Suete Jesu, bryht ant shene,
          Y preye the, thou here my bene,
          Thourh erndyng of the hevene quene,
          That my bone be nou sene.

45        Suete Jesu, berne best,
          With the Ich hope habbe rest;
          Whether Y be south other west,
          The help of the be me nest.

          Suete Jesu, wel may him be,
50        That the may in blisse se;
          After mi soule let aungles te,
          For me ne gladieth gome ne gle.

          Suete Jesu, hevene kyng,
          Feir ant best of alle thyng,
55        Thou bring me of this longing,
          Ant come to the at myn endyng.

          Suete Jesu, al folkes reed,
          Graunte ous, er we buen ded,

Sweet Jesus, king of earth,
You cause me to understand well
That my heart must experience
How sweet is your love-bond.

75va]   Sweet Jesus, my Lord,
26      My life, my heart is all yours;
        Open my heart and dwell therein,
        And shield me from the Devil's snare.

        Sweet Jesus, my soul's food,
30      Your works are both sweet and good;
        You bought me upon the cross;
        For me, you shed your blood.

        Sweet Jesus, I regret deeply
        Sins I've committed in the past;
35      Therefore I pray your mercy and pardon:
        "Mercy, Lord, I'll do it no more!"

        Sweet Jesus, Lord God,
        You bought me with your blood;
        Out of your heart flowed the flood;
40      Your mother saw it, who by you stood.

        Sweet Jesus, bright and shimmering,
        I pray you, hear my prayer,
        Through intercession of heaven's queen,
        That my request now be seen.

45      Sweet Jesus, best man,
        With you I hope to have rest;
        Whether I be south or west,
        May your help be next to me.

        Sweet Jesus, well may he be
50      Who you may see in paradise;
        Let angels come for my soul,
        For pleasures do not comfort me.

        Sweet Jesus, heaven's king,
        Fair and best of everything,
55      May you deliver me from this sadness,
        That I may come to you at my death.

        Sweet Jesus, all folks' wisdom,
        Grant us, before we are dead,

The underfonge in fourme of bred,
60    Ant seththe to heovene thou us led.


**Jesu Crist, heovene kyng** *strategic reading*                    [art. 51]

75va]    ¶ Jesu Crist, heovene kyng,
         Yef us alle god endyng —
             That bon biddeth the.


         At the biginnyng of mi song,
5        Jesu, Y the preye among,
             In stude, al wher Y be.
75vb]    For thou art kyng of alle,
         To the Y clepie ant calle:
             "Thou have merci of me!"


10       This ender day in o morewenyng,
         With dreri herte ant gret mournyng,
             On mi folie Y thohte.
         One that is so suete a thing,
         That ber Jesu, the hevene kyng,
15           Merci Y besohte.


         Jesu, for thi muchele myht,
         Thou graunte us alle hevene lyht,
             That us so duere bohtes.
         For thi merci, Jesu suete,
20       Thin hondywerk nult thou lete,
             That thou wel yerne sohtes.


         Wel Ichot, ant soth hit ys,
         That in this world nys no blys,
             Bote care, serewe, ant pyne.
25       Tharefore, Ich rede we wurchen so
         That we mowe come to
             The joye withoute fyne!


**Wynter wakeneth al my care** *strategic reading*                 [art. 52]

75vb]    ¶ Wynter wakeneth al my care;
         Nou this leves waxeth bare.
         Ofte Y sike ant mourne sare
             When hit cometh in my thoht
5            Of this worldes joie:
                 Hou hit geth al to noht!

60
To receive you in form of bread,
And lead us afterward to heaven.

**Jesus Christ, Heaven's King** *strategic reading*                    [art. 51]

75va]   ¶ Jesus Christ, heaven's king,
Give us all good ending —
That's the prayer you request.

At the beginning of my song,
5       Jesus, I pray to you all the while,
In place, wherever I be.
75vb]   Because you are king of all,
To you I cry out and call:
"You have mercy on me!"

10      This past day upon a morning,
With heavy heart and great mourning,
I reflected on my folly.
To the one who's so sweet a creature,
Who bore Jesus, the king of heaven,  *— Mary*
15          I besought mercy.

Jesus, for your powerful might,
Grant to us all of heaven's light,
Who bought us so dearly.
On account of your mercy, Jesus sweet,
20      Your handiwork you'll not abandon,
Which you most eagerly sought.

Well I know, and true it is,
That in this world is no bliss,
Just woe, sorrow, and pain.
25      Therefore, I advise that we act so
That we may come to
The joy without end!

**A Winter Song** *strategic reading*                    [art. 52]

75vb]   ¶ Winter awakens all my sorrow;
Now these leaves grow barren.
Often I sigh and sadly mourn
When it enters into my thought
5           Regarding this world's joy:
How it goes all to nought!

Nou hit is, ant nou hit nys,
Also hit ner nere, ywys!
That moni mon seith, soth hit ys:
10    Al goth bote Godes wille;
    Alle we shule deye,
      Thath us like ylle.

Al that gren me graveth grene;
Nou hit faleweth al bydene.
15   Jesu, help that hit be sene,
    Ant shild us from helle,
      For Y not whider Y shal,
        Ne hou longe her duelle.

**When Y se blosmes springe** *strategic reading*      [art. 53]

76r]   ¶ When Y se blosmes springe,
    Ant here foules song,
A suete love-longynge
    Myn herte thourhout stong
5   Al for a love newe
That is so suete ant trewe!
    That gladieth al my song:
Ich wot al myd iwisse
My joie ant eke my blisse
10    On him is al ylong.

When Y miselve stonde
    Ant with myn eyen seo:
Thurled fot ant honde
    With grete nayles threo —
15   Blody wes ys heued —
On him nes nout bileved
    That wes of peynes freo!
Wel wel ohte myn herte
For his love to smerte,
20    Ant sike ant sory beo.

Jesu, milde ant softe,
    Yef me streynthe ant myht
Longen sore ant ofte
    To lovye the aryht.
25   Pyne to tholie ant dreye
For the sone, Marye,
    Thou art so fre ant bryht!
Mayden ant moder mylde,

Now it is, and now it isn't,
As if it had never been, indeed!
What many a man says, true it is:
10      All passes except God's will;
    We all shall die,
        Though we dislike it.

All that seed men bury unripe;
Now it withers all at once.
15      Jesus, help that this be known,
    And shield us from hell,
      For I know not whither I'll go,
        Nor how long here dwell.

**A Spring Song on the Passion**  *strategic reading*                          [art. 53]

76r]    ¶ When I see blossoms spring,
    And hear birds' song,
A sweet love-longing
    Pierces through my heart
5       Entirely for a new love
Who is so sweet and true!
    That gladdens my song:
I know quite certainly
My joy and also my bliss
10      Wholly in him belongs.

When I myself stand
    And with my eyes see:
Pierced in foot and hand
    With three great nails —
15      Bloody was his head —
On him was nothing withheld
    That was of noble suffering!
Very truly ought my heart
Feel pain for his love,
20      And sigh and be sorry.

Jesus, mild and gentle,
    Give me strength and might
To desire deep and oft
    To love you truly.
25      And to suffer and endure pain
For your son, Mary,
    You are so free and bright!
Maiden and mother mild,

          For love of thine childe,
30          Ernde us heven lyht!

          Alas, that Y ne con
            Turne to him my thoht,
          Ant cheosen him to lemmon!
            So duere he us hath yboht
35        With woundes deope ant stronge,
          With peynes sore ant longe,
            Of love ne conne we noht!
          His blod that feol to grounde,
          Of hise suete wounde,
40          Of peyne us hath yboht.

          Jesu, milde ant suete,
            Y synge the mi song;
          Ofte Y the grete
            Ant preye the among:
45        "Let me sunnes lete,
          Ant in this lyve bete
            That Ich have do wrong."
          At oure lyves ende,
          When whe shule wende,
50          Jesu, us undefong.
            Amen.

### Ferroy chaunsoun                                    [art. 54]

76r]   ¶ Ferroy chaunsoun que bien doit estre oyé —
       De ma amie chaunterai qe m'ad deguerpié!
       Bien le sai e bien le voi,
       Qe ele ne me ayme mye,
5          E ele ayme un autre plus de moi,
           E si ad perdu la foy
           Que ele me out plevye!
             *Je pri a Dieu e seint Thomas*
             *Qe il la pardoigne le trespas,*
10           *E je si verroiement le fas*
               *Si ele "merci" me crye!*

       Il n'y a guere passé
       Que je ne la amay sauntz fauceté
       E tot sauntz trycherye —
15         Pur ce me tient ele fol e tot pleyn de folye!
           En verité, le vous dy,
           Si ma amie me ust garny,

For love of your child,
30      Obtain us heaven's light!

Alas, that I cannot
   Turn to him my thought,
And choose him as lover!     *— ab. CB has a similar notion of*
   So dearly he has us bought     *Jesus as a lover*
35   With wounds deep and strong,
With pains sore and long,
   By a love we understand not!
His blood that fell to ground,
From his sweet wound,
40      With pain has redeemed us.

Jesus, mild and sweet,
   I sing to you my song;
Often you I greet
   And pray you all the while:
45   "Let me abandon sins,
And in this life atone
   For what I have done wrong."
At our lives' end,
When we shall pass on,
50      Jesus, us receive.
         Amen.


**I Pray to God and Saint Thomas**                    [art. 54]

76r]    ¶ I'll compose a song that much needs to be heard —
I'll sing of my love who has left me!
Well I know it and well I see it,
How she doesn't love me at all,
5      And loves another more than me,
      And thus has broken the faith
      That she had pledged to me!
         *I pray to God and Saint Thomas*
         *That they forgive her her trespass,*
10         *And very truly will I give it*
            *Should she "mercy" beg me!*

Never has there been a time
That I've not loved her without lie
And completely without guile —
15   For this she deems me a fool and all full of folly!
      In truth, I tell you,
      Had my love welcomed me,

        Je usse pris amye!
          *Je pri a Dieu e seint Thomas*
20           *Qe il la pardoigne le trespas,*
          *E je si verroiement le fas*
            *Si ele "merci" me crye!*

        Certes uncore la ameray,
        Quei que l'em me dye,
25       E par taunt asayerai
        Si amour soit folie.
          Par cest chaunsoun salutz portez
          A ma tresdouce amye,
          Quar ne vueil autre message, quei que je me afye.
30           Si ele die rien de moi,
           Que me ayme en bone foy,
          Ja aylours ne ameroi
            Taunt come su en vie!
            *Je pri a Dieu e seint Thomas*
35           *Qe il la pardoigne le trespas,*
          *E je si verroiement le fas*
            *Si ele "merci" me crye!*

## Dum ludis floribus                                              [art. 55]

76r]    ¶ Dum ludis floribus velud lacivia,
        Le Dieu d'Amour moi tient en tiel angustia,
        Merour me tient de duel e de miseria,
        Si je ne la ay quam amo super omnia.

5       Eius amor tantum me facit fervere
        Qe je ne soi quid possum inde facere;
        Pur ly covent hoc seculum relinquere,
        Si je ne pus l'amour de li perquirere.

        Ele est si bele e gente dame egregia,
10      Cum ele fust imperatoris filia;
        De beal semblant e pulcra continencia,
        Ele est la flur in omni regis curia.

        Quant je la vey, je su in tali gloria,
        Come est la lune celi inter sidera!
15      Dieu la moi doint sua misericordia,
        Beyser e fere que secuntur alia.

        Scripsi hec carmina in tabulis.
        Mon ostel est enmi la vile de Paris.

I would have had a lover!
*I pray to God and Saint Thomas*
20 *That they forgive her her trespass,*
*And very truly will I give it*
*Should she "mercy" beg me!*

Certainly I'll love her still,
No matter what they say to me,
25 And by this I'll ascertain
Whether love be folly.
   May this song carry greetings
   To my dearest gentle love,
   For I won't send a different message, no matter how I'm received.
30      If she speaks of me at all,
     Saying she loves me faithfully,
     Then I'll never love elsewhere
       For as long as I live!
       *I pray to God and Saint Thomas*
35        *That they forgive her her trespass,*
       *And very truly will I give it*
        *Should she "mercy" beg me!*

**While You Play in Flowers**                 **[art. 55]**

76r]   ¶ While you play in flowers as if in wantonness,
The God of Love binds me in such anguish,
Holding for me a mirror of sorrow and misery,
Since I don't have her whom I love above all.

5 Love of her makes me burn so fervently
That I don't know what I can do about it;
For her I must give up this world,
If I can't be worthy of her love.

She's a lady so superbly beautiful and refined,
10 As if she were an emperor's daughter;
Of lovely appearance and beautiful demeanor,
She's the flower in every king's court.

When I see her, I'm in such ecstasy,
Like the moon among the stars of heaven!
15 May God grant her to me by his mercy,
To kiss and do the other things that follow.

I've written these songs on a tablet.
My lodging's amid the city of Paris.

May Y sugge namore, so wel me is;
20    Yef Hi deye for love of hire, duel hit ys!


**Quant fu en ma juvente**                                        [art. 56]

76v]    ¶ Quant fu en ma juvente
        E en ma volenté,
        Molt mis ma entente
        Certe a jolifté.
5       Molt fu pesaunt e lent
        A chescune bounté,
        Ne pensoi de la rente
        Que me serroit demaundé.


        Tut fut mon cuer mis
10      Certe a folour;
        Molt fu en verglis —
        Alas, a icel jour!
        Que trop en ay pris
        De terrien honour,
15      Jour e nuit ma pensé mis
        En trop fol amour.


        Certes, molt desirroi
        Aver lel amisté,
        Mes nule ne trovoi
20      Quant je le oy prové;
        Quant je bien regardoi,
        Ne vi qe vanité.
        Sovent dis "weylowoi"
        De quoi ai je pensé.


25      Un jour m'en aloi deduyre,
        Mon solas querant;
        Avynt par aventure
        Qe je oy un chaunt.
        A ce mis ma cure,
30      Si estois escotaunt —
        Certes, bone e pure
        La dite fut del chaunt!


        La dite du chaunt
        Vous dirroi, come je say;
35      Touz ceus qe vont pensant
        Pur quere amour verray,
        Attendent a mon chaunt!

I may say no more, as seems best;
20      Should I die for love of her, sad it is!


**Song on Jesus' Precious Blood**                          [art. 56]

76v]     ¶ When I was in my youth
         And at my will,
         I eagerly pursued my desire
         Wholly for amusement.
5        I was quite lethargic and slow
         Regarding any virtue,
         Nor did I think of the cost
         That would be exacted of me.

         All my heart was set
10       Entirely on folly;
         Truly I was on slippery ice —
         Alas, for that day!
         When I was over-concerned
         With earthly honor,
15       Day and night I set my mind
         On extremely foolish love.

         Indeed, I deeply desired
         To have true friendship,
         But I found none
20       When I had tried it;
         When I looked closely,
         I saw only vanity.
         Often I said "wailaway"
         About what I desired.

25       One day I went to be amused,
         Seeking my comfort;
         It happened by chance
         That I heard a song.
         To this I paid attention,
30       And I stood listening —
         Indeed, good and pure
         Were the words of the song!

         The words of the song
         I will tell you, as I can;
35       All those who go wishing
         To seek out true love,
         Listen to my song!

Je lur enseigneray
De un ami, fyn amaunt,
40      Bon, bel, e verray.

"Flur de tote bounté,
E de pureté auxi,
Fluret de tote leauté
E de clareté, vous dy,
45      Chescun manere de bounté
Puet um trover en ly.
Flur de tote pieté,
Molt est tresdouz amy.

"Tote manere de douçour
50      Est en cel lel amaunt;
Yl fiet de fyn amour
Plus qe nul vivaunt.
Roy e empereour
A ly sunt obeissaunt.
55      Molt ad il grant honour
Qe ad un tiel amant.

"Jesus est apelé,
Ycel y qe vous dy.
Yl nous ad bien mostré
60      Que il est lel amy,
Pusqe nous ad fourmé
Trestous aprés ly.
Cher nous ad achaté;
Pur nous la mort soffry.

65      "Pusqe nomé vous ay
Qe est cel lel amaunt,
Ne fetez nul delay —
Alez a ly coraunt!
Metez en asay
70      Si ce seit veir qe vous chaunt.
Nul amour, par foi,
Vers celi ne valt un gaunt.

"Pucele est la mere
De celi dount je chaunt.
75      Sur tote rien est lumere
Aprés son cher enfaunt.
Soun fitz est son pere,
Espous, e lel amaunt.

I will instruct them
About a friend, a pure lover,
40      Good, beautiful, and true.

"Flower of all goodness,
And of purity as well,
Little flower of all faithfulness
And brightness, I tell you,
45      Every sort of goodness
May one discover in him.
Flower of all mercy,
Truly he's a most kind friend.

"Every sort of sweet kindness
50      Exists in this true lover;
He pledges purer love
Than any who lives.
King and emperor
Are obedient to him.
55      He acquires very great honor
Who has such a lover.

"Jesus he is called,
Of whom I tell you.
He has shown us well
60      That he's a faithful friend,
Since he has fashioned us
Wholly in his image.
He has bought us dearly;
For us he suffered death.

65      "Since I've named for you
Who is this true lover,
Don't delay at all —
Go to him running!
Put to the test whether
70      What I sing to you be true.
No love, in faith,
Is worth a rag beside this one.

"A maiden is the mother
Of the one of whom I sing.
75      Above all she's the light
After her dear child.
Her son is her father,
Husband, and true lover.

Bonet seit tiele mere
80      E soun douz enfaunt!

"Mes ore vous oyez,
Qe desirrez amour,
Si vous aver volez
De touz amours la flour,
85      Molt covent qe seiez
Estable par tendrour,
E vostre cuer recreiez
De trop terrien honour.

77r]    "Si vous amer volez
90      Jesus enterement,
Chescun amour ohtes
Qe a folie apent,
Quar quanqe vous pensez,
Il siet veroiement
95      Molt covyent qe eyez
Net cuer e talent.

"La playe regardez
Que soffry vostre Creatour,
E le sang veiez
100     Que issist pur vostre amour.
De prier ne cessez
Par nuyt ne par jour;
Orez e plorez
Desque tu senz douçour.

105     "Si goute aver poez
De ce sang precious
Qe li duz Jesu espaundez
Pur vous,
Vostre cuer bien lavez
110     De verrois amours.
A vostre amy priez:
En ly troverez socours.

"Quant bien avez lavé
Vostre cuer de ce sang,
115     Plus pros de li alez
La croyz seiez beysaunt;
En la plaie entrez,
Que est si long e graunt,
Yleqe vous tenez,
120     Ne issez pur nul vivaunt.

        Blessed be such a mother
80       And her sweet child!

        "But now listen,
        You who desire love,
        If you wish to have
        The flower of all loves,
85       It's most fitting that you be
        Steadfast in affection,
        And that your heart refrain
        From excessive worldly honor.

77r]    "If you wish to love
90       Jesus entirely,
        Throw off each love
        That pertains to folly,
        For whatever you think,
        It is certainly
95       Most fitting that you have
        A clean heart and mind.

        "Look at the wound
        That your Creator suffered,
        And see the blood
100     That issued out for your love.
        Don't cease to pray
        By night and by day;
        Worship and cry
        Till you feel compassion.

105     "If you're able to taste
        This precious blood
        That sweet Jesus shed
        For you,
        Wash well your heart
110     With true love.
        Pray to your friend:
        In him you'll find aid.

        "When you've washed well
        Your heart in this blood,
115     Go closer to him
        By bowing to the cross;
        Enter into the wound,
        Which is long and large.
        Hold fast there,
120     Don't issue out for anyone living.

"Le cuer de vostre amy
Seisez e ferm tenez;
Ne dotez nul enymy
Taunt come la demorez.
125 Si tu es assayly,
Cel sang lur mostrez.
Sachez en bon foy
Trestouz les venkerez.

"Marie regardez, pres
130 De la croys esteaunt;
De sa dolour pensez
Come ele estut ploraunt.
Pur amour, la priez
Qe ele vous seit eydaunt.
135 Si amer la volez,
Ne seiez pas dotaunt.

"Parlez a la flur,
E a ly dites taunt:
'De vous nasqui cely
140 Qe soffry peyne graunt
Seiez nostre socour,
Pur soun precious sang;
Deliverez nous de le Enymy
Qe nous est deceyvant.'

145 "A cel seint sang ne puet
Enymy venyr,
Mes son poer fragrant
Qe vous dotez issyr.
Pres de vous ert esteant
150 Pur vous tot dis geytir.
Molt avera peyne grant
Quaunt de ly poez fuyr.

"Si toun cuer lavez
Bien de cet precious sang,
155 E pus estes entrez
En la playe graunt,
E la dame avez,
De nyent serrez dotaunt.
Tempté poez estre,
160 Mes vous averez garaunt.

"Seint Johan regardez,
Qe est le amy Jesu.

"The heart of your friend
Seize and hold tight;
Don't fear any enemy
As long as you dwell there.
125    If you're attacked,
Show them this blood.
Know with good faith
You'll vanquish them all.

"Look at Mary, close
130    To the cross standing;
Think of her sorrow
As she stands crying.
In love, pray to her
That she may help you.
135    If you wish to love her,
Be without fear.

"Talk to the flower,
And speak to her like this:
'From you was born that one
140    Who endured great pain.
Be our assistance,
For his precious blood;
Deliver us from the Enemy
Who is deceiving us.'

145    "Toward that holy blood
The Enemy's not able to come,
But he'll do his very best
To make you afraid to issue out.
Nearby you he's standing
150    To cast you down forever.
He'll suffer great agony
When you're able to flee him.

"If you wash your heart
Well with this precious blood,
155    And then you are entered
Into the great wound,
And you possess the lady,
You'll not fear anything.
You may be tempted,
160    But you'll have a protector.

"Look at Saint John,
Who is Jesus' friend.

          Molt est a ly privez,
          Apelé est soun dru.
165       Cely fust mostré,
          Quant Jesu fust pendu,
          Qe sa douce mere
          A ly baylé fu.

          "Pensez de la dolour
170       Qu'il out pur son amaunt.
          Priez la virgine
          Que ele vous seit aydaunt,
          A Jesu, nostre Creatour,
          Que est soun douz enfaunt,
175       Qe en totes peryls nous seit
          Escu e garaunt."
               Amen.


**Marie, mere al Salveour**                                        [art. 57]

77va]     ¶ Marie, mere al Salveour,
          De totes femmes estes flour.
          Vous estes pleyne de grant doçour.
          Vous estes refu al peccheour.

5         Dame, vous estes virgine e mere,
          Espouse a le haltisme piere.
          Vous estes pleyne de bounté.
          Vous estes dame de pieté.

          Toun fitz, Dame, est vostre pere,
10        E vous file e sa mere.
          Tres bele, tres noble, e tres chere:
          A tous peccheours estes lumere.

          De totes femmes estes la flour
          De pureté e de douz odour.
15        Mestresse estes de lel amour,
          Marie, mere al Salveour.

          Digne ne sui de estre oyé,
          Pur mon desert e ma folie,
          Mes par vous, qe estes douz e pié,
20        Espeir je bien aver la vie.

          Marie, pleyne de bounté,
          Marie, pleyne de charité,

|     | He is very close to him, |
|-----|--------------------------|
|     | He is called his beloved. |
| 165 | It was explained to him, |
|     | When Jesus was hanging, |
|     | That his sweet mother |
|     | Was entrusted to him. |

|     | "Think of the sorrow |
|-----|----------------------|
| 170 | That he felt for his love. |
|     | Pray to the virgin |
|     | That she may help you, |
|     | With Jesus, our Creator, |
|     | Her sweet child, |
| 175 | Who in all dangers may be for us |
|     | Shield and protector." |
|     |         Amen. |

**Mary, Mother of the Savior**                                    [art. 57]

| 77va] | ¶ Mary, mother of the Savior, |
|-------|-------------------------------|
|       | Of all women you are the flower. |
|       | You are full of great compassion. |
|       | You are refuge for the sinner. |

| 5 | Lady, you are virgin and mother, |
|---|----------------------------------|
|   | Spouse to the most exalted father. |
|   | You are full of goodness. |
|   | You are lady of mercy. |

|    | Your son, Lady, is your father, |
|----|---------------------------------|
| 10 | And you, daughter and his mother. |
|    | Very lovely, very noble, and very dear: |
|    | To all sinners you are the light. |

|    | Of all women you are the flower |
|----|---------------------------------|
|    | Of purity and sweet fragrance. |
| 15 | You are mistress of true love, |
|    | Mary, mother of the Savior. |

|    | I'm not worthy of being heard, |
|----|--------------------------------|
|    | For my deeds and my folly, |
|    | But through you, sweet and merciful, |
| 20 | I hope well to attain life. |

|    | Mary, full of goodness, |
|----|-------------------------|
|    | Mary, full of charity, |

Douce est vostre amysté:
De moi, cheitif, eiez pieté.

25      Ton fitz, Dame, me ad cher achaté
E grant amour a moi mostré.
Alas, trop poi le ay pensee,
Qe molt ay ver ly meserré.

Quant je regard mes pecchiez,
30      Bien quide certes estre dampnez.
Mes quant regard je vos grant bountez,
Grant espoir ay de salvetez.

Dame, pur nous devynt enfaunt
Ly douz Jesu, roi puissaunt.
35      Pur vous, Dame, nous ama taunt.
Dame, seiez nostre garaunt.

E nous, par vous, averum la vie,
Quar vous li estes si chere amye,
Qe nule rien a vous desdie.
40      Pensez de nous, douce Marie!

Ave, de totes la plus digne!
Ave, de totes la plus benigne!
Ave, de totes graces signe!
Pur moi priez que su indigne.

45      Mostrez, Dame, qe tu es mere
A toun fitz e a toun pere.
A ly portez ma priere
Qe je pus vere sa chere,
Tresdouce, Dame debonere.

50      Dame, moi donez vostre enfaunt,
Qe de vous si fust l'estaunt.
Par vostre douçour fetez taunt,
Autre chose ne vous demaunt.

**Dulcis Jesu memoria**                                    [art. 58]

77vb]    ¶ Jesu, suete is the love of the.
Nothing so suete may be:
Al that may with eyen se
Haveth no suetnesse ageynes the!

Sweet is your friendship:
On me, wretched, have mercy.

25     Your son, Lady, bought me dearly
And showed me a great love.
Alas, too little have I thought of him,
Having grievously sinned against him.

When I consider my misdeeds,
30     I expect surely to be damned.
But when I consider your utter goodness,
I have great hope of salvation.

Lady, for us became a child
The sweet Jesus, powerful king.
35     For you, Lady, he loved us so much.
Lady, be our protector.

And we will, through you, attain life,
Since you're so dear a friend to him,
He who denies you nothing.
40     Think of us, sweet Mary!

Hail, of all most worthy!
Hail, of all most mild!
Hail, of all graces the sign!
Pray for me who am unworthy.

45     Show, Lady, that you are mother
To your son and to your father.
To him carry my prayer
That I may see his face,
Very gentle, blessed Lady.

50     Lady, give to me your child,
Who through you was made to be.
By your compassion do this much,
No other thing do I ask of you.

**Jesus, Sweet Is the Love of You** [art. 58]

77vb]    ¶ Jesus, sweet is the love of you.
Nothing so sweet may be:
All who may with eyes see
Have no sweetness beside you!

5  Jesu, nothing may be suettere,
  Ne noht in eorthe blysfulere,
  Noht may be feled lykerusere
  Then thou, so suete a luviere.

  Jesu, thi love wes ous so fre
10  That we from hevene brohten the;
  For love thou deore bohtest me,
  For love thou hong on rode-tre.

  Jesu, for love thou tholedest wrong,
  Woundes sore ant pine strong;
15  Thine peynes rykene hit were long,
  Ne may hem tellen spel ne song.

  Jesu, for love thou dreyedest wo,
  Blody stremes ronne the fro,
  That thi bodi wes blake ant blo;
20  For oure sunnes hit wes so.

  Jesu, for love thou stehe on rode,
  For love thou yeve thin heorte blode;
  Love thou madest oure soule fode;
  Thi love us brohte to alle gode.

25  Jesu, mi lemman, thou art so fre
  That thou deyedest for love of me.
  Whet shal Y tharefore yelde the?
  Thar nys noht bote hit love be.

  Jesu my God, Jesu my kyng,
30  Thou ne askesd me non other thing
  Bote trewe love ant eke servyng
  Ant love-teres with suete mournyng.

  Jesu my lyf, Jesu my lyht,
  Ich love the, ant that is ryht;
35  Do me love the with al mi myht,
  Ant for the mournen day ant nyht.

  Jesu, do me so serven the
  That ever mi thoht upon the be;
  With thine suete eyen loke towart me,
40  Ant myldeliche myne, Y preie, al that thou se.

  Jesu, thi love be al my thoht,
  Of other thing ne recche Y noht.

5       Jesus, nothing may be sweeter,
         Or nothing on earth more blissful,
         Nothing may be felt more sensuous
         Than you, so sweet a lover.

         Jesus, your love for us was so gracious
10      That we drew you from heaven;
         For love you dearly purchased me,
         For love you hung on rood-tree.

         Jesus, for love you suffered wrong,
         Grievous wounds and hard pain;
15      To reckon your pains would be long,
         None may tell them by story or song.

         Jesus, for love you suffered agony,
         Bloody streams flowed from you,
         Until your body was black and pale;
20      For our sins it was so.

         Jesus, for love you climbed on rood,
         For love you gave your heart's blood;
         You made love our souls' food;
         Your love brought us to perfect good.

25      Jesus, my lover, you are so generous
         That you died for love of me.
         What shall I therefore give to you?
         There's nothing else but it be love.

         Jesus my God, Jesus my king,
30      You asked of me no other thing
         But true love and also service
         And love-tears with sweet mourning.

         Jesus my life, Jesus my light,
         I love you, and that is right;
35      Let me love you with all my might,
         And mourn for you day and night.

         Jesus, let me so serve you
         That always my thoughts be upon you;
         With your sweet eyes look toward me,
40      And mildly remember, I pray, all you see.

         Jesus, your love is my every thought,
         Of other things I care nothing.

Y yyrne to have thi wille ywroht,
For thou me havest wel deore yboht.


45      Jesu, thah Ich sunful be,
        Wel longe thou havest yspared me;
        The more oh Ich to lovie the
        That thou me havest ben so fre.


        . . . . . . . . . . . . . . . . . . . . . . . .
50      . . . . . . . . . . . . . . . . . . . . . . . .
        Thy bac of thornes, thy nayles thre,
        The sharpe spere that thourh-stong the.


78ra]   Jesu, of love-soth tocknynge:                        [quire 9]
        Thin armes spredeth to mankynde,
55      Thin heued doun-boweth to suete cussinge,
        Thin side al openeth to love-longynge.


        Jesu, when Ich thenke on the,
        Ant loke upon the rode-tre,
        Thi suete body totoren Y se;
60      Hit maketh heorte to smerte me.


        Jesu, the quene that by the stod,
        Of love-teres heo weop a flod;
        Thin woundes ant thin holy blod
        Made hire huerte of dreori mod.


65      Jesu, suete love the dude gretyn;
        Love the made blod to sueten;
        For love thou were sore ybeten;
        Love the dude thi lyf to leten.


        Jesu, fyf woundes Ich fynde in the;
70      Thy love-sprenges tacheth me;
        Of blod ant water the stremes be,
        Us to whosshe from oure fon thre.


        Jesu, my saule drah the to,
        Min heorte opene ant wyde undo,
75      This hure of love, to drynke so
        That fleysshliche lust be al fordo.


        Jesu Crist, do me love the so
        That, wher Y be ant what so Y do,
        Lyf ne deth, weole ne wo,
80      Ne do myn huerte the turne fro.

       I long to have your will done,
       For you have redeemed me most dearly.

45      Jesus, though I be sinful,
       Quite long you have spared me;
       The more ought I to love you
       For you have been so gracious to me.


       . . . . . . . . . . . . . . . . . . . . . . . . .
50      . . . . . . . . . . . . . . . . . . . . . . . .
       Your crown of thorns, your three nails,
       The sharp spear that pierced through you.

78ra]   Jesus, example of love-truth:                                **[quire 9]**
       Your arms spread out to mankind,
55      Your head bowed down for sweet kissing,
       Your side all open for love-longing.

       Jesus, when I think of you,
       And look upon the rood-tree,
       Your sweet body all torn I see;
60      It makes my heart feel pain.

       Jesus, the queen that stood by you,
       Of love-tears she wept a flood;
       Your wounds and your holy blood
       Made her heart feel sorrowful grief.

65      Jesus, sweet love did attack you;
       Love made you to bleed;
       For love you were cruelly beaten;
       Love caused you to lose your life.

       Jesus, five wounds I find on you;
70      Your love-fountains bind me;
       Of blood and water the streams are,
       To wash us from our three foes.

       Jesus, my soul ventures to you,
       Unfasten my heart open and wide,
75      In this hour of love, to drink so
       That fleshly desire is quite vanquished.

       Jesus Christ, let me love you so
       That, wherever I am and whatever I do,
       In life or death, weal or woe,
80      Let my heart never turn from you.

Marie, suete mayde fre,
For Jesu Crist, byseche Y the:
Thi suete sone do lovie me,
Ant make me worthi that Y so be.

85      Jesu, do me that, for thi name,
Me liketh to dreye pyne ant shame,
That is thy soule note ant frame,
Ant make myn herte milde ant tame.

Jesu, al that is fayr to se,
90      Al that to fleyhs mai likyng be,
Al worldes blisse to leten me —
Graunte for the love of the.

Jesu, in the be al my thoht —
Al other blisse ne recch Y noht —
95      When Ich of the mai felen oht,
Thenne is my soule wel ywroht.

Jesu, yef thou forletest me,
What may mi likyng of that Y se?
Mai no god blisse with me be —
100     O, that thou come ageyn to me!

78rb]   Jesu, yef thou bist yeorne bysoht —
When thou comest, ant elles noht —
No fleishliche lust ne wicked thoht
Into myn heorte ne be ybroht.

105     Jesu, mi soule is spoused to the;
Ofte Ych habbe misdon ageynes the;
Jesu, thi merci is wel fre.
"Jesu, merci!" Y crie to the.

Jesu, with herte thi love Y crave;
110     Hit bihoveth nede that ich hit have.
The deu of grace upon me lave,
Ant from alle harme thou me save.

Jesu, from me be al that thyng
That the may be to mislikyng;
115     Al that is nede thou me bryng;
To have thi love is my yyrnyng.

Jesu mi lif, of milde mod,
Mi soule hath gret neode of thi god;

Mary, sweet noble virgin,
For Jesus Christ, I beseech you:
Let your sweet son love me,
And make me so that I be worthy.

85      Jesus, let me, for your name,
Desire to suffer pain and shame,
[For] your soul's benefit and profit,
And make my heart mild and tame.

Jesus, all that is fair to see,
90      All that appeals to flesh,
All worldly bliss may I reject —
Grant this for the love of you.

Jesus, in you are all my thoughts —
I care nothing about all other joys —
95      When I may feel anything of you,
Then is my soul entirely complete.

Jesus, if you forsake me,
What sights may please me?
There would be no good joy for me —
100     O, that you come again to me!

78rb]   Jesus, if you are eagerly besought —
When you come, or else not —
No fleshly desire nor wicked thought
Into my heart can be brought.

105     Jesus, my soul is espoused to you;
Often I have sinned against you;
Jesus, your mercy is very generous.
"Jesus, mercy!" I cry to you.

Jesus, fervently I crave your love;
110     It is essential that I have it.
The dew of grace wash upon me,
And may you save me from all harms.

Jesus, withdraw everything from me
That may be to your displeasure;
115     All that's necessary bring to me;
To have your love is my longing.

Jesus my life, of gentle demeanor,
My soul has great need of your goodness;

Tak hire, treufole ant tholemod,
120     Ant ful hire of thi love-blod.

Jesu my soule, bidde Y the,
Everemore wel us be;
Jesu, almyhtful hevene kyng,
Thi love is a wel derne thing.

125     Jesu, wel mai myn herte se
That milde ant meoke he mot be;
Alle unthewes ant lustes fle
That felen wole the blisse of the.

Jesu, thah Ich be unworthi
130     To love the, Louerd almyhti,
Thi love me maketh to ben hardy,
Ant don me al in thin merci.

Jesu, thi mildenesse froreth me,
For no mon mai so sunful be,
135     Yef he let sunne ant to the fle,
That ne fynd socour at the.

For sunful folk, suete Jesus,
Thou lihtest from the heye hous;
Pore ant loye thou were for ous;
140     Thin heorte love thou sendest ous.

Jesu, forthi byseche Y the,
Thi suete love thou graunte me;
That ich thareto worthi be,
Make me worthi, that art so fre.

145     Jesu, thou art so god a mon!
Thi love Y yyrne al so Y con.
Tharefore ne lette me no mon,
Thah Ich for love be blac ant won.

78va]   Jesu al suete, Jesu al god,
150     Thi love drynketh myn heorte blod;
Thi love me maketh so swythe wod,
That Y ne drede for no flod.

Jesu, thi love is suete ant strong;
Mi lif is al on the ylong.
155     Tech me, Jesu, thi love song
With suete teres ever among.

Take her, obedient and submissive,
120    And fill her with your love's blood.

Jesus my soul, I pray you,
That we be well evermore;
Jesus, almighty king of heaven,
Your love is a very private thing.

125    Jesus, well may my heart see
How mild and meek one must be;
All wicked impulses must flee from
He who would feel the bliss of you.

Jesus, though I be unworthy
130    To love you, Lord almighty,
Your love makes me feel strong,
And sets me wholly in your mercy.

Jesus, your mildness comforts me,
For no one may be so sinful,
135    If he stops sin and turns to you,
That he cannot find succor in you.

For sinful people, sweet Jesus,
You alighted from your noble house;
Poor and humble you became for us;
140    You sent us your heart's love.

Jesus, for that cause I beseech you,
Grant me your sweet love;
So that I may be worthy of it,
Make me worthy, you who are so gracious.

145    Jesus, you are so good a man!
Your love I desire as much as I can.
Therefore don't let anyone hinder me,
Though I for love be pale and wan.

78va]    Jesus all sweet, Jesus all good,
150    Your love drinks my heart's blood;
Your love makes me so entirely enraptured,
That I have no fear of any change.

Jesus, your love is sweet and strong;
My life wholly belongs to you.
155    Teach me, Jesus, your love song
With sweet tears all the while.

Jesu, do me to serven the
Wher in londe so Y be;
When Ich the fynde, wel is me,
160    Yef thou ne woldest awey fle.

Jesu, yef thou be from me go,
Mi soule is fol of serewe ant wo.
Whet may I sugge bote "wolawo"
When mi lif is me atgo?

165    Jesu, thin ore! Thou rewe of me!
For whenne shal Ich come to the?
Jesu, thi lore biddeth me
With al myn herte lovie the.

Jesu mi lif, Jesu my kyng,
170    My soule haveth to the yyrnyng;
When thi wille is to the hire bryng,
Thou art suetest of alle thyng.

Jesu, that deore bohtest me,
Make me worthi come to the;
175    Alle mi sunnes foryef thou me,
That Ich with blisse the mowe se.

Jesu so feir, Jesu so briht,
That I biseche with al my myht,
Bring mi soule into the lyht,
180    Ther is day withoute nyht.

Jesu, thin help at myn endyng,
Ant ine that dredful outwendyng,
Send mi soule god weryyng,
That Y ne drede non eovel thing.

185    Jesu, thi grace that is so fre,
In siker hope do thou me
Atscapen peyne ant come to the,
To the blisse that ay shal be!

Jesu, Jesu, ful wel ben he
190    That yne thi blisse mowen be,
Ant fulliche habbe the love of the!
Suete Jesu, thou graunte hit me!

Jesu, thi love haveth non endyng;
Ther nis no serewe ne no wepyng,

Jesus, cause me to serve you
Wheresoever I am on earth;
When I find you, I am well,
160    If you wish not to turn away.

Jesus, if you are gone from me,
My soul is full of sorrow and woe.
What may I say but "wailaway"
When my life is gone from me?

165    Jesus, your pardon! Have pity on me!
For when shall I come to you?
Jesus, your teaching asks me
With all my heart to love you.

Jesus my life, Jesus my king,
170    My soul feels longing for you;
When your will is to bring her to you,
You are sweetest of everything.

Jesus, who dearly redeemed me,
Make me worthy to come to you;
175    Forgive of me all my sins,
So that I with bliss may see you.

Jesus so fair, Jesus so bright,
Whom I beseech with all my might,
Bring my soul into the light,
180    Where there is day without night.

Jesus, grant your help at my death,
And in that dreadful passage outward,
Send my soul good protection,
So that I fear no evil thing.

185    Jesus, by your grace so generous,
In certain hope may you cause me
To escape pain and come to you,
To the bliss that always shall be!

Jesus, Jesus, very well is he
190    Who in your bliss may reside,
And fully have the love of you!
Sweet Jesus, grant it to me!

Jesus, your love has no end;
There is no sorrow and no weeping,

195      Bote joie ant blisse ant lykyng!
         Suete Jesu, thareto us bryng!
              Amen.


         **Une petite parole**                                              [art. 59]

78vb]       ¶ Une petite parole, seigneurs, escotez!
            De ce que je vous counterai, ne me blamerez,
            Mes moltz des biens aprendre —
            Si vous volez entendre —
5           Trestous vous poez.


               Adam fust, premerement,
            Le premer fet de tote gent.
            Aprés Dieu meismes fust fourmé,
            Come en escrit nous est mostré.
10          E Eve de soun un costé,
            Come Dieu voleit, fust taillé,
            La quele primes fist pecchié,
            Dount nous fumes touz dampné.


               Ce vist Jesu le Salveour,
15          De tot le mound Creatour,
            Que en li fust nostre socour,
            Nostre eyde e nostre honour.
            Honme devynt e enfaunt,
            E pur nous soffry peyne graunt.
20          Molt nous fust verroi amaunt;
            Ne se feyna taunt ne quant
            En la croyz si fu mounté,
            E soun cuer parmi percé.
            Alas, qe tant serroit pené,
25          Cil qe unque ne fist pecchié!
            Des espines fust coronee,
            E d'escourges flaelé.
            Fel a boyvre ly fust doné.
            Molt devoms aver grant pieté
30          De sa benigne humilité.
            Ne fust orgoil en ly trové
            Que pout tendre a nul pecchié.


               Pur ce, vous pri remenbrez
            Quei il soffry pur nos pecchiez,
35          E de ly sovent pensez
            Quant vous estes rien temptez
            De pecchié fere ou folie,

195     Only joy and bliss and pleasure!
        Sweet Jesus, bring us there!
            Amen.


### Sermon on God's Sacrifice and Judgment                                    [art. 59]

78vb]       ¶ To just a few words, sirs, listen!
        For what I'm going to tell you, don't blame me,
        But learn many good things —
        If you'll pay attention —
5       As much as you can.

            Adam was, in the beginning,
        Created first of all people.
        Like God himself was he formed,
        As is shown to us in Scripture.
10      And Eve from one of his ribs,
        As God wished, was fashioned,
        She who first committed a sin,
        For which we were all damned.

            Jesus the Savior saw this,
15      Creator of the whole world,
        Who in himself was our aid,
        Our help and our honor.
        He became man and child,
        And for us he suffered deep agony.
20      Indeed he was for us a true lover;
        He didn't pretend the slightest bit
        When he had mounted on the cross,
        And his heart pierced through.
        Alas, that he was so tormented,
25      He who never committed a sin!
        With thorns he was crowned,
        And with scourges flogged.
        He was given gall to drink.
        Truly we ought to feel deep pity
30      For his meek humility.
        No pride was found in him
        That could point to any sin.

            For this, I ask you to remember
        What he suffered for our sins,
35      And think often on him
        When you are at all tempted
        To commit sin or folly,

             De averice ou envie,
             De hayne ou de lecherie,
40           De coveytise ou glotonie,
             Ou de orgoil ensement,
             Qe est racyne verroiement
             De tous mals ou de tous pecchiez.
             Pur Dieu, de ly vous bien gardez!
45           Quar Lucifer par cel pecchié —
             Que fust de Dieu molt bien amé,
             E en ciel molt halt mounté —
             En enfern chiet tot parfound,
             La ou touz remeyndrount
79ra]        Que en orguil sunt pris:
51           Yleque serrount il tot dis!


                 E, pur ce, si vous seiez
             En grant honour enhauncez,
             E de grant saver aournez,
55           Ou de grant force ou bealtez,
             De ce ne vous enorguyllez —
             Pensez de vous meismes salver!
             E quant temps est a Dieu servyr,
             Ne pas tousjours a gayner.
60           Ne facez pas come les uns fount,
             Que de Dieu rien ne pensount,
             Mes tot ount doné lur cuer,
             Nuit e jour, a lur gaigner.
             Des queux il fet a merviler:
65           De Dieu ne pensent ne de sa mort,
             Mes si il puissent rien a tort
             Gaygner par nulle faucine,
             Ou par robberie ou par ravyne;
             De averice sunt englywe,
70           Q'est un mortel pecchié.
             Jamés ne quident assez aver,
             Mes, come la terre, lur dust failer.
             De quele gent fet a doter
             Si il ne se vueillent amender.


75               Pur ce, vous pri je bonement
             Qe vous donez entendement,
             E ce, qe vous oiez counter,
             Afforcez vous de ce tener,
             E aprés cel trestouz overyr.
80           Ne coveitez pas autrui bienz
             A tort aver pur nulle rienz,
             Mes, qe dount vivre assez eyez,

By avarice or envy,
By hatred or by lust,
40  By covetousness or gluttony,
Or by pride as well,
Which is truly the root
Of all evils and of all sins.
By God, defend yourself from it well!
45  For by this sin Lucifer —
Who was of God much beloved,
And in heaven exalted very high —
Fell exceedingly far to hell,
Where all will remain
79ra]  Who are taken in pride:
51  There they will abide forever!

And, therefore, if you should be
Lifted up in great honor,
And adorned with great wisdom,
55  Or with great strength or beauty,
Do not pride yourself in this —
Think on saving yourself!
And when it's time to serve God,
Don't always [dwell] on profit.
60  Don't do as others do,
Who don't at all think on God,
But wholly have set their intent,
Night and day, on their own profit.
Of them, it is incredible:
65  They think not on God nor on his death,
But only on how they can wrongfully
Gain by some deceit,
Or by robbery or by theft;
They're defiled by avarice,
70  Which is a mortal sin.
They never believe they have enough,
But, like earth, it must fail them.
One must fear for such people
If they don't wish to amend.

75  Therefore, I ask in good faith
That you pay attention,
And that, of what you hear related,
You strive to adhere to it,
And afterward bring all of it about.
80  Don't covet to have wrongfully
In any way the goods of others,
But, that you may have enough to live,

Lealmentz travilez.
E si rien eiez a tort,
85      Purpensez vous devant la mort
Yce rendre, si vous poez,
A ly de qui vous le avyez.
Si il seit mort qe vous quidez,
Pur sa alme le donez,
90      Issi qe en peril ne seiez,
Pur ce qe, devant Jesu,
De respoundre sumes tenu
De quanqe nous avoms resçu.


Molt serra estroit acounte,
95      Molt en averunt il grant hounte
79rb]   Que lors serrunt accusez
E de lur pecchiez reprovez.
Touz nos faitz e touz nos ditz
Que en pecchié nous ount mys
100     Serrount en nos frountz escritz.
Yl n'y avera nul pleder,
Jour de amour ne acorder,
Ne nul qe purra acounter,
Pur argent ne pur or gaygner.
105     Alas, que froms nous ycel jour,
Quant Jesu vendra, le Salveour,
Trestot come il fust crucifié,
E come il fust des Gyws pené,
E come il fust al cuer naufré,
110     Piés e meyns parmi piercé?
Riant ne serra nul trové
Que ly averount regardé.
Molt serra hidous quant jugera.
N'y avera nul qe noise fra.
115     Chescun serra rewerdoné
Come il avera deservy gré:
En grant joie les bons irrount
E la sauntz fyn remeindrount
Ou totes maneres de joies sunt!


120     Pur ce, vous vueil je ore garnyr
Que vous pensez a Dieu servyr
E la joie graunde aver
Que nulle lange puet counter.
Ycel nous doint ly Salveour,
125     De cel e terre empereour.
Amen, amen, pur sa douçour.

Work faithfully.
And if you have anything wrongfully,
85 Resolve before your death
To return it, if you can,
To him from whom you had it.
If the one in question should be dead,
Donate it for his soul,
90 So that you not be in danger,
Because, before Jesus,
We are held to answer
For whatever we've received.

Narrow indeed will be the reckoning,
95 Truly they will have great shame
79rb] Who will then be accused
And punished for their sins.
All our deeds and all our words
That we've committed in sin
100 Will be written on our foreheads.
There will be no pleading,
Loveday or reconciliation,
Nor will any be able to render account,
To profit with silver or with gold.
105 Alas, what will we do that day,
When Jesus will come, the Savior,
Exactly as he was crucified,
And as he was tormented by the Jews,
And as he was wounded in heart,
110 Feet and hands pierced through?
None will be found laughing
Who has looked at him.
It will be truly horrible when he judges.
No one will make a sound.
115 Each one will be rewarded
As he has merited grace:
Into great joy the virtuous will go
And remain without end
Where all manner of joys abide!

120 Therefore, I wish to warn you now
To resolve to serve God
And possess the great joy
That no tongue can describe.
May the Savior give this to us,
125 The emperor of heaven and earth.
Amen, amen, for his sweet kindness.

**Stond wel, moder, under rode** *streategic reeardiy*                    [art. 60]

79rb] ¶ "Stond wel, Moder, under rode,                    **[Jesus]**
Byholt thy sone with glade mode;
   Blythe moder myht thou be."
"Sone, hou shulde Y blithe stonde?                    **[Mary]**
5    Y se thin fet, Y se thin honde
   Nayled to the harde tre."

"Moder, do wey thy wepinge.                    **[Jesus]**
Y thole deth for monkynde;
   For my gult thole Y non."
10   "Sone, Y fele the dede stounde.                    **[Mary]**
The suert is at myn herte grounde
   That me byhet Symeon."

79va] "Moder, merci! Let me deye                    **[Jesus]**
For Adam out of helle beye
15    Ant his kun that is forlore."
"Sone, what shal me to rede?                    **[Mary]**
My peyne pyneth me to dede;
   Lat me deye the byfore."

"Moder, thou rewe al of thy bern;                    **[Jesus]**
20   Thou wosshe awai the blody tern.
   Hit doth me worse then my ded."
"Sone, hou may Y teres werne?                    **[Mary]**
Y se the blody stremes erne
   From thin herte to my fet."

25   "Moder, nou Y may the seye,                    **[Jesus]**
Betere is that Ich one deye
   Then al monkunde to helle go."
"Sone, Y se thi bodi byswongen,                    **[Mary]**
Fet ant honden thourhout stongen —
30   No wonder thah me be wo."

"Moder, now Y shal the telle                    **[Jesus]**
Yef Y ne deye, thou gost to helle;
   Y thole ded for thine sake."
"Sone, thou art so meke ant mynde;                    **[Mary]**
35   Ne wyt me naht — hit is my kynde
   That Y for the this sorewe make."

"Moder, nou thou miht wel leren                    **[Jesus]**
Whet sorewe haveth that children beren,
   Whet sorewe hit is with childe gon."

## Stand Well, Mother, under Rood  *strategic reading*                    [art. 60]

| | | |
|---|---|---|
| 79rb] | ¶ "Stand well, Mother, under <u>rood</u>, | **[Jesus]** |
| | Behold your son with gladness; | |
| | Joyful mother may you be." | |
| | "Son, how may I stand happily? | **[Mary]** |
| 5 | I see your feet, I see your hands | |
| | Nailed to the hard tree." | |
| | | |
| | "Mother, cease your weeping. | **[Jesus]** |
| | I suffer death for mankind; | |
| | I suffer nothing for my own guilt." | |
| 10 | "Son, I feel your death's wound. | **[Mary]** |
| | The sword is piercing my heart | |
| | As Simeon promised me." | |
| | | |
| 79va] | "Mother, mercy! Let me die | **[Jesus]** |
| | In order to redeem Adam out of hell | |
| 15 | And his kindred who are lost." | |
| | "Son, what am I to do? | **[Mary]** |
| | My pain tortures me to death; | |
| | Let me die before you." | |
| | | |
| | "Mother, you suffer much for your child; | **[Jesus]** |
| 20 | Wash away your bloody tears. | |
| | It pains me worse than my death." | |
| | "Son, how may I hold back tears? | **[Mary]** |
| | I see the bloody streams flow | |
| | From your heart to my feet." | |
| | | |
| 25 | "Mother, now I may explain to you, | **[Jesus]** |
| | It's better that I die one day | |
| | Than for all mankind to go to hell." | |
| | "Son, I see your body tormented, | **[Mary]** |
| | Feet and hands pierced through — | |
| 30 | It's no wonder I'm distraught." | |
| | | |
| | "Mother, now I will tell you | **[Jesus]** |
| | That if I don't die, you'll go to hell; | |
| | I suffer death for your sake." | |
| | "Son, you are so gentle and kind; | **[Mary]** |
| 35 | Don't reproach me — it's my nature | |
| | That I express this grief for you." | |
| | | |
| | "Mother, now you may well know | **[Jesus]** |
| | What sorrow have they who bear children, | |
| | What sorrow it is to go with child." | |

40      "Sorewe, ywis, Y con the telle;                        **[Mary]**
        Bote hit be the pyne of helle,
            More serewe wot Y non!"

        "Moder, rew of moder kare,                              **[Jesus]**
        For nou thou wost of moder fare
45          Thou thou be clene mayden-mon."
        "Sone, help at alle nede,                               **[Mary]**
        Alle tho that to me grede,
            Maiden, wif, ant fol wymmon."

        "Moder, may Y no lengore duelle:                        **[Jesus]**
50      The time is come, Y shal to helle;
            The thridde day Y ryse upon."
        "Sone, Y wil with the founden;                          **[Mary]**
        Y deye, ywis, for thine wounden.
            So soreweful ded nes never non!"

55      When he ros, tho fel hire sorewe;                       **[Narrator]**
        Hire blisse sprong the thridde morewe:
            Blythe moder were thou tho!
79vb]   Levedy, for that ilke blisse,
        Bysech thi sone, of sunnes lisse;
60          Thou be oure sheld ageyn oure fo.

        Blessed be thou, ful of blysse;
        Let us never hevene misse
            Thourh thi suete sones myht.
        Louerd, for that ilke blod
65      That thou sheddest on the rod,
            Thou bryng us into hevene lyht!
                Amen.


        **Jesu, for thi muchele miht**                          **[art. 61]**


79vb]   ¶ Jesu, for thi muchele miht,
            Thou yef us, of thi grace,
        That we mowe, dai ant nyht,
            Thenken o thi face.
5       In myn herte hit doth me god
        When Y thenke on Jesu blod
            That ran doun bi ys syde,
        From is herte doun to is fot;
        For ous he spradde is herte blod —
10          His wondes were so wyde!

40   "Sorrow, indeed, I can tell to you;                    **[Mary]**
     Unless it be the pain of hell,
        More sorrow I cannot imagine!"

     "Mother, have pity for mothers' worry,                **[Jesus]**
     For now you know a mother's plight
45      Though you are a clean virgin."
     "Son, help all who are in need,                       **[Mary]**
     All of those who call to me,
        Maiden, wife, and sinful woman."

     "Mother, I may remain no longer:                      **[Jesus]**
50   The time has come, I will go to hell;
        Upon the third day I will rise."
     "Son, I wish to go with you;                          **[Mary]**
     I die, indeed, for your wounds.
        So sorrowful a death was never!"

55   When he arose, then her sorrow ceased;                **[Narrator]**
     Her bliss sprang up on the third morrow:
        Joyful mother were you then!
79vb] Lady, for that same bliss,
     Beseech your son, for joy of your son;
60      Be our shield against our foe.

     Blessed be you, full of bliss;
     Let us never heaven miss
        Through your sweet son's might.
     Lord, for that same blood
65   That you shed on the rood,
        Bring us into heaven's light!
           Amen.

**Jesus, by Your Great Might**                             **[art. 61]**

79vb] ¶ Jesus, by your great might,
        Grant us, of your grace,
     That we may, day and night,
        Think on your countenance.
5    In my heart it does me good
     When I think on Jesus' blood
        That flowed down by his side,
     From his heart down to his foot;
     For us he spilled his heart's blood —
10      His wounds were so wide!

When Y thenke on Jesu ded,
   Min herte overwerpes;
Mi soule is won so is the led
   For mi fole werkes.
15    Ful wo is that ilke mon
That Jesu ded no thenkes on,
   What he soffrede so sore.
For my synnes Y wil wete,
Ant alle Y wyle hem forlete,
20      Nou ant evermore.

Mon that is in joie ant blis,
   Ant lith in shame ant synne,
He is more then unwis
   That therof nul nout blynne.
25    Al this world, hit geth away;
Me thynketh hit neyyth Domesday;
   Nou man gos to grounde.
Jesu Crist that tholede ded,
He may oure soules to hevene led
30      Withinne a lutel stounde.

Thah thou have al thi wille,
   Thenk on Godes wondes,
For that we ne shulde spille.
   He tholede harde stoundes;
35    Al for mon he tholede ded,
Yyf he wyle leve on is red
   Ant leve his folie.
We shule have joie ant blis
More then we conne seien, ywys,
40      In Jesu compagnie!

Jesu, that wes milde ant fre,
   Wes with spere ystongen;
He was nailed to the tre,
   With scourges yswongen.
45    Al for mon he tholede shame,
Withouten gult, withouten blame,
   Bothe day ant other.
Mon, ful muchel he lovede the
When he wolde make the fre
50      Ant bicome thi brother.

When I think on Jesus' death,
   My heart is downcast;
My soul is ashen as lead
   On account of my sinful works.
15    Most woeful is that same man
Who thinks not on Jesus' death,
   What he suffered so grievously.
For my sins I will shed tears,
And I will wholly renounce them,
20     Now and evermore.

Man who is in joy and bliss,
   And lies in shame and sin,
He is more than unwise
   Who will not cease thereof.
25    All this world, it goes away;
I think it approaches Doomsday;
   Now man goes to ground.
Jesus Christ who suffered death,
He may lead our souls to heaven
30     Within a little while.

Though you have all your will,
   Think on God's wounds,
By which we will not perish.
   He endured hard pangs;
35    All for man he suffered death,
If man will believe in his command
   And leave behind his folly.
We will have joy and bliss
More than we can express, indeed,
40     In Jesus' company!

Jesus, who was mild and gracious,
   Was pierced with a spear;
He was nailed to the tree,
   With scourges flogged.
45    All for man he suffered shame,
Without guilt, without blame,
   Both day and other.
Man, he loved you very much
When he wished to make you free
50     And become your brother.

**I syke when Y singe** *strategic reading*                    [art. 62]

80ra]    ¶ I syke when Y singe
    For sorewe that Y se,
When Y, with wypinge,
    Biholde upon the tre
5    Ant se Jesu the suete:
Is herte blod forlete
    For the love of me;
Ys woundes waxen wete;
Thei wepen, stille ant mete.
10        Marie, reweth the.

Heye upon a doune
    Ther al folk hit se may,
A mile from uch toune,
    Aboute the midday,
15    The rode is up arered;
His frendes aren afered
    Ant clyngeth so the clay.
The rode stond in stone;
Marie stont hire one
20        Ant seith, "weylaway."

When Y the biholde
    With eyyen bryhte bo,
Ant thi bodi colde,
    Thi ble waxeth blo,
25    Thou hengest al of blode,
So heye upon the rode
    Bituene theves tuo —
Who may syke more?
Marie wepeth sore
30        Ant siht al this wo.

The naylles beth to stronge;
    The smythes are to sleye;
Thou bledest al to longe;
    The tre is al to heyye;
35    The stones beoth al wete!
Alas, Jesu the suete,
    For nou frend hast thou non
Both Seint Johan mournynde,
Ant Marie wepynde,
40        For pyne that the ys on.

**I Sigh When I Sing** *strategic reading*                                 [art. 62]

80ra]     ¶ I sigh when I sing
              For sorrow that I see,
          When I, with weeping,
              Look upon the tree
5         And see Jesus the sweet:
          His heart's blood shed
              For the love of me;
          His wounds grow wet;
          They weep, quiet and proper.
10            Mary, it grieves you.

          High upon a hill
              Where all folk may see it,
          A mile from any town,
              About midday,
15        The cross is raised up;
          His friends are afraid
              And recoil like the clay.
          The cross stands in stone;
          Mary stands alone
20            And says, "wailaway."

          When I behold you
              With both keen eyes,
          And see your body cold,
              Your face grows ashen pale,
25        You hang all blood-strewn,
          So high upon the cross
              Between two thieves —
          Who may sigh more?
          Mary weeps mournfully
30            And saw all this agony.

          The nails be too strong;
              The smiths are too skilled;
          You bleed all too long;
              The tree is all too high;
35        The stones be all wet!
          Alas, Jesus the sweet,
              For now you have no friend
          Except Saint John mourning,
          And Mary weeping,
40            For the pain that you are in.

Ofte when Y sike
   Ant makie my mon,
Wel ille thah me like,
   Wonder is hit non,
45     When Y se honge heye,
Ant bittre pynes dreye,
   Jesu, my lemmon!
His wondes sore smerte;
The spere al to is herte
50       Ant thourh is sydes gon.

Ofte when Y syke,
   With care Y am thourhsoht;
When Y wake, Y wyke;
   Of serewe is al mi thoht.
55     Alas, men beth wode
That suereth by the rode,
   Ant selleth him for noht!
That bohte us out of synne,
He bring us to wynne,
60       That hath us duere boht.

### Nou skrinketh rose ant lylie-flour [art. 63]

80rb]   ¶ Nou skrinketh rose ant lylie-flour
That whilen ber that suete savour
   In somer, that suete tyde;
Ne is no quene so stark ne stour,
5     Ne no levedy so bryht in bour,
   That ded ne shal byglyde.
Whose wol fleysh lust forgon
   Ant hevene blis abyde,
On Jesu be is thoht anon,
10       That therled was ys side.

From Petresbourh in o morewenyng,
As Y me wende o my pleyyyng,
   On mi folie Y thohte;
Menen Y gon my mournyng
15     To hire that ber the hevene kyng,
   Of merci hire bysohte:
"Ledy, preye thi sone for ous,
   That us duere bohte,
Ant shild us from the lothe hous
20       That to the Fend is wrohte!"

Often when I sigh
   And utter my lament,
Though I like it very ill,
   Wonder is it none,
45    When I see hung high,
And bitter pains suffered,
   Jesus, my lover!     — similar to art. 54
His wounds sorely hurt;
The spear all through his heart
50      And through his sides gone.

Often when I sigh,
   With care I am pierced through;
When I awake, I weaken;
   Of sorrow is all my thought.
55    Alas, men are crazed
Who swear by the cross,
   And sell him for nought!
He who redeemed us out of sin,
May he bring us to bliss,
60      Who has us dearly bought.

**An Autumn Song**                                                            [art. 63]

80rb]    ¶ Now wither rose and lily-flower
That once bore such sweet scent
   In summer, that sweet season;
There's no queen so mighty or strong,
5    Nor any lady so beautiful in bower,
   Whom death will not steal away.
Whoever will forego fleshly lust
   And wait for heaven's bliss,
On Jesus is forever his thought,
10      Whose side was pierced through.

From Peterborough one morning,
As I took my way for pleasure,
   I reflected on my folly;
I began to utter my lament
15    To her who bore the heaven's king,
   I besought her for mercy:
"Lady, pray to your son for us,
   He who bought us dearly,
And shield us from the loathsome house
20      That's made for the Devil!"

Myn herte of dedes wes fordred
Of synne that Y have my fleish fed,
    Ant folewed al my tyme,
That Y not whider I shal be led
25   When Y lygge on dethes bed,
    In joie ore into pyne.
On o Ledy myn hope is,
    Moder ant virgyne;
Whe shulen into hevene blis
30      Thurh hire medicine.

Betere is hire medycyn
Then eny mede or eny wyn;
    Hire erbes smulleth suete!
From Catenas into Dyvelyn,
35   Nis ther no leche so fyn
    Oure serewes to bete.
Mon that feleth eni sor
    Ant his folie wol lete,
Withoute gold other eny tresor
40      He mai be sound ant sete.

Of penaunce is his plastre al.
Ant ever serven hire Y shal,
    Nou ant al my lyve;
Nou is fre that er wes thral,
45   Al thourh that Levedy gent ant smal:
    Heried be hyr joies fyve!
Wherso eny sek ys,
    Thider hye blyve!
Thurh hire beoth ybroht to blis,
50      Bo mayden ant wyve.

For he that dude is body on tre
Of oure sunnes have piete,
    That weldes heovene boures!
Wymmon, with thi jolyfte,
55   Thah thou be whyt ant bryth on ble,
    Thou thench on Godes shoures!
.  .  .  .  .  .  .  .  .  .  .  .  .  .  .  .  .  .  .  .  .  .  .
    Falewen shule thy floures.
Jesu, have merci of us,
60      That al this world honoures.
        Amen.

My heart was terrified of deeds
Of sin by which I've fed my flesh,
   And pursued all my time,
So I don't know which way I'll be led
25 When I lie on death's bed,
   In joy or into pain.
On one Lady is my hope,
   Mother and virgin;
We will go into heaven's bliss
30    Through her medicine.

Better is her medicine
Than any mead or any wine;
   Her herbs smell sweet!
From Caithness to Dublin,
35 There's no physician so excellent
   To assuage our sorrows.
The one who feels any grief
   And will abandon his sin,
Without gold or other treasure
40    He may be sound and content.

His whole remedy consists of penance.
And always I shall serve her,
   Now and all my life;
Now he's free who once was thrall,
45 On account of that Lady noble and delicate:
   Praised be her five joys!
Wherever one is sick,
   Hasten there quickly!
He'll be brought to bliss through her,
50    Both maiden and wife.

May he who set his body on tree
Have mercy of our sins,
   He who rules heaven's bowers!
Women, with your joyfulness,
55 Though you be fair and lovely of face,
   Think on God's afflictions!
. . . . . . . . . . . . . . . . . . . . . . .
   Wither shall your flowers.
Have mercy on us, Jesus,
60    Whom all this world honors.
    Amen.

**My deth Y love, my lyf Ich hate** *strategic reading*       [art. 64]

80v]    ¶ "My deth Y love, my lyf Ich hate, for a levedy shene;       **[Clerk]**
        Heo is brith so daies liht, that is on me wel sene.
        Al Y falewe so doth the lef in somer when hit is grene,
        Yef mi thoht helpeth me noht, to wham shal Y me mene?

5        "Sorewe ant syke ant drery mod byndeth me so faste
        That Y wene to walke wod yef hit me lengore laste;
        My serewe, my care, al with a word he myhte awey caste.
        Whet helpeth the, my suete lemmon, my lyf thus forte gaste?"

        "Do wey, thou clerc! Thou art a fol! With the bydde Y noht chyde.       **[Girl]**
10      Shalt thou never lyve that day mi love that thou shalt byde.
        Yef thou in my boure art take, shame the may bityde;
        The is bettere on fote gon then wycked hors to ryde."

        "Weylawei! Whi seist thou so? Thou rewe on me, thy man!       **[Clerk]**
        Thou art ever in my thoht in londe wher Ich am.
15      Yef Y deye for thi love, hit is the mykel sham;
        Thou lete me lyve ant be thi luef, ant thou my suete lemman."

        "Be stille, thou fol — Y calle the ritht! Cost thou never blynne?       **[Girl]**
        Thou art wayted day ant niht with fader ant al my kynne.
        Be thou in mi bour ytake, lete they, for no synne,
20      Me to holde ant the to slon, the deth so thou maht wynne!"

        "Suete ledy, thou wend thi mod! Sorewe thou wolt me kythe?       **[Clerk]**
        Ich am al so sory mon so Ich was whylen blythe.
        In a wyndou ther we stod, we custe us fyfty sythe;
        Feir biheste maketh mony mon al is serewes mythe."

25      "Weylawey! Whi seist thou so? Mi serewe thou makest newe!       **[Girl]**
        Y lovede a clerk al par amours — of love he wes ful trewe;.
        He nes nout blythe, never a day, bote he me sone seye;
        Ich lovede him betere then my lyf! Whet bote is hit to leye?"

        "Whil Y wes a clerc in scole, wel muchel Y couthe of lore;       **[Clerk]**
30      Ych have tholed for thy love woundes fele sore,
        Fer from the, ant eke from men, under the wode-gore.
        Suete ledy, thou rewe of me! Nou may Y no more."

        "Thou semest wel to ben a clerc, for thou spekest so scille;       **[Girl]**
        Shalt thou never for mi love woundes thole grylle;
35      Fader, moder, ant al my kun ne shal me holde so stille
        That Y nam thyn, ant thou art myn, to don al thi wille."

**The Clerk and the Girl** *stanzgic reading*                    [art. 64]

80v]  ¶ "My death I love, my life I hate, because of a radiant lady;        **[Clerk]**
       She is as beautiful as daylight, which I can see so clearly.
       I shrivel completely like the leaf when it's green in summer,
       If my thoughts can't help me at all, to whom shall I complain?

5      "Sorrow and sighing and dejected mood bind me so tight
       That I expect to go mad if my state lasts any longer;
       My sorrow, my care, all with a word might she dispel.
       What does it help you, my sweet dear, to waste thus my life?"

       "Be off, you clerk! You're a fool! I don't want to argue with you.    **[Girl]**
10     You'll never live to that day you obtain my love.
       If you are caught in my room, may shame befall you;
       You're better to go on foot than ride a wicked horse."

       "Wailaway! Why say you so? Have pity on me, your man!                 **[Clerk]**
       You're always in my thought wherever I'm on ground.
15     If I die for your love, it's much to your shame;
       Let me live and be your love, and you my sweet dear."

       "Be still, you fool — I name you aright! Can't you ever cease?       **[Girl]**
       You're spied on day and night by father and all my kin.
       Were you caught in my room, they'll not refrain, for any sin,
20     To seize me and slay you, so that you'll have your death!"

       "Sweet lady, change your mind! Will you show me pity?                **[Clerk]**
       I am as sorrowful a man as once I was happy.
       In a window where we stood, we kissed fifty times;
       Fair promise makes many a man hide all his sorrow."

25     "Wailaway! What are you saying? You renew my sorrow!                  **[Girl]**
       I loved a clerk very deeply — in love he was quite true;
       He was not happy, never a day, unless he saw me soon;
       I loved him better than my life! What use is it to lie?"

       "When I was a clerk in school, well versed I was of love-lore;       **[Clerk]**
30     For your love I've suffered many wounds all hurtful,
       Far from you, and also from men, under the forest-skirt.
       Sweet lady, have pity on me! Now I may do no more."

       "You seem truly to be a clerk, for you speak so gently;              **[Girl]**
       You shall never for my love suffer dreadful wounds;
35     Father, mother, and all my kin shall not hold me so tightly
       That I can't be your own, and you be mine, to do all your desire."

**When the nyhtegale singes** *strategic reading*                    [art. 65]

80v]    ¶ When the nyhtegale singes, the wodes waxen grene;
        Lef ant gras ant blosme springes in Averyl, Y wene,
        Ant love is to myn herte gon with one spere so kene!
        Nyht ant day my blod hit drynkes. Myn herte deth me tene.

81r]    Ich have loved al this yer that Y may love namore;
6       Ich have siked moni syk, lemmon, for thin ore.
        Me nis love never the ner, ant that me reweth sore.
        Suete lemmon, thench on me — Ich have loved the yore!

        Suete lemmon, Y preye the of love one speche;
10      Whil Y lyve in world so wyde, other nulle Y seche.
        With thy love, my suete leof, mi blis thou mihtes eche;
        A suete cos of thy mouth mihte be my leche.

        Suete lemmon, Y preye the of a love-bene:
        Yef thou me lovest ase men says, lemmon, as Y wene,
15      Ant yef hit thi wille be, thou loke that hit be sene.
        So muchel Y thenke upon the that al Y waxe grene.

        Bituene Lyncolne ant Lyndeseye, Norhamptoun ant Lounde,
        Ne wot Y non so fayr a may as Y go fore ybounde.
        Suete lemmon, Y preye the, thou lovie me a stounde!
20          Y wole mone my song
            On wham that hit ys on ylong.


**Blessed be thou, Levedy**                                           [art. 66]

81r]    ¶ Blessed be thou, Levedy, ful of heovene blisse,
        Suete flur of parays, moder of mildenesse;
        Preyye Jesu, thy sone, that he me rede ant wysse
        So my wey forte gon that he me never misse.

5       Of the, suete Levedy, my song Y wile byginne;
        Thy deore suete sones love thou lere me to wynne.
        Ofte Y syke ant serewe among — may Y never blynne!
        Levedi, for thi milde mod, thou shilde me from synne.

        Myne thohtes, Levedy, maketh me ful wan;
10      To the Y crie ant calle — thou here me for thi man!
        Help me, hevene quene, for thyn ever Ych am.
        Wisse me to thi deore sone — the weies Y ne can!

**When the Nightingale Sings** *strategic reading*                                             [art. 65]

80v] ¶ When the nightingale sings, the woods grow green;
Leaf and grass and blossom flourish in April, I know,
And love goes to my heart with a spear so sharp!
Night and day it drinks my blood. My heart brings me pain.

81r] I've loved all this year so much that I may love no more;
6 I've sighed many a sigh, sweetheart, for your mercy.
Love is never the nearer to me, and that grieves me deeply.
Sweet dear, think about me — I've loved you a long time!

Sweet dear, I beg you for one word of love;
10 While I live in the world so wide, another I'll not seek.
With your love, my sweet dear, you can increase my bliss;
A sweet kiss of your mouth can be my physician.

Sweet dear, I beg of you a love-favor:
If you love me as they say, sweetheart, as I believe,
15 And if it be your will, make sure that it be openly known.
So constantly do I think on you that I become all pale.

Between Lincoln and Lindsey, Northampton and Lounde,
I know of no maiden so fair as she for whom I go fettered.
Sweet dear, I pray you, love me soon!
20 I will express my song
About the one on whom it depends.


**Blessed Are You, Lady**                                             [art. 66]

81r] ¶ Blessed are you, Lady, full of heaven's bliss,
Sweet flower of paradise, mother of mildness;
Pray Jesus, your son, that he may guide and teach me
How to go on my way so that he'll never forget me.

5 Of you, sweet Lady, my song I will begin;
Teach me how to win your dear sweet son's love.
Often I sigh and all the time lament — may I never cease!
Lady, for your gentle bearing, guard me from sin.

My thoughts, Lady, make me very pale;
10 To you I cry and call — hear me as your man!
Help me, heaven's queen, for I am ever yours.
Guide me to your dear son — the ways I cannot find!

Levedy Seinte Marie, for thi milde mod,
Soffre never that Y be so wilde ne so wod
15    That Ich her forleose the that art so god,
That Jesu me tobohte with is suete blod.

Bryhte ant shene, sterre cler, lyht thou me ant lere
In this false, fykel world myselve so to bere
That Y ner at myn endyng have the feond to fere.
20    Jesu, mid thi suete blod, thou bohtest me so dere!

81v]    Levedi Seinte Marie, so fair ant so briht,
Al myn help is on the bi day ant by nyht;
Levedi fre, thou shilde me so wel as thou myht,
That Y never forleose heveriche lyht.

25    Levedy Seinte Marie, so fayr ant so hende,
Preye Jesu Crist, thi sone, that he me grace sende
So to queme him ant the, er Ich henne wende,
That he me bringe to the blis that is withouten ende.

Ofte Y crie, "Merci!" Of mylse thou art welle.
30    Alle buen false that bueth mad bothe of fleysh ant felle!
Levedi suete, thou us shild from the pine of helle —
Bring us to the joie that no tonge hit may oftelle.

Jesu Crist Godes Sone, Fader, ant Holy Ghost,
Help us at oure nede, as thou hit al wel wost;
35    Bring us to thin riche, ther is joie most.
Let us never hit misse for non worldes bost!

**Ase Y me rod this ender day** *strategic reading*                [art. 67]

81va]    ¶ Ase Y me rod this ender day
By grene wode to seche play,
Mid herte Y thohte al on a may,
     Suetest of alle thinge.
5    Lythe, ant Ich ou telle may
     Al of that suete thinge.

This maiden is suete ant fre of blod,
Briht ant feyr, of milde mod —
Alle heo mai don us god
10       Thurh hire bysechynge;
Of hire he tok fleysh ant blod,
     Jesu, hevene kynge.

Lady Saint Mary, for your gentle bearing,
Let me not be so wayward nor so mad
15 That here I lose you who are so good,
For Jesus bought me with his sweet blood.

Fair and beautiful, clear star, illuminate and teach me
In this false, fickle world how to bear myself
So that I'll never at my end have to fear the fiend.
20 Jesus, with your sweet blood, you bought me so dearly!

81v] Lady Saint Mary, so fair and so bright,
All my help is fixed on you by day and by night;
Noble Lady, protect me as well as you are able,
So that I'll never lose the heavenly kingdom's light.

25 Lady Saint Mary, so fair and so gracious,
Pray Jesus Christ, your son, that he send me grace
So to please him and you, before I pass on hence,
That he may bring me to the bliss that's without end.

Oft I cry, "Mercy!" Of mercy you are the fount.
30 All is false that is made both of flesh and skin!
Lady sweet, shield us from the pain of hell —
Bring us to the joy that no tongue may express.

Jesus Christ God's Son, Father, and Holy Ghost,
Help us at our need, as you know it very well;
35 Bring us to your kingdom, where joy is fullest.
Let us never forfeit it for any worldly pride!

**The Five Joys of the Virgin** *strategic reading* [art. 67]

81va] ¶ As I rode out the other day
To seek pleasure by the green wood,
Fervently I thought wholly on a girl,
Sweetest of everything.
5 Listen, and I may tell you
All about that sweet thing.

This maiden is sweet and noble of birth,
Beautiful and fair, of gentle manner —
She may bring us only good
10 By our beseeching her;
Of her he took flesh and blood,
Jesus, heaven's king.

With al mi lif Y love that may;
He is mi solas nyht ant day,
15   My joie ant eke my beste play,
        Ant eke my love-longynge.
     Al the betere me is that day
        That Ich of hire synge!

     Of alle thinge Y love hire mest —
20   My dayes blis, my nyhtes rest!
     Heo counseileth ant helpeth best
        Bothe elde ant yynge.
     Nou Y may, yef Y wole,
        The fif joyes mynge.

25   The furst joie of that wymman:
     When Gabriel from hevene cam
     Ant seide God shulde bicome man
        Ant of hire be bore,
     Ant bringe up of helle pyn
30      Monkyn that wes forlore.

     That other joie of that may
     Wes o Cristesmasse day:
     When God wes bore on thoro lay,
        Ant brohte us lyhtnesse.
35   The ster wes seie byfore day;
        This, hirdes bereth wytnesse.

81vb]  The thridde joie of that levedy,
     That men clepeth the Epyphany:
     When the kynges come, wery,
40      To presente hyre sone
     With myrre, gold, ant encens,
        That wes mon bicome.

     The furthe joie we telle mawen:
     On Ester morewe wen hit gon dawen,
45   Hyre sone that wes slawen
        Aros in fleysh ant bon —
     More joie ne mai me haven,
        Wyf ne mayden non!

     The fifte joie of that wymman:
50   When hire body to hevene cam,
     The soule to the body nam,
        Ase hit wes woned to bene.

With all my life I love that girl;
She's my solace night and day,
15 My joy and also my best delight,
        And also my love-longing.
I always fare better on that day
        When I sing about her!

Of all things I love her most —
20 My day's bliss, my night's rest!
She counsels and helps best
        Both old and young.
Now I may, as I wish,
        The five joys call to mind.

25 The first joy of that woman:
When Gabriel came from heaven
And said God would become man
        And of her be born,
And raise up out of hell-pain
30        Mankind who was forlorn.

The next joy of that maiden
Occurred on Christmas day:
When God was born in perfect light,
        And brought us to enlightenment.
35 The star was visible before day;
        To this, shepherds bear witness.

81vb] The third joy of that lady,
Which men call the Epiphany:
When the kings came, weary,
40        To present her son
With myrrh, gold, and incense,
        Who had become man.

The fourth joy we may tell:
On Easter morn when it began to dawn,
45 Her son that was slain
        Arose in flesh and bone —
More joy may no man have,
        Nor wife nor maiden either!

The fifth joy of that woman:
50 When her body came to heaven,
The soul joined with the body,
        Where it was accustomed to be.

Crist, leve us alle, with that wymman,
   That joie al forte sene!

55    Preye we alle to Oure Levedy,
      Ant to the sontes that woneth hire by,
      That heo of us haven merci,
         Ant that we ne misse
      In this world to ben holy,
60       Ant wynne hevene blysse.
            Amen.


**Herkne to my ron**                                    [art. 68]

82ra]    ¶ Herkne to my ron,
         As Ich ou telle con
            Of Elde, al hou it ges,
         Of a mody mon
5        Hihte Maxumon,
            Soth, withoute les.
         Clerc he was, ful god,
         So moni mon understod —
            Nou herkne hou it wes.

10       Ys wille he hevede ynoh:
         Purpre ant pal he droh,
            Ant other murthes mo;
         He wes the feyrest mon
         Withouten Absolon
15          The seththe wes ant tho.
         Tho laste is lyf so longe
         That he bigan unstronge,
            As mony tides so.
         Him con rewe sore
20       Al is wilde lore,
            For Elde him dude so wo.

         So sone as Elde him com,
         Ys boc an honde he nom,
            Ant gan of reuthes rede.
25       Of his herte ord,
         He made moni word,
            Ant of is lyves dede
         He gan mene is mone.
         So feble were is bone,
30          Ys hew bigon to wede;
         So clene he was ygon,

Christ, grant us all, with that woman,
    To see that joy!

55      Pray we all to Our Lady,
    And to the saints that dwell near her,
    That she have mercy on us,
      And that we not fail
    In this world to be holy,
60        And win heaven's bliss.
      Amen.

## Maximian                      [art. 68]

82ra]    ¶ Hearken to my song,
    For I can tell you
      Of Age, all how it goes,
    And of a distraught man
5      Named Maximian,
      Truly, without lie.
    A clerk he was, quite good,
    As many a man understood —
      Now hearken how it was.

10      He'd fulfilled his will enough:
    Fine silks and robes he'd had,
      And other joys besides;
    He was the fairest man
    Since Absolon
15        Had been alive and thrived.
    Then lasted his life so long
    That he began to lose strength,
      As happens many times.
    He did sorely regret
20      All his willful ways,
      For Age so gave him woe.

    As soon as Age came to him,
    He took his book in hand,
      And began to read of regrets.
25      From his heart's treasure-store,
    He uttered many words,
      And regarding his life's deeds
    He began to say his lament.
    So feeble were his bones,
30        His hue began to fade;
    So wholly was he changed,

That heu ne hade he none;
   Ys herte gan to blede.


"Care ant kunde of Elde
35     Maketh mi body felde
   That Y ne mai stonde upriht,
Ant min herte unbolde,
Ant mi body to colde,
   That er thou wes so lyht,
40     Ant mi body thunne.
Such is worldes wunne!
   This day me thinketh nyht.


Riche Y was of londe,
Ant mon of fayrest honde —
45     That wes bote a stounde!
Mi meyn, that wes so strong,
Mi middel smal ant long,
   Ybroht it is to grounde.


82rb]  Forthi Y grunte ant grone,
50     When Y go myn one,
   Ant thenke on childes dede.
Al this wylde wone
Nis hit bote a lone —
   Her beth blisse gnede!
55     To wepen ant to grone,
To make muche mone,
   That we doth for nede;
Ant under the stone,
With fleish ant with bone,
60     Wormes shule we fede.


Ther Y stod in a snowe
Wel heye upon a lowe;
   Y was a wilde mon.
Hunten herd Y blowe,
65     Hertes gonne rowe;
   Stunte me ne ston.


"Nou hit nis nout so —
Y lerne forte go,
   Ant stonde ant syke sore;
70     My wele is went to wo!
Ant so beth other mo
   That lyved habbeth yore.
So litht as Y wes tho,

That color had he none;
   His heart began to bleed.

    "Sorrow and Age's nature
35    Cause my body to shrivel
     So I can't stand upright,
And my heart to be weak,
And my body to chill,
   Which before was so nimble,
40   And my body to grow thin.
Such is the world's joy!
   This day seems as night.

    "Rich I was in land,
And man of fairest hand —
45    That lasted but a moment!
My strength, it was so strong;
My waist small and long,
   Brought it is to ground.

82rb]   "Therefore I grunt and groan,
50    When I go on my own,
    And think on child's deeds.
All this willful dwelling
Is nothing but a loan —
   Here bliss is scarce!
55   To weep and to groan,
To make much moan,
   We do that for need;
And under the stone,
With flesh and with bone,
60    Worms we shall feed.

    "There I stood in snow
Very high on a hill;
   I was a willful man.
I heard hunters blow,
65   Harts were disturbed;
   No stone impeded me.

    "Now it is not so —
I learn how to walk,
   And stand and sorely sigh;
70   My weal has gone to woe!
And such are many others
   Who've lived very long.
So nimble was I then,

Ant wilde as eny ro,
75      Er Y bygon to hore.
Reuthful is my red,
Ne shulde me be gled —
    Me reweth swythe sore.


"With hunger Y am feed;
80      Heo seith Y 'spille breed,'
    My wif that shulde be.
Myn herte is hevy so led,
Me were levere be ded
    Then lyves forte be.
85      Hit is ful soth ysed,
The mon that haveth dred,
    His frendes wile him fle.


"Tho I was strong ant wis
Ant werede feir ant grys,
90      Ich havede frendes tho.
Fol soth iseid it ys,
The mon that is of pris,
    He haveth frendes mo.
My myht no wyht nys,
95      Ygon hit is, ywys;
    He bringe me of wo.
82rc]   Men wyste non, ywys,
That werede veyr ant gris
    (Ythryven ase Y was tho),
100    That havede more of his:
Nou hit so nout nys,
    Ah al hit is ago!


"So gentil ne so chis,
Ne mon of more pris —
105    Ful wo nou me may be!
The world wrechede is,
Ant that he wyten, ywis.
    My frendes nulleth me se.


"Fair Y was ant fre,
110    Ant semly forte se —
    That lasteth lutel stounde!
Gladdere mon with gle
Ne mihte never be,
    Thurh al Godes mounde.
115    Elde, unhende is he;
He chaungeth al my ble

And wild as any roe,
75       Before I began to gray.
Sorrowful is my thought,
Nor should I be happy —
       I'm so deeply regretful.

"With hunger I am fed;
80    She says I 'waste bread,'
       My wife that she should be.
My heart's as heavy as lead,
I rather would be dead
       Than alive so to be.
85    It's very truly said,
The man who carries fear,
       His friends from him will flee.

"When I was strong and wise
And wore splendid furs,
90       I had friends then.
Full truly said it is,
The man who has the praise,
       He has the more friends.
My might is not strong,
95    Gone it is, indeed;
       It makes me suffer woe.
82rc]  Men know not, indeed,
Who wear splendid furs
       (Thriving as I was then),
100   Who own many things:
Now it's as if it isn't,
       And everything is gone!

"So noble and so choice,
No man of higher praise —
105       Most sad now may he be!
The world is miserable,
And that he knows, indeed.
       My friends don't wish to see me.

"Fair I was and generous,
110   And comely to behold —
       That lasts a brief instant!
A gladder man with mirth
Might there never be,
       Through all God's power.
115   Age, discourteous is he;
He changes all my color

Ant bringeth me to grounde.
When Y shal henne te,
Y not whider Y fle;
120      Forthi Y sike unbestounde.

"Y sike ant sorewe sore;
Ne may Y be namore
      Mon as Y was tho.
Ys hit nowhith yore
125    That Y bigon to hore;
      Elde is nou my fo.
Y wake as water in wore!
Jesu Crist, thin ore,
      Why is me so wo?

130    "Thicke Y was ant riht,
Of wordes wis ant lyht,
      As Ich understonde;
Of belte Y wes briht,
Ant lovelyche ydiht,
135      Ant fayrest mon of londe.

"When foules singeth on rys,
Y mourne ant serewe, ywis,
      That unnethe Y go.
This world wicked is,
140    Ant that ye wyten, ywys,
      Hit is byfalle so.

82va]    "Reuthful is my red.
Hue maketh me selde gled,
      My wyf that shulde be.
145    Y dude as hue me bad,
Of me hue is asad —
      Evele mote hue the!
Hue clepeth me 'spille bred' —
Serewe upon hyre hed! —
150      For hue nul me yse.
Ych am hevy so led;
Betere me were ded
      Then thus alyve to be.

"Ase Ich rod thourh Rome
155    Richest alre home,
      With murthes as Ycholde,
Ledys wyht so swon,
Maidnes shene so bon,

And casts me to ground.
When I shall travel from hence,
I know not whither I'll flee;
120     Therefore I often sigh.

"I sigh and grieve sore;
I cannot be any more
   The man as I was then.
It's not very long ago
125   Since I began to gray;
   Age is now my foe.
I'm restless as waves on shore.
Jesus Christ, your mercy,
   Why am I so sad?

130   "Muscular I was and straight,
Of words wise and quick,
   As I understand;
With belt I was splendid,
And beautifully clothed,
135     And fairest man in land.

"When birds sing on limb,
I mourn and sorrow, indeed,
   So that scarcely may I walk.
This world wicked is,
140   And that you know, indeed,
   For it's befallen so.

82va]   "Sorrowful is my thought.
She makes me seldom happy,
   My wife that she should be.
145   I did as she bade me,
Yet with me she's unsatisfied —
   Evil may she thrive!
She calls me 'wasted bread' —
Sorrow upon her head! —
150     For she'll not look at me.
I'm as heavy as lead;
Better were I dead
   Than thus alive to be.

"As I rode through Rome
155   Richest of all men,
   With joys as I held,
Ladies white as swans,
Maidens bright as bone,

Me come to biholde.
160    Ant seyden on after on:
'Gent ryd Maximon
    With is burnes bolde!'
Nou nis non of the
That wolleth me yse,
165      In mine clothes olde.

"This world is wok ant les,
Y nam noht as Ych wes;
    Ych wot by myne chere.
For gent Ich wes ant chys,
170    Ant mon of muche pris,
    Ant leof to ben yfere.

"Ther nes clerc ne knyht
Ne mon of more myht
    That levere wes in londe.
175    Ystunt is al my syht,
This day me thuncheth nyht;
    Such is the world to fonde!

"Fair ich wes of hewe,
Ant of love trewe —
180      That lasteth lutel stounde!
They that me yknewe
Hem may sore rewe,
    Soth, hit is yfounde.

82vb]    "Of nothing that Y se
185    Ne gladieth me no gle;
    Myn herte breketh atuo!
For Ich wes on the
That woned wes glad to be,
    In londe that wes tho.
190    Nou Ich am liche a tre
That loren hath is ble;
    Ne groweth hit namo.
For thah Icholde fle,
Y not wyder te;
195      Elde me worcheth wo.

"Stunt is al mi plawe,
That Y wes woned to drawe
    Whil Y wes so lyht.

              Came to gaze at me.
160    And said one after one:
       'Nobly rides Maximian
          With his valiant men!'
       Now there's none of them
       Who will look at me,
165       In my old clothes.

       "This world is weak and false,
       I am not as I was;
          I know it by my face.
       For noble I was and choice,
170    And man of great praise,
          And dear to be among.

       "There was no clerk or knight
       Or man of greater might
          Who dearer was in land.
175    Blinded is all my sight,
       This day seems to me night;
          So does the world deceive!

       "Handsome I was of hue,
       And of love true —
180       That lasts a brief instant!
       They who knew me
       May feel deep pity,
          Truly, it is found.

82vb]  "Nothing that I see
185    Gladdens or brings me mirth;
          My heart breaks in two!
       For I was one of them
       Accustomed to be happy,
          Thriving upon earth.
190    Now I'm like a tree
       Having lost its color;
          It no longer grows.
       For though I would flee,
       I know not whither to go;
195       Age strikes me with woe.

       "Ended is all my play,
       Which I was wont to pursue
          While I was so nimble.

       "Y wolde Y were in rest,
200     Lowe leid in chest.
         My blisse is forloren!
       For mourne Y make mest
       The while that hit lest.
         Nou wo is me, therfore!
205     Ne gladieth me no gest;
       Ne murgeth me no fest;
         Alas, that Y wes bore!

       "This lond me thuncheth west;
       Deth Y doute mest:
210        Whider that Y shal te?
       Whet helpeth hit ytold?
       Y waxe blo ant cold;
         Of lyve Y wolde be.

       "When blosmes breketh on brere,
215     Murthes to me were,
         Ant blythe Y was of mod.
       Care ant kunde yfere
       Changeth al mi chere
         Ant mengeth al my blod.
220     To longe Ichave ben here,
       Bi mo then sixty yere,
         So Y me understod.
       Icholde that Ych were
       Al so Y never nere —
225        My lyf is nothyng god.

82vc]   "Myn neb that wes so bryht
       So eny sterre lyht,
         Falu is ant won.
       My body that wes so wyht
230     Styth hit stod upryht —
         Y wes a mody mon!
       My mayn ant eke my myht!
       Stunt is al my syht!
         Lerneth nou of thon:
235     Nis non so kene knyht
       That so ne byth ydyht
         When Elde him cometh on.

       "Mi body that wes strong,
       Mi middel, smal ant long,
240        Ybroht hit is to grounde!
       Nou nabbe Y nout that yong,

          "I wish I were at rest,
200      Laid low in coffin.
                My happiness is destroyed!
          For mostly I make mourning
          While time remains.
                Now woe is me, therefore!
205      No guest cheers me up;
          No feast gives me mirth.
                Alas, that I was born!

          "This land I think a waste;
          Death I fear most:
210            Whither shall I go?
          What helps if it were told?
          I grow dark and cold;
                Dead I'd like to be.

          "When flowers open on briar,
215      Pleasures came to me,
                And I was happy in spirit.
          Sorrow and nature together
          Wholly change my mood
                And agitate my passions.
220      Too long have I been here,
          By more than sixty years,
                As I have recalled.
          I wish that I were
          All as I never was —
225            My life's nothing good.

82vc]   "My nose that was as fine
          As any star's light,
                Is faded and discolored.
          My body that was so white
230      Sturdily stood upright —
                I was a worthy man!
          My strength and my might!
          Blinded is all my sight!
                Learn now from your life:
235      There's no knight so keen
          That he'll not be afflicted
                When Age comes to him.

          "My body that was strong,
          My waist, slender and long,
240            It is brought to ground!
          I have not now that youth,

That speche, ne that song;
   Mi lif nys bote a stounde!
Thah Y be men among,
245    Y gladie for no song
   Of haueke ne of hounde.

"My deth Icholde fle,
For Ich am on of the
   That deyeth boute wounde.
250    Ne con Y me no red;
Myn herte is hevi so led
   Ant wel faste ybounde.
Ich wes of feyre leynthe;
Agon is al my streynthe
255    In armes ant in honde.

"Er Ich were thus old,
Ich wes of speche bold,
   Ne recchi wo hit here;
Nou Ich am old ant cold,
260    Wet helpeth more ytold?
   Of lyve Ycholde Ich were.

"Gentil Ich wes ant freo,
Wildore then the leo
   Er Y bygon to hore,
265    Nou Y nam nout so,
My weole is turnd to wo,
   Ant hath ybe ful yore.

83r]   "Ant so bueth other mo
That lyveden nou ant tho,
270    Ne reccheth of weole ne wo.
Deth is that Y munne —
Me seggeth that hit is sunne —
   God brynge us out of tho."

    Amen, par charite,
275    Ant so mote hit be.

**Mayden, moder milde**            [art. 69]

83r]   ¶ Mayden, moder milde,
   Oiez cel oreysoun.
From shome thou me shilde,
   E de ly mal feloun;

That speech, nor that song;
  My life's but an instant!
Though I be among men,
245    I gladden for no song
  Of hawk or of hound.

"My death I would flee,
For I'm one of those
  Who die without wound.
250    Nor can I prepare myself;
My heart's as heavy as lead
  And very tightly bound.
I was of handsome height;
Gone is all my strength
255      In arms and in hand.

"Before I thus was old,
I was of speech bold,
  I cared not who it heard;
Now I am old and cold,
260    What helps it to say more?
  Dead I wish I were.

"Noble I was and free,
Wilder than the lion
  Before I began to gray,
265    Now I am not so,
My weal has turned to woe,
  And has been a long time.

83r]    "And so it is for many more
Who lived now and then,
270      Who care not for weal or woe.
Death is what I lament —
I say that it is sin —
  God bring us out of it."

      Amen, for charity,
275      And so may it be.

### Maiden, Mother Mild                    [art. 69]

83r]    ¶ Maiden, mother mild,
  Hear this prayer.
Shield me from disgrace,
  And from the evil villain;

5      For love of thine childe,
          Me menez de tresoun.
      Ich wes wod ant wilde;
          Ore su en prisoun.

      Thou art feyr ant fre,
10         E plein de douçour.
      Of the sprong the ble,
          Ly soverein Creatour.
      Mayde, byseche Y the
          Vostre seint socour.
15     Meoke ant mylde, be with me
          Pur le sue amour.

      Tho Judas Jesum founde,
          Donque ly beysa;
      He wes bete ant bounde,
20         Que nous tous fourma.
      Wyde were is wounde
          Qe le Gyw ly dona.
      He tholede harde stounde,
          Me poi le greva.

25     On ston ase thou stode,
          Pucele, tot pensaunt,
      Thou restest the under rode:
          Ton fitz veites pendant;
      Thou seye is sides of blode,
30         L'alme de ly partaunt.
      He ferede uch an fode
          En mound que fust vivaunt.

      Ys siden were sore;
          Le sang de ly cora.
35     That lond was forlore,
          Mes il le rechata.
      Uch bern that wes ybore
          En enfern descenda;
      He tholede deth therfore,
40         En ciel puis mounta.

      Tho Pilat herde the tydynge,
          Molt fu joyous baroun;
      He lette byfore him brynge
          Jesu Nazaroun.
45     He was ycrouned kynge
          Pur nostre redempcioun.

5       For love of your child,
            Lead me out of treachery.
        I was mad and wayward;
            Now I am in prison.

        You are fair and gracious,
10          And full of gentleness.
        From you sprang the radiance,
            The sovereign Creator.
        Maid, I ask of you
            Your holy succor.
15      Meek and mild, be with me
            For love of him.

        When Judas found Jesus,
            Then he kissed him;
        He was beaten and bound,
20          Who created us all.
        Wide were his wounds
            That the Jews gave him.
        He endured hard pangs,
            But little did it grieve him.

25      On stone as you stood,
            Virgin, all pensive,
        You pause under cross:
            You see your son hanging;
        You see his bloody sides,
30          The soul parting from him.
        He made whole each creature
            Who was living on earth.

        His sides were painful;
            The blood flowed from him.
35      That land was forlorn,
            But he redeemed it.
        Each child that was born
            Descended into hell;
        He suffered death for them,
40          Then rose into heaven.

        When Pilate heard the news,
            He was indeed a joyous lord;
        He ordered brought before him
            Jesus of Nazareth.
45      He was crowned king
            For our redemption.

Whose wol me synge
   Avera grant pardoun.


**The Geste of Kyng Horn**                                    [art. 70]

83r]      Her bygynneth the Geste of Kyng Horn.


    ¶ Alle heo ben blythe
That to my song ylythe.
A song Ychulle ou singe
Of Allof the gode kynge.
5    Kyng he wes by weste
The whiles hit yleste;
Ant Godylt his gode quene,
No feyrore myhte bene;
Ant huere sone hihte Horn,
10   Feyrore child ne myhte be born.
For reyn ne myhte byryne,
Ne sonne myhte shyne
Feyrore child then he was:
Bryht so ever eny glas,
15   So whit so eny lylye-flour,
So rose red wes his colour.
He wes feyr ant eke bold,
Ant of fyftene wynter old.
83v]  Nis non his yliche
20   In none kinges ryche!
    Tuelf feren he hadde
That he with him ladde,
Alle riche menne sones,
Ant alle suythe feyre gomes
25   Wyth him forte pleye.
Mest he lovede tueye:
That on wes hoten Athulf Chyld,
Ant that other Fykenyld.
Athulf wes the beste,
30   Ant Fykenyld the werste.
    Hyt was upon a someres day,
Also Ich ou telle may.
Allof the gode kyng
Rod upon ys pleyyyng
35   Bi the seeside
Ther he was woned to ryde.
With him ne ryde bote tuo —
Al to fewe hue were tho!
He fond by the stronde,

Whoever will sing with me
   Will have great pardon.


**King Horn**                                                                 [art. 70]

83r]    Here begins the romance of King Horn.

       ¶ They'll all be glad
    Who listen to my song.
    I'll sing you a song
    Of Allof the good king.
5      He was king in the west
    As long as it lasted;
    And Godild his good queen,
    No fairer might there be;
    And their son named Horn,
10    A fairer child was never born.
    For rain couldn't dampen,
    Nor the sun shine upon
    A fairer child than he:
    Brighter than any glass,
15    As white as any lily-flower,
    His color as red as a rose.

*← descriptions usually used for women*

    He was fair and also brave,
    And fifteen winters old.
83v]   None is his equal
20    In any king's realm!
      Twelve companions he had
    Under his leadership,
    All rich men's sons,
    And all such fair young men
25    To play with him.
    He most loved two:
    One named Athulf Child,
    And the other Fikenild.
    Athulf was the best,
30    And Fikenild the worst.

*- 12 followers and of whom is bad/ a squire possibly*

      It was on a summer's day,
    As I may tell you.
    Allof the good king
    Rode for his leisure
35    Along the seashore
    Where he normally rode.
    With him rode only two —
    All too few were they then!
    He encountered at the coast,

40      Aryved on is londe,
        Shipes fyftene
        Of Sarazynes kene.
        He askede whet hue sohten
        Other on is lond brohten.
45          A payen hit yherde
        Ant sone him onsuerede:
        "Thy londfolk we wolleth slon,
        That ever Crist leveth on,
        Ant the, we wolleth ryht anon,
50      Shalt thou never henne gon!"
            The kyng lyhte of his stede,
        For tho he hevede nede;
        Ant his gode feren tuo
        Mid ywis huem wes ful wo.
55      Swerd hy gonne gripe
        Ant togedere smyte.
        Hy smyten under shelde,
        That hy somme yfelde.


            ¶ The kyng hade to fewe
60      Ageyn so monie schrewe:
        So fele myhten ethe
        Bringe thre to dethe!
        The payns come to londe
        Ant nomen hit an honde.
65      The folk hy gonne quelle,
        Ant Sarazyns, to felle,
        Ther ne myhte libbe,
        The fremede ne the sibbe,
        Bote he is lawe forsoke
70      Ant to huere toke.
            Of alle wymmanne
        Werst wes Godyld thanne:
        For Allof hy wepeth sore
        Ant for Horn yet more.
75      Godild hade so muche sore
        That habbe myhte hue na more.
        Hue wente out of halle,
        From hire maidnes alle,
        Under a roche of stone
80      Ther hue wonede alone.
        Ther hue servede Gode
        Ageyn the payenes forbode;
        Ther hue servede Crist
        That the payenes hit nust,

- 15 ships of pagans arrive and take over the country.
  ↳ they oppress the people and force them to abandon
     Christ
  ↳ the queen secretly worships under a rock

ART. 70. KING HORN                                                          303

40    Arrived on his land,
      Fifteen ships
      Of fierce Saracens.
      He asked what they sought
      Or brought to his land.
45       A pagan heard it
      And soon answered him:
      "We plan to kill your people,
      Who firmly believe in Christ,
      And you, we'll make certain,
50    Shall never escape!"
         The king got off his horse,
      For then he was forced to;
      And his two good companions
      Were indeed very frightened.
55    They then gripped swords
      And struck against them.
      They struck under shields,
      Causing some to die.

         ¶ The king had too few
60    Against so many villains:
      So many could easily
      Bring three to death!
      The pagans came to land
      And seized control of it.
65    The people they then killed,
      And the Saracens, to oppress,
      Allowed no one to live,
      No stranger or relative,
      Unless he forsook his religion
70    And adopted theirs.
         Of all women
      The saddest then was Godild:
      She wept sorely for Allof
      And even more for Horn.

— why for Horn?

75    Godild bore so much sorrow
      That she couldn't bear more.
      She left the hall,
      Away from all her maidens,
      [To go] under a rock of stone
80    Where she dwelled alone.
      There she served God
      Against the pagans' edict;
      She served Christ there,
      So the pagans wouldn't know,

85      Ant ever hue bad for Horn Child,
        That Crist him wrthe myld.

            ¶ Horn wes in payenes hond
        Mid is feren of the lond.
        Muche wes the feyrhade
90      That Jesu Crist him made.
        Payenes him wolde slo,
        Ant summe him wolde flo;
        Yyf Hornes feyrnesse nere,
        Yslawe this children were.
95          Tho spec on admyrold,
        Of wordes he wes swythe bold:
        "Horn, thou art swythe kene,
        Bryht of hewe ant shene;
        Thou art fayr ant eke strong,
100     Ant eke eveneliche long.
        Yef thou to lyve mote go,
        Ant thyne feren also,
        That Y may byfalle
        That ye shule slen us alle.
84r]    Tharefore thou shalt to streme go,
106     Thou ant thy feren also;
        To shipe ye shule founde
        Ant sinke to the grounde!
        The see the shal adrenche,
110     Ne shal hit us ofthenche.
        For yef thou were alyve
        With suerd other with knyve,
        We shulden alle deye
        Thy fader deth to beye."
115         The children ede to the stronde,
        Wryngynde huere honde,
        Ant into shipes borde
        At the furste worde.
        Ofte hade Horn be wo,
120     Ah never wors then him wes tho!

            ¶ The see bygon to flowen,
        Ant Horn faste to rowen,
        Ant that ship wel suythe drof,
        Ant Horn wes adred therof!
125     Hue wenden mid ywisse
        Of huere lyve to misse.
        Al the day ant al the nyht,
        O that sprong the daylyht,
        Flotterede Horn by the stronde

85      And always she prayed for Horn Child,
        That Christ to him be mild.

           ¶ Horn was in the pagans' hands
        With his fellows of the land.
        Great was the beauty
90      Jesus Christ bestowed on him.
        The pagans planned to kill him,
        And some wished to flog him;
        Had Horn not been beautiful,
        These children would've been slain.
95          Then spoke a commander,
        Of speech he was most arrogant:
        "Horn, you're very brave,
        Good-looking and radiant;
        You're fair and also strong,
100     And also straight and tall.
        If you were to escape alive,
        And your fellows too,
        Then I'd be responsible
        Should you slay us all.
84r]    Therefore you shall go to sea,
106     You and your fellows too;
        You shall depart on a ship
        And sink to the bottom!
        The sea shall drown you,
110     And it won't grieve us.
        For were you to remain alive
        With sword or with knife,
        We'd all have to die
        To pay for your father's death."
115         The children went to the shore,
        Wringing their hands,
        And boarded the ship
        Upon the first command.
        Often had Horn been fearful,
120     But never worse than then!

           ¶ The sea began to flow,
        And Horn perforce to sail,
        And that ship traveled rapidly,
        And Horn was scared by that!
125     They believed with certainty
        They would lose their lives.
        All day and all night,
        Until daylight arose,
        Horn was tossed in the sea

130      Er he seye eny londe.
             "Feren," quoth Horn the yynge,
         "Y telle ou tydynge:
         Ich here foules singe
         Ant se the grases springe.
135      Blythe, be ye alyve!
         Ur ship is come to ryve."
             Of shipe hy gonne founde
         Ant sette fot to grounde
         By the seesyde.
140      Hure ship bigon to ryde.
             Thenne spec him Child Horn,
         In Sudenne he was yborn:
         "Nou, ship, by the flode,
         Have dayes gode!
145      By the see brynke,
         No water the adrynke.
         Softe mote thou sterye,
         That water the ne derye.
         Yef thou comest to Sudenne,
150      Gret hem that me kenne.
         Gret wel the gode
         Quene Godild mi moder!
         Ant sey thene hethene kyng,
         Jesu Cristes wytherlyng,
155      That Ich, hol ant fere,
         In londe aryvede here,
         Ant say that he shal fonde
         Then deth of myne honde!"

             ¶ The ship bigon to fleoten,
160      Ant Horn Child to weopen.
         By dales ant by dounes
         The children eoden to tounes.
         Metten hue Eylmer the kyng,
         Crist him geve god tymyng! —
165      Kyng of Westnesse,
         Crist him myhte blesse!
             He spec to Horn Child
         Wordes suythe myld:
         "Whenne be ye, gomen,
170      That bueth her alonde ycomen,
         Alle threttene
         Of bodye suythe kene?
         By God that me made,
         So feyr a felaurade
175      Ne seh Y never stonde

—the ship arrives safely on a shore and Horn and his
men leave the boat.
↳ the ship floats away and Horn tells it to greet his
mother if it reaches Sudenne.
—they walk into town and meet the king of
Westness.

ART. 70. KING HORN                                                        307

130     Before he saw any land.
            "Fellows," said Horn the young,
        "I have good news for you:
        I hear birds sing
        And see the grass grow.
135     Happily, you're alive!
        Our ship has come to shore."
            They began to leave the ship
        And set foot on ground
        Along the seashore.
140     Their ship floated away.
            Then spoke Child Horn,
        In Sudenne he was born:
        "Now, ship, by the wave,
        Have good day!
145     By the sea's edge,
        May no water drown you.
        Calmly may you steer,
        So that water doesn't harm you.
        If you come to Sudenne,
150     Greet them who know me.
        Greet well the good
        Queen Godild my mother!
        And tell your heathen king,
        Jesus Christ's enemy,
155     That I, whole and sound,
        Have arrived here on land,
        And say that he shall find
        Death thus by my hand!"

            ¶ The ship then floated away,
160     And Horn Child wept.
        By dale and by down
        The children walked to town.
        They met Aylmer the king,
        Christ give him good fortune! —
165     King of Westness,
        May Christ bless him!
            He spoke to Horn Child
        Words very kind:
        "Where are you from, lads,
170     Who've come ashore here,
        All thirteen
        So daring of body?
        By God who created me,
        So fine a fellowship
175     I've never seen stand

In Westnesse londe.
Say me whet ye seche."
Horn spec huere speche.

¶ Horn spac for huem alle,
180     For so hit moste byfalle —
He wes the wyseste
Ant of wytte the beste:
"We bueth of Sudenne,
Ycome of gode kenne,
185     Of Cristene blode,
Of cunne swythe gode.
Payenes ther connen aryve
Ant Cristine brohten of lyve,
Slowen ant todrowe
190     Cristine men ynowe.
So Crist me mote rede,
Ous hy duden lede
84v]    Into a galeye
With the see to pleye.
195     Day is gon ant other,
Withoute seyl ant rother,
Ure ship flet forth ylome,
Ant her to londe hit ys ycome.
Nou thou myht us slen ant bynde
200     Oure honde us bihynde,
Ah yef hit is thi wille,
Help us that we ne spille!"

¶ Tho spac the gode kyng,
He nes never nythyng:
205     "Sey, child, whet is thy name?
Shal the tide bote game."
The child him onsuerede
So sone he hit yherde:
"Horn Ych am yhote,
210     Ycome out of this bote
From the seeside.
Kyng, wel the bitide."
"Horn Child," quoth the kyng,
"Wel brouc thou thy nome, yyng.
215     Horn him goth so stille
Bi dales ant by hulles;
Horn hath loude soune
Thurhout uch a toune.
So shal thi nome springe
220     From kynge to kynge,

In the land of Westness.
Tell me what you seek."
Horn spoke their response.

¶ Horn spoke for them all,
180 For so it must be —
He was the wisest
And the best of wit:
"We are from Sudenne,
Come of good kin,
185 Of Christian blood,
From very good families.
Pagans arrived there
And bereft Christians of life,
Slew and cut to pieces
190 Many Christian men.
As Christ must guide me,
They did lead us
84v] Into a galley
To sport with the sea.
195 Day after another,
Without sail or rudder,
Our ship drifted on and on,
And here it's come ashore.
Now you might slay us and bind
200 Our hands behind us,
But if it be your will,
Help us that we not die!"

¶ Then spoke the good king,
He was never a coward:
205 "Say, child, what's your name?
Only play shall befall you."
The child answered him
As soon as he heard this:
"Horn I am called,
210 Come out of this boat,
From the seashore.
King, may you be well."
"Horn Child," said the king,
"Your name suits you, lad.
215 A horn sounds so gently
By dales and by hills;
A horn carries a loud sound
Through every town.
So shall your name spring
220 From king to king,

Ant thi feirnesse
Aboute Westnesse.
Horn, thou art so suete,
Ne shal Y the forlete."
225      Hom rod Aylmer the kyng,
Ant Horn with him, his fundlyng,
Ant alle his yfere
That him were so duere.
The kyng com into halle,
230      Among his knyhtes alle.
Forth he clepeth Athelbrus,
His stiward, ant him seide thus:
"Stiward, tac thou here
My fundling, forto lere,
235      Of thine mestere,
Of wode ant of ryvere;
Ant toggen o the harpe
With is nayles sharpe;
Ant tech him alle the listes
240      That thou ever wystest:
Byfore me to kerven,
Ant of my coupe to serven.
Ant his feren devyse
With ous other servise.
245      Horn Child, thou understond,
Tech him of harpe ant of song."

¶ Athelbrus gon leren
Horn ant hyse feren.
Horn mid herte lahte
250      Al that mon him tahte.
Withinne court ant withoute,
Ant overal aboute,
Lovede men Horn Child,
Ant most him lovede Rymenyld,
255      The kynges oune dohter,
For he wes in hire thohte.
Hue lovede him in hire mod,
For he wes feir ant eke god.
Ant thah hue ne dorste, at bord,
260      Mid him speke ner a word,
Ne in the halle,
Among the knyhtes alle,
Hyre sorewe ant hire pyne
Nolde never fyne
265      Bi daye ne by nyhte,
For hue speke ne myhte

And your fairness
All around Westness.
Horn, you're so sweet,
I'll not abandon you."
225    King Aylmer rode home,
And Horn with him, his foundling,
And all his companions
Who were very dear to him.
The king came into hall,
230    Among all his knights.
He calls forth Athelbrus,
His steward, and to him said thus:
"Steward, take here
My foundling, to be instructed,
235    According to your profession,
About wood and river;
And to pluck the harp
With his sharp nails;
And teach him all the arts
240    That you've ever known:
How to carve before me,
And to serve my cup.
And arrange for his fellows
To have other service with us.
245    Of Horn Child, you understand,
Teach him harp and song."

¶ Athelbrus began to teach
Horn and his fellows.
Horn learned willingly
250    All that man taught him.
In and out of court,
And everywhere,
People loved Horn Child,
And Rimenild loved him most,
255    The king's own daughter,
For he was on her mind.
She loved him passionately,
For he was fair and also good.
And though she dared not, at table,
260    Speak to him barely a word,
Nor in the hall,
Among all the knights,
Her sorrow and her pain
Would never cease
265    Day or night,
For she might not speak

With Horn, that wes so feir ant fre.
Tho hue ne myhte with him be,
In herte hue hade care ant wo,
270 Ant thus hue bithohte hire tho.
Hue sende hyre sonde
Athelbrus to honde,
85r] That he come hire to,
Ant also shulde Horn do,
275 Into hire boure,
For hue bigon to loure.
Ant the sonde sayde
That seek wes the mayde,
Ant bed him come suythe,
280 For hue nis nout blythe.

¶ The stiward wes in huerte wo,
For he nuste whet he shulde do,
What Rymenild bysohte.
Gret wonder, him thohte,
285 Aboute Horn the yinge,
To boure forte bringe.
He thohte on is mode
Hit nes for none gode.
He tok with him another:
290 Athulf, Hornes brother.
"Athulf," quoth he, "ryht anon
Thou shalt with me to boure gon
To speke with Rymenild stille,
To wyte hyre wille.
295 Thou art Hornes yliche —
Thou shalt hire bysuyke;
Sore me adrede
That hue wole Horn mysrede."
Athelbrus ant Athulf bo
300 To hire boure beth ygo.
Upon Athulf Childe
Rymenild con waxe wilde —
Hue wende Horn it were
That hue hade there.
305 Hue seten adoun stille
Ant seyden hure wille;
In hire armes tueye
Athulf he con leye.
"Horn," quoth heo, "wel longe
310 Y have loved the stronge;
Thou shalt thy treuthe plyhte
In myn hond, with ryhte,

- The princess pretends to be sick and asks for the steward
and Horn to her private apartments.
  ↳ The steward brings Horn's brother instead to trick her.
  ↳ She confesses her feelings to the brother.

ART. 70. KING HORN                                              313

With Horn, who was so fair and noble.
Since she might not be with him,
In heart she had care and pain,
270    And so she devised a plan then.
She sent her messenger
To summon Athelbrus,
85r]    That he should come to her,
And that Horn should come too,
275    Into her bower,
For she began to feel ill.
And so the messenger said
That the maiden was sick,
And bade him come quickly,
280    For she's not at all happy.

¶ The steward was concerned,
For he didn't know what he should do,
Or what Rimenild was after.
It was very strange, he thought,
285    Concerning Horn the young,
To bring him to her bower.
He decided in his mind
That it was for no good.
He took with him someone else:
290    Athulf, Horn's brother.
"Athulf," he said, "right now
You'll go with me to bower
To speak privately with Rimenild,
To understand her will.
295    You are like Horn —
You will trick her;
I am deeply worried
That she'll lead Horn astray."
Athelbrus and Athulf both
300    Have gone to her bower.
Toward Athulf Child
Rimenild then grew bold —
She thought it was Horn
Whom she had there.
305    She sat down softly
And revealed her will;
In her two arms
Athulf did lie.
"Horn," she said, "very long
310    I've loved you deeply;
You shall plight your troth
In my hand, properly,

Me to spouse welde
Ant Ich the louerd to helde."
315        So stille so hit were
Athulf seyde in hire eere:
"Ne tel thou no more speche,
May Y the byseche
Thi tale gyn thou lynne,
320    For Horn nis nout herynne,
Ne be we nout yliche,
For Horn is fayr ant ryche,
Fayrore by one ribbe
Then ani mon that libbe.
325    Thah Horn were under molde
Ant other ellewher he sholde
Hennes a thousent milen,
Y nulle him bigilen."

¶ Rymenild hire bywente,
330    Ant Athelbrus thus heo shende:
"Athelbrus, thou foule thef,
Ne worthest thou me never lef!
Went out of my boure!
Shame the mote byshoure,
335    Ant evel hap to underfonge
Ant evele rode on to honge!
Ne speke Y nout with Horne,
Nis he nout so unorne!"

¶ Tho Athelbrus, astounde,
340    Fel aknen to grounde:
"Ha, levedy myn owe,
Me lythe a lutel throwe,
Ant list werefore Ych wonde
To bringen Horn to honde.
345    For Horn is fayr ant riche —
Nis non his ylyche —
Aylmer the gode kyng
Dude him me in lokyng.
Yif Horn the were aboute,
350    Sore Ich myhte doute
With him thou woldest pleye,
Bituene ouselven tueye.
Thenne shulde withouten othe
The kyng us make wrothe.
85v]    Ah, forgef me thi teone,
356    My levedy ant my quene!
Horn Y shal the fecche,

- The weather reveals he is not Horn.
- She yells at the steward
- Steward explains that he would be responsible if something happened between them and then leaves to fetch

ART. 70. KING HORN   Horn.                                          315

To marry me as wife,
And I to hold you as lord."
315      As quietly as could be
Athulf whispered in her ear:
"Don't say any more,
I beg you,
You must end your speech,
320      For Horn isn't here,
Nor are we at all alike,
For Horn is fair and splendid,
Fairer by one rib
Than any man alive.
325      Though Horn were under ground
Or even somewhere
A thousand miles from here,
I'd never be false to him."

¶ Rimenild turned around,
330      And she rebuked Athelbrus thus:
"Athelbrus, you foul thief,
You'll never be dear to me!
Get out of my bower!
May shame fall on you,
335      And ill fortune seize you
And hang you on an evil cross!
I'm not speaking with Horn,
Nor is *he* so unattractive!"

¶ Then Athelbrus, perplexed,
340      Kneeled on the ground:
"Ah, my own lady,
Listen to me for a moment,
And hear why I hesitated
To bring Horn near you.
345      Because Horn's fair and splendid —
None is his equal —
Aylmer the good king
Placed him in my care.
If Horn were near you,
350      I might anxiously suspect
That you'd take pleasure with him,
Between your two selves.
Then assuredly would
The king be angry at us.
85v]      Ah, spare me your reproach,
356      My lady and my queen!
Horn I shall fetch for you,

Whamso hit yrecche."
　　Rymenild, yef heo couthe,
360　Con lythe with hyre mouthe;
Heo loh ant made hire blythe.
For wel wes hyre olyve!
"Go thou," quoth heo, "sone,
Ant send him after none,
365　A skuyeres wyse.
When the king aryse,
He shal myd me bileve
That hit be ner eve;
Have Ich of him mi wille —
370　Ne recchi whet men telle!"

　　¶ Athelbrus goth withalle;
Horn he fond in halle,
Bifore the kyng o benche,
Wyn forte shenche.
375　　"Horn," quoth he, "thou hende
To boure gyn thou wende
To speke with Rymenild the yynge,
Dohter oure kynge;
Wordes suythe bolde
380　Thin herte gyn thou holde,
Horn, be thou me trewe.
Shal the nout arewe."
　　He eode forth to ryhte
To Rymenild the bryhte.
385　Aknewes he him sette,
Ant suetliche hire grette.
Of is fayre syhte
Al that bour gan lyhte!
He spac faire is speche;
390　Ne durth non him teche:
"Wel thou sitte ant sothte,
Rymenild, kinges dohter,
Ant thy maydnes here,
That sitteth thyne yfere.
395　Kynges styward oure
Sende me to boure
Forte yhere, levedy myn,
Whet be wille thyn."
　　Rymenild up gon stonde
400　Ant tok him by the honde.
Heo made feyre chere,
Ant tok him bi the suere,
Ofte heo him custe,

Whatever anyone cares."
　　Rimenild, as well she might,
360　Then broke into a smile;
She laughed and grew happy.
She was ever so delighted!
"Go," she said, "at once,
And send him after noon,
365　Dressed as a squire.
When the king arises,
He'll remain with me
Until almost evening;
I'll have my will of him —
370　I don't care what people say!"

　　¶ Athelbrus left immediately;
He found Horn in the hall,
Before the king at table,
Ready to pour wine.
375　"Horn," he said, "politely
To the bower you must go
To speak with Rimenild the young,
Daughter of our king;
Words overly bold
380　You must hold in your heart,
Horn, as you're true to me.
You won't regret it."
　　He went forth directly
To Rimenild the bright.
385　On knees he set himself,
And sweetly greeted her.
By his fair countenance
All the bower was brightened!
He spoke his words eloquently;
390　No one needed to teach him:
"May you be well and true,
Rimenild, king's daughter,
And your maidens here,
Assembled around you.
395　Our king's steward
Sent me to your bower
In order to hear, my lady,
What may be your will."
　　Rimenild then stood up
400　And took him by the hand.
She behaved pleasantly,
And clasped him by the neck,
Often she kissed him,

      So wel hyre luste.
405    "Welcome, Horn," thus sayde
      Rymenild that mayde.
      "An even ant amorewe,
      For the Ich habbe sorewe
      That Y have no reste,
410    Ne slepe me ne lyste.
      Horn, thou shalt wel swythe
      Mi longe serewe lythe.
      Thou shalt, wythoute strive,
      Habbe me to wyve.
415    Horn, have of me reuthe,
      Ant plyht me thi treuthe."

       ¶ Horn tho him bythohte
      Whet he speken ohte.
      "Crist," quoth Horn, "the wisse
420    Ant geve the hevene blisse
      Of thine hosebonde,
      Who he be alonde.
      Ich am ybore thral,
      Thy fader fundlyng, withal;
425    Of kunde me ne felde
      The to spouse welde.
      Hit nere no fair weddyng
      Bituene a thral ant the kyng."
       Tho gon Rymenild mislyken,
430    Ant sore bigon to syken,
      Armes bigon unbowe,
      Ant doun heo fel yswowe.
      Horn hire up hente,
      Ant in is armes trente.
435    He gon hire to cusse,
      Ant feyre, forte wisse.
       "Rymenild," quoth he, "duere,
      Help me that Ych were
86r]   Ydobbed to be knyhte,
440    Suete, bi al thi myhte,
      To mi louerd the kyng —
      That he me geve dobbyng.
      Thenne is my thralhede
      Al wend into knyhthede;
445    Y shal waxe more,
      Ant do, Rymenild, thi lore."
       Tho Rymenild the yynge
      Aros of hire swowenynge:
      "Nou, Horn, to sothe,

- she wants to marry Horn; he says he is in essence a slave and therefore an unfit match.
⮡ He changes his mind and asks her to help him become a knight so he can marry her.

ART. 70. KING HORN                                                          319

As much as she pleased.
405   "Welcome, Horn," then said
Rimenild the maiden.
"By evening and morning,
Because of you I've had sorrow
Such that I find no rest,
410   Neither sleep nor pleasure.
Horn, you shall very soon
Assuage my long-held sorrow.
You shall, without resistence,
Have me as wife.
415   Horn, take pity on me,
And plight me your troth."

    ¶ Horn then considered
What he ought to say.
"Christ," Horn said, "guide you
420   And give you heaven's bliss
With your husband,
Whoever on earth he be.
I am born a slave,
Your father's foundling, too;
425   It doesn't fall to me by nature
To marry you as spouse.
There's no proper wedding
Between a thrall and the king."
    Then Rimenild was perturbed,
430   And began to sigh desperately,
Began to throw up her arms,
And she fell down in a swoon.
Horn caught her up,
And turned her in his arms.
435   He began to kiss her,
And sweetly, to tell the truth.
    "Rimenild," he said, "dear one,
Help me so that I may be
86r]   Dubbed as a knight,
440   Sweet one, by all your power,
Before my lord the king —
That he give me dubbing.
Then will my servitude
Wholly change to knighthood;
445   I shall grow greater,
And do, Rimenild, your bidding."
    Then Rimenild the young
Woke up from her swoon:
"Now, Horn, in truth,

450     Y leve the, by thyn othe.
        Thou shalt be maked knyht
        Er then this fourteniht.
        Ber thou her thes coppe,
        Ant thes ringes theruppe,
455     To Athelbrus the styward,
        Ant say him he holde foreward.
        Sey Ich him biseche,
        With loveliche speche,
        That he for the falle
460     To the kynges fet in halle,
        That he, with is worde,
        The knyhty with sworde.
        With selver ant with golde
        Hit worth him wel yyolde.
465     Nou Crist him lene spede
        Thin erndyng do bede."

            ¶ Horn toke is leve,
        For hit wes neh eve.
        Athelbrus he sohte
470     Ant tok him that he brohte,
        Ant tolde him thare
        Hou he hede yfare.
        He seide him is nede,
        Ant him bihet is mede.
475         Athelbrus so blythe
        Eode into halle swythe
        Ant seide: "Kyng, nou leste
        O tale mid the beste.
        Thou shalt bere coroune
480     Tomarewe in this toune.
        Tomarewe is thi feste —
        The bihoveth geste.
        Ich the rede mid al my myht
        That thou make Horn knyht
485     Thin armes do him welde.
        God knyht he shal the yelde."
            The kyng seide wel sone:
        "Hit is wel to done!
        Horn me wel quemeth;
490     Knyht him wel bysemeth.
        He shal have mi dobbyng
        Ant be myn other derlyng,
        Ant hise feren tuelve
        He shal dobbe himselve.
495     Alle Y shal hem knyhte

*— The steward is payed to, suggest the king unight Hoen. So the king says he will unight Hoen and the Hoen shall thight all his men.*

450     I believe you, by your oath.
        You shall be made knight
        Within this fortnight.
        Take here this cup,
        And these rings too,
455     To Athelbrus the steward,
        And tell him to keep his promise.
        Say that I beseech him,
        With gracious words,
        That for you he should bow
460     At the king's foot in hall,
        So that he should, with his oath,
        Knight you with sword.
        With silver and with gold
        He'll be well rewarded.
465     Now Christ lend him success
        In urging your business."

        ¶ Horn took his leave,
        For it was near evening.
        He sought Athelbrus
470     And gave him what he brought,
        And told him there
        How he had fared.
        He told him about his need,
        And promised him his reward.
475       Athelbrus ever so joyfully
        Walked quickly into the hall
        And said: "King, now listen
        To the best of stories.
        You shall bear the crown
480     Tomorrow in this town.
        Tomorrow is your feast —
        You need to host an event.
        I advise you wholeheartedly
        That you dub Horn knight
485     To have him wield your arms.
        A good knight he'll prove for you."
        The king said right away:
        "That's a good thing to do!
        Horn pleases me well;
490     Knighthood well suits him.
        He shall have my dubbing
        And be my other favorite,
        And his twelve comrades
        He himself shall dub.
495     I will knight them all

Byfore me to fyhte!"
   Al that the lyhte day sprong,
Aylmere thohte long.
The day bigon to springe.
500    Horn com byfore the kynge
With his tuelf fere,
Alle ther ywere.
Horn knyht made he
With ful gret solempnite,
505    Sette him on a stede
Red so eny glede.
Smot him a lute wiht
Ant bed him buen a god knyht.
Athulf vel akne ther
510    Ant thonkede Kyng Aylmer:

    ¶ "Nou is knyht Sire Horn,
That in Sudenne wes yborn.
Lord he is of londe
Ant of us, that by him stonde.
515    Thin armes he haveth ant thy sheld
Forte fyhte in the feld.
Let him us alle knyhte,
So hit is his ryhte."
    Aylmer seide ful ywis:
520    "Nou do that thi wille ys."
Horn adoun con lyhte
Ant made hem alle to knyhte.
86v]    For muchel wes the geste,
Ant more wes the feste!
525    That Rymenild nes nout there.
Hire thohte seve yere.
Efter, Horn hue sende.
Horn into boure wende.
He nolde gon is one —
530    Athulf wes hys ymone.

    ¶ "Rymenild welcometh Sire Horn
Ant Athulf, knyht him biforn:
"Knyht, nou is tyme
Forto sitte by me.
535    Do nou that we spake:
To thi wyf thou me take.
Nou thou hast wille thyne,
Unbynd me of this pyne!"
    "Rymenild, nou be stille.
540    Ichulle don al thy wille,

- Horn is knighted and given a red horse.
- Horn and his brethren go to Rimenild's apartments where she again asks for marriage.

ART. 70. KING HORN                                                  323

      To fight before me!"
        Until the daylight dawned,
      Aylmer pondered long.
      The day began to arise.
500     Horn came before the king
      With his twelve companions,
      All of them were there.
      He made Horn a knight
      With most great solemnity,
505     Placed him on a horse
      Red as any spark.
      He struck him a gentle blow
      And bade him be a good knight.
      Athulf fell to knee there
510     And thanked King Aylmer:

        ¶ "Now knighted is Sir Horn,
      Who was born in Sudenne.
      Lord he is of lands
      And of us, who stand by him.
515     He has your arms and shield
      To fight with in the field.
      Let him knight us all,
      For such is his right."
        Aylmer responded readily:
520     "Now do what you will."
      Horn then dismounted
      And dubbed them all knights.
86v]    Great indeed was the occasion,
      And even more the feast!
525     Rimenild was not there.
      It seemed to her seven years.
      Afterwards, she sent for Horn.
      Horn entered the bower.
      He wished not to go alone —
530     Athulf was his companion.

        ¶ Rimenild welcomes Sir Horn
      And Athulf, knight before him:
      "Knight, now it is time
      To sit next to me.
535     Do now what we spoke of:
      Take me as your wife.
      Now that you have your will,
      Release me from this pain!"
        "Rimenild, now be calm.
540     I shall do all your will,

Ah her hit so bitide,
Mid spere Ichulle ryde
Ant my knyhthod prove
Er then Ich the wowe.
545   We bueth nou knyhtes yonge,
Alle today yspronge,
Ant of the mestere
Hit is the manere:
With sum other knyhte
550   For his lemmon to fythte,
Er ne he eny wyf take,
Other wyth wymmon forewart make.
Today, so Crist me blesse,
Y shal do pruesse
555   For thi love, mid shelde,
Amiddewart the felde.
Yef Ich come to lyve,
Ychul the take to wyve."
    "Knyht, Y may yleve the,
560   Why, ant thou trewe be.

    ¶ "Have her this gold ring.
Hit is ful god to thi dobbyng.
Ygraved is on the rynge
'Rymenild, thy luef, the yynge.'
565   Nis non betere under sonne
That eny mon of conne.
For mi love thou hit were,
Ant on thy fynger thou hit bere.
The ston haveth suche grace
570   Ne shalt thou, in none place,
Deth underfonge
Ne buen yslaye with wronge,
Yef thou lokest theran
Ant thenchest o thi lemman.
575   Ant Sire Athulf, thi brother,
He shal han enother.
Horn, Crist Y the byteche,
Myd mourninde speche —
Crist the geve god endyng,
580   Ant sound ageyn the brynge!"
The knyht hire gan to cusse,
Ant Rymenild him to blesse.
    Leve at hyre he nom
Ant into halle he com.
585   Knyhtes eode to table,
Ant Horn eode to stable.

But before it happens thus,
I shall ride with a spear
And prove my knighthood
Before the time I woo you.

545 We are now young knights,
All risen up today,
And of the profession
This is the manner:
[One must] with some other knight

550 Fight for his beloved,
Before he take any wife,
Or with a woman make contract.
Today, may Christ bless me,
I shall do deeds of prowess

555 For your love, with shield,
In the midst of the field.
If I return alive,
I shall take you as wife."
    "Knight, I may trust you,

560 Why, if you be true.

    ¶ "Accept here this gold ring.
It is proper to your dubbing.
On the ring is engraved
'Rimenild, your beloved, the young.'

565 Under the sun there's none better
That anyone knows of.
Wear it for my love,
And bear it on your finger.
The stone has such power

570 That you'll not, in any place,
Be captured by death
Or slain unjustly,
Should you look upon it
And think of your beloved.

575 And Sir Athulf, your brother,
He shall have another.
Horn, I commend you to Christ,
With sorrowful lament —
May Christ give you success,

580 And bring you back sound!"
The knight kissed her,
And Rimenild blessed him.
    He took leave of her
And came into the hall.

585 Knights went to the table,
And Horn went to the stable.

Ther he toc his gode fole,
Blac so ever eny cole.
With armes he him sredde,
590        Ant is fole he fedde.
               The fole bigon to springe,
Ant Horn murie to synge.
Horn rod one whyle,
Wel more then a myle.
595        He seh a shyp at grounde
With hethene hounde.
He askede wet hue hadden,
Other to londe ladden.
An hound him gan biholde
600        Ant spek wordes bolde:
"This land we wolleth wynne
Ant sle that ther bueth inne!"
               Horn gan his swerd gripe
Ant on is arm hit wype.
605        The Sarazyn he hitte so
That is hed fel to ys to.
Tho gonne the houndes gone
Ageynes Horn ys one.
87r]       He lokede on is rynge
610        Ant thohte o Rymenyld the yynge.
He sloh therof the beste,
An houndred at the leste,
Ne mihte no mon telle
Alle that he gon quelle;
615        Of that ther were oryve,
He lafte lut olyve.


               ¶ Horn tok the maister heued,
That he him hade byreved,
Ant sette on is suerde,
620        Aboven o then orde.
He ferde hom to halle,
Among the knyhtes alle.
               "Kyng," quoth he, "wel thou sitte,
Ant thine knyhtes mitte.
625        Today Ich rod o my pleyyng
After my dobbyng.
Y fond a ship rowen
In the sound byflowen
Mid unlondisshe menne
630        Of Sarazynes kenne,
To dethe forte pyne
The ant alle thyne.

- Horn rides a black horse to the shore where he encounters
a heathen ship.
- As the heathens plan to invade, he slays 100 of them
- Horn takes the leader's head and presents it to

ART. 70. KING HORN  the king          327

There he took his good horse,
As black as any coal.
With weapons he armed himself,
590  And his horse he fed.
    The horse started to prance,
And Horn to sing merrily.
Horn rode for awhile,
Fully more than a mile.
595  He saw a ship moored
With heathen hounds.
He asked what they wanted
Or brought to land.
A hound began to look at him
600  And speak insolent words:
"This land we plan to conquer
And slay those who are in it!"
    Horn then gripped his sword
And wiped it on his arm.
605  He hit the Saracen so hard
That his head fell to his toes.
Then the hounds started to attack
Against Horn on his own.
87r]  He looked upon his ring
610  And thought of Rimenild the young.
He slew the best of them,
A hundred at least,
Nor might any man count
All that he did kill;
615  Of those who were ashore,
He left few alive.

    ¶ Horn took the leader's head,
Which he'd cut off of him,
And set it on his sword,
620  On top at the point.
He traveled home to hall,
Among all the knights.
    "King," he said, "well may you be,
And your knights with you.
625  Today I rode for my leisure
After my dubbing.
I found a ship steered
Into the flowing channel
By foreign men
630  Of Saracen race,
Intending to torment to death
You and all yours.

Hy gonne me asayly;
Swerd me nolde fayly!
635 Y smot hem alle to grounde
In a lutel stounde.
The heued Ich the brynge
Of the maister, Kynge.
Nou have Ich the yolde
640 That thou me knyhten woldeste."
     The day bigon to springe.
The kyng rod on hontynge
To the wode wyde
Ant Fykenyld bi is syde,
645 That fals wes ant untrewe,
Whose him wel yknewe.

     ¶ Horn ne thohte nout him on,
Ant to boure wes ygon.
He fond Rymenild sittynde
650 Ant wel sore wepynde,
So whyt so the sonne,
Mid terres al byronne.
     Horn seide: "Luef, thyn ore,
Why wepest thou so sore?"
655     Hue seide: "Ich nout ne wepe
Ah Y shal er Y slepe!
Me thohte o my metyng
That Ich rod o fysshyng.
To see my net Y caste,
660 Ant wel fer hit laste.
A gret fysshe at the ferste
My net made berste.
That fysshe me so bycahte
That Y nout ne lahte —
665 Y wene Y shal forleose
The fysshe that Y wolde cheose!"

     ¶ "Crist ant Seinte Stevene,"
Quoth Horn, "areche thy swevene:
No shal Y the byswyke,
670 Ne do that the mislyke.
Ich take the myn owe,
To holde ant eke to knowe
For everuch other wyhte.
Therto my trouthe Y plyhte."
675     Wel muche was the reuthe
That wes at thilke treuthe!
Rymenild wep wel ylle,

They began to attack me;
My sword didn't fail me!
635    I struck them all to ground
In a brief moment.
I bring to you the head
Of the leader, King.
Now have I repaid you
640    For making me a knight."
    The day began to dawn.
The king rode off to hunt
Into the wide woods
With Fikenild by his side,
645    Who was false and untrue,
Whoever knew him well.

    ¶ Horn thought not at all of him,
And went to the bower.
He found Rimenild sitting
650    And weeping very pitifully,
As white as the sun,
With tears all flowing.
    Horn said: "Dear one, your mercy,
Why do you weep so pitifully?"
655    She said: "I scarcely weep at all
As I shall before I sleep!
It seemed to me in my dream
That I rode to go fishing.
I cast my net to sea,
660    And quite long it held.
A big fish all of a sudden
Made my net burst.
That fish so got the better of me
That I could not capture it —
665    I think I shall lose
The fish I want to choose!"

    ¶ "By Christ and Saint Stephen,"
Said Horn, "understand your dream:
I will not deceive you,
670    Nor do what displeases you.
I take you as my own,
To hold and also to know
Before every other creature.
Thereto I plight my troth."
675    Great was the sorrow
That came with this troth!
Rimenild wept very hard,

Ant Horn let terres stille.
   "Lemmon," quoth he, "dere,
680    Thou shalt more yhere.
Thy sweven shal wende:
Summon us wole shende.
That fysshe that brac thy net —
Ywis, it is sumwet
685    That wol us do sum teone.
Ywis, hit worth ysene."

    ¶ Aylmer rod by Stoure,
Ant Horn wes yne boure.
Fykenyld hade envye
690    Ant seyde theose folye:
"Aylmer, Ich the werne,
Horn the wole forberne!
Ich herde wher he seyde,
Ant his suerd he leyde
695    To brynge the of lyve,
Ant take Rymenyld to wyve.
87v]   He lyht nou in boure,
Under covertoure,
By Rymenyld thy dohter,
700    Ant so he doth wel ofte.
Do him out of londe
Er he do more shonde."

    ¶ Aylmer gan hom turne,
Wel mody ant wel sturne.
705    He fond Horn under arme
In Rymenyldes barme.
"Go out!" quoth Aylmer the kyng.
"Horn, thou foule fundlyng,
Forth out of boures flore,
710    For Rymenild thin hore!
Wend out of londe sone!
Her nast thou nout to done —
Wel sone bote thou flette,
Myd suert Y shal the sette!"
715    Horn eode to stable,
Wel modi for that fable.
He sette sadel on stede;
With armes he gon him shrede.
His brunie he con lace,
720    So he shulde, into place.
His suerd he gon fonge;
Ne stod he nout to longe.

- Horn tells her her dream means someone will injure them.
- Fikenild tells the king Horn wants to kill him to marry his daughter and is currently sleeping w/ her
  - The king catches the couple embracing and tells

ART. 70. KING HORN ~~Horn to leave the kingdom.~~                     331

to Horn saddles his horse, arms himself and leaves.

And Horn stilled her tears.
  "Beloved," he said, "dear one,
680      You shall hear more.
         Your dream will come about:
         Someone will injure us.
         That fish that broke your net —
         Indeed, it is something
685      That will do us some harm.
         Indeed, it will come to pass."

         ¶ Aylmer rode by the Stour,
         And Horn was in the bower.
         Fikenild was envious
690      And spoke this nonsense:
         "Aylmer, I warn you,
         Horn will destroy you!
         I heard what he said,
         And he swore by his sword
695      To take your life,
         And take Rimenild to wife.
87v]     He lies now in bower,
         Under bedcovers,
         With Rimenild your daughter,
700      And so he does quite often.
         Exile him from the land
         Before he does more harm."

         ¶ Aylmer then turned home,
         So angry and so stern.
705      He found Horn embraced
         In Rimenild's bosom.
         "Get out!" said Aylmer the king.
         "Horn, you evil foundling,
         Be off from bower's floor,
710      From Rimenild your whore!
         Leave the land at once!
         You've no business here —
         Unless you flee right now,
         I'll strike you with sword!"
715      Horn went to the stable,
         Very offended at that lie.
         He put saddle on horse;
         With weapons he armed himself.
         He laced his coat of mail,
720      As he ought, in place.
         He grasped his sword;
         He didn't pause long at all.

To is suerd he gon teon.
Ne durste non wel him seon.
725      He seide: "Lemmon, derlyng,
Nou thou havest thy swevenyng.
The fysshe that thyn net rende,
From the me he sende.
The kyng with me gynneth strive;
730      Awey he wole me dryve.
Tharefore, have nou godneday!
Nou Y mot founde ant fare away
Into uncouthe londe
Wel more forte fonde.
735      Y shal wonie there
Fulle seve yere.
At the seve yeres ende,
Yyf Y ne come ne sende,
Tac thou hosebonde.
740      For me that thou ne wonde.
In armes thou me fonge
Ant cus me swythe longe!"
Hy custen hem a stounde,
Ant Rymenyld fel to grounde.

745      ¶ Horn toc his leve,
He myhte nout byleve.
He toc Athulf is fere
Aboute the swere
Ant seide: "Knyht, so trewe,
750      Kep wel my love newe.
Thou never ne forsoke
Rymenild to kepe ant loke."
His stede he bigan stryde,
Ant forth he con hym ryde.
755      Athulf wep with eyyen,
Ant alle that hit yseyyen.
   Horn forth him ferde.
A god ship he him herde
That him shulde passe
760      Out of Westnesse.
The wynd bigon to stonde
Ant drof hem upo londe.
   To londe that hy fletten,
Fot out of ship hy setten.
765      He fond bi the weye
Kynges sones tueye.
That on wes hoten Athyld,
Ant that other Beryld.

- Horn says he will go to a foreign land for seven years and that if he doesn't return, Rimenild should marry another man
- He tells his brethren to watch after Rimenild in his absence
- He sails to a new land and meets that land's king's

ART. 70. KING HORN  two sons.                    333

His sword he held on to.
He dared let no one see him.

725     He said: "Sweetheart, darling,
Now you have your dream.
The fish that tore your net,
He sends me away from you.
The king begins to fight me;

730    He plans to drive me away.
Therefore, have now farewell!
Now I must leave and go away
To a strange land
To experience much more.

735    I shall dwell there
Seven full years.
At the seventh year's end,
If I don't come or send a message,
Take yourself a husband.

740    Don't hesitate on my account.
Embrace me in your arms
And kiss me very long!"
They kissed for a while,
And Rimenild fell to ground.

745    ¶ Horn took his leave,
He could not delay.
He took Athulf his fellow
By the neck
And said: "Knight, so true,

750    Keep well my new love.
You've never failed
To keep and look after Rimenild."
He then mounted his horse,
And forth he did ride.

755    Athulf wept by eye,
And so did all who saw it.
Horn traveled forth.
He hired a good ship
That would carry him

760    Away from Westness.
The wind began to rise
And drove him onto land.
At land where he sailed,
He stepped from the ship.

765    He found on the road
Two king's sons.
One was called Athild,
And the other Berild.

*Joseph's story in the Bible had similar images/events.*

Beryld hym con preye
770 That he shulde seye
What he wolde there
Ant what ys nome were.

¶ "Godmod," he seith, "Ich hote,
Ycomen out of this bote,
775 Wel fer from byweste,
To seche myne beste."
Beryld con ner him ryde
Ant toc him bi the bridel:
"Wel be thou, knyht, yfounde.
780 With me thou lef a stounde.
Also, Ich mote sterve,
The kyng thou shalt serve!
Ne seh Y never alyve
So feir knyht her aryve!"
785 Godmod he ladde to halle.
Ant he adoun gan falle,
88r] Ant sette him a knelyng,
Ant grette thene gode kyng.
Tho saide Beryld wel sone:
790 "Kyng, with him thou ast done;
Thi lond tac him to werie.
Ne shal the no mon derye,
For he is the feyreste man
That ever in this londe cam."

795 ¶ Tho seide the kyng: "Wel dere
Welcome be thou here!
Go, Beryld, wel swythe,
Ant make hym wel blythe.
Ant when thou farest to wowen,
800 Tac him thine gloven!
Ther thou hast munt to wyve,
Awey he shal the dryve —
For Godmodes feyrhede,
Shalt thou nower spede!"
805 Hit wes at Cristesmasse,
Nouther more ne lasse.
The kyng made feste
Of his knyhtes beste.
Ther com in at none
810 A geaunt, suythe sone,
Yarmed of paynyme,
Ant seide thise ryme:
"Site, Kyng, bi kynge,

-Horn introduces himself as Godmod.
↳ The king's son says Horn shall serve his king as a
knight.
-The king is holding a christmas feast for his knights.

ART. 70. KING HORN ↳ a giant, armed like a pagan enters 335

Berild entreated him
770    That he should explain
What he wanted there
And what was his name.

¶ "Godmod," he said, "I'm called,
Come from this boat,
775    Very far from home,
To seek my best."
Berild then rode near him
And took him by the bridle:
"Well may you be found, knight.
780    Stay with me awhile.
Indeed, as I must die,
You shall serve the king!
I never saw alive
So fair a knight arrive here!"
785    He led Godmod to hall.
And then he bowed down,
88r]    Set himself on knee,
And greeted that good king.
Then said Berild at once:
790    "King, with him you ought to deal;
Use him to defend your land.
Then no one will do you harm,
For he's the fairest man
Who ever came to this land."

795    ¶ Then said the king: "Most dearly
Be you welcome here!
Go now, Berild, very swiftly,
And make him most glad.
And when you go to woo,
800    Challenge him with your glove!
Wherever you mean to propose,
He'll drive you off —
Because of Godmod's good looks,
You shall prosper nowhere!"
805    The time was Christmas,
Neither more nor less.
The king hosted a feast
For his best knights.
There came in at noon
810    A giant, quite suddenly,
Armed like a pagan,
Who said this rhyme:
"Sit, King, by king,

Ant herkne my tidynge.
815  Her bueth paynes aryve,
Wel more then fyve.
Her beth upon honde,
Kyng, in thine londe.
On therof wol fyhte
820  Togeynes thre knyhtes.
Yef oure thre sleh oure on,
We shulen of ore londe gon;
Yef ure on sleh oure thre,
Al this lond shal ure be.
825  Tomorewe shal be the fyhtynge
At the sonne upspringe."

      ¶ Tho seyde the Kyng Thurston:
"Godmod shal be that on,
Beryld shal be that other,
830  The thridde, Athyld is brother,
For hue bueth strongeste
Ant in armes the beste.
Ah wat shal us to rede?
Y wene we bueth dede!"
835      Godmod set at borde
Ant seide theose wordes:
"Sire Kyng, nis no ryhte
On with thre fyhte;
Ageynes one hounde,
840  Thre Cristene to founde.
Ah, Kyng, Y shal alone,
Withoute more ymone,
With my suerd ful ethe
Bringen hem alle to dethe."
845      The kyng aros amorewe;
He hade muche sorewe.
Godmod ros of bedde.
With armes he him shredde:
His brunye he on caste,
850  Ant knutte hit wel faste,
Ant com him to the kynge
At his uprysynge.
      "Kyng," quoth he, "com to felde
Me forte byhelde,
855  Hou we shule flyten
Ant togedere smiten."

      ¶ Riht at prime tide
Hy gonnen out to ryde.

*- The giant says if three of the knights can slay one of the giant inhabits they will leave the land, if not they'll claim the land.*

*- Horn volunteers to fight alone as three against one isn't fair.*

ART. 70. KING HORN

337

And heed my tiding.

815    Here do pagans arrive,
Well more than five.
They're here at hand,
King, in your land.
One means to fight

820    Against three knights.
If your three slay our one,
From your land we'll be gone;
If our one slays your three,
All this land ours shall be.

825    Tomorrow shall be the fighting
With the sun's uprising."

    ¶ Then said King Thurston:
"Godmod shall be one,
Berild shall be another,

830    The third, Athild his brother,
For they are strongest
And the best at arms.
But what shall avail us?
I fear we are dead!"

835    Godmod sat at table
And said these words:
"Sir King, it's not right
For one to fight three;
Against one hound,

840    Three Christians to fight.
So, King, I shall alone,
Without more companions,
Full readily with my sword
Bring them all to death."

845    The king arose the next day;
He bore deep sorrow.
Godmod rose out of bed.
With weapons he armed himself:
He put on his coat of mail,

850    And laced it very tightly,
And he came to the king
As he was arising.
"King," he said, "come to field
To behold me,

855    How we shall oppose
And strike each other."

    ¶ Just at the hour of prime
He began to ride out.

|        | Hy founden in a grene |
|--------|-----------------------|
| 860    | A geaunt swythe kene, |
|        | His feren him biside, |
|        | That day forto abyde. |
|        | Godmod then engaged — |
|        | Nolde he nout faylen! |
| 88v]   | He gef duntes ynowe; |
| 866    | The payen fel yswowe. |
|        | Ys feren gonnen hem withdrawe, |
|        | For huere maister wes neh slawe. |
|        | He seide, "Knyht, thou reste |
| 870    | Awhyle, yef the leste. |
|        | Y ne hevede ner of monnes hond |
|        | So harde duntes, in non lond, |
|        | Bote of the Kyng Murry, |
|        | That wes swithe sturdy. |
| 875    | He wes of Hornes kenne. |
|        | Y sloh him in Sudenne!" |

|        | ¶ Godmod him gon agryse, |
|--------|--------------------------|
|        | Ant his blod aryse. |
|        | Byforen him he seh stonde |
| 880    | That drof him out of londe |
|        | Ant fader his aquelde! |
|        | He smot him under shelde. |
|        | He lokede on is rynge |
|        | Ant thohte o Rymenild the yynge. |
| 885    | Mid god suerd, at the furste, |
|        | He smot him thourh the huerte. |
|        | The payns bigonne to fleon |
|        | Ant to huere shype teon — |
|        | To ship hue wolden erne! |
| 890    | Godmod hem con werne. |
|        | The kynges sones tweyne, |
|        | The paiens slowe beyne. |
|        | Tho wes Godmod swythe wo, |
|        | Ant the payens he smot so |
| 895    | That in a lutel stounde |
|        | The paiens hy felle to grounde. |
|        | Godmod ant is men |
|        | Slowe the payenes everuchen. |
|        | His fader deth ant ys lond |
| 900    | Awrek Godmod with his hond! |
|        | The kyng, with reuthful chere, |
|        | Lette leggen is sones on bere, |
|        | Ant bringen hom to halle. |
|        | Muche sorewe hue maden alle |

*- He wills a quint and almost wills the leader.*
*- The leader says he has never seen such a fighter accept*
*when he killed the king of Suddene (Horn's father)*
*- Godrod slays the leader and then all the pagens.*

ART. 70. KING HORN    *→ the pagens had slain the kings two sons*    339

He encountered on a green
860     A ferocious giant,
His companions beside him,
Expectant of that day.
Godmod then engaged them —
He would not fail!
88v]     He struck plenty of blows;
866     The pagan fell in a swoon.
His companions withdrew,
For their leader was almost slain.
    He said: "Knight, pause
870     Awhile, if you please.
I've never felt by anyone's hand
Such hard strokes, in any land,
Except from King Murry,   *← this king Allof, Horn's father*
Who was very powerful.
875     He was of Horn's kin.
I slew him in Sudenne!"

    ¶ Godmod began to tremble,
And his blood rose.
He saw stand before him
880     The one who'd exiled him
And killed his father!
He struck him under shield.
He looked upon his ring
And thought of Rimenild the young.
885     With his good sword, at once,
He struck him through the heart.
    The pagans started to flee
And withdraw to their ship —
To ship they wanted to run!
890     Godmod did hinder them.
The king's two sons,
The pagans slew them both.
Then Godmod was aggrieved,
And he smote the pagans so hard
895     That in a brief while
He felled them to ground.
Godmod and his men
Slew every pagan.
His father's death and his land
900     Godmod avenged with his hand!
    The king, with sad demeanor,
Had his sons laid on bier,
And had them brought into hall.
Great sorrow they all made

905    In a chirche of lym ant ston.
       Me buriede hem with ryche won.

           ¶ The kyng lette forth calle
       Hise knyhtes alle,
       Ant seide: "Godmod, yef thou nere,
910    Alle ded we were!
       Thou art bothe god ant feyr.
       Her Y make the myn heyr,
       For my sones bueth yslawe
       Any ybroht of lyfdawe.
915    Dohter Ich habbe one —
       Nys non so feyr of blod ant bone! —
       Ermenild that feyre may,
       Bryht so eny someres day.
       Hire wolle Ich geve the,
920    Ant her kyng shalt thou be."
           He seyde: "More Ichul the serve,
       Kyng, er then thou sterve.
       When Y thy dohter yerne,
       Heo ne shal me nothyng werne."

925        ¶ Godmod wonede there
       Fulle six yere,
       Ant the sevethe yer bygon.
       To Rymynyld sonde ne sende he non.
       Rymenyld wes in Westnesse
930    With muchel sorewenesse.
       A kyng ther wes aryve
       Ant wolde hyre han to wyve.
       At one were the kynges
       Of that weddynge.
935    The dayes were so sherte,
       Ant Rymenild ne derste
       Latten on none wyse.
       A wryt hue dude devyse —
       Athulf hit dude wryte,
940    That Horn ne lovede nout lyte.
       Hue sende hire sonde
       Into everuche londe
       To sechen Horn Knyhte
       Whesoer me myhte.
945    Horn therof nout herde,
       Til o day that he ferde
       To wode forte shete,
       A page he gan mete.
       Horn seide, "Leve fere,

- The king takes Godmod as his heir for saving the country.
- He also wants him to marry his daughter.
- Rimenild is set to marry a foreign king and hers Horn's brother sends out a messenger to find him throughout every land.
ART. 70. KING HORN                                                                      341
- Horn turns into a page in the woods while hunting.

905    In a church of lime and stone.
     They buried them with rich splendor.

       ¶ The king caused to be summoned
     All his knights,
     And said: "Godmod, had you not come,
910    We would all be dead!
     You're both good and fair.
     I make you here my heir,
     For my sons are slain
     And taken from life.
915    I have one daughter —
     None living is so fair! —
     Ermenild that fair maiden,
     Bright as any summer's day.
     I intend to give her to you,
920    And king here you shall be."
      He said: "More shall I serve you,
     King, before you die.
     When I desire your daughter,
     She'll refuse me nothing."

925      ¶ Godmod lived there
     Six full years,
     And the seventh year began.
     To Rimenild he sent no messenger.
     Rimenild remained in Westness
930    In deep sorrow.
     A king had arrived there
     And planned to marry her.
     The kings were in accord
     Regarding that wedding.
935    The time was so brief,
     And Rimenild dared not
     Resist in any way.
     She composed a letter —
     Athulf wrote it,
940    He who loved Horn dearly.
     She sent her messenger
     Into every land
     To seek Horn Knight
     Wherever one might.
945      Horn heard nothing of this,
     Until one day when he went
     To shoot in the woods,
     He came upon a page.
     Horn said, "Dear friend,

950     Whet dest thou nou here?"
89r]        "Sire, in lutel spelle
        Y may the sone telle:
        Ich seche from Westnesse
        Horn Knyht of Estnesse,
955     For Rymenild that feyre may
        Soreweth for him nyht ant day.
        A kyng hire shal wedde,
        A Sonneday to bedde,
        Kyng Mody of Reynis,
960     That is Hornes enimis.
        Ich habbe walked wyde
        By the seeside.
        Ne mihte Ich him never cleche
        With nones kunnes speche,
965     Ne may Ich of him here
        In londe fer no nere.
        Weylawey the while,
        Him may hente gyle!"

            ¶ Horn hit herde with earen
970     Ant spec with wete tearen:
        "So wel, grom, the bitide.
        Horn stond by thi syde.
        Ageyn to Rymenild turne,
        Ant sey that hue ne murne —
975     Y shal be ther bitime,
        A Sonneday er prime."
        The page wes wel blythe,
        Ant shipede wel suythe.
        The see him gon adrynke!
980     That Rymenil may ofthinke!
        The see him con ded throwe
        Under hire chambre wowe.
        Rymenild lokede wide
        By the seesyde
985     Yef heo seye Horn come
        Other tidynge of eny gome;
        Tho fond hue hire sonde,
        Adronque, by the stronde,
        That shulde Horn brynge.
990     Hire hondes gon hue wrynge!

            ¶ Horn com to Thurston the kynge
        Ant tolde him thes tidynge,
        Ant tho he was biknowe
        That Rymenild wes ys owe,

- The page says he is looking for Horn b/c Rimenild is
set to marry one of his enemies.
- Horn reveals himself and tells the messenger to tell
Rimenild he will come back in time.

ART. 70. KING HORN - The page drowns at sea before
reaching here.                                                    343

950    What are you doing now here?"
89r]      "Sir, in few words
        I can quickly tell you:
        From Westness I seek
        Horn Knight of Eastness,
955    For Rimenild that fair maiden
        Who grieves for him night and day.
        A king shall wed her,
        On Sunday take her to bed,
        King Mody of Reynes,
960    Who is Horn's enemy.
        I have walked far
        Along the seashore.
        I'm never able to find him
        By any kind of report,
965    Nor have I heard of him
        In lands far or near.
        Wailaway the while,
        Guile may overtake him!"

        ¶ Horn heard it with his ears
970    And spoke with wet tears:
        "Much good, man, come to you.
        Horn stands by your side.
        Return to Rimenild,
        And tell her not to mourn —
975    I'll be there on time,
        On Sunday before prime."
        The page was quite pleased,
        And set sail very quickly.
        The sea made him drown!
980    Rimenild may be sorry for it!
        The sea tossed his corpse
        Under her chamber window.
        Rimenild looked far off
        By the seashore
985    To see whether Horn came
        Or news came of any man;
        Then she found her messenger,
        Drowned, by the shore,
        He who should bring back Horn.
990    She began to wring her hands!

        ¶ Horn came to Thurston the king
        And told him this news,
        And then he revealed
        How Rimenild was his own,

995   Ant of his gode kenne,
      The kyng of Sudenne,
      Ant hou he sloh afelde
      Him that is fader aquelde.
      Ant seide: "Kyng, so wyse,
1000  Yeld me my service.
      Rymenild help me to wynne,
      Swythe, that thou ne blynne!
      Ant Y shal do to house
      Thy dohter wel to spouse,
1005  For hue shal to spouse have
      Athulf, my gode felawe.
      He is knyht mid the beste
      Ant on of the treweste."
         The kyng seide so stille,
1010  "Horn, do al thi wille."
      He sende tho by sonde
      Yend al is londe
      After knyhtes to fyhte
      That were men so lyhte.
1015  To him come ynowe
      That into shipe drowe.

         ¶ Horn dude him in the weye
      In a gret galeye.
      The wynd bigon to blowe
1020  In a lutel throwe.
      The see bigan with ship to gon,
      To Westnesse hem brohte anon.
      Hue striken seyl of maste
      Ant ancre gonnen caste.
1025  Matynes were yronge
      Ant the masse ysonge
      Of Rymenild the yynge
      Ant of Mody the kynge.
      Ant Horn wes in watere —
1030  Ne mihte he come no latere!
      He let is ship stonde
      Ant com him up to londe.
      His folk he made abyde
      Under a wode syde.

89v]     ¶ Horn eode forh alone
1036  So he sprong of the stone.
      On palmere he ymette
      Ant with wordes hyne grette.
      "Palmere, thou shalt me telle,"

*- Horn goes to the king, explains what has happened and asks for help to win his wife in exchange for setting up his daughter w/ his brother.*
*- The king sends for knights and a ship.*
*- Horn arrives after the wedding.*
*- Horn walks in the forest and meets a palmer.*

995     And he was of good family,
         Of the king of Sudenne,
         And how he slew in the field
         Him who'd killed his father.
         And he said: "King, so wise,
1000    Repay me my service.
         Help me win Rimenild,
         Quickly, don't delay!
         And I shall act to establish
         Well your daughter's marriage,
1005    For she shall have as husband
         Athulf, my good friend.
         He's of the best knights
         And one of the truest."
           The king said most humbly,
1010    "Horn, do all your will."
         He then sent by messenger
         Throughout all his land
         For battle-ready knights
         Who were very skilled men.
1015    Many came to him
         Who drew into a ship.

       ¶ Horn set out on his way
         In a great galley.
         The wind started to blow
1020    In a little while.
         The sea began to drive the ship,
         Bringing them soon to Westness.
         He lowered sail from mast
         And cast the anchor.
1025    Matins were rung
         And the mass sung
         For Rimenild the young
         And Mody the king.
         And Horn was in the water —
1030    He couldn't have come any later!
         He caused his ship to rest
         And came ashore.
         He made his men wait
         Beside a forest.

89v]      ¶ Horn walked forth alone
1036    As on the day he was born.
         He met a palmer
         And greeted him with words.
         "Palmer, you must tell me,"

1040    He seyde, "of thine spelle,
        So brouke thou thi croune —
        Why comest thou from toune?"
            Ant he seide on is tale:
        "Y come from a brudale,
1045    From brudale wylde
        Of maide Remenylde.
        Ne mihte hue nout dreye
        That hue ne wep with eye.
        Hue seide that 'hue nolde
1050    Be spoused with golde —
        Hue hade hosebonde,
        Thah he were out of londe.'
        Ich wes in the halle,
        Withinne the castel walle;
1055    Awey Y gon glide —
        The dole Y nolde abyde!
        Ther worth a dole reuly!
        The brude wepeth bitterly."
            Quoth Horn: "So Crist me rede,
1060    We wolleth chaunge wede.
        Tac thou robe myne,
        Ant ye schlaveyn thyne.
        Today Y shal ther drynke
        That summe hit shal ofthynke."
1065        Sclaveyn he gon doun legge,
        Ant Horn hit dude on rugge,
        Ant toc Hornes clothes —
        That nout him were lothe!


            ¶ Horn toc bordoun ant scrippe
1070    Ant gan to wrynge is lippe.
        He made foule chere
        Ant bicollede is swere.
        He com to the gateward,
        That him onsuerede froward.
1075    Horn bed undo wel softe,
        Moni tyme ant ofte,
        Ne myhte he ywynne
        Forto come therynne.
        Horn the wyket puste
1080    That hit open fluste.
        The porter shulde abugge —
        He threw him adoun the brugge,
        That thre ribbes crakede!
        Horn to halle rakede,
1085    Ant sette him doun wel lowe

- The palmer explains he came from the wedding and that Rimenild wouldn't stop crying.
- Horn asks to exchange clothes.
- Horn breaks down the door and throws the porter over the bridge.

ART. 70. KING HORN                                                    347

1040    He said, "your story,
    If you value your head —
    Why come you from town?"
      And he said in reply:
    "I come from a wedding,

1045    From the cruel wedding
    Of maiden Rimenild.
    She couldn't make dry
    What she wept from her eyes.
    She said 'she didn't want

1050    To be wedded with gold —
    She *had* a husband,
    Though he was away.'
    I was in the hall,
    Inside the castle wall;

1055    I slipped away —
    I couldn't stand the grief!
    There was piteous sorrow!
    The bride weeps bitterly."
      Horn said: "As Christ counsels me,

1060    We have to exchange clothes.
    Take my robe,
    And you [give me] your cloak.
    Today I shall there drink
    Such that some shall regret it."

1065    He laid down his cloak,
    And Horn put it on his back,
    And took Horn's clothes —
    He wasn't at all displeased!

      ¶ Horn took staff and wallet

1070    And twisted his lip.
    He formed an ugly face
    And blackened his neck.
    He came to the gatekeeper,
    Who answered him insolently.

1075    Horn gently asked to enter,
    Many times and oft,
    But he might not succeed
    In coming inside.
    Horn pushed the wicket door

1080    Till it flew open.
    The porter must pay —
    He threw him over the bridge,
    Cracking three ribs!
    Horn hastened to the hall,

1085    And set himself down low

In the beggeres rowe.
He lokede aboute
Myd is collede snoute.
Ther seh he Rymenild sitte
1090    Ase hue were out of wytte,
Wepinde sore,
Ah he seh nower thore
Athulf is gode felawe,
That trewe wes in uch plawe.

1095        ¶ Athulf wes o tour ful heh
To loke, fer ant eke neh,
After Hornes comynge,
Yef water him wolde brynge.
The see he seh flowe,
1100    Ah Horn nower rowe.
He seyde on is songe:
"Horn, thou art to longe!
Rymenild thou me bitoke,
That Ich hire shulde loke.
1105    Ich have yloked evere,
Ant thou ne comest nevere!"
    Rymenild ros of benche
The beer al forte shenche
After mete in sale,
1110    Bothe wyn ant ale.
An horn hue ber an honde
For that wes lawe of londe;
Hue dronc of the beere
To knyht ant skyere.
1115    Horn set at grounde;
Him thohte he wes ybounde.

        ¶ He seide, "Quene, so hende,
To me hydeward thou wende.
90r]    Thou shenh us with the vurste —                    **[quire 10]**
1120    The beggares bueth afurste."
    Hyre horn hue leyde adoune,
Ant fulde him, of the broune,
A bolle of a galoun.
Hue wende he were a glotoun.
1125    Hue seide: "Tac the coppe
Ant drync this ber al uppe.
Ne seh Y never, Y wene,
Beggare so kene!"
    Horn toc hit hise yfere,
1130    Ant seide: "Quene, so dere,

In the beggar's row.
He looked about
With his blackened snout.
There he saw Rimenild sit
1090    As though she were crazed,
Weeping pitifully,
But he saw nowhere there
Athulf his good friend,
True in every adventure.

1095        ¶ Athulf was quite high in a tower
To look out, far and also near,
For Horn's coming,
If the waves should carry him.
He saw the sea flowing,
1100    But Horn nowhere sailing.
He said in his song:
"Horn, you're too late!
You've entrusted Rimenild to me,
That I should look after her.
1105    I've looked out always,
And yet you never come!"
    Rimenild rose from the bench
In order to pour the beer
With food in the hall,
1110    Both wine and ale.
A horn she bore in hand
For that was the land's custom;
She drank of the beer
To [honor] knight and squire.
1115    Horn sat on the ground;
It seemed to him he was bound.

       ¶ He said: "Queen, so noble,
Come hither to me.
90r]    Pour to us right away —
1120    The beggars are first."
    Her horn she laid down,
And filled for him, from a brown vessel,
A bowl holding a gallon.
She thought he was a glutton.
1125    She said: "Take the cup
And drink this beer up.
I never saw, I think,
A beggar so bold!"
    Horn gave it to his fellows,
1130    And said: "Queen, so dear,

[quire 10]

No beer null Ich ibite
Bote of coppe white.
Thou wenest Ich be a beggere;
Ywis, Ich am a fysshere,
1135　　Wel fer come byweste
To seche mine beste.
Min net lyht her wel hende
Withinne a wel feyr pende.
Ich have leye there,
1140　　Nou is this the sevethe yere.
Ich am icome to loke
Yef eny fysshe hit toke.
Yef eny fysshe is therinne,
Therof thou shalt wynne.
1145　　For Ich am come to fysshe,
Drynke null Y of dysshe.
Drynke to Horn of horne,
Wel fer Ich have yorne."

　　　¶ Rymenild him gan bihelde.
1150　　Hire herte fel to kelde!
Ne kneu hue noht is fysshyng,
Ne himselve nothyng,
Ah wonder hyre gan thynke
Why for Horn he bed drynke.
1155　　Hue fulde the horn of wyne
Ant dronke to that pelryne.
Hue seide: "Drync thi felle,
Ant seththen thou me telle
Yef thou Horn ever seye
1160　　Under wode-leye."

　　　¶ Horn dronc of horn a stounde
Ant threu is ryng to grounde,
Ant seide, "Quene, thou thench
What Y threu in the drench."
1165　　　The quene eode to boure
Mid hire maidnes foure,
Hue fond that hue wolde:
The ryng ygraved of golde
That Horn of hyre hedde.
1170　　Fol sore hyre adredde
That Horn ded were,
For his ryng was there.
Tho sende hue a damoisele
After thilke palmere.
1175　　"Palmere," quoth hue, "so trewe,

No beer will I taste
Unless it be from a white cup.
You think I'm a beggar;
In fact, I'm a fisher,
1135   Come very far home
To seek my best.
My net lies quite near here
Inside a most fair shelter.
I have laid it there,
1140   Now is this the seventh year.
I am come to take a look
Whether it's caught any fish.
Should any fish be in it,
Of that you shall win.
1145   Since I am come to fish,
I'll not drink from a dish.
Drink to Horn from a horn,
So far have I traveled."

        ¶ Rimenild then beheld him.
1150   Her heart began to chill!
She knew nothing about his fishing,
And nothing about him,
But she started to wonder
Why to Horn he'd asked to drink.
1155   She filled the horn with wine
And drank to that pilgrim.
She said: "Drink your fill,
And afterwards tell me
If you ever saw Horn
1160   Under cover of woods."

        ¶ Horn drank a bit from the horn
And threw his ring in its bottom,
And said, "Queen, consider
What I threw into the drink."
1165       The queen went to her bower
With her four maidens.
She found what she desired:
The engraved ring of gold
That Horn received from her.
1170   She was terribly afraid
That Horn was dead,
For there was his ring.
Then she sent a maiden
After that palmer.
1175   "Palmer," she said, "so true,

"The ryng that thou yn threwe —
Thou sey wer thou hit nome,
Ant hyder hou thou come."
   He seyde: "By Seint Gyle,
1180  Ich eode mony a myle,
Wel fer yent byweste,
To seche myne beste,
Mi mete forte bydde,
For so me tho bitidde.
1185  Ich fond Horn Knyht stonde,
To shipeward at stronde;
He seide he wolde gesse
To aryve at Westnesse.
The ship nom into flode
1190  With me ant Horn the gode.
Horn bygan be sek ant deye,
Ant, for his love, me preye
To gon with the rynge
To Rymenild the yynge.
1195  Wel ofte he hyne keste.
Crist geve is soule reste."

    ¶ Rymenild seide at the firste:
"Herte, nou toberste!
Horn worth the no more,
1200  That haveth the pyned sore."
90v]  Hue fel adoun abedde
Ant after knyves gredde
To slein mide hire kyng lothe
Ant hireselve, bothe,
1205  Withinne thilke nyhte,
Come yef Horn ne myhte.
   To herte knyf hue sette.
Horn in is armes hire kepte.
His shurte lappe he gan take
1210  Ant wypede awey the foule blake
That wes opon his suere,
Ant seide, "Luef, so dere,
Ne const thou me yknowe?
Ne am Ich, Horn, thyn owe,
1215  Ich, Horn of Westnesse?
In armes thou me kesse!"
Yclupten ant kyste
So longe so hem lyste.
   "Rymenild," quod he, "Ich wende
1220  Doun to the wodes ende,
For ther bueth myne knyhte,

- Horn tells her he was on Horn's ship when he became
  sick and died.
- Rimenild tries to kill herself but Horn stops her and
  then reveals himself.

ART. 70. KING HORN                                      353

The ring you threw in —
Say where you got it,
And how you came hither."
   He said: "By Saint Giles,
1180   I traveled many a mile,
Far away from home,
To seek my best,
To beg for my food,
For such then was my lot.
1185   I found Horn Knight standing,
Headed to ship by a shore;
He said that he planned
To arrive in Westness.
The ship took to sea
1190   With me and Horn the good.
Horn began to sicken and die,
And, for his love, prayed me
To go with the ring
To Rimenild the young.
1195   So often he kissed it.
Christ give his soul rest."

    ¶ Rimenild said at once:
"Heart, now burst asunder!
You no longer have Horn,
1200   For whom you've pined sorely."
90v]   She fell down on her bed
And cried out for knives
To slay her hated king
And herself, too,
1205   On this very night,
If Horn could not come.
   She set a knife to her heart.
Horn restrained her in his arms.
His shirt's edge he then took
1210   And wiped away the foul black
That was on his neck,
And said: "Beloved, so dear,
Don't you know me?
Who I am, Horn, your own,
1215   I, Horn of Westness?
Kiss me in your arms!"
They embraced and kissed
As long as they wished.
   "Rimenild," he said, "I must go
1220   Down by the forest's edge,
For there are my knights,

Worthi men ant lyhte,
Armed under clothe.
Hue shule make wrothe
1225 The kyng ant hise gestes
That bueth at thise festes —
Today Ychulle huem cacche!
Nou Ichulle huem vacche."

¶ Horn sprong out of halle.
1230 Ys sclavin he let falle.
Rymenild eode of boure,
Athulf hue fond loure:
"Athulf, be wel blythe,
Ant to Horn go swythe —
1235 He is under wode bowe
With felawes ynowe."
Athulf gon froth springe
For that ilke tydynge;
Efter Horn he ernde —
1240 Him thohte is herte bernde!
He oftok him, ywisse,
Ant custe him with blysse.
Horn tok is preye
Ant dude him in the weye.
1245 Hue comen in wel sone,
The gates weren undone.
Yarmed suithe thicke
From fote to the nycke,
Alle that ther evere weren,
1250 Withoute is trewe feren.
Ant the Kyng Aylmare,
Ywis, he hade muche care!
Monie that ther sete,
Hure lyf hy gonne lete.
1255 Horn understondyng ne hede
Of Fykeles falssede.
Hue suoren alle ant seyde
That hure non him wreyede,
Ant suore othes holde
1260 That huere non ne sholde
Horn never bytreye,
Thah he on dethe leye.
Ther hy ronge the belle
That wedlak to fulfulle;
1265 Hue wenden hom with eyse
To the kynges paleyse.
Ther wes the brudale suete

*[Handwritten annotations at top:]*
- Rimenild tells Horn's brother to meet his men in the forest.
- Horn's men slay everyone except his 12 men and the king of westness.
- Horn and Rimenild marry and then go to the king's palace where a wedding feast is held.

Worthy and skilled men,
Armed under clothing.
They shall disturb
1225     The king and his guests
Who are at these feasts —
Today I'll catch them!
Now will I go fetch them."

    ¶ Horn rushed out of hall.
1230     He let fall his cloak.
Rimenild went out of bower,
And found Athulf frowning:
"Athulf, be cheerful,
And go swiftly to Horn —
1235     He's under the forest shade
With numerous friends."
    Athulf began to leap forth
Upon hearing that very news;
He longed for Horn —
1240     It seemed his heart burned!
He caught up with him, indeed,
And kissed him happily.
    Horn took his band
And set them on the path.
1245     They entered directly,
The gates were unlatched.
[They were] armed most heavily
From foot to neck,
All those who were there,
1250     Except for his true companions.
And then King Aylmer,
Assuredly, he had much care!
Many who sat there,
Their lives they did lose.
1255     Horn had no knowledge
Of Fikenild's falseness.
They all vowed and said
They would not betray him,
And swore loyal oaths
1260     That none of them would
Ever betray Horn,
Even if he lay dying.
There they rang the bell
To seal that wedlock;
1265     They went home with delight
To the king's palace.
The wedding feast was pleasing

For riche men ther ete.
Telle ne mihte no tonge
1270    The gle that ther was songe.

     ¶ Horn set in chayere
Ant bed hem alle yhere.
He seyde: "Kynge of londe,
Mi tale thou understonde.
1275    Ich wes ybore in Sudenne.
Kyng wes mi fader of kenne.
Thou me to knyhte hove;
Of knythod habbe Y prove.
Thou dryve me out of thi lond,
1280    Ant seydest Ich wes traytour strong.
Thou wendest that Ich wrohte
That Y ner ne thohte:
By Rymenild forte lygge.
Ywys, Ich hit withsugge!
91r]    Ne shal Ich hit ner agynne
1286    Er Ich Sudenne wynne.
Thou kep hyre me a stounde
The while that Ich founde
Into myn heritage.
1290    With this Yrisshe page,
That lond Ichulle thorhreche
Ant do mi fader wreche!
Ychul be kyng of toune,
Ant lerne kynges roune;
1295    Thenne shal Rymenild the yynge
Ligge by Horn the kynge."

     ¶ Horn gan to shipe drawe
With hyse Yrisshe felawe,
Athulf with him, his brother;
1300    He nolde habbe non other.
The ship bygan to croude;
The wynd bleu wel loude.
Wythinne dawes fyve
The ship bigan aryve
1305    Under Sudennes side.
Huere ship bygon to ryde
Aboute the midnyhte.
Horn eode wel rihte.
He nom Athulf by honde
1310    Ant ede up to londe.
Hue fonden under shelde
A knyht liggynde on felde;

For the richness they ate there.
No tongue might describe
1270    The merriment there sung.

¶ Horn sat on a throne
And summoned them all there.
He said: "King of the land,
You know my story.
1275    I was born in Sudenne.
A king was my father by blood.
You made me a knight;
Of knighthood am I proven.
You drove me out of your land,
1280    And said I was a fierce traitor.
You thought that I'd done
What I never considered:
To lie by Rimenild.
Indeed, I deny it!
91r]    Nor shall I ever undertake it
1286    Before I've won Sudenne.
Keep her for me awhile
Until I have entered
Into my heritage.
1290    With this Irish page,
I shall penetrate that land
And avenge my father!
I shall be king of that town,
And learn the language of kings;
1295    Then shall Rimenild the young
Lie by Horn the king."

¶ Horn began to board ship
With his Irish companion,
Athulf with him, his brother;
1300    He would have no other.
The ship began to move;
The wind blew loudly.
Within five days
The ship reached land
1305    Along Sudenne's coast.
Their ship came to rest
At around midnight.
Horn proceeded immediately.
He took Athulf by the hand
1310    And went upon land.
They found under a shield
A knight lying on the field;

O the shelde wes ydrawe
A croyz of Jesu Cristes lawe.
1315     The knyht him lay on slape
In armes wel yshape.

¶ Horn him gan ytake
Ant seide: "Knyht, awake!
Thou sei me whet thou kepest,
1320     Ant here whi thou slepest.
Me thuncheth, by crois liste,
That thou levest on Criste,
Bote thou hit wolle shewe,
My suerd shal the tohewe."
1325     The gode knyht up aros,
Of Hornes wordes him agros.
He seide: "Ich servy ille
Paynes togeynes mi wille —
Ich was Cristene sumwhile.
1330     Ycome into this yle
Sarazyns, lothe ant blake.
Me made Jesu forsake,
To loke this passage
For Horn that is of age,
1335     That woneth her by weste,
God knyht mid the beste!
Hue slowe mid huere honde
The kyng of thisse londe,
Ant with him mony honder.
1340     Therfore me thuncheth wonder
That he ne cometh to fyhte.
God geve him the myhte,
That wynd him hider dryve,
To don hem alle of lyve!
1345     Ant slowen Kyng Mury,
Hornes cunesmon hardy.
Horn of londe hue senten.
Tuelf children with him wenten.
With hem was Athulf the gode,
1350     Mi child, myn oune fode!
Yef Horn is hol ant sounde,
Athulf tit no wounde.
He lovede Horn with mihte,
Ant he him, with ryhte.
1355     Yef Y myhte se hem tueye,
Thenne ne roht I forte deye!"

On the shield was drawn
A cross of Jesus Christ's law.
1315    The knight lay asleep
In well-fashioned arms.

      ¶ Horn then shook him
And said: "Knight, wake up!
Tell me what you guard,
1320    And why you sleep here.
I assume, by the cross emblem,
That you believe in Christ,
But unless you prove it,
My sword will cut you to pieces."
1325    The good knight rose up,
Shuddering at Horn's words.
He said: "I wrongly serve
Pagans against my will —
I was once a Christian.
1330    Upon this island have come
Saracens, hideous and black.
They made me forsake Jesus,
To look out at this passage
For Horn who's of age,
1335    And dwells here to the west,
A good knight with the best!
They slew with their hands
The king of this land,
And with him many hundred.
1340    Therefore it seems to me strange
That he's not come to fight.
God give him the strength,
The wind drive him hither,
To kill them all!
1345    And they slew King Murry,
Horn's powerful kinsman.
They exiled Horn from the land.
Twelve children went with him.
With him was Athulf the good,
1350    My child, my own offspring!
If Horn is whole and sound,
Athulf suffers no wound.
He loved Horn deeply,
And he him, rightly.
1355    If I might see those two,
Then I don't care if I die!"

*[handwritten marginal note: arent Horn and Athulf brothers?]*

      ¶ "Knyht, be thenne blythe,
Mest of alle sythe
Athulf ant Horn is fere,
1360     Bothe we beth here!"
      The knyht to Horn gan skippe
Ant in his armes clippe.
Muche joye hue maden yfere
Tho hue togedere ycome were.
91v]    He saide with stevene thare:
1366     "Yunge men, hou habbe ye yore yfare?
Wolle ye this lond wynne
Ant wonie therynne?"
He seide: "Suete Horn Child,
1370     Yet lyveth thy moder Godyld.
Of joie hue ne miste
Olyve yef hue the wiste."
     Horn seide on is ryme:
"Yblessed be the time
1375     Ich am icome into Sudenne
With fele Yrisshemenne.
We shule the houndes kecche
Ant to the deye vecche!
Ant so we shulen hem teche
1380     To speken oure speche!"

      ¶ Horn gon is horn blowe.
Is folk hit con yknowe.
Hue comen out of hurne
To Horn swythe yurne.
1385     Hue smiten ant hue fyhten
The niht ant eke the ohtoun.
The Sarazyns hue slowe,
Ant summe quike todrowe;
Mid speres-ord hue stonge
1390     The olde ant eke the yonge.

      ¶ Horn lette sone wurche
Bothe chapel ant chyrche.
He made belle rynge,
Ant prestes masse synge.
1395     He sohte is moder halle
In the roche walle;
He custe hire ant grette,
Ant into the castel fette.
Croune he gan werie
1400     Ant make feste merye.

    ¶ "Knight, be then happy,
Most of all because
Athulf and Horn his friend,
1360    We both are here!"
     The knight then leapt to Horn
And clasped him in his arms.
Much joy they made at once
When together they'd come.
91v]    He spoke familiarly there:
1366    "Young men, how have you been?
Do you think to win this land
And dwell therein?"
He said: "Sweet Horn Child,
1370    Your mother Godild still lives.
She won't lack for joy
When she finds out you're alive."
    Horn said in his rhyme:
"Blessed be the time
1375    That I've come to Sudenne
With many Irishmen.
We will the hounds catch
And to the death fetch!
And them so shall we teach
1380    To converse in our speech!"

    ¶ Horn then blew his horn.
His people did know it.
They came out of hiding
To Horn most eagerly.
1385    They struck and they fought
All the night and also dawn.
They slew the Saracens,
And some they cut up alive;
With spear-point they pierced
1390    The old and also the young.

    ¶ Horn soon caused to be built
Both chapels and churches.
He had the bells rung,
And the priests sing masses.
1395    He sought out his mother's hall
In the rock's wall;
He kissed and honored her,
And established her in the castle.
He began to wear the crown
1400    And make merry feasts.

Murie he ther wrohte,
Ah Rymenild hit abohte.

¶ The whiles Horn wes oute,
Fikenild ferde aboute,
1405    The betere forte spede.
The riche he gef mede,
Bothe yonge ant olde,
With him forte holde.
Ston he dude lade,
1410    Ant lym therto he made:
Castel he made sette,
With water byflette,
That theryn come ne myhte
Bote foul with flyhte,
1415    Bote when the see withdrowe,
Ther mihte come ynowe.
Thus Fykenild gon bywende
Rymenild forte shende,
To wyve he gan hire yerne.
1420    The kyng ne durst him werne
Ant habbeth set the day
Fykenild to wedde the may.
Wo was Rymenild of mode;
Terres hue wepte of blode.
1425    Thilke nyht Horn suete
Con wel harde mete
Of Rymenild his make:
That into shipe wes take;
The ship gon overblenche —
1430    Is lemmon shulde adrenche!

¶ Rymenild mid hire honde
Swymme wolde to londe;
Fykenild ageyn hire pylte
Mid his suerdes hylte.
1435    Horn awek in is bed —
Of his lemmon he wes adred!
"Athulf," he seide, "felawe,
To shipe nou we drawe!
Fykenild me hath gon under
1440    Ant do Rymenild sum wonder!
Crist for his wondes fyve
Tonyht thider us dryve."

92r]    ¶ Horn gon to shipe ride,
His knyhtes bi his side.

Joyously he ruled there,
But Rimenild suffered for it.

¶ While Horn was away,
Fikenild schemed about,
1405    The better to succeed.
To the rich he gave rewards,
Both young and old,
So that they'd ally with him.
He had stone carried in,
1410    And lime made for that purpose:
He had a castle built,
Surrounded by water,
So that none might enter there
Except bird in flight,
1415    But when the sea withdrew,
Then many might come.
    Thus did Fikenild proceed
To harm Rimenild,
He aimed to marry her forcefully.
1420    The king dared not refuse him
And has set the day
For Fikenild to wed the maiden.
Rimenild was anxious of mind;
She wept tears of blood.
1425    This same night noble Horn
Dreamed nightmarishly
About Rimenild his mate:
That she was taken into a ship;
The ship began to capsize —
1430    His beloved would drown!

¶ Rimenild with her hands
Wanted to swim to land;
Fikenild thrust against her
With his sword's hilt.
1435    Horn awoke in his bed —
For his beloved he was afraid!
    "Athulf," he said, "friend,
Let's now draw to the ship!
Fikenild has deceived me
1440    And does some horror to Rimenild!
May Christ for his five wounds
Tonight drive us thither."

92r]    ¶ Horn then rode to his ship,
His knights by his side.

*[handwritten marginal note:]* seems predicting the future / seeing what is happening far away

1445    The ship bigon to sture
        With wynd god of cure.
          Ant Fykenild her the day springe
        Ferde to the kynge
        After Rymenild the brhyte,
1450    Ant spousede hyre by nyhte.
        He ladde hire, by derke,
        Into is newe werke.
        The feste hue bigonne
        Er then aryse the sonne.
1455       Hornes ship atstod in Stoure
        Under Rymenildes boure.
        Nuste Horn alyve
        Wher he wes aryve.
        Thene castel hue ne knewe
1460    For he was so newe.
          The see bigon to withdrawe.
        Tho seh Horn his felawe,
        The feyre knyht Arnoldyn,
        That wes Athulfes cosyn,
1465    That ther set in that tyde
        Kyng Horn to abide.
          He seide: "Kyng Horn, kynges sone,
        Hider thou art welcome.
        Today hath Sire Fykenild
1470    Yweddeth thi wif Rymenild.
        White the nou this while
        He haveth do the gyle.
        This tour he dude make
        Al for Rymenildes sake.
1475    Ne may ther comen ynne
        No mon with no gynne.

         ¶ "Horn, nou Crist the wisse,
        Rymenild that thou ne misse!"
          Horn couthe all the listes
1480    That eni mon of wiste.
        Harpe he gon shewe
        Ant toc him, to felawe,
        Knyhtes of the beste
        That he ever hede of weste.
1485    Oven o the sherte
        Hue gurden huem with suerde.
        Hue eoden on the gravele
        Towart the castele.
        Hue gonne murie singe,
1490    Ant makeden huere gleynge,

1445 The ship began to stir
   In a good healthy wind.
    And Fikenild before dawn
   Went to the king
   For Rimenild the bright,
1450 And wedded her by night.
   He brought her, in the dark,
   Into his new fortress.
   The feast they began
   Before the sun rose.
1455  Horn's ship halted in the Stour
   Under Rimenild's bower.
   She didn't know Horn was alive
   Nor where he'd arrived.
   She didn't know that castle
1460 Because it was so new.
    The sea then withdrew.
   Then Horn saw his friend,
   The fair knight Arnoldin,
   Who was Athulf's cousin,
1465 Stationed in that tide
   To await King Horn.
    He said: "King Horn, king's son,
   You are welcome here.
   Today Sir Fikenild has
1470 Wedded your wife Rimenild.
   Know now that in this time
   He has plotted against you.
   He's had this tower built
   Just for Rimenild's sake.
1475 No one may enter there
   By any contrivance.

    ¶ "Horn, now may Christ guide you,
   That you not lose Rimenild!"
    Horn knew all the tricks
1480 Of which anyone was aware.
   He brought out his harp
   And took with him, for company,
   The very best knights
   He'd ever had from the west.
1485 On top of their shirts
   They girded themselves with swords.
   They went on the sand
   Toward the castle.
   They began to sing merrily,
1490 And make their minstrelsy,

That Fykenild mihte yhere.
He axede who hit were.
Men seide hit were harpeirs,
Jogelers, ant fythelers.
1495    Hem me dude in lete.
At halle dore hue sete.
Horn sette him a benche;
Is harpe he gan clenche.
He made Rymenild a lay,
1500    Ant hue seide, "Weylaway!"

¶ Rymenild fel yswowe —
Tho nes ther non that lowe!
Hit smot Horn to herte;
Sore con him smerte.
1505    He lokede on is rynge
Ant o Rymenild the yynge.
He eode up to borde
Mid his gode suorde;
Fykenildes croune
1510    He fel ther adoune,
Ant alle is men arowe
He dude adoun throwe,
Ant made Arnoldyn kyng there,
After Kyng Aylmere,
1515    To be kyng of Westnesse
For his mildenesse.
The kyng ant is baronage
Geven him truage.

¶ Horn toc Rymenild by honde
1520    Ant ladde hire to stronde,
Ant toc with him Athelbrus,
The gode stiward of hire fader hous.
92v]    The see bigan to flowen,
Ant hy faste to rowen.
1525    Hue aryveden under reme
In a wel feyr streme.
Kyng Mody wes kyng in that lond.
That Horn sloh with is hond.
Athelbrus he made ther kyng
1530    For his gode techyng;
For Sire Hornes lore,
He wes mad kyng thore.

¶ Horn eode to ryve;
The wynd him con wel dryve.

So that Fikenild might hear it.
He asked who it was.
Men said that it was harpers,
Jugglers, and fiddlers.
1495    They then let them in.
They sat at the hall door.
Horn sat down on a bench;
His harp he began to pluck.
He sang a lay for Rimenild,
1500    And she said, "Wailaway!"

¶ Rimenild fell in a swoon —
Then no one was laughing!
It struck Horn to the heart;
He was deeply pained.
1505    He looked upon his ring
And upon Rimenild the young.
He went up to the table
With his good sword;
Fikenild's head
1510    He there struck down,
And all his men in a row
He did overthrow,
And made Arnoldin king there,
After King Aylmer,
1515    To be king of Westness
On account of kindness.
The king and his baronage
Offered him tribute.

¶ Horn took Rimenild by the hand
1520    And led her to the shore,
And took with him Athelbrus,
The good steward of her father's house.
92v]    The sea then flowed,
And he quickly sailed.
1525    They arrived in a realm
By a most favorable current.
King Mody was king of that land,
Whom Horn slew with his hand.
He made Athelbrus king there
1530    For his good teaching;
On account of Lord Horn's learning,
He was made king there.

¶ Horn went to sea;
The wind drove him well.

1535 He aryvede in Yrlonde
   Ther Horn wo couthe er fonde.
   He made ther Athulf Chyld
   Wedde mayden Ermenyld.
    Ant Horn com to Sudenne
1540 To is oune kenne.
   Rymenild he made ther is quene,
   So hit myhte bene.
   In trewe love hue lyveden ay,
   Ant wel hue loveden Godes lay.
1545 Nou hue beoth bothe dede.
   Crist to heovene us lede!
    Amen.

1535 He arrived in Ireland
   Where Horn had once felt grief.
   He there had Athulf Child
   Wed maiden Ermenild.
    And Horn came to Sudenne
1540 To his own family.
   Rimenild he made there his queen,
   As it should happen.
   They lived always in true love,
   And they loved well God's law.
1545 Now they're both dead.
   Christ lead us to heaven!
    Amen.

**ABBREVIATIONS:** ***AND***: *Anglo-Norman Dictionary*; ***ANL***: *Anglo-Norman Literature: A Guide to Texts and Manuscripts* (R. Dean and Boulton); **BL**: British Library (London); **Bodl.**: Bodleian Library (Oxford); **CCC**: Corpus Christi College (Cambridge); **CUL**: Cambridge University Library (Cambridge); ***IMEV***: *The Index of Middle English Verse* (Brown and Robbins); ***IMEV Suppl.***: *Supplement to the Index of Middle English Verse* (Robbins and Cutler); ***MED***: *Middle English Dictionary*; ***MWME***: *A Manual of the Writings in Middle English, 1050–1500* (Severs et al.); ***NIMEV***: *A New Index of Middle English Verse* (Boffey and Edwards); **NLS**: National Library of Scotland (Edinburgh).

## BOOKLET 3

### ABC A FEMMES / ABC OF WOMEN [ART. 8]

The *ABC of Women* provides an alphabetic list of the virtues of women. The narrator claims he wants to protect women from the slanders of misogynistic and deceptive men: such men, he says, debase their breeding whenever they speak ill of women. Literate women are asked to convey this message to other women who cannot read so as to spread the truth that women, who are ever honorable and good, deserve men's respect. The speaker directs his argument, however, mainly at men, wishing to convince them it is wrong to disparage women's nature. The central rationale is that God chose a woman, that is, Mary, by whom to be born. Therefore Jesus and his mother offer the perfect model for understanding the abundant worth of women.

The piece has a playful tone that deftly equates the sexual pleasure women hold for men with the heavenly delight, healing, and salvation ushered in by Mary's role in God's incarnation. Several stanzas operate in a double register, blending the amorous play of lovers with the religious comfort God worked by entering Mary's body. Maintaining this light tone, the author eventually draws several brief, sharp vignettes of women suffering the risks and pains of pregnancy and labor, acting selflessly on our behalf (*pur nous*), much as Jesus suffered on the cross *pur nous*.

R. Dean suggests that this poem was composed to be sung "to the accompaniment of a stringed instrument" (*ANL* 201). For further commentary, see Revard 2007, pp. 103–04; and Kuczynski 2000, pp. 155–56. For comparisons to its analogue in Middle English, *Alphabetical Praise of Women*, see Dove 2000, pp. 331–36; and Pickering, pp. 287–304. The two poems are related, but it is not known which one was written first.

[Fols. 49r–50v. *ANL* 201. Långfors, p. 310. Vising §280. **Scribe:** B (Ludlow scribe). **Quire:** 5. **Initials:** Opening *Q* and *A–Z* stanza initials are each two lines high; initials of last two stanzas — *A* (*Ave*) and *A* (*Amen*) — are marked with paraphs and slightly enlarged. **Meter:** Thirty 11–line stanzas, abababadcc. Lines 1–8 are octosyllabic. Line 9 is two or three syllables. Lines 10–11 (proverbial in tone) have, together, twelve or fourteen syllables with the caesura marked. **Layout:** No columns, each stanza is copied on five lines, lines 1–8 bracketed, ninth line written to the right. **Editions:** Wright 1842, pp. 1–13 (no. 1); Holthausen; Dove 1969, pp. 95–102; Kennedy, pp. 74–94 (no. 5). **Other MSS:** None. **Middle English Version:** *Alphabetical Praise of Women*, in the Auchinleck MS (Edinburgh, NLS MS Advocates 19.2.1), fols. 324ra–325vb (ed. Kölbing, pp. 101–10; Holthausen, pp. 288–301; Burnley and Wiggins, online facsimile). **Translation:** Kennedy, pp. 74–94.]

23          *entame*. Literally, "harms, injures," and figuratively, "opens (a wound, heart, discussion, etc.)." The verb implies that the speaker's heart, wounded by love and now open, thus urges him to write about the wrongs women suffer.

111         *honme*. "Man," translated "Infant" because the *ABC* requires here a word beginning with *I*.

161–65      The coy, teasing language suggests double entendre; the speaker compliments a woman's mouth and perhaps a different bodily *bel doun*, which he leaves unnamed. Compare this stanza to *Annot and John* (art. 28), lines 21–30.

192–98      The speaker refers to women suffering through childbirth and its mortal dangers, a theme he will increasingly develop in the remainder of the poem. At the end of this stanza, *joye* "descends" from women, in the way they give birth.

221         *Tryacle*. A medicinal elixir. Compare *Annot and John* (art. 28), line 32. It is here compared to breast milk.

235         *bone aprise*. "Highly praiseworthy, estimable, excellent." For the sense of this phrase, used also at line 264, see *MED*, *ap(p)rise* (n.(2)), and *ap(p)risen* (v.), both derived from OF *aprisier* (v.).

254         *Ysope*. The herb hyssop, spelled in the translation "yssop" because the *ABC* requires here a word beginning with *Y*. See *MED*, *isope* (n.(1)).

313         *Jesum*. On this Latin accusative form in French verse, compare *Prayer to the Three Kings* (art. 108a), line 1.

322–27      The repetitions of *pur nous*, "on our behalf," for God's sacrifice, draw a likeness to the sacrifice women undergo in birthing humans, for which the same phrase is often repeated.

## DE L'YVER ET DE L'ESTÉ / DEBATE BETWEEN WINTER AND SUMMER                [ART. 9]

In *Debate between Winter and Summer* nature's seasonal renewal is made "un grand estrif" that ends with Winter banished and Summer ascendent. As each season argues for its advantages over the other, each also speaks in its own idiom: Winter debates in octosyllabic couplets against an opponent who utters lyrical tail-rhyme stanzas. They go three rounds, each longer than the last, till Summer finally wins. In the closing argument Summer discloses that his opponent dwells with Lucifer, while he hails from paradise. The debate thus gains a moral dimension, associating Winter with sin and evil, Summer with grace and comfort. Several have suggested that the author is Nicholas Bozon, a fourteenth-century English Franciscan who wrote a large number of religious poems in Anglo-Norman, as well as the antifeminist poem *Women and Magpies* (art. 78), appearing in Harley's quire 12 (see Jeffrey and Levy, pp. 14–16).

Debate poems are a late medieval form that might have been inspired by and modeled on Virgil's *Eclogues*. The earliest known European example addresses the same theme treated here: *Conflictus Veris et Hiemis*, commonly attributed to Alcuin (?735–804), an English scholar who became a leading teacher at Charlemagne's court. A tradition of setting Winter in debate with Summer continued with vigor in medieval Latin verse. The seasons in monumental debate also appear in medieval English folk celebrations of May Day, where there survive "vestiges of a once fully fledged ritual depicting the struggle between the representatives of Winter and those of Summer" (Matthews, p. 403). Numerous Harley lyrics align mood and morals with seasonal change (e.g., arts. 43, 52, 53, 63).

For commentary on the poem, see Bossy, pp. 162–63; Reichl 2000, pp. 220–26 (who presents Latin analogues); Revard 2007, pp. 105–08; and Cartlidge, pp. 248–52.

[Fols. 51ra–52va. *ANL* 146. Långfors, p. 423. Vising §366. **Scribe:** B (Ludlow scribe). **Quire:** 5. **Meter:** For Winter, octosyllabic couplets; for Summer, 6- and 9-line tail-rhyme stanzas, aabaab(aab), octosyllabic a-lines, tetrasyllabic b-lines. **Layout:** Double columns, speaker changes marked by paraphs. **Editions:** Jubinal, 2:40–49; Dove 1969, pp. 174–79; Bossy, pp. 2–14; (in error, Ker, p. x, lists Wright as editor). **Other MSS:** None. **Translation:** Bossy, pp. 3–15.]

89   *vous lou je bien*. "I well advise you." Forms of this idiom occur elsewhere at the end of the disputants' speeches. See also lines 146 and 190.

136–41  This stanza refers to meat preserved by salt- and smoke-curing.

150   *lerroy*. "Failed to mention"; see *AND, laier* (v.), "to omit, leave out."

156   *danz Poydras, Maymont, Sweyn*. These followers of Summer have names evocative of summer frivolity. I adopt here the translation given by Reichl for *Poydras*, "Littlecloth" (2000, p. 221), but see also *MED, peudreas* (n.), "dusty," a derogatory epithet drawn from the OF word for "dust, dirt."

176   *peus*. "Supported, sustained." See *MED, puen* (v.), from OF *puiier* (v.).

229   *a val*. This phrase, as found in the manuscript, does not rhyme on -*aunt*; it seems to link, instead, with the b-rhyme of the next stanza.

254   In this stanza Summer shifts the address from Winter to Winter's followers.

## VORTE MAKE CYNOPLE / HOW TO MAKE RED VERMILION     [ART. 10]

Eight recipes have been inserted by the manuscript's third scribe, whose work in a cramped hand is not much later than that of Scribe B. Seven recipes are for paints used by book illuminators, and one is for keeping an artist's metal instruments in good working order. The punctuation for arts. 10–17 is guided by the pause marks provided by the scribe. The first recipe explains the method for making red vermilion, which could be used for rubrication as well as for images.

[Fol. 52va. *MWME* 10:3685 [416]. **Scribe:** C. **Quire:** 5. **Layout:** Prose added to blank lower left column. **Editions:** Wright 1844, p. 64; Keller, p. 96. **Other MSS:** None. **Analogues:** See Fein 2013, p. 44 n. 28.]

incipit       *cynople*. See *MED*, *sinopre* (n.), "A red ocher used in making a vermilion coloring material; also the color vermilion, red."

1             *brasyl*. See *MED*, *brasile* (n.), sense (b), "a dye, dye-solution, or pigment from brazilwood."

              *seoth*. This verb refers to the process of reducing a liquid by boiling it down. See *MED*, *sethen* (v.(1)).

## VORTE TEMPRENE ASURE / HOW TO TEMPER AZURE                                    [ART. 11]

    This item is a recipe for making blue paint to be applied in manuscripts. Earwax is a recommended additive if the product develops bubbles.

[Fol. 52va. *MWME* 10:3685 [416]. **Scribe:** C. **Quire:** 5. **Layout:** Prose added to blank lower left column. **Editions:** Wright 1844, pp. 64–65; Keller, p. 96. **Other MSS:** None. **Analogues:** See Fein 2013, p. 44 n. 28. ]

incipit       *asure*. Blue pigment or paint; see *MED*, *asur* (n.(1) & adj.).

6             *gleyr*. "Egg white, glair." See *MED*, *glaire* (n.), sense (a), "the white of an egg," and sense (b), "a preparation made from the whites of eggs for tempering pigments." Glair was used for its binding properties in gesso painting and book binding. See art. 15 on the gluing of silver and goldfoil.

9             *gummet-water*. "Gum-water," that is, the water in which gum has been dissolved. See *MED*, *gommen* (v.).

## VORTE MAKE GRAS-GRENE / HOW TO MAKE GRASS-GREEN                               [ART. 12]

    This item is a recipe for making manuscript paint of a bright green color, perhaps with a tinge of blue. It combines mineral and plant matter.

[Fol. 52vb. *MWME* 10:3685 [416]. **Scribe:** C. **Quire:** 5. **Layout:** Prose added to blank right column. **Editions:** Wright 1844, p. 65; Keller, p. 96. **Other MSS:** None. **Analogues:** See Fein 2013, p. 44 n. 28.]

1             *verdigres*. See *MED*, *verdegrece* (n.), sense (d), "a green or blue-green pigment," made by applying acetic acid obtained from ripe apples to the green oxide that

forms on weathered copper or brass, from which the powdered dye was then distilled. See art. 13.

### VORTE MAKEN ANOTHER MANER GRENE / HOW TO MAKE . . . GREEN          [ART. 13]

The green made by this paint recipe is probably of a hue between the preceding and succeeding recipes, hence, a lighter green than *gras-grene*. It is made by adding rotten apple juice to the verdigris.

[Fol. 52vb. *MWME* 10:3685 [416]; **Scribe:** C. **Quire:** 5. **Layout:** Prose added to blank right column. **Editions:** Wright 1844, p. 65; Keller, p. 96. **Other MSS:** None. **Analogues:** See Fein 2013, p. 44 n. 28.]

### YET FOR GAUDE-GRENE / ANOTHER FOR YELLOW-GREEN          [ART. 14]

The green indicated here, *gaude-grene*, would be a yellow-green associated with the color of a rosary's counting beads.

[Fol. 52vb. *MWME* 10:3685 [416]. **Scribe:** C. **Quire:** 5. **Layout:** Prose added to blank right column. **Editions:** Wright 1844, p. 65; Keller, p. 96. **Other MSS:** None. **Analogues:** See Fein 2013, p. 44 n. 28.]

incipit    *gaude-grene*. See *MED*, *gaudi* (adj.), "yellowish green color or pigment."

1          *peniwort*. See *MED*, *wort* (n.(1)), sense 3.(e).

           *gladene*. A plant of the iris family. See *MED*, *gladene* (n.).

### VORTE COUCHE SELVERFOYL / HOW TO APPLY SILVERFOIL          [ART. 15]

After explaining how to make silverfoil, the author of this recipe details the delicate method for applying silverfoil to a manuscript illumination. He then explains how the technique for applying goldfoil is similar except that one should use glue of a reddened hue.

[Fol. 52vb. *MWME* 10:3685 [416]. **Scribe:** C. **Quire:** 5. **Layout:** Prose added to blank right column. **Editions:** Wright 1844, p. 65; Keller, pp. 96–97. **Other MSS:** None. **Analogues:** See Fein 2013, p. 44 n. 28.]

1          *gumme arabuk*. See *MED*, *gomme* (n.), "a gum from a certain species of acacia."

3          *pinsel*. See *MED*, *pencel* (n.(2)), "a small brush used for painting, manuscript illumination, etc.; also, a pointed straw or stick of similar use."

7          *thac*. "Pat, stroke, or dab"; see *MED*, *thakken* (v.).

9          *sise*. Glue. See *MED*, *sise* (n.(2)), "A sticky fluid used to prepare a surface before applying gold or silver overlay," and *assise*, sense 10.(c) (the form that appears in line 12).

11         *radel*. See *MED*, *radel* (n.), "Red ochre used as a pigment."

VORTE MAKEN IREN AS HART AS STEL / HOW TO MAKE IRON AS HARD AS STEEL    [ART. 16]

This item appears to be a recipe for painters and illuminators who must keep their metal implements hard and in good working order. The compound is prepared on a cloth, which is then wrapped around the implement. The instrument is next thrown into a fire, where it is hardened by the melted compound.

[Fol. 52vb. *MWME* 10:3685 [416]. **Scribe:** C. **Quire:** 5. **Layout:** Prose added to blank right column. **Editions:** Wright 1844, p. 65; Keller, p. 97. **Other MSS:** None. **Analogues:** See Fein 2013, p. 44 n. 28.]

1            *argul*. See *MED*, *argoille* (n.), "a tartar." Wright notes that "It appears, by the explanation the writer gives, that this was a word of only very restricted use" (1844, p. 65).

2–3          *Cluppe the egge of thi lome*. See *MED*, *clippen* (v.(1)), sense 2(b); *egge* (n.(2)); and *lome* (n.), sense (a), "an implement, tool."

VORTE MAKEN BLANKPLUM / HOW TO MAKE WHITE LEAD                          [ART. 17]

This elaborate recipe explains the process for deriving white lead (a paint substance) from lead. It requires a gallon-size vessel, altered so as to have pegs making rungs upon which to hang the lead in thin sheets. The vessel must have a tight lid. The chemical process requires vinegar and a setting of the vessel in horse dung for nine nights.

[Fol. 52vb. *MWME* 10:3685 [416]. **Scribe:** C. **Quire:** 5. **Layout:** Prose added to blank right column. **Editions:** Wright 1844, p. 65–66; Keller, p. 97. **Other MSS:** None. **Analogues:** See Fein 2013, p. 44 n. 28.]

incipit      *blankplum*. "White lead." See *MED*, *blaunk plum* (phr.).

10           *vleote*. See *MED*, *fleten* (v.(1)), sense 2.(a), "To flow, to be in a fluid or volatile state."

20           *undefiyet*. "Undissolved." See *MED*, *undefien* (v.).

## BOOKLET 4

INCIPIT VITA SANCTI ETHELBERTI / THE LIFE OF SAINT ETHELBERT          [ART. 18]

Saint Ethelbert [Æthelberht], martyred king of the East Angles (d. ca. 792–94), is the patron saint of the city of Hereford. The cathedral there is formally known as "The Cathedral Church of St. Mary the Virgin and Saint Ethelbert the King." Ethelbert's martyrdom is intertwined with the history of the cathedral because his body was brought to its site soon after he died, as explained in this legend. His murder occurred in a palace of King Offa at Sutton, near Marden, four miles north of Hereford. By legend, a well sprang up at the martyrdom site; Ethelbert's feast day on May 20 commemorates the event. The saint's body was buried at Hereford, but centuries later his head was exhumed and reburied at Westminster. Eventually his original tomb at Hereford was destroyed; a shrine was reerected there in 2007.

According to the legend (which merges with history), Ethelbert is the young king of East Anglia who intends to marry Alfrida, daughter of the powerful King Offa of Mercia. Offa holds an ambition to rule all of England. Another royal heiress, Sindritha, is first considered, for she already has her inheritance, but Ethelbert prefers Alfrida. The desire seems mutual, for when Ethelbert is murdered, Alfrida declares herself unsuited for marriage and departs the court to live as an anchoress in Croyland. Initially, Offa's position regarding the alliance is presented as uncertain, but he grows strongly opposed when his queen Cynethryth meddles to have Ethelbert treacherously destroyed. She does this because Ethelbert spurns her own illicit, lustful advances. Offa goes along with this plot perhaps because the marriage could threaten his own dominance if Ethelbert were to secure a claim as his successor. When Ethelbert enters Offa's palace in suit of Alfrida, an ally of Offa named Gwinbert beheads him, betraying a long-standing trust that had existed between himself and Ethelbert. In penance for this deed — and to retain power — Offa sponsors the canonization of Ethelbert.

This Harley 2253 vita of an Anglo Saxon martyr-king is an abridged version of the oldest form of the story. The source legend — represented here and in CCC MS 308 — comes from Hereford. As James notes, it appears to be the work of a local churchman composed for reading on St. Ethelbert's Day (pp. 218–19). Later accounts by Gerald of Wales (a canon of Hereford) and John Capgrave derive from Osbert of Clare's more prolix expansion of the source legend. In the twelfth century Osbert was a prior and eventually abbot of Westminster, where Ethelbert's head was a relic.

The Harley text has not been previously edited. It contains several passages that deviate from the longer version found in CCC MS 308. For further details on the legend in its various forms, see James, pp. 214–22; Jones, pp. 125–29; Blair 2002a, pp. 505–06, and 2002b, pp. 480, 483–84; Finberg, pp. 221–23; and *Murder of King Ethelbert*. On the depiction of kingship in this text and in MS Harley 2253 in general, see Corrie 2003, pp. 67–73. There are two other Latin tales of Anglo-Saxon saints in the Harley manuscript: *The Legend of Saint Etfrid, Priest of Leominster* and *The Martyrdom of Saint Wistan* (arts. 98, 116); on their presence, see Kuczynski 2000, pp. 138–40. The translation printed here is by Jan Ziolkowski, prepared for this edition.

[Fols. 53ra–54vb. Hardy 1:494–95 (no. 1054). **Scribe:** B (Ludlow scribe). **Quire:** 6. **Layout:** Double columns; large initials mark the beginning of each new section. **Editions:** None. **Other MS:** A longer version appears in CCC MS 308, fols. 1r–8r (ed. James, pp. 236–44). **Analogue:** Capgrave's fifteenth-century adaptation of Osbert's expansion (ed. Horstmann 1901, 1:412–19). **Translations:** None.]

2    *sanctus Beda*. Bede mentions Ethelbert's ancestor, Redwald (d. ?637), king of East Anglia, more than once. See, especially, Bede, p. 107.

4    *Leofruna*. James, p. 218, notes how the proper names found in this version represent older forms: Leofruna, Eglan (line 24), and Sindritha (line 25).

59   *Sottone*. Sutton, north of Hereford and near Marden, the site of a palace used by the Mercian King Offa. See *Murder of King Ethelbert*.

72ff.       The story of Queen Cynethryth's spurned advances turning to revenge against
            Ethelbert allows direct responsibility for the murder to be deflected somewhat
            from King Offa. A biblical model for this episode is the story of Joseph and
            Potiphar's wife (Genesis 39:7–20), a version of which is told by the Ludlow scribe
            in *Old Testament Stories* (art. 71).

117         *Stratum Waye fluminis*. James comments: "it seems not unreasonable to regard
            *Stratus waye* as meaning the street of the Wye, and as equivalent to Hereford" (p.
            219). CCC MS 308 reads: "propter ripam fluminis Wæge situm" (James, p. 242).

## ANIMA CHRISTI, SANCTIFICA ME / SOUL OF CHRIST, SANCTIFY ME                    [ART. 19]

This work is a familiar hymn and prayer used in liturgy and also accorded power as
conveying an indulgence — and sometimes an amulet invoking the body and blood of Christ
(Skemer, p. 191 n. 45). It is generally attributed to Pope John XXII (1316–34) and dated
around 1330. For commentary, see Kuczynski 2000, p. 140; Duffy 2006, p. 28; and Wilmart,
pp. 367–68.

[Fol. 54vb. Chevalier, p. 67 (no. 1090). Daniel 1:345. **Scribe:** B (Ludlow scribe). **Quire:** 6.
**Layout:** Copied as prose, filling a portion of a blank column; text opens with large initial
*A*. **Edition:** Valois, p. 532.]

10          *Et pone me iuxta te*. "And set me beside you" (Job 17:3). This line replaces the
            prayer's usual phrase "Et iube me venire ad te," "And bid me to come to you."

## QUANT VOY LA REVENUE D'YVER / A GOLIARD'S FEAST                               [ART. 20]

*A Goliard's Feast* is a comic monologue by a glutton who feasts and drinks with gusto
through the winter months, savoring especially the gourmand delights of Christmas, Lent,
and Easter. Despite its scant manuscript record, it probably had lively oral currency, for a
version exists in Old French as well. R. Dean calls it a "Tavern Song" (*ANL* 150). Both versions
have highly irregular stanzas, suggesting the changes, line displacements, and ad libs that
would have occurred in performance.

If the original poem had stanzas of uniform length, they appear to have been of ten
lines with three rhymes aaaabbacca, allowing for a 4-rhyme variant, abbaccadda. The basic
3-rhyme pattern is found in the French poem, lines 1–10, and in Harley's Anglo-Norman
version, lines 29–38, 57–66, with traces of it detectable elsewhere. There are also hints of
an interruptive 8-line stanza used to list delectable foods, in the form aabbccdd in short,
mostly 4-syllable lines. It seems loosely preserved at lines 67–74 (edible birds) and lines
95–100 (baked goods and more birds). Dove, too, detects stanzas of variable length (2000,
pp. 330–31).

The stanza was probably too challenging to be well sustained in actual minstrel practice.
The Ludlow scribe copies the piece evidently from a performance script or from memory,
omitting line breaks and filling a full recto page. The stanza breaks that are detectable by
rhyme and content usually correspond to the scribe's paraphs and capitals. For another
performance piece with unusual metrics, compare the English poem *Maximian* (art. 68).

Elsewhere the same scribe preserves numerous items of comic monologue in English (e.g., arts. 40, 81) and comic dialogue in French (e.g., arts. 37, 75). For commentary on this poem and its French analogue, see Revard 2005b, and 2007, p. 107.

[Fol. 55ra–b. *ANL* 150. Vising §242. **Scribe:** B (Ludlow scribe). **Quire:** 6. **Meter:** Though what is here preserved is quite irregular, the original meter was probably aaaabbacca, with four to six syllables per line; see explanatory note to lines 57–66. Stanzas of eight 4-syllable lines, aabbccdd, seem sometimes to intervene between 10-line stanzas. **Layout:** Double columns. **Editions:** Wright 1842, pp. 13–18 (no. 2); Revard 2005b, pp. 858–67. **Other MSS:** None. **Old French Version:** Bern, Burgerbibliothek, cod. 354, fols. 112v–114r (ed. and trans. Revard 2005b, pp. 858–67). **Translation:** Revard 2005b, pp. 858–67].

7   *Feu de souche meisné.* Literally "Household fire of large logs." Revard reads the last word as *meisue* and translates it "mossy" (2005b, p. 859). This reading helps the rhyme but does not resemble the word for "moss" (see *AND, mos*), nor does it seem likely. The word is more probably *meisné*, "household," which, compounded with *feu*, seems to mean "hearth fire." For *souche*, see the French-based words in the *MED, zouche* (n.), "large log," and *souche* (n.), "?a chimney-shaft."

57–66   These lines seem to preserve the original meter: 6aaaa 4bb 6a 4cc 6a.

61   *gavigaut.* The spice galingale. As Revard explains, this spelling in MS Harley 2253 is an odd error for what should be *garingal* (as in the Bern manuscript), a standard spelling for the spice galingale (2005b, p. 861).

62   *cetewaut.* The spice zedoary. See *AND, cedewale,* and *MED, setewale* (n.).

69   *chanevaus.* "On canvas [i.e., strained]." Canvas, a thick cloth, was used to strain boiled or braised foods. See *MED, canevas* (n.), sense 2(a), and examples given there from recipes. This meaning is, however, uncertain. The canvasback duck is not meant: it is found only in North America. If the word is a mistake for *chanetans,* then "ducklings" (French *canetons*) was intended. On this crux, see also Revard 2005b, p. 862.

105–10   These lines are hard to follow, but they may mean that the speaker habitually sleeps late after his feasting and drinking, and the innkeeper (his landlord?) recommends chestnuts as a nighttime remedy for his hangover.

139   *la sesoun retrere.* Winter and the privations of Lent draw to a close, and the speaker grows less quiet, that is, more active.

148   *En verynz.* "On weekdays, feria"; see *MED, feria* (n.), and *AND, ferial* (adj.). The word is another indication of the calendar day, with *v* substituted for *f.* Uncertain of the meaning of *verynz,* Revard tentatively proposes "[in a glass dish??]" (2005b, p. 866).

## ALLE HERKNETH TO ME NOU / HARROWING OF HELL                                    [ART. 21]

*Harrowing of Hell* is an interlude designed for performance. Halliwell names it a "miracle-play" and associates with other works of medieval drama that feature biblical characters speaking apocryphally. Its parts lend themselves to dramatic reading, possibly within a household, with parts taken by family members and guests, including older children. Alternatively, it could have been written for an abbey. Nothing is certain about how it was originally designed to be performed, whether by multiple speakers or by a single performer who adopted dramatic voices. In MS Harley 2253 the anticipated use seems to have been for a secular household, for the scribe is here collecting texts for a patron with an eye to their value as entertainment and instruction. The script holds good dramatic potential: loud excitement at the gates of hell, a hubristic villain in Satan (who is eventually tied up), and biblical characters made vivid (perhaps bearing props and wearing costumes) by which children could learn the doctrine of Christ harrowing hell.

There are nine speaking roles not counting the narrator. The lengthiest ones belong to Christ and Satan. Most speech markers are provided by the scribe, set in the margin and underlined. A character's speech usually begins with a capital. The first speaking part, at line 43, does not have a marker, but it opens a column of text and displays a prominent initial *H*. Hulme prints the three versions in parallel, and Böddeker, pp. 264–84, offers a critical edition that collates the three texts. For background on the Harrowing of Hell tradition, see MacCulloch; and Tamburr, esp. pp. 113–19. For commentary on this Harley article, see Kuczynski 2000, pp. 134–35; and Nelson 2013. For another item in the Harley manuscript marked for performance by means of speech markers, see *Gilote and Johane* (art. 37).

[Fols. 55va–56vb. *IMEV*, *NIMEV* 185. *MWME* 2:449 [313]. **Scribe:** B (Ludlow scribe). **Quire:** 6. **Meter:** Tetrameter couplets. **Layout:** Double columns, speech markers in margins. **Editions:** Halliwell, pp. 13–33; Hulme, pp. 3–23. **Other MS:** Auchinleck MS (NLS Advocates 19.2.1), fols. 36r–v, begins imperfectly (ed. Burnley and Wiggins, online facsimile). **Older Version:** Bodl. MS Digby 86, fol. 119r–120v (Tschann and Parkes, p. xxv [item 40]; *IMEV* 1258, *NIMEV* 1850.5).]

2        *strif*. The *MED* defines the word in this context as "battle, war," but the contest recounted is also intensely verbal and legalistic.

5        *hys*. "His own." Possessive pronouns (*his, mine, thine*), used as substantives and bandied between Jesus and Satan, are a recurring feature of their debate over who possesses jurisdiction over the virtuous souls who currently reside in hell. This device underscores the legal argument: Who has robbed whom? Who rightfully holds dominion over the souls? What belongs judicially to Jesus and what to Satan?

36       *losen us from the qued*. This line bears a double sense: "to deliver us from evil" and "to release us from the contract." See *MED*, *quede* (n.(1)), "evil, wickedness," and *quede* (n.(2)), "promise, agreement, contract."

43       The speech marker does not appear in the manuscript. For the sense of this line, see *MED*, *gon* (v.), sense 10(b), and *gate* (n.(2)), sense 2(e).

52       *woh*. "Wickedness, depravity, transgression"; see *MED*, *wough* (n.(2).

69       *lay*. "Domain, region." See *MED*, *lei* (n.), sense 1.(a), which cites this line: "the area or region governed by a system of law; domain, country."

79       *bilevest*. "Give up, abandon"; see *MED*, *bileven* (v.(1)), sense 1.(b).

81  *Par ma fey*. Satan speaks French in mock courtesy, and the phrase "by my faith" is itself sarcastic when uttered by the devil.

83  *Resoun*. This word carries an array of legal meanings: justice; fundamental principle; reckoning; compensation or payment. See *MED*, *resoun* (n.(2)), especially senses 4, 5, and 6.

88  *Monrade*. See *MED*, *man-reden* (n.), "a pledge of service, homage."

108  *ambes aas*. Double aces, that is, a low score; misfortune. See *MED*, *amber-as* (n.).

134  *yonge*. Even though the first letter is a *y*, not a yogh or a *g*, the intended word is *gonge*, "gone"; compare *Debate between Body and Soul* (art. 22), line 78: *Up hit shal aryse anon ant to the dom gonge*.

166  *froryng*. "Comfort, solace"; see *MED*, *frouring* (ger.).

229  *bete*. "Atone for, make amends for"; see *MED*, *beten* (v.(2)), sense 2.

231  *hihte*. "Ordered, commanded"; see *MED*, *hoten*, (v.(1)), sense 3a.(e). The patriarchal sequence moves from Adam's infraction of God's command to Moses's upholding of the law.

238  The reminder of Doomsday links this work to the next item, the body-and-soul debate.

**IN A THESTRI STUDE Y STOD / DEBATE BETWEEN BODY AND SOUL**   **[ART. 22]**

Set in a dreamlike place of darkness, *Debate between Body and Soul* is another poem of vivid debate, much like *Debate between Winter and Summer* (art. 9) and its companion in quire 6, *Harrowing of Hell* (art. 21). At the end of the quire, the theme will lightly reemerge in the moralistic *Three Foes of Man* (art. 27). The motif itself has a wide and lengthy history in medieval literature across numerous languages. Utley identifies fourteen distinct forms of the debate in Middle English (*MWME* 3:692–95). The version here is preserved in two more books, both of which predate MS Harley 2253.

Frequent internal rhyme suggests that the original was composed in septenary quatrains that rhymed in an octave pattern: $(a_4b_3)(a_4b_3)(a_4b_3)(a_4b_3)$. Lines 1–4 make plain the pattern of internal rhymes. The stanzaic forms that survive, however, show great variation, with many clearly not accidental. In the Harley version, for example, the fifth day in the week before Doomsday is described in a 6-line stanza of shorter lines, $aabbcc_4$ (lines 69–74).

While the poem does not contain speech markers in MS Harley 2253, the shifts in speakers are readily indicated by the names appearing internally near the heads of stanzas. Body and Soul speak alternate stanzas, back and forth, until line 49, when Soul takes over and enumerates the signs before Doomsday. Jesus utters an important line, reported by Soul, announcing his victory over hell (line 92) and also, thereby, providing retroactive linkage to the preceding text, *Harrowing of Hell* (art. 21). Both parties suffer a miserable fate: Soul goes to hell, and Body rots endlessly in the earth (lines 99–100).

On the Harley version, see Reichl 2000, pp. 227–28; and Phillips, pp. 252–59. For commentary on the Digby version, see Conlee, pp. 10–11; and Raskolnikov, pp. 70–104.

Reichl edits the three versions in parallel (1973, pp. 339–65). On the tradition in general, see Lambdin and Lambdin, pp. 140–49.

[Fols. 57r–58v. *IMEV, NIMEV* 1461. *MWME* 3:693 [18(f)]. **Scribe:** B (Ludlow scribe). **Quire:** 6. **Meter:** Roughly thirty 4-line stanzas, aaaa$_{6-7}$, with irregular stanzas of two, three, and five lines. **Layout:** No columns, one line per manuscript line. **Editions:** Wright 1841, pp. 346–49; Böddeker, pp. 235–43; Dove 1969, pp. 220–39; Reichl 1973, pp. 345–65. **Other Versions:** Bodl. MS Digby 86, fols. 195v–197v (Tschann and Parkes, pp. xxx–xxxi [item 68]; ed. Conlee, pp. 10–11; trans. Raskolnikov, pp. 203–06); Cambridge, Trinity College, MS B.14.39, fols. 29v–32r.]

6          *chaunge two for fyve*. That is, cheat and swindle.

15         *purpris*. "Worldly goods." See *MED, purprise* (n.), sense (b), which cites this line
           as the only instance of this meaning for a word that normally means "enclosure,
           domain."

92         *genge*. "Hole of hell"; see *MED, gang, gong* (n.), sense 3.(b).

## SITTETH ALLE STILLE ANT HERKNETH TO ME / A SONG OF LEWES                        [ART. 23]

*A Song of Lewes* is the earliest surviving English *sirventes*, that is, a poem made to mock a beaten enemy. The rowdy refrain seems to call for loud singing by a group of like-minded partisans, everyone chiming in to deride "Richard the trichard." Scattergood notes that the rhyme naming Richard of Cornwall a traitor had widespread valence (2000a, pp. 180, 183). This song and the Anglo-Norman one that comes next relive decisive moments in the Second Barons' War (1264–67). Both focus on the exploits of Simon de Montfort, Earl of Leicester and leader of the barons against the forces of Henry III. *A Song of Lewes* celebrates the baronial victory over Richard, the king's brother, at Lewes on May 14, 1264. This win prompted shows of exultation. The song's refrain ends every stanza on the word *nevermore*, declaring that the royalists will never recover, but this assertion was mistaken.

The song must have been composed somewhat later than the battle itself, that is, after Henry's son Edward was imprisoned at Dover (January 1265) but yet before Montfort's fall at the Battle of Evesham (August 4, 1265), the event lamented in the next poem. Therefore its period of composition occupies a narrow window of only seven months (the first half of 1265). Although highly partisan and selective, the poet is also well-informed, for the details he introduces corroborate accounts found in Latin chronicles (Brown 1932, pp. 222–24). Crowned German king in 1257, Richard of Cornwall had become unpopular on account of his foreign schemes of ambition. When the king's party had been defeated, he ignominiously took shelter in a windmill, from whence he was captured and then imprisoned till September 1265. The poet's invectives tend to spare the ruling monarch Henry III (referred to as "Windsor"), but they scathingly accuse his brother of thievery, debauchery, oath-breaking, and cowardice. Lesser targets of scorn are Lord Edward, John de Warenne, and Sir Hugh Bigot.

The events of 1264–67 hold great importance for English constitutional history. As the barons fought what was seen as royal oppression, many contemporaries read God's presence in the victory at Lewes. Many celebrated Montfort and his fellows as heroes united in faith and courage, prepared to die for country, as they fought for English rights against a misdirected monarchy. A long Latin poem, *The Battle of Lewes*, sets out the legal principle they championed: "law is above the king, and in principle a weak or bad king can be forced by his subjects to obey the law" (A. Taylor 2002, p. 124). *The Battle of Lewes* appears in MS Harley 978, a book probably owned by William of Winchester, a monk of Reading who in 1280 was subprior at Leominster, a dependency of Reading in Herefordshire. The Ludlow scribe of MS Harley 2253 displays an avowed interest in Leominster by his inclusion of *The Legend of Saint Etfrid, Priest of Leominster* (art. 98).

For comment on this item and its historical background, see Scattergood 2000a, pp. 178–85, esp. pp. 182–83; Jeffrey 2000, p. 263; and A. Taylor 2002, pp. 93, 110–26. For background on Montfort, see Labarge; and Maddicott.

[Fols. 58v–59r. *IMEV, NIMEV* 3155. *MWME* 5:1404 [25]. **Scribe:** B (Ludlow scribe). **Quire:** 6. **Meter:** Eight 8-line stanzas with refrain, $aaa_4b_3C_1C_3B_4$; the last stanza contains two extra lines before the refrain, $aaa_4b_3a_4b_3C_1C_3B_4$. **Layout:** No columns, line 5 of each stanza written to right. The refrain (lines 6–8) is also written to the right, in full for stanzas 1–2, abbreviated for stanzas 3–8. The poem appears on a verso opposite *Lament for Simon de Montfort*, in diptych fashion. **Editions:** Wright 1839, pp. 68–71; Ritson 1877, pp. 11–13; Böddeker, pp. 98–100; Brandl and Zippel, p. 129; Brown 1932, pp. 131–32, 222–24 (no. 72). **Other MSS:** None. **Cognate Latin Works:** Three Latin pro-baronial poems are ed. and trans. Wright 1839, pp. 72–125; the longest is *The Battle of Lewes*, in London, BL MS Harley 978, fols. 75a–117v (ca. 1275–1300; ed. Kingsford).]

| | |
|---|---|
| 2 | *bi mi leaute*. "On my honor; by my word." For this idiom, see *MED, leaute* (n.), sense (e). The *Kyng of Alemaigne* refers to Richard, 1st Earl of Cornwall (1209–1272), brother of Henry III, who was crowned German king from 1257. He joined King Henry in fighting against Simon de Montfort's rebels in the Second Barons' War (1264–67). |
| 7 | *trichard*. "Traitor." As Brown notes, "It was charged that Richard broke the oath which he had taken at Canterbury to abide by the provisions of the Statutes of Oxford" (1932, p. 223). |
| 11 | *Walingford*. After Richard of Cornwall was captured at Lewes, he was imprisoned in his own castle of Wallingford. |
| 12 | A proverbial phrase: "to drink as one brews." See *MED, drinken* (v.), sense 3. |
| 13 | *Wyndesore*. That is, King Henry III, brother of Richard of Cornwall. |
| 19 | *grounde the stel*. "Secured their position." For this figurative meaning, see *MED, stele* (n.(3)). |
| 26 | *mulnepost*. The supporting shaft of a windmill. After the decisive royalist defeat at Lewes, Richard took refuge in a windmill, was discovered, and imprisoned until September 1265. |
| 33 | *synne*. Cannon notes the moral quality of this word: "the projection of 'synne' (rather than merely wrong) onto the other side follows the logic [of partisanship]. . . . This poem is . . . keen to embrace the various sorts of passion — the self- |

satisfaction as well as the threats — licensed by the insistence that virtue lies only on one side" (p. 88).

34      *Erl of Warynne.* John de Warenne, 7th Earl of Surrey (1231–1304). Warenne started as a strong supporter of the king, switched to support for the barons from 1260 to 1263, and then returned to the royalist party. After the battle, which was fought near his castle at Lewes, he fled to the Continent, where he remained for about a year. He returned to fight in the campaign culminating in the Battle of Evesham and the siege of Kenilworth Castle.

41      *Sire Simond de Mountfort.* Simon de Montfort, Earl of Leicester, charismatic leader of the barons against royalist forces during the Second Barons' War (1264–67). His victory at the Battle of Lewes (May 14, 1264) is here celebrated; his defeat at Evesham in 1265 is mourned in art. 24.

50      *Sire Hue de Bigot.* Hugh Bigot was chief justice of England from 1257 to 1260 and one of the original seven rebels. He and Warenne escaped from Lewes to France.

51      *scot.* "Royal tax." See *MED*, *scot* (n.(2)), sense 2.(a).

52      *with his fot pot.* Literally "kick with his foot," but with the broader implication of inflicting violent force. See *MED*, *poten* (v.), sense 1.(a), "push, shove, cast (oneself)."

57      *Sire Edward.* Lord Edward, who was later King Edward I. Here he is attacked in direct terms. Elsewhere in MS Harley 2253, Edward is named in *Lament for Simon de Montfort* (art. 24), line 29, and in *The Execution of Sir Simon Fraser* (art. 25), lines 232–33. His death is mourned in *The Death of Edward I* (art. 47).

58      *sporeles o thy lyard.* The terms here mock Lord Edward's public shame. As Scattergood notes, "The giving of spurs was part of the institution of knighthood and to be deprived of them was axiomatically a disgrace. And 'lyard' was a derogatory term for a horse — certainly not the sort of mount a 'kyng' ought to have" (2000a, p. 183).

59      *Dovere-ward.* Along with Richard of Cornwall, Lord Edward was captured at the Battle of Lewes. First imprisoned at Wallingford Castle, he was moved to Dover in early 1265. Lines 57–59 "fix the composition of the poem after Jan. 1265" (Brown 1932, p. 223).

63      *Forsoke thyn emes lore.* Simon de Montfort was Lord Edward's uncle by marriage. As Scattergood comments: "The allusion to ignoring an uncle's teaching takes one back to the traditional notion in heroic society of a close relationship between uncles and nephews" (2000a, p. 183).

## CHAUNTER M'ESTOIT / LAMENT FOR SIMON DE MONTFORT                                    [ART. 24]

This Anglo-Norman song laments the death of Simon de Montfort, Earl of Leicester, slain at the Battle of Evesham in Worcestershire on Tuesday, August 4, 1265. The forces of Lord Edward, Henry III's son, caught Montfort and his army by surprise, and there the baronial cause suffered a severe defeat. Comparing Montfort's death to Thomas Becket's martyrdom, the poet grieves for him and for the other slaughtered nobles, mentioning by name Montfort's son Henry and Hugh Despenser, justice of England. As an ardent partisan of the extremist rebel side, the poet shows disdain for the Earl of Gloucester, who, in advocating for a more moderate baronial position, defected at Evesham. Aspin sets the likeliest time for the poem's composition as 1267–68, that is, well after the battle. Shields argues persuasively, however, that it was written within just weeks of the defeat: the poem "is not so much a document seeking to influence the course of politics as a voice expressing popular reaction to an event of history which had intensely human interest" (pp. 205–06).

The scribe's inclusion of this item after *A Song of Lewes* shows a formal plan for this portion of MS Harley 2253. The two poems work as a diptych, facing each other on verso and recto. It also exhibits an attentiveness to the events of the Second Barons' War, particularly to Montfort as an illustrious man. The poem promotes arguments made in an ultimately unsuccessful effort to have Montfort canonized. This campaign was forwarded by a group of Franciscans who styled Montfort in death as a second Saint Thomas who fought for Holy Church against royal impieties. As the poet notes, Montfort was found wearing a hair shirt when he died, as was Beckett. Simon de Montfort's name was brandished everywhere in the 1260s, and many did regard him as a saint.

In western England this attitude lingered well into the next century. To account for the Montfortian poems in MS Harley 2253, Turville-Petre notes that they must have "reflected the interests of the patrons and their circle. Any family of significance in the south-west midlands is certain to have been involved in some of the events described"; local families would have "taken sides in the battle of nearby Evesham," and the attack on Gloucester "will not have displeased his rivals" (1996, p. 197). Parallel interests appear in MS Harley 978 (see explanatory note to art. 23). Among Montfort's prominent adherents were the Franciscans Robert Grosseteste and Adam Marsh, as well as the Oxford chancellor Walter Cantilupe, who was the uncle of Thomas Cantilupe, bishop of Hereford. These are provocative associations in the context of MS Harley 2253.

Looking beyond the praise of Montfort, one senses, too, how the scribe wishes to issue a warning on earthly pride: he juxtaposes Montfort's dramatic rise at Lewes (art. 23) with his sudden fall at Evesham. He then caps the Montfortian poems with epitaphs on vanity in three tongues, a universalizing touch that displays the Ludlow scribe's moralistic sensibility (arts. 24a, 24a*, 24b). According to Carter Revard (by personal communication), the other extant copy of the poem, in Dublin, Trinity College, MS 347, is similarly situated next to a Wheel of Life diagram with an "ashes to ashes" reminder issued for the last stage of life. For further comments on this item and its pairings with other items, see Aspin, pp. 24–35; Scattergood 2000a, pp. 183–85; Jeffrey 2000, p. 263; Fein 2007, pp. 77–78; and Revard 2007, pp. 109–10. For background on Simon de Montfort, see A. Taylor 2002, pp. 122–23; Labarge; and Maddicott.

[Fol. 59r–v. *ANL* 84. **Scribe:** B (Ludlow scribe). **Quire:** 6. **Meter:** Nine 18-line stanzas built of three 6-line units, with lines 13–18 repeated as refrain: 4a4a6b4c4c6b|4d4d6e4f4f6e|4G4G6H4I4I6H (syllable counts somewhat irregular). Four-syllable lines have masculine rhymes; 6-syllable lines have feminine rhymes. **Layout:** No columns; three lines per manuscript line. The refrain is written out for stanzas 1, 7; elsewhere it is abbreviated and written on the right. The poem appears on a recto opposite *A Song of Lewes*, in diptych fashion. **Editions:** Wright 1839, pp. 125–27; Ritson 1877, pp. 13–16; Aspin, pp. 24–35 (no. 3). **Other MS:** Dublin, Trinity College, MS 347 (C.5.8), fols. 2v–3r (ed. Shields). **Old French**

**Versions:** See *ANL* 84. **Latin Analogue:** See Aspin, p. 27. **Translations:** Wright 1839, pp. 125–27; Ritson 1877, pp. 16–19 (in verse, by George Ellis); Aspin, pp. 32–33.]

7–8      Aspin believes that these lines refer to the pacification achieved later, at the Parliament of Marlborough in November 1267 (p. 26). She uses these lines to date the poem's composition in 1267–68. But see also Shields, pp. 205–06, who dates the poem within mere weeks or months of the battle.

16       *Ly quens Mountfort.* Simon de Montfort, Earl of Leicester, eulogized here and named also in *A Song of Lewes* (art. 23), line 41.

20       *un mardi.* The Battle of Evesham was fought on Tuesday, August 4, 1265.

24       Welsh infantry were present, but they fled (Aspin, p. 34).

29       *Sire Edward.* Lord Edward, Henry III's son (and the future Edward I). He led the royalist forces at Evesham. Compare *A Song of Lewes* (art. 23), line 57, and explanatory note.

40–41    *ly martyr / De Caunterbyr.* Thomas Beckett, to whom Simon de Montfort was compared by those who wished to see him canonized. This poem may have been written as part of that effort.

55–56    *Sire Hue le fer / Ly Despencer.* Hugh Despenser (1223–1265), chief justice of England (1260–61, 1263–65), sided with the barons and was killed at Evesham.

61       *Sire Henri.* Simon de Montfort's son. The poet singles out Montfort, his son Henry, and Hugh Despenser as the most prominent losses among the many dead at Evesham.

66       *le cuens de Gloucestre.* The Earl of Gloucester led the moderates on the baronial side, defecting to the royalist cause at Evesham. The poet blames him for the defeat.

91–93    The discovery of the hair shirt again links Montfort's piety to that of Thomas Beckett.

112      *l'enfant.* An apparent reference to Montfort's youngest son, Amaury (Aspin, p. 34).

120      This line alludes to the clergy who sided ardently with the baronial cause and wanted to make Montfort a saint.

136–38   Of these lines on the flatterer and the fool, Aspin comments: "No particular individuals seem to be indicated. The phrase may be meant to emphasize the contrast between the honest bluntness and strict respect for the law, attributed to Montfort and his supporters, and the insincerity imputed to the royalist victors" (p. 34).

154–56   This mention of prisoners "presumably [refers to] those captured at Evesham, of whom Guy de Montfort, Simon's third son, was one. He escaped to France in April or May 1266" (Aspin, p. 34).

**CHARNEL AMOUR EST FOLIE / CARNAL LOVE IS FOLLY**                          [ART. 24A]

In the sequence of arts. 24a, 24a*, and 24b, the scribe creates a trilingual meditation on "dust to dust," which falls between laments for the heroically ill-fated traitors Simon de Montfort and Simon Fraser. *Carnal Love Is Folly*, consisting of a single stanza in Anglo-Norman, is yoked with a Latin tag (art. 24a*) and then followed by the English riddle-poem *Earth upon Earth* (art. 24b). Only the last item was recorded by Wanley (2:586), and he did not see it as separate from art. 24. Variants of this French moralization appear as the second stanza of a longer poem:

> Charnel amur est folie: ke vuet amer sagement
> Eschue, kar brieve vie ne let durer lungement.
> Ja tant la char n'ert florie, ke a puriture ne descent;
> E bref delit est lecherie, mes sans fin dure le turment! (*Cuard est,* MS Douce 137, fol. 111r)

For commentary on its presence in MS Harley 2253, see Turville-Petre 1996, p. 199; Kuczynski 2000, p. 143–44; Fein 2007, p. 78; and Revard 2007, p. 110.

[Fol. 59v. *ANL* 913. **Scribe:** B (Ludlow scribe). **Quire:** 6. **Meter:** Eight heptasyllabic lines in alternating rhyme, abababab. **Layout:** No columns, written two lines per manuscript line; matched paraphs for this item and *Earth upon Earth*. **Edition:** Dove 1969, p. 295. **Other MSS:** None, but for the variant stanza in *Cuard est,* see *ANL* 913 and these editions: Jeffrey and Levy, pp. 268–71 (no. 52) (Oxford, Bodl. MS Douce 137, fol. 111r); Dove 1969, p. 296 (Herebert MS [London, BL MS Add. 46919], fol. 74v). **Translations:** None.]

**MOMENTANEUM EST QUOD DELECTAT / WHAT ALLURES IS MOMENTARY**          [ART. 24A*]

*What Allures Is Momentary* is a Latin tag that serves as the source for lines 7–8 of art. 24a. A paraphrase occurs, as well, in the last item of quire 6, *The Three Foes of Man* (art. 27), lines 14–15. Commonly used by preachers, this moral saying is attributed to Saint Augustine of Hippo (Homily 250) and sometimes also to Saint Gregory. The tag was not given an article number by Ker, p. x. Turville-Petre (1996, p. 199) and Revard (2007, p. 110) comment on its aptness at this point in MS Harley 2253.

[Fol. 59v. **Scribe:** B (Ludlow scribe). **Quire:** 6. **Meter:** One Latin couplet. **Layout:** No columns, written on one manuscript line, intervening between *Carnal Love Is Folly* and *Earth upon Earth*. **Edition:** Dove 1969, p. 295. **Translation:** Turville-Petre 1996, p. 199.]

**ERTHE TOC OF ERTHE / EARTH UPON EARTH**                                   [ART. 24B]

In MS Harley 2253 *Earth upon Earth* concludes the Ludlow scribe's trilingual meditation on mortality, which begins with the Anglo-Norman quatrain admonishing one to avoid earthly vanity (art. 24a) followed by a Latin couplet (art. 24a*). This pithy lyric is presumed to be the oldest type for the "Erthe on erthe" category of poems. Variants fall into four types spread across forty-one manuscripts. Belonging to the gnomic A-Version, *Earth upon Earth* joins longer formulations found in the Kildare manuscript (seven 6-line stanzas) and John

Grimestone's preaching book (four quatrains). The A-Version precedes the three other, more openly didactic versions.

Aside from the broad tradition documented by later texts, the brevity of the Ludlow scribe's version is remarkably suited to the multilingual context it is given here. The scribe is probably responsible for this creative assemblage of texts, and maybe also for constructing from a folk aphorism this enigmatic version of *Earth upon Earth*. The Harley lyric riddles by means of dense, repetitive, often bewildering puns upon *erthe* (dust, flesh, woman, world, mankind, incarnate Christ), offering a mind-teasing elaboration of the Ash Wednesday liturgy: "Memento, homo, quod cinis es et in cinerem reverteris" (Remember, man, that thou art dust and to dust thou shalt return).

For comment on the poem, see Peck 1975, pp. 465–66 (who detects in it at least four different meanings); Kuczynski 2000, pp. 143–44; Boklund-Lagopoulou, p. 43; Fein 2007, p. 78; Fuller, pp. 269–70; and the descriptive bibliography provided in *MWME* 11:4317–18.

[Fol. 59v. *IMEV, NIMEV* 3939. *MWME* 9:3019 [263], 11:4172 [1]. **Scribe:** B (Ludlow scribe). **Quire:** 6. **Meter:** Four lines, aaaa₄; the word *erthe* receives the first three stresses of every line. **Layout:** No columns; matched paraphs for this item and *Carnal Love Is Folly* (art. 24a). **Editions:** Ritson 1877, p. 13; H. M. R. Murray, p. 1; Brown 1932, p. 132 (no. 73); Brook, p. 29 (no. 1); Treharne, p. 568. **Other MSS:** Version A: Kildare MS (London, BL MS Harley 913), fols. 62r–63v; Grimestone MS (Edinburgh, NLS MS Advocates 18.7.21), fol. 87v. For Versions B and C, see *IMEV, NIMEV* 703, 704, 3940, 3985; *MWME* 9:3019 [264–66]; and H. M. R. Murray.]

## LYSTNETH, LORDYNGES! A NEWE SONG ICHULLE BIGYNNE / THE EXECUTION . . . [ART. 25]

In characterizing this poem, Scattergood aptly cites Foucault on the show of political power that is a public execution: it "is to be understood not only as a judicial, but also as a political ritual. It belongs, even in minor cases, to the ceremonies by which power is manifested" (2000a, pp. 175–76). *The Execution of Sir Simon Fraser* is a poem about viewing events of national import, hearing them recounted in vivid detail, and, especially, taking notice of them. The author writes as if he were actually present in London during the executions of Wallace and Fraser. Adopting the style of an oral performer, he certifies an authority as witness and truthful reporter. The account itself is up-to-date and well-informed.

As background, the poet describes the August 1305 capture, execution, and quartering of Sir William Wallace, termed a traitor from Scotland. The second half of the poem narrates the June 1306 capture and September execution of Sir Simon Fraser (or Frisel), another Scottish traitor, taken at the Battle of Methven (or Kirkencliff). The gruesome details of each man's public death are dwelt on. Each torture is performed according to the new fashion of drawing and disemboweling the victim while still alive. Wallace and Fraser are transformed from dangerous men into sobering public examples, purveyors of a grim moral and political message. The point is to warn everyone — Scots, French, even fellow English — of the state's ultimate power in quelling uprisings and unrest. At beginning and end, the author paints a picture of proud Wallace and Fraser brought low in public view, their severed heads displayed on London Bridge.

The tone of the piece is vigorously nationalistic and anti-Scots. Scattergood 2000a places its composition in the autumn of 1306, close to the events described (p. 174). Revard notes how the portrait of Edward undergoes some alterations in MS Harley 2253: "By 1305 the English Prince Edward, scorned and mocked in the ME *sirventes* of 1264 [art. 23], has become the great and pious king who rightly punishes Scots rebels" (2007, p. 110). *The Execution of Sir Simon Fraser* concludes with a warning to the French and the Scots to beware so long as Edward of the "longe shonkes" is alive. By 1306, Edward I was ill and had not long to live; notably, the roles in suppressing the Scots taken by Edward of Carnarvon (the future Edward II) and by Sir Aymer de Valence (Edward's guardian) are the ones spotlighted here.

The scribe's interesting arrangement of material conveys many messages in itself. The trilingual meditation on mortality (arts. 24a, 24a*, 24b) points forward to this poem of public execution as well as backward to the death in battle of Simon de Montfort, who was also dismembered. Thus do two Simons die ignobly, one French, one Scottish, both enemies of the Crown. The scribe also connects the ending of this poem to the opening of the next one, a comic satire. One of the closing rhymes (*strif/knyf/lyf*) is reprised at the start of *On the Follies of Fashion* (art. 25a).

For further commentary on this poem, see Robbins 1959, pp. 252–56; Turville-Petre 1996, pp. 12–13, 21, 196–97; Scattergood 2000a, pp. 174–77; Revard 2007, pp. 110–11; and Cannon, p. 89. For another Harley item with Scottish concerns, see *The Prophecy of Thomas of Erceldoune* (art. 90).

[Fols. 59v–61v. *IMEV, NIMEV* 1889. *MWME* 5:1405 [28]. **Scribe:** B (Ludlow scribe). **Quire:** 6. **Meter:** Twenty-nine 8-line stanzas, aabb$_4$c$_1$ddc$_{2-3}$ (rhymes a and b are frequently combined), in non-iambic, tumbling rhythm; the last stanza contains an extra line with d-rhyme. **Layout:** No columns, lines 6–8 of each stanza are written as one line, bob written to the right of lines 1–4. **Editions:** Wright 1839, pp. 212–23; Ritson 1877, pp. 25–34; Böddeker, pp. 126–34; Brandl and Zippel, pp. 129–33; Robbins 1959, pp. 14–21 (no. 4). **Other MSS:** None.]

1        *newe*. According to Scattergood (2000a, pp. 174–75), this adjective refers to not only the national "news" reported in the poem but also to the new method of execution used against the Scots. See explanatory notes to lines 18–21 and 185–89.

10      *heuedes*. The heads are those of both Wallace and Fraser, foreshadowing the content of the poem. Fraser's capture and execution are recounted in the poem's second half (lines 105–216). Compare lines 201–02.

18–21    Sir William Wallace was executed on August 23, 1305, by the particularly gruesome method detailed here. It was a new technique, used by the English for the first time on this occasion (Scattergood 2000a, p. 175). Robbins 1959, p. 253, lists contemporary accounts and provides Stow's 1615 historical description.

19      *Al quic*. See note to line 186.

25      *Sire Edward*. Edward I (1239–1307), king of England from 1272 to 1307.

27      The four quarters of Wallace's body were sent to Newcastle, Berwick, Perth, and Aberdeen (Robbins 1959, p. 253).

36      *res*. See *MED*, *res* (n.), sense 4.(c), "an occasion, ?also, a crisis, an emergency," citing this line.

| | |
|---|---|
| 37 | *Thrye*. "At all times," literally, "three times." Robbins calls the word an intensive and translates it "in every respect" (1959, p. 253), a definition not listed in the *MED*. |
| 39 | *temed*. "Tamed, brought under control, restrained"; see *MED, tamen* (v.(1)), sense 2. The word is used ironically. |
| 49 | *The Bisshop of Glascou*. "Robert of Wishart (d. 1316), who swore allegiance to Edward I, but later supported Bruce" (Robbins 1959, p. 253). |
| 50 | *The Bisshop of Seint Andre*. "William Lamberton (d. 1328), swore repeated fealty to Edward, but assisted in the coronation of Bruce" (Robbins 1959, p. 253), as mentioned in line 65. |
| 51 | *The Abbot of Scon*. Identified only as "Thomas" by Robbins 1959, p. 253. |
| 65–80 | *Kyng Hobbe in the mures*. These stanzas mock Robert Bruce, king of Scotland, as a weak, unimpressive ruler, "really just a temporary, holiday king from a summer game. . . . Despite his coronation, says the poet, 'Kyng Hobbe' is a fugitive, living a hunted and marginalized existence on the 'mures' (lines 73–74), which is derogative in a punning way — 'Hobbe' being both a familiar diminutive form of Robert and a generic name for a rustic or clown and a hobgoblin or sprite" (Scattergood 2000a, p. 176). See also the note by Robbins 1959, p. 254. |
| 76 | *on Englysshe to pype*. This line recalls the linguistic distance and likeness between the Scots and the English. For a discussion of this line in terms of English national identity, see Turville-Petre 1996, pp. 21–22. |
| 80 | *O brede ant o leynthe*. "Far and wide, everywhere"; see *MED, brede* (n.(2)), sense 5.b. |
| 81 | *Sire Edward of Carnarvan*. Edward, Prince of Wales (1284–1327), later Edward II, King of England from 1307 to 1327. Robbins notes that "Since Edward I was ill, he entrusted the task of suppression to his son, whom he had knighted on Whitsunday" (1959, p. 254). See also *The Death of Edward I* (art. 47), line 73, and *The Flemish Insurrection* (art. 48), line 133 (and the explanatory notes to those lines). |
| 82 | *Sire Emer de Valence*. Aymer de Valence, Earl of Pembroke (ca. 1275–1324), who defeated Bruce at Methven in 1306. He was loyal to Edward I and Edward II throughout his career. |
| 84 | *false contree*. That is, Scotland. |
| 87 | *alast*. "On the last occasion, lastly"; see *MED, a-last* (adv. (& phrase)), sense (b). |
| 89 | Robbins calls this the line of a professional minstrel (1959, p. 253). |
| 91 | *batayle of Kyrkenclyf*. This term refers to the Battle of Methven, near Perth, June 1306, where Aymer de Valence defeated Robert Bruce, and Simon Fraser (here called Frisell) was captured. |
| 99 | *Sire Johan of Lyndeseye*. "John Lindsay, later bishop of Glasgow (1323–35), active in church and politics" (Robbins 1959, p. 254). |

105      *Seint Bartholomeus Masse*. August 25, 1306.

107      *Sire Thomas of Multoun*. The judge for Fraser's trial, a noble from Cumberland; on his pedigree, see Robbins's note (1959, p. 254).

108      *Sire Johan Jose*. Another noble active in the custody and execution of Fraser; see Robbins (1959, pp. 254–55).

129      *Sire Herbert of Morham*. A knight of French origin. Robbins provides a contemporary Latin account of his ill-fated wager (1959, p. 255).

137      *anon-ryht*. "At once, instantly, immediately"; see *MED*, *anon-rightes* (adv. & conj.).

141      *So Y bate*. "So my courage ends." See *MED*, *baten* (v.(1)), sense 4, "?To stop, come to the end (of one's story)," with this line cited, but see also sense 3.(b), "lose one's courage or composure." Robbins (1959, p. 255) provides an idiomatic definition: "So I assure (you)."

145      *Oure Levedy Even*. September 7, 1306.

148      *Sire Rauf of Sondwyche*. "Ralph of Sandwich (d. 1308), knight and judge, Constable of the Tower on several occasions under Edward I" (Robbins 1959, p. 255).

149      *Sire Johan Abel*. A name not recorded elsewhere.

162      *lordswyke*. "Traitor, perjurer," a somewhat archaic term that "looked backward to an heroic past" (Green 1999, p. 209).

185–89      The description of Fraser's execution on September 7, 1306, is virtually identical to the stanza on Wallace's execution (lines 18–21). As Scattergood notes, "the poet uses the same rhymes and much of the same vocabulary. But the repetition is part of the point: it establishes the pattern of shame ('shonde') and humiliation to which the 'traytours of Scotland' (lines 2, 225) are subjected" (2000a, p. 175).

186      *Al quic*. The pun in this phrase (latent possibly in line 19 too) is made explicit by the second half of the line. It means both "still alive" and "very quickly." Still conscious, Fraser felt his beheading, and to him it did not seem quick.

196–200      Scattergood calls these lines "a revealing passage" in which "the poet tries to define the appropriate public reaction, that is, to define the response of his audience under the guise of describing it," and he concludes that "the triumphalism of this poem may be qualified by a degree of anxiety" about "an English populace that was becoming increasingly lawless and restive" (2000a, p. 177).

201      *tu-brugge*. "Drawbridge"; see *MED*, *tou* (n.(2)). Lines 201–02 return to the opening image of two heads displayed on London Bridge (line 10), thereby "closing the circle of the poem's action" (Scattergood 2000a, p. 175).

209–33      Scattergood characterizes the final lines as three "triumphalist stanzas on more general political matters" (2000a, p. 175).

218      *the Erl of Asseles*. John de Strathbolgie (or de Asceila), who was also judged a traitor; because he was related to Edward I, his execution involved only hanging and

beheading, not drawing and quartering. He too was captured after the Battle of Methven, and his head was also placed on London Bridge. See Robbins's note (1959, p. 256).

227        *Charles of Fraunce.* Charles the Fair (1294–1328), later Charles IV, king of France from 1322 to 1328.

229        This line is sarcastic. Charles's help and support for the Scots will amount to nothing.

230        *Tprot.* An exclamation of contempt.

230–32     The rhyme on *strif, knyf,* and *lyf* will be repeated in the opening lines of the next item. This is a common device used by the Ludlow scribe to link juxtaposed works.

233        *longe shonkes.* A popular name for Edward I. Scattergood notes the historical circumstance in 1306: Edward I "was ill when this poem was written (he dies the following year) — hence, perhaps the stress given to the achievements of Edward of Caernavon, Aymer de Valence, Earl of Pembroke, and others. The poet appears to be trying to persuade himself and his audience that even without Edward I England would have war leaders capable of destroying its enemies and of securing it against foreign aggression" (2000a, pp. 176–77). For other instances of Edward I named in MS Harley 2253, see explanatory note to *A Song of Lewes* (art. 23), line 57.

## LORD THAT LENEST US LYF / ON THE FOLLIES OF FASHION                    [ART. 25A]

   This satire on women's dress is first and foremost a comic piece that defuses the tension brought on by the preceding item on the execution of Scottish traitors — a piece that had dramatically raised an audience's disquieting fear of border wars and rebellions. In juxtaposition to that poem, this one delivers a funny vernacular satire, a tour de force of alliterative humor on the trivial subject of how foolish English girls aspire to affect the French fashions of Anglo-Norman noblewomen.

   *On the Follies of Fashion* begins by repeating the *lyf/knyf/strif* rhyme that had concluded *The Execution of Sir Simon Fraser* (art. 25), with *wyf* now added as a rhyme-word. God is told that he may withdraw his knife and withhold strife, because all folks know the law and hold a properly fearful respect for his power, as they have since Adam and Eve (evoking, coyly, the point of origin for human dress). Meanwhile, pride is still a problem, as the example of women's fashion will illustrate. Girls make themselves strumpets and unwitting targets of the devil in their vain desire to imitate the rich and noble. The object of particular ridicule is an extreme hairstyle of large buns worn over each ear, which make the bearer seem a "slat swyn," a baited pig (line 36). This outrageous fashion is in fact a throne for the devil, an invitation for him to hold court on the foolish girl's head and secure her entrapment.

   Critics tend to take this piece more seriously than is necessary. It does indeed share some of the antifeminist strains found elsewhere in MS Harley 2253 (see, for example, Bozon's *Women and Magpies* [art. 78]), but only if its comedic performance value (with its huge dollop of social humor) is heard first. Turville-Petre remarks how the abuse of dress skewered here is "grounded in the disparity between French elegance and English plainness" (1996, p. 202), a disparity reenacted in colorful English idiom. Readers often hear stern moralism in the satire. Scattergood, for example, identifies an essentially conservative viewpoint: fashionable dress is critiqued as "conducive to lechery, hence the accusation that the woman is a whore in the company of dissolute people"; the poem is therefore "driven by the author's perception that these new fashions are a threat to social order" (2000a, p. 200). Sumptuary laws of the time dictated what could lawfully be worn by rank and income. Fashions worn by ladies were not permissible for the lowborn.

The primary motive of the piece is, however, to entertain a sophisticated audience. The butts of the joke are an exaggerated fashion and the misguided creature trying to attain it in an obviously tasteless manner. As Revard remarks, the invectives grow "increasingly vituperative" as the poem proceeds; he attaches the poem's content to its political/moral context in the manuscript: "The proud women, like the proud Scots, and perhaps like the proud rebel barons, have over-reached and been made fools by the powers of the world, the flesh, and the devil" (2007, p. 111). Maybe so, but the target here is small, like the gossip in church (whom, by long comic/moral tradition, the devil also entraps), and pleasure outweighs seriousness. Every stanza ends with a surprise, a punch line, revealing this poem as an English script for a performer of precise linguistic skill and impeccable comic timing.

[Fol. 61v. *IMEV, NIMEV* 1974. *MWME* 5:1407 [32]. **Scribe:** B (Ludlow scribe). **Quire:** 6. **Meter:** Five alliterative 11-line stanzas, $a_3b_2a_3b_2a_3b_2a_3b_2c_1cc_4$. **Layout:** No columns, two lines per manuscript line, bob written to the right (compare art. 27). **Editions:** Wright 1839, pp. 153–53; Böddeker, pp. 106–7; Brown 1932, pp. 133–34 (no. 74); Turville-Petre 1989, pp. 12–13. **Other MSS:** None.]

3       *cocke with knyf.* This phrase means literally "fight with a knife"; see *MED, cokken* (v.(1)). This invocation depicts God as ready to act belligerently, indeed, somewhat like a common brawler. On the verbal echoes between this opening and the juxtaposed ending of *The Execution of Sir Simon Fraser* (art. 25), see Stemmler 2000, p. 116; and Revard 2007, pp. 110–11. The opening also quietly parallels the first and last stanzas of *The Three Foes of Man* (art. 27), as the texts of quire 6 will soon close upon the subject of God's moral bidding and final judgment.

9       *In wunne.* "In bliss," that is, in the garden of Eden.

19      *drahtes wol drawe.* For the idiom here, *drawen draught*, meaning "to play a trick," see *MED, draught* (n.), sense 3.(e).

22      *smoke.* The smock is her necessary underwear. The speaker laments that these underclass girls dress themselves up without modestly tending first to having proper undergarments. Attendant sexual laxity is implied.

24      *boses.* Fashionable hair buns worn over each cheek; see *MED, boce* (n.), sense 2. "The total result looked remarkably like a pig with drooping ears" (Turville-Petre 1989, p. 12).

38      *joustynde gyn.* The phrase appears to be a comic insult over the size of the hair buns: they are like targets to joust at. See *justen* (v.), sense 3.(a). In resembling either a baited pig or a target, the hairstyle seems always to be a conspicuous lure by which to attract the devil's attention.

40–42     The joke in these lines lies in the proverbial saying on mutability, "all comes to decline," applied to a hair fashion that literally hangs low about the ears. It comically reprises the moralisms of the preceding poems: *Lament for Simon de Montfort* (art. 24), lines 130–35, and *The Execution of Sir Simon Fraser* (art. 25), lines 169–70. For Scattergood, the lines reveal the poet's attitude of resistance to social change: "this sense of things going to the bad is characteristic of the political and quasi-political verses in the manuscript. Old certainties were being questioned, and a new order was emerging in all sorts of areas — political, economic, and social" (2000a, p. 201).

43–44     The fashion invites the devil to hold court on the girl's head, with the irony being that she sets herself up as vulnerable to his decree. The word *halymotes* may carry latinate inflection; see *MED*, *halimot* (n.).

47–48     Commentators often suppose that the "worse" liquid is urine (Turville-Petre 1989, p. 13; Revard 2007, p. 111), an alkaline solution like lye. Another possibility is that it is spit. Turville-Petre speculates that the original word was *wouse*, "plant sap."

49          The words *bout* and *barbet* are not recorded elsewhere in Middle English.

51          *fauce*. "False," indicating that the cloth is not of the silk quality worn by ladies.

54–55     Between these lines there is a comic pause and reversal of meaning.

## ENSEIGNEMENT SUR LES AMIS / LESSON FOR TRUE LOVERS                              [ART. 26]

*The Lesson for True Lovers* lays out the rules of pure true love, which is called by the poet "fyn amour verroie"(line 108). In the introductory stanza the poet explains that the listener ought to examine his own heart and begin to read there. The song merely puts into words — in plain French (*en romauns*) — what the true lover already comprehends perfectly because he is so entirely devoted to love. The poet readily allies himself with the tradition of *fin amour*, which modern scholars often call "courtly love," a concept explored and amplified by writers of romance like Chrétien de Troyes and Marie de France.

Aside from the first and last stanzas, each stanza expounds a rule. The twelve rules may be summarized as follows:

(1) A true lover does not abandon one who falls into poverty.
(2) A true lover loyally ignores slanders said about the beloved.
(3) A true lover turns to the beloved when advice or assistance is needed.
(4) A true lover loyally confides private thoughts to the beloved.
(5) A true lover admonishes the beloved only in private.
(6) A true lover compliments the beloved to others but does not flatter the beloved in person.
(7) Equality of good sense, courtesy, love, and graciousness exists between lovers.
(8) A true lover will defend the beloved, even from a strike or blow.
(9) A true lover does not ask more of the beloved than that person can do.
(10) A true lover will never divulge secrets of the beloved.
(11) If one's beloved sins in private, a true lover does not tell anyone.
(12) A true lover tells the beloved what is true to his/her honor.

What many of these rules express might also be termed *derne* love, that is, the intimate workings of a private love shared by two people. This phrase appears in some English secular love lyrics in MS Harley 2253 (e.g., arts. 28, 93), and it is warned against in the first stanza of the next item, *The Three Foes of Man* (art. 27). In the end, the poet declares that the dictates of true love are to be followed, and all should acknowledge this — laity and clergy — for a loyal heart loves correctly. A closing allusion to liturgical prayer seems to move the piece toward religious parody, but it is probably also meant to suggest that true love is aligned with God's mercy.

*Lesson for True Lovers* is somewhat analogous to the brief Anglo-Norman prose *Rules of Friendship*, which offers twelve rules (*ANL* 144). This work survives in three manuscripts, with the best text appearing in a book owned by the Ludlow scribe of MS Harley 2253. The book in question is MS Harley 273, where *Rules of Friendship* occurs on fol. 85ra–va (ed. Hunt, pp. 9–11), and it survives as well in MS Digby 86 and MS Longleat 26. Though the version found in MS Harley 273 was copied by someone else, it is nonetheless among works known to be in the scribe's possession, which include others on courtesy and friendship. As a poem on friendship and love, this secular text is comparable to the mystical *Song on Jesus' Precious Blood* (art. 56). For some commentary on *Lesson for True Lovers*, see Revard 2007, p. 111.

[Fols. 61v–62v. *ANL* 144. Långfors, p. 69. **Scribe:** B (Ludlow scribe). **Quire:** 6. **Meter:** Fourteen 8-line stanzas, with alternating masculine and feminine rhymes in lines of eight or six syllables: 8a 6b 8a 6b 8a 6b 8a 6b. **Layout:** No columns; two lines per manuscript line. **Editions:** Wright 1842, pp. 18–22 (no. 3); Kennedy, pp. 15–23 (no. 3). **Other MS:** Oxford, Corpus Christi College MS 154, fols. 400v–401v (13th cent.); ed. Jeffrey and Levy, pp. 260–67 (no. 51). **Translation:** Kennedy, pp. 15–23.]

| | |
|---|---|
| 16 | *sa.* "Her." In this translation the beloved one is gendered feminine. The speaker seems to be a man giving advice to other men. Kennedy uses masculine gender for the beloved, a choice that paints the topic as more generally about friendship than about romantic love, or else as advice to women. |
| 17 | *Si toun ami as esprové.* Kennedy notes how "the poet alternates second person plural and singular without apparent purpose. In reference to the lovers as a couple, he always uses the plural; but in speaking to the individual lover, that is, the reader, he uses both forms: 'toun ami' (17), 'ton consail' (30), 'vostre . . . ami' (33), 'vostre consail' (37), etc." (p. 16). |
| 65 | *fyn amour.* Here and in line 108 the poet uses a term frequently used by Provençal and French poets to refer to refined secular love. |
| 97 | *pas.* According to Kennedy, "this word has the double meaning of 1) the literal passages in the poem and 2) the figurative steps or way of practice of 'fyn amour.' It is the second sense which leads into the next stanza with its reference to the 'droite voie'" (p. 22). See also the explanatory note to line 107. |
| 107 | *prenge le travers.* According to Kennedy, this phrase "has both the literal meaning of 'take a short-cut' . . . and the figurative meaning of 'take amiss,' or 'take something wrong.' Thus it relates to both meanings of *pas* (97)" (p. 23). See the explanatory note to line 97. |

111      *"Tu autem"*. The Latin phrase ends the poem with an imitation of liturgical ritual. A common way to close a prayer from the pulpit is "Tu autem, Domine, miserere nobis" (But thou, O Lord, have mercy on us). The poet-cum-preacher concludes the *Lesson for True Lovers* by asking for a "respounz" (a liturgical term) from the audience. Kennedy suggests an alternate meaning, believing that the phrase alludes to Matthew 6:6, where Christ instructs believers to pray the Pasternoster in private: "Tu autem cum oraveris, intra in cubiculum tuum, et clauso ostio, ora Patrem tuum in abscondito" (But thou, when thou shalt pray, enter into thy chamber, and having shut the door, pray to thy Father in secret: [and thy Father, who seeth in secret, will reward thee]). According to Kennedy, "the full quote suggests the courtly convention of secrecy" (p. 23).

## MIDDELERD FOR MON WES MAD / THE THREE FOES OF MAN          [ART. 27]

*The Three Foes of Man* delivers an alliterative, penitential homily against humankind's three chief temptations: Flesh, World, Devil. In the first stanza the poet preaches that private sin is always exposed in the soul, a message that inverts the virtues of secrecy between lovers, which was exalted in *Lesson for True Lovers* (art. 26). This final item in quire 6 introduces the subject of God's all-seeing judgment, creating a decisively moral ending for the texts gathered here, which begin with Ethelbert's martyrdom (art. 18) and then offer *memento mori* portraits of other worldly men cast down (arts. 23, 24, 25). The theme of Judgment Day rounds out, as well, the quire's earlier enactments of the Harrowing of Hell and the body and soul in debate (arts. 21, 22), both events being steps within salvational history (one for humankind, the other for the individual).

Explaining how secret sin will slay the soul, the poet edges his message with pessimism and more than a little misogyny, for woman is identified with Flesh. In the fourth stanza, worldly marriage is analogized to the warring of soul (man) with body (woman), and the likeness dramatizes how all of life is a conflict for the sinner who may never rest easy. An anxious weariness over having to struggle against relentless temptation animates the poem's aesthetic seriousness. The preacher's rhetorical stance deftly shifts from admonition to personal remorse, and then to a final communal bowing before the Lord, who will enable "ryhtwyse men to aryse" (line 77). The poet adopts a style that is densely alliterative, frequently doubling lines upon one alliterative sound. Verbal repetition links the last and first lines of adjacent stanzas. The 11-line alliterative stanza is unique among Middle English poems, and some scholars have called it a precursor to the 12-line form of *Pearl*. Among Harley's penitential poems, *The Three Foes of Man* and *An Old Man's Prayer* (art. 45) most resemble the secular Harley lyrics in metrical and lexical complexity. For treatments of similar themes, see *The Sayings of Saint Bernard* (art. 74) and *Jesus, Sweet Is the Love of You* (art. 58), line 72.

For commentary on this poem, see Kuczynski 2000, pp. 144–45; Revard 2007, pp. 111–12; and the bibliography in *MWME* 11:4318–19.

[Fol. 62v. *IMEV, NIMEV* 2166. *MWME* 11:4172 [2]. **Scribe:** B (Ludlow scribe). **Quire:** 6. **Meter:** Seven 11-line stanzas with strongly alliterative ornament, $abababab_4cbc_3$, linked by concatenation. **Layout:** No columns, two lines per manuscript line, bob written to the right (compare art. 25a). **Editions:** Wright 1842, pp. 22–25 (no. 4); Böddeker, pp. 181–84; Brown 1932, pp. 134–36 (no. 75); Brook, pp. 29–31 (no. 2). **Other MSS:** None.]

| | |
|---|---|
| 3 | *Hedy.* See *MED, edi* (adj.), sense 2.(b), "Blessed One (God or Christ)." |
| 4 | *hem.* That is, mankind. |
| 14–15 | These lines rephrase the proverbial sentiment of *Carnal Love Is Folly* (art. 24a) and *What Allures Is Momentary* (art. 24a\*). |
| 24 | *Yef.* "So that"; see *MED, if* (conj.), sense 3., introducing a clause of purpose. |
| 31 | *fyve.* That is, the five senses, with Flesh representing touch. |
| 39 | *under felde.* "Under earth, underground," though some editors gloss the phrase "on earth." The idea seems to be that there are men now dead (and also living?) who endured (and endure?) life mated to their worst enemy, their wife — just as body and soul are yoked, forever and often in contention. Translation of lines 39–40 is difficult because of shifts in tense and pronoun number. |
| 41 | *gelde.* Other editors translate the word as "destitute, deprived, lacking," but the blatant sense "gelded" suits the bitter tone. |
| 57 | *sully.* "Extremely; also, wondrously, strangely"; see *MED, selli* (adv.). |
| 58 | *meint.* Emended from *meind* for rhyme. See *MED, mengen* (v.), sense 1.(c), "blend, temper, alloy, moderate, combine, taint." |
| 67–77 | Revard characterizes this stanza as the "moving finale" of all of quire 6 (2007, p. 112). |
| 72 | *umbe throwe.* "At times, sometimes"; see *MED, umbe* (prep.), sense (b), ~ *throu.* |
| 74 | *bonnyng.* "Summoning" ; see *MED, banning* (ger.). |

## BOOKLET 5

### ICHOT A BURDE IN A BOUR ASE BERYL SO BRYHT / ANNOT AND JOHN [ART. 28]

Set at the head of booklet 5, *Annot and John* is the first of the English love lyrics to appear in the Harley manuscript. The Ludlow scribe has grouped it with two more amorous poems on fol. 63r–v (arts. 29, 30). Stanza by stanza, John compares his lady Annot to precious stones, flowers, birds, spices, and famous people. Deliriously love-struck, he celebrates her gemlike appeal; beauty as vibrant as choice flowers; a name that evokes avian music; a fragrance as sweet as spices; and a capacity to heal that exceeds celebrated heroines of romance. Reveling in his experience of *derne* (secret) love, John paints the joy it gives him while (paradoxically) airing it publicly. His myriad similes recall lists in lapidaries and herbals. Densely piled on, they replicate his lady's decorative lushness. Riddling on her name ("an note," line 29), John also conjures her superlative virtues. In sharing such secrets with an audience, John dispenses her rich plentitude. For the long history of commentary on *Annot and*

*John*, one of the best-known Harley lyrics, see the bibliography in *MWME* 11:4319–21, to which may be added Turville-Petre 1996, pp. 207–08; and Scattergood 2005, pp. 58–59.

[Fol. 63r–v. *IMEV*, *NIMEV* 1394. *MWME* 11:4173 [3]. **Scribe:** B (Ludlow scribe). **Quire:** 7. **Meter:** Five 10-line alliterative stanzas, rhyming aaaaaaaabb$_{4-5}$, with concatenation joining lines 8 and 9. **Layout:** No columns. **Editions:** Wright 1842, pp. 25–27 (no. 5); Böddeker, pp. 145–47; Brown 1932, pp. 136–38 (no. 76); Brook, pp. 31–32 (no. 3); Stemmler 1970, pp. 29–30; Turville-Petre 1989, pp. 14–16; Millett, online edition. **Other MSS:** None.]

10        *charbocle*. "A precious stone, a gem." See *MED*, *carbuncle* (n.).

15        *cunde*. This word is a playful pun on "nature" and "cunt," meant as an enthusiastic compliment. The naming of a private body part matches the directness found in the Harley fabliaux; see the explanatory note to *The Knight Who Made Vaginas Talk* (art. 87), line 12. In English, the pun is possible and allows the coarser word to adopt a facade of decorum, as in *The Life of Saint Marina* (art. 32), line 217 (see explanatory note). On the interpretation and the critical history of this line, see Fein 2000c, p. 356.

18        *celydoyne*. Celandine, a plant used medicinally. See *MED*, *celidoine* (n.(1)), and, elsewhere in MS Harley 2253, *Heliotrope and Celandine* (art. 112).

20        *solsecle*. The marigold. This flower is also used to describe a woman's beauty in *Blow, Northern Wind* (art. 46), line 67, and it appears as an herbal item in *Heliotrope and Celadine* (art. 112; see explanatory note).

              *sauve*. "Heal, cure." For the verb here and at line 34, see *MED*, *saven* (v.), sense 11.(a), and compare *salven*, (v.).

21–30    The stanza on birds seems filled with playful sexual innuendo, as each bird is "in" something and seems willing to frolic with the speaker. Compare the refrain of *A Beauty White as Whale's Bone* (art. 36). For the translation of *in pyn* in line 21, I accept Hough's interpretation, "in a pine" (pp. 174–75), instead of the standard editorial interpretation "for pain, for torment."

23        *thrustle*. See explanatory note to *A Beauty White as Whale's Bone* (art. 36), burden.

29        *an note*. The riddle's answer in plain sight is that her name is Annot. Her name is a fitting conclusion to the stanza on birds. For a similar flattering, perhaps erotic analogy of women to birds, see *ABC of Women* (art. 8), lines 161–65 (and explanatory note). For antifeminist analogies, see *The Blame of Women* (art. 77), lines 41–45; and *Women and Magpies* (art. 78).

34        *saveth*. See explanatory note to line 20.

35        *bayeth*. The verb is *baithen*, "to inquire, ask, grant," and the word here is often emended to *baytheth* by editors.

36        *in dayne*. "In daytime." Brown 1932 is the only editor who reads the phrase as the word *indayne*, "unworthy," which the *MED* follows; see *indigne* (adj.).

41        *medicyne*. The emendation is adopted by Brook and by Turville-Petre 1989. The
          *MED* accepts the manuscript reading of *medierne* (as do several editors), even
          though it is poorly attested. See *med-yern* (adj.) ~ *might*, "?desirous of power."

42–48     The identities of these names are obscure, but they appear to be taken from
          Scandinavian or Celtic romance lore.

48–49     *me . . . me*. The word means "one, mankind in general." See *MED*, *me* (pron.(1)),
          and compare *Song of the Husbandman* (art. 31), line 19 and the explanatory note.
          By line 49, the word could mean "me," having shifted in sense from the general
          to the specific.

50        *Jonas*. Breeze suggests that the original reading was *Iason*, referring to Jason of
          the Argonauts (2004).

          *Jon*. This word names the speaker and poet.

## BYTUENE MERSH ANT AVERIL / ALYSOUN                                                     [ART. 29]

*Alysoun* is a spirited song of youthful love in springtime. Longing for a girl of particular
beauty, the impassioned speaker praises her delectable charms: brown hair, black eyes,
swan-white neck, and sweet English name. The infectious refrain of this lyric trips its own
tune, the delirious lover declaring how his desire is fixed by happy fortune on one named
Alysoun. The name *Alysoun* carries connotations of beauty and pleasure, being related to Old
French *alis*, "smooth, delicate, soft, slim (of waist)" (as mentioned in line 16), and to Middle
English *lisse* (n.), "comfort, ease, joy, delight." Though the lover's affection has not been returned, the girl's very existence brings him pleasure. He is optimistic and yet weary with
anticipation. The lyric's gaiety sets off his desperation, spurring one to dance while the lover
suffers. Commentators frequently note how the homespun heroine of this lyric resembles her
namesakes in Chaucer: the Miller's lively heroine and the effervescent Wife of Bath
(Donaldson, pp. 23–24). In MS Harley 2253 *Alysoun* is one of three English love poems copied
on fol. 63r–v. Characterizing love's frenzy, they project a continuum of emotion — joy to
despair — as experienced by an aspirant male: his love requited (art. 28), hoped for (art.
29), or rebuffed (art. 30). For some of the rich and varied commentary on this popular,
much-anthologized lyric, see the bibliography and discussion in *MWME* 11:4174–75,
4321–24; and also Turville-Petre 1996, pp. 204–05; Scattergood 2005, p. 56; and Lerer
2008, pp. 241–43.

[Fol. 63v. *IMEV, NIMEV* 515. *MWME* 11:4174 [4]. **Scribe:** B (Ludlow scribe). **Quire:** 7.
**Meter:** Four 8-line stanzas, ababbbb$_{3-4}$c$_3$, each followed by a lilting 4-line refrain, DDD$_4$C$_3$,
tied by rhyme to the stanza. **Layout:** No columns. **Editions:** Wright 1842, pp. 27–29 (no. 6);
Morris and Skeat, pp. 43–44; Ritson 1877, pp. 49–50; Böddeker, pp. 147–48; Brown 1932,
pp. 138–39 (no. 77); Brook, p. 33 (no. 4); Stemmler 1970, pp. 13–14; Silverstein, pp. 85–87
(no. 66); Millett, online edition; Treharne, pp. 568–69. **Other MSS:** None.]

4         *lud*. "Language, tongue, speech." The lyric begins with the separate language of
          birds, playing up its own musicality.

8          *baundoun.* "Power to control, rule, dispose of," a word of French origin. See *MED*,
           *bandoun* (n.), and the discussion by Lerer of this word "located in the register of
           Anglo-French regnal power" (2008, p. 242).

11         *lent.* "Withdrawn, be removed." See *MED*, *lenden* (v.), sense 2.(e).

12         The name *Alysoun* is sometimes used in English love lyrics to playfully echo the
           liturgical invocation *Kyrie eleyson*, "Lord have mercy." See D'Arcy, p. 317.

30         *bounte.* "Goodness, virtue." Lerer discusses the effect of this French-derived word
           amid a predominately English lexicon: "It is perfectly possible that this Harley
           Lyric is using the word, if not for the very first time in English verse, then certainly
           at a time when it would have been widely recognized as a distinctively French
           word, unabsorbed into the English poetic lexicon" (2008, p. 242).

38         *wore.* "Seashore, beach"; see *MED*, *wore* (n.). The sense of weariness seems to be
           compared to constant wave movement. Compare, too, the sense of *were* (n.(1)),
           "a dam, a weir," that is, water obstructed and restrained. On this phrase, see also
           *Maximian* (art. 68), line 127. Lerer comments that the phrase "seems to recall an
           ancient Anglo-Saxon idiom; but there are no Old English poems that contain it"
           (2008, p. 243).

43         *Geynest under gore.* On this suggestive phrase as a running motif in quire 7, see
           Fein 2000c, pp. 351–70.


## WITH LONGYNG Y AM LAD / THE LOVER'S COMPLAINT                                    [ART. 30]

    *The Lover's Complaint* is a lament from a wooer with scant hope of success. Its abrupt
trimeter lines mirror the speaker's mood of distracted, restless despair. Mired in bleakness,
the lover pleads self-pityingly for the lady's mercy while also swearing fidelity to his sad cause.
Calling on the lady directly, he accuses her of heartlessness: he loves mightily, loses sleep,
and all for no reward! He yearns to be made whole through carnal satisfaction, but comfort
is out of reach. Doomed by the lady's nonresponse, feeling deprived, the speaker remains
stuck in complaint. An unrequited lover may only lament and pursue. Like most of the English
love lyrics in MS Harley 2253, *The Lover's Complaint* survives only here, where it resides in
a triad of verse on fol. 63r–v examining passionate male desire (arts. 28, 29, 30). For the
range of commentary on *The Lover's Complaint*, see the bibliography in *MWME* 11:4324–25,
to which may be added Birkholz, pp. 175–80, 202–08.

[Fol. 63v. *IMEV, NIMEV* 4194. *MWME* 11:4175 [5]. **Scribe:** B (Ludlow scribe). **Quire:** 7.
**Meter:** Four 10-line stanzas, aabaabbaab₃; most lines and many line-pairs alliterate. **Layout:**
No columns; written as prose. **Editions:** Wright 1842, pp. 29–30 (no. 7); Morris and Skeat,
pp. 44–46; Böddeker, pp. 149–50; Brown 1932, pp. 139–40 (no. 78); Brook, p. 34 (no. 5);
Bennett and Smithers, pp. 111–12; Stemmler 1970, pp. 14–15. **Other MSS:** None.]

23         *menske.* "Love or honor as mistress or wife." See *MED*, *mensken* (v.), sense 3.

38–40      Woolf calls this ending "an extravagant but probably conventional hyperbole"
           (1970, p. 287). It resembles the endings of *Alysoun*, *The Fair Maid of Ribblesdale*,

and *A Beauty White as Whale's Bone* (arts. 29, 34, 36). On the phrase *brihtest under bys*, see Fein 2000c, p. 357.

## ICH HERDE MEN UPO MOLD / SONG OF THE HUSBANDMAN                    [ART. 31]

Set amid love lyrics, this item of English peasant complaint is usually labeled historical or political, and then occluded from consideration with the lyrics that occur near it in quire 7. However, its tones of discontent and thwarted desire complement the immediate context (Fein 2000c, pp. 357–58, 368). Generically, *Song of the Husbandman* belongs with a distinctive set of Harley poems in English alliterative verse that lodge protest by means of earthy vernacular idiom. These poems tend to be vivid monologues (e.g., arts. 25a, 40, 81, 88). Here, the anonymous poet gives voice to English farmers who find themselves impoverished and victimized by oppressive taxation and extortion. As in *Satire on the Consistory Courts* (art. 40), illiteracy is wielded as a weapon against the speaker. Of the tax collector's hated bill, which the husbandman cannot read, Scattergood observes that those "who collected the king's taxes were exploiting their literacy and the illiteracy of the peasantry by not entering records for payment, appropriating what was paid for their own use, and demanding the money all over again on the strength of the 'writ'" (2000b, p. 41). What illiterate farmers could read all too well was the fearsome sign of green wax sealing the document (Green 1999, p. 200).

*Song of the Husbandman* aligns with other works in MS Harley 2253 that vociferously register moral objection to oppressive, corrupt taxation: the Latin *All the World's a Chess Board* and the French/Latin *Against the King's Taxes* (arts. 109, 114). These combined selections would seem to reflect the compiler's own attitude about authoritarian abuse of power. Meanwhile, this poem's dense alliterative lines deliver hints of biting moral allegory, rather like *Piers Plowman* (Newhauser). In ways resembling *Trailbaston* and *Satire on the Retinues of the Great* (arts. 80, 88), the poet adopts a tone of legal plaint. For further commentary, see Turville-Petre 1996, p. 197; Scattergood 2000a, pp. 188–89; Fein 2007, pp. 91–93; and Scase 2007, pp. 33–41.

[Fol. 64r. *IMEV Suppl.*, *NIMEV* 1320.5. *MWME* 5:1404 [26]. **Scribe:** B (Ludlow scribe). **Quire:** 7. **Meter:** Six 12-line stanzas in alliterative long lines, rhymed ababababcdcd. **Layout:** No columns; written two lines per ruled line. **Editions:** Wright 1839, pp. 149–53; Böddeker, pp. 102–05; Brandl and Zippel, pp. 134–35; Robbins 1959, pp. 7–9 (no. 2); Turville-Petre 1989, pp. 17–20; J. M. Dean, pp. 251–53. **Other MSS:** None.]

| | |
|---|---|
| 3 | Böddeker begins the quotation at this line instead of at line 5. I take this line as direct speech, with the full speech beginning at line 5. |
| 19 | *me.* "They." This pronoun, which appears several times in this poem, is indefinite in meaning and refers to the generalized "they" who victimize the husbandman. See *MED*, *me* (pron. (1)), and compare *Annot and John* (art. 28), line 48. |
| 41 | That the roast hens are extorted as bribes is strongly implied. |
| 47 | The speaker complains of the disrespect he receives: he is called a *foul cherl* even when he makes payment. |
| 53 | *munten.* See *MED*, *munten* (v.), sense 1.(b) ~ *mede*, "propose or offer a bribe." |

55        *under gore.* "To the quick," literally, "under robes." See *MED*, *gore* (n.(2)), sense
          3.(b), and Fein 2000c, pp. 357–58.

64        *lith.* See *MED*, *leie* (adj.), "fallow, uncultivated."

68–69     *ruls.* This word does not appear elsewhere. The *MED*, s.v. *ruls* (n. or adj.), suggests
          that it means "ʔoverripe, rotten" or "ʔrubbish, something useless," and that it
          may be related to an Icelandic term.

## HERKETH HIDEWARD ANT BEOTH STILLE / THE LIFE OF SAINT MARINA                    [ART. 32]

*The Life of Saint Marina* is a curious tale that mixes the genre of holy saint's life with
profane comedy. The main plot follows the life of a female saint (Marina), who is cross-
dressed as a man in order to pass as a monk (Marin). The switch is made by her father, a
widower turned monk, when Marina is a mere child, leaving her wholly innocent of the ruse,
which takes place in a monastery — a celibate setting that at its spiritual ideal ought to be
unconcerned with gender. But this is a tale obsessed with sexual difference, its focus fixed on
Marin/a's hidden gender under clothes, an interest similarly found in many of the surrounding love lyrics (Fein 2000c). As a young monk, Marina is accused of rape by a dairyman's
daughter, in actuality made pregnant by a passing knight. Marina proves her sanctity by
accepting a harsh penance for this sin that she cannot possibly have committed, the nature
of which she has no knowledge of. Ultimately, she dies of this unwarranted penance. At her
death, the full truth is revealed by a miracle that is both sublime and comic: the monks gaze,
awestruck, at Marina's naked body.

A secondary miracle then takes place in the tale's denouement. This one bears earthy
parallel to the first one, centering on the monk's female accuser. Upon learning that the
young monk was in fact a girl, the dairyman's daughter goes mad. This tragedy prompts
Marina to work her first posthumous miracle: she restores the girl's *womones cunde* (her
rationality and "woman's nature") expressed in a way that invites a bawdy double meaning.

An English saint's life refashioned from hagiographical analogues but adding a goliard's
wit, this tale is comparable to other comic, mixed-genre works in the Harley manuscript, more
typically in French, such as *Gilote and Johane* and *The Jongleur of Ely and the King of England*
(arts. 37, 75). Numerous Harley poems debate the qualities and nature of women, while the
fabliaux often operate by plots that expose private parts of the body (e.g., arts. 75a, 84, 87).
Simultaneously, the Ludlow scribe inscribed three Latin saints' tales of considerably more
decorum (arts. 18, 98, 116), while Scribe A's portion of the book includes the French lives of
John the Evangelist, John the Baptist, Bartholomew, and Peter (arts. 4, 5, 6, 7).

[Fols. 64va–65vb. *IMEV, NIMEV* 1104. **Scribe:** B (Ludlow scribe). **Quire:** 7. **Meter:** Iambic
tetrameter couplets, with a final 6-line tail-rhyme stanza, aa$_4$b$_3$aa$_4$b$_3$. **Layout:** Double columns.
**Editions:** Horstmann 1878, pp. 171–73; Böddeker, pp. 256–63. **Other MSS:** None. **Middle
English Analogue:** From *Northern Homily Cycle* (*IMEV, NIMEV* 89; ten manuscripts,
including Vernon MS, fols. 179vb–180rb (ed. Horstmann 1876, pp. 259–61). **Anglo-Norman
Analogue:** From AN *Vitas patrum* (Clugnet, pp. 288–311). **Old French Analogue:** Christine
de Pizan, *Book of the City of Ladies*, trans. Richards, pp. 241–43. **Latin Analogues:** From *Vitas
patrum* (Patrologia Latina 73:692–96); Jacobus de Voragine, *Golden Legend*, trans. Ryan,
1:324–25.]

4      *Maryne*. The scribe carefully spells the feminine form with a final *-e* (Marina), the masculine without it (Marin).

10     *soule fode*. The phrase's primary meaning is "spiritual sustenance, soul's comfort, salvation"; see *MED, fode* (n.(1)), and compare *Swete Jesus, King of Bliss* (art. 50), line 29, and *Debate between Body and Soul* (art. 22), line 90. In the context of this tale, however, there is probably a pun on *fode* (n.(2): "a young child, offspring, daughter or son." The man loved his soul's comfort, both his salvation and his child. Note how the poem ends on the love of Mary for her child (line 232).

75–76  The author's pronoun for the child changes from *she* to *it* upon the child's entrance into the monastery, and from *it* to *he* when the child becomes the monk Marin.

89–90  Here the genre of *pastourelle* intrudes upon the saint's life. A *pastourelle* is a secular lyric, commonly in French, wherein a nobleman seduces or tries to seduce a lowborn woman. *The Meeting in the Wood* (art. 35) is one of the few extant English *pastourelles*.

106    *leh*. For the meaning "trust, depend on" with the preposition *on*, see *MED, leien* (v.(1)), sense 9.(b).

109    *wareisoun*. "Endowment, treasure, wealth." See *MED, warisoun* (n.).

110    *eny-kunnes gersoun*. See *MED, ani-kinnes* (phrase), "any kind(s) of," and *gersume* (n.), "treasured object, valuable possession."

127–34 The baby (whose gender is never named) seems to fade out of the narrative. I have translated *he* as "they" in line 127, but by lines 132 and 134, the pronoun seems to be singular again: "*he*, Marine."

145    *prisoun*. "Prisoner, captive, wretch." See *MED, prisoun* (n.), sense 7.

158    *eny-cunnes*. See explanatory note to line 110.

164    *ydyht*. "Changed, transformed." See *MED, dighten* (v.), sense 3b.(a).

166    This profoundly ambiguous line showcases the teller's comic wit, which blends celibate innocence with carnal thinking. It may mean either "No one is capable of seeing (or expressing) the joy Marina received from God," or "No man ever enjoyed Marina." See Fein 2000c, pp. 363–65.

175    *A* is written for *Ha*, "they" (Böddeker, p. 262).

184    *ord ant ende*. "Beginning and end." For this idiom, see *MED, ord* (n.), sense (c).

202    *shute*. Though the meaning is that confusion and injury have afflicted the woman's mind, this word is difficult to identify. Perhaps it is a nominal form of "shut" or a mistake for *MED, shathe* (n.), sense 2.(a), "Harm, injury, damage."

217    *womones cunde*. "Woman's nature," that is, her rational self, but with a sly pun on "cunt," denoting her sexualized woman's nature, which she now finally acknowledges. On the wordplay, see Fein 2000c, pp. 364–65, and the explanatory note

to *Annot and John* (art. 28), line 15. On such terms in fabliaux, see the explanatory note to *The Knight Who Made Vaginas Talk* (art. 87), line 12.

232          The final six lines form a coda in tail-rhyme. On the theme of parental love for the child, see explanatory note to line 10.

## WEPING HAVETH MYN WONGES WET / THE POET'S REPENTANCE                    [ART. 33]

The poet of *The Poet's Repentance* might be "Dunprest," the name written in the right margin. Whoever he was, he shows himself an adept wordsmith. Reveling in alliteration, pararhyme, and concatenation, the speaker assumes a contritional pose that repents of slandering women. His verses are, however, so infused with playful duplicity and hyperbole that his sincerity has to be questioned. He audaciously yokes repentance, veiled misogyny, Marian compliment, and broad overstatement (i.e., women have not been wicked since Christ's birth). The play of elements that alternately praise and taunt women resembles the French texts in the Harley manuscript — especially in booklet 6 — that comment variously on woman's nature (arts. 8, 76, 77, 78, 83). The poem may be a witty, masked act of courtship, or it may be have been produced in competition with a poet named Richard, cited in the last stanza. The speaker sets himself in humble subordination to Richard, a paragon in the art of praising and pleasing women. The poet thus buries his actual intent in banter, double-talk, and humor, as if the lyric was composed to lob a volley in an ongoing game between the sexes or between rival male poets. This mock repentance follows the mock saint's tale *The Life of Saint Marina* (art. 32) (Fein 2000c, pp. 358, 366). This poet's duplicitous wit on the topic of women's nature — a ploy for wooing one — may also be compared to *Advice to Women* (art. 44). For recent commentary on this poem, see the bibliography in *MWME* 11:4325–26; Turville-Petre 1996, pp. 205–06, 214; Birkholz, pp. 206–07, 210–16; and Choong, pp. 28–31.

[Fol. 66r. *IMEV, NIMEV* 3874. *MWME* 11:4176 [6]. **Scribe:** B (Ludlow scribe). **Quire:** 7. **Meter:** Six 12-line stanzas, ababababₐcdcd₃, with concatenation at lines 8 and 9 and between stanzas. Prolific alliteration typically extends across two lines, with rhyme words consonantally matched at both ends (i.e., *wet/wit/bet/bit*). **Layout:** No columns; written two line per ruled line. **Editions:** Wright 1842, pp. 30–33 (no. 8); Böddeker, pp. 151–54; Brown 1932, pp. 141–43 (no. 79); Brook, pp. 35–36 (no. 6); Stemmler 1970, pp. 30–32; Turville-Petre 1989, pp. 21–24; Millett, online edition. **Other MSS:** None.]

1          *Dunprest*. This word is written to the right of the line, in the manner of a speech marker. It could be the name of the poet or the assumed persona of a performer. Hall suggests that the name, which he reads *dimprest*, is that of the compiler (p. viii).

2          *wone*. "Absence, lack, deficiency, shortage"; see *MED, wane* (n.(1)).

4          *Bruches broken*. "Broken breaches"; see *MED: bruche* (n.), "transgression, offense, sin." In a phrase such as this, a breach is doubly broken. On this lyric's slippery language, see Margherita, pp. 71–75.

13         *a wyf*. That is, Eve.

| | |
|---|---|
| 16 | The allusion is to a popular legend in the Middle Ages, wherein Aristotle allowed himself to be saddled and bridled like a horse so that a girl he loved foolishly could ride on his back. See Brook, p. 77. |
| 17 | *stythye*. "Excellent one," that is, Mary; see *MED*, *stithie* (n.(2)). |
| 27 | *last of lot*. "Blameful conduct." See *MED*, *last*, (n.(3)), sense (c), "grounds for blame," and *lote* (n.), sense 2, "virtuous or vicious behavior." |
| 38 | *teme*. "Vouch, warrant (something)"; see *MED*, *temen* (v.(2)), sense 2. |
| 48 | *warp*. "Casts out, expels, drives out (something)"; see *MED*, *warpen* (v.), sense 4.(a). |
| 62 | *Rykening*. "Paragon"; see *MED*, *rekeninge* (ger.), sense 4.(a), "moral discernment, also ?judgment, standard." |
| 68 | *thin hap is on*. "Follows your fortune," literally, "in on your fortune." |

## MOST I RYDEN BY RYBBESDALE / THE FAIR MAID OF RIBBLESDALE [ART. 34]

*The Fair Maid of Ribblesdale* is a secular lyric that describes the lady in terms of her physical attributes. Its distinctive feature is hyperbole. The portrait moves from the head downward, dwelling on each of her parts and growing incrementally more exaggerated so as to suggest, ultimately, that the maid can hardly be mortal: she must be a fairy or else the speaker is so smitten he cannot perceive her otherwise. The lyric dissolves into fantasized ecstasy that ultimately conflates physical eroticism and mystical experience: the man so favored by Christ as to lie one night beside the Ribblesdale maid will attain heaven there. As Turville-Petre comments, "Divine love and sensual love are now indistinguishable, so that earth has become heaven and Christ died on the Cross in order that a lover might spend the night in the arms of his mistress" (1996, p. 216). A similar ending is found in *The Lover's Complaint* (art. 30).

Two other Harley lyrics match this one in stanza form and extensive alliteration — *Spring* and *Advice to Women* (arts. 43, 44) — but they differ in vocabulary. The scribe may be grouping this lyric with the two that follow it: *The Meeting in the Wood* and *A Beauty White as Whale's Bone* (arts. 35, 36). He copies them together in one opening, fols. 66v–67r. The first two have *chanson d'aventure* openings, and all three open in praise of a woman's beauty (Stemmler 2000, p. 117). For further recent commentary, see the bibliography in *MWME* 11:4326–28, to which may be added Turville-Petre 1996, pp. 214–16; Kinch, pp. 143–46; Scattergood 2005, pp. 57–58; and Choong, pp. 17–21.

[Fol. 66v. *IMEV*, *NIMEV* 1449. *MWME* 11:4180 [8]. **Scribe:** B (Ludlow scribe). **Quire:** 7. **Meter:** Five 8-line and two 4-line stanzas, abab(abab)$_{3-4}$, with verbal and alliterative linking of stanzas' last and first lines. Each line possesses two to four alliterating syllables. **Layout:** No columns; written two lines per ruled line. **Editions:** Wright 1842, pp. 33–36 (no. 9); Böddeker, pp. 154–60; Brook, pp. 39–40 (no. 8); Bennett and Smithers, pp. 113–15; Stemmler 1970, pp. 16–18; Millett, online edition. **Other MSS:** None.]

| | |
|---|---|
| 2 | *wale*. This word is glossed in the *MED*, s.v. *walen* (v.(1)) under sense (d), "to be found, also ?seek, ?find," but the usage here best fits the word's primary meaning, sense (a), "to make a choice, choose." |

31–33   The speaker imagines the maiden's hair flowing loose, causing her to seem more beautiful and festive. For the idiom *mongen with mirthe*, see *MED, mongen* (v.(2)). The verb *breden* (v.(2)) means "to spread out over" (sense 2). For lines 31–32, compare *Blow, Northern Wind* (art. 46), lines 13, 15.

45   *That freoly ys to fede.* This line follows the description of teeth and neck, how the lady possesses beautiful instruments of eating (*to fede*), after lines 37–39 articulate the lady's beautiful mouth for speaking (*to mele*). For *freoly*, see *MED, freli* (adj.), used as a noun.

50   *lef.* The word means either "dear one, beloved, precious treasure" or, metaphorically, "leaf" to denote the hand's fragile beauty.

55   *feir to folde.* The idiom here, of fingers "fair to fold," carries the suggestion of matrimony.

61   *bete gold.* "Gold hammered thin, gold leaf." See *MED, beten* (v.(1)), sense 2a.(b).

63   *triketh.* This verb is attested here only. See *MED, triken* (v.), "to hang down, fall in a flowing manner."

65   *Withinne corven.* See *MED, kerven* (v.), sense 9b. The adverb *withinne* refers to the intricacy of the artistic ornamentation.

82   For the idiom *Christ me se*, see *MED, sen* (v.(1)), sense 23(a), "to look after, protect, care for."

## IN A FRYHT AS Y CON FARE FREMEDE / THE MEETING IN THE WOOD                    [ART. 35]

*The Meeting in the Wood* is the earliest extant English *pastourelle*, a poem of amorous encounter, often seduction, between a nobleman and a lowborn girl. The poem opens in *chanson d'aventure* fashion, with the male narrator recounting a past event, but it closes on the maiden's musing thoughts. By the end the maiden seems ready to acquiesce to the narrator's advances, but this is not altogether certain. Indeterminacy and ambiguity are inherent features of this lyric, which enacts a form of debate (Reichl 2000, pp. 233–35). The speech markers are editorial and do not appear in the manuscript. Different scholars have posed various ways to assign lines to the two speakers (for a summary, see *MWME* 3:726–27 [53]). The markers given here follow internal indicators and avoid emendation. It may be that in an earlier version each character spoke full stanzas in alternating turn.

A particularly intriguing feature of this lyric is the way it states social realities and a woman's psychological dilemma, an inversion of the generic *pastourelle* seduction formula, which normally maintains a male perspective. The clothing trope further signals the poet's awareness of this ambiguity, of how a wooing narrator/poet would dress the woman (corporeally, rhetorically) versus how the sharp-witted woman reacts to this proposed reconstruction of who she is. Another Harley poem that resembles a *pastourelle* is *The Clerk and the Girl* (art. 64). A typical *pastourelle* narrative of a knight seducing a dairyman's daughter occurs, as well, in *The Life of Saint Marina* (art. 32), lines 89–90. For commentary on *The Meeting in the Wood*, see the bibliography in *MWME* 11:4328–30; and Scattergood 2005, pp. 60–61.

[Fols. 66v–67r. *IMEV, NIMEV* 1449. *MWME* 3:726–27 [53], 11:4180 [8]. **Scribe:** B (Ludlow scribe). **Quire:** 7. **Meter:** Five 8-line and two 4-line stanzas in septenary rhythm, $a_4b_3a_4b_3(a_4b_3a_4b_3)$, with verbal and alliterative linking of stanzas' last and first lines. Each line possesses two to four alliterating syllables. **Layout:** No columns; written two lines per ruled line. Speech markers are not in the manuscript and have been added editorially. **Editions:** Wright 1842, pp. 36–38 (no. 10); Böddeker, pp. 158–60; Brook, pp. 39–40 (no. 8); Bennett and Smithers, pp. 116–17; Stemmler 1970, pp. 32–34; Turville-Petre 1989, pp. 25–27. **Other MSS:** None.]

| | |
|---|---|
| 4 | *gome.* The word is normally specific to men. The *MED* lists this line as the only seeming application of the word to a woman. See *gome* (n.(1)), sense 4(b). |
| 5 | *kenede.* The narrator's wondering involves curiosity as to her kinship and family relations, with the sense being "who in the world gave birth to, or engendered, her?" The girl's initial golden, glistening appearance (as perceived by the narrator) and her final musings about her own ordinary mortality play off a recurrent, inquisitive examination of what her origins are, fairy or mortal, noble or low. |
| 21 | *Of munnyng ne munte.* For these verbs, see *MED, moninge* (ger.), "remembering," and *minten* (v.), sense 2(a), "to think." |
| 25–26 | These lines highlight the brief transience of the encounter. He asks her why she does not believe him any longer than the time in which he has fixed his "love" on her. The comparison underlines the flighty casualness of his feelings and the falseness of his pledges. |
| 37–40 | The word "yet" is added to the translation of line 37 because here there is a shift in the girl's thinking, a shift that corresponds with the opening of a new stanza. Turville-Petre assigns lines 37–40 to the man, emending the pronoun *me* in line 40 to *þe* (1989, p. 26). |
| 43–44 | The man's cavalier attitude toward troth-making is that, despite a verbal promise, no one can change or foresee what God decrees. His attitude evades honor and future responsibility for his own actions. |
| 45 | *ashunche.* "Be altered." The word is attested here only, and the *MED* defines it as "frighten": *ashunchen* (v.). But compare *shunchen* (v.), sense (b), "to cause (something) to turn aside." |

## A WAYLE WHYT ASE WHALLES BON / A BEAUTY WHITE AS WHALE'S BONE            [ART. 36]

*A Beauty White as Whale's Bone* is a boisterous love song in carol form, goliardic in spirit. Recapturing its original structure requires a reordering of the stanzas as they are found in MS Harley 2253. Written at the end of the poem are its incipit, first two stanzas, and lively refrain (lines 1–22). The error was apparently caused by the scribe copying a double-sided song sheet in reverse order (Degginger, pp. 84–90; Duncan, pp. 4–6). Here, the text has been reconstructed. For the actual manuscript arrangement, see textual notes.

The male speaker declares in the refrain that he wishes he were a bird hidden between the lady's kirtle and smock, with a erotic pun playing on the rhyme words *threstelcok* and *lavercok*. His desire becomes funnier by rollicking repetition. The poem is a parody of *derne* love set in a bourgeois world: the lady is a woman of the town, and she is apparently married; the lover faces her hostility and also her husband's. Undaunted, however, he declares himself wounded by her eyes, feels himself dying before his time, and dreams of how kissing her would be *murthe*. In the final stanza, the hyperbole of love verse turns absurdly mercantile: to have his lady, the lover swears he would trade, without haggling, three ladies for one, for there is, from heaven to hell, from sun to sea, none so prudent as himself.

For commentary on *A Beauty White as Whale's Bone*, see the bibliography in *MWME* 11:4330–31; and also Ransom, pp. 69–70; D'Arcy, p. 318; and Scattergood 2005, pp. 58–59.

[Fol. 67r. *IMEV, NIMEV* 105. *MWME* 11:4181[9]. **Scribe:** B (Ludlow scribe). **Quire:** 7. **Meter:** In reconstructed form, there are eight 6-line stanzas, $a_{2-4}aa_4b_2a_4b_2$, with a 5-line burden, $CC_4D_2C_4D_2$. The last stanza has an added seventh line, $aaa_4b_2a_4ba_2$. **Layout:** No columns; written as prose with line breaks marked. (The order of stanzas has been altered according to the reconstruction proposed by Degginger, pp. 88–90.) **Editions:** Wright 1842, pp. 38–40 (no. 11); Böddeker, pp. 161–63; Brook, pp. 40–41 (no. 9); Bennett and Smithers, pp. 117–19; Stemmler 1970, pp. 18–20; Millett, online edition. **Other MSS:** None.]

incipit       *Wose wole of love be trewe, do lystne me*. Omitting this line from his text, Degginger explains it as a heading to the song when it was inscribed on a single leaf. This explanation makes sense. The line ought to be included with the poem, however: as the incipit, it demonstrates how a minstrel expected to call out to his audience, commanding silence and attention, even before the opening *Herkneth me* of his song.

burden      In form, this poem is a carol. As reconstructed here, the first five unnumbered lines constitute the burden, that is, the carol's external refrain, which was sung at the beginning of each stanza. See also art. 46.

           *threstelcok*. The bird named is a male song thrush. See *MED, throstel-cok* (n.), and also *Spring* (art. 43), line 7. The translation here is "throstle-cock" to retain the playful pun. The female of the species is named in *Annot and John* (art. 28), line 23.

38          *ybrad*. Here translated "entangled," but the meaning "tormented" is also possible. The line is cited under both senses in the *MED*; see *breden* (v.(1)), sense 2, and *breiden* (v.(1)), sense 9(d).

48          *thryven ant thro*. "Excellent one." For this expression, see *MED, thriven* (v.), sense 1(e).

84          *Ne half so freo*. Degginger omits this line in his reconstructed poem, but an extrametrical line in a final stanza is not uncommon in the lyrics of MS Harley 2253. They reveal how jongleurs liked to close a musical or declamatory performance with a rhetorical flourish.

## GILOTE E JOHANE / GILOTE AND JOHANE               [ART. 37]

As a performance piece *extraordinaire*, *Gilote and Johane* offers riotous comedy by exploiting the genres of debate, *chanson d'aventure*, and sermon; using the bawdy diction and plot motifs of fabliaux; and serving up witty satire on gender roles, societal conventions, and religious pilgrimage. At its close, it is geographically situated and dated, rather like a legal document: it was performed or composed (*fet*) in Winchester in the twenty-ninth year of the reign of King Edward I, on September 15, 1301. Because of this claim's specificity and because the Harley copyist has inserted several (but not all) speech markers, scholars accept that the piece was played before an audience. Referring to the Westminster statutes promulgated in 1275 and 1285 by Edward I ("statutes defining marriage, adultery, and the dowry and property rights involved in these"), Revard suggests that the original Winchester audience consisted of lawyers and clerics (2004, p. 135 n. 16).

Besides the undoubtedly male narrator and the young knight who eavesdrops (line 2), the interlude's three principal characters are women: Gilote, Johane, and Wife (*Uxor*). The poem works somewhat as a debate in which the dominant force is Gilote (promiscuity), who coerces and converts Johane (virginity) to her ways. As Reichl notes, "Gilote has an answer for everything" (2000, p. 230). Now a pair, Gilote and Johane proselytize sexual freedom to other women and eventually come to counsel young Wife (marriage) on the best way to take a lover and still retain her dowry from a wealthy old husband. The material for this comedy borrows richly from arguments found in traditional debates on women and marriage, especially anti-marriage debates like *Against Marriage* (art. 83). Such material is here uproariously refracted through a constructed female perspective (like Chaucer's giving voice to the Wife of Bath), so that women themselves come to enact and speak the very stereotypes made by men about women's nature and waywardness, and, as they do so, to break free from all strictures of proper behavior. Texts in this playful, normally androcentric tradition are abundant in MS Harley 2253; see, for example, in French, arts. 8, 76, 77, 78, and in English, arts. 32, 44, 93.

The bawdy content of *Gilote and Johane* aligns it with the four Harley fabliaux (arts. 75a, 82, 84, 87), while its manner of witty repartee and entertaining debate greatly resembles *The Jongleur of Ely and the King of England* (art. 75), itself also a script for performance. The only other Harley text possessing speech markers inserted by the scribe conveys a very different tone of debate, the English *Harrowing of Hell* (art. 21). In voicing a woman's pragmatic point of view within limited options, *Gilote and Johane* is also like *The Meeting in the Wood* (art. 35), wherein the girl considers which is better: a churlish peasant husband or a transient noble lover. *Gilote and Johane* also holds a spot in a long string of works in quire 7, ending "on a rollicking, comic note . . . [a] sequential obsession with feminine secrets under clothes" (Fein 2000c, p. 366). As this series closes, the Harley compiler transfers to a new subject — pilgrimage (arts. 38, 39) — a theme comically bridged by *Gilote and Johane* when the female pair travel northward to preach to and convert women throughout England and Ireland.

For further commentary on *Gilote and Johane*, see Revard 1982, 2004; Reichl 2000, pp. 230–31; Dove 2000, pp. 336–37, 347–48; and Fein 2000c, pp. 359–60, 366–68. The translation printed here is indebted to an unfinished translation made by the late Barbara Nolan.

[Fols. 67va–68va (there is an extra leaf, fol. 67*, between fols. 67 and 68). *ANL* 193. Vising §256. **Scribe:** B (Ludlow scribe). **Quire:** 7. **Meter:** Anglo-Norman rhyming couplets chiefly in decasyllabic lines, but with variations. One line is comically in Middle English (line 245). **Layout:** Double columns, speech markers in margins. **Editions:** Jubinal 2:28–39; Kennedy, pp. 146–77 (no. 10); Dove 1969, pp. 180–87; Revard 2004, pp. 125–32. **Other MSS:** None. **Translations:** Kennedy, pp. 146–77; Revard 2004, pp. 125–32.]

1–5    For a later manifestation of this comic trope of a naive young man overhearing what women *really* think of men, see William Dunbar's "Tretis of the Tua Mariit Wemen and the Wedo" (*Complete Works*, pp. 198–214).

182    *soun voler*. This phrase has been translated "her will," but it might mean, alternatively, "his will."

245    *Alas, alas, for Godes deth, such womon is yshent!* Gilote comically lapses into English. What motivates the outburst is pity for the defrauded woman whose husband cannot satisfy her libido. Compare the similar surprise effect of affective English in *While You Play in Flowers* (art. 55), lines 19–20.

337    *juer a talevas devant*. Literally, "to play before the shield." A bawdy sense is clearly intended, apparently with a crude euphemism for a woman's genital parts. The word (spelled *talevace*) recurs as a derogatory term for an old woman in *The Knight and the Basket* (art. 82), line 37. See Kennedy, p. 175; and Revard 2004, pp. 135–36 n. 18.

340    *Pount-Freint*. The term means "broken bridge," a literal translation of the Latin Pontefract, a town near Leeds in Yorkshire. To walk from Winchester in the south to Pontefract in the north means, in effect, to traverse the whole country, moving northward to Ireland. Revard points out that Pontefract, castle site for the earls of Lancaster, was the place where Thomas, Earl of Lancaster, who led the 1321–22 baronial uprising against the Despensers and Edward II, was taken and beheaded in 1322 (2004, pp. 134–35 n. 13). Popularly regarded as a near-saint, Thomas of Lancaster is memorialized as a martyr in another manuscript containing the hand of the Ludlow scribe, London, BL MS Royal 12.C.12 (ca. 1323–26; ed. Wright 1839, pp. 268–72).

345    *vyntenuefyme*. "Twenty-ninth." This word was mistakenly read *vyntennesyme* ("twentieth") by Jubinal, followed by Dove 1969 and *ANL* 193. The error was corrected by Kennedy (pp. 176–77), followed by Revard (2004, p. 132) and Reichl (2000, p. 231).

## LES PELRINAGES . . . EN LA SEINTE TERRE / PILGRIMAGES IN THE HOLY LAND     [ART. 38]

This item, dated 1258–63, offers a travel guide to Christian pilgrimage routes and destinations in the Holy Land. Heading south to Jerusalem from Acre via the coastline, it passes through Caesarea and Jaffa. Reaching the Holy City, the author dwells for a time on the places to be toured there, especially the Church of the Holy Sepulcher, with highlights of other churches, the city gates, the Mount of Olives, and so on. The route continues southward to Bethlehem and then stretches north, inland, to Nazareth, eventually returning to the coastline north of Acre, in Tyre and Sidon. By the end the traveler is pointed northward in the direction of Beirut.

The pilgrimage sites are often joined to biblical events, especially to places central to the Nativity and Passion stories. Several visual and tactile icons of Christ's existence are named, such as a handprint upon a stone. The sites include Hebron, homeland and burial cave of the Old Testament patriarchs and their wives. Locations associated with the prophet Elijah and his New Testament counterpart, John the Baptist, are prominent in the itinerary, from beginning to end; these references draw on the traditional lineage of prophets proceeding from Elijah to the Baptist (Luke 9:7–9, John 1:25), to Jesus, and even to Saint George. See also the explanatory notes for *Reasons for Fasting on Friday* (art. 106).

Articles 38 and 39 are likely written by the same author. For related Anglo-Norman items, see *ANL* 334–35. Among English texts, this itinerary of Holy Land sites may be compared to that described in *Mandeville's Travels*, dated 1357 (Seymour 1993, pp. 5–7), which exists in many forms in Middle English (see the several editions by Seymour listed in the bibliography). The best modern source on specific destinations in the Crusader Kingdom of Jerusalem is the four-volume study by Pringle (1993–2009).

[Fols. 68va–70rb. *ANL* 336. **Scribe:** B (Ludlow scribe). **Quires:** 7–8 (fol. 70 opens quire 8). **Layout:** Prose in double columns. **Edition:** Michelant and Raynaud, pp. xxx–xxxi, 227–35 (no. 12). **Other MSS:** None. **Translation:** Pringle 2012, pp. 229–34.]

2      *SEYNT ELYE*. On this monastery of St. Elijah, see Pringle 1998, 2:224–26 (no. 202).

3      la *CAVE SEYNT ELYE a la CARME*. See Pringle 1998, 2:226–29 (no. 203).

4      *SEINT JOHAN DE TYR*. On this church, see Pringle 1998, 2:369–72 (nos. 272–73).

6–7      le *CHASTIEL PELRYN*. 'Atlit. See Pringle 1993, 1:69–81 (nos. 26–27).

7      *MERLE*. Tantura; see Pringle 1998, 2:257. The city associated with Andrew in the Bible is Bethsaida (John 1:44).

8–9      la *CAVE la ou Nostre Dame se mussa ov son fitz pur doute des Gyws*. See Pringle 1998, 2:257.

10      *NOSTRE DAME DE MARREIS*. A pilgimage chapel "for people from Caesarea and for travellers proceeding south along the coast road from 'Alit"; see Pringle 1998, 2:257–58 (no. 214).

11      *CESARIE*. The medieval pilgrimage sites in Caesarea are described in Pringle 1993, 1:166–83 (nos. 68–76).

12      *JAPHET*. Medieval Jaffa is described in Pringle 1993, 1:264–73 (nos. 109–20).

     le *PEROUN SEINT JAKE*. This stone was said to be the place where the martyred apostle's body lay prior to its transport to Galicia in Spain. See Pringle 1993, 1:268.

13      une *CHAPELE ou seint Abakuc soleint meindre*. The Abbey Church of St. Habakkuk. See Pringle 1993, 1:283–85 (no. 127).

14      *RAMES*. On the Church of St. George in Ramla, see Pringle 2:195–99 (no. 189). However, the saint's cult and martyrdom were centered at the nearby Cathedral Church of St. George in Lydda (Pringle 1998, 2:9–27 [no. 137]).

15      *BETYNOBLE*. Bait Nuba; see Pringle 1993, 1:102–3 (no. 34).

16      *EMAUS*. Abu Ghosh. See Map 8 in Pringle 1998, 2:425. According to Luke, Jesus appeared before Cleophas and another follower on the road to Emmaus after his resurrection.

18          *MONT JOIE*. Rama, or Nabi Samwil, also known as "Mount Joy" or "Mons
            Gaudii," the location of the Abbey Church of St. Samuel. See Pringle 1998,
            2:85–97 (no. 159).

21          la *PORTE ou seint Estevene fust lapidé*. On St. Stephen's Gate, or Damascus Gate,
            in Jerusalem, see Pringle 2007, 3:478 (map 2). The Church of St. Stephen was
            located outside this gate (Pringle 2007, 3:372–79 [no. 359], 3:477 [map 1]). Lion's
            Gate in the old city of Jerusalem was also called St. Stephen's Gate (Boas, p. 50),
            and there was a tradition that the stoning occurred here, though it probably hap-
            pened at Damascus Gate.

22          *SEINT SEPULCRE*. On the history and sacred significance of the Church of the
            Holy Sepulcher for medieval pilgrims, see Pringle 2007, 3:6–73 (no. 283). It was
            initially a basilica constructed by Constantine in the fourth century.

23          *peroun*. Stone, the "omphalos." The meaning of the stone reflects ancient Jewish
            tradition that named Jerusalem the "navel" of the world. By medieval cosmology
            the city was set at the earth's true center, both spiritually and geographically, as
            on a T and O map.

25          *MOUNT CALVARIE*. On the location of Calvary and Golgotha in the Church of the
            Holy Sepulcher, see Pringle 2007, 3:7–9, 3:39 (floor plan).

28          *Godefroy de Boylloun*. Godfrey of Bouillon (ca. 1060–1100) was the first Latin ruler
            of Jerusalem, a standing that made him (alongside Charlemagne and Arthur)
            a Christian "worthy" in the celebrated roster of Nine Worthies. A Frankish knight,
            Godfrey helped lead the First Crusade from 1096 until his death. After Jerusalem
            was won in 1099, he was elected Lord of Jerusalem; he refused the title "king,"
            claiming that kingship belonged to God alone. He was buried in the Church of
            the Holy Sepulcher, and his tomb remained there until it was destroyed in the
            nineteenth century.

31          *treis Maries*. On the chapel of the Three Marys, see Pringle 2007, 3:30.

32          la *trova seinte Eleyne la seinte Croyz*. To Saint Helena, mother of Emperor
            Constantine, was attributed the discovery of the wood of the Holy Cross several
            hundred years after its burial. See Jacobus de Voragine, *The Golden Legend*, trans.
            Ryan, 1:277–84; Pringle 2007, 3:9; and Boas, p. 33. Described here is the way
            to the chapel dedicated to Saint Helena in the Church of the Holy Sepulcher
            (Pringle 2007, 3:39 [map], 44).

33          la *CHAPELE GRYFFOUNE*. The chapel indicated by this name is unclear.

35          le *HOSPITAL SEINT JOHAN* . The Church and Hospital of St. John the Baptist,
            located south of the Church of the Holy Sepulcher. See Pringle 2007, 3:192–207
            (nos. 322–23); and Boas, pp. 26–27.

36          la *EGLISE SEINT CARYOUT*. The Monastery Church of Saint Chariton, located
            near the northeast corner of the Church of the Holy Sepulcher. See Pringle
            2007, 3:158–60 (no. 310); and Boas, p. 128. The odd spelling indicates a scribal
            misreading of "toū" as "out."

la LATYNE. The Abbey Church of St. Mary Latin in Jerusalem, located just south of the Church of the Holy Sepulcher; see Pringle 2007, 3:236–53 (no. 334); and Boas, pp. 121–26.

38    TEMPLUM DOMINI. For the Abbey Church of the Templum Domini (the Jewish Temple of Jerusalem), see Pringle 2007, 3:397–417 (no. 367), 3:479 (map 3); and Boas, pp. 109–10.

42    The prophecy of Zachary concerns the birth of John the Baptist (Luke 1:13).

48    JERUSALEM. The Jerusalem Gate, named in a few other early records, is either the "portico on the eastern side of the upper platform on the Temple Mount" or the "inner (western) gate of the Golden Gate" (Boas, pp. 63–64). In the Bible the actions of Peter and John occur at the gate called "Speciosa" (Beautiful) (Acts 3:2, 10).

49    PARAYS. No gate is identified by this name in Pringle or in Boas. Pringle's map 5 (3:479) shows three northern gates of the Temple Precinct. The southern Triple Gate was also called the Spring Gate (Pringle 2007, 3:419). The repeated phrase est apele parays could be scribal error (dittography).

51    SPECIOUSE. For some of the associations surrounding this gate (also called Bab as-Silsila), see Pringle 2007, 3:405, 420–21, 432; and Boas, p. 64.

52    PORTE ORRYENE. On the history and associations of this gate, see Pringle 2007, 3:103–09 (no. 293), 3:479 (map 3); and Boas, pp. 63–64.

55    PROBATICA PISCINA. For the Chapel of the Sheep Pool, see Pringle 2007, 3:389–97 (no. 366), 3:479 (map 3); and Boas, p. 175.

57    TEMPLE SALOMON. The Templar Chapel in the Templum or Palatium Salomonis and the adjacent Church of the Templars; see Pringle 2007, 3:417–35 (nos. 368–69), 3:481 (map 5).

59    TOUR DAVID. David's Tower, the Citadel of Jerusalem (Pringle 2007, 3:480 [map 4]).

59–60    une CHAPELE, e leynze est seint Johan bouche orriene. A relic of a portion of John the Baptist's head was reportedly housed in a crypt below the Church of Saint John the Baptist; see Pringle 2007, 3:201.

60–61    une EGLYSE ou seint Jame fust decolé. The Armenian Cathedral Church of St. James the Great; see Pringle 2007, 3:168–82 (no. 318), 3:480 (map 4).

61    le MOUNT SYON. A district on the southwest side of Jerusalem, in which is located the Abbey Church of St. Mary of Mount Sion; see Pringle 2007, 3:261–87 (no. 336), 3:480 (map 4).

68    la PRETORIE CAYPHAS. See Pringle 2007, 3:131 and the explanatory note to line 61.

70    la CAVE GALYGANT. The Church of St. Peter of the Cock Crow on Mount Sion was reportedly the site of the house of Caiaphas and where Peter denied knowing Christ. The original site was a cave known as "Gallicantus." See Pringle 2007, 3:346–49 (no. 352), 3:480 (map 4).

71      *la NATORYE SYLOE*. Exegetes frequently linked the episode of Jesus bringing sight
        to the man born blind at the Pool of Siloam to passages from Isaiah. See
        especially Isaiah 8:6, 12:3, 29:18, and 35:5. There is no direct reference to
        Isaiah's death and burial in the Bible.

73      *ACHELDEMAC*. Where Judas hanged himself. In the Vulgate the place is
        "Haceldama" and defined as "ager sanguinis," field of blood.

74      *le VAL DE JOSAPHAT*. As described, the Valley of Jehoshaphat lies to the east of
        Jerusalem, between the city and the Mount of Olives. See Pringle 2007, 3:477
        (map 1), 3:479 (map 3).

75      *SEINT ANNE*. The Abbey Church of St. Anne; see Pringle 2007, 3:142–56 (no.
        305), 3:479 (map 3); and Boas, pp. 114–19.

78–79   *une EGLISE DE SEINT SALVEOUR*. The Church of St. Savior in Gethsemane; see
        Pringle 2007, 3:358–72 (no. 357), 3:479 (map 3).

89      *BETHPHAGE*. On the medieval pilgrimage sites in Bethphage, see Pringle 1993,
        1:157–59 (no. 64).

93      *BETHANYE*. The medieval pilgrimage sites of Bethany are described in Pringle
        1993, 1:122–37 (nos. 59–60). The chief destinations for the faithful were the
        houses of Lazarus and Simon (associated with Mary Magdalen).

94      *evesque de Marcille*. By tradition, Lazarus served as the first bishop of Marseilles.
        Lazarus's tomb was one of the destinations in Bethany.

96      *la QUARANTEYNE*. On the medieval priory of Quarantena, see Pringle 1993,
        1:252–58 (nos. 104–07).

98      *JERICO*. On the pilgrimage sites in Jericho, see Pringle 1993, 1:275–76 (no. 123).

102     *SEINTE ELYE*. The Monastery of St. Elijah. See Pringle 1998, 2:224–26 (no. 202),
        2:425 (map 8).

105     *SEINT RACHEL*. On the site of Rachel's Tomb between Jerusalem and Bethlehem,
        see Pringle 1998, 2:176–78, 2:425 (map 8).

106     *BEDLEHEM*. On the pilgrimage sites in Bethlehem, see Pringle 1993, 1:137–57
        (nos. 61–63).

110     *apparust le aungel as berchers*. On the location of Shepherds' Fields, see Pringle
        1998, 2:315–16 (no. 232), 2:425 (map 8).

112     *SEINT HABRAHAM*. On Hebron, a major pilgrimage site, and especially the
        Cathedral Church of St. Abraham, see Pringle 1993, 1:223–39 (no. 100).

113     *SPELUNCA DUPPLICI*. The double tombs of the married patriarchs were
        discovered and announced in 1119. See Pringle: "The status of the sanctuary at
        Hebron was enhanced considerably between June and October 1119 . . . when
        a way into the cave beneath it was accidentally discovered and the supposed
        bodies of the Patriarchs were found inside" (1993, 1:225; see also 1:235–39).

| 119 | *SEINT JOHAN DE BOYS*. On this church and its associations with John the Baptist's birth and childhood, see Pringle 1993, 1:38–46 (no. 8). |
|---|---|
| 121 | *NAPLES*. On the pilgrimage sites in Nablus, see Pringle 1998, 2:94–115 (no. 160–67). |
| | *PUYTZ JACOB*. On this site, named in the Bible at John 4:6, see Pringle 1993, 1:258–64 (no. 108). |
| 123 | *BASQUE*. Sebaste, location of the Cathedral Church and Monastery Church of St. John the Baptist, reputed to be the site of the saint's beheading, see Pringle 1998, 2:283–301 (nos. 225–26). The name in the manuscript is a corrupt form. |
| 125 | *MOUNT HERMON*. A place associated both with the ascent of Elijah to heaven and with the baptism of Jesus; see the description of the Monastery Church of St. John the Baptist in Pringle 1998, 2:240–41 (no. 209). |
| 126 | *NAMES*. The village of Na'im, or (in the Bible) Nain. The manuscript spelling *James* is a scribal error. On the site and Mount Tabor, see Pringle 1998, 2:115–16 (no. 168). |
| 128 | *MOUNT TABOUR*. On the pilgrimage sites of Mount Tabor, see Pringle 1998, 2:63–85 (nos. 155–58). The church referred to is the Abbey Church of the Savior, or the Transfiguration of the Lord (no. 155). |
| 131 | *BEBIE*. On the pilgrimages sites in Tiberias, on the eastern shore of the Sea of Galilee, see Pringle 1998, 2:351–66 (nos. 255–68). |
| 136 | *la CHASTIEL MAGDALON*. The Church of St. Mary Magdalen (or Mary of Bethany), in Tiberias; see Pringle 1998, 2:359 (no. 262). |
| 137 | *NAZAREZ*. On the pilgrimage sites in Nazareth, see Pringle 1998, 2:116–50 (nos. 169–73). The first place described here is the Cathedral Church of the Annunciation (no. 169). |
| 140 | *une FONTEYNE DE SEINT GABRIEL*. The Church of St. Gabriel in Nazareth; see Pringle 1998, 2:140–44 (no. 170). |
| 146 | *ZAPHORY*. On the Galilee city of Saffuriya, traditionally thought to be the birthplace of Saint Anne, and its church probably dedicated to her, see Pringle 1998, 2:209–18 (no. 196). |
| 148 | *la CANE GALYLEE*. On this site, see Pringle 1998, 2:162–64 (no. 181). The name "Architelin" does not appear in the Bible. |
| 151 | *la EGLISE DE SEINT SOFFROUN*. This unlocated church is discussed by Pringle 1998, 2:302 (no. 227). It seems to have existed in Shafa 'Amur, also called Saffran or Sapharanum. A scribe may have confused the place-name with Saint Sophronia of Tarentum, a female recluse of the fourth century. |
| 153 | *la EGLISE SEINT NYCHOLAS*. There were many Holy Land churches dedicated to Saint Nicholas; see, for example, the one at the Monastery of St. Sabas, which contained the skulls of monks martyred in the seventh century (Pringle 1998, 2:264–66 [no. 217]). |

155     *KOKET.* A region called Kuwaikat, Coquet, or Cochetum. See Pringle 1998, 2:32, 4:163.

156     It was John the Baptist who pronounced Jesus the Lamb of God (John 1:29, 36).

158     *SUR.* On the pilgrimage sites of Tyre, see Pringle 2009, 4:177–230 (nos. 454–79).

162     *PUTEUS AQUARUM* . The location of this well is uncertain; it may be named for Canticles 4:15, "puteus aquarum viventium" (well of living waters).

163     *SERPHENT.* On the pilgrimage site in Sarepta and its associations with the prophet Elijah, see Pringle 1998, 2:281–82 (no. 224).

165     *SEETE.* On the pilgrimage sites of Sidon, see Pringle 1998, 2:317–29 (nos. 236–45).

        *une EGLISE DE SEINT SALVEOUR.* The location of this church in Sidon is unknown. See Pringle 1998, 2:321–22 (no. 238).

168     *BARUTH.* On the pilgrimage sites of Beirut, see Pringle 1993, 1:111–19 (nos. 42–55), 2:316 (no. 234).

169     *un ymage de Nostre Seignour.* The author refers to the bleeding icon of Beirut. In around the year 765 an icon of Christ began to give forth blood after being subjected, as the story says, to ritual humiliation by the Jews. In 932 the icon was taken to Constantinople and housed in the Hagia Sophia. Feasts in celebration of it were popular in France and Spain. This reference shows that the story was also disseminated in England. See Vincent, pp. 46–48; and Pfaff, pp. 116–26. This icon is also mentioned in *The Land of the Saracens* (art. 95), lines 45–46.

174     *Sardayné.* The Monastery Church of Sardenay in Saidnaiya, a pilgrimage destination because it was the site of a legendary icon of the Virgin Mary said to have been painted by Saint Luke. See Pringle 1998, 2:219–21 (no. 198). The site is more fully described in *The Land of the Saracens* (art. 95).

## LES PARDOUNS DE ACRES / THE PARDONS OF ACRE                                    [ART. 39]

In 1040 during the First Crusade, Acre was the chief port in the Holy Land for crusaders. Articles 38 and 39 indicate how it remained an entry point for pilgrims. Dated 1258–63, *The Pardons* contains a unique listing of the shrines and holy houses (churches, hospitals, monasteries, etc.) that a pilgrim to Acre should plan to visit — and perhaps lodge at — during a stay there. The document specifies the indulgence a pilgrim will obtain upon visiting each sanctuary. In some cases, it is stated that an extended stay will bring added benefit. This text is closely allied with the preceding pilgrimage text (art. 38). For a helpful map of medieval Acre that pinpoints these sites, see Pringle 2009, 4:16–17.

[Fol. 70rb–v. *ANL* 337. **Scribe:** B (Ludlow scribe). **Quire:** 8. **Layout:** Prose in double columns, with final portion on fol. 70v written without columns. **Edition:** Michelant and Raynaud, pp. xxx–xxxi, 235–36 (no. 12). **Other MSS:** None. **Translations:** Pringle 2009, 4:22; Pringle 2012, pp. 15–17, 235–36.]

3      *Seint Nicholas*. Identified by Pringle as the Cemetery Chapel of St. Nicholas, which was outside the walls of the city (2009, 4:151–55 [no. 438]). See also the Church of St. Nicholas of the Field of the English (2009, 4:155–56 [no. 439]).

4      *Alemayns*. Church and Hospital of St. Mary of the Germans, Acre; see Pringle 2009, 4:131–36 (no. 425).

5      *Seint Leonard*. Abbey Church of St. Leonard, Acre; see Pringle 2009, 4:124–25 (no. 419).

6      *Seint Romaunt*. Church of St. Romanus in the Gardens, Acre; see Pringle 2009, 4:158 (no. 442).

7      *Seint Estevene*. Church and Hospital of St. Stephen, Acre; see Pringle 2009, 4:160–61 (no. 445).

8      *Seint Samuel*. Abbey Church of St. Samuel, Acre; see Pringle 2009, 4:158–60 (no. 443).

9      *Seint Lazer de Bethayne*. Church and Monastery of St. Lazarus of Bethany, Acre; see Pringle 2009, 4:120–21 (no. 417).

10      *Sepulcre*. Church of the Holy Sepulcher, Acre; see Pringle 2009, 4:52–53 (no. 384).

11      *Nostre Dame de Chevalers*. Church of St. Mary of the Knights, Acre; see Pringle 2009, 4:136–37 (no. 426).

12      *Nostre Dame de Sur*. Abbey Church of the Sisters of St. Mary of Tyre, Acre; see Pringle 2009, 4:142–44 (no. 431).

13      *Seinte Croyz*. Cathedral Church of the Holy Cross, Acre; see Pringle 2009, 4:35–40 (no. 371).

14      *Seint Marc de Venyse*. Parish Church of St. Mark of the Venetians, Acre; see Pringle 2009, 4:125–29 (no. 420).

15      *Seint Lorenz*. Identified by Pringle as the Parish Church of St. Laurence of the Genoese, Acre (2009, 4:117–19 [no. 415]). There is also tentative evidence for a Church of St. Laurence of the Knights in medieval Acre (Pringle 2009, 4:120 [no. 416]).

16      *Josaphat*. Abbey Church of St. Mary of the Valley of the Jehoshaphat, Acre; see Pringle 2009, 4:144–47 (no. 432).

17      *la Latyne*. Abbey Church of St. Mary Latin, Acre; see Pringle 2009, 4:139–40 (no. 428).

18      *Seint Pere de Pyse*. Church of St. Peter of the Pisans, Acre; see Pringle 2009, 4:156–57 (no. 440).

19      *Seint Anne*. Abbey Church of St. Anne, Acre; see Pringle 2009, 4:70–71 (no. 395).

20      *Seint Espyrit*. Hospital of the Holy Spirit, Acre; see Pringle 2009, 4:54–55 (no. 386).

21      *Bedlehem*. Hospital of the Brothers and/or Sisters of Bethlehem, Acre; see Pringle 2009, 4:44–45 (no. 377).

22          *Seint André*. Church of St. Andrew, Acre; see Pringle 2009, 4:63–69 (nos. 393).

23          *Temple*. Church and Castle of the Templars, Acre; see Pringle 2009, 4:166–72 (no. 451).

            *vj vintaines jours*. Six score, or 120, days. The scribe abbreviates *vintaine* by super-scripting *xx* after *vj*.

24          *Frere Prechours*. Church of the Dominicans (Preaching Friars), Acre; see Pringle 2009, 4:46–48 (no. 380).

25          *Seint Michel*. Parish Church of St. Michael, Acre; see Pringle 2009, 4:149–50 (nos. 436).

26          *Freres de Sake*. House of the Friars of the Sack, Acre; see Pringle 2009, 4:50 (no. 382).

27          *le Hospital Seint Johan*. Church and Hospital of St. John, Acre; see Pringle 2009, 4:82–114 (nos. 410–11).

29          *Seint Gyle*. Church and Hospital of St. Giles, Acre; see Pringle 2009, 4:80–81 (no. 408).

30          *la Magdaleyne*. Abbey Church of St. Mary Magdalen (Cistercian nuns), Acre; see Pringle 2009, 4:147–48 (no. 388).

31          *la Katerine*. Hospital of St. Katherine of the Battlefield, Acre; see Pringle 2009, 4:73 (no. 399).

32          *la Trinité*. House of the Holy Trinity and Captives, Acre; see Pringle 2009, 4:56–57 (no. 387).

33          *Seinte Bryde*. Church and Hospital of St. Brigid, Acre; see Pringle 2009, 4:72 (no. 398).

34          *Seint Martin de Bretons*. Hospital of St. Martin of the Bretons, Acre, founded in August 1254; see Pringle 2009, 4:129–30 (no. 421).

35          *Lazer de Chevalers*. Church and Hospital of St. Lazarus of the Knights, Acre; see Pringle 2009, 4:121–23 (no. 418).

36          *Seint Thomas*. Church and Hospital of St. Thomas the Martyr, Acre; see Pringle 2009, 4:161–64 (no. 447).

37          *Seint Bartholomeu*. Leper Hospital of St. Bartholomew of Beirut, Acre; see Pringle 2009, 4:72 (no. 397).

38          *Seint Antoyne*. Church and Hospital of St. Antony, Acre; see Pringle 2009, 4:71–72 (no. 396).

39          *Frere Menours*. House of the Franciscans (Friars Minor), Acre; see Pringle 2009, 4:48–50 (no. 381).

40          *Repentires*. House of the Magdalenes (the Penitents), Acre; see Pringle 2009, 4:58–59 (no. 388).

41      *Seint Denys*. Church and Hospital of St. Denis, Acre; see Pringle 2009, 4:76–77 (no. 403).

42      *Seint George*. Church of St. George of Lydda, Acre; see Pringle 2009, 4:77–78 (no. 405; see also nos. 406, 407, 415).

## NE MAI NO LEWED LUED LIBBEN . . . / SATIRE ON THE CONSISTORY COURTS     [ART. 40]

This richly comic satire complements a host of works found elsewhere in MS Harley 2253: the antifeminist French poems, the alliterative English monologues set for dramatic performance, and the many items that voice a person's needs, frustrated desires, or oppressed victimization at the hands of authoritative officialdom. In itself, the poem presents a biting satire of the ecclesiastical court system. It is here copied by a man with legal and clerical training, who himself performed duties as a legal scrivener (Revard 2000b).

The anonymous poet's awareness of the power of literacy is striking. He fashions a bewildered, angry, entrapped speaker who finds himself destroyed by books, "disempowered by a culture controlled by a clerical and intellectual elite, based on writing and documentation, which is alien to him" (Scattergood 2000b, p. 39). He has been hauled into court to face a judge ("an old cherl in a blake hure," line 19) and a row of smug, self-important summoners. Books are open, wherein are recorded his name and crime. He is in this predicament for what is, to his thinking, a trivial act: sexual dalliance with a girl on the ground (line 4). The girl takes the matter quite seriously, however, and demands justice in the form of marriage — something the narrator may have casually promised in the act of seduction. Because this is a comic monologue, the whole scene is constructed and colored through the lens of the speaker — an aggrieved, *lewed* man with disdain for a court system that would side (for its own extortionist gain) with a foolish woman. A riotous scene unfolds, one "alive with noise and movement: the bustle of the judicial officers, the jilted, bedraggled women vulgarly bawling their accusation across the courtroom" (Turville-Petre 1996, pp. 201–02). The accuser called to bear witness is summoned by two generic names, Maggie and Moll, which probably does not connote more than one accuser but does suggest the repetitive nature of such a scene in the ecclesiastical courts, where loose morals become grist and income for corrupt judicial officers.

As an English alliterative satiric complaint constructed as a dramatic monologue, this item is comparable to Harley arts. 25a, 31, 45, 81, 88. There is metrical similarity as well to *An Old Man's Prayer* (art. 45). *Satire on the Consistory Courts* is also sensitively counterpoised with the item that follows it, *The Laborers in the Vineyard* (art. 41), which is copied in parallel columns. *Laborers* handles similar themes in contrastive, nuanced ways. For commentary on *Satire on the Consistory Courts*, see Turville-Petre 1997; Scase 2007, pp. 38 n. 130, 143; and Scattergood 2000a, pp. 197–99, and 2000b, pp. 27–42. For this poem and English ecclesiastical statutes on marriage, see McCarthy, pp. 78–82, 210–13.

[Fols. 70va, 71ra, 71va. *IMEV, NIMEV* 2287. *MWME* 5:1406 [30]. **Scribe:** B (Ludlow scribe). **Quire:** 8. **Meter:** Five 18-line alliterative stanzas, rhyming aabccbddbeebfgggf, with concatenation at lines 12–13 and a complex metrical pattern. Lines rhyming a, c, d, and e are long, 4-stress lines. Lines rhyming b are short, 2-stress lines. Lines 11–17 form a wheel in 2-stress lines with a final bob (line 18) that rhymes with line 13 and alliterates with line 17.

**Layout:** Written in left columns of double-column pages. **Editions:** Wright 1839, 155–59; Böddeker, pp. 109–12; Robbins 1959, pp. 24–27 (no. 6); Turville-Petre 1989, pp. 28–31. **Other MSS:** None.]

2          *hyrt.* "Ecclesiastical court"; see *MED, hired* (n.), sense 1.(a), which provides this meaning for the word in line 56. It bears the same meaning here, even though the *MED* glosses *hyrt* here as "company of people, crowd" (sense 3.(c)), and Scattergood defines it as "retinue" (2000b, p. 33).

           *haver of honde.* "Skilled of hand." See *MED, honde* (n.), sense 5.(b), "manual skill" and *haver* (adj.), "skillful, willing, ready." Scattergood sees here a contrast between the illiterate man, who works with his hands, and the bookish men of the court (2000a, p. 199; 2000b, p. 33). The context indicates, however, the view that the *lewed* must keep up with the *lerede* by *haver of honde*, that is, they must be able to outwit them to survive, so the implied meaning is "cunning, handily skilled or clever." Moreover, the act of writing, which is constantly performed here against the narrator, is another kind of manual act.

3          *biledes.* "Leads, directs," but often also with a contextual sense of "mislead, abuse." See *MED, bileden* (v), senses 1 and 2.

4          *mote.* Despite its lack of a specific verb, the phrase *on molde mote with a mai* clearly implies sexual play. Perhaps the verb *mote* is a variant spelling of *mete*; see *MED, meten* (v.(4)), sense 6, "to have sexual intercourse." Line 5 plays off the sense of this line, inverting the man's agency to victimhood: "if I *lie* with a girl, I must bow before them and learn their *lay.*" For the phrase *on molde*, see the explanatory note to line 52.

7          *on folde.* "In the enclosure," that is, the court session, but in terms of a captured animal.

12–13      These are difficult lines. The translation of line 12 follows Robbins 1959, p. 258, and the *MED, umbreiden* (v.). For line 13, see *MED, unbreded* (ppl.), "unopened, obscure, unread," but "unclasped" seems more likely; the books are unclasped and ready to be (or already are) opened, threatening the speaker. For *wendeth*, I follow Turville-Petre's gloss, "turn over" (1989, p. 259).

23         *breven.* This word and *breved* in line 26 indicate the specific vocabulary of the lettered elite, that is, those who know how to write (Scattergood 2000b, p. 38). *Brevia* are notes made upon parchment to record a proceeding.

25         The image of the court clerks' stabbing on parchment suggests the way in which the plaintiff feels victimized, as it alludes to the devotional metaphor of Christ's tortured flesh as inscribed parchment.

31–32      A sharp rhetorical question and answer is a comic feature of stanzas 2–4, always occurring at the stanza's thirteenth and fourteenth lines.

34         *bacbite.* The narrator feels attacked from behind (Scattergood 2000b, p. 39). John Gower cites backbiting as one of the children of Envy and links it to the

spreading of false accusations behind one's back (*Confessio Amantis* 2:1604–12, 3140–51). Compare "mysnotinde men," line 38.

38      *by here evene*. "By their appearance, likeness, or character"; see *MED*, *even* (adj.), sense 12.(e).

41      *polketh*. For this verb, see *MED*, *pilken* (v.), "to deprive (sb.) of goods by exercise of power."

42      *clastreth*. "Enclose, (fig.) enslave." This is the only instance of the verb recorded in the *MED*. *Colle* means "net," so the sense is of ensnarement (*calle* (n.)). Editors have defined *colle* as the less well-attested *cole* (n.), sense (b), "trickery," but the repetition of the net figure in reference to women in line 60 seems an artful play in the poem that juxtaposes again the man's temptation and his punishment.

44      *bugge*. The verb here is *bien*, "to purchase, pay off."

46      *countene*. Turville-Petre glosses this word as "shire," i.e., "of the county" (1989, p. 225), while Robbins defines the phrase *countene court* as "court of accounts." (1959, p. 259).

50–54      According to Scattergood (2000b, p. 41), the poet alludes here to the figure of demonic scribes, with the narrator hoping for their damnation because of their association with writing.

52      *folht*. "Filth," and here "filthy girl, wanton woman, strumpet"; see *MED*, *filth* (n.), sense 3c. This epithet is comically literalized in the simile of line 58, and it was initiated when the narrator himself lay with her "on molde" (line 4). The *MED* is incorrect in defining the word as "sacrament of baptism" (*fulloght* (n.)).

57      *"Magge!" ant "Malle!"* Because there seems to be only one plaintiff, the apparent naming of two women has been seen as a problem. Turville-Petre views the situation as that of "a man accused of making promises of marriage to both Margaret and Mary" (1996, p. 201). Scattergood suggests that the second woman is a witness in the case (2000b, pp. 33–34). But both names may apply to a single woman, perhaps by Christian name and surname; both are generic and vernacular, denoting a common "any woman" lodging a common female grievance.

58      *bymodered*. "Covered with mud." On this image, see the explanatory note to line 52.

60      This line comically reverses what would be a typical, flattering phrase of love verse, *comely under calle*.

70      *forswat*. "Sweaty"; see *MED*, *forswat*, "covered with sweat," and *sweten* (v.(1)). The word contributes to allusions that cast the men of the court as hellish (see explanatory note to lines 50–54) and to others that suggest how these men "labor."

71      *hat*. The judicial order is to marry the woman.

73      *chapitre*. This word reverberates in many ways. First, it alliteratively echoes the *chaffare* bought at the market (*chepe*), so it puns as a new variety of marketplace. More literally, it references the ecclesiastical court as a monastic chapter house, and it also adds a bookish allusion to chapters of Scripture and canon law, used

here by the literate, clerical elite to censure and punish the narrator. See *MED*, *chapitre* (n.).

74        *unthenfol to be*. "To come to grief." This reading corrects previous editors, who have struggled to make sense of a problematic reading: *unpeufol*. For the adjective *unthenfol*, compare *MED*, *unthen* (v.), "fail to thrive, not prosper, come to grief." Turville-Petre 1989 defined *unpeufol* as "feeble" (1989, p. 258). The *MED* suggests "?ill-behaved, ?vicious"; see *untheuful* (adj.), and compare *theuful* (adj.).

82        On this punishment, see Turville-Petre, 1989, p. 31; and Scattergood 2000a, p. 198.

90        *ware*. The noun connotes the thing purchased or acquired, continuing the commercial image of the stanza, but it also holds the sexual meaning of a woman's private parts; see Turville-Petre 1989, p. 31; Scattergood 2000a, p. 198; and *MED*, *ware* (n.(2)), senses 1.(a) and 3. The term is applied to husbands in a later Middle English satiric poem; see "A Talk of Ten Wives on Their Husband's Wares" (*Trials and Joys of Marriage*, ed. Salisbury, pp. 95–98).

## OF A MON MATHEU THOHTE / THE LABORERS IN THE VINEYARD                    [ART. 41]

The Ludlow scribe inserted this poem, *The Laborers in the Vineyard*, after adjacent material — *Satire on the Consistory Courts* (art. 40) — had already been copied. He set this poem parallel to that one, in right-hand columns. Addressing themes of law and literate authority, fairness and judgment, these English works — a comic satire, a biblical homily — create a subtle and fascinating pair. In translating Matthew 20:1–16, the poet follows the scriptural narrative until the last stanza, where he turns the parable to a penitential lesson. The Harley lyric is notable as a precursor to the *Pearl* poet's exegetical use of the parable (*Pearl*, lines 497–600; ed. Gordon, pp. 18–22). Stemmler suggests that the scribe groups this poem with arts. 43, 44, and 45 because of their common stanzas of twelve lines (2000, p. 117), but only arts. 43 and 44 are alike in stanza form. *The Laborers in the Vineyard* utilizes a taut 3-rhyme tetrameter stanza that is more like the stanzas of variable length found in *Maximian* (art. 68).

For further commentary, see the bibliography in *MWME* 11:4331–32; Green 1999, p. 373; Fein 2007, pp. 79–80, 91; and Kerby-Fulton et al.

[Fols. 70vb, 71rb. *IMEV, NIMEV* 2604. *MWME* 2:398 [45], 11:4182 [10]. **Scribe:** B (Ludlow scribe). **Quire:** 8. **Meter:** Five 12-line isometric stanzas with three rhymes, aabaabccbccb$_3$, except for the last stanza, which has four rhymes, aabaabccbddb$_3$. **Layout:** Written in right columns of double-column pages. **Editions:** Wright 1842, pp. 41–43 (no. 12); Morris and Skeat, pp. 46–48; Böddeker, pp. 184–86; Brown 1932, pp. 143–45 (no. 80); Brook, pp. 42–43 (no. 10). **Other MSS:** None.]

5        *under*. "Undren," that is, nine o'clock in the morning.

7        *mydday ant at non*. "Midday and at none," that is, at noon and three o'clock.

9        *hoc*. If we are to imagine a vineyard, then the implement is probably "a sharp hook for cutting or tearing"; see *MED*, *hok* (n.), sense 4.(a). The definition

provided for this line, however, suggests an implement for an English field harvest: "a sickle for cutting grain; a reaping hook, a scythe" (sense 4.(c)).

13    *evesong*. The sixth canonical hour, that is, evening vespers.

42    *ase foreward wees*. "According to the agreement, pledge, or bargain." See the idiom under *MED, fore-ward* (n.), sense 3.(b).

45    *lees*. The word has a range of meaning: "untruthful"; "faithless, disloyal"; and "?unjust" (the definition chosen by the *MED* for this line). See *lese* (adj), sense 1a.(c).

48    *wraththelees*. "Without anger." This is the only attested instance of the word, according to the *MED*.

## LENTEN YS COME WITH LOVE TO TOUNE / SPRING     [ART. 43]

This famous lyric exemplifies at its best the Middle English *reverdie*, a song celebrating spring. The vitality of the new season quickens every line of *Spring* and animates its dancing rhythm. Metrically, the poem is similar to *The Fair Maid of Ribblesdale* and (aside from dialect) *Advice to Women* (arts. 34, 44). The latter poem is its partner in MS Harley 2253: the scribe sets the two works in parallel columns on fol. 71v, pairing them for meter and content. Linkages between the two poems exist in their shared springtime openings and in a few verbal echoes in the last stanza of *Spring* and the first one of *Advice*.

Other Middle English analogues to *Spring* are worth noting. Joyous birdsong, lively mood, and natural setting are evoked in the fine lyrics *Somer is i-cumen in* and *Foweles in the frith* (*IMEV, NIMEV* 3223, 864). In addition, the bird debate *The Thrush and the Nightingale* (*IMEV, NIMEV* 3222) closely corresponds to *Spring* in how it opens on the same line, substituting the word *Somer* for *Lenten*. Because *Thrush* is also composed in a 12-line, 3-rhyme tail-rhyme stanza, it seems clearly related to *Spring*. When grouped with *Advice*, this triad of poems exhibits a shared theme: men's desire for women brings pleasure and pain.

In *Spring*, the speaker's conflicted emotions produce an inherent tension. The language conveys spring's lush fullness by means of vivid, finely distilled detail, while the speaker, whose love is unrequited, feels at odds with the season's pleasures. In the end, he can endure only so much of the sensual life buzzing around him, and he flees from it in self-imposed exile. For commentary on *Spring*, see the bibliography in *MWME* 11:4332–35; Turville-Petre 1996, pp. 206–07; D'Arcy, pp. 314–16; Fuller, pp. 262–63; and Scattergood 2005, p. 55.

[Fol. 71va. *IMEV, NIMEV* 1861. *MWME* 11:4183 [10]. **Scribe:** B (Ludlow scribe). **Quire:** 8. **Meter:** Three 12-line tail-rhyme stanzas, $aa_4b_3cc_4b_3dd_4b_3ee_4b_3$, with regular alliterative ornament. **Layout:** Left side of double-column page. **Editions:** Wright 1842, pp. 43–44 (no. 13); Morris and Skeat, pp. 48–49; Böddeker, pp. 164–65; Brown 1932, pp. 145–46 (no. 81); Brook, pp. 43–44 (no. 11); Stemmler 1970, pp. 20–21; Millett, online edition; Treharne, pp. 569–70. **Other MSS:** None.]

7    *threstelcoc*. See explanatory note to *A Beauty White as Whale's Bone* (art. 36), burden.

36    This line can be read different ways depending on whether *wyht* is seen as a noun ("creature, man") or an adverb ("quickly"); *fleme* as a noun ("fugitive") or

a verb ("be banished"); and *wode* as "woods" or "madness." An alternate meaning is: "And be banished as a madman."

## IN MAY HIT MURGETH WHEN HIT DAWES / ADVICE TO WOMEN                [ART. 44]

Sharing the same meter and page, *Advice to Women* is the scribe's companion to *Spring* (art. 43). Longer than *Spring* by one stanza, it also contains a bit of extra patterning in the repetition of the word *wymmen* at the head of three stanzas. The poet's rhetoric of hidden intent resembles what is found in *The Poet's Repentance* (art 33): the language is witty and playful. It slyly exposes itself as potentially duplicitous while both explaining and enacting the love maneuvers that men use to woo women. The speaker expounds the ground rules of love talk:

(1) women are by nature free and may choose a lover freely;

(2) men will strive to bind them and will use words — often deceptively — to do so;

(3) many women are false, but they become so by foolishly succumbing to the false promises of treacherous men; and

(4) a woman who is tricked into being deflowered loses both freedom and truth, but the woman wooed by the speaker, if she submits, will gain true happiness.

The speaker's argument is thus stitched with mock-serious ambiguity. By warning women of men's often deceitful intentions, he avows himself a trustworthy informant, yet shows himself to be actively wooing a particular lady. So ultimately the poem strives to be an instrument of verbal persuasion. But yet, by the speaker's own argument, should he not be received with skepticism? If the lady should choose to accept him and be wrong, she will have only herself to blame, especially after having been so well warned.

The verbal wit of *Advice to Women* compliments women's mental agility while exposing men's duplicity. It plays off the old theme of women praised and blamed — a theme abundantly aired in Harley's French texts, especially in booklet 6 (see arts. 76, 77, 78, 83, and compare art. 8). The presence of lyrics like *Advice to Women* and *The Poet's Repentance* displays well-bred parlor discourse at its sophisticated best. These English texts and the others in French indicate, at some time and place, a mixed-gender audience that liked a joke that cut both ways between the sexes. For further commentary on *Advice to Women*, see the bibliography in *MWME* 11:4335–36; and also Scattergood 2005, pp. 56–57; Dane; Fein 2007, p. 72; and Choong, pp. 25–27.

[Fols. 71vb–72ra. *IMEV, NIMEV* 1504. *MWME* 9:2997 [153], 11:4185 [12]. **Scribe:** B (Ludlow scribe). **Quire:** 8. **Meter:** Four 12-line tail-rhyme stanzas, aa$_4$b$_3$cc$_4$b$_3$dd$_4$b$_3$ee$_4$b$_3$, with regular alliterative ornament. **Layout:** Right side of double-column page, with last stanza on next folio. **Editions:** Wright 1842, pp. 45–46 (no. 14); Ritson 1877, pp. 58–60; Böddeker, pp. 166–67; Brown 1932, pp. 146–47 (no. 82); Brook, pp. 44–45 (no. 12); Bennett and Smithers, pp. 119–21; Stemmler 1970, pp. 21–22; Treharne, pp. 570–71. **Other MSS:** None.]

9          *With love*. This phrase points two ways: ladies who are bright with love, and the poet who would bind one of them with love.

17         *lastes bed*. "Offer them vices, that is, tempt them to sin." See *MED, last* (n.(3)), sense (c), for the phrase.

| 30 | *Lounde*. The place is either Lound or London. |
|----|------|

| 33 | *stevenyng*. "Tryst." This line is the only instance attested in the *MED*; see *stevening* (n.(2)), "an assignation, appointment." |

| 35 | *yeynchar*. "Turning back"; see *MED*, *yenchar* (n.). |

| 41 | *ou*. "You," as accepted by all editors except Wright 1842. Wright's reading, *on*, "one," is also plausible, both in sense and as a reading of the manuscript. |

| 44 | *liht byleyn*. "Lies deflowered." The repeated word *liht* recalls the nature opening, especially lines 3–4. |

| 45 | *that he lahte*. The phrase seems to mean "what she got," but it may have a double sense as well: "what he took." See *MED*, *lacchen* (v.(1)), sense 4.(a). |

| 47–48 | The last two lines seems to be male sweet talk that aims to have the lady ignore the poet's own advice and be won over by his advances. |

## HEYE LOUERD, THOU HERE MY BONE / AN OLD MAN'S PRAYER [ART. 45]

*An Old Man's Prayer* is a penitential lyric that poignantly expresses contrition mixed with nostalgia for days gone by. Composed in a sophisticated, challenging stanza, the lyric features dense alliterative ornament, pararhyme, and concatenation. All but one stanza is linked by alliteration. The only break in the pattern occurs after the fifth stanza, where the speech is charged with emotion: here the old man confronts and abruptly addresses "Dreadful Deth" (line 86). Framed as a prayerful utterance, the poem seems suited for moving dramatic performance. In recalling his youth, the speaker revisits its pleasures and evokes a sad sense of the gulf between past vigor and present enfeeblement. He confesses in colorful figures that the seven sins were once his close companions: Lechery was his mistress, Liar his interpreter, Sloth and Sleep his bedfellows, and so on (lines 52–68). As the lyric closes, the speaker approaches death in a state of penitential dread and hope. The anonymous poet constructs a fictional self-portrait of psychological subtlety and insight.

Among English Harley lyrics, an analogue to *An Old Man's Prayer* is *Maximian* (art. 68), another complaint by an old man. The elaborateness of the stanza also invites comparison to the intricate metrical patterning of *Satire on the Consistory Courts* (art. 40). For commentary on *An Old Man's Prayer*, see the bibliography in *MWME* 11:4336–37, as well as Scattergood 2000b, pp. 15–26; Fuller, p. 261; and Treharne, pp. 571–72.

[Fol. 72ra–va. *IMEV, NIMEV* 1216. *MWME* 9:3034 [335], 11:4186 [13]. **Scribe:** B (Ludlow scribe). **Quire:** 8. **Meter:** Six 17-line stanzas with five rhymes in a complex pattern, $aa_4b_3aa_4b_3cc_4b_3cc_4b_3d_4e_3dd_4e_3$, and one final 5-line stanza, $a_4b_3aa_4b_3$. (Stanza 4 substitutes two c-rhymes for two a-rhymes.) Regular features of the stanza include pararhyme, alliteration, stanza-linking, and concatenation at lines 12–13. Lines 13–17 form a wheel. **Layout:** Double columns. **Editions:** Wright 1842, pp. 47–51 (no. 15); Böddeker, pp. 187–90; Patterson, pp. 61–64; Brown 1952, pp. 3–7 (no. 6); Brook, pp. 46–48 (no. 13); Treharne, pp. 572–74. **Other MSS:** None.]

3    *of murthes munne.* Either "salvation-minded" or "pleasure-minded." The ambiguity aptly begins this poem of regret over sin and hope for redemption.

9–10   These lines are about the old man's spent assets of character. His wise proverbs constituted a portion of his virtuous capital.

17    *waynoun-wayteglede.* On this term of derision, see *MED, wainoun* (n.) and *waiten* (v.), sense 1b.(a). This line is the only attested instance of *wainoun*, "lazy dog, worthless person," in the *MED*.

21    *no fynger folde.* The idiom refers to being able to love a woman. Compare the phrasing in *The Fair Maid of Ribblesdale* (art. 34), line 55, and *Blow, Northern Wind* (art. 46), line 31.

42    *atgoht.* "Gone, vanished, slipped away"; see *MED, atgon* (v.), sense 1.(a).

55    *plowe-fere.* A very common term for "playmate." See *MED, pleie* (n.), sense 10.(a), "companion, playmate, friend; also, paramour."

56    *lavendere.* Lechery was his laundress, implying she was his mistress.

63–64   The link word *weneth/whene* has an interesting range of meaning: "entertain, amuse," and also "exhaust." See *MED, wenen* (v.(1)), sense 2 (citing this line), and sense 3.

65    This line is repeated at line 80, and it echoes the idea stated in line 3 (see explanatory note). The speaker focuses on his own incapacity to exchange worldly happiness in society for spiritual happiness in heaven. For the verb *meten,* see *MED, meten* (v.(4)), sense 1.(b), "to encounter, experience, be afflicted by." Compare, too, the idiom *meten with mirth,* "be saved, attain salvation"; see *MED, mirthe* (n.), sense 2.(b).

## Ichot a Burde in Boure Bryht / Blow, Northern Wind    [ART. 46]

  Like *A Beauty White as Whale's Bone* (art. 36), *Blow, Northern Wind* is a love lyric in carol form. The burden is almost certainly older in origin than the poem. Appealingly direct and simple, the burden carries the air of a popular folk song. In its "evocative inconsequence" (Woolf 1970, p. 287), it breathes a natural, spirited plea for the north wind to blow the speaker's "suetyng" to him. The poem differs from the burden in its overall reliance on love-lyric formulas. Obviously designed for singing, the stanzas provide a conventional catalogue of the lady's beauties, and they occasionally seem little connected from one to the next. As in *The Fair Maid of Ribblesdale* (art. 34), the description moves down the woman's body from head to toe (stanzas 2–4). A musical medium would seem to lend itself to rhetorical repetition within some stanzas (see stanzas 2, 6, 9). Similes and expressions of emotion tend to be uncomplicated and standard, as in the metaphors on gems and flowers in stanza 6.

  Some interesting phrases or figures do stand out, however. In a startling conceit in stanza 2, the speaker calls upon Christ to honor his dear lady (lines 19–20). In lines 73–104, an allegory arises: Love's three knights, Sighing, Sorrowing, and Thought, have brought the poor lover into bale, against the power of Peace, and the speaker makes his complaint to Love. Viewed whole, the lyric's ten stanzas convey a rise-and-fall movement based in hyperbole:

the lady's incomparable essence (1); her beauty enumerated (2–4); superlative praise (5–6); the allegory of Love (7–9); and the lover's incomparable love-mourning (10). For further commentary on *Blow, Northern Wind*, see the bibliography in *MWME* 11:4337–39; and especially Greene 1962, pp. 252–54, and 1977, pp. 483–84; Boklund-Lagopoulou, pp. 29–30; Scattergood 2005, pp. 59–60; Scase 2007, pp. 170–73; and Choong, pp. 22–24.

[Fols. 72va–73rb. *IMEV, NIMEV* 1395. *MWME* 6:1750 [445], 11:4187 [14]. **Scribe:** B (Ludlow scribe). **Quire:** 8. **Meter:** Ten 8-line stanzas, aaa$_{3-4}$b$_3$ccc$_{3-4}$b$_3$, attached to a 4–line burden, CDED$_3$. **Layout:** Double columns, with the burden written at head and signaled after stanzas 1 and 2. **Editions:** Wright 1842, pp. 51–54 (no. 16); Ritson 1877, pp. 50–53; Böddeker, pp. 168–71; Brandl and Zippel, pp. 127–28; Brown 1932, pp. 148–50 (no. 83); Brook, pp. 48–50 (no. 14); Bennett and Smithers, pp. 121–24; Stemmler 1970, pp. 22–25; Silverstein, pp. 89–91 (no. 68) (omits stanzas 3–4); Greene 1977, pp. 268–69 (no. 440); Treharne, pp. 574–76. **Other MSS:** None.]

| | |
|---|---|
| burden | The form of this poem is a carol, and the first four unnumbered lines (written by the scribe) constitute the burden, that is, the external refrain. It is to be sung at the beginning and after each stanza. See also art. 36. |
| 13–15 | On the phrasing, compare *The Fair Maid of Ribblesdale* (art. 34), lines 31–32. |
| 31 | A line suggestive of matrimonial desire. Compare *The Fair Maid of Ribblesdale* (art 34), line 55, and *An Old Man's Prayer* (art. 45), line 21. |
| 67 | *solsecle*. See explanatory note to *Annot and John* (art. 28), line 20. |

## ALLE THAT BEOTH OF HUERTE TREWE / THE DEATH OF EDWARD I         [ART. 47]

*The Death of Edward I* is a poem in praise and remembrance of King Edward I, who died July 7, 1307, in Carlisle, while in pursuit of the Scots under Bruce and his brothers. His body was interred at Westminster Abbey. Calling upon a popular audience (*al Englond*), the poet participates in spreading the fame (*nome*) that springs from a great king who now lies low (stanza 2). This elegy exists in another version written in Anglo-Norman, the evident source. Both versions laud Edward as the flower of Christendom, a ruler who would have been a mighty crusader had he had the opportunity. Regrettably, however, according to both versions, the French obstructed him. The poet of the Anglo-Norman version is evidently a churchman. The English poet conveys an emphatic sense of England the nation and of building a legend around the deceased king. For a comparative analysis of the two poems, see Aspin, pp. 80–82; De Wilde; and the additional comments offered by Scattergood 2000a, pp. 169–71; and Treharne, p. 576.

[Fol. 73r–v. *IMEV, NIMEV* 205. *MWME* 5:1405–06 [29]. **Scribe:** B (Ludlow scribe). **Quire:** 8. **Meter:** Ten 8-line stanzas, most with three rhymes, ababbcbc$_4$, plus a closing, extended 12-line stanza, ababbcdcdef$_4$de$_2$. Stanzas 3 and 4 vary slightly with four and two rhymes, respectively. De Wilde attributes the irregular stanzas to the scribe's alteration of an original northern dialect (p. 240). **Layout:** No columns; written two lines per ruled line. **Editions:** Wright 1839, pp. 246–50; Böddeker, pp. 140–43; Robbins 1959, pp. 21–24 (no. 5); Treharne, pp. 576–78. **Other MS:** Cambridge, CUL Addit. MS 4407, art. 19 (a fragment;

ed. Skeat, pp. 149–50). **Anglo-Norman Source:** *Seignurs oiez, pur Dieu le grant,* from Cambridge, CUL MS Gg.1.1, fols. 489rb–vb (ed. Wright 1839, pp. 241–45; Böddeker, pp. 453–55; Aspin, pp. 79–89).]

12          *Yent.* "Throughout, everywhere." See *MED, yond* (prep.).

25–32       On Edward's well-documented intention to undertake a crusade, see Aspin, who notes that "Edward himself blamed the Scottish wars, not the king of France, for preventing him from going to the Holy Land" (p. 88).

41–48       This account of Pope Clement V's reaction to the news of Edward's death is historically plausible. A Vatican manuscript contains a 1307 sermon delivered as a eulogy on Edward to Pope Clement V (Clanchy, pp. 286–87). Further comment is provided by Aspin, pp. 88–89; and Scattergood 2000a, p. 170.

54          That is, perform the service in memory of Edward and on behalf of his soul, which follows in the next stanzas.

73          *Edward of Carnarvan.* King Edward II (1307–27), son of Edward I. He was crowned at Westminster on February 25, 1308. He is also mentioned in a hopeful fashion at the end of *The Flemish Insurrection* (art. 48), line 133. See also *The Execution of Sir Simon Fraser* (art. 25), line 81 (and explanatory note).

81–82       These lines are faintly reminiscent of either *Aeneid* 6.625–27 (Scattergood 2000a, p. 169) or 1 Corinthians 13:1 (Aspin, p. 82).

## LUSTNETH, LORDINGES, BOTHE YONGE ANT OLDE / THE FLEMISH INSURRECTION [ART. 48]

*The Flemish Insurrection* records a remarkable defeat of the French at the hands of the Flemish, which occurred five years before the death of Edward I (commemorated in art. 47). The anonymous English poet exults that the burghers of Bruges led by cloth-weaver Peter de Conyng were victorious over the French . The occupying French garrison was overcome by means of a revolt. Soon thereafter the professional French army suffered full-scale humiliation at the Battle of Courtrai on July 11, 1302. On the English poet's siding with the Flemish, Robbins comments, "At this date, before the development of the native cloth industry, the English could feel sympathy for their Flemish customers of wool" (1959, p. 251). The poet's rabid anti-French sentiment is allied in partisan mood with *The Death of Edward I* (art. 47), and it also suits the political climate during the making of the Harley manuscript. The copyist wants to emphasize and "demonstrate how the flower of French chivalry was humiliated by 'an fewe fullaris' (48.112), an encouraging example for the English as they prepare to encounter the French in the late 1330s" (Turville-Petre 1996, p. 196). In addition, the poem's inclusion reflects Ludlow's vital engagement with the wool trade, a regional interest that surfaces, too, in *Against the King's Taxes* (art. 114) (Revard 2000b, pp. 28–29).

The conflict depicted here is given literary and social meaning as a watershed moment when two sets of values collided: those of the down-to-earth local townsmen versus those of the imperious French aristocrats who claim sovereignty and moral superiority: "What astonished contemporaries about the battle of Courtrai was that a well-equipped army, led by aristocrats — the natural *bellatores* of their society — could be defeated by Flemish city militias. . . . [T]he lack of military sophistication of the citizen militias is used as a stick to beat the French" (Scattergood 2000a, pp. 172–73). The French expect courtly rules of war to be upheld, whereby nobles are captured and then ransomed, but the men of Bruges deride such customs and summarily execute the leader of the French armies, Robert, Count of Artois (lines 89–96). For further details on the historical circumstances and political climate, see Robbins 1959, pp. 250–52; and Scattergood 2000a, pp. 171–74.

[Fols. 73v–74v. *IMEV, NIMEV* 1894. *MWME* 5:1405 [27]. **Scribe:** B (Ludlow scribe). **Quire:** 8. **Meter:** Seventeen 8-line stanzas, aaa$_{5-7}$b$_3$ccc$_{5-7}$b$_3$. **Layout:** No columns. **Editions:** Wright 1839, pp. 187–95; Ritson 1877, pp. 44–48; Böddeker, pp. 116–21; Robbins 1959, pp. 9–13 (no. 3). **Other MSS:** None.]

11      *arewe*. "Resent, feel a grievance." See *MED, areuen* (v.), sense 3.

15      *anonen*. "Immediately, at once, soon"; see *MED, an-on* (adv. & conj.), sense 1(a).

17      *fullaris*. "The fullers beat the cloth to clean and thicken it" (Robbins 1959, p. 251).

19      *Conyng*. The surname puns in at least two ways. The first is a play on "king," derived from Old English *cyning*, a pun expressed in this line. The second is on "rabbit"; see the explanatory note to line 69. A possible third wordplay is on the gerund *conninge*, "skill, knowledge, cleverness." Peter de Conyng was master of the cloth-weavers in Bruges and a leader of the revolt against the French garrison.

20      *cheveuteyn*. "Ringleader." See *MED, chevetaine* (n.), sense 3.(b).

26      *destaunce*. "Civil strife, rebellion." See *MED, distaunce* (n.), sense 2.

30      *avowerie*. "Offical sanction, authorization, permission." See *MED, avouerie* (n.), sense 2.

36      *mounde*. "Military force, body of troops." See *MED, mounde* (n.(1)), sense 3.(f).

38      *basyns*. "Basins used as gongs." See *MED, bacin* (n.), sense 1.(b), and Robbins's note (1959, p. 251).

39      *todryven*. "To beat, smash to pieces." See *MED, todriven* (v.), sense (d).

65      Rauf de Nel is the name of the Earl of Bologne. Wright 1839 and Robbins 1959 mistakenly place the name inside the earl's speech.

66–67    The noble speaks a full line in French, and the word *assoygne*, "excuse, delay," also slips in. Compare, too, the insertion of French at lines 50, 56, and 61. On various instances of linguistic mockery in this poem, see Scattergood 2000a, pp. 172–74.

68      This line completes, with an English idiom, the sense of French line 66: "We won't leave any alive, at all!"

69      The line puns on *coning*, "rabbit"; see *MED, coning* (n.), sense 1.(a), and also sense 1.(b), figuratively, "a soldier as quick as a rabbit" (citing this line). They will prepare Coning like a roast rabbit. See also the explanatory note to line 19, and Scattergood 2000a, p. 172. But it is the French who will be caught like rabbits (line 81).

81            *so the hare*. See explanatory note to line 69.

85            *dabbeth*. This is the only attestation of this word with the military meaning "strike
              on the head, defeat"; see *MED*, *dabben* (v.).

87            *doddeth*. See *MED*, *dodden* (v.), sense 2(c) ~ *of*, "cut off (someone's head)."

89–92         The tone taken by the French noble is imperious and haughty, explaining to
              Coning how he ought to act if he is to be honorable.

91            *vylte*. "Dishonor, disgrace, vulgarity, ignominy." See *MED*, *vilte* (n.), sense 2.(a).
              The word is of French origin.

93            *leaute*. The French word spoken by either Coning or his partner John Breydel
              (master of the butchers) conveys the sarcasm of his response. The word *bocher*
              may indicate that the speaker is Breydel, who is not elsewhere mentioned. See
              Robbins 1959, p. 251, and Scattergood 2000a, pp. 172–73.

95–96         The implication is that the earl's life is not worth the expense of feeding him in
              prison.

97–104        I agree with Wright that line 97 depicts the mass grave of the French army
              (1839, p. 193). A different interpretation is offered, however, by the glossary of
              Robbins 1959: "There they were defeated in the ambush." The *MED* follows
              Robbins: *knillen* (v), sense (d), and *pit-falle* (n.), sense (b). However, the other
              meaning is available in *pit-falle*, sense (a). Böddeker seeks to improve the order
              of ideas by transposing lines 99–100 with lines 103–04.

106           The French king's gesture figuratively imitates the literal beheading of his nobles.

113           "The poet reminds Pope Boniface VIII of his degradation of two cardinals of the
              Colonna family in 1294 [and] advises him to go to Rome to put things right"
              (Scattergood 2000a, p. 174). See also Robbins 1959, p. 252.

133           *Prince of Walis*. Edward of Carnarvon, the future Edward II, also mentioned at
              the end of *The Death of Edward I* (art. 48), line 73. See also *The Execution of Sir
              Simon Fraser* (art. 25), line 81 (and explanatory note).

## Marie, pur toun enfaunt / The Joys of Our Lady                                    [Art. 49]

   *The Joys of Our Lady* is an elegant Anglo-Norman prayer by the Five Joys for protection
against the devil (named at start and finish). Its stanzas are symmetrically patterned: two
open the petition, five enumerate the Joys, two close the petition. The Joys named here are
identical to those cited in another French work in Harley, *Prayer on the Five Joys of Our Lady*
(art. 104): Annunciation, Nativity, Resurrection, Assumption, and Coronation. Noting the
lyric's idiom of servitude, fidelity, and elegant compliment, Jeffrey and Levy characterize
*The Joys of Our Lady* as a "courtly-feudal gesture of homage" (p. 48). A slightly different set
of Joys is given in the English lyric *Five Joys of the Virgin* (art. 67), and the motif is mentioned
without enumeration in *An Autumn Song* (art. 63), line 46. On the juxtaposition of this poem
with *Sweet Jesus, King of Bliss* (art. 50), compare the similar placement of *Mary, Mother of the*

*Savior* (art. 57) as prelude before *Jesus, Sweet Is the Love of You* (art. 58). For recent commentary on this item, see Durling, pp. 277–78, 286.

[Fol. 75ra–b. *ANL* 743. Långfors, p. 215. **Scribe:** B (Ludlow scribe). **Quire:** 8. **Meter:** Nine 6-line stanzas in tail-rhyme, aabaab. With some irregularities, a-lines have seven or eight syllables, b-lines have five or six. **Layout:** Double columns. **Editions:** Wright 1842, pp. 54–56 (no. 17); Dove 1969, pp. 290–92; Jeffrey and Levy, pp. 44–48 (no. 4). **Other MSS:** None. **Translation:** Jeffrey and Levy, pp. 45–47.]

## SUETE JESU, KING OF BLYSSE / SWEET JESUS, KING OF BLISS                [ART. 50]

*Sweet Jesus, King of Bliss*, a hymn of praise on the name of Jesus, consists in MS Harley 2253 of fifteen stanzas, each stanza starting with the phrase *Suete Jesu*. The first three stanzas correspond to a shorter, older poem found in MS Digby 86. The Harley version is, therefore, an expansion of the Digby poem. Later versions of *Sweet Jesus, King of Bliss* blend its stanzas with those of *Jesus, Sweet Is the Love of You* (art. 58), an intriguing fact because both poems appear in MS Harley 2253. These lyrics are among the earliest hymns upon the Holy Name, and they bear a relationship to lyrics ascribed to the Yorkshire mystic Richard Rolle (Ogilvie-Thomson, pp. lxxxv–xci; see also *MWME* 9:3063, 3422 [12]). As expanded versions of earlier renderings, both suggest an active literary background for texts appearing in the Harley manuscript. The lyrics occur fairly near each other, separated by seven items. *Sweet Jesus, King of Bliss* is set beside *Jesus Christ, Heaven's King* (art. 51), another prayer to Jesus in a more penitential mood. For fuller commentary on this lyric, see the manuscript affiliations and bibliography in *MWME* 11:4339–41, to which may be added Durling, p. 278.

[Fol. 75rb–va. *IMEV, NIMEV* 3236. *MWME* 9:3061–63 [12], 11:4189 [15]. **Scribe:** B (Ludlow scribe). **Quire:** 8. **Meter:** Fifteen monorhymed quatrains, aaaa$_4$, each stanza beginning *Suete Jesu*. **Layout:** Double columns. **Editions:** Wright 1842, pp. 57–59 (no. 18); Böddeker, pp. 191–93; Horstmann 1896, 2:9–11; Brown 1952, pp. 7–9 (no. 7); Brook, pp. 51–52 (no. 15). **Other MSS:** MS Harley 2253 is one of sixteen manuscripts that preserve this lyric in different forms; its copy is the oldest of the Version B texts. For Versions A–D, see *MWME* 11:4339–40. **Older Version (Version A):** Oxford, Bodl. MS Digby 86, fol. 134v (Tschann and Parkes, p. xxvi [item 48]; ed. Brown 1932, pp. 91–92 [no. 50]).]

16      *dreem.* "Singing, song"; see *MED*, *drem* (n.(1)), sense c.

35      *mylse ant ore.* "Mercy and pardon." These synonyms are often said together; see *MED*, *milce* (n.) and *ore* (n.(2)).

43      *erndyng.* "Intercession"; see *MED*, *erendinge* (n.), sense (a).

51      For this idiom, see *MED*, *ten* (v.(1)), sense (d), ~ *after min soule*, "come for my soul."

55      *longing.* For the negative senses of this word, see *MED*, *longinge* (ger.(1)), sense (e), "sorrow, sadness, distress, anxiety."

JESU CRIST, HEOVENE KYNG / JESUS CHRIST, HEAVEN'S KING                    [ART. 51]

In *Jesus Christ, Heaven's King*, the speaker seeks a good outcome for his soul beyond this sad world of "care, serewe, ant pyne" (line 24). The poet of this verse prayer does not wish to construct a dramatic monologue such as is found in the similarly penitential *An Old Man's Prayer* (art. 45). The *chanson d'aventure* opening at line 10 ("This ender day in o morewenyng") begins to situate the speaker in a specific moment, but, lacking narrative development, it remains a simple device imported from secular lyric style. A similar but more developed instance occurs in *An Autumn Song* (art. 63), lines 11–13. The scribe sets *Jesus Christ, Heaven's King* in a thematic sequence on fols. 75–76 (arts. 49–53) (Revard 1982, p. 134–36). For commentary, see the bibliography in *MWME* 11:4341–42; and Durling, p. 278.

[Fol. 75va–b. *IMEV, NIMEV* 1678. *MWME* 11:4190 [16 ]. **Scribe:** B (Ludlow scribe). **Quire:** 8. **Meter:** Four 6-line tail-rhyme stanzas, aa₄b₃cc₄b₃, with a prefacing 3-line prayer, aa₄b₃, which could attach to stanza 1. **Layout:** Double columns. **Editions:** Wright 1842, pp. 59–60 (no. 19); Böddeker, pp. 193–94; Patterson, pp. 88–89; Brown 1952, pp. 9–10 (no. 8); Brook, pp. 52–53 (no. 16). **Other MSS:** None.]

10–11     The wordplay on *morewenyng* and *mournyng* also occurs at the beginning of *The Four Leaves of the Truelove*, another poem that opens as a *chanson d'aventure*. See Fein 1998, pp. 166, 180. Compare also *An Autumn Song* (art. 36), lines 11–14.

14        *Jesu*. No earlier editor has adopted this emendation of scribal *jesse*, but Brown notes that the manuscript reading is "[c]learly a scribal error for *iesu*" (1952, p. 245). The emendation is needed for sense, and it also softens the meditative shift from Mary to Jesus.

WYNTER WAKENETH AL MY CARE / A WINTER SONG                    [ART. 52]

Highly regarded and widely anthologized, this superb English lyric offers an emotional reflection upon mutability and mortality as inspired by the signs of winter. Its haunting tones have been taken as possible evidence of Franciscan piety (or its influence) within a song genuinely inspired by nature while at the same time evangelical in purpose, as the lyric "moves without effort from an acute apprehension of physical reality to a personal reflection which is metaphysical and ultimately theological" (Jeffrey 1975, p. 257). The Harley compiler has juxtaposed the poem with *A Spring Song on the Passion* (art. 53). In both lyrics, contrastive natural seasons inspire transcendent religious feelings. Winter awakens a speaker's grief over his own mortality; springtime elicits love-longing for Christ. For commentary on *A Winter Song*, see the bibliography in *MWME* 11:4342–43; and Scattergood 2000b, pp. 63–68, and 2005, pp. 63–68.

[Fol. 75vb. *IMEV, NIMEV* 4177. *MWME* 9:3028 [310], 11:4190–91 [17]. **Scribe:** B (Ludlow scribe). **Quire:** 8. **Meter:** Three 6-line stanzas, aaab₄cb₂₋₃. A strong pause ends unrhymed line 5 before an emphatic line 6. **Layout:** Right column of a double-column page. **Editions:** Wright 1842, pp. 60–61 (no. 20); Ritson 1877, p. 56; Böddeker, p. 195; Brown 1952, p. 10 (no. 9); Brook, p. 53 (no. 17); Silverstein, pp. 52–53 (no. 30). **Other MSS:** None.]

13      *Al that gren me graveth grene.* "All that seed men bury unripe." This line is com-
        pressed in sense and somewhat difficult. For *graveth*, see *MED*, *graven* (v.(1)),
        sense 1.(b), "to put something under the ground, cover with earth; bury; plant."
        There is no *MED* gloss for *gren*, a much-discussed crux, sometimes emended to
        *grein*, "grain, seed" (suggestive of John 12:24–25: "Amen, amen I say to you, unless
        the grain of wheat falling to the ground die, itself remaineth alone. But if it die,
        it bringeth forth much fruit"). This reading is accepted here; emendation is
        unnecessary.

## WHEN Y SE BLOSMES SPRINGE / A SPRING SONG ON THE PASSION  [ART. 53]

In the mode of a secular lyric, the narrator of *A Spring Song on the Passion* suffers the pain
of "suete" love-longing and delays revealing his beloved's identity until the second stanza,
where it is disclosed gradually by an image of Christ on the cross. Stung to the quick by
viewing flowers burst into bloom and hearing birds erupt with song, the poet expresses a
lyrical sweetness and sadness. The method suggests, as in *A Winter Song* (art. 52), an origin or
influence in meditational piety. Two texts of the poem survive: the 5-stanza Harley version and
a 6-stanza version in an earlier manuscript. The extra stanza falls between Harley stanzas 1
and 2. On how the scribe has situated this poem above two others on the same page, both of
which deal with passion for a lady, see the explanatory note for *While You Play in Flowers* (art.
55). For commentary, see the bibliography in *MWME* 11:4343–44; Kinch, pp. 142–43; and
Durling, pp. 280–81.

[Fol. 76r. *IMEV*, *NIMEV* 3963. *MWME* 11:4191 [18]. **Scribe:** B (Ludlow scribe). **Quire:** 8.
**Meter:** Five 10-line isometric stanzas, ababccbddb₃. **Layout:** No columns; written as prose.
**Editions:** Wright 1842, pp. 61–63 (no. 21); Böddeker, pp. 196–98; Brook, pp. 54–55 (no.
18); Millett, online edition. **Other MS:** London, BL MS Royal 2.F.8, fol. 1v (ed. Brown 1932,
pp. 120–22 [no. 63]).]

16      *bileved.* The verb is *bileven* (v.(1)), "to remain, hold back, or turn from," not
        "believe" as glossed by Brook. The line expresses the superlative depth of Jesus'
        suffering.

## FERROY CHAUNSOUN / I PRAY TO GOD AND SAINT THOMAS  [ART. 54]

This Anglo-Norman secular song is a *departie*, that is, a lament from an anguished lover
whose lady does not return his passion. Ready to try again to win her, he pledges his fidelity.
Bearing an infectious refrain, this lyric in French is like the exuberant English *Alysoun* (art.
29). In its theme of unrequited love, it resembles *The Lover's Complaint* and *The Way of Woman's
Love* (arts. 30, 93). The poet's line lengths and rhymes are a bit eccentric, causing Jeffrey
and Levy to comment that "Although it is plain that this song does not obey the rules of formal
structure, it seems to be a deliberate play-on-metre rather than the work of a mere amateur
or incompetent, a conscious (sometimes, perhaps, even perverse) seeking after variations
of structural dimensions" (p. 254). By the lyric's placement on fol. 76r between two other
poems, it participates in a trilingual dialogue on passion in both the religious and the
secular sense (Fein 2007, p. 83). For recent commentary on this item, see Durling, p. 281.

[Fol. 76r. *ANL* 127. **Scribe:** B (Ludlow scribe). **Quire:** 8. **Meter:** Three stanzas, two of seven lines, one of eleven lines, irregular in meter and rhyme scheme. A catchy 4-line refrain, 8ccc 6b, follows each stanza. **Layout:** No columns; written as prose with line divisions marked. Large capitals mark the initials of each stanza. **Editions:** Wright 1842, pp. 63–64 (no. 22); Kennedy, pp. 10–11 (no. 1); Jeffrey and Levy, 251–54 (no. 48). **Other MSS:** None. **Translations:** Kennedy, pp. 10–11; Jeffrey and Levy, pp. 252–53.]

## DUM LUDIS FLORIBUS / WHILE YOU PLAY IN FLOWERS                                    [ART. 55]

Aside from *Song on the Times* (ed. Wright 1839, pp. 251–52), *Dum ludis floribus* is the earliest known lyric to blend Latin, Anglo-Norman, and English. Its first four stanzas combine French half-lines with Latin conclusions. The last stanza opens with a Latin verse followed by an Anglo-Norman one. Only the last two verses are in English, and the linguistic shift delivers a climactic surprise, "the shock for which nothing before has prepared the reader" (Turville-Petre 1996, p. 203). Identifying himself as a student in Paris, the poet writes in praise of his beloved while in the throes of desperate love-longing. His sigh of love-anguish, uttered in the vernacular, ends his elegant appeal with a bluntly native lament. To literalize the poet's final stanza, he writes in Latin, lodges in France, but in the depth of despair moans in English.

In miniature, *Dum ludis floribus* reflects the trilingual fluency of the Harley compilation. The poem is sometimes viewed as evidence for a class of poet, the so-called wandering student, who would readily import Latin and French poetic conventions into vernacular English verse. The lyric's position on folio 76r below *A Spring Song on the Passion* and *I Pray to God and Saint Thomas* (arts. 53, 54) seems a calculated exercise in displaying various forms of passion (Turville-Petre 1996, pp. 212–13; Lerer 2003, pp. 1255–59; Fein 2007, pp. 72–73, 83). For the Latin translation, I acknowledge the assistance of Radd Ehrman, classics professor at Kent State University. For further commentary on *Dum ludis floribus*, see the bibliography in *MWME* 11:4344–45; Scattergood 2005, pp. 53–54; Lerer 2008; Durling, pp. 281–83; and Birkholz, p. 218.

[Fol. 76r. *ANL* 134. Långfors, p. 109. *IMEV Suppl.*, *NIMEV* 694.5. *MWME* 11:4191–92 [19]. **Scribe:** B (Ludlow scribe). **Quire:** 8. **Meter:** A macaronic lyric in five monorhymed alexandrine quatrains, alternating Latin and Anglo-French, until the last two lines, which are in Middle English. **Layout:** No columns, written as prose. **Editions:** Wright 1842, pp. 64–65 (no. 23); Kennedy, pp. 12–14 (no. 2); Brook, p. 55 (no. 19); Stemmler 1970, p. 25; Jeffrey and Levy, pp. 248–50 (no. 47); Millett, online edition; Lerer 2008, pp. 249–50. **Other MSS:** None. **Translations:** Kennedy, pp. 12–14; Jeffrey and Levy, pp. 248–50; Millett, online translation; Lerer 2008, pp. 250.]

1          *lacivia*. The traditional reading *lacinia*, "border or fringe of a garment," has led to many difficulties in translating this line. Stemmler 1970 and Lerer 2008 prefer the reading *lacivia*, which I accept here; *velud lacivia* means "as in wantonness." The poem's opening line seems to address a male friend who loves many women ("flowers"), while the speaker loyally pines for his beloved, a peerless flower (line 12). Lerer adopts this reading as better than *lacinia*, yet advocates emendation to *luscinia*, "nightingale" (2008, pp. 245–48).

17        *Scripsi*. All editors emend the manuscript word *Scripsit*, "he has written," to *Scripsi*, "I have written."

19–20     Compare the similar surprise effect of affective English in *Gilote and Johane* (art. 37), line 245.

## QUANT FU EN MA JUVENTE / SONG ON JESUS' PRECIOUS BLOOD        [ART. 56]

This Anglo-Norman poem on mystical friendship exhorts the reader to find his true love and firm security against the devil in the blood of Jesus. It begins with a narrator's love-longing that cannot find fulfillment. At the end of a five-stanza prologue, the disconsolate, lethargic speaker is comforted by a song (*dite*) that seems to arrive miraculously without known cause. He will sing it now for the reader. It tells of the loyal, pure friendship of Jesus for the one who would seek him through his heart's wound. Just as Jesus' blood issued out of this wound, so is the believer to enter it, cling to Jesus' heart, and wash his own heart in this holy blood. By meditating on Jesus' wound in such a latently erotic way, true love is to be found. The wound is like an eye (compare *I Sigh When I Sing* [art. 62], line 9, where Jesus' wounds "weep"). Looking outward from within Jesus' wound, the reader is also urged to envision and feel sorrow with Mary his mother and Saint John his friend, Jesus' compassionate companions at the Passion. By devotion to God's blood, the reader will gain true love and be ever shielded from danger. As a poem that dwells on the subject of friendship, this text becomes a mystical counterpart to the Anglo-Norman *Lesson for True Lovers* (art. 26). For its focus on Christ's blood, compare *The Way of Christ's Love* (art. 92). One of the final items in MS Harley 2253 is a mediation on Christ's Passion, *Seven Hours of the Passion of Jesus Christ* (art. 115). For recent commentary on this item, see Durling, pp. 283–84.

[Fols. 76v–77r. *ANL* 911. Sinclair 1988, no. 6490. Långfors, p. 301. **Scribe:** B (Ludlow scribe). **Quire:** 8. **Meter:** Twenty-two 8-line stanzas, in alternating rhyme, abababab, six syllables per line (with some irregularity). **Layout:** No columns. **Edition:** Dove 1969, pp. 299–301. **Other MSS:** None. **Translations:** None.]

## MARIE, MERE AL SALVEOUR / MARY, MOTHER OF THE SAVIOR        [ART. 57]

*Mary, Mother of the Savior*, an Anglo-Norman salutation to Mary, is situated between a French poem that honors the blood of Jesus and an English one that honors the name of Jesus (arts. 56, 58). Its metrics resemble the English one. Moreover, its idiom of compliment to Mary's goodness, mercy, and sweetness (*douçour*) flows seamlessly into the next poem's praise of Jesus' sweetness. The poem enacts the medieval Christian's belief in Mary as intercessor, addressing God's mother as a preliminary step to uttering praise directly to Jesus. A similar juxtaposition of address, first to Mary and then to Jesus, occurs in *The Joys of Our Lady* and *Sweet Jesus, King of Bliss* (arts. 49, 50). It is interesting how, in each instance, Mary is approached in French before Jesus is named, petitioned, and praised in English.

[Fol. 77va. *ANL* 795. Långfors, p. 215. Vising §184/*78*. **Scribe:** B (Ludlow scribe). **Quire:** 8. **Meter:** Thirteen monorhymed quatrains, 8aaaa. Stanza 2 has two rhymes, 8aabb, and stanza 12 has a fifth line. **Layout:** Right side of a double-column page. **Editions:** Wright 1842, pp. 65–67 (no. 24); Dove 1969, pp. 288–89. **Other MSS:** None. **Translations:** None.]

DULCIS JESU MEMORIA / JESUS, SWEET IS THE LOVE OF YOU                              [ART. 58]

Like *Sweet Jesus, King of Bliss* (art. 50), this religious lyric is a hymn of praise on the name
of Jesus. The scribe supplies the underlined title *Dulcis Jesu memoria* in the upper margin,
a title that associates it with a well-known Latin hymn ascribed to Bernard of Clairvaux
(Daniel 1:227). One editor notes that the poem "has just 50 stanzas, so it was probably
meant to form a rosary" (Horstmann 1896, 2:11), but this count is not correct: the Harley
poem has forty-eight and a half stanzas (lines 49–50 are lost or never existed). In the Ludlow
scribe's arrangement of matter, *Mary, Mother of the Savior* (art. 57) serves as prelude to this
poem. *Jesus, Sweet Is the Love of You* belongs to a cluster of related English lyrics in the same
4-line meter that names Jesus at the head of each stanza. Stanzas from these deeply
devotional lyrics were freely extracted, blended, and multiplied. Elsewhere, this lyric is
yoked to *Sweet Jesus, King of Bliss* to make a long poem that survives in Vernon and other
manuscripts (*IMEV, NIMEV* 3238; ed. Furnivall, pp. 449–62). On the affiliation of these
malleable lyrics with the school of Richard Rolle, see the explanatory note to art. 50. For
recent commentary on this item, see Durling, pp. 285–86.

[Fols. 77vb–78va. *IMEV, NIMEV* 1747 (compare *NIMEV* 3238). Compare *MWME* 9:3061–63
[12], 11:4340 [15, Version C]. **Scribe:** B (Ludlow scribe). **Quires:** 8–9 (fol. 78 opens quire
9). **Meter:** Forty-nine monorhymed quatrains, aaaa$_4$, each stanza beginning *Jesu*. Stanza 13,
written at the base of a column, lacks two lines (lines 49–50, here numbered). **Layout:**
Double columns; title is provided and underlined by the scribe. **Editions:** Wright 1842, pp.
68–76 (no. 25); Böddeker, pp. 198–205; Horstmann 1896, 2:11–24. **Other MSS:** Three
other MSS contain versions of this lyric; see *NIMEV* 1747.]

8           *a luviere.* Wright 1842 and Böddeker read these words as *alumer,* a word that has
            entered the *MED* as a nonce word: "One who enlightens." But see also *lovere*
            (n.(2)), sense 1.(a), the variant found in Glasgow, University of Glasgow, MS
            Hunterian 512.

49–52       The first two lines of this stanza are missing. Horstmann 1896 suggests a gap of
            six lines here. Wright 1842 prints lines 45–52 as a 6-line stanza. The half-stanza
            of lines 51–52 was probably invented by the scribe: "To create a balanced look
            to the page [beside the column containing *Mary Mother of the Savior*], the scribe
            topped column b with the title and inserted two unmetrical lines at the base of
            that column" (Fein 2007, p. 84 n. 45).

51          *bac.* "Crown (of thorns)." The word appears to derive from Old French *bague,*
            "bundle." It is the only attestation listed in the *MED.*

53          *tocknynge.* "Example, model." See *MED, tokninge* (ger.), sense 7.(b).

54–56       The depiction is of Christ on a crucifix, arms spread out, head down, with his
            posture reinterpreted, in mystically erotic terms, as the welcome of a lover.

65          *gretyn.* "Attack, strike." This word is emended from manuscript *gredyn* ("call out,
            shout"), which suits neither context nor rhyme. See *MED, greten* (v.(2)), sense 2.(b).

66          *blod to sueten.* "To bleed," literally, "to sweat blood." See *MED, sweten* (v.(1)),
            sense 1.(c).

| | |
|---|---|
| 70 | *tacheth*. "Bind, arrest," with a legal connotation; see *MED*, *tachen* (v.(1)), sense 2.(b). |
| 72 | *fon thre*. The three foes are the Flesh, the World, and the Devil. Compare *The Three Foes of Man* and *The Sayings of Saint Bernard* (arts. 27, 74). |
| 74 | *opene*. The *MED* reads this word as a verb, but it is an adverb. |
| 87 | The general import of this line is obscure. See *MED*, *note* (n.(2)), sense 1.(a), "benefit, profit, advantage," and *frame* (n.(1)), sense 1, "profit, benefit, advancement." |
| 100 | *O*. I interpret this word as an interjection; Horstmann defines it "till" (1896, 2:19). |
| 119 | *treufole ant tholemod*. "Obedient and submissive"; see *MED*, *treuful* (adj.), sense (a), and *thole-mode* (adj.), sense (a). |
| 121–24 | Because of the mixed rhyme in this stanza, Horstmann 1896 thinks lines may be missing here. |
| 133 | *froreth*. "Comforts, cheers, encourages"; see *MED*, *frovren, -ien* (v.). |
| 148 | *blac*. "Pale, livid"; see *MED*, *blak* (adj.), sense 6.(a). |
| 150 | Note the reversal in who drinks whose blood. |
| 152 | *drede for no flod*. The idiom here is revealed in the *MED* Middle English term *flod-drede* (n.), "dread of change or instability." |
| 183 | *weryyng*. "Protection"; see *MED*, *weringe* (ger.(1)). |
| 187 | *Atscapen*. "To escape," a verbal form attested only here; see *MED*, *atscapen* (v.) |

## UNE PETITE PAROLE / SERMON ON GOD'S SACRIFICE AND JUDGMENT [ART. 59]

This wide-ranging verse sermon, covering Creation to Doomsday, delivers with such direct simplicity its lessons on basic doctrine that it seems best suited for children. After a 5-line prologue, the speaker moves with broad strokes from Adam's creation and Eve's sin to Christ's expiation for human sinning upon the cross. Then an account of the seven sins leads to the example of Lucifer's fall for pride. The lesson next turns to the sin of avarice, preaching an economic pragmatism similar in kind to that of the courtesy texts found later in MS Harley 2253 (arts. 79, 89, 94). Here, though, the warning remains moralistic and religious. Virtue means never taking anything wrongfully and striving before you die to return what you ought not possess, so as to ensure that you have squared all accounts before the final reckoning. For recent commentary on this item, see Durling, pp. 286–87.

[Fols. 78vb–79rb. *ANL* 608. Sinclair 1988, no. 6802. Vising §148. **Scribe:** B (Ludlow scribe). **Quire:** 9. **Meter:** This poem has 120 lines, basically octosyllabic but with irregularities, rhyming sometimes by couplets but often with three, four, or more lines on the same rhyme. **Layout:** Columns. **Editions:** Wright 1842, pp. 76–80 (no. 26); Dove 1969, pp. 292–94. **Other MSS:** None. **Translations:** None.]

88      *qe vous quidez.* "the one in question." The phrase means literally "the one whom you imagine."

## STOND WEL, MODER, UNDER RODE / STAND WELL, MOTHER, UNDER ROOD    [ART. 60]

*Stand Well, Mother, under Rood* is a richly moving lyric modeled directly on the 11-stanza Latin sequence *Stabat juxta Christi crucem.* It survives in six manuscripts, but only Harley and two others preserve the full eleven stanzas. The piece also appears in MS Digby 86, where it lacks the last two stanzas. Two manuscripts preserve the song with music: Cambridge, St. John's College, MS 111, and London, BL MS Royal 12.E.1. Editors Dobson and Harrison date the lyric no earlier than 1250. A range of dialects shows that the English hymn was widely dispersed.

In form, the first nine stanzas set Christ in dialogue with his mother, three lines allotted to each speaker. Their tender speeches are intensely intimate, elegaic, and suffused harmoniously with suffering and love. Through their exchanges, "extreme emotion . . . is conveyed sharply and tightly" (Gray, p. 136) in a delicate balance of meditation, *planctus,* and debate. The English poem displays, according to Woolf, "a warmth not characteristic of Latin hymns" (1968, p. 245). The last two stanzas expound for Mary the joyous outcome of the Passion, and the poem ends with the narrator petitioning for mercy. Christ and Mary display in dialogue a symbiotic kind of suffering, constructed by the poet in palpable detail. What Christ experiences as God Mary may feel ever more feelingly as human mother. Her show of natural emotion softens his dogmatic exposition of doctrine. Their joint suffering becomes the true labor pains (prelude to humanity's rebirth) that the Virgin and Son did not experience at the Nativity (stanza 7). For the rich range of commentary on *Stand Well, Mother, under Rode,* see the bibliography in *MWME* 11:4345–47, to which may be added Durling, pp. 287–88.

[Fol. 79rb–vb. *IMEV, NIMEV* 3211. *MWME* 3:676–77 [1(r)], 11:4192 [20]. **Scribe:** B (Ludlow scribe). **Quire:** 9. **Meter:** Eleven 6-line stanzas, aabccb$_4$. In the Harley version, stanza 6 is moved to third position. **Layout:** Double columns. Speech markers are not in the manuscript and have been added editorially. **Editions:** Wright 1842, pp. 80–83 (no. 27); Böddeker, pp. 206–8; Brook, pp. 56–57 (no. 20).**Other MSS:** Oxford, Bodl. MS Digby 86, fol. 127r–v (9 stanzas) (Tschann and Parkes, p. xxvi [item 45]); Cambridge, St. John's College, MS 111, fol. 106v (4½ stanzas with music); London, BL MS Royal 8.F.2, fol. 180r (1 stanza); London, BL MS Royal 12.E.1, fols. 193r–194v (11 stanzas with music); Dublin, Trinity College MS 201, fol. 194r (11 stanzas). **Critical Edition (Manuscripts and Music):** Dobson and Harrison, pp. 152–60, 254–55, 301.]

11–12    Mary asserts that the spear prophesied by Simeon has figuratively struck her heart, a reference to Luke 2:35.

13    Jesus' pleading to his mother for mercy is a striking moment of reversal.

23    *erne.* "Flow"; see *irennen* (v.), sense 2.(b).

28    *byswongen.* "Tormented, afflicted"; see *MED, biswingen* (v.).

47          Anachronistically, Mary sees herself as an intercessor even at the scene of the
            Passion.

48          *fol wymmon.* "Sinful woman." The word *fol* opens a semantic range: "foolish,
            stupid, ignorant, lecherous, wanton, impious, imprudent." On this phrase in this
            line, see *MED, fol* (adj.), sense 3, "prostitute, wanton woman"; and Dobson and
            Harrison: "'foolish', doubtless in the sense 'morally loose'" (p. 159).

61–67       The last stanza reverses the order of the stanza-by-stanza dialogues when the
            speaker prays first to Mary and then to Jesus.


## JESU, FOR THI MUCHELE MIHT / JESUS, BY YOUR GREAT MIGHT                            [ART. 61]

As a verse meditation on the Passion, *Jesus, by Your Great Might* belongs with the manuscript's series of religious lyrics on Mary and the Passion that began with the Anglo-Norman
*Song on Jesus' Precious Blood* (art. 56). Its meditative focus is fixed on divine and human
incarnation. The penitent contemplates Christ's wounds and physical death, setting these
beside his own desire to remain whole after death and beyond Doomsday. An English lyric of
similar metrics and theme is *On leome is in þis world ilist* (*IMEV, NIMEV* 293; ed. Brown 1932,
pp. 34–37). For commentary, see the bibliography in *MWME* 11:4347; and Durling, p. 288.

[Fol. 79vb. *IMEV, NIMEV* 1705. *MWME* 11:4194 [21]. **Scribe:** B (Ludlow scribe). **Quire:** 9.
**Meter:** Five 10-line stanzas, $a_4b_3a_4b_3cc_4d_3ee_4d_3$. **Layout:** Right side of a double-column page;
lines 1–4 of each stanza are written as two lines, as in next poem. **Editions:** Wright 1842, pp.
83–85 (no. 28); Böddeker, pp. 208–10; Brown 1932, pp. 150–52 (no. 84); Brook, pp. 57–59
(no. 21). **Other MSS:** None.]


12          *overwerpes.* Of the heart, "to sink, be downcast"; see *MED, overwerpen* (v.), sense
            (b).

18          *wete.* "Shed tears"; see *MED, weten* (v.), sense 3.(c).

34          *stoundes.* "A time of trial or suffering, pangs of woe"; see *MED, stounde* (n.), sense
            3.


## I SYKE WHEN Y SINGE / I SIGH WHEN I SING                                          [ART. 62]

Called by Woolf the "most moving of the Harley Passion lyrics" (1968, p. 65), *I Sigh
When I Sing* conveys heartfelt grief and religious longing. In the delicate, anguished tones
of this lyric, one feels the subtle influence of secular love poetry. An older version appears
in MS Digby 2, *Hi sike, al wan hi singe.* Editors often prefer the Digby version because it preserves some lost rhyme words and presents a finely modulated lament in its final lines.
Stanzas appear in different order in the two versions with the fourth and fifth stanzas transposed. The Harley arrangement concentrates the Crucifixion image at the center of the poem,
with a visionary sense of entry and exit from a deeply ocular meditation. Intimate, second-
person addresses to Christ, called *lemmon,* emerge at the height of the depicted Crucifixion.
In the Digby version, the speaker approaches the divine lover more slowly, reaching second-

person address only in the fifth stanza. For the history of commentary on this lyric, see the bibliography in *MWME* 11:4348–49, to which may be added Durling, p. 288–90.

[Fol. 80ra. *IMEV, NIMEV* 1365. *MWME* 11:4194–95 [22]. **Scribe:** B (Ludlow scribe). **Quire:** 9. **Meter:** Six isometric 10-line stanzas, ababccbddb$_3$. **Layout:** Left side of a double-column page; lines 1–4 of each stanza are written as two lines, as in preceding poem. **Editions:** Wright 1842, pp. 85–87 (no. 29); Böddeker, pp. 210–12; Brook, pp. 59–60 (no. 22); Saupe, pp. 109–10 (no. 47); Millett, online edition; Treharne, pp. 579–80. **Other MSS:** Oxford, Bodl. MS Digby 2, fol. 6r (ed. Brown 1932, pp. 122–24 [no. 64]).]

9          The wounds weep as wounds and eyes. Compare the explanatory note for *Song on Jesus' Precious Blood* (art. 56).

17         *clyngeth.* "Recoil, shrink in fear or sorrow, be disheartened"; see *MED, clingen* (v.), sense 3.

32         This line may refer to an apocryphal legend of the smiths who forged the nails for the Crucifixion. See *MWME* 11:4194, 4348.

## NOU SKRINKETH ROSE ANT LYLIE-FLOUR / AN AUTUMN SONG                    [ART. 63]

   *An Autumn Song* offers a sensitive meditation on mortal decay and spiritual health. An unusual feature is the embedded *chanson d'aventure* formula that occupies the second through fifth stanzas. A similar though less-developed device occurs in *Jesus Christ, Heaven's King* (art. 51). The curative balm for the sinner rests in Mary, whom the speaker seeks as he thinks on his folly. He ventures out in Peterborough upon a *morewenyng* in a mood of sad rumination and lament. The echoic "mournyng" in line 14 yokes setting and mood by means of pun. The same pun exists in *Jesus Christ, Heaven's King* (art. 51), lines 10–11, and also in the opening of the alliterative *Four Leaves of the Truelove* (*IMEV, NIMEV* 1453), a poem about seeking and finding spiritual remedy (Fein 1998, pp. 166, 180). Here, the speaker depicts Mary's curative medicine: herbs of sweet smell that offer the way to heaven, prefigured in the faded *suete savour* of real flowers. The poet brilliantly merges the starkly contrastive fairness of ladies and the pierced side of Christ. The evocative first line, a *reverdie* stung by autumnal nostalgia, establishes a mood of elegiac sadness because floral beauty (of rose and lily) is beset with decay. The flowers, conventional for describing women's complexions, deftly come to denote the certainty of death, and then, in what seems a spontaneous transition, fleshly renunciation and Jesus' torn body. The poem thus quietly abjures the secular lyric's celebration of women's love by converting the floral image to meanings of transience and *memento mori*. In fearing death, the speaker meditates on Jesus' death on the cross and birth in Mary's flesh, and finds therein a female physician's "cure" for his mourning, thoroughly transforming the trouvères' concept of the lady as healer.
   Homage to the Virgin's Five Joys (line 46) connects this lyric to other works in MS Harley 2253 (arts. 49, 67, 104). Topical and verbal links (the brightness of a lady, the wilting of a petal or leaf) join the ending to the beginning of the next item (Stemmler 2000, pp. 118–19). In the sequence of English lyrics on fols. 79r–81r, this poem culminates a religious sequence (arts. 60–63) and forms a bridge to the secular songs (arts. 64, 65) that follow. For

further commentary, see the bibliography in *MWME* 11:4349–50; Scattergood 2005, pp. 65–66; Fein 2007, pp. 84–85; and Durling, p. 289.

[Fol. 80rb. *IMEV, NIMEV* 2359. *MWME* 11:4195 [23]. **Scribe:** B (Ludlow scribe). **Quire:** 9. **Meter:** Six 10-line stanzas, aa$_4$b$_3$aa$_4$b$_3$c$_4$b$_3$c$_4$b$_3$. The final stanza lacks line 7. **Layout:** Right side of a double-column page; lines 7–10 of each stanza are written as two lines.. **Editions:** Wright 1842, pp. 87–89 (no. 30); Böddeker, pp. 213–15; Patterson, pp. 98–100; Brown 1952, pp. 11–12 (no. 10); Brook, pp. 60–62 (no. 23); Silverstein, pp. 47–48 (no. 27); Saupe, pp. 149–50 (no. 78); Millett, online edition; Treharne, pp. 580–82. **Other MSS:** None.]

6      *byglyde.* "Steal away, pass away"; see *MED, bigliden* (v.), which cites this line as the only instance.

40      *sete.* "Content, at ease"; see *MED, sete* (adj.), sense c.

46      On the theme of the Five Joys in the Harley manuscript, see the English *Five Joys of the Virgin* (art. 67) and the French *Joys of Our Lady* and *Prayer on the Five Joys of Our Lady* (arts. 49, 104).

55–56      The order of the lines is reversed in the manuscript. The emendation follows Brown 1952.

59      *us.* The rhyme scheme indicates that a line is missing. Lines 54–56, 58–60 are written at the base of a column in a crowded fashion. Brook emends *us* to *me*, reading the last stanza as a 9-line variant with a rhyme scheme requiring this restoration: aa$_4$b$_3$a$_4$b$_3$a$_4$b$_3$a$_4$b$_3$. Brook's emended pronoun maintains the speaker's inward penitential musings, while the manuscript reading (retained here) directs the thought outward in a pastoral fashion. Brown 1952 suggests that a copyist transposed lines 55–56 and left out the next line, which rhymed with *us*. A few Harley poems conclude with variant stanzas, for example, *A Beauty White as Whales Bone* and *When the Nightingale Sings* (arts. 36, 65).

## MY DETH Y LOVE, MY LYF ICH HATE / THE CLERK AND THE GIRL      [ART. 64]

A variant of the *pastourelle* in which a lover pleads at the lady's window, *The Clerk and the Girl* is often linked to another Harley *pastourelle*, *The Meeting in the Wood* (art. 35). The oxymorons of the first line might also be meant to connect it to the opening of the preceding *Autumn Song* (art. 63), wherein lovely women betoken death and death on the cross betokens life. While that poem is religious, this one — a dialogue with debate elements — is secular. The clerk speaks the first two stanzas, and the remaining ones alternate speakers. The girl has the final word. The clerk seems at first to be talking to himself, bemoaning unrequited love, but then it becomes clear he is addressing the girl. She answers in blunt colloquial tones that puncture the pretensions of his speech: "Do wey, thou clerc! Thou art a fol!" (line 9). In the rich colors of parody, a no-nonsense girl mocks a poet-lover's self-absorbed airs and even the class disparity of the traditional *pastourelle*: it is better to go on foot than ride a wicked horse, she says, playing off the sexual meaning too. The two argue as opposites in diction (his elevated love talk versus her down-to-earth colloquialisms) and in stance (his wooing persistence versus her stubborn reluctance). Class is less an issue here than in the traditional *pastourelle*: the couple evokes a rustic village pairing of equals. Dispute yields eventually to reconciliation, as in many medieval debates. While the woman at first shows surprise, disgust, and alarm at the man's persistence, she eventually seems to know him as her long-lost love once he reveals that they kissed fifty times before at her window.

Many analogues and influences have been proposed for this lyric. Two are from popular ballad: the enmity-of-kin theme as found in *Clerk Saunders* (Child, no. 69; *MWME* 6:1798); and the returned-sailor theme as in *The Kitchie Boy* (Child, no. 252), wherein the lover returns after an absence and tests his beloved's fidelity by posing as a new suitor. A resemblance to *The Nut-Brown Maid* is also sometimes cited (*MWME* 3:730–33 [61]). Woolf compares the piece to a German *Fensterlieder*, in which a lover pleads at a window for admission (1970, p. 285). Conlee calls it "the finest example of a 'night-visit' dialogue in Middle English" (p. xxxvi). It appears to be darkness of night that hides the speaker's identity. He compliments the lady as a source of light, "briht so daies liht," while he is like a sun-blighted summer leaf (lines 2–3). Thus does a clerk maddened by sorrow wander under *wode-gore* and find his way back to radiant love.

*The Clerk and the Girl* appears to be grouped, by layout and meter, with the two poems that come next (arts. 65, 66). It is not to be confused with an English interlude known by a similar title, *De Clerico et Puella* (*IMEV, NIMEV* 668; *MWME* 5:1324 [6]; ed. Brandl and Zippel, p. 203). For further commentary, see the bibliography in *MWME* 11:4350–52, and also Turville-Petre 1996, pp. 209–10; Scattergood 2000b, pp. 43–62, and 2005, pp. 63–64; and Hines, pp. 99–100.

[Fol. 80v. *IMEV, NIMEV* 2236. *MWME* 3:727 [54], 11:4196–98 [24]. **Scribe:** B (Ludlow scribe). **Quire:** 9. **Meter:** Nine 4-line stanzas in septenary meter, aaaa$_7$, with some internal rhymes. **Layout:** No columns. Speech markers are not in the manuscript and have been added editorially. **Editions:** Wright 1842, pp. 90–91 (no. 31); Böddeker, pp. 172–73; Brown 1932, pp. 152–54 (no. 85); Brook, pp. 62–63 (no. 24); Bennett and Smithers, pp. 124–26; Stemmler 1970, pp. 26–27; Silverstein, pp. 91–92 (no. 69). **Other MSS:** None.]

18          *wayted*. "Spied on, secretly"; see *MED, waiten* (v.), sense 5.(b).

24          *mythe*. "Hide, conceal (emotions, actions, etc.)"; see *MED, mithen* (v.(1)), sense (a).

31          *under the wode-gore*. This phrase reflects the often sexualized *under gore* motif found in many Harley lyrics. See the explanatory notes to *Alysoun* (art. 29), line 43, and *Song of the Husbandman* (art. 31), line 55.

## WHEN THE NYHTEGALE SINGES / WHEN THE NIGHTINGALE SINGS [ART. 65]

In the Harley manuscript this secular love poem sits between two poems of identical meter (arts. 64, 66). With a *reverdie* opening as in *Spring* (art. 43), the poet celebrates the season of renewal before revealing how its stabs him with pangs of unfulfilled longing. As the landscape waxes green, the speaker goes ill (*grene*, line 16) with love-longing. A kiss bestowed by his lady would heal him. The lyric represents the type of English love song — courtly sentiment modulated with vernacular idiom — most prone to be adapted by religious poets. The final stanza of this lyric adds a flourish to the final rhyme, much like the metrically extended ending of *A Beauty White as Whale's Bone* (art. 36). Brook suspects the influence of the *envoi* in these final variant stanzas (p. 86). The dialect is east or northeast Midland, and the place-names Lindsey, Lincoln, Northampton, and Lound map out an approximate geographical area. For further commentary, see the bibliography in *MWME* 11:4352–53; and Scattergood 2005, pp. 55–56.

[Fols. 80v–81r. *IMEV, NIMEV* 4037. *MWME* 11:4198 [25]. **Scribe:** B (Ludlow scribe). **Quire:** 9. **Meter:** Five 4-line stanzas in septenary meter, aaaa$_7$, with frequent internal rhyme. The last stanza plays a variation, aaa$_7$b$_3$b$_4$. The irregular internal rhymes lead some to print this poem in octaves, a$_4$b$_3$c$_4$b$_3$d$_4$b$_3$e$_4$b$_3$ (e.g., Duncan, Davies). **Layout:** No columns. **Editions:** Wright 1842, p. 92 (no. 32); Ritson 1877, pp. 53–54; Böddeker, p. 174; Brown 1932, p. 154 (no. 86); Brook, p. 63 (no. 25); Bennett and Smithers, p. 126; Stemmler 1970, p. 27; Silverstein, p. 93 (no. 70). **Other MSS:** None.]

| | |
|---|---|
| 6 | *lemmon, for thin ore*. This phrase is formulaic. Gerald of Wales, a canon of Hereford, repeats it in the story of a priest who embarrassed himself (*Jewel of the Church*, 1.43). Hearing it sung repeatedly by outdoor revelers the night before, it became stuck in his head, and he mistakenly sang it as the Host was elevated. The anecdote helps to place *When the Nightingale Sing*s in the tradition of popular verse. |
| 16 | *grene*. "Green, that is, lovesick." See *MED*, *grene* (adj.), sense 1.(b), "pale, colorless," and *grene* (n.(2)), "desire, sexual passion." |
| 17 | *Lounde*. Probably Lound, not London. Compare *Advice to Women* (art. 44), line 30. |

## BLESSED BE THOU, LEVEDY / BLESSED ARE YOU, LADY [ART. 66]

*Blessed Are You, Lady* is a dignified prayer to the Virgin that also survives in MS Egerton 613, a book older than MS Harley 2253. The two versions each have two unique stanzas and many phrasal variations, and after lines 1–8 the stanzas are not in the same order. The lyric was probably copied from memory for at least one of the two texts. The Harley scribe has clustered three poems in the same meter (arts. 64, 65, 66) on two facing leaves (fols. 80v–81r) (Solopova, pp. 377–79). The grouping may indicate that they are to be sung to the same music. Moreover, the placement of this prayer item with the others seems to make deliberate contrast between secular and religious love, which the scribe clearly does elsewhere (compare arts. 92, 93). For the history of commentary on *Blessed Are You, Lady*, see the bibliography in *MWME* 11:4353–54, to which may be added Durling, p. 290.

[Fol. 81r–v. *IMEV, NIMEV* 1407. *MWME* 11:4199 [26]. **Scribe:** B (Ludlow scribe). **Quire:** 9. **Meter:** Nine 4-line stanzas, aaaa$_{6-7}$, with some internal rhyme. Compared to the Egerton version, the Harley lyric tends to reduce regular septenary meter to six stresses. **Layout:** No columns. **Editions:** Wright 1842, pp. 93–94 (no. 33); Böddeker, pp. 216–17; Brook, pp. 64–65 (no. 26); Saupe, pp. 127–28 (no. 64). **Other MS:** London, BL MS Egerton 613, fol. 2r (ed. Brown 1932, pp. 111–13 [no. 55]).]

17    *shene, sterre cler.* This epithet for Mary corresponds to the *Ave Maris Stella* hymns of the fourteenth century (compare *IMEV, NIMEV* 1082, 1235; ed. Brown 1952, pp. 58–59 [no. 45], 22–23 [no. 20]).

32    *oftelle.* "Express, speak of, mention"; see *MED, oftelle* (v).

## ASE Y ME ROD THIS ENDER DAY / THE FIVE JOYS OF THE VIRGIN [ART. 67]

*The Five Joys of the Virgin* has been called the "purest example in English of a love song to the Virgin" (Woolf 1968, p. 137). The poet's amorous thoughts of his Lady yield to devotion on her Five Joys and eventually to a petition for participation in her transcendent joyfulness. Expressing himself in the manner of a courtly singer, the poet permits an erotic subtext to develop: in asking Christ to grant Mary's intimate mediation (line 52), he hopes to advance toward a heavenly state of sublime pleasure.

A well-known secular poem with the refrain *Nou sprinkes the sprai* (*IMEV, NIMEV* 360; ed. Brown 1932, pp. 119–20 [no. 62]) shares this poem's first line but not its meter. The imitator here is apparently the religious poet, who has adapted a familiar opening to evoke the eroticized circumstance of a *pastourelle* encounter. For the phenomenon of turning a secular song or phrase to religious purpose, one can compare the Ludlow scribe's pairing of *The Way of Christ's Love* and *The Way of Women's Love* (arts. 92, 93) and the conversion of a phrase from *When the Nightingale Sings* (art. 65; see explanatory note to line 6). Like the narrator of *Nou sprinkes the sprai*, the speaker of *The Five Joys of the Virgin* is intent on *play*, his thoughts focused on a beloved *may* (lines 2–3). The secular ploy continues until the maiden is identified as Mary and her Five Joys contemplated: Annunciation, Nativity, Epiphany, Resurrection, and Ascension. The inclusion of the Epiphany is unusual but not unique among English poems; here it replaces the traditional fifth Joy, the Assumption (subsumed in the Ascension).

Elsewhere in the Harley manuscript the same theme is addressed in the French *Joys of Our Lady* and *Prayer on the Five Joys of Our Lady* (arts. 49, 104), and it is referenced in the English *An Autumn Song* (art. 63). In more than a dozen extant Middle English lyrics on the subject, Mary's Joys are usually five in number, although formulations on seven, eight, twelve, or fifteen joys also occur. For further commentary, see the bibliography in *MWME* 11:4354–55.

[Fol. 81va–b. *IMEV, NIMEV* 359. *MWME* 11:4200 [27]. **Scribe:** B (Ludlow scribe). **Quire:** 9. **Meter:** Ten 6-line stanzas, aaa$_4$b$_3$a$_4$b$_3$. **Layout:** Double columns. **Editions:** Wright 1842, pp. 94–96 (no. 34); Böddeker, pp. 218–19; Brown 1952, pp. 13–14 (no. 11); Brook, pp. 65–66 (no. 27); Saupe, pp. 147–48 (no. 77); Millett, online edition. **Other MSS:** None.]

33    *thoro lay.* "Perfect light"; see *MED, thurgh* (adj.), sense (e), and *leie* (n.(2)), sense (f).

34    *lyhtnesse.* "Enlightenment, spiritual insight"; see *MED, lightnesse* (n.(1)), sense 2.(b).

## HERKNE TO MY RON / MAXIMIAN [ART. 68]

This English poem is a loose paraphrase of a familiar Latin work, the first *Elegy* of Maximian. It has been seldom edited and printed because an earlier, better version survives in MS Digby 86. There the scribe sets it under a French title, *Le Regret de Maximian.* The

Harley version of *Maximian* has thirty-one stanzas of variable length. The more regular Digby version has twenty-two 12-line stanzas and one apparently defective 9-line stanza. The level of variation and reordering between the two versions is quite freewheeling.

Like *An Old Man's Prayer* (art. 45), *Maximian* laments old age within the "signs of death" tradition. The specific debt here is to the *Elegies* attributed to Maximianus, an elusive sixth-century Latin poet whose utterances may in fact derive from more than one person. In his verse he claimed to be a friend of Boethius, whose *Consolation of Philosophy* also spawned poetic exercises, sometimes on the same theme (see Ziolkowski 1998, pp. 126–29, 311–13 [no. 50]). The *Elegies* were frequently used in the Middle Ages to teach Latin to schoolboys, and they were therefore popular among medieval writers, Chaucer included. After beginning didactically, naming Maximian a handsome and rich man in his youth, the poet constructs a dramatic monologue of mournful lament, which becomes, especially in Harley, "excessively disordered in thought" (Woolf 1968, p. 105). Repeated stanza units suggest delivery by memory or even, perhaps, a performance that seeks to reenact an old man's rambling forgetfulness. Scattered throughout the poem are *Elegy*-derived signs of aging and impending death: loss of strength, faded beauty, sexual impotency, bent stature, and so on. The speaker dwells bitterly on the contrast between youth and age, his loss of the former, and the contemptible state he is now in. He exemplifies the conventional moral warning that Death awaits everyone, and he utters this truth with the experiential knowledge of old age.

For commentary on *Maximian*, see Woolf 1968, pp. 102–15; and Tristram, pp. 63–64. For other Harley works with corresponding Digby versions, see the explanatory notes for *Harrowing of Hell*; *Debate between Body and Soul*; *Sweet Jesus, King of Bliss*; *Stand Well, Mother, under Rood*; *The Sayings of Saint Bernard*; *The Blame of Women*; *Hending*; and *Prayer on the Five Joys of Our Lady* (arts. 21, 22, 50, 60, 74, 77, 89, 104). On the broad correspondences between MSS Harley 2253 and Digby 86, see Corrie 2000. A Harley poem with a similar though more regular meter is *The Laborers in the Vineyard* (art. 41).

[Fols. 82ra–83r. *IMEV, NIMEV* 1115. *MWME* 9:3034–35 [336]. **Scribe:** B (Ludlow scribe). **Quire:** 9. **Meter:** Thirty-one stanzas of typically six, nine, or twelve lines, built of 3-line tail-rhyme segments, $aab_3$, with a final prayer couplet, $aa_3$. The Digby version has twenty-two 12-line stanzas, $aabaabaabaab_3$, and one 9-line stanza. Some stanzas in the Harley version possess more than two rhymes. **Layout:** Triple columns. **Editions:** Wright and Halliwell, 1:119–25; Böddeker, pp. 245–53. **Other MS:** Oxford, Bodl. MS Digby 86, fols. 134va–136vb (Tschann and Parkes, p. xxvi [item 49]; ed. Brown 1932, pp. 92–100 [no. 51]).]

| | |
|---|---|
| 11 | *droh.* "To get (something), obtain"; See *MED*, *drauen* (v.), sense 2d.(a). |
| 15 | *tho.* "Thrived"; see *MED*, *then* (v.), sense 1.(a). |
| 20 | *lore.* "Conduct, behavior"; see *MED*, *lore* (n.(2)), sense 8. |
| 30 | *wede.* "Fade, become pale"; see *MED*, *waden* (v.), sense 4. |
| 42 | This line is similar to line 176. |
| 44 | *fayrest honde.* Perhaps this phrase is an idiom for "generous." |
| 46–48 | These lines are very similar to lines 238–40. |
| 54 | *gnede.* "Scanty, scarce"; see *MED*, *gnede* (adj.), sense 2.(a). |

65        *rowe*. "Be disturbed"; see *MED*, *reuen* (v.(1), sense 1.(b).

70        *My wele is went to wo.* Here and in line 266 an image of the Wheel of Fortune is implicit.

76        *Reuthful is my red.* "Sorrowful is my thought." For *red* as "state of mind, thought process," see *MED*, *red* (n.(1)), sense 2a.(d).

76–81     These lines are similar to lines 142–48.

114       *mounde* "Power, might"; see *MED*, *mounde* (n.(1)), sense 3.(a).

124       *nowhith*. "Not very long, a short span of time, a brief period"; see *MED*, *wight* (n.), sense 2.(d).

127       *wore*. "Shore." The same phrase occurs in *Alysoun* (art. 29), line 38 (see explanatory note).

130       *Thicke*. "Muscular, stout"; see *MED*, *thikke* (adj.), sense 6.

142–48    These lines are similar to lines 76–81.

142       *red*. In context, the provider of "counsel, advice," is gendered female. The speaker is not receiving the kind of fond speech from a woman that he remembers.

150       *yse*. "Look at, gaze upon"; see *MED*, *isen* (v.(1)), sense 4a. There could be a sexual connotation; see sense 6, "consort with, visit." The next stanza will contrast this state with the speaker's memories of past attentions from women.

175       *Ystunt*. "Blinded"; see *MED*, *istinten* (v.), sense (b). This line is similar to line 233.

176       This line is similar to line 42.

177       *fonde*. "Deceive, mislead"; see *MED*, *fonnen* (v.), sense 2.

219       *mengeth al my blod.* "Agitate my passions, provoke my feelings"; for this idiom, see *MED*, *mengen* (v.), sense 6.(c).

222       *So Y me understod.* "As I have recalled"; for this reflexive construction, see *MED*, *understonden* (v.), sense 7.(b).

223–24    Literally, "I wish that I were all as I never was." This existential expression reflects a desire both to relive the past and to have never existed.

228       *Falu*. "Sallow, faded"; see *MED*, *falwe* (adj.(2)), sense (a).

233       This line is similar to line 175.

234       *thon*. "Thine," that is, "your own life or experience."

238–40    These lines are very similar to lines 46–48.

250       *red*. "Prepare"; see *MED*, *reden* (v.(1)), sense 14.(a).

266       *My weole is turnd to wo.* See explanatory note to line 70.

MAYDEN, MODER MILDE / MAIDEN, MOTHER MILD                                        [ART. 69]

*Maiden, Mother Mild* is an elegant macaronic prayer to Mary that serves as an opening invocation for *King Horn*, the long romance that follows it on fol. 83r. The lyric's conclusion is linked verbally to *Horn*'s beginning by repetition of the thematic rhyme words *synge* and *kynge*. Its linguistic fluidity is remarkable: the poet's "heartfelt simplicity of the English combines with the gracious euphony of the French" (Turville-Petre 1996, p. 202). The poem's final stanza alludes to the *Acta Pilati* or *Gospel of Nicodemus*, and it seems to break the lyric's sequence of Passion events, which run from the legend of the Instantaneous Harvest (perhaps) to the scene of Resurrection. In terms of Harley's contents to this point, before the Ludlow scribe has copied the long romance of *King Horn*, the closing references to the Harrowing and Nicodemus's Gospel create a rounding-out in the book, a reiteration of Marian praise and of Christ's descent, as found much earlier, in the French *ABC of Women* and the English *Harrowing of Hell* (arts. 8, 21). It should be noted, too, that the apocryphal *Gospel of Nicodemus* in French prose (art. 3) appeared even earlier in Scribe A's portion of the book. Another literary relationship for *Maiden, Mother Mild* exists in how a Middle English adapter fashioned its first stanza to provide a verse conclusion to Dan Michael of Northgate's *Ayenbite of Inwit* (*MWME* 7:2258–59 [4]). For commentary on this poem, see *MWME* 11:4355–56; Fein 2007, pp. 86–87; Archibald, pp. 279–80; and Durling, pp. 290–91.

[Fol. 83r. *IMEV, NIMEV* 2039. *MWME* 11:4201 [28]. *ANL* 809. Sinclair 1979, no. 3166. Vising §184/*78*. **Scribe:** B (Ludlow scribe). **Quire:** 9. **Meter:** Macaronic lyric in six 8-line stanzas that alternate Middle English with Anglo-Norman, abababab. English a-rhyme lines are tetrameter; French b-rhyme lines have six syllables. **Layout:** No columns. **Editions:** Wright 1842, pp. 97–98 (no. 35); Böddeker, pp. 220–22; Brown 1932, pp. 155–56 (no. 87); Brook, pp. 66–68 (no. 28); Silverstein, pp. 49–50 (no. 28); Jeffrey and Levy, pp. 41–43 (no. 3); Saupe, pp. 135–36 (no. 70); Millett, online edition. **Other MSS:** None. **Translation:** Jeffrey and Levy, pp. 41–42.]

11      *ble*. "Radiance"; see *MED*, *ble* (n.), sense 1(b). The word conveys a range of meanings, including "person" (sense 3(b)), cited for this line in the *MED* and chosen by Saupe (p. 135). Brook glosses it "noble person" (p. 92), and Jeffrey and Levy translate it "blossom" (p. 42). On the word as possibly meaning "corn, wheat, cornfield," creating an allusion to the legend of the Instantaneous Harvest, see Breeze 1992, pp. 150–52.

12      *Creatour*. As Saupe notes (p. 254), the word means both "creator" and "creature." The word *soverein* is either adjective or noun; Jeffrey and Levy gloss the phase "king of creation" (p. 42).

25      *ston*. The word in the manuscript is either *ston* or *stou* ("place"). Editors disagree on which word is written here, and both readings are reasonable in context. Both alliterate with *stode* in this line and with *stounde* in the preceding English line. Compare *ston*, a rhyme-word in a similar context, in *I Sigh When I Sing* (art 62), line 18.

31      *ferede*. "Healed, made whole"; see *MED*, *feren* (v.(4), *fer* (n.(3)), and *fer* (n.(4)). Others have read this verb as *feren* (v.(1)), "cause fear in."

32          *En mound que fust vivaunt*. Jeffrey and Levy interpret this line as referring to
            Christ: "in the world where He had lived" (p. 42).


## THE GESTE OF KYNG HORN / KING HORN                                              [ART. 70]

MS Harley 2253 is one of three manuscripts to preserve the famous Matter of England
romance *King Horn*, considered the oldest romance in Middle English (ca. 1225–75). An
earlier copy survives in Cambridge, CUL, MS Gg.4.27.2, and that version has become the
text of choice by most editors, as in the editions or partial editions produced by French and
Hale (1930); Sands (1966); Gibbs (1966); Allen (1984, a critical edition); Garbáty (1984);
and Herzman, Drake, and Salisbury (1999). Even though Cambridge holds the best-known
version, two modern editors have featured the Harley text: Dunn and Byrnes (1973) and
Treharne (2010). The Harley version was also chosen for treatment by the antiquarian
Joseph Ritson, who printed it in 1829. (References given here to Ritson's edition are taken
from the second edition of Goldsmid's 1877 revision, published in 1885.)

The third surviving version of the Middle English *King Horn* resides next to the other
major Matter of England romance, *Havelok the Dane*, copied by the same hand in Oxford,
Bodl. MS Laud Misc. 108, a codex famous for its preservation of a large collection of saints'
lives, the *South English Legendary* (*SEL*), in its earliest known form. The juxtaposition of *Havelok*
and *Horn* in the second part of that manuscript suggests a compiler or readership that viewed
these tales of secular heroic chosenness as correspondent to some saints' lives, especially
those with nationalistic valence, as in the lives of the king-saints of England. The Oxford
text has been printed only in the two parallel-text editions that give all three versions, that
is, by McKnight (1901; a revision of an 1866 edition by J. Rawson Lumby), and by Hall
(1901), the standard edition for *Horn*. Recent research on *Horn* in this context appears in
Bell and Couch, particularly in the essays by Liszka, A. Taylor 2011, Lynch, and Bell.

What influences and causes might explain the inclusion of *Horn* in MS Harley 2253?
Wiggins considers its appeal within the secular setting we imagine as most likely to have been
the incubator for Harley: "*King Horn*, which recounts the trial by sea of the young Horn and
his eventual marriage to maiden Rymenild, was regarded as suitable reading material for
the trilingual Herefordshire household for whom Harley 2253 was compiled in the 1330s"
(p. 251). Such a predominately French-speaking household might also have known the
older Anglo-Norman *Romance of Horn* by Mestre Thomas (ca. 1170; *ANL* 151). Moreover,
in the scribe's immediate vicinity there certainly existed a late Anglo-Norman romance,
*Fouke le Fitz Waryn* (ca. 1280), which like *Horn* is a tale of enforced exile, daring return, and
restored inheritance. The Ludlow scribe copied the sole extant version of *Fouke* (ca. 1330)
into MS Royal 12.C.xii. He might in fact be its author, for it is evidently a prose reworking
of a verse original. Crane has deftly delineated the Anglo-Norman baronial milieu,
"tenaciously legalistic yet adaptable and practical," in which such romances were made,
read, and disseminated (p. 21). We glimpse more of this milieu — now specific to the
scribe's world — in the *Old Testament Stories* (art. 71) that follow *Horn*, written in an Anglo-
Norman prose style much like the prose of *Fouke*. This string of stories seems also to be the
scribe's own authorial product; in it, we see more of his fascination with narrative. His
interest in romance also turns up in his other books, where, besides *Fouke*, he has copied the
Anglo-Norman *Purgatoire s. Patrice* (in MS Harley 273) and the *Short Metrical Chronicle* (in
MS Royal 12.C.12) (see Rock).

Other clues embedded in the Harley context for *Horn* exhibit a clear understanding that this romance is here being preserved as a performance piece. If much of the stylistic variation in the Harley text may be credited to the Ludlow scribe (as often seems the case), he here shows himself to be "well-versed in the tradition of romance diction and formulaic style" (Allen, p. 62). Beyond his mastery of the minstrel idiom, he stages an aural reading or singing of the romance by fashioning for it a preface. What precedes *Horn* in MS Harley 2253 (and only there) is the macaronic *Maiden, Mother Mild* (art. 69), a prayer-poem that brings listeners to a mood of reverence and receptivity for the *Horn* performance (Fein 2007, pp. 86-87, 94). Rhyme words found in its first stanza resonate through the romance: *mylde/childe*. Until he is knighted, the hero is perpetually termed Horn *Child*, and when his mother Queen Godild prays that Christ protect her son in exile, she invokes the term *myld* (line 86). Her request is fulfilled when King Aylmer welcomes the vulnerable child: "He spec to Horn Child / Wordes suythe *myld*" (lines 167–68). The prayer also names the betrayal of Judas, exemplar for wicked Fikenild in Horn's band of twelve friends. Most tellingly, the last lines of *Maiden, Mother Mild* enunciate the same rhyme that powers the first ones of the romance: *synge/kynge*. The scribe apparently envisioned a performance of *Horn* for which the elegant prayer to Mary would commence the occasion, and the final line ("Crist to heovene us lede. Amen") would aptly end it. Moreover, the act of beginning *Horn* with a Marian lyric parallels other moments in Harley 2253 where a French poem to Mary introduces an English lyric on Jesus' name (arts. 49–50, 57–58). It confirms that Horn was seen by contemporary readers as a type for Christ.

Numerous thematic threads tie *Horn* to other works copied by the Ludlow scribe. Phillips connects *Horn*'s two important "sea-centered dreams" to the scribe's evident interest in interpretation of dreams (*A Book of Dreaming* [art. 85]) and their moral valence as seen in the quasi-dream poem *Debate between Body and Soul* (art. 22) (see also Corrie 2003, pp. 67–73). The Harley lyrics' recurrent interest in exploring male/female love relationships is realized narratively in the romance. One can readily imagine how *Horn* would have appealed viscerally to adolescent boys in a well-to-do household, where such entertainment would have helped to inculcate social skills and good morals in prospective heirs. Horn's own exciting travels enact a paradigm of maturation from child to knight to king, with examples of eloquence before royalty and ladies fitted neatly in among scenes of combat and suspenseful disguise. The romance charts Horn's gradual departure from youthful play among boys, to the pitfalls of *derne* love, and then to a full sense of how character is proven by deeds, by responsible married love, and by wise governance of oneself and others.

Much has been written about the fuzzy geography of the place-names in Horn. One cannot identify exactly where Horn's homeland is. It has the name Sudenne (defined as *by weste* in line 5), and once it is called Eastness (line 954), which seems to indicate merely that it is east of everywhere else in the poem. It appears to refer to some portion of England, south as well as east. Westness — "Westerness" in the Cambridge text — is somewhere west of Sudenne, perhaps the Wirral in Cheshire. It may be that poets, scribes, and readers from the West Midlands would have vaguely imagined it to be of their own region. Notably, Westness is the key intermediate location for all of Horn's adventures: his fostering by King Aylmer, his education by Athelbrus, his romance with Rimenild, and his rescues of her from two ill-conceived marriages. It has been suggested that the westward movements of Horn, after he leaves Sudenne, mark his entrance into Celtic worlds. Such is true of his third destination, which is oddly specific in how it has a real place-name: Ireland. Horn's adventures in Ireland, where he encounters and kills his father's murderer, mark the most westward point in his travels. For the scribe's immediate Herefordshire audience, the Irish references were likely to resonate with the real admixture of Anglo-Hiberno business dealings by powerful local magnate families. On such active cross-cultural commerce as an illuminating backdrop to the contents of MS Harley 2253 and its sister manuscripts, see Thompson 2007, who reminds us that the families who owned most of Ludlow were the Mortimers and the de Verduns, both of whom managed extensive holdings and interests in Ireland (2007, pp. 125–26). One may recall that a binding fragment in MS Harley 2253 is from the account rolls of a Mortimer household in Trim, County Meath (Ker, p. xxii). For further new research in this direction, see Bell, pp. 268–74, who examines the expansionist efforts to colonize Ireland under Edward I, connecting this history (or its aftermath) to the events in *Horn*. Bell comments that "Horn's embrace of the Irish also brings two of the Irish *sanctorale* poems [found in the Oxford MS], *St. Patrick and his Purgatory* and *St. Brendan the Navigator*, more fully into the *SEL*'s sphere of English sanctity" (p. 273). It is also worth recalling that the Anglo-Norman *Le Purgatoire de s. Patrice* (*ANL* 55) is another narrative collected and copied by the Ludlow scribe. Consequently, there are several intriguing leads, awaiting further study, between the geographical mapping of the *Horn* narrative and the sociopolitical interests of its various compilers in different manuscripts, including MS Harley 2253.

[Fols. 83r–92v. *IMEV, NIMEV* 166. *MWME* 1:18 [1]. **Scribe:** B (Ludlow scribe). **Quires:** 9–10. **Meter:** Couplets, predominately aa$_3$, "with numerous two- and four-stress lines intermixed and with feminine rhymes far outnumbering the masculine" (Sands, p. 16). **Layout:** No columns; one couplet per line. Sections are headed with paraphs. **Editions:** Ritson 1885, 2:100–147; McKnight, pp. 1–69; Hall, pp. 1–88; Dunn and Byrnes, pp. 114–49; Treharne, pp. 583–614. **Other MSS:** Cambridge, CUL MS Gg.4.27.2, fols. 6ra–13rb; Oxford, Bodl. MS Laud Misc. 108, fols. 219v–228r.]

4           *Allof.* The King of Sudenne is named Murry (Mory, Moy) in the Cambridge and Oxford versions. The Harley version names Horn's father Allof in its opening setup, but confuses the matter by naming Murry his father later on; see explanatory notes to lines 873 and 1345.

5           *by weste.* The phrase serves to define Sudenne, that is, vaguely, "England," a place to the west of the Continent, named an island at line 1330. The phrase will return as a marker of Horn's homeland and also of his travels further westward. See explanatory note to line 775.

10–18     On the intensity of Horn's "numinous beauty," see Bradbury 2010, pp. 297–99.

11          *byryne.* "Dampen." The verb word is recorded only in *King Horn*. See *MED*, *birinen* (v.).

21          *Tuelf.* The MS reading is *tueye*. The text elsewhere (and in other versions) clearly indicates that Horn has twelve companions, like the number of Christ's disciples. *Tweye* therefore seems a mistake for *twelve*, caused perhaps by an anticipation of the two soon-to-be-named companions Athulf and Fikenild, or even by aural elision with *feren*, allowing *tweye* to sound like *twelf*. Other editors retain *tweye*, but McKnight glosses it "twelve."

| | |
|---|---|
| 66 | *Sarazyns*. Dunn and Byrnes's and Treharne's emendation to *cherches for* is based on the readings found in the other two manuscripts: *And churchen for to felle* (Cambridge) and *Cherches he gonnen gelle* (Oxford). The Harley version, though awkward, has an intelligible sense and is retained. |
| 165 | *Westnesse*. The place-name *Westness* appears in the Harley and Oxford versions. In Cambridge, King Aylmer's realm is named *Westerness*. |
| 197 | *ylome*. "On and on, for a long time." See *MED*, *ilome* (adv.), "frequently, often." |
| 214 | *brouc*. "Suit, be fitting, do credit to." For this idiom, see *MED*, *brouken* (v.), sense 4. |
| 311–14 | For the terms of legal marriage expressed in these lines of private betrothal, see *MED*, *welden* (v.), sense 7. |
| 362 | For the idiomatic sense of this line, see *MED*, *alive* (adv. & adj.), sense 3(a). |
| 379–80 | Athelbrus's warning cuts two ways and shows political acumen: Horn must be cautious in how he converses with the impetuous Rimenild, and he must also be secretive because the king does not know of the meeting. |
| 383 | *to ryhte*. For the meaning "directly," see *MED*, *right* (n.), sense 8(c). |
| 492 | *myn other derlyng*. "My other favorite." Aylmer seems to be saying that Horn will join Athelbrus in his inner circle at court. This concept fits with the pattern of paired comrades in the poem: for Allof, the two who are killed with him; for Horn, Athulf and Fikenild; later for Horn in Ireland, Berild and Athild. It is interesting that Aylmer later goes hunting with Fikenild. It seems that the treacherous friend fills in for Horn with the king, in parallel to the way Athulf often stands in for Horn in matters pertaining to Rimenild. |
| 569–74 | On the power of the ring, symbol of Horn and Rimenild's love, see the interesting discussion by Cooper, pp. 149–50, 153–54. Observing that the ring itself seems less than magical, Cooper identifies its *grace* as the strength generated whenever Horn thinks upon his lady. She notes how "the condition of thinking of his lady to make the magic work . . . becomes the focus of the story" (p. 150). |
| 589 | *sredde*. "Clothed, dressed, armed (oneself).": for this verb, which is repeated a few times in *King Horn*, see *MED*, *shriden* (v.) |
| 732–34 | In this farewell to Rimenild, Horn the "foundling" repeats the word *fo(u)nde*, drawn from different verbs: "to depart" and "to seek, to experience"; see *MED*, *founden* (v.(1)) and *finden* (v.). |
| 773 | *Godmod*. Horn's disguise name in the other versions is Cuthbert or Cutberd. On this name borrowed from a saint and specifically attached to Horn's Irish adventure, see Bell, pp. 264–65. The name Godmod, "good or godly in spirit," counterpoints Horn's enemy, King Mody, whose name denotes arrogant pride. |
| 775 | *from byweste*. "from home." The phrase puns on the direction of Horn's travels. He has journeyed west to Ireland, so the phrase indicates literal travel from east to west; see *MED*, *bi west(en* (phrase, adv., prep.) and *west* (n.), sense 1.(b). But |

the poet has also expanded the meaning of the phrase *by weste* — first used unambiguously in line 5 to refer to Sudenne — to embrace its homonym, the OE-derived *biwist* (n.), "a dwelling place, home; a way or condition of life" (*MED*). The phrase — key to the meanings behind Horn's movements — has confused many commentators. See, for example, Garbáty: "the author, minstrel, or scribe seems to have a predilection for blundering around the compass in odd directions" (p. 161). Compare lines 1135, 1181, and 1335.

813       *Site, Kyng, bi kynge*. In this version, the pagan giant names himself a king in his challenge to King Thurston: "Sit, King, beside another king." The other versions read: *Syte knythes by þe king* (Oxford) and *Site stille, sire kyng* (Cambridge).

862       *day*. The variant in the Cambridge manuscript is *deþ*. Compare line 1378.

873       *Kyng Murry*. The maker of this version seems to have forgotten that he named Horn's father Allof earlier in the poem. Murry is his name in other versions; see explanatory notes to lines 4 and 1345.

954       *Estnesse*. This place-name (a seeming synonym for Sudenne) does not occur in the Cambridge version, but it is found in the Oxford version. Horn is from Sudenne, which is east of Westness. In traveling to Ireland, land of King Thurston, he has traveled even further west.

1036      *So he sprong of the stone*. For this proverbial saying, see *MED*, *ston* (n.), sense 1.(j). Other instances cited there verify that the meaning is: "as alone and barren (of goods) as when he was born." The proverb might allude to the myth of Deucalion and his wife Pyrrha throwing stones over their backs, from whence sprung people (Ovid, *Metamorphoses*, 1:390–415). See also McKnight's proposed meaning: "The simile is one of quickness[,] that of a spark from the stone of striking a light, like modern 'quick as a flash'" (p. 144, note to line 1102).

1072      *bicollede*. "Blackened with coal or soot." The verb is attested only in *King Horn*. See *MED*, *bicolwen* (v.).

1116      *ybounde*. The semantic range of this past participle is rich, especially in this context. See *MED*, *binden* (v.). It could mean that Horn feels trapped or constrained in his disguised situation. It could mean that he is captivated and spellbound as he looks upon Rimenild. It may suggest that he is now ensnared in her net, in fulfillment of her dream. It also suggests his sense of obligation to her, in marriage and in sworn troth. The word also suggests that Horn faces his destiny and feels a compulsion to act.

1135      *byweste*. The phrase riddles on three meanings: "from the west" (i.e, from Ireland), "from Sudenne" (designated *by weste*, line 5), and "home" beside his wife Rimenild (see explanatory note to line 775).

1136      *beste*. Literally, "my best." This word adds to the riddle. It means: "fortune" or "my best action" or "my best person" (i.e., Rimenild). Lines 1135–36 echo words spoken by Horn when he arrived in Ireland (lines 775–76), and similar riddling occurs at lines 1181–82. See *MED*, *beste* (adj. as n.), senses 1 and 2.

1148      *have yorne*. "Have traveled rapidly." The verb is the past participle of *MED*, *runnen* (v.(1)).

1154      *for Horn*. The line puns on drinking from the horn and drinking to Horn. Rimenild is bewildered that the beggar has asked to drink from the horn, requesting an honor reserved for knights and nobles, and also that he has asked her to drink to Horn.

1179      *Seint Gyle*. The saint's name puns on "guile" as it is uttered by the disguised Horn.

1181–82      See explanatory notes to lines 775, 1135, and 1136.

1202      *gredde*. This verb, "cried out" (*MED*, *greden* (v.)), obscures an important detail found in the other versions, both of which indicate that Rimenild has hidden a knife or knives in her bower for the purpose of slaying herself and King Mody, should Horn not come. The Oxford version reads *hauede knyues leyd* and the Cambridge version reads *heo knif hudde*.

1230      *sclavin*. This emendation of MS *brunie* (coat of mail), taken by Dunn and Byrnes and by Treharne, agrees with the reading found in the other two versions, and it makes better sense of the passage: Horn removes his disguise, the pilgrim's cloak.

1291      *thorhreche*. "Penetrate, or seize." For the range of this rare verb of violent action, see *MED*, *thurghrechen* (v.).

1335      *woneth her by weste*. This phrase means either "dwells here to the west" or "is from this western place" (i.e., Sudenne). See explanatory notes to lines 5 and 775.

1345      *Kyng Mury*. See the explanatory notes to lines 4 and 873.

1355–56      These words spoken by Athulf's father may be meant to lightly recall the Nunc dimittis, or Canticle of Simeon. Promised by the Holy Ghost that he would not die before he had seen the Savior, Simeon rejoiced when he beheld infant Jesus with Mary (Luke 2:29–32).

1378      *deye*. The word means "death," and yogh (*deȝe*) is substituted for thorn (*deþe*). Compare the explanatory note to line 862.

1401      *Murie*. One might suspect wordplay here: Horn reestablishes his father's *murie* kingdom. See also line 1489, where Horn brings this spirit to Westness.

1412      *byflette*. "Surrounded (by water)." This is the only instance of the word recorded in the *MED*; see *biflette* (v. (p.t.)). It appears in the Cambridge and Harley versions.

1429      *overblenche*. "Overturn, capsize." This word is known only in *King Horn*.

1448      *Ferde*. Dunn and Byrnes, as well as Treharne, read the manuscipt word as *seide*, "asked," but the correct reading is *ferde*, attested by McKnight and Hall and also found in the other versions.

1456      *Rymenildes*. The reading in Harley and Oxford is *Fykenildes*. The emendation, adopted from the Cambridge version, is made because Rymenild's bower is a symbolic constant in the poem, and because this line marks a shift to the heroine's point of view.

1489        *murie*. See explanatory note to line 1401.

1525        *under reme*. "At a realm," as in the Oxford version (*in a reaume*); the term is omitted in the Cambridge version. Dunn and Byrnes, and later Treharne, translate the phrase "at Reynis," that is, the land of King Mody. Compare line 959.

# TEXTUAL NOTES

ABBREVIATIONS: **As:** Aspin; **Bö:** Böddeker; **Bos:** Bossy; **Br:** Brook; **BS:** Bennett and Smithers; **BZ:** Brandl and Zippel; **B13:** Brown 1932; **B14:** Brown 1952; **DB:** Dunn and Byrnes; **Deg:** Degginger; **Do:** Dove 1969; **Gr:** Greene 1977; **Ha:** Halliwell; **Hal:** Hall; **Hol:** Holthausen; **Hor[1]:** Horstmann 1878; **Hor[2]:** Horstmann 1896; **Hu:** Hulme; **JL:** Jeffrey and Levy; **Ju:** Jubinal; **Kel:** Kelle r; **Ken:** Kennedy; **Le:** Lerer 2008; **Mc:** McKnight; **Mi:** Millett; **MR:** Michelant and Raynaud; **Mo:** Morris and Skeat; **MS:** MS Harley 2253; **Mu:** H. M. R. Murray; **Pa:** Patterson; **Pr:** Pringle 2009; **Rei:** Reichl 1973; **Rev[1]:** Revard 2004; **Rev[2]:** Revard 2005b; **Ri[1]:** Ritson 1877; **Ri[2]:** Ritson 1885; **Ro:** Robbins 1959; **Sa:** Saupe; **Si:** Silverstein; **St:** Stemmler 1970; **Tr:** Treharne; **Tu:** Turville-Petre 1989; **Ul:** Ulrich; **W[1]:** Wright 1839; **W[2]:** Wright 1841; **W[3]:** Wright 1842; **W[4]:** Wright 1844; **WH:** Wright and Halliwell.

## BOOKLET 3

### ABC A FEMMES                                                    [ART. 8]

| | |
|---|---|
| 5 | *qe.* So MS, Do, Ken. W[3], Hol: *que.* |
| | *eit.* So MS, W[3], Hol, Ken. Do: *est.* |
| 7 | *forbanys.* So MS, Do, W[3], Hol. Ken: *forbayns.* |
| 23 | *femme.* So MS, W[3], Hol, Ken. Do: *femmes.* |
| 24 | *enveysure.* So MS, W[3], Hol, Do. Ken: *enuoysure.* |
| 25 | *femme.* So MS, W[3], Hol, Ken. Do: *femmes.* |
| 39 | *E.* So MS, W[3], Hol, Ken. Do: omitted. |
| 40 | *qe en.* So MS, Do, Ken. W[3], Hol: *que en.* |
| 45 | *honme.* So MS, W[3], Hol, Ken. Do: *homme.* |
| 52 | *porte qe.* So MS, Do. W[3], Hol, Ken: *porte que.* |
| 56 | *Dyamaund.* So MS, W[3], Hol, Ken. Do: *Dyamand.* |
| 58 | *sunt.* So MS, W[3], Hol, Ken. Do: *sount.* |
| 79 | *E.* So MS, W[3], Hol, Ken. Do: omitted. |
| | *faucoun.* So MS, W[3], Hol, Do. Ken: *faucon.* |
| 88 | *vyleynie.* So MS, W[3], Hol, Ken. Do: *vileynie.* |
| 89 | *femme.* So MS, W[3], Hol, Ken. Do: *femmes.* |
| 94 | *pust.* So MS, W[3], Hol, Do. Ken: *oust.* |
| 98 | *qe.* So MS, Do, Ken. W[3], Hol: *que.* |
| 99 | *N'out.* So MS, W[3], Hol, Do. Ken: *n'eut.* |
| 102 | *sount.* So W[3], Hol, Do. MS, Ken: *fount.* |
| 111 | *honme.* So MS, W[3], Ken. Hol, Do: *homme.* |
| 124 | *fenme.* So MS, W[3], Hol, Ken. Do: *femme.* |

| | |
|---|---|
| 127 | *soffry.* So MS, Ken, Do. W³, Hol: *suffry.* |
| 150 | *qe.* So MS, Do, Ken. W³, Hol: *que.* |
| 154 | *Qe.* So MS, Do, Ken. W³, Hol: *que.* |
| 160 | *honme.* So MS, W³, Hol, Ken. Do: *homme.* |
| 164 | *Dieu fist.* So MS, Do, Ken. W³, Hol: *diensist.* |
| 168 | *honme.* So MS, W³, Ken. Hol, Do: *homme.* |
| 171 | *L'anguisse.* So MS, Ken. W³, Hol, Do: *languisse.* |
| 177 | *pris.* So MS, Hol, Do, Ken. W³: *de pris.* |
| 178 | *autre.* So MS, W³, Hol, Do. Ken: omitted. |
| 182 | The rhyme scheme indicates that this line is missing. |
| 186 | *en ly.* So MS, W³, Hol, Do. Ken: omitted. |
| 213 | *um.* So MS, W³, Hol, Do. Ken: *un.* |
| 217 | *countrepleyder.* So MS, W³, Hol, Do. Ken: *countreplayder.* |
| 220 | *qe.* So MS, Do, Ken. W³, Hol: *que.* |
| 245 | *vyleynye.* So MS, W³, Hol, Ken. Do: *vyleynie.* |
| 274 | *se.* So MS, W³, Hol, Do. Ken: *sa.* |
| 279 | *ou.* So MS, W³, Hol, Ken. Do: *ne.* |
| 293 | *honme.* So MS, W³, Ken. Do: *homme.* |
| 312 | *chaunbre.* So MS, W³, Hol, Ken. Do: *chambre.* |
| 314 | *Qe.* So MS, Do, Ken. W³, Hol: *que.* |
| | *en.* So MS, W³, Ken. Hol: *in.* Do: *ou.* |
| 316 | *qe.* So MS, Do, Ken. W³, Hol: *que.* |

## DE L'YVER ET DE L'ESTÉ                                        [ART. 9]

| | |
|---|---|
| 3 | *queux.* So MS, Do. Ju, Bos: *quieux.* |
| 4 | *oncke.* So MS (*e* abbrev). Ju, Bos: *onckes.* Do: *onck.* |
| 16 | *E.* So MS, Do. Ju, Bos: *Et.* |
| 17 | *cotiver.* So MS, Do. Ju, Bos: *coliner.* |
| 29 | *E.* So MS, Do. Ju, Bos: *Et.* |
| 65 | *E.* So MS, Do. Ju, Bos: *Et.* |
| 86 | *countree.* So MS, Ju, Do. Bos: *contree.* |
| 94 | *De.* So MS, Do, Bos. Ju: *E.* |
| 113 | *ay.* So MS, Ju, Bos. Do: *aye.* |
| 150 | *seignurye.* So MS, Do. Ju, Bos: *seignurie.* |
| 156 | *Maymont.* So MS, Ju, Bos. Do: *Maymout.* |
| | *Sweyn.* So MS, Do. Ju, Bos: *Swyn.* |
| 160 | *feyteez.* So MS, Do. Ju, Bos: *scytees.* |
| 161 | *e.* So MS, Do. Ju, Bos: *et.* |
| 167 | *Je.* So MS, Do. Ju, Bos: *Ge.* |
| 171 | *guyree.* So Ju, Bos. MS, Do: *quyree.* |
| 172 | *Ycele.* So MS, Ju, Bos. Do: *Ytele.* |
| 180 | *molt.* So MS (*o* abbreviated), Ju, Bos. Do: *mult.* |
| 182 | *sourveyl.* So MS. Ju, Bos, Do: *sourneyl.* |
| 196 | *Son.* So MS, Ju, Bos. Do: *soun.* |
| 218 | *Quanqe.* So MS, Ju. Do, Bos: *Quanque.* |
| 220 | *e.* So MS, Do. Ju, Bos: *et.* |

| | |
|---|---|
| 228 | *futes.* So MS, Ju, Bos. Do: *futez.* |
| 237 | *nous.* So MS. Ju, Bos: *nus.* Do: *vus.* |
| 239 | *parais.* So MS, Ju, Bos. Do: *parays.* |
| 257 | *dy.* So MS, Ju, Bos. Do: *di.* |
| 260 | *nasquid.* So MS, Do. Ju, Bos: *nasquit.* |
| 262 | *frez.* So MS, Ju, Do. Bos: *ferez.* |

## VORTE TEMPRENE ASURE [ART. 11]

| | |
|---|---|
| title | *temprene.* So MS (*m* and final *e* abbreviated), W⁴. Kel: *tempren.* |
| 5 | *grynnt.* So MS (*n* abbreviated). W⁴, Kel: *grynt.* |
| 10 | *seyde.* So MS, W⁴. Kel: *sede.* |

## VORTE COUCHE SELVERFOYL [ART. 15]

| | |
|---|---|
| 7 | *wit.* So MS, W⁴. Kel: *with.* |

## VORTE MAKEN BLANKPLUM [ART. 17]

| | |
|---|---|
| 14 | *seththen.* So MS (*n* abbreviated), Kel. W⁴: *seththe.* |
| | *nethermoste.* So MS (*r* abbreviated), Kel. W⁴: *nethemoste.* |

# BOOKLET 4

## INCIPIT VITA SANCTI ETHELBERTI [ART. 18]

| | |
|---|---|
| 34 | *Regine.* MS: *Regine no.* |
| 74 | *plurimum.* MS: *plurium.* |
| 76 | *ut.* MS: *utri* (*ri* abbreviated). |
| 90 | *scelere.* MS: *sceleri.* |
| 101 | *paludem.* MS: *palude.* |
| 117 | *Stratum Waye.* MS: *statum Waye.* |
| 122 | *Perrexerunt.* MS: *Porexerunt.* |

## ANIMA CHRISTI, SANCTIFICA ME [ART. 19]

| | |
|---|---|
| 5 | *conforta.* MS: *corforta.* |

## QUANT VOY LA REVENUE D'YVER [ART. 20]

| | |
|---|---|
| 7 | *meisné.* So MS. W³: *meis ne.* Rev²: *meisue.* |
| 27 | *blaunchys.* So MS, Rev². W³: *braunchys.* |
| 36 | *vou.* So MS, Rev². W³: *von.* |
| 38 | *Qe.* So MS, Rev². W³: *que.* |
| | *dees.* So MS, W³. Rev²: *deez.* |
| 50 | *noreture.* So MS, Rev². W³: *norture.* |

58          *qe.* So MS. $W^3$, $Rev^2$: *que.*
61          *gavigaut.* So MS, $Rev^2$. $W^3$: *ganigant.*
62          *cetewaut.* So MS, $Rev^2$. $W^3$: *cetewant.*
63          *chaudee peveré.* So MS, $Rev^2$. $W^3$: *chandee peneré.*
64          *fet.* So MS, $Rev^2$. $W^3$: *fit.*
67          *Oues.* So MS, $Rev^2$. $W^3$: *Ques.*
69          *chanevaus.* So MS, $Rev^2$. $W^3$: *chavenans.*
71          *pouns.* So MS, $W^3$. $Rev^2$: *poons.*
72          *Grues.* So MS, $Rev^2$. $W^3$: *Groues.*
            *heyrouns.* So MS, $W^3$. $Rev^2$: *heirouns.*
73          *Cerceles.* So MS, $Rev^2$. $W^3$: *Terceles.*
76          *entrelardé.* So MS, $W^3$. $Rev^2$: *entrelardee.*
77          *cele.* So MS, $W^3$. $Rev^2$: *cerf.*
80          *deym.* So MS, $W^3$. $Rev^2$: *daym.*
            *velee.* So MS, $Rev^2$. $W^3$: *ne lée.*
85          *tonne.* So MS, $Rev^2$. $W^3$: *toune.*
87          *fosoyne.* So MS, $Rev^2$. $W^3$: *foysoyne.*
89          *encine.* So MS, $Rev^2$. $W^3$: *en cive.*
94          *pui.* So $Rev^2$. MS, $W^3$: *pur.*
97          *doreez.* So $Rev^2$. MS, $W^3$: *dorrez.*
98          *Perdryz.* So MS, $W^3$. $Rev^2$: *perdriz.*
105         *quant.* So MS. $W^{3.}$: *grant.* $Rev^2$: *quaunt*
            *noune.* So MS, $W^3$. $Rev^2$: *noun.*
111         *Lentre.* So MS. $Rev^2$, $W^3$: *l'entre.*
113         *enversee.* So MS, $Rev^2$. $W^3$: *enversé.*
120         *flamiche.* So MS, $Rev^2$. $W^3$: *flaunche.*
124         *veudie.* So MS, $Rev^2$. $W^3$: *vendie.*
129         *crevice.* So $Rev^2$. MS, $W^3$: *creinte.*
135         *Mout.* So MS, $W^3$. $Rev^2$: *m'ont.*
136         *repoire.* So MS, $Rev^2$. $W^3$: *repeire.*
139         *sesoun.* So MS, $W^3$. $Rev^2$: *saison.*
147         *pucynz.* So MS, $W^3$. $Rev^2$: *pucyns.*
154         *desployré.* So MS, $Rev^2$. $W^3$: *despleyre.*
161         *m'envoys.* So MS, $Rev^2$. $W^3$: *m'ennoys.*

**Alle Herkneth to Me Nou**                                    [ART. 21]

14          *Crist.* So MS, Hu. Ha: *Christ.*
16          *Crist.* So MS, Hu. Ha: *Christ.*
19          *Ant.* So Hu. MS: *An.* Ha: *And.*
20          *Cristes.* So MS, Hu. Ha: *Christes.*
            *oune.* So MS, Hu. Ha: *onne.*
21          *the.* So Ha, Hu. MS: *þ.*
22          *Crist.* So MS, Hu. Ha: *Christ.*
26          *then.* So MS, Hu. Ha: *than.*
28          *Y.* So MS, Hu. Ha: *I.*
29          *Crist.* So MS, Hu. Ha: *Christ.*

| 41 | *Then.* MS, Ha, Hu: *þe.* |
|---|---|
| 42 | *Alse.* So MS. Ha, Hu: *Asse.* |
| | *Y.* So MS, Hu. Ha: *i.* |
| 43 | *Harde.* So MS, Hu. Ha: *Hard.* |
| | *hav Y.* So MS. Ha, Hu: *havy.* |
| | *Dominus.* As in Auchinleck MS (Hu, p. 5). MS: *omitted.* |
| 70 | *woll Y.* So MS, Hu. Ha: *wolly.* |
| 197 | *[David].* A modern hand has written *David* in the right margin. |
| 207 | *Crist.* So MS, Hu. Ha: *Christ.* |
| 213 | *Crist.* So MS, Hu. Ha: *Christ.* |
| 220 | *everuch.* So Ha, Hu. MS: *overuch.* |
| 231 | *Ich.* So MS, Hu. Ha: *I.* |
| 232 | *thou.* So MS (*þou*), Hu. Ha: *thon.* |
| 244 | *Crist.* So MS, Hu. Ha: *Christ.* |

## IN A THESTRI STUDE Y STOD                                [ART. 22]

| 4 | *wrht.* So MS, Do, Rei. W²: *wrth.* Bö: *wurht.* |
|---|---|
| 7 | *wrohstes.* So MS, W², Do, Rei. Bö: *wrohtes.* |
| 8 | *me.* So MS, W², Do, Rei. Bö: *þe.* |
| 10 | *Was.* So MS, W², Do, Rei. Bö: *Wit.* |
| 13 | *spake.* So MS (*e* abbreviated). W², Bö, Rei: *spak.* Do: *spac.* |
| 15 | *palefreis.* So MS, W², Bö, Rei. Do: *palefrois.* |
| 19 | *am.* So MS (*ay am*, with *ay* marked for deletion), W², Bö, Rei. Do: *ay am.* |
| 25 | *wen.* So MS, W², Rei. Bö, Do: *wend.* |
| | *strift.* So MS. W²· Bö: *strist.* Do, Rei: *strif.* |
| 30 | *bete.* So MS, W², Do, Rei. Bö: *beten.* |
| 31 | *threte.* So MS, W², Do, Rei. Bö: *threten.* |
| 32 | *ete.* So MS, W², Do, Rei. Bö: *eten.* |
| 35 | *ete.* So MS, W², Do, Rei. Bö: *eten.* |
| 57 | *hire forestond.* So MS, W², Do, Rei. Bö: *hit forestondes.* |
| 58 | *hire forewonde.* So MS, W², Do, Rei. Bö: *hit forewondes.* |
| 60 | *aren.* So MS, Bö, Do, Rei. W²: *arene.* |
| 61 | *hyle.* So Bö. MS, W², Do, Rei: *hylen.* |
| 62 | *flume.* So MS, Bö, Do. W²: *flunie.* Rei: *fluuie.* |
| | *hit.* So MS, Bö, Do, Rei. W²: *it.* |
| 72 | Line omitted by Do. |
| 78 | *anon.* MS, W², Bö, Rei. Do: omitted. |
| 82 | *holde.* So MS, W², Do, Rei. Bö: *to holde.* |
| 89 | *schowen.* So MS, W², Do, Rei. Bö: *schowend.* |
| 92 | *the.* So MS, W², Do, Rei. Bö: *þou.* |
| 111 | *corteis.* So MS, W², Bö, Rei. Do: *curteis.* |
| 117 | *stoude.* So MS, W² (who suggests *proude*), Bö, Do, Rei. |
| 124 | *worldes.* So Bö, Rei. MS, W², Do: *wolrdes.* |
| 126 | *that.* So MS (*a* abbreviated), W², Do, Rei. Bö: *not.* |

**Sitteth alle stille ant herkneth to me**                                    [Art. 23]

| | |
|---|---|
| 2 | *Kyng.* So Ri[1], Bö, BZ. MS, W[1], B13: *kyn.* |
| 15–16 | *ever trichard . . . nevermore.* So MS, Bö, B13. W[1], Ri[1], BZ: *ever &c.* |
| 22–24 | MS, W[1], Ri[1], Bö, BZ, B13: *Richard &c.* |
| 27 | *prude.* So MS, W[1], Bö, BZ, B13. Ri[1]: *pride.* |
| 28 | *mony.* So MS, W[1], Bö, BZ, B13. Ri[1]: *moni.* |
| 30–32 | MS, W[1], Ri[1], Bö, BZ, B13: *Richard &c.* |
| 34 | *over.* So W[1], Ri[1], Bö, BZ, B13. MS: *ever.* |
| 35 | *the fenne.* So W[1], Ri[1], BZ, B13. MS, Bö: *þ fenne.* |
| 38–40 | MS, W[1], Ri[1], Bö, BZ, B13: *Richard &c.* |
| 46–48 | MS, W[1], Ri[1], Bö, BZ, B13: *Richard &c.* |
| 49 | *top.* So MS, Bö, B13. W[1], BZ: *cop.* Ri[1]: *fot.* |
| 51 | *quite.* So MS, W[1], Bö, BZ, B13. Ri[1]: *grant.* |
| 52 | *fot.* So MS, W[1], Bö, BZ, B13. Ri[1]: *sot.* |
| 54–56 | MS, Ri[1], W[1], Bö, BZ, B13: *Richard &c.* |
| 63 | *Forsoke* So MS, W[1], Ri[1], Bö, B13. BZ: *Forsake.* |
| 64–66 | MS, W[1], Bö, BZ, B13: *Richard &c.* Ri[1]: omitted. |

**Chaunter m'estoit**                                                       [Art. 24]

| | |
|---|---|
| 16 | *Mountfort.* So MS, Ri[1], As. W[1]: *Montfort.* |
| 18 | *en plorra.* So MS, W[1], As. Ri[1]: *emplorr.* |
| 31–36 | MS, W[1], Ri[1], As: *Ore est ocis &c.* |
| 42 | *sa.* So MS, W[1], As. Ri[1]: *la.* |
| 49–54 | MS, W[1], Ri[1], As: *Ore est ocys &c.* |
| 67–72 | MS, W[1], Ri[1], As: *Ore est ocis &c.* |
| 74 | *mentenir.* So MS, W[1], As. Ri[1]: *mentenyr.* |
| 85–90 | MS, W[1], Ri[1], As: *Ore est &c.* |
| 102 | *sonme.* So MS, W[1]. Ri[1], As: *soume.* |
| 103–08 | MS, W[1], Ri[1], As: *Ore est &c.* |
| 121–26 | MS: written out by scribe. So W[1]. Ri[1], As: *Ore est ocis etc.* |
| 139–44 | MS, W[1], Ri[1], As: *Ore est ocis &c.* |
| 157–62 | MS, W[1], Ri[1], As: *Ore est ocys &c.* |

**Momentaneum est quod delectat**                                            [Art. 24a*]

| | |
|---|---|
| 2 | *cruciat.* So MS (*ru* abbreviated). Do: *conciat.* |

**Erthe toc of erthe**                                                       [Art. 24b]

| | |
|---|---|
| 3 | *erthene.* So MS, Mu, Br, B13, Tr. Ri[1]: *erthe ne.* |

**Lystneth, lordynges! A newe song Ichulle bigynne**                         [Art. 25]

| | |
|---|---|
| 20 | *wes.* So MS, W[1], Bö, BZ. Ri[1]: *was.* Ro: *wos.* |
| 23 | *wes.* So MS, W[1], Bö, BZ, Ro. Ri[1]: *was.* |

| | |
|---|---|
| 37 | *Thrye.* So MS, W¹, Ri¹, Bö, BZ. Ro: *þryes.* |
| 40 | *Weht.* So MS, W¹, Ri¹, Ro. Bö, BZ: *whet.* |
| 54 | *Hii.* So MS, W¹, Bö, BZ, Ro. Ri¹: *Hu.* |
| 66 | *ne.* So MS, W¹, Ri¹, BZ. Ro. Bö: *no.* |
| 75 | *gripe.* So MS, W¹, Bö, BZ, Ro. Ri¹: *grype.* |
| 84 | *contree.* So MS, W¹, Ri¹, Bö, BZ. Ro: *contre.* |
| 91 | *wes.* So MS, W¹, Bö, BZ. Ri¹, Ro: *was.* |
| 107 | *Multoun.* So MS (*n* abbreviated). W¹, Ri¹, Bö, BZ, Ro: *Multone.* |
| 116 | *ydyht.* So MS, W¹, Ri¹, BZ, Ro. Bö: *wes ydyht.* |
| 129 | *Morham.* So MS, W¹, Ro. Ri¹, Bö, BZ: *Norham.* |
| 132 | *smhyte.* So MS, W¹, Ri¹, Ro. Bö, BZ: *smyte.* |
| 133 | *Wat.* So MS, W¹, Ri¹, BZ, Ro. Bö: *what.* |
| 134 | *wes.* So MS, W¹, Ri¹, Bö, BZ. Ro: *wos.* |
| 147 | *Multoun.* So MS (*n* abbreviated). W¹, Ri¹, Bö, BZ, Ro: *Multone.* |
| 148 | *told.* So MS, W¹, Bö, BZ, Ro. Ri¹: *hold.* |
| | *pris.* So MS, W¹, Bö, BZ, Ro. Ri¹: *prys.* |
| 166 | *Wickednesse.* So MS, W¹, Ri¹, Ro. Bö, BZ: *Wikednesse.* |
| 177 | *todrawe.* So MS, W¹, Bö, BZ, Ro. Ri¹: *todrowe.* |
| 196 | *loketh.* So MS, Bö, BZ, Ro. W¹, Ri¹: *laketh.* |
| 204 | *Wet.* So MS, W¹, Ri¹, BZ, Ro. Bö: *whet.* |
| 211 | *gaste.* So Ro, Bö, BZ. MS, W¹, Ri¹: *garste.* |
| 212 | *tuenti.* So MS, Ri¹, Bö, Ro. W¹, BZ: *twenti.* |

**LORD THAT LENEST US LYF**                                [ART. 25A]

| | |
|---|---|
| 10 | *monkune.* So MS, W¹, B13, Tu. Bö: *monkunne.* |
| 16 | *lyne.* So MS, W¹, B13, Tu. Bö: *lyue.* |
| 19 | *wol.* MS, W¹, Bö, B13, Tu.: *wl.* |
| 29 | *shrewe.* So MS, W¹, Bö, B13. Tu: *schrewe.* |
| 45 | *Yef.* So MS (*ʒef*), W¹, Bö, Tu. B13: *ʒof.* |
| 47 | *worse.* So MS, W¹, B13, Tu. Bö: *forse.* |
| | *wet.* So MS, W¹, B13, Tu. Bö: *fet.* |
| 48 | *lac.* So Bö, B13, Tu. MS, W¹: *lat.* |

**ENSEIGNEMENT SUR LES AMIS**                                [ART. 26]

| | |
|---|---|
| 68 | *n'ert.* So MS, Ken. W³: *n'est.* |
| 69 | *dolour.* So MS, W³. Ken: *doulour.* |
| 78 | *puet.* So MS, Ken. W³: *peut.* |
| 106 | *chaut qe l'oye.* So MS, Ken. W³: *chant qe loye.* |
| 112 | *respounz.* So MS W³. Ken: *repounz.* |

**MIDDELERD FOR MON WES MAD**                                [ART. 27]

| | |
|---|---|
| 3 | *Hedy hath.* So MS, W³, B13, Br. Bö: *hendy hap.* |
| 14 | *I telle.* So MS, B13, Br. W³, Bö: *itelle.* |
| 18 | *liveth.* So MS, Bö, B13, Br. W³: *livith.* |

| | |
|---|---|
| 19 | *hete*. MS, W³, B13, Br. Bö: *hede*. |
| 21 | *thrivene*. MS, W³, B13, Br. Bö: *vn þriuene*. |
| 25 | *brotherli*. So B13, Br. MS: *broerli*. W³, Bö: *broerh*. |
| 26 | *best*. So MS, W³, B13, Br. Bö: *beþ*. |
| 28 | *Is*. So MS, W³, B13, Br. Bö: *ist*. |
| 29 | *Fyth*. So MS, W³, B13. Bö, Br: *fyht*. |
| | *darth*. So MS (*darþ*), W³, Bö, B13. Br: *darf*. |
| | *fleo*. So Bö, W³, B13. MS, Br: *floe*. |
| 30 | *faunyng*. So MS, W³, Bö, Br. B13: *fannyng*. |
| | *foreode*. So MS, W³, Bö, Br. B13: *fortode*. |
| 37 | *belde*. So MS, Bö, B13, Br. W³: *bel*. |
| 38 | *Y sugge*. So MS, W³, B13, Br. Bö: *ysugge*. |
| 39 | *beeth*. So MS. W³, Bö, Br, B13: *beoth*. |
| 48 | *Y tolde*. So MS, W³, B13, Br. Bö: *ytolde*. |
| 57 | *sully*. So MS, Br. W³, Bö, B13: *fully*. |
| 58 | *meint*. So MS, W³, Bö, B13, Br: *meind*. |
| 70 | *lustes*. So MS, W³, B13, Br. Bö: *lastes*. |
| 74 | *bonnyng*. So MS, Br. W³, Bö, B13: *bounyng*. |
| | *him*. So MS, W³, B13, Br. Bö: *hem*. |

## BOOKLET 5

### ICHOT A BURDE IN A BOUR ASE BERYL SO BRYHT [ART. 28]

| | |
|---|---|
| 5 | *on*. So MS, W³, B13, Br, St, Tu, Mi. Bö: omitted. |
| 6 | *diamaund*. So MS, Bö, B13, Br, St, Tu, Mi. W³: *diamaunde*. |
| 9 | *mai*. So MS, Bö, B13, Br, St, Tu, Mi. W³: *may*. |
| 10 | *ches*. So MS, W³, B13, Br, St, Tu, Mi. Bö: *chos*. |
| 13 | *peruenke*. So MS (*er* abbreviated; an *e* before the *u* is marked for deletion), B13, Br, St, Tu, Mi. W³: *parvenke*. Bö: *paruenke*. |
| 20 | *sauve*. MS, Br, St, Tu, Mi: *sauue*. W³, Bö, B13: *sanne*. |
| 22 | *To*. So MS, W³, B13, Br, St, Tu, Mi. Bö: *þou*. |
| 23 | *in*. So MS, W³, Bö, B13, Br, St, Mi. Tu: *ant*. |
| 25 | *dernest*. So MS, W³, B13, Br, St, Tu, Mi. Bö: *derrest*. |
| 30 | *roune*. So MS, Bö, B13, Br, St, Tu, Mi. W³: *ronne*. |
| 31 | *thourh*. So Bö, B13, Br, St, Tu. MS, W³: *þouh*. Mi: *thorh*. |
| 33 | *Lyne*. So MS, B13, Br, St, Tu, Mi. W³: *lyve*. Bö: *lyue*. |
| 34 | *saveth*. So MS, W³, Bö, Tu. B13, Br, St, Mi: *saneþ*. |
| 35 | *bayeth*. So MS, Bö, B13. W³, Br, St, Tu, Mi: *bayþeþ*. |
| 36 | *dede is in dayne*. So MS, W³. B13: *dede is indayne*. Bö: *dedis in dayne*. Br, St, Tu, Mi: *dedis in day*. |
| 37 | *in greve*. So MS (*re* abbreviated), B13, Br, St, Tu, Mi. W³, Bö: *in grene*. |
| 41 | *medicyne*. So Br, Mi. MS, W³, Bö, B13: *medierne*. St, Tu: *medicine*. |
| 43 | *Tegeu*. So MS, B13, Br, St, Tu, Mi. W³, Bö: *Tegen*. |
| 44 | *oft*. So B13, Br, St, Tu, Mi. MS, W³: *of*. Bö: omitted. |
| 47 | *carf*. So MS, W³, B13, Br, St, Tu, Mi. Bö: *þat carf*. |

50          *heo*. So MS, B13, Br, St, Tu, Mi. W³, Bö: *he*.

## BYTUENE MERSH ANT AVERIL                                        [ART. 29]

2           *springe*. So MS (*ri* abbreviated), W³, Mo, Ri¹, Bö, B13, Br, St, Si, Mi. Tr:
              *sprynge*.
8           *baundoun*. So MS, W³, Mo, Bö, B13, Br, St, Si, Mi, Tr. Ri¹: *banndoun*.
10          *from*. So MS, W³, Mo, Bö, B13, Br, St, Si, Mi, Tr. Ri¹: *form*.
21–24       MS, W³, Mo, Ri¹, Bö, B13, Br, St, Si, Mi, Tr: *An hendy hap &c.*
33–36       MS, W³, Mo, Ri¹, Bö, B13, Br, St, Si, Mi, Tr: *An hendi &c.*
40          *Ychabbe*. So MS, W³, Mo, Bö, B13, Br, St, Si, Mi, Tr. Ri¹: *Ychal*.
45–48       MS, W³, Mo, Ri¹, Bö, B13, Br, St, Si, Mi, Tr: *An hendi &c.*

## WITH LONGYNG Y AM LAD                                          [ART. 30]

19          *nul Y*. So MS, BS. W³, Mo, Bö, B13, Br, St: *nuly*.

## ICH HERDE MEN UPO MOLD                                         [ART. 31]

7           *bid*. So MS, W¹, Ro, Dea. Bö, BZ, Tu: *bit*.
16          *bockneth*. So MS, W¹, Bö, BZ, Ro, Dea. Tu: *beckneth*.
17          *wo*. So MS, W¹, BZ, Ro, Tu, Dea. Bö: *who*.
22          *en*. So MS, W¹, BZ, Ro, Tu, Dea. Bö: *an*.
24          *is*. So MS, W¹, Ro, Tu, Dea. Bö, BZ: *hap*.
26          *me*. So MS, Ro, Tu, Dea. W¹: omitted. Bö, BZ: *men*.
28          *biddyng*. So W¹, Bö, BZ, Ro, Tu, Dea. MS: *bddyng*.
29          *Meni*. So MS, W¹, Ro, Dean. Bö, BZ, Tu: *Men*.
35          *hale*. So MS, W¹, Bö, Ro, Tu, Dea. BZ: *halle*.
41          *Ych*. So MS, W¹, Ro, Tu. Bö, BZ, Dea: *ich*.
42          *fyhshe-day*. So MS (*e* abbreviated). W¹: *fyhshe day*. Ro, Dea: *fyhsh day*. Tu: *fyhsh-
              day*. Bö, BZ: *fysh day*.
55          *Thus*. So MS (*us* abbreviated), Bö, BZ, Ro, Tu, Dea. W¹: *Ther*.
56          *doth*. So MS, W¹, Bö, Ro, Tu, Dea. BZ: *dep*.
57          *doth*. So Ro, Tu, Dea. MS, W¹: *doh*. Bö, BZ: *doht*.
58          *tek*. So MS, W¹, Ro, Dea. Bö, BZ, Tu: *tok*.
59          *boded*. So MS, W¹, BZ, Ro, Tu, Dea. Bö: *biden*.
              *fulle*. So MS, Bö, BZ, Tu. W¹, Ro, Dea: *sulle*.
70          *broke*. So MS (*e* abbreviated), Tu, Dea. W¹, Bö, BZ: *brok*. Ro: *brokes*.
72          *is*. So MS, W¹, Bö, BZ, Tu, Dea. Ro: *in*.

## HERKETH HIDEWARD ANT BEOTH STILLE                              [ART. 32]

1           *Herketh*. So MS, Hor¹. Bö: *Herkneth*.
18          *yelden*. So MS (*n* abbreviated), Hor¹. Bö: *ȝelde*.
49          *susteined*. So MS, Bö. Hor¹: *sustened*.
51          *Wether*. So MS, Hor¹. Bö: *wheþer*.
97          *on*. So MS, Hor¹. Bö: *ou*.

98              *Y.* So MS, Bö. Hor¹: *Yn.*
104             *The.* So MS, Hor¹ (who suggests *þo*). Bö: *þat.*
131             *anhyse.* So MS, Hor¹. Bö: *an hyrse.*
137             *doh.* So MS, Hor¹ (who suggests *doþ*). Bö: *doht.*
146             *wet.* So MS, Hor¹. Bö: *whet.*
152             *him.* So MS, Hor¹. Bö: *hem.*
154             *o.* So MS, Bö. Hor¹: *a.*
163             *his.* So MS, Hor¹. Bö: *hire.*
172             *whosshen.* So MS, Hor¹. Bö: *wosshen.*
192             *ther.* So MS, Hor¹. Bö: *þat þer.*
209             *ther.* So MS (*er* abbreviated), Hor¹. Bö: *þus.*

## WEPING HAVETH MYN WONGES WET                                    [ART. 33]

1               *Dunprest.* So MS, written in right margin in the manner of the speaker
                names in art. 21.
13              *wyf.* So MS, W³, B13, Br, St, Tu, Mi. Bö: *wif.*
16              *durthe.* So MS, W³, Tu. Bö: *durste.* B13: *durre.* Br, St, Mi: *durfte.*
28              *hake.* So MS (*e* abbreviated), W³, Bö. B13, Br, St, Mi: *hauk.* Tu: *hauke.*
31              *fleishe.* So MS (*e* abbreviated), W³. Bö, B13, Br, Tu, Mi: *fleish.* St: *fleisch.*
32              *feld.* So MS, W³, B13, Br, St, Tu, Mi. Bö: *fold.*
40              *Our.* So Bö, B13, Tu. MS: *or* (stroke over *r*). W³, Br, St, Mi: *Or.*
41              *roune.* So MS, W³, Bö, B13, Br, St, Mi. Tu: *to roune.*
42              *hem.* So MS (*m* abbreviated), Bö, B13, Br, St, Tu, Mi. W³: *he.*
44              *mene.* So B13, Br, St, Tu, Mi. MS, W³: *me ne.* Bö: *ne.*
70              *hendelec.* So MS, B13, Br, St, Tu, Mi. W³: *hende let.* Bö: *hendelek.*
71              *him.* So Bö, B13, Br, St, Tu, Mi. MS, W³: *hem.*

## MOST I RYDEN BY RYBBESDALE                                    [ART. 34]

2               *wilde.* So MS, W³, Br, BS, St, Mi. Bö: *wil.*
3               *wuch.* So MS, W³, BS, Mi. Bö, Br, St: *whuch.*
12              *fyldor.* So MS, Br, BS, St, Mi. W³: *fyld or.* Bö: *fyld her.*
17              *That.* So W³, Br, BS, St, Mi. MS, Bö: *þ.*
20              *leneth.* So MS, Bö, Br, BS, St, Mi. W³: *leveth.*
30              *spredes.* So Bö, Br, BS, St. MS, W³, Mi: *spredeþ.*
32              *For.* So MS, W³, Br, BS, St, Mi. Bö: *fol.*
33              *hit.* So MS, W³, Br, BS, St, Mi. Bö: *heo.*
36              *roser.* So MS, Br, BS, St, Mi. W³: *rosen.* Bö: *rose.*
44              *Y mette.* So MS, Br, BS, St, Mi. W³, Bö: *ymette.*
48              *Stythes.* So MS, W³, St. Bö: *stype.* Br, BS, Mi: *stypest.*
51              *mihte.* So MS, Bö, Br, BS, St, Mi. W³: *myhte.*
53              *Baloygne mengeth.* So MS, Br, BS, St, Mi. W³: *Baloynge mengeth.* Bö: *bolnynge
                men seþ.*
64              *whith.* So MS, W³, Mi. Bö, Br, BS, St: *wiþ.*

**IN A FRYHT AS Y CON FARE FREMEDE** [ART. 35]

| | |
|---|---|
| 8 | *henyng*. So MS, W³, Br, BS, St, Tu. Bö: *heþyng*. |
| 18 | *be*. So MS, W³, Bö, Br, Tu. BS, St: *beþ*. |
| 31 | *tho*. So MS, W³. Bö, Br, BS, St, Tu: *þou*. |
| 33 | *hongren*. So Bö, Br, BS, St, Tu. MS, W³: *hengren*. |
| 36 | *clevyen*. So MS, Br, BS, St, Tu. W³, Bö: *clenyen*. |
| 37 | *yclothe*. So MS, W³, Bö. Br, St, Tu: *y cloþe*. BS: *ycloþed*. |
| 39 | *ywedded*. So MS, W³, Bö, Br, St, Tu. BS: *Y wedded*. |
| 40 | *me*. So MS, W³, Bö, Br, BS, St. Tu: *þe*. |
| | *myht I*. So BS. MS, W³, Bö, Br, St: *myhti*. Tu: *myhtu*. |
| 44 | *mey non* . So MS, Br, BS, St, Tu. W³: *me y-nou*. Bö: *mey*. |
| 45 | *ne mey hit*. So MS, W³, Br, BS, St, Tu. Bö: *me mey*. |
| 47 | *that*. So MS, W³, Bö, Br, BS, St. Tu: *þah*. |
| | *ofthunche*. So MS, W³, Bö, St, Tu. Br, BS: *ofthuncheþ*. |

**A WAYLE WHYT ASE WHALLES BON** [ART. 36]

| | |
|---|---|
| burden | ¶ *A wayle whyt ase whalles bon / A grein in golde that godly shon / A tortle that min herte is on / In tounes trewe / Hire gladshipe nes never gon / While Y may glewe / When heo is glad / Of al this world namore Y bad / Then beo with hire myn one bistad / Withoute strif / The care that Ich am yn ybrad / Y wyte a wyf / A wyf nis non so worly wroht / When heo ys blythe to bedde ybroht / Wel were him that wiste hire thoht / That thryven ant thro / Wel Y wot heo nul me noht / Myn herte is wo / Hou shal that lefly syng / That thus is marred in mournyng / Heo me wol to dethe bryng / Longe er my day / Gret hire wel that swete thing / With eyenen gray / Hyre heye haveth wounded me ywisse / Hire bende browen that bringeth blisse / Hire comely mouth that mihte cusse / In muche murthe he were / Y wolde chaunge myn for his / That is here fere / Wolde hyre fere beo so freo / Ant wurthes were that so myhte beo / Al for on Y wolde geve threo / Withoute chep / From helle to hevene ant sonne to see / Nys non so yeep / Ne half so freo / Wose wole of love be trewe do lystne me / Herkneth me Y ou telle / In such wondryng for wo Y welle / Nys no fur so hot in helle / Al to mon / That loveth derne ant dar nout telle / Whet him ys on / Ich unne hire wel ant heo me wo / Ych am hire frend and heo my fo / Me thuncheth min herte wol breke atwo / For sorewe ant syke / In Godes greting mote heo go / That wayle whyte / Ich wolde ich were a threstelcok / A bountyng other a lavercoke / Swete bryd / Bituene hire curtel ant hire smoke / Y wolde ben hyd.* |
| incipit | *Wose*. So MS, BS. W³, Bö, Br, St: *Whose*. Mi: *Wo-se*. Deg's reconstruction omits this line. |
| 24 | *godly*. So MS, W³, Br, Deg, BS, St, Mi. Bö: *goldly*. |
| 61 | *eyenen*. So MS (*eȝenen*), W³, Bö, BS, Mi. Br, Deg, St: *eȝen*. |
| 84 | *Ne half so freo*. Deg's reconstruction omits this line. |

**GILOTE E JOHANE** [ART. 37]

| | |
|---|---|
| 2 | *chivaler*. So MS, Ju, Ken, Do. Rev¹: *cheualer*. |

| 10 | *que.* So MS, Ju, Ken, Do. Rev[1]: *qe.* |
| 11 | *beal.* So MS, Ju, Ken, Do. Rev[1]: *bel.* |
| 15 | *lele.* So MS, Ken, Do, Rev[1]. Ju: *tele.* |
| 20 | *e.* So MS, Ken, Do, Rev[1]. Ju: *et.* |
| 24 | *d'enconbrer.* So MS, Ken, Do, Rev[1]. Ju: *d'encombrer.* |
| 25 | *estez.* So MS, Ju, Ken, Rev[1]. Do: *estes.* |
| 30 | *su.* So MS, Ju, Ken, Rev[1]. Do: *fu.* |
| 31 | *Pus qe.* So MS, Ju, Ken. Do, Rev[1]: *Pus ce qe.* |
| 34 | *Pus qe.* So MS, Ju, Ken. Do, Rev[1]: *Pus ce qe.* |
| 37 | *virginité.* So MS, Ju, Ken, Do. Rev[1]: *virginitee.* |
| 42 | *aparteynaunce.* So MS, Ju, Do, Rev[1]. Ken: *aparceynaunce.* |
| 52 | *vyt.* So Do, Rev[1]. MS: *xyt.* Ju: *uyt.* Ken: *eyt.* |
| 57 | *pris.* So MS, Ju, Do, Rev[1]. Ken: *pres.* |
| 58 | *Desolé.* So MS, Ju, Do, Rev[1]. Ken: *defole.* |
| 65 | *quaunt.* So MS, Ju, Do. Ken, Rev[1]: *quant.* |
| 70 | *mesfetz.* So MS, Ken, Do, Rev[1]. Ju: *meffetz.* |
| 73 | *lele.* So MS, Ken, Do, Rev[1]. Ju: *tele.* |
| 88 | *su.* So MS, Ju, Ken, Rev[1]. Do: *fu.* |
| 89 | *salvacioun.* So MS, Ju, Do, Rev[1]. Ken: *salvatioun.* |
| 90 | *E.* So MS, Ken, Do, Rev[1]. Ju: *Et.* |
| 96 | *en.* So Do, Rev[1]. MS, Ju, Ken: *e.* |
|  | *je.* So MS, Ju, Do, Rev[1]. Ken: omitted. |
| 98 | *ensaunple.* So MS, Ken, Do, Rev[1]. Ju: *ensample.* |
| 101 | *salvacioun.* So MS, Ju, Do, Rev[1]. Ken: *salvatioun.* |
| 113 | *E.* So MS, Ken, Do, Rev[1]. Ju: *Et.* |
| 118 | *soume.* So MS, Ken, Rev[1]. Ju, Do: *somme.* |
| 119 | *Dieu.* So Ken, Rev[1]. MS, Ju, Do: *Bien.* |
|  | *ne.* So MS, Ken, Do, Rev[1]. Ju: *de.* |
| 121 | *mesfet.* So MS, Ken, Do, Rev[1]. Ju: *meffet.* |
| 137 | *destaunce.* So MS, Ju, Do, Rev[1]. Ken: *distaunce.* |
| 141 | *cristen.* So MS (*crist* abbreviated), Do, Rev[1]. Ju, Ken: *cristien.* |
| 148 | *meynz.* So MS, Ken, Do, Rev[1]. Ju: *mynz.* |
|  | *l'escole.* So MS, Ju, Ken, Do. Rev[1]: *le scole.* |
| 156 | *serra.* So MS, Ju, Ken. Do, Rev[1]: *ferra.* |
| 157 | *avez.* So MS, Ken, Do, Rev[1]. Ju: *arez.* |
| 171 | *me ussez.* So MS, Ken, Do, Rev[1]. Ju: *m'eussez.* |
| 174 | *nulle.* So MS Ju, Ken, Rev[1]. Do: *nule.* |
| 191 | *seme.* So Ken. MS, Ju, Do, Rev[1]: *seine.* |
| 197 | *e.* So MS, Ken, Do, Rev[1]. Ju: omitted. |
| 198 | *su.* So MS, Ju, Ken, Rev[1]. Do: *fu.* |
| 199 | *e.* So MS, Do, Rev[1]. Ju, Ken: *et.* |
| 209 | *deveyer.* So MS, Do, Rev[1]. Ju, Ken: *deneyer.* |
| 214 | *E.* So MS, Ken, Do, Rev[1]. Ju: *Et.* |
| 217 | *l'autrer.* So MS, Ken, Do, Rev[1]. Ju: *l'autr'er.* |
| 218 | *Johane.* So MS, Ken, Do, Rev[1]. Ju: *Jehane.* |
| 232 | *tienk.* So MS, Ken, Do, Rev[1]. Ju: *tient.* |
| 239 | *rien.* So MS, Ju, Do, Rev[1]. Ken: *bien.* |

| | |
|---|---|
| 243 | *honme*. So MS, Ken. Ju, Do: *homme*. Rev[1]: *houme*. |
| 245 | *womon*. So MS, Do, Rev[1]. Ju: *coomoun*. Ken: *woman*. |
| | *yshent*. So MS, Ken, Do, Rev[1]. Ju: *y-sheent*. |
| 247 | *jeouene*. So MS, Do, Rev[1]. Ju: *geouene*. |
| | *clerjoun*. So Rev[1]. MS, Ken, Do: *clerioun*. Ju: *clersoun*. |
| 255 | *predicacioun*. So MS, Do, Rev[1]. Ju, Ken,: *predicatioun*. |
| 256 | *e*. So MS, Ken, Do, Rev[1]. Ju: *et*. |
| 263 | *medicine*. So MS, Ju, Ken, Do. Rev[1]: *medecine*. |
| 265 | *par*. So MS (*ar* abbreviated), Ken, Do. Ju, Rev[1]: *pur*. |
| 269 | *lettre*. So MS (*ett* abbreviated), Ju, Ken, Do. Rev[1]: *letre*. |
| 273 | *lyws*. So MS, Ken, Do, Rev. Ju: *luus*. |
| 275 | *eyn de gré*. So MS, Ju. Ken, Do, Rev[1]: *eyndegre*. |
| 276 | *honme*. So MS, Ken. Ju: *homme*. Do, Rev[1]: *houme*. |
| 278 | *ov*. So MS, Ju, Ken, Rev[1]. Do: *en*. |
| 279 | *an enter*. So MS, Ken, Do, Rev[1]. Ju: *anenter*. |
| 280 | *mis*. So MS, Ju, Ken, Do. Rev[1]: *mys*. |
| 281 | *enterré*. So MS, Ju, Ken, Rev[1]. Do: *en terre*. |
| 283 | *cas*. So MS, Ju, Ken, Do. Rev[1]: *case*. |
| 287 | *accion*. So MS, Ju, Ken, Do. Rev[1]: *action*. |
| 298 | *vylenye*. So MS, Ju, Do, Rev[1]. Ken: *vylynye*. |
| 300 | *pernez*. So MS (*er* abbreviated), Ju, Do, Rev[1]. Ken: *prenez*. |
| 301 | *promistes*. So MS, Ju, Ken, Do. Rev[1]: *promiste*. |
| 302 | *a dreyture*. So MS (*ur* abbreviated), Ju, Ken, Do. Rev[1]: *dreyte*. |
| 310 | *Recevez*. So MS, Ju, Do, Rev[1]. Ken: *receudez*. |
| 323 | *moster*. So MS, Ken, Do, Rev[1]. Ju: *mostrer*. |
| 325 | *desputerent*. So MS, Ju, Do, Rev[1]. Ken: *disputerent*. |
| 327 | *comunement*. So MS (*mun* abbreviated), Ju. Ken, Do, Rev[1]: *communement*. |
| 328 | *e*. So MS, Ken, Do, Rev[1]. Ju: *et*. |
| 331 | *bosoignes*. So MS, Ju, Ken, Do. Rev[1]: *besoignes*. |
| 337 | *Qe*. So MS, Ken, Do, Rev[1]. Ju: *Que*. |
| | *siet*. So MS Ju, Ken, Do. Rev[1]: *fiet*. |
| 338 | *Engletere*. So MS, Ken, Do. Ju, Rev[1]: *Engleterre*. |
| 341 | *tornerent*. So MS, Ju, Ken, Do. Rev[1]: *tornererent*. |
| 345 | *vyntenuefyme*. So MS, Ken, Rev[1]. Ju, Do: *vyntennesyme*. |

## LES PELRINAGES COMMUNES QUE CRESTIENS FOUNT EN LA SEINTE TERRE [ART. 38]

| | |
|---|---|
| 7 | *Eufemie*. So MS. MR: *Eufenie*. |
| 8 | *nasquy*. So MS. MR: *nasquis*. |
| 12 | *um*. So MS. MR: *wn*. |
| 15 | *maveis*. So MS. MR: *maweis*. |
| 18 | *yleqe*. So MS. MR: *yleque*. |
| 20 | *de bel*. So MR. MS: *de de bel*. |
| 21 | *pus*. So MS (*us* abbreviated). MR: *puis*. |
| 24 | *mounde*. So MS. MR: *monde*. |
| 28 | *Delees*. So MS. MR: *deleis*. |
| 31 | *Pashe*. So MS (*e* abbreviated). MR: *Pask*. |

| 36 | *EGLISE*. So MS. MR: *esglise*. |
| 38 | *dedenz*. So MS. MR: *dedeinz*. |
| 42 | *par cele*. So MS (*ar* abbreviated). MR: *per cele*. |
| | *fitz, qe*. So MS. MR: *fitz qi*. |
| 67 | *liw*. So MS. MR: *lew*. |
| | *d'espynes*. So MS. MR: *d'esspynes*. |
| 70 | *GALYGANT*. So MS. MR: *Galygant*. |
| 71 | *le um*. So MS. MR: *um*. |
| 77 | *deis*. So MS. MR: *dois*. |
| 79 | *piere*. So MS. MR: *pere*. |
| 90 | *Jerusalem*. So MS (abbreviated). MR: *Iherusalem*. |
| 101 | *par*. So MS. MR: *pur*. |
| 102 | *Jerusalem*. So MS (abbreviated). MR: *Iherusalem*. |
| 103 | *Jerusalem*. So MS (abbreviated). MR: *Iherusalem*. |
| 106 | *une*. So MS. MR: *.j.* |
| 112 | *Jerusalem*. So MS (abbreviated). MR: *Iherusalem*. |
| 114 | *EVE*. So MS. MR: *Ewe*. |
| 115 | *lyw*. So MS. MR: *lywe*. |
| 118 | *Jerusalem*. So MS (abbreviated). MR: *Iherusalem*. |
| | *le lyw*. So MS. MR: *la lywe*. |
| 121 | *Jerusalem*. So MS (abbreviated). MR: *Iherusalem*. |
| 126 | *NAMES*. So MR. MS: *James*. |
| 129 | *Johan*. So MS. MR: *Jehan*. |
| 134 | *feseient*. So MS. MR: *fesoient*. |
| 136 | *MAGDALEYNE*. So MS. MR: *Magdalyne*. |
| 142 | *comaunderent*. So MS. MR: *commanderent*. |
| 148 | *la*. So MR. MS: *lar*. |
| 150 | *apartement*. So MS (*ar* abbreviated). MR: *apertement*. |
| 164 | *delyverer*. So MS. MR: *delyvrer*. |
| 165 | *EGLISE*. So MS. MR: *esglise*. |
| 168 | *BARUTH*. So MS. MR: *Baruch*. |
| | *par*. So MS (*ar* abbreviated). MR: *per*. |

## LES PARDOUNS DE ACRES [ART. 39]

| 6 | *Romaunt*. So MS. MR, Pr: *Romant*. |
| 13 | *Croyz*. So MS (*croyʒ*), Pr. MR: *Croy*. |
| 20 | *Espyrit*. So MS, MR. Pr: *Esprit*. |
| 23 | *iiij*. So MS. MR: *viij*. Pr: *8*. |
| 24 | *Prechours*. So MS. MR, Pr: *preschours*. |
| 26 | *de Sake*. So MS (*e* abbreviated). MR, Pr: *desakes*. |
| 28 | *digmange*. So MS. MR, Pr: *digmangt*. |
| 30 | *Magdaleyne*. So MS, MR. Pr: *Magdalene*. |
| 34 | *Martin*. So MS, MR. Pr: *Martyn*. |
| 35 | *xv karantaines*. So MS. Pr: *2 years 70 days*. |
| 37 | *iiij aunz*. So MS, MR. Pr: *3 years*. |
| 39 | *ccc*. So MS, MR. Pr: *1 year 35 days*. |

**NE MAI NO LEWED LUED LIBBEN IN LONDE**                                    [ART. 40]

| | |
|---|---|
| 12 | *unbredes*. So MS, W$^1$, Ro, Tu. Bö: *on bredes*. |
| 13 | *unbrad*. So MS, W$^1$, Ro, Tu. Bö: *on brad*. |
| 17 | *yt*. So MS, Bö, Ro, Tu. W$^1$: *it*. |
| 22 | *heme*. So MS, W$^1$, Ro, Tu. Bö: *hemed*. |
| 24 | *songe*. So MS, W$^1$, Ro, Tu. Bö: *sonke*. |
| 31 | *er*. So W$^1$, Bö, Ro, Tu. MS: *euer* (*er* with mark over *e*). |
| 33 | *wreint*. So MS, W$^1$, Bö, Ro. Tu: *wreit*. |
| 41 | *polketh*. So MS, W$^1$, Ro, Tu. Bö: *pelteþ*. |
| 42 | *clastreth*. So MS, W$^1$, Ro, Tu. Bö: *clattreþ*. |
| | *wyth*. So MS, Bö, Ro, Tu. W$^1$: *with*. |
| 74 | *unthenfol*. So MS, W$^1$. Bö: *vnþenkfol*. Ro, Tu: *untheufol*. |
| 78 | *Heore*. So MS, W$^1$, Ro, Tu. Bö: *henne*. |
| 86 | *whissheth*. So MS, W$^1$, Ro, Tu. Bö: *wissheþ*. |

**OF A MON MATHEU THOHTE**                                    [ART. 41]

| | |
|---|---|
| 2 | *whrohte*. So MS, W$^3$, Mo, B13. Bö, Br: *wrohte*. |
| 24 | *nyht*. So MS, W$^3$, Mo, B13, Br. Bö: *noht*. |
| 39 | A mark at the foot of column 70vb matches one at the top of 71rb, indicating how the reader is to skip over the left-hand column of the facing page to find the remainder of the poem. |
| 52 | *doh*. So MS, W$^3$, B13. Bö: *doht*. Mo, Br: *doþ*. |

**LENTEN YS COME WITH LOVE TO TOUNE**                                    [ART. 43]

| | |
|---|---|
| 11 | *wynter*. So MS, W$^3$, Mo, Bö, B13, St, Si, Tr. Br, Mi: *wynne*. |
| 22 | *doh*. So MS, W$^3$, B13. Bö: *doht*. Mo, Br, St, Si, Mi, Tr: *doþ*. |
| 28 | *Deawes*. So MS, Mo, Bö, B13, Br, St, Si, Mi, Tr. W$^3$: *Deowes*. |
| 29 | *with*. So MS (*wiþ*), W$^3$, Mo, Bö, B13, Br, St, Mi, Tr. Si: *wis'th* (i.e., *wiseth*). |

**IN MAY HIT MURGETH WHEN HIT DAWES**                                    [ART. 44]

| | |
|---|---|
| 8 | *bour*. So MS, Ri$^1$, Bö, B13, Br, BS, St, Tr. W$^3$: *boure*. |
| 21 | *tricherie*. So MS (*ri* abbreviated), W$^3$, Bö, B13, Br, BS, St, Tr. Ri$^1$: *trecherie*. |
| 22 | *trichour*. So MS (*ri* abbreviated), W$^3$, Bö, B13, Br, BS, St, Tr. Ri$^1$: *trechour*. |
| 31 | *trichour*. So MS (*ri* abbreviated), W$^3$, Bö, B13, Br, BS, St, Tr. Ri$^1$: *trechour*. |
| 34 | *levedis*. So MS, W$^3$, Bö, B13, Br, BS, St, Tr. Ri$^1$: *levedies*. |
| | *onwar*. So MS, W$^3$, Bö, B13, Br, BS, St, Tr. Ri$^1$: *ou war*. |
| 39 | *trichour*. So MS (*ri* abbreviated), W$^3$, Bö, B13, Br, BS, St, Tr. Ri$^1$: *trechour*. |
| 41 | *me*. So MS, W$^3$, Bö, B13, Br, BS, St, Tr. Ri$^1$: *men*. |
| | *ou*. So MS, Ri$^1$, Bö, B13, Br, BS, St, Tr. W$^3$: *on*. |
| 43 | *send*. So MS (*seind* with *i* deleted), W$^3$, B13, Br, BS, St, Tr. Ri$^1$: *seind*. Bö: *lend*. |
| 45 | *lahte*. So MS, W$^3$, Bö, B13, Br, BS, St, Tr. Ri$^1$: *hahte*. |
| 47 | *levely*. So MS, Ri$^1$, Bö, B13, Br, BS, St, Tr. W$^3$: *lovely*. |

### HEYE LOUERD, THOU HERE MY BONE                                    [ART. 45]

| | |
|---|---|
| 18 | *wille.* So MS, W³, B14, Br, Tr. Bö, Pa: *wille &.* |
| 23 | *Yleved.* So MS, W³, B14, Br, Tr. Bö, Pa: *y leued.* |
| 27 | *Thar.* So MS, W³, Br. Bö, Pa, B14, Tr: *That.* |
| 28 | *Y swyke.* So MS, W³, B14, Br, Tr. Bö, Pa: *yswyke.* |
| 55 | *plowe-fere.* So MS, W³, B14, Br, Tr. Bö, Pa: *plawe fere.* |
| 62 | *bedyver.* So MS, B14, Br, Tr. W³, Bö, Pa: *bedyner.* |
| 63 | *unbe-while.* So MS, W³, Bö, Pa, B14, Tr. Br: *umbewhile.* |
| 64 | *whene.* So MS, W³, Bö, Pa, Tr. Br, B14: *wene.* |
| 67 | *me.* So MS, W³, B14, Br,Tr. Bö, Pa: *mi.* |
| 76 | *Y wroht.* So MS, W³, B14, Br, Tr. Bö, Pa: *ywroht.* |
| 83 | *Y sugge.* So MS, W³, B14, Br, Tr. Bö, Pa: *ysugge.* |
| 85 | *heued.* So MS, W³, B14, Br, Tr. Bö, Pa: *heueþ.* |

### ICHOT A BURDE IN BOURE BRYHT                                    [ART. 46]

| | |
|---|---|
| burden | Written at the head of the poem. The repetition after each stanza is signaled by the scribe after lines 8 and 20. See also art. 36. |
| 2 | *sully.* So MS, Br, BS, St, Si. W³, Ri¹, Bö, BZ, B13, Gr, Tr: *fully.* |
| 9–12 | MS, W³, Ri¹, Bö, B13, Br, BS, St, Si, Tr: *Blow &c.* BZ, Gr: omitted. |
| 10 | *Sent.* So MS, W³, Bö, BZ, B13, Br, BS, St, Si, Gr, Tr. Ri¹: *Send.* |
| 14 | *fonde.* So MS, W³, Bö, BZ, B13, Br, BS, St, Si, Gr, Tr. Ri¹: *fonge.* |
| 20 | *leflich.* So MS, W³, Bö, BZ, B13, Br, BS, St, Si, Gr, Tr. Ri¹: *leflych.* |
| 21–24 | MS, W³, Ri¹, Bö, B13, Br, BS, St, Si, Tr: *Blou &c.* BZ, Gr: omitted. |
| 44 | *heste.* So MS, W³, Ri¹, Bö, BZ, Br, BS, St, Gr, Tr. B13: *beste.* |
| 54 | *bi west.* So MS, W³, Bö, BZ, B13, Br, BS, St, Si, Gr, Tr. Ri¹: *by west.* |
| 55 | *fiele.* So MS, W³, BZ, B13, Br, BS, St, Si, Tr. Ri¹: *ficle.* Bö, Gr: *fiþele.* |
| 63 | *clannesse.* So MS, W³, Bö, BZ, B13, Br, BS, St, Si, Gr, Tr. Ri¹: *clairnesse.* |
| 67 | *solsecle.* So MS, W³, Ri¹, BZ, B13, Br, BS, St, Si, Tr. Bö: *selsecle.* Gr: *salsecle.* |
| 73 | *leflich.* So MS, W³, Ri¹, Bö BZ, Br, BS, St, Si, Gr. B13, Tr: *loflich.* |
| 97 | *Hire.* So MS, W³, Ri¹, B13, Br, BS, St, Si, Gr, Tr. Bö, BZ, Gr: omitted. |
| 101 | *bisecheth.* So MS, W³, Ri¹, Bö, B13, Br, BS, St, Si, Gr, Tr. BZ: *biseche.* |

### ALLE THAT BEOTH OF HUERTE TREWE                                    [ART. 47]

| | |
|---|---|
| 12 | *springe.* So MS (*ri* abbreviated), W¹, Bö, Ro. Tr: *sprynge.* |
| 16 | *Cristendome.* So MS (*ri* abbreviated), Bö, Ro. W¹, Tr: *Christendome.* |
| 28 | *pris.* So MS (*ri* abbreviated), Bö, Ro, Tr. W¹: *prys.* |
| 30 | *Agein.* So MS, Bö, Ro, Tr. W¹: *Aȝeyn.* |
| 40 | *heveriche.* So MS, Bö, Tr. W¹, Ro: *hevenriche.* |
| 43 | *hond.* So MS, W¹, Bö, Ro. Tr: *bond.* |
| 48 | *Cristendome.* So MS (*ri* abbreviated), Bö, Ro. W¹, Tr: *Christendome.* |
| 49 | *chaumbre.* So W¹, Bö, Ro, Tr. MS: *chaunbre.* |
| 52 | *Cristes.* So MS (*ri* abbreviated), W¹, Bö, Ro. Tr: *Christes.* |
| 61 | *lene.* So MS, W¹, Ro, Tr. Bö: *leue.* |
| 69 | *fol.* So MS, W¹, Ro. Bö, Tr: *ful.* |

71   *crie*. So MS (*ri* abbreviated), W¹, Bö, Ro. Tr: *crye*.

79   *Engelond*. So MS, W¹, Bö, Tr. Ro: *engeland*.

### LUSTNETH, LORDINGES, BOTHE YONGE ANT OLDE    [ART. 48]

6   *Flemmysshe*. So MS, W¹, Ro. Ri¹: *Flemmyssh*. Bö: *flemmyshe*.

15   *anonen*. So MS, Bö. W¹, Ri¹: *an oven*. Ro: *anouen*.

20   *cheveuteyn*. So MS, Ro. W¹, Ri¹, Bö: *cheuenteyn*.

33   *hou*. So W¹, Ri¹, Bö, Ro. MS: *hout*.

57   *Phelip*. So MS, W¹, Bö, Ro. Ri¹: *Philip*.

63   *with*. So W¹, Ri¹, Bö, Ro. MS: omitted.

65   *de Nel*. So MS, Ro. W¹, Ri¹, Bö: *Deuel*.

67   *ritht*. So MS (*riþt*), W¹, Ri¹, Ro. Bö: *riht*.

    *assoygne*. So MS, W¹, Ri¹, Ro. Bö: *assoyne*.

73   *eorles*. So MS, W¹, Bö, Ro. Ri¹: *eorls*.

74   *Fiftene*. So MS, W¹, Ri¹, Bö. Ro: *Fyftene*.

87   *doddeth*. So MS, W¹, Bö, Ro. Ri¹: *deddeth*.

99–104  So MS, W¹, Ri¹, Ro. Bö: lines 99–100 transposed with lines 103–04.

101   *knyhtes*. So MS, W¹, Bö, Ro. Ri¹: *kynhtes*.

107   *springe*. So MS (*ri* abbreviated), W¹, Bö, Ro. Ri¹: *sprynge*.

114   *meste*. So MS, W¹, Bö, Ro. Ri¹: *mest*.

127   *hy*. So MS, W¹, Bö, Ro. Ri¹: *by*.

129–30  So MS, W¹, Ri¹, Ro. Bö: *the bataille thus bigon* (line 129) transposed with *hou hue weren fon* (line 130).

131   *heden*. So MS, W¹, Bö, Ro. Ri¹: *hedeu*.

133   *Yef*. So W¹, Ri¹, Bö, Ro. MS: *Ʒe*.

### MARIE, PUR TOUN ENFAUNT    [ART. 49]

36   *la*. So MS, W², Do. JL: *le*.

### SUETE JESU, KING OF BLYSSE    [ART. 50]

12   *leve*. So MS, B14, Br. W³, Bö, Hor²: *lene*.

19   *me*. So MS, W³, B14, Br. Hor², Bö: *we*.

20   *wete*. So Bö, Hor², B14, Br. MS, W³: *wepe*.

22   *fer*. So MS, W³, B14, Br. Bö: *for*. Hor²: *for to*.

34   *wrotht*. So MS (*wroþt*), W³. Bö, Hor², B14, Br: *wroht*.

46   *the*. So Hor², B14, Br. MS, W³, Bö: omitted.

### JESU CRIST, HEOVENE KYNG    [ART. 51]

6   *al wher*. So MS, W³, B14, Br. Bö, Pa: *aiwher*.

14   *Jesu*. MS, W³, Bö, Pa, B14, Br: *jesse*.

21   *sohtes*. So Bö, Pa, Br. MS, W³, B14: *sohtest*.

**Wynter wakeneth al my care** [ART. 52]

12       *Thath*. So MS (*þaþ*), W³. Ri¹, Bö, B14, Br: *þah*. Si: *That*.
13       *gren*. So MS, W³, Ri¹, Bö. B14, Br, Si: *grein*.

**When Y se blosmes springe** [ART. 53]

2       *foules*. So MS, Bö, Br, Mi. W³: *soules*.
19       *smerte*. So MS, Bö, Br, Mi. W³: *swerte*.
26       *the*. So MS (*þe*), W³, Br. Bö, Mi: *thi*.
         *sone*. So MS, W³, Bö. Br: *swete*. Mi: *suete*.
31       *con*. So Bö. Br, Mi. MS, W³: *couþe*.
32       *Turne*. So MS, Bö, Br, Mi. W³: word printed at end of line 31.
40       *yboht*. So MS, W³, Bö, Br. Mi: *ybroht*.

**Ferroy chaunsoun** [ART. 54]

5       *E ele*. So MS, W³, Ken. JL: *Cele*.
9       *la*. So MS, W³, JL. Ken: omitted.
15       *fol*. MS: a line break mark appears after this word. W³, Ken, JL: divided as two lines.
19–22       So JL. MS, W³, Ken: *Je pri a Dieu &c.*
27       *salutz portez*. Emended for rhyme. MS, W³, Ken, JL: *portez salutz*.
27–28       So Ken. MS: no line break indicated. W³, JL: combined as one line.
34–37       So JL. MS, W³, Ken: *Je pri a Dieu &c.*

**Dum ludis floribus** [ART. 55]

1       *lacivia*. So MS, St (considers *lacinia*). W³, Br, Ken (considers *lacivia*), JL, Mi: *lacinia*. Le: *luscinia*.
17       *Scripsi*. So W³, Br, Ken, St, JL, Mi, Le. MS: *Scripsit*.
18       *ostel*. So MS, W³, Br, St, JL, Mi, Le. Ken: *hostle*.

**Quant fu en ma juvente** [ART. 56]

11       *en verglis*. So MS. Do: *enveoglise*.
51       *fiet*. So MS. Do: *siet*.
79       *Bonet*. So MS. Do: *Benet*.
107       *espaundez*. So MS (*ez* abbreviated). Do: *espaundi*.
125       *assayly*. So MS. Do: *affayly*.
149       *esteant*. So MS. Do: *esteaunt*.

**Marie, mere al Salveour** [ART. 57]

30       *quide*. So MS (abbreviation mark on *d*), W³, Do.

**DULCIS JESU MEMORIA** [ART. 58]

| | |
|---|---|
| 3 | *may.* So MS, W³, Bö. Hor²: *me may.* |
| 8 | *a luviere.* So MS. W³, Bö: *alumere.* Hor²: *a lover.* |
| 14 | *pine.* So MS, W³, Hor². Bö: *þine.* |
| 22 | *yeve.* Suggested by Hor². MS, W³, Bö, Hor²: *seʒe.* |
| 23 | *thou madest.* So MS, W³, Bö, Hor² (who suggests *þe made*). |
| 30 | *askesd.* So MS, W³. Bö, Hor²: *askest.* |
| 41 | *my.* So MS, Bö, Hor². W³: *mi.* |
| 62 | *heo.* So MS, Bö, Hor². W³: *he.* |
| 65 | *gretyn.* So Hor². MS, W³, Bö: *gredyn.* |
| 72 | *whosshe.* So MS, W³, Hor². Bö: *wosshe.* |
| 87 | *thy.* So MS, W³, Bö. Hor²: *þe.* |
| 98 | *mi likyng.* So MS, W³. Bö: *me like.* Hor²: *me likyn.* |
| | *Y se.* So MS, Hor². W³: *y-se.* Bö: *yse.* |
| 109 | *thi love.* So MS, W³, Bö. Hor²: *bi-leue.* |
| 114 | *the.* So Hor². MS, W³, Bö: *me.* |
| 119 | *Tak.* So MS, W³, Bö. Hor²: *mak.* |
| | *treufole.* So MS, Bö, Hor². W³: *trenfole.* |
| 120 | *love-blod.* So MS, W³, Bö. Hor²: *loue-flod.* |
| 130 | *almyhti.* So MS, W³, Hor². Bö. *almihti.* |
| 138 | *the.* So MS, W³, Bö. Hor²: *þi.* |
| 144 | *me.* So W³, Bö, Hor². MS: *mere* (*er* abbreviated). |
| 151 | *me maketh.* So MS, Bö, Hor². W³: *maketh me.* |
| | *swythe.* So MS, W³, Bö, Hor² (who suggests *swete*). |
| 173 | *bohtest.* So Bö, Hor². MS, W³: *bostest.* |
| 176 | *with.* So MS, W³, Bö, Hor² (who suggests *in*). |
| 193 | *thi.* So MS, Bö, Hor² (who suggests *þer*). W³: *thy.* |

**UNE PETITE PAROLE** [ART. 59]

| | |
|---|---|
| 3 | *aprendre.* So W³, Do. MS: *apredre.* |
| 18 | *Honme.* So MS, W³. Do: *Hounme.* |
| 21 | *quant.* So MS, Do. W³: *quaunt.* |
| 22 | *croyz.* So MS, Do. W³: *croiz.* |
| 44 | *bien.* So MS, Do. W³: *Dieu.* |
| 55 | *ou.* So MS, Do. W³: *on.* |
| 83 | *Lealmentz.* So MS, W³. Do: *lealment.* |

**STOND WEL, MODER, UNDER RODE** [ART. 60]

| | |
|---|---|
| 8 | *monkynde.* So MS, Bö, Br. W³: *mankynde.* |
| 28 | *byswongen.* So Bö. MS, Br, W³: *byswngen.* |
| 29 | *honden.* So MS, W³, Br. Bö: *honde.* |

**JESU, FOR THI MUCHELE MIHT** [ART. 61]

42   *ystongen.* So Br. MS, W³, Bö, B13: *ystonge.*
44   *yswongen.* So MS, W³, B13, Br. Bö: *yswonge.*

**I SYKE WHEN Y SINGE** [ART. 62]

38   *mournynde.* So MS, Bö, Br, Sa, Mi, Tr. W³: *to-mournynde.*
47   *my.* So MS, W³, Bö, Br, Sa. Mi, Tr: *mi.*
48   *smerte.* So MS, Bö, Br, Sa, Mi, Tr. W³: *swerte.*

**NOU SKRINKETH ROSE ANT LYLIE-FLOUR** [ART. 63]

1   *skrinketh.* So Bö, Pa, Br, Sa, Mi, Tr. MS, Si: *skrnkeþ.* W³: *skruketh.* B14: *skrynkeþ.*
27   *o.* So MS, W³, Br, Si, Sa, Mi, Tr. Bö, Pa, B14: *a.*
29   *Whe.* So MS, W³, Si. Bö, Br, Pa, B14, Sa, Mi, Tr: *we.*
55–56  These lines are transposed in the MS. The emendation follows B14.
55   *bryth.* So MS, W³, B14, Si, Sa, Mi, Tr. Bö, Pa, Br: *bryht.*
57   The rhyme scheme indicates that a line is missing. See explanatory note.
59   *us.* So MS, W³, Bö, Pa, B14, Sa, Mi, Tr. Br, Si: *me.*

**MY DETH Y LOVE, MY LYF ICH HATE** [ART. 64]

2   *brith.* So MS, W³, BS. Bö, B13, Br, St, Si: *briht.*
17   *ritht.* So MS (*riþt*), W³. Bö, B13, Br, BS, St, Si: *riht.*
20   *the deth.* So MS, W³, Bö, B13, BS, Br, St. Si: *thi deth.*
31   *the₁.* So BS. MS: omitted. W³, Bö, Br, St, Si: *hom.* B13: *bour.*
33   *scille.* So MS, B13, Si. W³, Bö, Br, BS, St: *stille.*

**WHEN THE NYHTEGALE SINGES** [ART. 65]

12   *mouth.* So W³, Ri¹, Bö, B13, Br, BS, St, Si. MS: *mouerth* (*er* abbreviated).
13   *preye.* So W³, Ri¹, Bö, B13, Br, BS, St. MS: *preeȝe* (*re* abbreviated). Si: *preeye.*

17   *Lyndeseye.* So MS, W³, Bö, B13, Br, BS, St, Si. Ri¹: *Lyndesey.*
18   *fore.* So MS, W³, Bö, B13, Br, BS, St, Si. Ri¹: *sore.*
20   Ri¹ substitutes an invented line: *els to al that ys on grounde.*

**BLESSED BE THOU, LEVEDY** [ART. 66]

3   *Preyye.* So W³, Bö, Br. MS: *prereyȝe* (first *re* abbreviated). Sa: *Preyghe.*
16   *suete.* So MS, Bö, Br, Sa. W³: *to suete.*
29   *welle.* So MS, W³, Bö, Br. Sa: *well.*
30   *felle.* So MS, W³, Bö, Br. Sa: *fell.*

## ASE Y ME ROD THIS ENDER DAY [ART. 67]

5     *Lythe.* So MS, Bö, B14, Br, Sa, Mi. W³: *Kythe.*

12    *Jesu.* So MS (abbreviated *ihc* with stroke through *h*). W³: *Jhesu.* B14, Sa: *ihesus.* Br, Mi: *Iesus.* Bö: *iesu crist.*

14    *He.* So MS, W³, Bö, Br, Sa, Mi. B14: *heo.*

25    *wymman.* So Bö, B14, Br, Sa, Mi. MS, W³: *wynman.*

33    *thoro.* So MS, B14, Br, Sa, Mi. W³: *thore.* Bö: *þorwe.*

35    *The ster.* So B14, Br, Sa, Mi. MS: *þe stri* (*ri* abbreviated). W³, Bö: *þestri.*

44    *wen.* So MS, W³, B14, Sa. Bö, Br, Mi: *when.*

## HERKNE TO MY RON [ART. 68]

3     *ges.* So MS, Bö. WH: *gos.*

14    *Absolon.* So MS, Bö. WH: *Absalon.*

36    *upriht.* So MS, Bö. WH: *upright.*

73    *litht.* So MS (*liþt*), WH. Bö: *liht.*

77    *Ne.* So WH. MS: *he.* Bö: *hou.*

96    *bringe.* So MS (*ri* abbreviated), Bö. WH: *buge.*

97    *ywys.* So MS, Bö. WH: *ywis.*

98    *gris.* So MS, Bö. WH: *grys.*

101   *nys.* So MS, WH. Bö: *ys.*

107   *he.* So MS, WH. Bö: *ȝe.*

117   *bringeth.* So MS (*ri* abbreviated), Bö. WH: *bugeth.*

124   *nowhith.* So MS (*nowhiþ*), WH. Bö: *no wiht.*

157   *wyht.* So MS, WH. Bö: *whyt.*

167   *noht.* So Bö, WH. MS: *nolt.*

170   *pris.* So MS, Bö. WH: *prys.*

175   *Ystunt.* So MS, WH. Bö: *ystund.*

194   *te.* So WH, Bö. MS: *tt.*

197   *wes.* So MS, Bö. WH: *was.*

218   *Changeth.* So MS, Bö. WH: *Chaungeth.*

228   *Falu.* So MS, WH. Bö: *falu hit.*

230   *Styth.* So MS. WH, Bö: *Styf.*

231   *Y.* So MS, Bö. WH: *I.*

233   *my.* So MS, Bö. WH: *mi.*

237   *him.* So MS, Bö. WH: *hym.*

258   *wo.* So MS, WH. Bö: *who.*

260   *Wet.* So MS, WH. Bö: *Whet.*

## MAYDEN, MODER MILDE [ART. 69]

1     *Mayden.* So MS, W³, B13, Br, Si, JL, Sa, Mi. Bö: *Maiden.*

3     *shome.* So MS, W³, B13, Br, Si, JL, Sa, Mi. Bö: *shame.*

25    *ston.* So MS, Bö, B13. W³, Br, Si, JL, Sa, Mi: *stou.*

47    *me.* So MS, W³, B13, Br, Si, JL, Sa, Mi. Bö: *mo.*

THE GESTE OF KYNG HORN [ART. 70]

| | |
|---|---|
| 8 | *myhte*. So MS, Mc, Hal, DB, Tr. Ri²: *myghte*. |
| 10 | *myhte*. So MS, Mc, Hal, DB, Tr. Ri²: *myghte*. |
| 15 | *So whit so*. So MS, Ri², Mc, Hal, DB. Tr: *Is so whit so*. |
| 21 | *Tuelf*. MS, Ri², Mc, Hal: *Tueye*. DB, Tr: *Tweye*. See explanatory note. |
| 24 | *suythe*. So MS (*suyþe*), Ri², Mc, Hal. DB, Tr: *swyþe*. |
| 26 | *tueye*. So MS, Ri², Mc, Hal. DB, Tr: *tweye*. |
| 37 | *tuo*. So MS, Ri², Mc, Hal. DB, Tr: *two*. |
| 38 | *to*. So MS, Ri², Mc, Hal. DB, Tr: *too*. |
| 45 | *yherde*. So MS, Ri², Mc, Hal, DB. Tr: *yherd*. |
| 46 | *onsuerede*. So MS, Ri², Mc, Hal, Tr. DB: *onswerede*. |
| 47 | *londfolk*. So MS, Ri², Mc, Hal, DB. Tr: *landfolk*. |
| 49 | *the*. So MS (*þe*), Ri², Mc, Hal. DB, Tr: *þee*. |
| 53 | *tuo*. So MS, Ri², Mc, Hal, Tr. DB: *two*. |
| 59 | *to*. So MS, Ri², Mc, Hal, DB. Tr: *too*. |
| 66 | *Sarazyns*. So MS, Ri², Mc, Hal. DB, Tr: *cherches for*. See explanatory note. |
| 67 | *myhte*. So MS, Mc, Hal, DB, Tr. Ri²: *myghte*. |
| 86 | *wrthe*. So MS (*wrþe*), Ri², Mc, Hal. DB, Tr: *wurþe*. |
| 94 | *this*. So MS (*þis*), Mc, Hal, DB, Tr. Ri²: *thise*. |
| 112 | *suerd*. So MS, Ri², Mc, Hal, Tr. DB: *swerd*. |
| 123 | *suythe*. So MS (*suyþe*), Ri², Mc, Hal. DB, Tr: *swyþe*. |
| 153 | *sey thene*. So MS (*sey þene*), Mc, Hal, DB, Tr. Ri²: *seythene*. |
| 161 | *dounes*. So MS, Ri², Mc, Hal. DB, Tr: *doune*. |
| 162 | *children*. So MS, Ri², Mc, Hal. DB, Tr: *chidren*. |
| | *tounes*. So MS, Ri², Mc, Hal. DB, Tr: *toune*. |
| 166 | *Crist*. So Ri², Mc, Hal, DB, Tr. MS: *est*. |
| 168 | *suythe*. So MS (*suyþe*), Ri², Mc, Hal. DB, Tr: *swyþe*. |
| 172 | *suythe*. So MS (*suyþe*), Ri², Mc, Hal. DB, Tr: *swyþe*. |
| 174 | *felaurade*. So MS, Mc, Hal. Ri²: *felanrade*. DB, Tr: *felawrade*. |
| 175 | *seh Y never*. So MS, Ri², Mc, Hal, DB. Tr: *seh Ich ynever*. |
| 198 | *londe*. So MS, Ri², Mc, Hal, DB. Tr: *lande*. |
| 199 | *Nou*. So MS, Ri², Mc, Hal. DB, Tr: *Now*. |
| 202 | *spille*. So MS, Mc, Hal, DB, Tr. Ri²: *spylle*. |
| 207 | *onsuerede*. So MS, Ri², Mc, Hal, Tr. DB: *onswerede*. |
| 214 | *brouc*. So MS, Mc, Hal, DB, Tr. Ri²: *brouk* (reads *bront* or *brout*). |
| 216 | *dales*. So MS, Mc, Hal, DB, Tr. Ri²: *dale*. |
| | *hulles*. So MS, Mc, Hal, DB, Tr. Ri²: *hille* (reads *halles*). |
| 218 | *Thurhout*. So MS, Mc, Hal, DB, Tr. Ri²: *Thurghout*. |
| 219 | *springe*. So MS (*ri* abbreviated), Mc, Hal, DB, Tr. Ri²: *sprynge*. |
| 223 | *suete*. So MS, Ri², Mc, Hal, Tr. DB: *swete*. |
| 230 | *knyhtes*. So MS, Mc, Hal, DB, Tr. Ri²: *knyghtes*. |
| 234 | *fundling*. So MS, Ri², Hal, Tr. Mc, DB: *fundlyng*. |
| 240 | *wystest*. So MS, Mc, Hal, DB, Tr. Ri²: *wystes*. |
| 255 | *kynges*. So MS, Mc, Hal, DB, Tr. Ri²: *kinges*. |
| 256 | *thohte*. So MS (*þohte*), Mc, Hal, DB, Tr. Ri²: *thote*. |
| 273 | *hire*. So MS, Ri², Hal, DB, Tr. Mc: *hue*. |

279      *suythe*. So MS (*suyþe*), Ri², Mc, Hal. DB, Tr: *swyþe*.

307      *tueye*. So MS, Ri², Mc, Hal. DB, Tr: *tweye*.

309      *heo*. So MS, Ri², Hal, DB, Tr. Mc: *he*.

326      *Ant other*. So MS (& *oþer*), Ri², Mc, Hal. DB, Tr: *Other*.

335      *underfonge*. So MS, Mc, Hal, DB, Tr. Ri²: *undersonge*.

338      *so*. So MS, Mc, Hal, DB, Tr. Ri²: *sa*.

340      *aknen*. So MS, Ri², Mc. Hal, DB, Tr: *akneu*.

352      *Bituene*. So MS, Ri², Mc, Hal. DB, Tr: *Bitwene*.

           *tueye*. So MS, Ri², Mc, Hal. DB, Tr: *tweye*.

363      *thou*. So MS (*þou*), Ri², Hal, DB, Tr. Mc: *þon*.

379      *suythe*. So MS (*suyþe*), Ri², Mc, Hal. DB, Tr: *swyþe*.

380      *herte*. So MS, Ri². Mc, Hal, DB, Tr: *horte*.

385      *Aknewes*. So MS, Mc, Hal, DB, Tr. Ri²: *A kne wes*.

386      *suetliche*. So MS, Ri², Mc, Hal, Tr. DB: *swetliche*.

389      *spac*. So MS, Ri², Mc, Hal. DB, Tr: *spak*.

391      *sothte*. So MS (*soþte*), Mc. Ri²: *sothta*. Hal, DB, Tr: *softe*.

402      *suere*. So MS, Ri², Mc, Hal. DB, Tr: *swere*.

413      *wythoute*. So MS (*wyþoute*), Ri², Mc, Hal. DB, Tr: *withoute*.

425      *felde*. So MS, Mc, Hal, DB, Tr. Ri²: *selde*.

428      *Bituene*. So MS, Ri², Mc, Hal. DB, Tr: *Bitwene*.

440      *Suete*. So MS, Ri², Mc, Hal, Tr. DB: *Swete*.

454      *ringes*. So MS, Ri², Mc, Hal. DB, Tr: *ringe*.

493      *tuelve*. So MS, Ri², Mc, Hal, Tr. DB: *twelve*.

499      *springe*. So MS (*ri* abbreviated), Mc, Hal, DB, Tr. Ri²: *sprynge*.

501      *tuelf*. So MS, Ri², Mc, Hal, Tr. DB: *twelf*.

534      *by me*. So MS, Ri², DB, Tr. Mc, Hal: *byme*.

550      *fythte*. So MS (*fyþte*), Ri², Mc, Hal. DB, Tr: *fyhte*.

560      *ant*. So MS, Ri², Hal, DB, Tr. Mc: *aut*.

578      *Myd*. So MS, Ri², Hal. Mc, DB, Tr: *Mid*.

580      *sound*. So MS, Mc, Hal, DB, Tr. Ri²: *found*.

589      *sredde*. So MS, Mc, Hal, DB, Tr. Ri²: *fredde*.

619      *suerde*. So MS, Ri², Mc, Hal, Tr. DB: *swerde*.

627      *Y*. So MS, Ri², Mc, Hal. DB, Tr: *I*.

637      *brynge*. So MS, Ri², Hal. Mc, DB, Tr: *bringe*.

640      *woldeste*. So MS. Ri²: *wolde*. Mc, Hal, DB, Tr: *woldest*.

659      *Y caste*. So MS. Ri², Mc, Hal, DB, Tr: *ycaste*.

666      *The*. So MS (*þe*), Ri², Mc, Hal, DB. Tr: *Þat*.

667      *Seinte*. So MS, Mc, Hal, DB, Tr. Ri²: *seint*.

694      *suerd*. So MS, Ri², Mc, Hal. DB, Tr: *swerd*.

714      *suert*. So MS, Ri², Mc, Hal. DB, Tr: *swert*.

721      *suerd*. So MS, Ri², Mc, Hal, Tr. DB: *swerd*.

722      *to*. So MS, Ri², Mc, Hal, Tr. DB: *too*.

723      *suerd*. So MS, Ri², Mc, Hal, Tr. DB: *swerd*.

744      *Ant*. So MS (&), Ri², Mc, Hal, DB. Tr: *An*.

750      *my love*. So MS, Ri², Hal, DB, Tr. Mc: *loue*.

764      *hy*. So MS, Mc, Hal, DB, Tr. Ri²: *by*.

765      *bi*. So MS, Mc, Hal, DB, Tr. Ri²: *by*.

| | |
|---|---|
| 766 | *tueye*. So MS, Ri², Mc, Hal, Tr. DB: *tweye*. |
| 778 | *bridel*. So MS, Mc, Hal, DB, Tr. Ri²: *bride*. |
| 796 | *be*. So MS, Ri², Hal, DB, Tr. Mc: *þe*. |
| 804 | *nower*. So MS, DB, Tr. Ri²: *newer*. Mc, Hal: *no wer*. |
| 809 | *com*. So MS, Mc, Hal, DB, Tr. Ri²: *come*. |
| 810 | *suythe*. So MS (*suyþe*), Ri², Mc, Hal. DB, Tr: *swyþe*. |
| 821 | *oure thre*. So MS (*oure þre*), Mc, Hal. Ri²: *ure thre*. DB, Tr: *eure þre*. |
| 822 | *ore*. So MS, Mc, Hal. Ri²: *ure*. DB, Tr: *eure*. |
| 823 | *oure*. So MS, Ri², Mc, Hal. DB, Tr: *eure*. |
| 843 | *suerd*. So MS, Ri², Mc, Hal. DB, Tr: *swerd*. |
| 864 | *faylen*. So MS, Mc, Hal, DB, Tr. Ri²: *saylen*. |
| 871 | *ner*. So MS, Mc, Hal, DB, Tr. Ri²: omitted. |
| 885 | *suerd*. So MS, Ri², Mc, Hal. DB, Tr: *swerd*. |
| 890 | *con*. So MS, Mc, Hal, DB, Tr. Ri²: *gon*. |
| 913 | *yslawe*. So MS, Ri², Hal, Tr. Mc, DB: *yflawe*. |
| 916 | *Nys*. So MS, Ri², Mc, Hal, Tr. DB, Tr: *Nis*. |
| 917–18 | In MS this couplet is added in the right margin. |
| 926 | *Fulle*. So MS, Ri², Mc, Hal, DB. Tr: *Full*. |
| 932 | *hyre*. So MS, Ri², Mc, Hal, DB. Tr: *byre*. |
| 978 | *suythe*. So MS (*suyþe*), Ri², Mc, Hal. DB, Tr: *swyþe*. |
| 981 | *see*. So Mc, Hal, DB, Tr. MS, Ri²: omitted. |
| | *throwe*. So MS (*þrowe*), Mc, Hal, DB, Tr. Ri²: *thhrowe*. |
| 1014 | *were*. So MS, Mc, Hal, DB, Tr. Ri²: *wer*. |
| 1062 | *ye*. So MS (*ȝe*), Ri², Mc, Hal. DB: Y. Tr: *I*. |
| 1070 | *wrynge*. So MS, Mc, Hal, DB, Tr. Ri²: *wringe*. |
| 1074 | *onsuerede*. So MS, Ri², Mc, Hal, Tr. DB: *onswerede*. |
| 1077 | *ywynne*. So MS, Mc, Hal, DB, Tr. Ri²: *ywinne*. |
| 1083 | *thre*. So MS (*þre*), Mc, Hal, DB, Tr. Ri²: *the*. |
| 1118 | *hydeward*. So MS, Ri², Mc, Hal, DB, Tr: *hyderward*. |
| 1119 | *shenh*. So MS, Mc, Hal, DB, Tr. Ri²: *shench*.(reads *shenk*). |
| 1131 | *null Ich ibite*. So MS, Ri², Hal, DB. Mc, Tr: *nullich I bite*. |
| 1136 | *beste*. So Ri², Hal, DB, Tr. MS, Mc: *bestee*. |
| 1169 | *hyre*. So MS, Ri², Mc, Hal, Tr. DB: *her*. |
| 1201 | *Hue*. So MS, Ri², Mc, Hal, DB. Tr: *Hoe*. |
| 1211 | *suere*. So MS, Mc, Hal. Ri²: *fuere*. DB, Tr: *swere*. |
| 1230 | *sclavin*. So DB, Tr. MS, Ri², Mc, Hal: *brunie*. |
| 1237 | *froth*. So MS, Mc, DB, Tr. Ri², Hal: *forth*. |
| 1247 | *suithe*. So MS (*suiþe*), Ri², Mc, Hal. DB, Tr: *swiþe*. |
| 1252 | *he*. So MS, Ri², Mc, Hal. DB, Tr: *hue*. |
| 1257 | *suoren*. So MS, Ri², Mc, Hal. DB, Tr: *sworen*. |
| 1259 | *suore*. So MS, Ri², Mc, Hal. DB, Tr: *swore*. |
| 1267 | *suete*. So MS, Ri², Mc, Hal, Tr. DB: *swete*. |
| 1295 | *yynge*. So MS (*ȝynge*), Mc, Hal, DB, Tr. Ri²: *yinge*. |
| 1297 | *shipe*. So MS, Ri², Mc, Hal. DB, Tr: *ship*. |
| 1301 | *croude*. So MS, Mc, Hal, DB, Tr. Ri²: *cronde*. |
| 1302 | *loude*. So MS, Mc, Hal, DB, Tr. Ri²: *londe*. |
| 1303 | *Wythinne*. So MS (*wyþinne*), Mc, Hal, DB, Tr. Ri²: *Withinne*. |

| | |
|---|---|
| 1304 | *bigan.* So MS, Ri², Tr, Hal. Mc, DB: *began.* |
| 1312 | *liggynde.* So MS, Mc, Hal, DB, Tr. Ri²: *liggunde.* |
| 1315 | *knyht.* So MS, Mc, Hal, DB, Tr. Ri²: knyght. |
| 1321 | *thuncheth.* So MS (*þuncheþ*), Mc, Hal, DB, Tr. Ri²: *thinkes.* |
| 1324 | *suerd.* So MS, Ri², Mc, Hal, Tr. DB: *swerd.* |
| 1325 | *knyht.* So MS, Mc, Hal, DB, Tr. Ri²: *knyght.* |
| 1331 | *Sarazyns.* So MS, Mc, Hal, DB, Tr. Ri²: *Sarazynes.* |
| 1332 | After this line DB insert 2 lines from the Oxford version: *God, on wam Y leve, / Tho hue makeden me reve.* |
| 1345 | *Ant slowen.* So MS, Ri², Mc, Hal. DB: *Hue slowen.* Tr: *Ant hue slowen.* |
| 1346 | *Hornes cunesmon.* So MS, Mc, Hal, DB, Tr. Ri²: *Horn es com es mon.* |
| 1348 | *Tuelf.* So MS, Ri², Mc, Hal. DB, Tr: *Twelf.* |
| 1355 | *tueye.* So MS, Ri², Mc, Hal, Tr. DB: *tweye.* |
| 1369 | *Suete.* So MS, Ri², Mc, Hal, Tr. DB: *Swete.* |
| 1382 | *folk.* So MS, Ri², Hal. Mc, DB, Tr: *folc.* |
| 1390 | *The.* So MS (*de þe, de* marked for deletion), Mc, Hal, DB, Tr. Ri²: *De the.* |
| 1398 | *fette.* So MS, Mc, Hal, DB, Tr. Ri²: *sette.* |
| 1417 | *Thus.* So MS (*þus* with *us* abbreviated), Mc, Hal, DB, Tr. Ri²: *Ther.* |
| 1419 | *gan.* So MS, Mc, Hal, DB, Tr. Ri²: *gen.* |
| 1423 | *Rymenild.* So MS, Ri², Mc, Hal, DB. Tr: *Rymenhild.* |
| 1425 | *nyht.* So MS, Mc, Hal, DB, Tr. Ri²: *nyhte.* |
| | *suete.* So MS, Ri², Mc, Hal, Tr. DB: *swete.* |
| 1430 | *adrenche.* So MS, Ri², Mc, Hal, DB. Tr: *drenche.* |
| 1434 | *suerdes.* So MS, Ri², Mc, Hal, Tr. DB: *swerdes.* |
| 1448 | *Ferde.* So MS, Mc, Hal. Ri²: *Sende.* DB, Tr: *Seide.* |
| 1449 | *brhyte.* So MS, Mc, Hal. Ri², DB, Tr: *bryhte.* |
| 1456 | *Rymenildes.* MS, Ri², Mc, Hal, DB, Tr: *Fykenildes.* See explanatory note. |
| 1462 | *Horn.* So Ri², Hal, Mc, DB, Tr. MS: *horns.* |
| 1466 | *abide.* So MS, Mc, Hal, DB, Tr. Ri²: *abyde.* |
| 1467 | *kynges sone.* So MS, Mc, Hal, DB, Tr. Ri²: *kyngsone.* |
| 1470 | *Yweddeth.* So MS (*yweddeþ*), Ri², Mc, Hal, Tr. DB: *Y-wedded.* |
| 1476 | *no.* So MS, Mc, Hal, DB, Tr. Ri²: *na.* |
| 1482 | *toc.* So MS (*toc* or *tot*), Ri², Mc (reads *tot*), Hal, DB, Tr. |
| 1485 | *Oven.* So MS, Mc, Hal, DB, Tr. Ri²: *Onen.* |
| 1486 | *suerde.* So MS, Ri², Mc, Hal, Tr. DB: *swerde.* |
| 1493 | *harpeirs.* So MS, Mc, DB, Tr. Ri², Hal: *harperis.* |
| 1500 | *weylaway.* So MS, Ri², Hal. Mc, DB, Tr: *weylawey.* |
| 1508 | *suorde.* So MS, Ri², Mc, Hal, Tr. DB: *sworde.* |
| 1539 | *com.* So MS, Ri², Mc, Hal, DB. Tr: *corn.* |

# APPENDIX: FULL CONTENTS OF MS HARLEY 2253

**BOOKLET 1 (quires 1–2, Scribe A)**

| | | | |
|---|---|---|---|
| 1. | fols. 1ra–21vb | French verse | The Lives of the Fathers |
| 1a. | fols. 21vb–22ra | French verse | The Story of Thais |

**BOOKLET 2 (quires 3–4, Scribe A)**

| | | | |
|---|---|---|---|
| 2. | fols. 23ra–33rb | French verse | Herman de Valenciennes, The Passion of Our Lord |
| 3. | fols. 33va–39rb | French prose | The Gospel of Nicodemus |
| 3a. | fol. 39rb | French prose | The Letter of Pilate to Tiberias |
| 3b. | fols. 39va–41va | French prose | The Letter of Pilate to Emperor Claudius |
| 4. | fols. 41va–43vb | French prose | The Life of Saint John the Evangelist |
| 5. | fols. 43vb–45vb | French prose | The Life of Saint John the Baptist |
| 6. | fols. 45vb–47vb | French prose | The Life of Saint Bartholomew |
| 7. | fols. 47vb–48vb | French prose | The Passion of Saint Peter |

**BOOKLET 3 (quire 5, Scribes B and C)**

| | | | |
|---|---|---|---|
| 8. | fols. 49r–50v | French verse | ABC of Women |
| 9. | fols. 51ra–52va | French verse | Debate between Winter and Summer |
| 10. | fol. 52va | English prose | How to Make Red Vermilion |
| 11. | fol. 52va | English prose | How to Temper Azure |
| 12. | fol. 52vb | English prose | How to Make Grass-Green |
| 13. | fol. 52vb | English prose | How to Make Another Kind of Green |
| 14. | fol. 52vb | English prose | Another for Yellow-Green |
| 15. | fol. 52vb | English prose | How to Apply Silverfoil |
| 16. | fol. 52vb | English prose | How to Make Iron as Hard as Steel |
| 17. | fol. 52vb | English prose | How to Make White Lead |

**BOOKLET 4 (quire 6, Scribe B)**

| | | | |
|---|---|---|---|
| 18. | fols. 53ra–54vb | Latin prose | The Life of Saint Ethelbert |
| 19. | fol. 54vb | Latin verse | Soul of Christ, Sanctify Me |
| 20. | fol. 55ra–b | French verse | A Goliard's Feast |
| 21. | fols. 55va–56vb | English verse | Harrowing of Hell |
| 22. | fols. 57r–58v | English verse | Debate between Body and Soul |
| 23. | fols. 58v–59r | English verse | A Song of Lewes |
| 24. | fol. 59r–v | French verse | Lament for Simon de Montfort |

| 24a. | fol. 59v | French verse | Carnal Love Is Folly |
| 24a*. | fol. 59v | Latin verse | What Allures Is Momentary |
| 24b. | fol. 59v | English verse | Earth upon Earth |
| 25. | fols. 59v–61v | English verse | The Execution of Sir Simon Fraser |
| 25a. | fol. 61v | English verse | On the Follies of Fashion |
| 26. | fols. 61v–62v | French verse | Lesson for True Lovers |
| 27. | fol. 62v | English verse | The Three Foes of Man |

BOOKLET 5 (quires 7–11, Scribe B)

| 28. | fol. 63r–v | English verse | Annot and John |
| 29. | fol. 63v | English verse | Alysoun |
| 30. | fol. 63v | English verse | The Lover's Complaint |
| 31. | fol. 64r | English verse | Song of the Husbandman |
| 32. | fols. 64va–65vb | English verse | The Life of Saint Marina |
| 33. | fol. 66r | English verse | The Poet's Repentance |
| 34. | fol. 66v | English verse | The Fair Maid of Ribblesdale |
| 35. | fols. 66v–67r | English verse | The Meeting in the Wood |
| 36. | fol. 67r | English verse | A Beauty White as Whale's Bone |
| 37. | fols. 67va–68va | French verse | Gilote and Johane |
| 38. | fols. 68va–70rb | French prose | Pilgrimages in the Holy Land |
| 39. | fol. 70rb–v | French prose | The Pardons of Acre |
| 40. | fols. 70va/71ra/71va | English verse | Satire on the Consistory Courts |
| 41. | fols. 70vb/71rb | English verse | The Laborers in the Vineyard |
| 43. | fol. 71va | English verse | Spring |
| 44. | fols. 71vb–72ra | English verse | Advice to Women |
| 45. | fol. 72ra–va | English verse | An Old Man's Prayer |
| 46. | fols. 72va–73rb | English verse | Blow, Northern Wind |
| 47. | fol. 73r–v | English verse | The Death of Edward I |
| 48. | fols. 73v–74v | English verse | The Flemish Insurrection |
| 49. | fol. 75ra–b | French verse | The Joys of Our Lady |
| 50. | fols. 75rb–va | English verse | Sweet Jesus, King of Bliss |
| 51. | fol. 75va–b | English verse | Jesus Christ, Heaven's King |
| 52. | fol. 75vb | English verse | A Winter Song |
| 53. | fol. 76r | English verse | A Spring Song on the Passion |
| 54. | fol. 76r | French verse | I Pray to God and Saint Thomas |
| 55. | fol. 76r | Trilingual verse | While You Play in Flowers |
| 56. | fols. 76v–77r | French verse | Song on Jesus' Precious Blood |
| 57. | fol. 77va | French verse | Mary, Mother of the Savior |
| 58. | fols. 77vb–78va | English verse | Jesus, Sweet Is the Love of You |
| 59. | fols. 78vb–79rb | French verse | Sermon on God's Sacrifice and Judgment |
| 60. | fol. 79rb–vb | English verse | Stand Well, Mother, under Rood |
| 61. | fol. 79vb | English verse | Jesus, by Your Great Might |
| 62. | fol. 80ra | English verse | I Sigh When I Sing |
| 63. | fol. 80rb | English verse | An Autumn Song |
| 64. | fol. 80v | English verse | The Clerk and the Girl |
| 65. | fols. 80v–81r | English verse | When the Nightingale Sings |
| 66. | fol. 81r–v | English verse | Blessed Are You, Lady |
| 67. | fol. 81va–b | English verse | The Five Joys of the Virgin |
| 68. | fols. 82ra–83r | English verse | Maximian |
| 69. | fol. 83r | French & English verse | Maiden, Mother Mild |

| 70. | fols. 83r–92v | English verse | King Horn |
| 71. | fols. 92v–105r | French prose | Ludlow Scribe, Old Testament Stories |
| 72. | fol. 105va–b | Latin prose | Names of the Books of the Bible |

BOOKLET 6 (quires 12–14, Scribe B)

| 73. | fol. 106r | English verse | God Who Wields All This Might |
| 74. | fols. 106ra–107rb | English verse | The Sayings of Saint Bernard |
| 75. | fols. 107va–109vb | French verse | The Jongleur of Ely and the King of England |
| 75a. | fol. 110ra–va | French verse | The Three Ladies Who Found a Prick |
| 76. | fols. 110vb–111rb | French verse | The Song on Women |
| 77. | fol. 111rb–vb | French verse | The Blame of Women |
| 78. | fol. 112ra–b | French verse | Nicholas Bozon, Women and Magpies |
| 79. | fols. 112rc–113vc | French verse | Urbain the Courteous |
| 80. | fols. 113vb–114v | French verse | Trailbaston |
| 81. | fols. 114v–115r | English verse | The Man in the Moon |
| 82. | fols. 115va–117ra | French verse | The Knight and the Basket |
| 83. | fols. 117ra–118rb | French verse | Against Marriage |
| 84. | fol. 118rb–vb | French verse | The Wager, or The Squire and the Chambermaid |
| 85. | fols. 119ra–121ra | English verse | A Book of Dreaming |
| 86. | fols. 121ra–122va | French verse | The Order of Fair Ease |
| 87. | fols. 122vb–124va | French verse | The Knight Who Made Vaginas Talk |
| 88. | fols. 124va–125r | English verse | Satire on the Retinues of the Great |
| 89. | fols. 125ra–127ra | English verse | Hending |
| 90. | fol. 127rb–va | English prose | The Prophecy of Thomas of Erceldoune |
| 91. | fol. 127va–b | French prose | Distinguishing Features of the Bodily Form of Jesus Christ Our Lord |
| 92. | fol. 128r | English verse | The Way of Christ's Love |
| 93. | fol. 128r–v | English verse | The Way of Woman's Love |
| 94. | fols. 128v–129v | French prose | The Teachings of Saint Louis to His Son Philip |
| 95. | fols. 129v–130v | French prose | The Land of the Saracens |
| 96. | fol. 131r | French prose | Heraldic Arms of Kings |
| 97. | fols. 131v–132r | Latin prose | Letter for Pilgrims on the Relics at Oviedo |
| 98. | fols. 132r–133r | Latin prose | The Legend of Saint Etfrid, Priest of Leominster |
| 99. | fol. 133v | French & Latin prose | Prayer for Protection |

BOOKLET 7 (quire 15, Scribe B)

| 100. | fol. 134r | French prose | Occasions for Angels |
| 101. | fol. 134r | French prose | Occasions for Psalms in French |
| 102. | fol. 134v | French verse | Glory to God in the Highest in French |
| 103. | fol. 134v | Latin prose | Prayer of Confession |
| 104. | fol. 134v–135r | French verse & prose | Prayer on the Five Joys of Our Lady |
| 105. | fol. 135r | Latin prose | Prayer for Contrition |
| 106. | fol. 135r | French prose | Reasons for Fasting on Friday |
| 107. | fol. 135r | French prose | Seven Masses to Be Said in Misfortune |

| 108. | fol. 135v | French prose | Seven Masses in Honor of God and Saint Giles |
| 108a. | fol. 135v | French prose | Prayer to the Three Kings |
| 109. | fols. 135v–136r | Latin prose | All the World's a Chess Board |
| 109a. | fol. 136r | French prose | Three Prayers That Never Fail |
| 110. | fol. 136r–v | Latin prose | Occasions for Psalms in Latin |
| 111. | fols. 136v–137r | French prose | Occasions for Psalms Ordained by Saint Hilary of Poitiers |
| 112. | fol. 137r | Latin prose | Heliotrope and Celandine |
| 113. | fol. 137r–v | Latin prose | Saint Anselm's Questions to the Dying |
| 114. | fols. 137v–138v | French & Latin verse | Against the King's Taxes |
| 115. | fols. 138v–140r | French prose | Seven Hours of the Passion of Jesus Christ |
| 116. | fol. 140v | Latin prose | The Martyrdom of Saint Wistan |

**VOLUME 2: INDEX OF FIRST LINES**

This index lists first lines, titles, and incipits. Titles that differ from the first line or incipit are in italics.

|  | *Page* |
|---|---|
| *ABC a femmes* [art. 8] | 18 |
| *ABC of Women* [art. 8] | 19 |
| *Advice to Women* [art. 44] | 197 |
| Alle herkneth to me nou [art. 21] | 66 |
| Alle that beoth of huerte trewe [art. 47] | 210 |
| *Alysoun* [art. 29] | 123 |
| *Autumn Song, An* [art. 63] | 273 |
| Anima Christi, sanctifica me [art. 19] | 58 |
| *Annot and John* [art. 28] | 121 |
| *Another for Yellow-Green* [art. 14] | 49 |
| Ase Y me rod this ender day [art. 67] | 280 |
| *Beauty White as Whale's Bone, A* [art. 36] | 151 |
| *Blessed Are You, Lady* [art. 66] | 279 |
| Blessed be thou, Levedy [art. 66] | 278 |
| *Blow, Northern Wind* [art. 46] | 205 |
| Blow, northerne wynd [art. 46] | 204 |
| Bytuene Mersh ant Averil [art. 29] | 122 |
| *Carnal Love Is Folly* [art. 24a] | 97 |
| Ces sunt les pardouns de Acres [art. 39] | 184 |
| Ces sunt les pelrinages communes [art. 38] | 172 |
| Charnel amour est folie [art. 24a] | 96 |
| Chaunter m'estoit [art. 24] | 88 |
| *Clerk and the Girl, The* [art. 64] | 277 |
| Cyl qe vodra oyr mes chauns [art. 26] | 112 |
| *De l'Yver et de l'Esté* [art. 9] | 34 |
| *Death of Edward I, The* [art. 47] | 211 |
| *Debate between Body and Soul* [art. 22] | 79 |
| *Debate between Winter and Summer* [art. 9] | 35 |
| *Dulcis Jesu memoria* [art. 58] | 246 |
| Dum ludis floribus [art. 55] | 234 |
| *Earth upon Earth* [art. 24b] | 97 |
| En may par une matyné, s'en ala juer [art. 37] | 156 |
| *Enseignement sur les amis* [art. 26] | 112 |

| | *Page* |
|---|---|
| Erthe toc of erthe [art. 24b] | 96 |
| *Execution of Sir Simon Fraser, The* [art. 25] | 99 |
| *Fair Maid of Ribblesdale, The* [art. 34] | 145 |
| Ferroy chaunsoun [art. 54] | 232 |
| *Five Joys of the Virgin, The* [art. 67] | 281 |
| *Flemish Insurrection, The* [art. 48] | 215 |
| *Geste of Kyng Horn, The* [art. 70] | 300 |
| *Gilote and Johane* [art. 37] | 157 |
| *Gilote e Johane* [art. 37] | 156 |
| Gloriosus ac summo regi acceptus rex Ethelbertus [art. 18] | 50 |
| *Goliard's Feast, A* [art. 20] | 59 |
| *Harrowing of Hell* [art. 21] | 67 |
| Her bygynneth the Geste of Kyng Horn [art. 70] | 300 |
| Herketh hideward ant beoth stille [art. 32] | 130 |
| Herkne to my ron [art. 68] | 284 |
| Heye Louerd, thou here my bone [art. 45] | 198 |
| *How to Apply Silverfoil* [art. 15] | 49 |
| *How to Make Another Kind of Green* [art. 13] | 49 |
| *How to Make Grass-Green* [art. 12] | 49 |
| *How to Make Iron as Hard as Steel* [art. 16] | 51 |
| *How to Make Red Vermilion* [art. 10] | 47 |
| *How to Make White Lead* [art. 17] | 51 |
| *How to Temper Azure* [art. 11] | 47 |
| *I Pray to God and Saint Thomas* [art. 54] | 233 |
| *I Sigh When I Sing* [art. 62] | 271 |
| I syke when Y singe [art. 62] | 270 |
| Ich herde men upo mold [art. 31] | 128 |
| Ichot a burde in a bour ase beryl so bryht [art. 28] | 120 |
| Ichot a burde in boure bryht [art. 46] | 204 |
| In a fryht as Y con fare fremede [art. 35] | 148 |
| In a thestri stude Y stode a lutel strif to here [art. 22] | 78 |
| In May hit murgeth when hit dawes [art. 44] | 196 |
| Incipit vita sancti Ethelberti [art. 18] | 50 |
| Jesu Crist, heovene kyng [art. 51] | 228 |
| Jesu, for thi muchele miht [art. 61] | 266 |
| Jesu, suete is the love of the [art. 58] | 246 |
| *Jesus, by Your Great Might* [art. 61] | 267 |
| *Jesus Christ, Heaven's King* [art. 51] | 229 |
| *Jesus, Sweet Is the Love of You* [art. 58] | 247 |
| *Joys of Our Lady, The* [art. 49] | 223 |
| *King Horn* [art. 70] | 301 |
| *Laborers in the Vineyard, The* [art. 41] | 193 |
| *Lament for Simon de Montfort* [art. 24] | 89 |
| Lenten ys come with love to toune [art. 43] | 194 |
| *Les pardouns de Acres* [art. 39] | 184 |
| *Les pelrinages communes que crestiens fount en la Seinte Terre* [art. 38] | 172 |

| | Page |
|---|---|
| *Lesson for True Lovers* [art. 26] | 113 |
| *Life of Saint Ethelbert, The* [art. 18] | 51 |
| *Life of Saint Marina, The* [art. 32] | 131 |
| Lord that lenest us lyf [art. 25a] | 108 |
| *Lover's Complaint, The* [art. 30] | 127 |
| Lustneth, lordinges, bothe yonge ant olde [art. 48] | 214 |
| Lystneth, lordynges! A newe song Ichulle bigynne [art. 25] | 98 |
| *Maiden, Mother Mild* [art. 69] | 297 |
| Marie, mere al Salveour [art. 57] | 244 |
| Marie, pur toun enfaunt [art. 49] | 222 |
| *Mary, Mother of the Savior* [art. 57] | 245 |
| *Maximian* [art. 68] | 285 |
| Mayden, moder milde [art. 69] | 296 |
| *Meeting in the Wood, The* [art. 35] | 149 |
| Middelerd for mon wes mad [art. 27] | 116 |
| Momentaneum est quod delectat [art. 24a*] | 96 |
| Most I ryden by Rybbesdale [art 34] | 144 |
| My deth Y love, my lyf Ich hate [art. 64] | 276 |
| Ne mai no lewed lued libben in londe [art. 40] | 188 |
| Nou skrinketh rose ant lylie-flour [art. 63] | 272 |
| Of a mon Matheu thohte [art. 41] | 192 |
| *Old Man's Prayer, An* [art. 45] | 199 |
| *On the Follies of Fashion* [art. 25a] | 109 |
| *Pardons of Acre, The* [art. 39] | 185 |
| *Pilgrimages in the Holy Land* [art. 38] | 173 |
| *Poet's Repentance, The* [art. 33] | 141 |
| Quant fu en ma juvente [art. 56] | 236 |
| Quant voy la revenue l'yver [art. 20] | 58 |
| Quy a la Dame de parays [art. 8] | 18 |
| *Satire on the Consistory Courts* [art. 40] | 189 |
| *Sermon on God's Sacrifice and Judgment* [art. 59] | 259 |
| Sitteth alle stille ant herkneth to me [art. 23] | 86 |
| *Song of the Husbandman* [art. 31] | 129 |
| *Song on Jesus' Precious Blood* [art. 56] | 237 |
| *Song of Lewes, A* [art. 23] | 87 |
| *Soul of Christ, Sanctify Me* [art. 19] | 59 |
| *Spring* [art. 43] | 195 |
| *Spring Song on the Passion, A* [art. 53] | 231 |
| *Stand Well, Mother, under Rood* [art. 60] | 265 |
| Stond wel, moder, under rode [art. 60] | 264 |
| Suete Jesu, king of blysse [art. 50] | 224 |
| *Sweet Jesus, King of Bliss* [art. 50] | 225 |
| Tac a vessel of eorthe [art. 17] | 50 |
| Tac argul [art. 16] | 50 |
| Tac brasyl [art. 10] | 46 |
| Tac gumme arabuk [art. 15] | 48 |

|  | *Page* |
|---|---|
| Tac jus of a rotet appel [art. 13] | 48 |
| Tac peniwort [art. 14] | 48 |
| Tac verdigres [art. 12] | 48 |
| *Three Foes of Man, The* [art. 27] | 117 |
| Un grant estrif oy l'autrer [art. 9] | 34 |
| Une petite parole [art. 59] | 258 |
| Vorte couche selverfoyl [art. 15] | 48 |
| Vorte make cynople [art. 10] | 46 |
| Vorte make gras-grene [art. 12] | 48 |
| Vorte maken another maner grene [art. 13] | 48 |
| Vorte maken blankplum [art. 17] | 50 |
| Vorte maken iren as hart as stel [art. 16] | 50 |
| Vorte temprene asure [art. 11] | 46 |
| *Wayle whyt ase whalles bon, A* [art. 36] | 150 |
| Weping haveth myn wonges wet [art. 33] | 140 |
| *What Allures Is Momentary* [art. 24a*] | 97 |
| When Y se blosmes springe [art. 53] | 230 |
| *When the Nightingale Sings* [art. 65] | 279 |
| When the nyhtegale singes [art. 65] | 278 |
| *While You Play in Flowers* [art. 55] | 235 |
| *Winter Song, A* [art. 52] | 229 |
| With longyng Y am lad [art. 30] | 126 |
| Wose wole of love be trewe, do lystne me [art. 36] | 150 |
| Wynter wakeneth al my care [art. 52] | 228 |
| Yef thin asure is fine [art. 11] | 46 |
| Yet for gaude-grene [art. 14] | 48 |

**VOLUME 2: INDEX OF MANUSCRIPTS CITED**

**Bern**

Burgerbibliothek cod. 354   379 (art. 20)

**Cambridge**

CCC MS 308   377–78 (art. 18)
CUL Addit. MS 4407, art. 19   427 (art. 47)
CUL MS Gg.1.1   427 (art. 47)
CUL MS Gg.4.27.2   448–54 (art. 70)
CUL MS Gg.5.35 (*Cambridge Songs* MS)   1 n. 1 (intro)
St. John's College MS 111   438 (art. 60)
St. John's College MS N. 16   1 n. 1 (intro)
St. John's College MS N. 17   1 n. 1 (intro)
Trinity College MS B.14.39   382 (art. 22)

**Dublin**

Trinity College MS 201   438 (art. 60)
Trinity College MS 347 (C.5.8)   385 (art. 24)

**Edinburgh**

NLS MS Advocates 18.7.21 (Grimestone MS)   388 (art. 24b)
NLS MS Advocates 19.2.1 (Auchinleck MS)   1 n. 1 (intro); 372 (art. 8); 380 (art. 21)

**Glasgow**

University of Glasgow MS Hunterian 512   436 (art. 58)

**London**

BL MS Add. 46919 (Herebert MS)   12 n. 34 (intro); 387 (art. 24a)
BL MS Cotton Nero A.x (*Pearl* MS)   1 n. 1 (intro)
BL MS Cotton Vitellius A.xv (*Beowulf* MS)   1 n. 1 (intro)
BL MS Egerton 613   443 (art. 66)
BL MS Harley 273   9 (intro); 395 (art. 26); 448 (art. 70)
BL MS Harley 913 (Kildare MS)   1 n. 1 (intro); 387–88 (art. 24b)
BL MS Harley 978   383 (art. 23)
BL MS Royal 2.F.8   433 (art. 53)
BL MS Royal 8.F.2   438 (art. 60)
BL MS Royal 12.C.12   4 n. 13, 9, 9 n. 22, 10, 11 (intro); 410 (art. 37); 448 (art. 70)
BL MS Royal 12.E.1   438 (art. 60)

**Marquess of Bath, Longleat House, Wiltshire**
MS Longleat 26   395 (art. 26)

**Oxford**
Bodl. MS Ashmole 61   1 n. 1, 8 (intro)
Bodl. MS Digby 2   439–40 (art. 62)
Bodl. MS Digby 86   9 (intro); 380 (art. 21); 381 (art. 22); 395 (art. 26); 431 (art. 50); 438 (art. 60); 444–45 (art. 68)
Bodl. MS Douce 137   387 (art. 24a)
Bodl. MS Douce 302 (Audelay MS)   1 n. 1 (intro)
Bodl. MS Eng. Poet. A.1 (Vernon MS)   1 n. 1 (intro); 402 (art. 32); 436 (art. 58)
Bodl. MS Laud Misc. 108   448, 450–54 (art. 70)
Corpus Christi College MS 154   395 (art. 26)

# VOLUME 2: INDEX OF PROPER NAMES

This index lists proper names found in the articles of MS Harley 2253. Each entry is listed by variant spellings (if any), article number, and line. Translated forms are indicated by italic font. Excluded from this list are terms for God ("Creatour," "Crist," "Dieu," "Jesu," "Salveour," etc.), terms for Mary ("Marie," Nostre Dame," etc.), and titles ("Child," "cuens," "Bisshop," "E(o)rl," "Kyng," "Seint(e)," etc.).

**Aaron** (*Aaron*): art. 38.44

**Abakuc** (*Habakkuk*): art. 38.13

**Abel**. *See* Johan Abel

**Abraham, Habraham** (*Abraham*): art. 18.56; art. 21; art. 38.114. *See also* Seint Habraham

**Absolon** (*Absolon*): art. 68.14

**Acheldemac** (*Field of Blood*): art. 38.73

**Acres** (*Acre*): art. 38.2, 155; art. 39. 1, 43; art. 48.71

**Adam** (*Adam*): art. 8.112; art. 21; art. 37.34; art. 38.112, 116; art. 59.6; art. 60.14

*Age*. *See* Elde

**Alemaigne, Alemayne** (*Germany*): art. 23.2, 9, 17, 25, 28

**Alemayns [Acre]** (*Germans, [Church and Hospital of St. Mary of the]*): art. 39.4

**Allof** (*Allof*): art. 70.4, 33, 73

**Alysoun** (*Alysoun*): art. 29.12, 24, 36, 48

**Amour**. *See* Dieu d'Amour; Love

**André** (*Andrew*): art. 38.8, 134. *See also* Seint André [Acre]; Seint Andre, Bisshop of

*Anger*. *See* Onde

**Anglie** (*Anglia*): art. 18.23, 31

**Anglorum** (*Angles*): art. 18.2, 3, 9

**Anne** (*Anne*): art. 38.146. *See also* Seint Anne [Acre]; Seint Anne [Jerusalem]

**Annote, Anote (riddle)** (*Annot*): art. 28.28, 29

**Annunciacioun** (*Annunciation*): art. 38.138

**Antoyne**. *See* Seint Antoyne [Acre]

*April*. *See* Averil

**Aquarum**. *See* Puteus Aquarum

**Architelin** (*Architelin*): art. 38.149

**Arnoldyn** (*Arnoldin*): art. 70.1463, 1513

**Artois, Artoys** (*Artois*): art. 48.51, 89

**Asseles** (*Asceila*): art. 25.218

**Athelbrus** (*Athelbrus*): art. 70

**Athulf** (*Athulf*): art. 70

**Athyld** (*Athild*): art. 70.767, 830

**Ave Maria** (*Ave Maria*): art. 8.309

**Averil, Averyl** (*April*): art. 29.1; art. 65.2

**Aylmer(e), Eylmer, Aylmare** (*Aylmer*): art. 70

*Aymer de Valence*. *See* Emer de Valence

*Bait Nuba*. *See* Betynoble

**Baltazar** (*Balthazar*): art. 38.107

**Baptist**. *See* Johan (the Baptist)

**Bartholomeu**. *See* Seint Bartholomeu [Acre]; Seint Bartholomeus Masse

**Baruth** (*Beirut*): art. 38.168

Basque (*Sebaste*): art. 38.123
*Beautiful. See* Speciouse
Bebie (*Tiberias*): art. 38.131
Beda (*Bede*): art. 18.2
Bedlehem, Bedleheem (*Bethlehem*): art. 38.102, 106; art. 50.15
Bedlehem [Acre] (*Bethlehem, [Hospital of the Brothers and/or Sisters of]*): art. 39.21
*Beirut. See* Baruth
Beryld (*Berild*): art. 70.768, 769, 777, 789, 797, 829
Bethanye (*Bethany*): art. 38.93
*Bethlehem. See* Bedlehem.
Bethphage (*Bethphage*): art. 38.89
Betynoble (*Bait Nuba*): art. 38.15
Bigot. *See* Hue de Bigot
*Blood, Field of. See* Acheldemac
Boc. *See* Bok(e)
Body (*Body*): art. 22
Bok(e), Boc (*Book, Bible*): art. 33.4. *See also* Byble; escripture
Boloyne (*Bologne*): art. 48.65
*Book. See* Bok(e)
Boylloun. *See* Godefroy de Boylloun
Boys. *See* Seint Johan de Boys
Bretons. *See* Seint Martin de Bretons [Acre]
*Brigid. See* Seinte Bryde [Acre]
Britanniam (*Britain*); art. 18.9
*Brithfrid. See* Brythfrid(us)
*Bruce. See* Robert the Bruyts
Bruges (*Bruges*): art. 48.11, 35, 95
Bruyts. *See* Robert the Bruyts
Bryde. *See* Seinte Bryde [Acre]
Brythfrid(us) (*Brithfrid*): art. 18.115
Byble (*Bible*) art. 37.147. *See also* Bok(e); escripture
Byrne (*Byrne*): art. 28.44

*Caesarea. See* Cesarie
*Caiaphas. See* Pretorie Cayphas
*Caithness. See* Catenas
Calvarie: art. 22.88. *See also* Mount Calvarie
*Cana Galilee. See* Cane Galylee
Cananee (*Canaanite*): art. 38.166

*Candlemas Day. See* Chandelour
Cane Galylee (*Cana Galilee*): art. 38.148
*Canterbury. See* Caunterbyr
Carme (*Carmel*): art. 38.3, 4
Carnarvan (*Carnarvon*). *See* Edward [II]
Caryout (*Chariton*): art. 38.36
Catenas (*Caithness*): art. 63.34
Caunterbyr (*Canterbury*): art. 24.41
Cave (*Cave [of Adam]*): art. 38.116
Cave (*Cave [of Our Lady]*): art. 38.8
Cave Galygant (*Gallicant Cave*): art. 38.70
Cave Seynt Elye (*St. Elijah's Cave*): art. 38.3
*Cayphas. See* Pretorie Cayphas
Cesarie (*Caesarea*): art. 38.11
Champ Flory (*Field of Flowers*): art. 38.103
Chandelour (*Candlemas Day*): art. 38.40
Chapele (*Chapel [of St. Habakkuk]*): art. 38.13
Chapele (*Chapel [of St. John the Baptist]*): art. 38.59
Chapele Gryffoune (*Griffin Chapel*): art. 38.33
*Chariton. See* Caryout
Charles [IV] of Fraunce (*Charles of France*): art. 25.227
Chastiel Magdalon (*Magdalen Castle*) art. 38.136
Chastiel Pelryn (*Pilgrims' Castle*): art. 38.6–7
Cheepe (*Cheapside*): art. 25.181
Chevalers. *See* Lazer de Chevalers [Acre]; Nostre Dame de Chevalers [Acre]
*Christendom. See* Cristendome
*Christian(s). See* Cristene
*Christmas. See* Cristesmasse; Noal
*Church. See* Eglyse; seint Eglise
*Church, Holy. See* seint Eglise
*Church of St. Chariton. See* Eglise Seint Caryout

*Church of St. Nicholas*. *See* Eglise Seint Nycholas

*Church of St. Saffran*. *See* Eglise de Seint Soffroun

*Church of the Holy Savior*. *See* Eglise de Seint Salveour [Jerusalem]; Eglise de Seint Salveour [Sidon]

**Cleophas** (*Cleophas*): art. 38.16

**Clerk (speaker)** (*Clerk*): art. 64

**Coloyne** (*Cologne*): art. 48.70

**Conyng, (Peter)** (*Coning, (Peter)*): art. 48.19, 69, 90

*Coquet*. *See* Koket

**Coveytise** (*Covetousness*): art. 45.58

**Cradoc** (*Cradoc*): art. 28.47

**Cristendome** (*Christendom*): art. 47.16, 48

**Cristene, Cristine** (*Christian(s)*): art. 37.120, 141; art. 70.185, 188, 190, 840, 1329

**Cristesmasse** (*Christmas*): art. 67.32; art. 70.805. *See also* Noal

**Crois**. *See* Holy Crois; seinte Croyz

*Croyland*. *See* Cruland

**Croyz**. *See* Holy Crois; seinte Croyz; Seinte Croyz [Acre]

**Cruland** (*Croyland*): art. 18.106

*Cynedrida*. *See* Kynedryda

**David, Davyd** (*David*): art. 21.19, 197, 203

*David's Tower*. *See* Tour David

**Denys**. *See* Seint Denys [Acre]

**Despencer**. *See* Hue le . . . Despencer

**Deth** (*Death*): art. 45.86; art. 47.3, 7

**Devel** (*Devil*): art. 21.7; art. 25a.43. *See also* Enymy; Fend; Fo; Lucifer; Sathan

**Dieu d'Amour** (*God of Love*): art. 55.2. *See also* Love

**digmange** (*Sunday*): art. 39.28. *See also* Sonneday

**Domesday, Domesdai** (*Doomsday*): art. 21.128, 148, 238; art. 22.50; art. 27.6; art. 61.26

*Dominicans*. *See* Frere Prechours

**Donbar** (*Dunbar*): art. 25.31

*Doomsday*. *See* Domesday

*Double Cave*. *See* Spelunca Dupplici

**Dovere** (*Dover*): art. 23.59

*Dublin*. *See* Dyvelyn

**Dunbar**. *See* Donbar

**Dunprest** (*Dunprest*): art. 33.margin

*Dupplici*. *See* Spelunca Dupplici

**Dyvelyn** (*Dublin*): art. 63.34

*East Anglia*. *See* Estanglia

*Easter*. *See* Ester; Pasche

*Eastness*. *See* Estnesse

**Edward [I]** (*Edward*): art. 23.57, 62; art. 24.29; art. 25.25, 41, 233 (longe shonkes); art. 37.345; art. 47

**Edward [II] of Carnarvan** (*Edward of Carnarvon*): art. 25.81; art. 47.73. *See also* Walis

**Egipciene** (*Egyptian*): art. 38.34

**Eglan** (*Eglan*): art. 18.24

**Eglise**. *See* seint Eglise

**Eglise** (*Church [of St. Peter and St. John]*): art. 38.128

**Eglise de Seint Salveour [Gethsemane]** (*Church of the Holy Savior*): art. 38.78–79

**Eglise de Seint Salveour [Sidon]** (*Church of the Holy Savior*): art. 38.165

**Eglise de Seint Soffroun** (*Church of St. Saffran*): art. 38.151

**Eglise Seint Caryout** (*Church of St. Chariton*): art. 38.36

**Eglise Seint Nycholas** (*Church of St. Nicholas*): art. 38.153

**Eglyse** (*Church [of St. James]*): art. 38.60

**Egmund(us)** (*Egmund*): art. 18.122

*Egyptian*. *See* Egipciene

**Elde** (*Age*): art. 68

**Eleyne** (*Helena*): art. 38.32

*Elfrida*. *See* Elphryda

*Elijah*. *See* Elye

**Elphryda** (*Elfrida*): art. 18.35, 74, 103

**Elye** (*Elijah*): art. 38.163. *See also* Cave Seynt Elye; Seinte Elye

Emaus (*Emmaus*): art. 38.16

Emer de Valence (*Aymer de Valence*):
art. 25.82

*Emmaus*. *See* Emaus

*England*. *See* Engletere; Englond

Englesshe, Englysshe (*English*): art.
25.76; art. 38.89

Engletere (*England*): art. 24.12; art.
37.338; art. 38.172

Englond, Engelond(e) (*England*):
art. 23.35; art. 25.75, 182, 226;
art. 47.9, 21, 38, 74, 79

*Envy*. *See* Nithe

Enymy (*Enemy*): art. 56.143, 146. *See
also* Devel; Fend; Fo; Lucifer;
Sathan

Epyphany (*Epiphany*): art. 67.38

Ermenild, Ermenyld (*Ermenild*): art.
70.917, 1538

escripture, escriptour, escrit
(*Scripture*): art. 37.119, 136; art.
59.9. *See also* Bok(e); Byble

Espyrit. *See* Seint Espyrit

Estanglia, Esstanglia, Estanglie (*East
Anglia*): art. 18.2, 18, 56

Esté (*Summer*): art. 9. *See also*
Somere, Kyng of

Ester: art. 67.44. *See also* Pasche

Estevene. *See* Stevene

Estnesse (*Eastness*): art. 70.954

Ethelbertus (*Ethelbert*): art. 18

Ethelredus (*Ethelred*): art. 18.4, 28, 88

Eufemie (*Euphemia*): art. 38.7

*Evangelist*. *See* Johan (le Ewangelie)

Eve (*Eve*): art. 8.112; art. 21; art.
59.10

*Eve's Sepulcher*. *See* Sepulture Eve

Ewangelie (*Evangelist*). *See* Johan (le
Ewangelie)

Eylmer. *See* Aylmer(e)


Falsshipe (*Falsehood*): art. 31.32

Fend (*Fiend*): art. 27.62; art. 32.13;
art. 50.28; art. 63.20. *See also*
Devel; Enymy; Fo; Lucifer; Sathan

*Field of Blood*. *See* Acheldemac

*Field of Flowers*. *See* Champ Flory

*Fiend*. *See* Fend

*Fikenild*. *See* Fykenyld

Flaundres (*Flanders*): art. 48.10, 81,
130, 131

Fleish, Fleyshe (*Flesh*): art. 22.97;
art. 27.30

Flem(m)isshe, Flem(m)ysshe
(*Flemish*): art. 48

*Flesh*. *See* Fleish

Floyres (*Floyres*): art. 28.46

Flum Jordan (*River Jordan*) art.
21.208; art. 38.99

Fo (*Foe*): art. 42.53. *See also* Devel;
Enymy; Fend; Lucifer; Sathan

Fonteyne de Seint Gabriel (*Well of St.
Gabriel*): art. 38.140

*France*. *See* Fraunc(e)

*Franciscans*. *See* Frere Menours

*Fraser*. *See* Symond Frysel

Fraunc(e) (*France*): art. 25.204; art.
38.171; art. 48

Fraunce, Kyng of (*France, King of*):
art. 47.33; art. 48. *See also* Charles
[IV] of Fraunce; Phelip [IV]

Frens(s)he, Freinsshe, Vrenshe,
fraunceis (*French*): art. 9.97,
106; art. 48.2, 7, 78, 81, 131. *See
also* romauns

Frere Menours [Acre] (*Friars Minor,
[House of the]*): art. 39.39

Frere Prechours [Acre] (*Preaching
Friars, [Church of the]*): art. 39.24

Freres de Sack [Acre] (*Friars of the
Sack, [House of the]*): art. 39.26

Frisel, Frysel. *See* Symond Frysel

Fykeles (*Fikenild's*): art. 70.1256

Fykenyld, Fikenild (*Fikenild*): art. 70


Gabbe (*Gossip*): art. 45.57, 73

Gabriel (*Gabriel*): art. 67.26. *See also*
Fonteyne de Seint Gabriel

*Gallicant Cave*. *See* Cave Galygant

Galylee. *See* Mer de Galylee

Gaste. *See* Gost

*Gate*. *See* Jerusalem; Parays; Porte;
Porte Orryene; Speciouse

*Gatekeeper*. *See* Ianitor

George (*George*): art. 38.14. *See also*
　　Seint George [Acre]
*Germans. See* Alemayns
*Germany. See* Alemaigne
*Gethsemane. See* Jessemany
*Giles. See* Gyle
Gilote (*Gilote*): art. 37
Girl (*Girl*) (speaker): art. 64
*Giwz. See* Gyw(s)
Glascou (*Glasgow*): art. 25.49
Glotonie (*Gluttony*): art. 45.53
Gloucestre (*Gloucester*): art. 24.66
*Gluttony. See* Glotonie
Godefroy de Boylloun (*Godfrey of
　　Bouillon*): art. 38.28
Godild, Godyld, Godylt (*Godild*):
　　art. 70.7, 72, 75, 152, 1370
Godmod (*Godmod*): art. 70
*Golden Gate. See* Porte Orryene
Golgatha (*Golgotha*): art. 38.26
*Gossip. See* Gabbe
Gost, Gaste (*Soul*): art. 22
*Griffin Chapel. See* Chapele Gryffoune
*Guile. See* Gyle
Gwynbertus (*Gwinbert*): art. 18.86,
　　99, 100
Gyle (*Giles*): art. 70.1179. *See also*
　　Seint Gyle [Acre]
Gyle (*Guile*): art. 45.57
Gyw(s), Giwz (*Jew(s)*): art. 38.9, 142,
　　169, 170; art. 59.108; art. 69.22

*Habakkuk. See* Abakuc
Habraham. *See* Abraham
Hebreus (*Hebrew*): art. 38.91
*Helena. See* Eleyne
Henri (*Henry [de Montfort]*): art.
　　24.61
Henry [III] (*Henry*): art. 37.346
Herbert of Morham (*Herbert of
　　Morham*): art. 25.129
Hereford. *See* Wye
Hermon. *See* Mount Hermon
Hilde (*Hilde*): art. 28.48
Hobbe, Kyng (*Hob, King*): art. 25.73
*Holy Church. See* seint Eglise
Holy Crois (*Holy Cross*): art. 47.63.

*See also* seinte Croyz
Holy Londe (*Holy Land*): art. 47.36,
　　39. *See also* Seinte Terre
*Holy Savior. See* Eglise de Seint Salveor
*Holy Sepulcher. See* Seint Sepulc(h)re;
　　Sepulcre
*Holy Spirit. See* Seint Espyrit
Horn (*Horn*): art. 70
Hospital Seint Johan [Jerusalem]
　　(*Hospital of St. John [the
　　Baptist]*): art. 38.35
Hospital Seint Johan [Acre] (*Hospital
　　of St. John [the Baptist, Church
　　of]*): art. 39.27
Hue de Bigot (*Hugh of Bigot*): art.
　　23.50
Hue le . . . Despencer (*Hugh [the]
　　Despenser*): art. 24.55–56

Ianitor (*Gatekeeper*): art. 21.141
*India. See* Ynde
Innocens (*Innocents*): art. 38.109
*Ireland. See* Yrlaund
*Irish. See* Yrisshe
*Irishmen. See* Yrisshemenne
Irlond. *See* Yrlaund
*Isaac. See* Ysaac
*Isaiah. See* Ysaye
Iunius (*June*): art. 18.113

Jacob (*Jacob*): art. 38.41, 114. *See also*
　　Puytz Jacob
*Jacob's Well. See* Puytz Jacob
*Jacques. See* Jakes
*Jaffa. See* Japhet
*Jake. See* Jame
Jakes (de Seint Poul) (*Jacques (de St.
　　Pol)*): art. 48.33, 45, 61
Jame (*James*): art. 38.61, 152; art.
　　48.126. *See also* Peroun Seint Jake
Japhet (*Jaffa*): art. 38.12
Jaspar (*Jaspar*): art. 38.107
*Jehoshaphat. See* Josaphat [Acre]; Val
　　de Josaphat
Jerico (*Jericho*): art. 38.98
Jerusalem (*Jerusalem*): art. 38; art.
　　47.65

**Jerusalem** (*Jerusalem*) (**gate**): art. 38.48

**Jessemany** (*Gethsemane*): art. 38.77

*Jew(s)*. *See* Gyw(s)

**Joachyn** (*Joachim*): art. 49.39

**Johan** (**le Ewangelie**) (*John (the Evangelist)*): art. 32.96, 178; art. 38.45 (le Ewangelie), 46, 90, 129, 151; art. 56.161; art. 62.38

**Johan** (**the Baptist, le Baptistre**) (*John (the Baptist)*): art. 21.21, 207, 219; art. 38.5, 59–60 (bouche orriene), 99, 119, 123

**Johan Abel** (*John Abel*): art. 25.149

**Johan de Boys**. *See* Seint Johan de Boys

**Johan de Tyr**. *See* Seint Johan de Tyr

**Johan Jose** (*John Jose*): art. 25.108

**Johan of Lyndeseye** (*John of Lindesay*): art. 25.99

**Johane** (*Johane*): art. 37

*John*. *See* Johan, Johon

*John of the Woods*. *See* Seint Johan de Boys

*John of Tyre*. *See* Seint Johan de Tyr

**Johon, Jon** (**lyric speaker**) (*John*): art. 28.30, 50

*Joie*. *See* Mont Joie

**Jonas** (*Jonas*): art. 28.50

**Jordan**. *See* Flum Jordan

**Josaphat**. *See* Val de Josaphat

**Josaphat [Acre]** (*Jehoshaphat, [Abbey Church of St. Mary of the Valley of]*): art. 39.16

*Jose*. *See* Johan Jose

*Joy*. *See* Mont Joie

**Judas** (*Judas*): art. 22.96; art. 69.17

*June*. *See* Iunius.

**Katerine [Acre]** (*Katherine [of the Battlefield, Hospital of St.]*): art. 39.31

*Kirkencliff*. *See* Kyrkenclyf

**Koket** (*Coquet*): art. 38.155

**Kynedryda** (*Cynedrida*): art. 18.36, 73

**Kyng**. *See specific name*

**Kyng of Fraunce**. *See* Fraunce, Kyng of

**Kyrkenclyf** (*Kirkencliff*): art. 25.91

**Latyne [Acre]** (*Latin, [Abbey Church of St. Mary]*): art. 39.17

**Latyne [Jerusalem]** (*Latin, [Abbey Church of St. Mary]*): art. 38.36

*Laurence*. *See* Seint Lorenz [Acre]

**Lawe** (*Law*): art. 31.23. *See also* Olde Lawe

**Lazer** (*Lazarus*): art. 38.93. *See also* Lazer de Chevelers [Acre]; Seint Lazer de Bethayne [Acre]

**Lazer de Chevalers [Acre]** (*Lazarus of the Knights, [Church and Hospital of St.]*): art. 39.35

**Lecherie** (*Lechery*): art. 45.56

*Leicester*. *See* Leycestre

**Lentre, Lenten** (*Lent*): art. 20.111; art. 43.1

**Leofruna** (*Leofruna*): art. 18.4, 37

**Leonard**. *See* Seint Leonard [Acre]

**Leycestre** (*Leicester*): art. 44.30

**Leycestre, cuens de** (*Leicester, Earl of*): art. 24.63. *See also* Simond de Mountfort

*Liar*. *See* Lyare

*Lincoln*. *See* Lyncolne

*Lindsey*. *See* Johan of Lyndeseye; Lyndeseye

*Littlecloth*. *See* Poydras

**Londe**. *See* Holy Londe

**Londone, Loundres** (*London*): art. 9.161; art. 25.114. *See also* Londone Brugge; Tour (of Londone)

**Londone Brugge** (*London Bridge*): art. 25.10, 188, 195

**Lone** (*Lune*): art. 28.33

**Lorenz**. *See* Seint Lorenz [Acre]

**Lounde** (*Lounde*): art. 44.30; art. 65.17

**Loundres**. *See* Londone

**Love** (*Love*): art. 46.73, 85, 97. *See also* Dieu d'Amour

**Lucifer** (*Lucifer*): art. 9.230, 238; art. 59.45. *See also* Devel; Enymy; Fend; Fo; Sathan

**Lugge (*Lugg*)**: art. 18.101
*Lune*. *See* Lone
**Lyare (*Liar*)**: art. 45.61
**Lyncolne (*Lincoln*)**: art. 65.17
**Lyndeseye (*Lindsey*)**: art. 65.17. *See also* Johan of Lyndeseye
**Lyne (*Lynn*)**: art. 28.33

*Magdalen*. *See* Magdaleyne
*Magdalen Castle*. *See* Chastiel Magdalon
*Magdalenes*. *See* Repentires
**Magdaleyne (*Magdalen*)**: art. 37.125; art. 38.95, 136. *See also* Magdaleyne [Acre]
**Magdaleyne [Acre] (*Magdalen, [Abbey Church of St. Mary]*)**: art. 39.30
**Magge (*Maggie*)**: art. 40.57
**Maid (*Maid*) (speaker)**: art. 35.13, 29, 45
**Malle (*Moll*)**: art. 40.57
**Man (*Man*) (speaker)**: art. 35.9, 21, 41
*Marc*. *See* Seint Marc de Venyse [Acre]
*March*. *See* Mersh
**Marcille, evesque de (*Marseilles, bishop of*)**: art. 38.94
**Maries, treis (*Marys, three*)**: art. 38.31, 36
*Marin; Marina*. *See* Maryn; Maryne
**Mark**. *See* Seint Marc de Venyse [Acre]
**Marreis**. *See* Nostre Dame de Marreis
**Martin**. *See* Seint Martin de Bretons [Acre]
*[Mary] Magdaleyne*. *See* Magdaleyne; Magdaleyne [Acre]
**Maryn (*Marin*)**: art. 32
**Maryne, Marine (*Marina*)**: art. 32
*Marys, three*. *See* Maries, treis
**Matheu (*Matthew*)**: art. 41.1, 55
**Maximon, Maxumon (*Maximian*)**: art. 68.5, 161
**May, may (*May, Maytime*)**: art. 8.156; art. 25.42; art. 37.1; art. 44.1. *See also* art. 18.113
**Maymont (*Mayhill*)**: art. 9.156
**Melchyor (*Melchior*)**: art. 38.103

**Menours**. *See* Frere Menours [Acre]
**Mer de Galylee (*Sea of Galilee*)**: art. 38.131
**Mercie, Merciam (*Mercia*)**: art. 18.32, 42, 56
**Mercenses, Merciorum, Mercensibus (*Mercians*)**: art. 18.33, 34, 38, 39, 59
**Merle (*Tantura*)**: art. 38.7
**Mersh (*March*)**: art. 29.1
**Michel (*Michael*)**. *See* Seint Michel [Acre]
**Mody (of Reynis), (*Mody (of Reynes)*)**: art. 70.959, 1028, 1527
*Moll*. *See* Malle
**Mont Joie (*Mount Joy*)**: art. 38.18
**Mont Synay (*Mount Sinai*)**: art. 38.174. *See also* Synay
**Montfort**. *See* Simond de Mountfort
**Morham**. *See* Herbert of Morham
*Moses*. *See* Moyses
**Mount Calvarie (*Mount Calvary*)**: art. 38.25. *See also* Calvarie
**Mount (de) Olyvete (*Mount of Olives*)**: art. 38.74, 80
**Mount Hermon (*Mount Hermon*)**: art. 38.125
*Mount Joy*. *See* Mont Joie
*Mount Sinai*. *See* Mont Synay
**Mount Syon (*Mount Zion*)**: art. 38.61, 64
**Mount Tabour (*Mount Tabor*)**: art. 38.128
*Mount Zion*. *See* Mount Syon
**Mountfort**. *See* Simond de Mountfort
**Moyses (*Moses*)**: art. 21.23, 223, 225, 231; art. 38.44
**Murry, Mury (*Murry*)**: art. 70.873, 1345

**Nablus (*Naples*)**: art. 38.121
**Names (*Names*)**: art. 38.126
*Naples*. *See* Nablus
**Natorye Syloe (*Pool of Siloam*)**: art. 38.71
**Nazarez, Nazaroun (*Nazareth*)**: art. 38.137, 146; art. 69.44

**Nel**. *See* Rauf de Nel
**Newegate (*Newgate*)**:  art. 25.115
**Nicholas, Nycholas**. *See* Eglise Seint
  Nycholas; Seint Nicholas [Acre]
**Nithe (*Envy*)**:  art. 45.59
**Noal (*Christmas*)**:  art. 20.65. *See also*
  Cristemasse
**Norhamptoun (*Northampton*)**:  art.
  65.17
**Nostre Dame (cave)**. *See* Cave
**Nostre Dame de Chevalers [Acre]**
  (*St. Mary of the Knights, [Church
  of]*)*:  art. 39.11
**Nostre Dame de Marreis (*Our Lady
  of the Marshes*)**:  art. 38.10
**Nostre Dame de Sur [Acre] (*St. Mary
  of Tyre, [Abbey Church of the the
  Sisters of]*)**:  art. 39.12
**Nycholas**. *See* Nicholas

**Offa (*Offa*)**:  art. 18
**Olde Lawe (*Old Law*)**:  art. 21.232
**Olyvete**. *See* Mount (de) Olyvete
**Omer (*Omer*)**:  art. 48.126
**Onde (*Anger*)**:  art. 45.59
**Orryene**. *See* Porte Orryene
**Oswaldus (*Oswald*)**:  art. 18.31, 66
*Our Lady of the Marshes*. *See* Nostre
  Dame de Marreis
**Oure Levedy Even (*Our Lady's Eve*)**:
  art. 25.145

**Paleis de malades [Acre] (*Palace of
  the Sick*)**:  art. 39.27–28
**Palmes, jour de (*Palm Sunday*)**:  art.
  38.90
**Parays (*Paradise*) (gate)**:  art. 38.49
**Paris (*Paris*)**:  art. 48.52; art. 55.18
**Pasche, Pashe (*Easter*)**:  art. 20.136;
  art. 38.31, 87. *See also* Ester
**Pater Nostre (*Paternoster*)**:  art. 38.86
**Pees (*Peace*)**:  art. 46.80
*Penitents*. *See* Repentires
**Pentecoste (*Pentecote*)**:  art. 38.69
**Pere, Piere (*Peter*)**:  art. 38.46, 47, 70,
  129, 134. *See also* Seint Pere de
  Pyse [Acre]

**Peroun Seint Jake (*St. James's Rock*)**:
  art. 38.12
*Peter*. *See* Pere
**Peter Conyng**. *See* Conyng
**Petresbourh (*Peterborough*)**:  art.
  63.11
**Peyters (*Poitiers*)**:  art. 47.57
**Phelip (*Philip*)**:  art. 38.90
**Phelip [IV] (*Philip*)**:  art. 48.57. *See
  also* Fraunce, Kyng of
**Piere**. *See* Pere
**Pilat (*Pilate*)**:  art. 69.41
*Pilgrims' Castle*. *See* Chastiel Pelryn
*Pisans*. *See* Seint Pere de Pyse [Acre]
*Piscina*. *See* Probatica Piscina
*Poitiers*. *See* Peyters
*Pontefract*. *See* Pount-Freint
*Pool of Siloam*. *See* Natorye Syloe
**Porte (*Gate [of St. Stephen]*)**:  art.
  38.21
**Porte Orryene (*Golden Gate*)**:  art.
  38.52
**Poul**. *See* Jakes (de Seint Poul)
**Pount-Freint (*Pontefract*)**:  art.
  37.340
*Poverty*. *See* Wondred
**Poydras (*Littlecloth*)**:  art. 9.156
**Prechours**. *See* Frere Prechours [Acre]
**Pretorie Cayphas (*Praetorium of
  Caiaphas*)**:  art. 38.68
*Pride*. *See* Prude
**Prince of Walis**. *See* Walis
**Probatica Piscina (*Sheep Pool*)**:  art.
  38.55
**Prude (*Pride*)**:  art. 45.55
**Put (*Well*)**:  art. 38.108
**Puteus Aquarum (*Well of Waters*)**:
  art. 38.162
**Puytz Jacob (*Jacob's Well*)**:  art.
  38.121
**Pyse (*Pisans*)**. *See* Seint Pere de Pyse
  [Acre]

**Quaranteyne (*Quarantena, [Priory
  of]*)**:  art. 38.96

**Rachel**. *See* Seint Rachel

*Ralph*. *See* Rauf

**Rames (*Ramath*)**: art. 38.14

**Rauf de Nel (*Rauf de Nel*)**: art. 48.65

**Rauf of Sondwyche (*Ralph of Sandwich*)**: art. 25.148

**Redwald(us) (*Redwald*)**: art. 18.2

**Regnas (*Regnas*)**: art. 28.42

**Repentires [Acre] (*Penitents, [House of] the*)**: art. 39.40

*Reynis*. *See* Mody (of Reynis)

*Ribblesdale*. *See* Rybbesdale

**Richard (poet) (*Richard*)**: art. 33.60, 61

**Richard (*Richard [of Cornwall]*)**: art. 23

*Rimenild*. *See* Rymenild

**River Jordan**. *See* Flum Jordan

**Robert the Bruyts (*Robert the Bruce*)**: art. 25.58, 217

**romauns (*French*)**: art. 26.5. *See also* Frens(s)he

*Romaunt*. *See* Seint Romaunt [Acre]

**Rome (*Rome*)**: art. 34.47; art. 38.171; art. 48.117; art. 68.154

**Rybbesdale (*Ribblesdale*)**: art. 34.1

**Rymenild, Rymenyld, Rymynyld, Rymenil (*Rimenild*)**: art. 70


*Sack*. *See* Freres de Sack [Acre]

*Saffran*. *See* Soffroun

*Saffuriya*. *See* Zaphory

*Saint*. *See specific name*

**Salomon**. *See* Temple Salomon

**Samaritane (*Samaritan*)**: art. 38.122

**Samuel (*Samuel*)**: art. 38.18. *See also* Seint Samuel [Acre]

**Sarazyn(e)(s) (*Saracens*)**: art. 70.42, 66, 605, 630, 1331, 1387

**Sardayné (*Sardenay*)**: art. 38.174

*Sarepta*. *See* Serphent

**Sathan, Sathanas (*Satan*)**: art. 21; art. 22.91. *See also* Devel; Enymy; Fend; Fo; Lucifer

*Saxony*. *See* Sesoyne

**Scon (*Scone*)**: art. 25.51

**Scot, Scottes (*Scotsman, Scotsmen*)**: art. 25.9, 44

**Scotlond(e) (*Scotland*)**: art. 25.2, 17, 46, 86, 112, 146, 203, 206, 225

**Scottyshe (*Scottish*)**: art. 211

*Scripture*. *See* escripture.

*Sea of Galilee*. *See* Mer de Galylee

*Sebaste*. *See* Basque

**Seete (*Sidon*)**: art. 38.165

**Seint**. *See specific name*

**Seint André [Acre] (*St. Andrew, [Church of]*)**: art. 39.22

**Seint Andre, Bisshop of (*St. Andrew, Bishop of*)**: art. 25.49

**Seint Anne [Acre] (*St. Anne, [Abbey Church of]*)**: art. 39.19

**Seint Anne [Jerusalem] (*St. Anne*)**: art. 38.75

**Seint Antoyne [Acre] (*St. Anthony, [Church and Hospital of]*)**: art. 39.38

**Seint Bartholomeu [Acre] (*St. Bartholomew [of Beirut, Leper Hospital of]*)**: art. 39.37

**Seint Bartholomeus Masse (*St. Bartholomew's Mass*)**: art. 25.105

**Seint Caryout**. *See* Eglise Seint Caryout

**Seint Denys [Acre] (*St. Denis, [Church and Hospital of]*)**: art. 39.41

**seint Eglise (*Holy Church*)**: art. 24.45; art. 37.289, 290, 346; art. 38.49–50

**Seint Espyrit [Acre] (*Holy Spirit, [Hospital of the]*)**: art. 39.20

**Seint Estevene [Acre] (*St. Stephen, [Church and Hospital of]*)**: art. 39.7

**Seint Gabriel**. *See* Fonteyne de Seint Gabriel

**Seint George [Acre] (*St. George [of Lydda, Church of]*)**: art. 39.42

**Seint Gyle [Acre] (*St. Giles, [Church and Hospital of]*)**: art. 39.29

**Seint Habraham (*St. Abraham, [Cathedral Church of]*)**: art. 38.112

**Seint Jake**. *See* Peroun Seint Jake

**Seint Johan de Boys** (*St. John of the Woods, [Church of]*): art. 38.119

**Seint Johan de Tyr** (*St. John of Tyre, [Church of]*): art. 38.4

**Seint Lazer de Bethayne [Acre]** (*St. Lazarus of Bethany, [Church and Monastery of]*): art. 39.9

**Seint Leonard [Acre]** (*St. Leonard, [Abbey Church of]*): art. 39.5

**Seint Lorenz [Acre]** (*St. Laurence [of the Genoese, Parish Church of]*): art. 39.15

**Seint Marc de Venyse [Acre]** (*St. Mark of the Venetians, [Parish Church of]*): art. 39.14

**Seint Martin de Bretons [Acre]** (*St. Martin of the Bretons, [Hospital of]*): art. 39.34

**Seint Michel [Acre]** (*St. Michael, [Parish Church of]*): art. 39.25

**Seint Nicholas [Acre]** (*St. Nicholas, [Cemetery Chapel of]*): art. 39.3

**Seint Nycholas.** *See* Eglise Seint Nycholas

**Seint Pere de Pyse [Acre]** (*St. Peter of the Pisans, [Church of]*): art. 39.18

**Seint Poul.** *See* Jakes (de Seint Poul)

**Seint Rachel** (*St. Rachel, [Tomb of]*): art. 38.105

**Seint Romaunt [Acre]** (*St. Romanus [in the Gardens, Church of]*): art. 39.6

*Seint Salveor.* *See* Eglise de Seint Salveour

**Seint Samuel [Acre]** (*St. Samuel, [Abbey Church of]*): art. 39.8

**Seint Sepulc(h)re [Jerusalem]** (*Holy Sepulcher*): art. 38.22, 23, 35

**Seint Soffroun.** *See* Eglise de Seint Soffroun

**Seint Thomas [Acre]** (*St. Thomas [the Martyr, Church and Hospital of]*): art. 39.36

**Seinte Bryde [Acre]** (*St. Brigid, [Church and Hospital of]*): art. 39.33

**seinte Croyz, seinte Croiz** (*Holy Cross*): art. 38.32, 118. *See also* Holy Crois

**Seinte Croyz [Acre]** (*Holy Cross, [Cathedral Church of the]*): art. 39.13

**Seinte Elye, Seynt Elye** (*St. Elijah, [Monastery of]*): art. 38.2, 102

**Seinte Terre** (*Holy Land*): art. 38.1. *See also* Holy Londe

**septembre** (*September*): art. 37.344

*Sepulcher.* *See* Seint Sepulc(h)re; Sepulcre; Sepulture Eve

**Sepulcre [Acre]** (*Sepulcher, [Church of the Holy]*): art. 39.10

**Sepulture Eve** (*Eve's Sepulcher*): art. 38.114

**Serewe, Sorewyng** (*Sorrow, Sorrowing*): art. 46.78, 89

**Serphent** (*Sarepta*): art. 38.163

**Sesoyne** (*Saxony*): art. 48.71

*Sheep Pool.* *See* Probatica Piscina

*Sidon.* *See* Seete

*Sighing.* *See* Sykyng

*Siloam.* *See* Natorye Syloe

*Simeon.* *See* Symeon

*Simon.* *See* Symond

*Simon Fraser.* *See* Symond Frysel

**Simond de Mountfort** (*Simon de Montfort*): art. 23.41; art. 24

*Sinai.* *See* Synay; Mont Synay

**Sindritha** (*Sindritha*): art. 18.25

**Slep** (*Sleep*): art. 45.62

**Sleuthe** (*Sloth*): art. 45.62

**Soffroun** (*Saffran*): art. 38.151

*Solomon's Temple.* *See* Temple Salomon

**Somere, Kyng of** (*Summer, King of*): art. 25.66. *See also* Esté

**Sondwyche.** *See* Rauf of Sondwyche

**Sonneday** (*Sunday*): art. 70.958, 976. *See also* digmange

*Sorrow, Sorrowing.* *See* Serewe

*Soul.* *See* Gost

**Speciouse** (*Beautiful*) **(gate)**: art. 38.51

**Spelunca Dupplici (*Double Cave*):** art. 38.113

*St. Abraham*. *See* Seint Habraham

*St. Andrew*. *See* Seint André [Acre]; Seint Andre, Bisshop of

*St. Anne*. *See* Seint Anne [Acre]; Seint Anne [Jerusalem]

*St. Anthony*. *See* Seint Antoyne [Acre]

*St. Bartholomew*. *See* Seint Bartholomeu [Acre]

*St. Bartholomew's Mass*. *See* Seint Bartholomeus Masse

*St. Brigid*. *See* Seinte Bryde [Acre]

*St. Chariton*. *See* Eglise Seint Caryout

*St. Denis*. *See* Seint Denys [Acre]

*St. Elijah*. *See* Seinte Elye

*St. Elijah's Cave*. *See* Cave Seynt Elye

*St. Gabriel*. *See* Fonteyne de Seint Gabriel

*St. George*. *See* Seint George [Acre]

*St. Giles*. *See* Seint Gyle [Acre]

*St. James's Rock*. *See* Peroun Seint Jake

*St. John of the Woods*. *See* Seint Johan de Boys

*St. John of Tyre*. *See* Seint Johan de Tyr

*[St.] Katherine [of the Battlefield]*. *See* Katerine

*St. Laurence*. *See* Seint Lorenz [Acre]

*St. Lazarus of Bethany*. *See* Seint Lazer de Bethayne [Acre]

*[St.] Lazarus of the Knights*. *See* Lazer de Chevalers

*St. Leonard*. *See* Seint Leonard [Acre]

*St. Mark of the Venetians*. *See* Seint Marc de Venyse [Acre]

*St. Martin of the Bretons*. *See* Seint Martin de Bretons [Acre]

*[St. Mary] Latin*. *See* Latyne [Acre]; Latyne [Jerusalem]

*[St. Mary] Magdaleyne*. *See* Magdaleyne [Acre]

*[St. Mary of the] Germans*. *See* Alemayns [Acre]

*St. Mary of the Knights*. *See* Nostre Dame de Chevalers

*St. Mary of Tyre*. *See* Nostre Dame de Sur

*St. Michael*. *See* Seint Michel [Acre]

*St. Nicholas*. *See* Eglise Seint Nycholas; Seint Nicholas [Acre]

*St. Peter of the Pisans*. *See* Seint Pere de Pyse [Acre]

*St. Pol*. *See* Jakes (de Seint Poul)

*St. Rachel*. *See* Seint Rachel

*St. Romanus*. *See* Seint Romaunt [Acre]

*St. Saffran*. *See* Eglise de Seint Soffroun

*St. Samuel*. *See* Seint Samuel [Acre]

*St. Stephen*. *See* Seint Estevene [Acre]

*St. Thomas*. *See* Seint Thomas [Acre]

**Stevene, Estevene (*Stephen*):** art. 38.21; art. 70.667. *See also* Seint Estevene [Acre]

*Stirling*. *See* Strivelyn

**Stoure (*Stour*):** art. 70.687, 1455

**Stratum (*Street*):** art. 18.117

**Strivelyn (*Stirling*):** art. 25.93

**Sudenne (*Sudenne*):** art. 70

*Summer*. *See* Esté

*Sunday*. *See* digmange; Sonneday

**Sur (*Tyre*):** art. 38.158, 163. *See also* Nostre Dame de Sur [Acre]; Seint Johan de Tyr

**Sweyn (*Swain*):** art. 9.156

**Sykyng (*Sighing*):** art. 46.78, 86

**Syloe**. *See* Natorye Syloe

**Symeon (*Simeon*):** art. 38.40; art. 60.12

**Symond (*Simon*):** art. 38.94

**Symond Frysel, Frisel (*Simon Fraser*):** art. 25

**Synay (*Sinai*):** art. 21.224

**Syon**. *See* Mount Syon

*Tabour*. *See* Mount Tabour

*Tantura*. *See* Merle

**Tegeu (*Tegeu*):** art. 28.43

**Temple [Acre] (*Templars, [Church and Castle of the]*):** art. 39.23

**Temple Salomon (*Solomon's Temple*):** art. 38.57

**Templum Domini (*Templum Domini*):** art. 38.38

**Terre**. *See* Seinte Terre

**Thoht** (*Thought*): art. 46.78, 87

**Thomas** (*Thomas*): art. 24.44; art. 38.65; art. 54.8, 19, 34. *See also* Caunterbyr; Seint Thomas [Acre]

**Thomas de Boys** (*Thomas de Bois*): art. 25.139

**Thomas of Multoun** (*Thomas of Multon*): art. 25.107, 147

*Thought. See* Thoht

*Three Kings. See* Trois (Treis) Rois

*Three Marys. See* Maries, treis

**Thurston** (*Thurston*): art. 70.827, 991

*Tiberias. See* Bebie

**Tour (of Londone)** (*Tower (of London)*): art. 25.144, 178

**Tour David** (*David's Tower*): art. 38.59

*Tower. See* Tour

**Trinité [Acre]** (*Trinity [and Captive, House of the Holy]*): art. 39.32

**Trois (Treis) Rois** (*Three Kings*): art. 38.106, 108-09

**Tu autem** (*Tu autem*): art. 26.111

*Tyre. See* Seint Johan de Tyr; Nostre Dame de Sur; Sur

**Uxor (speaker)** (*Wife*): art. 37.210, 224, 250, 270

**Uxores (speakers)** (*Wives*): art. 37.327

**Val de Josaphat** (*Valley of Jehoshaphat*): art. 38.62–63, 74. *See also* Josaphat [Acre]

**Valence**. *See* Emer de Valence

**Venyse** (*Venetians*). *See* Seint Marc de Venyse [Acre]

**Waleis** (*Wallace*): art. 25.18, 202

*Wales. See* Walis

**Walingford** (*Wallingford*): art. 23.11

**Walis, Prince of** (*Wales, Prince of*): art. 48.133. *See also* Edward [II]

*Wallace. See* Waleis

*Wallingford. See* Walingford

**Waryn(ne)** (*Warenne*): art. 23.34, 42

**Waye**. *See* Wye

**Wednesday** (*Wednesday*): art. 48.4

**Wee** (*Woe*): art. 31.71

*Well. See* Put

*Well of St. Gabriel. See* Fonteyne de Seint Gabriel

*Well of Waters. See* Puteus Aquarum

**Westnesse** (*Westness*): art. 70.165, 176, 929, 1022, 1188, 1215, 1515

*Weye. See* Wye

*Wife. See* Uxor

**Wil** (*Will*): art. 31.23, 31

*Winchester. See* Wyncestre

*Windsor*. See Wyndesore

*Winter. See* Yver

*Wirral. See* Wyrhale

*Wives. See* Uxores

*Woe. See* Wee

**Wondred** (*Poverty*): art. 31.31, 71

**Worlde** (*World*): art. 27.49

**Wye, Waye** (*Wye*): art. 18.117; art. 28.27

**Wylcadoun** (*Wylcadoun*): art. 28.45

**Wyncestre** (*Winchester*): art. 37.203, 343

**Wyndesore** (*Windsor*): art. 23

**Wyrhale** (*Wirral*): art. 28.27

**Wyrwein** (*Wyrwein*): art. 28.43

**Ynde** (*India*): art. 44.12

**Yrisshe** (*Irish*): art. 70.1290, 1298

**Yrisshemenne** (*Irishmen*): art. 70.1376

**Yrlaund, Yrlonde, Irlond** (*Ireland*): art. 37.338; art. 44.12; art. 70.1535

**Ysaac** (*Isaac*): art. 38.114

**Ysaye** (*Isaiah*): art. 38.72

**Yver** (*Winter*): art. 9

**Zacarie** (*Zachary*): art. 38.42

**Zaphory** (*Saffuriya*): art. 38.146

**Zabulon** (*Zebulon*): art. 8.265

*Zion. See* Mount Syon

# BIBLIOGRAPHY

Adams, Jenny. *Power Play: The Literature and Politics of Chess in the Late Middle Ages*. Philadelphia: University of Pennsylvania Press, 2006.

Allen, Rosamund, ed. *King Horn: An Edition Based on Cambridge University Library MS Gg. 4.27 (2)*. New York: Garland, 1984.

Andrew, Malcolm, and Ronald Waldron, eds. *The Poems of the Pearl Manuscript: Pearl, Cleanness, Patience and Gawain and the Green Knight*. Fifth edition. Exeter: University of Exeter Press, 2007.

*Anglo-Norman Dictionary* (*AND*). Online at http://www.anglo-norman.net.

Anselm of Canterbury. "*Admonitio morienti et de peccatus suis nimium formidanti*." In Patrilogia cursos completus . . . series latina. Ed. J.-P. Migne. Paris, 1844–64. 158:685–88.

Archibald, Elizabeth. "Macaronic Poetry." In *Companion to Medieval Poetry*. Ed. Corinne Saunders. Oxford: Blackwell Publishing, 2010. Pp. 277–88.

Ashley, Kathleen, trans. "The French *Enseignemenz a Phelippe* and *Enseignement a Ysabel* of Saint Louis." In *Medieval Conduct Literature: An Anthology of Vernacular Guides to Behaviour for Youth, with English Translations*. Ed. Mark D. Johnston. Toronto: University of Toronto Press, 2009. Pp. 3–16.

Aspin, Isabel S. T., ed. *Anglo-Norman Political Songs*. Anglo-Norman Texts 11. Oxford: Basil Blackwell, 1953.

Baker, Benedict, trans. *Vitae Patrum: Lives of the Desert Fathers*. 2004. Online at http://www.vitae-patrum.ork.

Barton, Simon, and Richard Fletcher, trans. *The World of El Cid: Chronicles of the Spanish Reconquest*. Manchester: Manchester University Press, 2000.

Bede. *A History of the English Church and People*. Trans. Leo Sherley-Price. Second edition. Rev. R. E. Latham. Harmondsworth: Penguin, 1968.

Beer, Jeanette, trans. *Master Richard's Bestiary of Love and Response*. Berkeley: University of California Press, 1986.

Bell, Kimberly K. "'holi mannes liues': England and Its Saints in Oxford, Bodleian Library, MS Laud Misc. 108's *King Horn* and *South English Legendary*." In *The Texts and Contexts of Oxford, Bodleian Library, MS Laud Misc. 108: The Shaping of English Vernacular Narrative*. Ed. Kimberly K. Bell and Julie Nelson Couch. Leiden: Brill, 2011. Pp. 251–74.

Bell, Kimberly K., and Julie Nelson Couch, eds. *The Texts and Contexts of Oxford, Bodleian Library, MS Laud Misc. 108: The Shaping of English Vernacular Narrative*. Leiden: Brill, 2011.

Bennett, J. A. W., and G. V. Smithers. *Early Middle English Verse and Prose*. Oxford: Clarendon, 1966.

Bennett, Janice. *Sacred Blood, Sacred Image. The Sudarium of Oviedo: New Evidence for the Authenticity of the Shroud of Turin*. Littleton, CO: Libri de Hispania, 2001.

Best, Michael R., and Frank H. Brightman, eds. *The Book of Secrets of Albertus Magnus of the Virtues of Certain Herbs, Stones, and Beasts, also A Book of the Marvels of the World*. Oxford: Clarendon, 1973.

Bevington, David, ed. *Medieval Drama*. Boston: Houghton Mifflin, 1975.

Biggs, Frederick M. "A Bared Bottom and a Basket: A New Analogue and a New Source for the *Miller's Tale*." *Notes and Queries* 254 (2009), 340–41.

Birkholz, Daniel. "Harley Lyrics and Hereford Clerics: The Implications of Mobility, c. 1300–1351." *Studies in the Age of Chaucer* 31 (2009), 175–230.

Blair, John (2002a). "A Handlist of Anglo-Saxon Saints." In *Local Saints and Local Churches in the Early Medieval West*. Ed. Alan Thacker and Richard Sharpe. Oxford: Oxford University Press, 2002. Pp. 495–565.

———— (2002b). "A Saint for Every Minster? Local Cults in Anglo-Saxon England." In *Local Saints and Local Churches in the Early Medieval West*. Ed. Alan Thacker and Richard Sharpe. Oxford: Oxford University Press, 2002. Pp. 454–94.

Blamires, Alcuin, ed. *Woman Defamed and Woman Defended: An Anthology of Medieval Texts*. Oxford: Clarendon Press, 1992.

Bloch, R. Howard. *The Scandal of the Fabliaux*. Chicago: University of Chicago Press, 1986.

Boas, Adrian J. *Jerusalem in the Time of the Crusades: Society, Landscape and Art in the Holy City under Frankish Rule*. London: Routledge, 2001.

Böddeker, Karl, ed. *Altenglische Dichtungen des MS. Harl. 2253*. Berlin: Weidmannsche, 1878.

Boffey, Julia. "Middle English Lyrics and Manuscripts." In *A Companion to the Middle English Lyric*. Ed. Thomas G. Duncan. Cambridge: D. S. Brewer, 2005. Pp. 1–18.

Boffey, Julia, and A. S. G. Edwards. *A New Index of Middle English Verse*. London: British Library, 2005.

Boklund-Lagopoulou, Karin. *'I have a yong suster': Popular Song and the Middle English Lyric*. Dublin: Four Courts Press, 2002.

Bonnard, Jean. *Les Traductions de la bible en vers français au moyen âge*. Geneva: Slatkine Reprints, 1884.

Bossuat, Robert. *Manuel bibliographique de la littérature française du moyen âge*. Melun: Librairie d'Argences, 1951.

Bossy, Michel-André, ed and trans. *Medieval Debate Poetry: Vernacular Works*. New York: Garland, 1987.

Boulton, Maureen (1996–97). "Le langage de la dévotion affective en moyen français." *Le moyen français* 39–41 (1996–97), 53–63.

———— (2009). "The Lives of the Virgin by Wace and Herman de Valenciennes: Conventions of Romance and Chanson de Geste in Religious Narratives." In *Church and Vernacular Literature in Medieval France*. Ed. Dorothy Kullmann. Toronto: Pontifical Institute of Mediaeval Studies, 2009. Pp. 109–23.

Bradbury, Nancy Mason (2008). "Rival Wisdom in the *Latin Dialogue of Solomon and Marcolf*." *Speculum* 83 (2008), 331–65.

———— (2010). "Popular Romance." In *A Companion to Medieval Poetry*. Ed. Corinne Saunders. Oxford: Blackwell Publishing, 2010. Pp. 289–307.

Bradbury, Nancy Mason, and Scott Bradbury, eds. *The Dialogue of Solomon and Marcolf: A Dual-Language Edition from Latin and Middle English Printed Editions*. Kalamazoo, MI: Medieval Institute Publications, 2012.

Brandl, A., and O. Zippel, eds. *Middle English Literature*. Second edition. New York: Chelsea, 1949. repr. 1965.

Brereton, G. E. "*La riote du monde*: A New Fragment." *Medium Ævum* 4 (1935), 95–99.

Breeze, Andrew (1992). "The Instantaneous Harvest and the Harley Lyric *Mayden Moder Milde*." *Notes and Queries* 237 (1992), 150–52.

———— (2004). "Jonas, Jason, and the Harley Lyric *Annot and John*." *Notes and Queries* 249 (2004), 237–38.

Brook, G. L., ed. *The Harley Lyrics: The Middle English Lyrics of Ms. Harley 2253*. Fourth edition. Manchester: Manchester University Press, 1968.

Brown, Carleton (1916, 1920). *Register of Middle English Religious and Didactic Verse*. 2 vols. Oxford: Bibliographical Society, 1916, 1920.

———— (1932), ed. *English Lyrics of the XIIIth Century*. Oxford: Clarendon, 1932.

———— (1952), ed. *Religious Lyrics of the XIVth Century*. Oxford: Clarendon, 1924. Second edition. Rev. G. V. Smithers. Oxford: Clarendon, 1952.

Brown, Carleton, and Rossell Hope Robbins. *The Index of Middle English Verse*. New York: Columbia University Press, 1943.

Burnley, David, and Alison Wiggins, eds. *Auchinleck Manuscript*. Edinburgh: National Library of Scotland, 2003. Online at http://auchinleck.nls.uk/editorial/project.html.

Butterfield, Ardis. "English, French and Anglo-French: Language and Nation in the Fabliau." In *Mittelalterliche Novellistik im europaischen Kontext: Kulturwissenschaftliche Perspektiven*. Ed. Mark Chinca, Timo Peuvekamp-Felber, and Christopher Yound. Berlin: Erich Schmidt, 2006. Pp. 238–59.

Cable, Thomas. "Foreign Influence, Native Continuation, and Metrical Typology in Alliterative Lyrics." In *Approaches to the Metres of Alliterative Verse*. Ed. Judith Jefferson and Ad Putter. Leeds Texts and Monographs, new series 17. Leeds: University of Leeds, 2009. Pp. 219–34.

Cannon, Christopher. *Middle English Literature: A Cultural History*. Cambridge: Polity Press, 2008.

Cartlidge, Neil. "Medieval Debate-Poetry and *The Owl and the Nightingale*." In *A Companion to Medieval Poetry*. Ed. Corinne Saunders. Oxford: Blackwell Publishing, 2010. Pp. 237–57.

Cartlidge, David R., and J. Keith Elliott. *Art and the Christian Apocrypha*. London: Routledge, 2001.

Cazelles, Brigitte, trans. *The Lady as Saint: A Collection of French Hagiographic Romances of the Thirteenth Century*. Philadephia: University of Pennsylvania Press, 1991.

Chaucer, Geoffrey. *The Riverside Chaucer*. Ed. Larry D. Benson et al. Third edition. Boston: Houghton Mifflin, 1987.

Chevalier, Ulysse. *Repertorium hymnologicum: Catalogue des chants, hymnes, proses, séquences, tropes en usage dans l'église latine Depuis les origines jusqu'a nos jours*. Tome 1. Louvain: Lefever, 1892.

Child, Francis James. *The English and Scottish Popular Ballads*. 5 vols. 1882–98. repr. New York: Dover, 1965.

Choong, Kevin Teo Kia. "Bodies of Knowledge: Embodying Riotous Performance in the Harley Lyrics." In *"And Never Know the Joy": Sex and the Erotic in English Poetry*. Ed. C. C. Barfoot. Amsterdam: Rodopi, 2006. Pp. 13–32.

Christine de Pizan. *The Book of the City of Ladies*. Trans. Earl Jeffrey Richards. New York: Persea Books, 1982.

Clanchy, M. T. *England and Its Rulers: 1066–1307*. Third edition. Oxford: Blackwell, 2006.

Clugnet, Léon, ed. "Vie de sainte Marine." *Revue de l'Orient Chrétien* 8 (1903), 288–311.

Coleman, Janet. *Medieval Readers and Writers 1350–1400*. New York: Columbia University Press, 1981.

Conlee, John W., ed. *Middle English Debate Poetry: A Critical Anthology*. East Lansing, MI: Colleagues Press, 1991.

Connolly, Margaret. "Compiling the Book." In *The Production of Books in England 1350–1500*. Ed. Alexandra Gillespie and Daniel Wakelin. Cambridge: Cambridge University Press, 2011. Pp. 129–49.

Cooke, Thomas D. "Pornography, the Comic Spirit, and the Fabliaux." In *The Humor of the Fabliaux: A Collection of Critical Essays*. Ed. Thomas D. Cooke and Benjamin L. Honeycutt. Columbia: University of Missouri Press, 1974. Pp. 137–62.

Cooper, Helen. *The English Romance in Time: Transforming Motifs from Geoffrey of Monmouth to the Death of Shakespeare*. Oxford: Oxford University Press, 2004.

Corrie, Marilyn (2000). "Harley 2253, Digby 86, and the Circulation of Literature in Pre-Chaucerian England." In *Studies in the Harley Manuscript: The Scribes, Contents, and Social Contexts of British Library MS Harley 2253*. Ed. Susanna Fein. Kalamazoo, MI: Medieval Institute Publications, 2000. Pp. 427–43.

——— (2003). "Kings and Kingship in British Library MS Harley 2253." *Yearbook of English Studies* 33 (2003), 64–79.

Crane, Susan. *Insular Romance: Politics, Faith, and Culture in Anglo-Norman and Middle English Literature*. Berkeley: University of California Press, 1986.

Cross, J. E. "The Sayings of St. Bernard and *Ubi Scount Qui Nos Fuerount*." *Review of English Studies*, n.s. 9 (1958), 1–7.

Da Rold, Orietta, Takako Kato, Mary Swan, and Elaine Treharne, eds. *The Production and Use of English Manuscripts 1060 to 1220*. Leicester: University of Leicester 2010. Online at http://www.le.ac.uk/ee/em1060to1220.

Dane, Joseph A. "Page Layout and Textual Autonomy in Harley MS 2253: 'Lenten Ys Come wiþ Loue to Toune.'" *Medium Ævum* 68 (1999), 32–41.

Daniel, Hermann Adalbert. *Thesaurus Hymnologicus sive Hymnorum Canticorum Sequentiarum Circa Annum MD Usitatarum Collectio Amplissima*. 5 vols. Leipzig: J. T. Loeschke, 1855–56.

Dante Alighieri. *La Divina Commedia*. Ed. G. H. Grandgent. Rev. Charles S. Singleton. Cambridge, MA: Harvard University Press, 1972.

D'Arcy, Anne Marie. "The Middle English Lyrics." In *Readings in Medieval Texts: Interpreting Old and Middle English Literature*. Ed. David F. Johnson and Elaine Treharne. Oxford: Oxford University Press, 2005. Pp. 306–22.

D'Arcy, Anne Marie, and Alan J. Fletcher, eds. *Studies in Late Medieval and Early Renaissance Texts in Honour of John Scattergood: The Key of All Good Remembrance*. Portland, OR: Four Courts Press, 2005.

Davies, R. T., ed. *Medieval English Lyrics: A Critical Anthology*. London: Faber and Faber, 1963.

De Wilde, Geert. "The Stanza Form of the Middle English *Lament for the Death of Edward I*: A Reconstruction." *Anglia* 123 (2005), 230–45.

Dean, James M., ed. *Medieval English Political Writings*. Kalamazoo, MI: Medieval Institute Publications, 1996.

Dean, Ruth J., with Maureen B. M. Boulton. *Anglo-Norman Literature: A Guide to Texts and Manuscripts*. London: Anglo-Norman Text Society, 1999.

Degginger, Stuart H. L. "'A Wayle Whyt Ase Whalles Bon': Reconstructed." *Journal of English and Germanic Philology* 53 (1954), 84–90.

Dobson, E. J., and F. Ll. Harrison, eds. *Medieval English Songs*. New York: Cambridge University Press, 1979.

Dobson, R. B., and J. Taylor. *Rymes of Robin Hood: An Introduction to the English Outlaw*. Pittsburgh, PA: University of Pittsburgh Press, 1976.

Donaldson, E. Talbot. *Speaking of Chaucer*. Durham, NC: Labyrinth, 1983.

Dove, Mary (1969). *A Study of Some of the Lesser-Known Poems of British Museum Ms. Harley 2253*. D.Phil. dissertation. Cambridge: Girton College, 1969.

——— (2000). "Evading Textual Intimacy: The French Secular Verse." In *Studies in the Harley Manuscript: The Scribes, Contents, and Social Contexts of British Library MS Harley 2253*. Ed. Susanna Fein. Kalamazoo, MI: Medieval Institute Publications, 2000. Pp. 329–49.

Dubin, Nathaniel E., trans. *The Fabliaux*. New York: Liveright, 2013.

Duffy, Eamon (1992). *The Stripping of the Altars: Traditional Religion in England c.1400–c.1580*. New Haven, CT: Yale University Press, 1992.

——— (2006). *Marking the Hours: English People and Their Prayers 1240–1570*. New Haven, CT: Yale University Press, 2006.

Dunbar, William. *The Complete Works*. Ed. John Conlee. Kalamazoo, MI: Medieval Institute Publications, 2004.

Duncan, Thomas G., ed. *Medieval English Lyrics: 1200–1400*. Harmondsworth: Penguin, 1995.

Dunn, Charles W. "I. 1. Romances Derived from English Legends." In Severs et al. Pp. 17–37, 206–24.

Dunn, Charles W., and Edward T. Byrnes, eds. *Middle English Literature*. New York: Harcourt, 1973.

Durling, Nancy Vine. "British Library MS Harley 2253: A New Reading of the Passion Lyrics in Their Manuscript Context." *Viator* 40 (2009), 271–307.

Edgar, Swift, ed. *The Vulgate Bible*. Volume 1, *The Pentateuch; Douay-Rheims Translation*. Cambridge, MA: Harvard University Press, 2010.

Elliott, J. K., trans. *The Apocryphal New Testament: A Collection of Apocryphal Christian Literature in an English Translation*. Oxford, Clarendon, 1993.

Fein, Susanna (1998), ed. *Moral Love Songs and Laments*. Kalamazoo, MI: Medieval Institute Publications, 1998.

——— (2000a), ed. *Studies in the Harley Manuscript: The Scribes, Contents, and Social Contexts of British Library MS Harley 2253*. Kalamazoo, MI: Medieval Institute Publications, 2000.

——— (2000b). "British Library MS Harley 2253: The Lyrics, the Facsimile, and the Book." In *Studies in the Harley Manuscript: The Scribes, Contents, and Social Contexts of British Library MS Harley 2253*. Ed. Susanna Fein. Kalamazoo, MI: Medieval Institute Publications, 2000. Pp. 1–20.

——— (2000c). "A Saint 'Geynest under Gore': Marina and the Love Lyrics of the Seventh Quire." In *Studies in the Harley Manuscript: The Scribes, Contents, and Social Contexts of British Library MS Harley 2253*. Ed. Susanna Fein. Kalamazoo, MI: Medieval Institute Publications, 2000. Pp. 351–76.

——— (2005). "XXVII. The Lyrics of MS Harley 2253." In Severs et al. Pp. 4168–4206, 4311–4361.

——— (2006). "Harley Lyrics." In *The Oxford Encyclopedia of British Literature*. Ed. David Scott Kastan and Gail McMurray Gibson. 5 vols. Oxford: Oxford University Press, 2006. 2:519–22.

——— (2007). "Compilation and Purpose in MS Harley 2253." In *Essays in Manuscript Geography: Vernacular Manuscripts of the English West Midlands from the Conquest to the Sixteenth Century*. Ed. Wendy Scase. Turnhout: Brepols, 2007. Pp. 67–94.

——— (2009), ed., *John the Blind Audelay, Poems and Carols (Oxford, Bodleian Library MS Douce 302)*. Kalamazoo, MI: Medieval Institute Publications, 2009.

——— (2013). "The Four Scribes of MS Harley 2253." *Journal of the Early Book Society* 16 (2013), 27–49.

——— (2014). "Of Judges and Jewelers: *Pearl* and the Life of Saint John." *Studies in the Age of Chaucer* 36 (2014), forthcoming.

——— (2015). "Literary Scribes: The Harley Scribe and Robert Thornton as Case Studies." In *Insular Books: Vernacular Miscellanies in Late Medieval Britain*. Ed. Margaret Connolly and Raluca Radulescu. Proceedings of the British Academy. London: British Academy, 2015 (forthcoming).

Finberg, H. P. R. *The Early Charters of the West Midlands*. Leicester: Leicester University Press, 1961.

Fisher, Matthew. *Scribal Authorship and the Writing of History in Medieval England*. Columbus: Ohio State University Press, 2012.

Flood, Victoria. "Imperfect Apocalypse: Thomas of Erceldoune's Reply to the Countess of Dunbar in MS Harley 2253." *Marginalia* (October 2010), 11–27. Online at http://www.marginalia.co .uk/journal/10apocalypse.

Ford, Alvin E., ed. *L'Evangile de Nicodème. Les versions courtes en ancien françaises et en prose*. Publications romanes et françaises 125. Geneva: Librairie Droz, 1973.

Förster, M. "Beiträge zur mittelalterliche Volkskunde." *Archiv für das studium der neueren Sprachen und Literaturen* 127 (1911), 31–84.

Foster, Frances A. "V. Saints' Legends. 6. Legends of Jesus and Mary." In Severs et al. Pp. 447–51, 639–44.

Fowler, David C. "XV. Ballads." In Severs et al. Pp. 1753–1808, 2019–70.

Frankis, John. "The Social Context of Vernacular Writing in Thirteenth Century England: The Evidence of the Manuscripts." In *Thirteenth Century England: Proceedings of the Newcastle upon Tyne Conference 1985*. Ed. P. R. Coss and S. D. Lloyd. Woodbridge: Boydell, 1986. Pp. 175–84.

French, Walter Hoyt, and Charles Brockway Hale, eds. *Middle English Metrical Romances*. New York: Prentice-Hall, 1930.

Fulk, R. D., ed. and trans. *The Beowulf Manuscript*. Cambridge, MA: Harvard University Press, 2010.

Fuller, David. "Lyrics, Sacred and Secular." In *A Companion to Medieval Poetry*. Ed. Corinne Saunders. Oxford: Blackwell Publishing, 2010. Pp. 258–76.

Furnivall, F. J., ed. *The Minor Poems of the Vernon MS. Part II*. EETS o.s. 117. London: Kegan Paul, Trench, Trübner, 1901.

Garbáty, Thomas J., ed. *Medieval English Literature*. Lexington, MA: D. C. Heath and Co., 1984.

Gerald of Wales. *The Jewel of the Church: A Translation of Gemma Ecclesiastica by Giraldus Cambrensis*. Trans. John J. Hagen. Leiden: Brill, 1979.

Gibbs, A. C., ed. *Middle English Romances*. London: Edward Arnold, 1966.

Goering, Joseph, ed. *William de Montibus (c. 1140–1213): The Schools and the Literature of Pastoral Care*. Toronto: Pontifical Institute of Mediaeval Studies, 1992.

Gordon, E. V., ed. *Pearl*. Oxford: Clarendon, 1953.

Gower, John. *Confessio Amantis*. Ed. Russell A. Peck, with Latin translations by Andrew Galloway. 3 vols. Kalamazoo, MI: Medieval Institute Publications, 2000–06.

Gray, Douglas. *Themes and Images in the Medieval English Religious Lyric*. London: Routledge and Kegan Paul, 1972.

Green, Richard Firth (1989). "The Two 'Litel Wot Hit Any Mon' Lyrics in Harley 2253." *Mediaeval Studies* 51 (1989), 304–12.

——— (1999). *A Crisis of Truth: Literature and Law in Ricardian England*. Philadelphia: University of Pennsylvania Press, 1999.

Greene, Richard Leighton (1962), ed. *A Selection of English Carols*. Oxford: Clarendon, 1962.

——— (1977), ed. *The Early English Carols*. Second edition. Oxford: Clarendon, 1977.

——— (1980). "XIV. Carols." In Severs et al. Pp.1743–52, 1940–2018.

Hall, Joseph, ed. *King Horn: A Middle-English Romance Edited from the Manuscripts*. Oxford: Clarendon, 1901.

Halliwell, James Orchard, ed. and trans. *The Harrowing of Hell, A Miracle Play Written in the Reign of Edward the Second*. London: John Russell Smith, 1840.

Hanna, Ralph. "The Matter of Fulk: Romance and the History of the Marches." *Journal of English and Germanic Philology* 110 (2011), 337–58.

Hardy, T. D. *Descriptive Catalogue of Materials Relating to the History of Great Britain and Ireland to the End of the Reign of Henry VII*. 3 vols. London: Longman, Green, Longman, and Roberts, 1862–71; repr. New York: Kraus, 1966.

Harris, Julie A. "Redating the Arca Santa of Oviedo." *Art Bulletin* 77 (1995), 82–93.

Harriss, G. L. *King, Parliament, and Public Finance in Medieval England to 1369*. Oxford: Clarendon, 1975.

Hathaway, E. J., P. T. Ricketts, C. A. Robson, and A. D. Wilshere, eds. *Fouke le Fitz Waryn*. Anglo-Norman Texts 26–28. Oxford: Basil Blackwell, 1975.

Hellman, Robert, and Richard O'Gorman, trans. *Fabliaux: Ribald Tales from the Old French*. London: Arthur Barker, 1965.

Herzman, Ronald B., Graham Drake, and Eve Salisbury, eds. *Four Romances of England: King Horn, Havelok the Dane, Bevis of Hampton, Athelston*. Kalamazoo, MI: Medieval Institute Publications, 1999.

Hindley, Alan, Frederick W. Langley, and Brian J. Levy, eds. *Old French Dictionary*. Cambridge: Cambridge University Press, 2000.

Hines, John. *Voices in the Past: English Literature and Archaeology*. Cambridge: D. S. Brewer, 2004.

Holbrook, Richard. "The Printed Text of Four Fabliaux in the *Recueil général et complet des fabliaux* Compared with the Readings in the Harleian ms., 2253." *Modern Language Notes* 20 (1905), 193–97.

Holthausen, F., ed. "Die Quelle des mittelenglischen Gedichtes 'Lob der Frauen.'" *Archiv für das Studium der neueren Sprachen und Literaturen* 108 (1902), 288–301.

Honeycutt, Benjamin L. "The Knight and His World as Instruments of Humor in the Fabliaux." In *The Humor of the Fabliaux: A Collection of Critical Essays*. Ed. Thomas D. Cooke and Benjamin L. Honeycutt. Columbia: University of Missouri Press, 1974. Pp. 75–92.

Horobin, Simon. "Manuscripts and Scribes." In *Chaucer: Contemporary Approaches*. Ed. Susanna Fein and David Raybin. University Park: Pennsylvania State University Press, 2010. Pp. 67–82

Horstmann, Carl (1876), ed. "Die Evangelien-Geschichten der Homiliensammlung des Ms. Vernon." *Archiv für das Studium der neueren Sprachen und Literaturen* 57 (1876), 241–316.

——— (1878), ed. *Sammlung Altenglischer Legenden*. Heilbronn: Von Gebr. Henninger, 1878; repr. Hildesheim: Georg Olms, 1969.

——— (1895, 1896), ed. *Yorkshire Writers: Richard Rolle of Hampole and His Followers*. 2 vols. London: Swan Sonnenschein, 1895, 1896.

——— (1901), ed. *Nova Legenda Anglie: As Collected by John of Tynemouth, John Capgrave, and Others, and First Printed, with New Lives, by Wynkyn de Worde a.d. mdxui*. 2 vols. Oxford: Clarendon, 1901.

Hough, Carole. "A Note on Harley Lyric No. 3 Line 21." *Review of English Studies* 214 (2003), 173–77.

Hrothsvitha. *Paphnutius*. Trans. Mary Marguerite Butler, R.S.M. In *Medieval and Tudor Drama*. Ed. John Gassner. 1963; repr. New York: Applause, 1987.

Hulme, William Henry, ed. *The Middle-English Harrowing of Hell and Gospel of Nicodemus*. EETS e.s. 100. London: Oxford University Press, 1907.

Hunt, Tony. "Anglo-Norman Rules of Friendship." *French Studies Bulletin* 30 (1989), 9–11.

Hunt, Tony, ed., and Jane Bliss, trans. *"Cher alme": Texts of Anglo-Norman Piety*. Tempe: Arizona Center for Medieval and Renaissance Studies, 2010.

Izydorczyk, Zbigniew. *Manuscript of the Evangelium Nicodemi: A Census*. Subsidia Mediaevalia 21. Toronto: Pontifical Institute of Mediaeval Studies, 1993.

Jacobus de Voragine. *The Golden Legend: Readings on the Saints*. Trans. William Granger Ryan. 2 vols. Princeton: Princeton University Press, 1993.

James, M. R. (1917). "Two Lives of St. Ethelbert, King and Martyr." *English Historical Review* 32 (1917), 214–44.

———— (1924), trans. *The Apocryphal New Testament, Being the Apocryphal Gospels, Acts, Epistles, and Apocalypses with Other Narratives and Fragments*. Oxford: Clarendon, 1924.

Jeffrey, David L. (1975). *The Early English Lyric and Franciscan Spirituality*. Lincoln: University of Nebraska Press, 1975.

———— (2000). "Authors, Anthologists, and Franciscan Spirituality." In *Studies in the Harley Manuscript: The Scribes, Contents, and Social Contexts of British Library MS Harley 2253*. Ed. Susanna Fein. Kalamazoo, MI: Medieval Institute Publications, 2000. Pp. 261–70.

Jeffrey, David L., and Brian J. Levy, eds. *The Anglo-Norman Lyric: An Anthology*. Toronto: Pontifical Institute of Mediaeval Studies, 1990.

Jennings, J. C. "The Writings of Prior Dominic of Evesham." *English Historical Review* 77 (1962), 298–304.

Jones, Trefor. *The English Saints: East Anglia*. Norwich: Canterbury Press, 1999.

Jordan, Richard, ed. "Kleinere Dichtungen der Handschrift Harley 3810." *Englische Studien* 41 (1910), 253–66.

Jubinal, Achille, ed. *Nouveau Recueil de contes, dits, fabliaux et autres pièces inedites des xiii$^e$, xiv$^e$ et xv$^e$ siècles*. Paris: Eduoard Pannier, 1839, 1842.

Keiser, George R. "XXV. Works of Science and Information." In Severs et al. Pp. 3593–3967.

Keller, Von Henning. "Die me. Rezepte des Ms. Harley 2253." *Archiv für das studium der neueren Sprachen und Literaturen* 207 (1971), 94–100.

Kemble, John M., ed. *The Dialogue of Salomon and Saturn, with an Historical Introduction*. London: Ælfric Society, 1848.

Kennedy, Thomas Corbin. *Anglo-Norman Poems about Love, Women, and Sex from British Museum MS. Harley 2253*. Ph.D. dissertation. New York: Columbia University, 1973.

Ker, N. R. Intro. to *Facsimile of British Museum MS. Harley 2253*. EETS o.s. 255. London: Oxford University Press, 1965.

Kerby-Fulton, Kathryn, Maidie Hilmo, and Linda Olson. *Opening Up Middle English Manuscripts: Literary and Visual Approaches*. Ithaca, NY: Cornell University Press, 2012.

Kinch, Ashby. "Dying for Love: Dialogic Response in the Lyrics of BL MS Harley 2253." In *Courtly Literature and Clerical Culture*. Ed. Christoph Huber and Henrike Lähnemann. Tübingen: Attempto, 2002. Pp. 137–47.

Kingsford, C. L., ed. *The Song of Lewes*. Oxford: Clarendon, 1890.

Kölbing, E., ed. "Klein Publicationen aus der Auchinleck-Hs. I. Lob der frauen." *Englische Studien* 7 (1884), 101–25.

Kremer, Eugen, ed. *La Bible von Hermann de Valenciennes*. Teil IV (Von der Speisung der fünftausend bis zum einzug in Jerusalem). Greifswald, 1914.

Krueger, Roberta L. "Introduction: Teach Your Children Well: Medieval Conduct Guides for Youths." In *Medieval Conduct Literature: An Anthology of Vernacular Guides to Behaviour for Youth, with English Translations*. Ed. Mark D. Johnston. Toronto: University of Toronto Press, 2009. Pp. ix–xxxiii.

Kuczynski, Michael P. (1995). *Prophetic Song: The Psalms as Moral Discourse in Late Medieval England*. Philadelphia: University of Pennsylvania Press, 1995.

—— (2000). "An 'Electric Stream': The Religious Contents." In *Studies in the Harley Manuscript: The Scribes, Contents, and Social Contexts of British Library MS Harley 2253*. Ed. Susanna Fein. Kalamazoo, MI: Mediaeval Institute Publications, 2000. Pp. 123–61.

—— (2012). "An Unpublished Middle English Version of the *Epistola Lentuli*: Text and Contexts." *The Mediaeval Journal* 2 (2012): 35–57.

Kuehne, Oswald Robert. *A Study of the Thaïs Legend with Special Reference to Hrothsvitha's "Paphnutius."* Philadelpha: University of Pennsylvania, 1922.

Kuralyk, Ewa. *Veronica and Her Cloth: History, Symbolism, and Structure of a "True" Image."* Oxford: Basil Blackwell, 1991.

Labarge, Margaret Wade. *Simon de Montfort*. London: Eyre and Spottiswoode, 1961.

Lacy, Norris. *Reading Fabliaux*. New York: Garland, 1993.

Lagorio, Valerie M., and Michael G. Sargent, with Ritamary Bradley. "XXIII. English Mystical Writings." In Severs et al. Pp. 3049–3137, 3405–71.

Lambdin, Laura Cooner, and Robert Thomas Lambdin. "Debate Poetry." In *A Companion to Old and Middle English Literature*. Ed. Laura Cooner Lambdin and Robert Thomas Lambdin. Westport, CT: Greenwood Press, 2002. Pp. 118–53.

Långfors, Arthur. *Les Incipit des poèmes français antéreurs au XVIᵉ siècle: Répertoire bibliographique*. 1917; repr. New York: Burt Franklin, 1970.

Lerer, Seth (2003). "Medieval English Literature and the Idea of the Anthology." *PMLA* 118 (2003), 1251–67.

—— (2008). "'Dum ludis floribus': Language and Text in the Medieval English Lyric." *Philological Quarterly* 87 (2008), 237–55.

Liszka, Thomas R. "Talk in the Camps: On the Dating of the *South English Legendary*, *Havelok the Dane*, and *King Horn* in Oxford, Bodleian Library, MS Laud Misc. 108." In *The Texts and Contexts of Oxford, Bodleian Library, MS Laud Misc. 108: The Shaping of English Vernacular Narrative*. Ed. Kimberly K. Bell and Julie Nelson Couch. Leiden: Brill, 2011. Pp. 31–50.

Little, A. G. *Studies in English Franciscan History*. Manchester: Manchester University Press, 1917.

Louis, Cameron. "XXII. Proverbs, Precepts, and Monitory Pieces." In Severs et al. Pp. 2957–3048, 3349–3404.

Lucas, Angela M., ed. and trans. *Anglo-Irish Poems of the Middle Ages*. Dublin: Columba Press, 1995.

Lynch, Andrew. "Genre, Bodies, and Power in Oxford, Bodleian Library, MS Laud Misc. 108: *King Horn*, *Havelok*, and the *South English Legendary*." In *The Texts and Contexts of Oxford, Bodleian Library, MS Laud Misc. 108: The Shaping of English Vernacular Narrative*. Ed. Kimberly K. Bell and Julie Nelson Couch. Leiden: Brill, 2011. Pp. 177–96.

Lyons, W. H. "Doctrinal Logic and Poetic Justice in the Twelfth Century: The Case of Herman de Valeniennes, Solomon and Henry II." In *Currents of Thought in French Literature: Essays in Memory of G. T. Clapton*. Ed. J. C. Ireson. Oxford: Basil Blackwell, 1965. Pp. 21–32.

MacCulloch, J. A. *The Harrowing of Hell: A Comparative Study of an Early Christian Doctrine*. Edinburgh: T. & T. Clark, 1930.

Macray, William Dunn, ed. *Chronicon abbatiae de Evesham ad annum 1418.* London: Longman, Green, Longman, Roberts, and Green, 1863.

Maddicott, J. R. *Simon de Montfort*. Cambridge: Cambridge University Press, 1994.

Margherita, Gayle. *The Romance of Origins: Language and Sexual Difference in Middle English Literature*. Philadelphia: University of Pennsylvania Press, 1994.

Martin, Ernst, ed. *La Bible von Hermann de Valenciennes*. Teil V (Von Christi einzug in Jerusalem bis zur himmelfahrt). Greifswald, 1914.

Martin, Lawrence T., ed. *Somniale Danielis: An Edition of a Medieval Latin Dream Interpretation Handbook*. Frankfurt am Main: Peter D. Lang,

Marx. C. W[illiam] (1995). *The Devil's Rights and the Redemption in the Literature of Medieval England*. Cambridge: D. S. Brewer, 1995.

———— (1997). "The *Gospel of Nicodemus* in Old English and Middle English." In *The Medieval Gospel of Nicodemus: Texts, Intertexts, and Contexts in Western Europe*. Ed. Zbigniew Izydorczyk. Tempe, AR: Medieval and Renaissance Texts and Studies, 1997. Pp. 207–59.

———— (2013), ed. *The Middle English Liber Aureus and Gospel of Nicodemus Edited from London British Library, MS Egerton 2658*. Heidelberg: Winter, 2013.

Marx. C. William, and Jeanne F. Drennan, eds. *The Middle English Prose Complaint of Our Lady and Gospel of Nicodemus ed. from Cambridge, Magdalene College, MS Pepys 2498*. Heidelberg: Carl Winter, 1987.

Matthews, John. "The Games of Robin Hood." In *Robin Hood: Anthology of Scholarship and Criticism*. Ed. Stephen Knight. Cambridge: D. S. Brewer, 1999. Pp. 393–410.

Maulsby, Stephen C. "The Harley Lyrics Revisited: A Multilingual Textual Community." Ph.D. dissertation, Catholic University of America, 2008.

McCarthy, Conor, ed. *Love, Sex and Marriage in the Middle Ages: A Sourcebook*. London: Routledge, 2004.

McKitterick, David, ed. *The Trinity Apocalypse (Trinity College Cambridge, MS R.16.2)*. London: The British Library, 2005.

McKnight, George H., ed. *King Horn, Floriȝ and Blauncheflur, The Assumption of our Lady*. EETS o.s. 14. London: Oxford University Press, 1901; repr. 1962.

McSparran, Frances. "The Language of the English Poems: The Harley Scribe and His Exemplars." In *Studies in the Harley Manuscript: The Scribes, Contents, and Social Contexts of British Library MS Harley 2253*. Ed. Susanna Fein. Kalamazoo, MI: Medieval Institute Publications, 2000. Pp. 391–426.

Menner, Robert J. "The Man in the Moon and Hedging." *Journal of English and Germanic Philology* 48 (1949), 1–14.

Meyer, Paul (1895). "Notice sur le manuscrit fr. 24862 de la Bibliothèque nationale contenant divers ouvrages composés ou éscrits en Angleterre." *Notices et extraits* 35 (1895), 131–68.

———— (1889). "Notice du ms. Egerton 2710 de Musée britannique." *Bulletin de la Société des anciens textes français* 15 (1889), 72–95.

———— (1903). "Les manuscripts français de Cambridge." *Romania* 32 (1903), 18–120.

Michelant, Henri, and Gaston Raynaud, eds. *Itinéraires à Jérusalem et descriptions de la Terre Sainte rédigés en français aux XI^e, XII^e & XIII^e siecles*. Preface by Comte Riant. Publications de la Société de l'Orient latin, Série Géographique 3: Itinéraires français. Geneva: Jules-Guillaume Fick, 1882.

*Middle English Dictionary (MED)*. Online at http://quod.lib.umich.edu/m/med.

Migne, J.-P., ed. *Patrologiae cursus completus . . . series latina*. Paris, 1844–64.

Mill, Anna J. "XII. Dramatic Pieces. 1. The Miracle Plays and Mysteries." In Severs et al. Pp. 1315–56, 1557–98.

Millett, Bella. *Wessex Parallel WebTexts*. 2003. Online at http://www.soton.ac.uk/~wpwt/.

Monda, Joseph B. "'The Sayings of Saint Bernard' from MS Bodleian Additional E 6." *Mediaeval Studies* 32 (1970), 299–307.

Montaiglon, Anatole de, and Gaston Raynaud, eds. *Recueil général et complet des fabliaux des XIII^e et XIV^e siècles*. 6 vols. Paris, 1872–90; repr. New York, 1964.

Mooney, Linne, Simon Horobin, and Estelle Stubbs. *Late Medieval English Scribes*. York: University of York, 2011. Online at http://www.medievalscribes.com.

Mooney, Linne, and Estelle Stubbs. *Scribes and the City: London Guildhall Clerks and the Dissemination of Middle English Literature 1375–1425*. York: York Medieval Press, 2013.

Morris, Richard, and Walter W. Skeat, eds. *Specimens of Early English. Part II: From Robert of Gloucester to Gower, A.D. 1298–A.D. 1393*. Second edition. Oxford: Clarendon, 1873.

Muir, Lawrence. "IV. Translations and Paraphrases of the Bible, and Commentaries." In Severs et al. Pp. 1385–1536, 1631–1725.

*The Murder of King Ethelbert of East Anglia — 794 AD*. http://www.herefordwebpages.co.uk/ethel.shtml.

Murray, H. J. R. *A History of Chess*. Oxford: Oxford University Press, 1913.

Murray, Hilda M. R., ed. *The Middle English Poem, Erthe upon Erthe, Printed from Twenty-Four Manuscripts*. EETS o.s. 141. 1911; Oxford: Oxford University Press, 1964.

Murray, James A. H., ed. *The Romance and Prophecies of Thomas of Erceldoune*. EETS 61. London: N. Trüber, 1875; repr. Felinbach: Llanerch,1991.

Muscatine, Charles. *The Old French Fabliaux*. New Haven, CT: Yale University Press, 1986.

Nelson, Ingrid Lynn (2010). "The Lyric in England, 1200–1400." Ph.D. dissertation, Harvard University, 2010.

——— (2013). "The Performance of Power in Medieval English Households: The Case of the *Harrowing of Hell*." *Journal of English and Germanic Philology* 112 (2013), 48–69.

Newhauser, Richard. "Historicity and Complaint in *Song of the Husbandman*." In *Studies in the Harley Manuscript: The Scribes, Contents, and Social Contexts of British Library MS Harley 2253*. Ed. Susanna Fein. Kalamazoo, MI: Medieval Institute Publications, 2000. Pp. 203–17.

Nicholls, Jonathan. *The Matter of Courtesy: Medieval Courtesy Books and the Gawain-Poet*. Woodbridge: D. S. Brewer, 1985.

Nichols, Stephen G., and Siegfried Wenzel, eds. *The Whole Book: Cultural Perspective on the Medieval Miscellany*. Ann Arbor: University of Michigan Press, 1996.

Nolan, Barbara. "Anthologizing Ribaldry: Five Anglo-Norman Fabliaux." In *Studies in the Harley Manuscript: The Scribes, Contents, and Social Contexts of British Library MS Harley 2253*. Ed. Susanna Fein. Kalamazoo, MI: Medieval Institute Publications, 2000. Pp. 289–327.

Noomen, Willem, and Nico van den Boogard, eds. *Nouveau recueil complet des fabliaux*. 10 vols. Assen: Van Gorcum, 1983–98.

Nykrog, Per. *Les Fabliaux: Nouvelle édition*. Geneva: Librairie Droz, 1973.

O'Connell, David, ed. *The Teachings of Saint Louis: A Critical Text*. Chapel Hill: University of North Carolina Press, 1972.

O'Connor, Br. Basilides Andrew, ed. *Henri D'Arci's* Vitas Patrum*: A Thirteenth-Century Anglo-Norman Rimed Translation of the* Verba Seniorum. Washington, DC: The Catholic University of America, 1949.

O'Farrell-Tate, Una, ed. *The Abridged English Metrical Brut Edited from London, British Library MS Royal 12.C.XII*. Heidelberg: C. Winter, 2002.

Ogilvie-Thomson, S. J., ed. *Richard Rolle: Prose and Verse, Edited from MS Longleat 29 and Related Manuscripts*. EETS o.s. 293. Oxford: Oxford University Press, 1988.

O'Gorman, Richard. "The *Gospel of Nicodemus* in the Vernacular Literature of Medieval France." In *The Medieval Gospel of Nicodemus: Texts, Intertexts, and Contexts in Western Europe*. Ed. Zbigniew Izydorczyk. Tempe, AR: Medieval and Renaissance Texts and Studies, 1997. Pp. 103–31.

O'Rourke, Jason (2000). "British Library MS Royal 12 C. xii and the Problems of Patronage." *Journal of the Early Book Society* 3 (2000), 216–25.

——— (2005). "Imagining Book Production in Fourteenth-Century Herefordshire: The Scribe of British Library, Harley 2253 and His 'Organizing Principles.'" In *Imagining the Book*. Ed. Stephen Kelly and John J. Thompson. Turnhout: Brepols, 2005. Pp. 45–60.

Ovid. *Metamorphoses*. Trans. David Raeburn. London: Penguin, 2004.

Parkes, M. B. *English Cursive Book Hands 1250–1500*. Oxford: Clarendon Press, 1969.

Parsons, H. Rosamond. "Anglo-Norman Books of Courtesy and Nurture." *PMLA* 44 (1929), 383–455.

Patterson, Frank Allen, ed. *The Middle English Penitential Lyric: A Study and Collection of Early Religious Verse*. New York: Columbia University Press, 1911.

Pearcy, Roy J. (1978). "Chansons de Geste and Fabliaux: 'La Gageure' and 'Berenger au long cul.'" *Neuphilologische Mitteilungen* 79 (1978), 76–83.

——— (2007). *Logic and Humour in the Fabliaux: An Essay in Applied Narratology*. Cambridge: D. S. Brewer, 2007.

Pearsall, Derek. *Old English and Middle English Poetry*. London: Routledge and Kegan Paul, 1977.

Peck, Russell A. (1970). "Theme and Number in Chaucer's *Book of the Duchess*." In *Silent Poetry: Essays in Numerological Analysis*. Ed. Alastair Fowler. London: Routledge, 1970. Pp. 73–115.

——— (1975). "Public Dreams and Private Myths: Perspective in Middle English Literature." *PMLA* 90 (1975), 461–68.

———— (1991), ed. *Heroic Women from the Old Testament in Middle English Verse*. Kalamazoo, MI: Medieval Institute Publications, 1991.

Perman, R. C. D., ed. "Henri d'Arci: The Shorter Works." In *Studies in Medieval French Presented to Alfred Ewert in Honour of His Seventieth Birthday*. Ed. E. A. Francis. Oxford: Clarendon, 1961. Pp. 279–321.

Pfaff, R. W. *New Liturgical Feasts in Later Medieval England*. Oxford: Clarendon, 1970.

Phillips, Helen. "Dreams and Dream Lore." In *Studies in the Harley Manuscript: The Scribes, Contents, and Social Contexts of British Library MS Harley 2253*. Ed. Susanna Fein. Kalamazoo, MI: Medieval Institute Publications, 2000. Pp. 241–59.

Pickering, Oliver. "Stanzaic Verse in the Auchinleck Manuscript: *The Alphabetical Praise of Women*." In *Studies in Late Medieval and Early Renaissance Texts in Honour of John Scattergood*. Ed. Anne Marie D'Arcy and Alan J. Fletcher. Dublin: Four Courts Press, 2005. Pp. 287–304.

Pringle, Denys (1993, 1998, 2007, 2009). *The Churches of the Crusader Kingdom of Jerusalem: A Corpus*. 4 vols. Cambridge: Cambridge University Press, 1993, 1998, 2007, 2009.

———— (2012). *Pilgrimage to Jerusalem and the Holy Land, 1187–1291*. Crusade Texts in Translation, 23. Burlington, VT: Ashgate, 2012.

Ransom, Daniel J. *Poets at Play: Irony and Parody in the Harley Lyrics*. Norman, OK: Pilgrim Books, 1985.

Raskolnikov, Masha. *Body against Soul: Gender and* Sowlehele *in Middle English Allegory*. Columbus: Ohio State University Press, 2009.

Raymo, Robert R. "XX. Works of Religious and Philosophical Instruction." In Severs et al. Pp. 2255–2378, 2467–2582.

Reichl, Karl (1973), ed. *Religiöse Dichtung im Englischen Hochmittelalter*. Munich: Wilhelm Fink, 1973.

———— (2000). "Debate Verse." In *Studies in the Harley Manuscript: The Scribes, Contents, and Social Contexts of British Library MS Harley 2253*. Ed. Susanna Fein. Kalamazoo, MI: Medieval Institute Publications, 2000. Pp. 219–39.

Reimer, Stephen R., ed. *The Works of William Herebert, OFM*. Toronto: Pontifical Institute of Mediaeval Studies, 1987.

Revard, Carter (1982). "*Gilote et Johane*: An Interlude in B. L. MS. Harley 2253." *Studies in Philology* 79 (1982), 122–46.

———— (2000a). "From French 'Fabliau Manuscripts' and MS Harley 2253 to the *Decameron* and the *Canterbury Tales*." *Medium Ævum* 69 (2000), 261–78.

———— (2000b). "Scribe and Provenance." In *Studies in the Harley Manuscript: The Scribes, Contents, and Social Contexts of British Library MS Harley 2253*. Ed. Susanna Fein. Kalamazoo, MI: Medieval Institute Publications, 2000. Pp. 21–109.

———— (2004). "*The Wife of Bath's Grandmother*: or How Gilote Showed Her Friend Johane That the Wages of Sin Is Worldly Pleasure, and How Both Then Preached This Gospel throughout England and Ireland." *Chaucer Review* 39 (2004), 117–36.

———— (2005a). "Four Fabliaux from London, British Library MS Harley 2253, Translated into English Verse." *Chaucer Review* 40 (2005), 111–40.

———— (2005b). "*A Goliard's Feast* and the Metanarrative of Harley 2253." *Revue Belge de Philologie et d'Histoire* 83 (2005), 841–67.

———— (2005c). "The Outlaw's Song of Trailbaston." In *Medieval Outlaws: Twelve Tales in Modern English Translation*. Ed. Thomas H. Ohlgren. Second edition. West Lafayette, IN: Parlor Press, 2005. Pp. 151–64.

———— (2007). "Oppositional Thematics and Metanarrative in MS Harley 2253, Quires 1–6." In *Essays in Manuscript Geography: Vernacular Manuscripts of the English West Midlands from the Conquest to the Sixteenth Century*. Ed. Wendy Scase. Turnhout: Brepols, 2007. Pp. 95–112.

Rézeau, Pierre. *Les Prières aux saints en française à la fin du moyen âge*. 2 vols. Geneva: Droz, 1982–83.

Rigg, A. G. (1986), ed. *Gawain on Marriage: The Textual Tradition of the "De coniuge non ducenda" with Critical Edition and Translation*. Toronto: Pontifical Institute of Mediaeval Studies, 1986.

———— (1992). *A History of Anglo-Latin Literature 1066–1422*. Cambridge: Cambridge University Press, 1996.

Ritson, Joseph (1877), ed. *Ancient Songs and Ballads from the Reign of King Henry the Second to the Revolution*. Third edition. Rev. W. Carew Hazlitt. London: Reeves and Turner, 1877.

———— (1884, 1885), ed. *Ancient English Metrical Romances*. Second edition. Rev. Edmund Goldsmid. 2 vols. Edinburgh: E & G Goldsmid, 1884, 1885.

Robbins, Rossell Hope (1959), ed. *Historical Poems of the XIVth and XVth Centuries*. New York: Columbia University Press, 1959.

———— (1975). "XIII. Poems Dealing with Contemporary Conditions." In Severs et al. Pp. 1385–1536, 1631–1725.

Robbins, Rossell Hope, and John L. Cutler. *Supplement to the Index of Middle English Verse*. Lexington: University of Kentucky Press, 1955.

Rock, Catherine A. *Romances Copied by the Ludlow Scribe*: Purgatoire Saint Patrice, Short Metrical Chronicle, Fouke le Fitz Waryn, *and* King Horn. Ph.D. dissertation. Kent, OH: Kent State University, 2008.

Rohde, Eleanour Sinclair. *The Old English Herbals*. London: Longmans, Green, 1922.

Rosenthal, Constance. *The Vitae Patrum in Old and Middle English Literature*. Philadelphia: University of Pennsylvania, 1936. repr. Folcroft, PA: Folcroft Library Editions, 1974.

Russell, Delbert W., ed. (1976). *La Vie de Saint Laurent: An Anglo-Norman Poem of the Twelfth Century*. Anglo-Norman Texts 34. London: Anglo-Norman Text Society, 1976.

———— (1989). *Légendier apostolique anglo-normand: édition, critique, introduction et notes*. Montreal: Les Presses del'Université de Montréal, 1989.

Russell, Norman, trans. *The Lives of the Desert Fathers*. Kalamazoo: Cistercian Publications, 1981.

Salisbury, Eve, ed. *The Trials and Joys of Marriage*. Kalamazoo, MI: Medieval Institute Publications, 2002.

Salter, Elizabeth. *Fourteenth-Century English Poetry: Contexts and Readings*. Oxford: Clarendon, 1983.

Samuels, M. L. "The Dialect of the Scribe of the Harley Lyrics." In *Middle English Dialectology: Essays on Some Principles and Problems*. Ed. Angus McIntosh, M. L. Samuels, and Margaret Laing. Aberdeen: Aberdeen University Press, 1989. Pp. 256–63.

Sands, Donald B., ed. *Middle English Verse Romances*. New York: Holt, Rinehart and Winston, 1966.

Saupe, Karen, ed. *Middle English Marian Lyrics*. Kalamazoo, MI: Medieval Institute Publications, 1998.

*Sayings of the Desert Fathers*. Online at www.orthodoxwiki.org/Sayings_of_the_Desert_Fathers.

Scahill, John. "Trilingualism in Early Middle English Miscellanies: Languages and Literature." *Yearbook of English Studies* 33 (2003), 18–52.

Scase, Wendy (2005). "*Satire on the Retinues of the Great* (MS Harley 2253): Unpaid Bills and the Politics of Purveyance." In *Studies in Late Medieval and Early Renaissance Texts in Honour of John Scattergood*. Ed. Anne Marie D'Arcy and Alan J. Fletcher. Dublin: Four Courts Press, 2005. Pp. 305–20.

———— (2007). *Literature and Complaint in England 1272–1553*. Oxford: Oxford University Press, 2007.

Scase, Wendy, ed., and Nick Kennedy, software. *A Facsimile Edition of the Vernon Manuscript, Oxford, Bodleian Library MS. Eng. poet. a. 1*. Bodleian Digital Texts 3. DVD-ROM. Oxford: Bodleian Library, University of Oxford, 2012.

Scattergood, John (2000a). "Authority and Resistance: The Political Verse." In *Studies in the Harley Manuscript: The Scribes, Contents, and Social Contexts of British Library MS Harley 2253*. Ed. Susanna Fein. Kalamazoo, MI: Medieval Institute Publications, 2000. Pp. 163–201.

———— (2000b). *The Lost Tradition: Essays on Middle English Alliterative Poetry*. Dublin: Four Courts Press, 2000.

———— (2005). "The Love Lyric before Chaucer." In *A Companion to the Middle English Lyric*. Ed. Thomas G. Duncan. Cambridge: D. S. Brewer, 2005. Pp. 39–67.

———— (2010). "Alliterative Poetry and Politics." In *A Companion to Medieval Poetry*. Ed. Corinne Saunders. Oxford: Blackwell Publishing, 2010. Pp. 349–66.

Schleich, G. "Die Sprichwörter Hendings und die Prouerbis of Wysdom." *Anglia* 51 (1927), 220–78.

Schmitt, P. Franciscus Salesius, ed. *Ein Neues Unvollendetes Werk des HL. Anselm von Canterbury.* Münster: Aschendorffschen, 1936.

Severs, J. Burke, Albert E. Hartung, and Peter G. Beidler, eds. *A Manual of the Writings in Middle English, 1050–1500.* 11 vols. New Haven: Connecticut Academy of Arts and Sciences, 1967–2005. [For specific chapters cited in the explanatory notes, see: Dunn (vol. 1), Fein 2005 (vol. 11), Foster (vol. 2), Fowler (vol. 6), Greene 1980 (vol. 6), Keiser (vol. 10), Lagorio and Sargent (vol. 9), Louis (vol. 9), Mill (vol. 5), Raymo (vol. 7), Robbins 1975 (vol. 5), and Utley (vol. 3).]

Seymour, M. C. (1963), ed. *The Bodley Version of Mandeville's Travels.* EETS o.s. 253. London: Oxford University Press, 1963.

———— (1973), ed. *The Metrical Version of Mandeville's Travels.* EETS o.s. 269. London: Oxford University Press, 1973.

———— (1993). *Sir John Mandeville.* Authors of the Middle Ages 1. Aldershot: Variorum, 1993.

———— (2002), ed. *The Defective Version of Mandeville's Travels.* EETS o.s. 319. Oxford: Oxford University Press, 2002.

———— (2010), ed. *The Egerton Version of Mandeville's Travels.* EETS o.s. 336. Oxford: Oxford University Press, 2010.

Shields, Hugh. "*The Lament for Simon de Montfort*: An Unnoticed Text of the French Poem." *Medium Ævum* 41 (1972), 202–07.

Short, Ian, trans. "Translation of the Life of St John and the Apocalypse." In *The Trinity Apocalypse (Trinity College Cambridge MS R.16.2).* Ed. David McKitterick, Nigel Morgan, Ian Short, and Teresa Webber. CD-ROM. London: The British Library, 2005. CD81–CD94.

Short, Ian, and Roy Pearcy, eds. *Eighteen Anglo-Norman Fabliaux.* ANTS Plain Texts Series 14. London: Anglo-Norman Text Society, 2000.

Shuffelton, George, ed. *Codex Ashmole 61: A Compilation of Popular Middle English Verse.* Kalamazoo, MI: Medieval Institute Publications, 2008.

Silverstein, Theodore, ed. *Medieval English Lyrics.* London: Edward Arnold, 1971.

Sims-Williams, Patrick. *Religion and Literature in Western England 600–800.* Cambridge: Cambridge University Press, 1990.

Sinclair, Keith V. (1979). *French Devotional Texts of the Middle Ages: A Bibliographic Manuscript Guide.* Westport, CT: Greenwood Press, 1979.

———— (1982). *French Devotional Texts of the Middle Ages: A Bibliographic Manuscript Guide, First Supplement.* Westport, CT: Greenwood Press, 1982.

———— (1988). *French Devotional Texts of the Middle Ages: A Bibliographic Manuscript Guide. Second Supplement.* New York: Greenwood Press, 1988.

———— (1997). "The Translations of the *Vitas patrum*, *Thaïs*, Antichrist, and *Vision de saint Paul.* Made for Anglo-Norman Templars: Some Neglected Literary Considerations." *Speculum* 72 (1997), 741–62.

Skeat, W. W., ed. "'Elegy on the Death of King Edward I' from a New MS." *Modern Language Review* 7 (1912), 149–50.

Skemer, Don C. *Binding Words: Textual Amulets in the Middle Ages.* University Park: Pennsylvania State University Press, 2006.

Spiele, Ina, ed. *Li Romanz de Dieu et sa mere d'Herman de Valenciennes chanoine et prêtre (XIIe siècle).* Leyde: Presse Universitaire de Leyde, 1975.

Solopova, Elizabeth. "Layout, Punctuation, and Stanza Patterns in the English Verse." In *Studies in the Harley Manuscript: The Scribes, Contents, and Social Contexts of British Library MS Harley 2253.* Ed. Susanna Fein. Kalamazoo, MI: Medieval Institute Publications, 2000. Pp. 377–89.

Stemmler, Theo (1970), ed. *Medieval English Love-Lyrics.* Tübingen: Max Niemeyer, 1970.

———— (2000). "Miscellany or Anthology? The Structure of Medieval Manuscripts: MS Harley 2253, for Example." In *Studies in the Harley Manuscript: The Scribes, Contents, and Social Contexts of British Library MS Harley 2253.* Ed. Susanna Fein. Kalamazoo, MI: Medieval Institute Publications, 2000. Pp. 111–21.

Suchier, Walther. *L'Enfant Sage (Das Gespräch des Kaisers Hadrian mit dem klugen Kinde Epitus)*. Dresden: Max Niemeyer, 1910.

Swanson, Jenny. *John of Wales: A Study of the Works and Ideas of a Thirteenth–Century Friar*. Cambridge: Cambridge University Press, 1989.

Tamburr, Karl. *The Harrowing of Hell in Medieval England*. Cambridge: D. S. Brewer, 2007.

Taylor, Andrew (2002). *Textual Situations: Three Medieval Manuscripts and Their Readers*. Philadelphia: University of Pennsylvania Press, 2002.

—— (2011). "'Her Y Spelle': The Evocation of Minstrel Performance in a Hagiographical Context." In *The Texts and Contexts of Oxford, Bodleian Library, MS Laud Misc. 108: The Shaping of English Vernacular Narrative*. Ed. Kimberly K. Bell and Julie Nelson Couch. Leiden: Brill, 2011. Pp. 71–86.

Taylor, Mark N. "Chaucer's Knowledge of Chess." *Chaucer Review* 38 (2004), 299–313.

Thompson, John J. (1997). "The Governance of the English Tongue: The *Cursor Mundi* and Its French Tradition." In *Individuality and Achievement in Middle English Poetry*. Ed. O. S. Pickering. Cambridge: D. S. Brewer, 1997. Pp. 19–37.

—— (2000). "'Frankis rimes here I redd, / Communlik in ilk[a] sted . . .': The French Bible Stories in Harley 2253." In *Studies in the Harley Manuscript: The Scribes, Contents, and Social Contexts of British Library MS Harley 2253*. Ed. Susanna Fein. Kalamazoo, MI: Medieval Institute Publications, 2000. Pp. 271–88.

—— (2007). "Mapping Points West of West Midlands Manuscripts and Texts: Irishness(es) and Middle English Literary Culture." In *Essays in Manuscript Geography: Vernacular Manuscripts of the English West Midlands from the Conquest to the Sixteenth Century*. Ed. Wendy Scase. Turnhout: Brepols, 2007. Pp. 113–28.

Thorndike, Lynn. "All the World's a Chess-Board." *Speculum* 6 (1931), 461–65.

Travis, Peter W. *Disseminal Chaucer: Rereading the Nun's Priest's Tale*. Notre Dame, IN: University of Notre Dame Press, 2010.

Treharne, Elaine, ed. *Old and Middle English c.890–c.1450*. Third edition. Chichester: Wiley-Blackwell, 2010.

Tristram, Philippa. *Figures of Life and Death in Medieval English Literature*. New York: New York University Press, 1976.

Tschann, Judith, and M. B. Parkes. Introduction to *Facsimile of Oxford, Bodleian Library, MS Digby 86*. EETS s.s. 16. Oxford: Oxford University Press, 1996.

Tucker, Samuel Marion. *Verse Satire in England before the Renaissance*. New York: Columbia University Press, 1908; repr. New York: AMS, 1966.

Turville-Petre, Thorlac (1989), ed. *Alliterative Poetry of the Later Middle Ages: An Anthology*. Washington, DC: Catholic University of America Press, 1989.

—— (1996). *England the Nation: Language, Literature, and National Identity, 1290–1340*. Oxford: Clarendon, 1996.

—— (1997). "English Quaint and Strange in 'Ne mai no lewed lued.'" In *Individuality and Achievement in Middle English Poetry*. Ed. O. S. Pickering. Cambridge: D. S. Brewer, 1997. Pp. 73–83.

Tyson, Diana B. "'Against the King's Taxes': The Second Manuscript." *Nottingham Medieval Studies* 54 (2010), 73–92.

Ulrich, J. "La riote du monde." *Zeitschrift für Romanische Philologie* 8 (1884), 275–89.

Utley, Francis Lee. "VII. Dialogues, Debates, and Catechisms." In Severs et al. Pp. 669–756, 829–902.

Valois, Noël. "Jacques Duèse, pape sous le nom de Jean XXII." *Histoire littéraire de la France* 34 (1914), 391–630.

Van Deusen, Nancy, ed. *The Place of the Psalms in the Intellectual Culture of the Middle Ages*. Albany: State University of New York Press, 1999.

Varnhagen, Hermann. "Zu mittelenglischen Gedichten. XI. Zu den sprichwörtern Hending's." *Anglia* 4 (1881), 180–210.

Vincent, Nicholas. *The Holy Blood: King Henry III and the Westminster Blood Relic*. Cambridge: Cambridge University Press, 2001.

Vising, Johan. *Anglo-Norman Language and Literature*. London: Oxford University Press, 1923.

Voragine. See Jacobus de Voragine.

Walker, Ian W. *Mercia and the Making of England*. Stroud, Gloucestershire: Sutton, 2000.

Walpole, Ronald N., ed. *The Old French Johannes Translation of the Pseudo-Turpin Chronicle: Supplement*. Berkeley: University of California Press, 1976.

Wanley, Humfrey, D. Casley et al. *A Catalogue of the Harleian Manuscripts in the British Museum*. 1759; rev. and repr. in 4 vols., London, 1808–12.

Ward, Benedicta, trans. *The Sayings of the Desert Fathers: The Alphabetical Collection*. Kalamazoo, MI: Cistercian Publications, 1975.

Waters, Claire M., ed. and trans. *Virgins and Scholars: A Fifteenth-Century Compilation of the Lives of John the Baptist, John the Evangelist, Jerome, and Katherine of Alexandria*. Turnhout: Brepolis, 2008.

Whatley, E. Gordon, ed., with Anne B. Thompson and Robert K. Upchurch. *Saints' Lives in Middle English Collections*. Kalamazoo, MI: Medieval Institute Publications, 2004.

Whiting, Bartlett Jere, with Helen Wescott Whiting. *Proverbs, Sentences, ands Proverbial Phrases from English Writings Mainly before 1500*. Cambridge, MA: Belknap Press of Harvard University Press, 1968.

Wiggins, Alison. "Middle English Romance and the West Midlands." In *Essays in Manuscript Geography: Vernacular Manuscripts of the English West Midlands from the Conquest to the Sixteenth Century*. Ed. Wendy Scase. Turnhout: Brepols, 2007. Pp. 239–55.

Wilmart, André. *Auteurs spirituels et textes dévots du moyen âge latin*. 1932; repr. Paris: Études augustiennes, 1971.

Wilshere, A. D. (1982), ed. *Miroir de Seinte Eglise (St. Edmund of Abingdon's Speculum Ecclesiae)*. Anglo-Norman Texts 40. London: Anglo-Norman Text Society, 1982.

——— (1988). "The Anglo-Norman Bible Stories in MS Harley 2253." *Forum for Modern Language Studies* 24 (1988), 78–89.

Wogan-Browne, Jocelyn, Carolyn Collette, Maryanne Kowaleski, Linne Mooney, Ad Putter, and David Trotter, eds. *Language and Culture in Medieval Britain: The French of England, c.1100–c.1500*. Woodbridge: York Medieval Press, 2009.

Woolf, Rosemary (1968). *The English Religious Lyric in the Middle Ages*. Oxford: Clarendon, 1968.

——— (1970). "Later Poetry: The Popular Tradition." In *The Middle Ages*. Ed. W. F. Bolton. London: Barrie & Jenkins, 1970. Pp. 263–311.

Woolgar, C. M., ed. *Household Accounts from Medieval England*. Part 1: *Introduction, Glossary, Diet Accounts (I)*. Records of Social and Economic History n.s. 17. Oxford: Oxford University Press for The British Academy, 1992.

Wright, Thomas (1839), ed. *Political Songs of England, from the Reign of John to That of Edward II*. 1839; repr. with an intro. by Peter Coss. Cambridge: Cambridge University Press, 1996.

——— (1841), ed. *The Latin Poems Commonly Attributed to Walter Mapes*. London: John Bowyer Nichols and Son (for the Camden Society), 1841; repr. New York: AMS Press, 1968.

——— (1842), ed. *Specimens of Lyric Poetry, Composed in England in the Reign of Edward the First*. Percy Society, 1842; repr. New York: Johnson Reprint Corporation, 1965.

——— (1844), ed. "Early English Receipts for Painting, Gilding, &c." *Archaeological Journal* 1 (1844), 64–66.

Wright, Thomas, and James Orchard Halliwell, eds. *Reliquiae Antiquae*. 2 vols. London: John Russell Smith, 1845.

Yorke, Barbara. *Kings and Kingdoms of Early Anglo-Saxon England*. London: Seaby, 1990.

Ziolkowski, Jan M. (1998), ed. and trans. *The Cambridge Songs (Carmina Cantabrigiensia)*. Tempe, AR: Medieval & Renaissance Texts and Studies, 1998.

——— (2008). *Solomon and Marcolf*. Cambridge, MA: Harvard University Press, 2008.

## ✒ MIDDLE ENGLISH TEXTS SERIES

*The Floure and the Leafe, The Assembly of Ladies, The Isle of Ladies*, edited by Derek Pearsall (1990)

*Three Middle English Charlemagne Romances*, edited by Alan Lupack (1990)

*Six Ecclesiastical Satires*, edited by James M. Dean (1991)

*Heroic Women from the Old Testament in Middle English Verse*, edited by Russell A. Peck (1991)

*The Canterbury Tales: Fifteenth-Century Continuations and Additions*, edited by John M. Bowers (1992)

Gavin Douglas, *The Palis of Honoure*, edited by David Parkinson (1992)

*Wynnere and Wastoure and The Parlement of the Thre Ages*, edited by Warren Ginsberg (1992)

*The Shewings of Julian of Norwich*, edited by Georgia Ronan Crampton (1994)

*King Arthur's Death: The Middle English Stanzaic Morte Arthur and Alliterative Morte Arthure*, edited by Larry D. Benson, revised by Edward E. Foster (1994)

*Lancelot of the Laik and Sir Tristrem*, edited by Alan Lupack (1994)

*Sir Gawain: Eleven Romances and Tales*, edited by Thomas Hahn (1995)

*The Middle English Breton Lays*, edited by Anne Laskaya and Eve Salisbury (1995)

*Sir Perceval of Galles and Ywain and Gawain*, edited by Mary Flowers Braswell (1995)

*Four Middle English Romances: Sir Isumbras, Octavian, Sir Eglamour of Artois, Sir Tryamour*, edited by Harriet Hudson (1996; second edition 2006)

*The Poems of Laurence Minot, 1333–1352*, edited by Richard H. Osberg (1996)

*Medieval English Political Writings*, edited by James M. Dean (1996)

*The Book of Margery Kempe*, edited by Lynn Staley (1996)

*Amis and Amiloun, Robert of Cisyle, and Sir Amadace*, edited by Edward E. Foster (1997; second edition 2007)

*The Cloud of Unknowing*, edited by Patrick J. Gallacher (1997)

*Robin Hood and Other Outlaw Tales*, edited by Stephen Knight and Thomas Ohlgren (1997; second edition 2000)

*The Poems of Robert Henryson*, edited by Robert L. Kindrick with the assistance of Kristie A. Bixby (1997)

*Moral Love Songs and Laments*, edited by Susanna Greer Fein (1998)

John Lydgate, *Troy Book Selections*, edited by Robert R. Edwards (1998)

Thomas Usk, *The Testament of Love*, edited by R. Allen Shoaf (1998)

*Prose Merlin*, edited by John Conlee (1998)

*Middle English Marian Lyrics*, edited by Karen Saupe (1998)

John Metham, *Amoryus and Cleopes*, edited by Stephen F. Page (1999)

*Four Romances of England: King Horn, Havelok the Dane, Bevis of Hampton, Athelston*, edited by Ronald B. Herzman, Graham Drake, and Eve Salisbury (1999)

*The Assembly of Gods: Le Assemble de Dyeus, or Banquet of Gods and Goddesses, with the Discourse of Reason and Sensuality*, edited by Jane Chance (1999)

Thomas Hoccleve, *The Regiment of Princes*, edited by Charles R. Blyth (1999)

John Capgrave, *The Life of Saint Katherine*, edited by Karen A. Winstead (1999)

John Gower, *Confessio Amantis*, Vol. 1, edited by Russell A. Peck; with Latin translations by Andrew Galloway (2000; second edition 2006); Vol. 2 (2003; second edition 2013); Vol. 3 (2004)

*Richard the Redeless and Mum and the Sothsegger*, edited by James M. Dean (2000)

*Ancrene Wisse*, edited by Robert Hasenfratz (2000)

Walter Hilton, *The Scale of Perfection*, edited by Thomas H. Bestul (2000)

John Lydgate, *The Siege of Thebes*, edited by Robert R. Edwards (2001)

*Pearl*, edited by Sarah Stanbury (2001)

*The Trials and Joys of Marriage*, edited by Eve Salisbury (2002)

*Middle English Legends of Women Saints*, edited by Sherry L. Reames, with the assistance of Martha G. Blalock and Wendy R. Larson (2003)

*The Wallace: Selections*, edited by Anne McKim (2003)

Richard Maidstone, *Concordia (The Reconciliation of Richard II with London)*, edited by David R. Carlson, with a verse translation by A. G. Rigg (2003)

*Three Purgatory Poems: The Gast of Gy, Sir Owain, The Vision of Tundale*, edited by Edward E. Foster (2004)

William Dunbar, *The Complete Works*, edited by John Conlee (2004)

*Chaucerian Dream Visions and Complaints*, edited by Dana M. Symons (2004)

*Stanzaic Guy of Warwick*, edited by Alison Wiggins (2004)

*Saints' Lives in Middle English Collections*, edited by E. Gordon Whatley, with Anne B. Thompson and Robert K. Upchurch (2004)

*Siege of Jerusalem*, edited by Michael Livingston (2004)

*The Kingis Quair and Other Prison Poems*, edited by Linne R. Mooney and Mary-Jo Arn (2005)

*The Chaucerian Apocrypha: A Selection*, edited by Kathleen Forni (2005)

John Gower, *The Minor Latin Works*, edited and translated by R. F. Yeager, with *In Praise of Peace*, edited by Michael Livingston (2005)

*Sentimental and Humorous Romances: Floris and Blancheflour, Sir Degrevant, The Squire of Low Degree, The Tournament of Tottenham, and The Feast of Tottenham*, edited by Erik Kooper (2006)

*The Dicts and Sayings of the Philosophers*, edited by John William Sutton (2006)

*Everyman and Its Dutch Original, Elckerlijc*, edited by Clifford Davidson, Martin W. Walsh, and Ton J. Broos (2007)

*The N-Town Plays*, edited by Douglas Sugano, with assistance by Victor I. Scherb (2007)

*The Book of John Mandeville*, edited by Tamarah Kohanski and C. David Benson (2007)

John Lydgate, *The Temple of Glas*, edited by J. Allan Mitchell (2007)

*The Northern Homily Cycle*, edited by Anne B. Thompson (2008)

*Codex Ashmole 61: A Compilation of Popular Middle English Verse*, edited by George Shuffelton (2008)

*Chaucer and the Poems of "Ch,"* edited by James I. Wimsatt (revised edition 2009)

William Caxton, *The Game and Playe of the Chesse*, edited by Jenny Adams (2009)

John the Blind Audelay, *Poems and Carols*, edited by Susanna Fein (2009)

*Two Moral Interludes: The Pride of Life and Wisdom*, edited by David Klausner (2009)

John Lydgate, *Mummings and Entertainments*, edited by Claire Sponsler (2010)

*Mankind*, edited by Kathleen M. Ashley and Gerard NeCastro (2010)

*The Castle of Perseverance*, edited by David N. Klausner (2010)

Robert Henryson, *The Complete Works*, edited by David J. Parkinson (2010)

John Gower, *The French Balades*, edited and translated by R. F. Yeager (2011)

*The Middle English Metrical Paraphrase of the Old Testament*, edited by Michael Livingston (2011)

*The York Corpus Christi Plays*, edited by Clifford Davidson (2011)

*Prik of Conscience*, edited by James H. Morey (2012)

*The Dialogue of Solomon and Marcolf: A Dual-Language Edition from Latin and Middle English Printed Editions*, edited by Nancy Mason Bradbury and Scott Bradbury (2012)

*Croxton Play of the Sacrament*, edited by John T. Sebastian (2012)

*Ten Bourdes*, edited by Melissa M. Furrow (2013)

*Lybeaus Desconus*, edited by Eve Salisbury and James Weldon (2013)

## ✒ COMMENTARY SERIES

Haimo of Auxerre, *Commentary on the Book of Jonah*, translated with an introduction and notes by Deborah Everhart (1993)

*Medieval Exegesis in Translation: Commentaries on the Book of Ruth*, translated with an introduction and notes by Lesley Smith (1996)

*Nicholas of Lyra's Apocalypse Commentary*, translated with an introduction and notes by Philip D. W. Krey (1997)

Rabbi Ezra Ben Solomon of Gerona, *Commentary on the Song of Songs and Other Kabbalistic Commentaries*, selected, translated, and annotated by Seth Brody (1999)

John Wyclif, *On the Truth of Holy Scripture*, translated with an introduction and notes by Ian Christopher Levy (2001)

*Second Thessalonians: Two Early Medieval Apocalyptic Commentaries*, introduced and translated by Steven R. Cartwright and Kevin L. Hughes (2001)

*The "Glossa Ordinaria" on the Song of Songs*, translated with an introduction and notes by Mary Dove (2004)

*The Seven Seals of the Apocalypse: Medieval Texts in Translation*, translated with an introduction and notes by Francis X. Gumerlock (2009)

*The "Glossa Ordinaria" on Romans*, translated with an introduction and notes by Michael Scott Woodward (2011)

## 🖋 Documents of Practice Series

*Love and Marriage in Late Medieval London*, selected, translated, and introduced by Shannon McSheffrey (1995)

*Sources for the History of Medicine in Late Medieval England*, selected, introduced, and translated by Carole Rawcliffe (1995)

*A Slice of Life: Selected Documents of Medieval English Peasant Experience*, edited, translated, and with an introduction by Edwin Brezette DeWindt (1996)

*Regular Life: Monastic, Canonical, and Mendicant "Rules,"* selected and introduced by Douglas J. McMillan and Kathryn Smith Fladenmuller (1997); second edition, selected and introduced by Daniel Marcel La Corte and Douglas J. McMillan (2004)

*Women and Monasticism in Medieval Europe: Sisters and Patrons of the Cistercian Reform*, selected, translated, and with an introduction by Constance H. Berman (2002)

*Medieval Notaries and Their Acts: The 1327–1328 Register of Jean Holanie*, introduced, edited, and translated by Kathryn L. Reyerson and Debra A. Salata (2004)

*John Stone's Chronicle: Christ Church Priory, Canterbury, 1417–1472*, selected, translated, and introduced by Meriel Connor (2010)

## 🖋 Medieval German Texts in Bilingual Editions Series

*Sovereignty and Salvation in the Vernacular, 1050–1150*, introduction, translations, and notes by James A. Schultz (2000)

*Ava's New Testament Narratives: "When the Old Law Passed Away,"* introduction, translation, and notes by James A. Rushing, Jr. (2003)

*History as Literature: German World Chronicles of the Thirteenth Century in Verse*, introduction, translation, and notes by R. Graeme Dunphy (2003)

Thomasin von Zirclaria, *Der Welsche Gast (The Italian Guest)*, translated by Marion Gibbs and Winder McConnell (2009)

*Ladies, Whores, and Holy Women: A Sourcebook in Courtly, Religious, and Urban Cultures of Late Medieval Germany*, introductions, translations, and notes by Ann Marie Rasmussen and Sarah Westphal-Wihl (2010)

## 🖋 Varia

*The Study of Chivalry: Resources and Approaches*, edited by Howell Chickering and Thomas H. Seiler (1988)

*Studies in the Harley Manuscript: The Scribes, Contents, and Social Contexts of British Library MS Harley 2253*, edited by Susanna Fein (2000)

*The Liturgy of the Medieval Church*, edited by Thomas J. Heffernan and E. Ann Matter (2001; second edition 2005)

Johannes de Grocheio, *Ars musice*, edited and translated by Constant J. Mews, John N. Crossley, Catherine Jeffreys, Leigh McKinnon, and Carol J. Williams (2011)

## 🖋 To Order Please Contact:

Medieval Institute Publications
Western Michigan University
Kalamazoo, MI 49008-5432
Phone (269) 387-8755
FAX (269) 387-8750
http://www.wmich.edu/medieval/mip/index.html

Typeset in 10/13 New Baskerville
and Golden Cockerel Ornaments display
Manufactured by Cushing-Malloy, Inc.

Medieval Institute Publications
College of Arts and Sciences
Western Michigan University
1903 W. Michigan Avenue
Kalamazoo, MI 49008-5432
http://www.wmich.edu/medieval/mip

 WESTERN MICHIGAN UNIVERSITY